SAVAGE & STEVENS ARMS

COLLECTOR'S HISTORY

Legendary
American Arms
Manufacturers of
Sporting and Target
Rifles, Shotguns, Pistols
and Accessories Since
the Late 1800's

Arthur Savage
1857-1941

Joshua Stevens
1814-1907

JAY KIMMEL

CoryStevens Publishing, Inc.

SAVAGE & STEVENS ARMS

 Collector's History

First Printing October, 1990
Second (Revised) Printing August, 1991
Third (Revised) Printing June, 1993
Fourth Printing January, 1997

Fifth (Revised) Printing February, 2004

Copyright © 1990 by Jay Kimmel

Library of Congress Catalog Card Number: 90-085046

ISBN: 0-942893-00-X

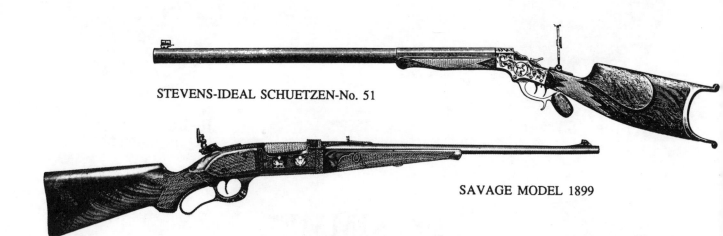

STEVENS-IDEAL SCHUETZEN-No. 51

SAVAGE MODEL 1899

CoryStevens Publishing, Inc.
15350 N.E. Sandy Blvd.
Portland, OR 97230
(503) 328-9339
VISA & MasterCard Accepted

SAVAGE & STEVENS ARMS

NSUMER CATALOG
NO. 1-53

SAVAGE · STEVENS · FOX
SHOTGUNS & RIFLES

SAVAGE ARMS CORPORATION
Chicopee Falls, Massachusetts

SAVAGE & STEVENS ARMS

Collector's History

Dedication

To my daughters, Emily & Julie, and their grandfather, Kenneth M. Kimmel (1912-1949), who had the foresight and good judgment to leave behind two Stevens rifles—a Model 70, slide action .22 and a 12 gauge double barrel shotgun. The disappearance of both led to a search and interest in Stevens & Savage Arms that continues to this date. This book is also dedicated to all who collect and cherish rather than reject and destroy. In this publication a tribute is being made to two great American companies—Savage Arms & Stevens Arms.

Special thanks are extended to the following contributors for assistance in making this book possible: Ed Mason, Frank de Haas, Mike Nesbitt, Daniel K. Stern, Susan Kimmel, Emily Kimmel, Don Simmons, John Wootters, Corporate officers of Savage Arms, Inc., Westfield, MA, William Parkerson, III, Editor, *The American Rifleman* (NRA), Oregon Arms Collectors, Rose City Arms Collectors, Dave Moreton, Jay Hard, Editor, *Guns & Ammo*, Philip B. Sharpe, Herschel C. Logan, Walter Wolk, James. E. Serven, Editors of *Outdoor Life*, Stoeger Arms Corporation, Chicopee Public Library, Springfield Armory, and others identified within the text. Special thanks to Roe. S. Clark for additional corrections to the third printing.

Author's Background

JAY KIMMEL, B.A., M.S., Author, Publisher & Realtor. Former Certified Rehabilitation Counselor & Office Manager for 15 years. Active member of National Rifle Association, Oregon Arms Collectors and Rose City Arms Collectors. Savage & Stevens collector since 1973. Previous publications include *Real Estate Investment* (Cornerstone/Simon & Schuster), *Money Strategy* (Conifer Publishing) and the following books by CoryStevens Publishing: *Custer, Cody & the Last Indian Wars*, *HomeWork: Starting & Growing a Business at Home*, and *U.S. NAVY SEABEES: Since Pearl Harbor*.

Jay Kimmel with Model 71 Savage/Stevens Commemorative

Forward

WHY STEVENS ARMS SET WORLD SHOOTING RECORDS

In my opinion, Joshua Stevens was a first class toolmaker in addition to being a distinctive manufacturer of sporting arms.

The quality of his rifle barrels were outstanding examples of craftmanship and contributed to world record shooting marks set year after year. His trigger pulls were consistently light and reliable. The light trigger pulls were obtained by positioning the mainspring, hammer and trigger so the full cock notch was nearly on dead center. The natural result was minimal pressure on the sears, yet enough pressure on the firing pin for good ignition.

ARMS COLLECTING

It is assumed that a majority of this book's readers will already possess an intense interest in arms collecting. Maybe for strictly personal reasons, much interest will be focused on Savage & Stevens firearms, paraphenalia and factual references not readily available in traditional marketplaces.

Some readers may already possess an expert's knowledge of firearms; others may be attempting to appraise a family inheritance, or learn more about a firearm possessed since childhood. Some readers may seek new information out of pure curiosity and the "sport" of seeking facts about special interests. Other readers may want to become more acquainted with the mechanical workings of a firearm; its repair, its value, its best uses, or some other personal reason.

Arms collectors often share many related interests and are usually generous about sharing information relevant to collecting. Ultimately, like the caretaker of valued objects and prized stories, certain readers will someday be able to pass on their enthusiasm and acquisitions to others who will hopefully expand and preserve this appreciation of firearms.

MY FIRST STEVENS

In 1924 I had some traps set to catch skunks, opossums and badgers for their pelts and wild rabbits for the meat. We had catalogs from Hill Brothers in Missouri that gave estimates of fur prices and contained both guns and traps for sale. I mailed them three dried skunk pelts, one dried opossum pelt along with the catalog page showing the Stevens Favorite for $10, Marksman for $7.50 and Crackshot for $6.50. By return mail Hill Brothers sent back #12 Stevens Marksman which I used extensively. In 1955, after searching everywhere, I was able to buy back that original gun at a barn sale. Many, many Stevens later I've never purchased a Stevens as an investment, but rather because I wanted it for its shooting ability, or to discover the reason for its performance. I have never seen a poor shooting Stevens firearm.

FINDING GUNS

In 1975 a friend in Montana told me about a distinctive small rifle a woman had brought with her to a Missoula shooting range. The rifle was for sale but she was unable to put a price on it. My friend referred her to Phil Judd, a well known gun collector in Butte. Mr. Judd remembered the rifle but was unable to make a certified appraisal or set a sales price because he could find no published information about it in his reference library. Actually, the rifle was a No. 14 Stevens Ladies Rifle in fine condition. I was ultimately able to purchase it at a fair price. I stayed in Butte for a period of time and helped Mr. Judd identify Stevens firearms in his huge building. He had one of the finest Colt, Sharps and Winchester collections in the world. He asked me, however, why I collected Stevens. The answer I gave him was that real collectors such as himself already possessed the best firearms. So, instead of searching for a needle in a haystack, I made a collection of the hay. *Ed Mason, October, 1990.*

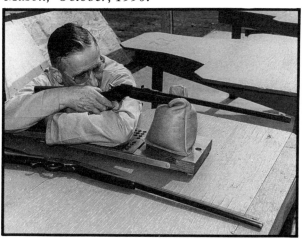

Ed Mason test firing a Model 71 Commemorative and Stevens Favorite (See article in Guns & Ammo, 1971).

The most recent hundred years have been the most dramatic period for change for any like period in recorded history. Social, economic and environmental changes have been occurring at what appear to be geometric rates. There's little surprise that lifestyle and occupational changes have radically altered the firearm market as well.

In 1890 most of the American population was rural based and/or had easy access to rural areas. Farmers, ranchers and "country-dwellers" were inclined to view firearms as essential tools. Outdoor publications were filled with competing ads for firearms and related accessories. Virtually every pre-teen male aspired to owning and using a small caliber firearm. A good, but inexpensive rifle could be readily obtained by selling a minimum number of magazine subscriptions. Men who were coming of age in the 1920's and 1930's often learned to shoot and at the same time earned bounties for bagging "pest" varmints that were viewed as interfering with agricultural pursuits. Getting out in the open country to hunt or target shoot with friends had the same peer pressure as learning to drive a car or excelling at Nintendo does now.

Now, virtually all of the American population is strictly urban-based. Wildlife habitats are severely endangered and risk becoming marginal lands. Rural access is severely limited for most Americans. Areas that will allow shooting are severely curtailed and may require private membership, or exorbitant travel. Both youngsters and oldsters devote as much time to non-aerobic television as either work or school.

Dramatic changes are also apparent in the laws of the land. Extended product liability insurance, ruinous taxes and lawsuit costs combine with manufacturing and sale costs to make it nearly impossible for a company in the precision machine trades, especially firearms manufacture, to survive. This publication is therefore intended in part to be a tribute to those persons who have historically & presently crafted Savage & Stevens arms.

Looking at a complex subject matter extending back for a century or more in time definitely produces many questions as well as answers. Example: Did fortuitous timing and craftsmanship account for Stevens Arms' growth from a one horse and one wagon company in 1864 to twelve acres of manufacturing space by 1902? Was it *politics* that forced Stevens Arms—then the largest sporting arms manufacturer in the world—to be sold to [New England] Westinghouse Electric to produce 1.5 million Russian rifles during World War I? After the war, why was Irving Page unable to buy back Stevens Arms? Why didn't Stevens Arms use a cumulative serial number on each firearm? Part of that answer is that Stevens typically used assembly numbers to insure that disassembled parts were fitted back properly, not to establish a perfect sequence. Actually, it was not until 1968 that arms manufacturers in the U.S. were required to stamp each firearm produced with a cumulative serial number. Savage Arms, in fact, voluntarily utilized a "final inspecton stamp" (not a serial number) from 1949 to 1968 that began with the letter A and proceeded through the alphabet with only the ambiguous letters O & Q missing before starting over again. Stevens Arms *did stamp* the caliber on both pistols and rifles if other than .22 (most arms were .22 caliber rimfires). The inexpensive Little Krag and the Little Scouts No. 14 and 14 1/2 were the only guns without assembly or final inspection stamps. The inexpensive Gem pistol was the only gun not stamped with the company name.

A common question that a collector will have is, "how old is this firearm?" Being able to accurately identify a specific firearm is greatly enhanced by reliable stamping and numbering that may also reflect the total numbers produced and the likely position within that production run. Issues of overall quality, however, are of a much more subjective nature and are certainly enhanced by increased knowledge of a particular firearm's evolution, history and relationship to other firearms. It's the intent of this omnibus publication to provide as much useful information about Savage & Stevens Arms history as may be found within any single reference.

Jay Kimmel, 1990, 1993.

SAVAGE & STEVENS ARMS
CONTENTS

SAVAGE & STEVENS ARMS

Hunters' Pet.

July 1, 1875.

Shot Guns.

Breech-Loading

Descriptive Circular and Retail Price List

—OF—

J. STEVENS & CO'S

POPULAR AND WELL KNOWN

Patent Breech-Loading Fire Arms,

CHICOPEE FALLS, MASS., U. S. A.

☞ *Sent by Express to all parts of the World, on Receipt of Price.*

Breech-Loading

Sporting Rifles.

Old Model Pocket Rifle.

A REMARKABLE little Fire-arm—a "Breech-loading Pocket Rifle"—weight only eleven ounces, yet shoots with great accuracy and power from 30 to 100 yards or more. Can be loaded and fired five times a minute—can be carried in a side pocket while working in the fields, ready to bring down game at short notice. Exceedingly convenient in new countries as a defensive weapon, or for picking off game, and useful generally upon the farm where wild animals, large or small, are common.

A Beautiful Little Piece for Amusement in Target Practice.

Breech-Loading

PocketRifles.

COVER PAGE FIRST STEVENS CATALOG, 1875

J. Stevens Arms Company
Historical Summary

- 1864-1888 J. Stevens & Co.
  Chicopee Falls, Mass.

- 1888-1915 J. Stevens Arms & Tool Co.
  Chicopee Falls, Mass. USA
  (or J. Stevens A & T Co.)

- 1916-1960 J. Stevens Arms Co.
  Chicopee Falls, Mass. USA

- 1960-to date J. Stevens Arms Co.
  SAVAGE ARMS
  Westfield, Mass. USA
      or
  STEVENS Model ———
  SAVAGE ARMS
  Westfield, Mass. USA

Joshua Stevens, a New England Yankee, was born in Chester, Massachusetts in 1814. He apprenticed as a machinist in 1834 and by 1838 was employed by famed gunmaker Cyrus B. Allen of Springfield, Massachusetts. Later he was to accept contractual employment with Samuel Colt at his fledgling revolver factory in Hartford, Connecticut. While employed there, and together with several other machinists, Stevens worked on revolver design improvement without Colt's full knowledge and consent because they thought Colt would be unable to afford the necessary retooling. A disagreement followed and Stevens' employment contract was terminated.

Shortly afterwards Joshua Stevens accepted employment with Edwin Wesson who was currently working on a patented revolver design. However, Wesson died unexpectedly and Stevens continued working on the pistol and obtained his own patents to several changes. J. Stevens obtained patents on percussion revolvers in 1850, 1853 & 1855 while employed by the Massachusetts Arms Company

By 1849 Stevens moved to Chicopee Falls, Massachusetts and began working for the Massachusetts Arms Company which had been formed in December, 1849. Based on design features patented in connection with the Edwin Wesson revolver, the Massachusetts Arms Company began to produce a revolver which did not acknowledge the Stevens name.

Samuel Colt, noted for being a litigious individual, sued the Massachusetts Arms Company for obscure patent infringement and Colt prevailed. Massachusetts Arms Company was obligated to pay Colt $15,000, almost enough to destroy the company, but they were able to eventually recoup their losses after purchasing the rights to manufacture the Maynard rifle. J. Stevens remained with the Massachusetts Arms Company until 1864.

In 1864 Joshua Stevens, now a master machinist, gunmaker and toolmaker, founded the company, which bears his name, with little more than a horse, a wagon, an old gristmill and about twenty employees. The original structure was a three-way partnership composed of Joshua Stevens, James E. Taylor and William B. Fay— all important individuals in the growth of a company that would ultimately become the largest sporting arms company in the world.

Joshua Stevens, more a talented craftsman, with thirty years of New England gunmaking experience, than a theoretical designer, obtained patent number 44123 dated September 6, 1864, which launched the company. This very basic, breech-loading tip-up (similar to the action of a modern shotgun) became the basis for all but two of the 14 Stevens single-shot pistols. The same tip-up design was also utilized for making Stevens rifles from 1869 until he designed the 1885 Sporting Rifle—a forerunner of the extremely popular "Favorite" single-shot rifle.

The high quality (accuracy and reliability compared to cost) of Stevens' typically inexpensive single-shots contributed directly to the company's 1912 claim of being the largest sporting arms company in the world. Stevens Arms' major contribution in the development and promotion of the .22 long rifle cartridge (world's most popular) also added to the positive image.

With optimism and tenacity, Joshua Stevens decided to manufacture small arms (Old Model Pocket Pistol and Vest Pocket Pistol) in the midst of an intensely crowded market. In forming his company near the end of the Civil War, he had to contend with a glut of surplus firearms being dumped on the U.S. market. A glut which contributed to the demise of many new and established arms makers of the time. Typically (not always) low cost and high quality workmanship were company standards and J. Stevens & Co. survived with two basically sound but inexpensive single-shot pistols. These proved to have sustained popularity at a time when large portions of the adult American population felt undressed without one or more concealed weapons on their person.

By 1867 the company was employing about 30 persons to manufacture firearms and machinists' tools. The official name of the company was J. Stevens & Company, Chicopee Falls, Massachusetts. The January 9, 1886 issue of *American Field* included the following comment: The old and popular firm of J.

Stevens & Company of Chicopee Falls, Massachusetts, manufacturers of the celebrated firearms and fine machinists' tools, have sold out their business to the new business just formed under the name of J. Stevens Arms & Tool Company with the following officers: Joshua Stevens, president; William B. Fay, Joshua Stevens, George S. Taylor, directors; Irving H. Page, secretary; James E. Taylor, agent and treasurer. The above took possession of the business January 1, 1886.

From 1875 to 1895 Stevens firearms and machinists' tools were manufactured in a three story frame structure. William Fay, one of the original three partners and long term factory manager died in 1893. In December 1895 Joshua Stevens retired at the age of 81 years. He lived another eleven years and could clearly see the extensive legacy of his creative works.

Irving H. Page, who was long associated with the business, bought out the interests of Joshua Stevens and James E. Taylor effective January 1, 1896. Also, Charles P. Fay, son of William B. Fay, who had inherited his father's interest, became the vice president and general superintendent.

In 1895 the company had approximately 17,000 square feet and employed about 44 persons. With the new management, effective January 1, 1896, floor space was increased to 34,000 square feet and the number of employees to 150. Popularity, promotions and growth in the small calibre, single-shot market was now growing at a geometric rate. By 1900, for example, there were over 900 employees. In the following year another 180,000 square feet was added which increased the total to over 10.25 acres. This plant was purchased from the Overman Wheel Company and for a brief time Stevens A & T Company continued to complete the assembly of bicycles in progress. It was during this time that Harry M. Pope, the internationally famous barrel maker, agreed to be contractually associated with Stevens Arms & Tool Company. It was Mr. Pope who laid the foundations for the target and sporting rifles that would become world famous for accuracy. Later an additional 85,000 square feet would be added; bringing the total plant area from 12.5 to 14 acres. All growth having limits, international warfare and the public demand for high-powered, repeating weapons had a suddenly chilling effect on that growth.

For reasons perhaps relating to Joshua Stevens' unwillingness to manufacture military arms for the Civil War or Spanish American War, J. Stevens Arms & Tool Company did not pursue lucrative arms contracts to supply the World War in Europe. Instead, the Stevens management, in May 1915, sold out all interest in their mammouth production facilities to the New England Westinghouse Company. The latter then used the facilities to produce approximately 1,500,000 Russian military rifles (bolt action "Nagant" 7.62 mm) in response to the patriotic demand to support English allies "at a distance." However, by 1917 Czar Nicholas II was assassinated and the mistrusted Bolshevik Revolution was underway. As a result the "Nagant" rifle contract was not completed and, with the assistance of the N.R.A, large numbers were sold as surplus or used by U.S. troops.

By July, 1916 the radically different company changed it's name to "J. Stevens Arms Company." Irving Page, after a long and successful Stevens career, retired. New officers of the Westinghouse-owned corporation included L.A. Osborne, president; E.M. Herr, vice president; and H.F. Baetz, treasurer. Limited production of Stevens Arms was continued in addition to the Nagant rifles. Much more attention was focused on shotgun production because of the market's distinct trend away from single-shots.

In April 1920, Savage Arms Corporation purchased all interests in J. Stevens Arms Company, retained that name and essentially the then current Stevens' focus under Savage Arms direction. By 1926 J. Stevens Arms Company would claim to be the *largest shotgun manufacturer in the world.* In 1936 Stevens was converted from a separate entity owned by Savage Arms to a division of Savage Arms.

During World War II most of the Stevens Arms facilities were committed to production of the British Lee Enfield No. 4 Mark 1 rifle. In 1960 the Chicopee Falls manufacturing plants were all closed and all assets and personnel were absorbed within the Savage Arms Corporation which is currently located in Westfield, MA (see history of Savage Arms Corp).

Extract from *"Economic History of a Factory Town, A Study of Chicopee, Massachusetts"* by Vera Shlakman, Smith College Studies in History, Northhampton, Mass., Vol. XX, Nos. 1-4, October, 1934-July, 1935.

Inasmuch as the Stevens Arms Company had been organized on a modest scale toward the end of the war, and had therefore not been subjected to such rapid expansion as some of the other companies, the firm was able to get off to a good start, and expanded its business slowly, without experiencing any setbacks. In 1867, 20 men were employed in the manufacture of pistols, calipers, dividers, and pruning shears. The half time services of a traveling salesman were secured and in 1868 the plant was enlarged somewhat [*see: Taylor Diary, Aug. 17, 1867; Springfield Republican, Jan. 13, Feb 10, 1868*]. In 1872 the company started the manufacture of a breech-loading shot gun, and 40 men found employment in the shops [*Springfield Republican, Jan. 3, 1873*]. It was soon necessary to install a larger water wheel in order to secure more power. This was just before the panic of 1873. No doubt business fell off during the next few years, but by 1877-78 orders were plentiful, and it was necessary to start night work in order to keep up with the demand for sporting rifles during the current "rifle shooting craze." With the general improvement of business in 1880-81 it was planned to double the existing productive capacity.

In 1885 the company was incorporated with a capital of $40,000, as the J. Stevens Arms and Tool Company. Joshua Stevens and W. B. Fay each subscribed to 120 shares of stock in the new corporation. Fay had been a gunsmith and had held a position of importance in the company for some years preceding its incorporation; possibly he had been a member of the firm. George S. Taylor, one time merchant, and now connected with the Belcher and Taylor Company took 10 shares. His brother, James, who had also been a merchant and had later been employed in the original Stevens Company, subscribed to 110 shares and was appointed treasurer of the firm. I. H. Page, the bookkeeper of the company took 40 shares. At the time of incorporation, the company employed 40 workers. End.

SAVAGE & STEVENS ARMS

SOME THOUGHTS ON STEVENS

Joshua Stevens was 50 years old when he started his gun and machinist tool manufacturing in 1864. He used a water-wheel for power, and daylight, oil lamps and candles for light. He may have been among the first American factories to use female help. In 1886 he made his partners stockholders in the corporation. He changed the name of the corporation in 1886 to Stevens Arms and Tool Co. and was making sporting rifles, gallery rifles, tip-up pistols and shotguns in addition to his complete line of machinist's tools with about 50 employees. In 1896 Irving Page started directing the operation. Shop space increased from 17,000 square feet to 275,000 square feet and almost 1,000 employees. By 1900 he had the largest sporting arms manufacturing plant in the world. Joshua Stevens died in 1907 at the age of 92, leaving the largest sporting arms business in the world. *Ed Mason, Spring, 1993.*

Joshua Stevens

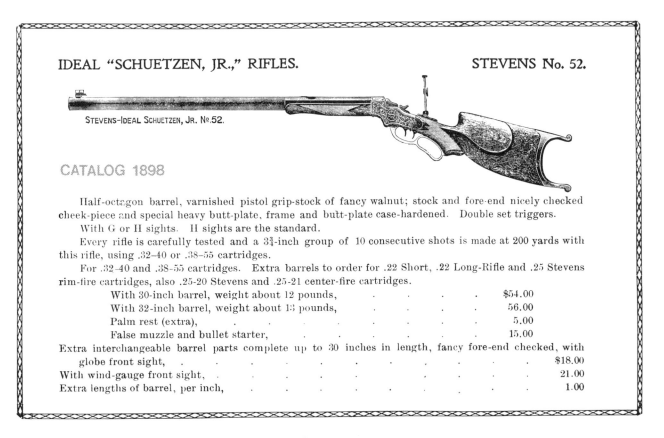

IDEAL "SCHUETZEN, JR.," RIFLES.   STEVENS No. 52.

STEVENS-IDEAL SCHUETZEN, JR. No.52.

CATALOG 1898

Half-octagon barrel, varnished pistol grip-stock of fancy walnut; stock and fore-end nicely checked cheek-piece and special heavy butt-plate, frame and butt-plate case-hardened. Double set triggers.

With G or H sights. H sights are the standard.

Every rifle is carefully tested and a 3¾-inch group of 10 consecutive shots is made at 200 yards with this rifle, using .32–40 or .38–55 cartridges.

For .32–40 and .38–55 cartridges. Extra barrels to order for .22 Short, .22 Long-Rifle and .25 Stevens rim-fire cartridges, also .25-20 Stevens and .25-21 center-fire cartridges.

With 30-inch barrel, weight about 12 pounds,	$54.00
With 32-inch barrel, weight about 13 pounds,	56.00
Palm rest (extra),	5.00
False muzzle and bullet starter,	15.00
Extra interchangeable barrel parts complete up to 30 inches in length, fancy fore-end checked, with globe front sight,	$18.00
With wind-gauge front sight,	21.00
Extra lengths of barrel, per inch,	1.00

THE J. STEVENS ARMS AND TOOL COMPANY,

MANUFACTURERS OF

Fine Single-Shot Target and Sporting Rifles,

SINGLE-SHOT PISTOLS, SHOTGUNS, SIGHTS, ETC.

FINE MECHANICAL TOOLS.

CHICOPEE FALLS, MASS., U. S. A.

February, 1898.   New York Office: 318 Broadway, Cor. Prince St.

RELIABLE POCKET RIFLES.   STEVENS No. 42.

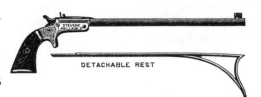

Round barrel, globe and peep sights, with detachable shoulder rest, frame nickeled, weight one pound.

For .22 Long-Rifle R. F.

With 10-inch barrel, plated rest,   .   .   . $8.25

TIP-UP PISTOL.

STEVENS No. 41.

Full nickel-plated, 3½-inch barrel.   In two calibres only.

.22 Short R. F., ...   Price, $2.50
.30 Short R. F., ...   Price, 2.50

HUNTERS' PET.   STEVENS No. 34.

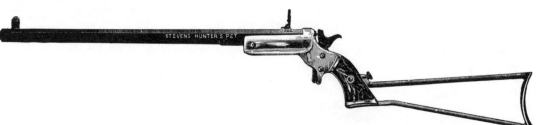

REAR SIGHT.
Price, $1.75.

Octagon barrel, Stevens combination sights, with detachable skeleton stock; frame and stock nickel-plated.   Made in three calibres for the following cartridges:

.22 Long-Rifle R. F., .25 R. F. and .32 Long R. F.

With 18-inch barrel, weight 5¾ pounds, ... $13.50

FRONT SIGHT.
Price, $1.50.

14

OPEN SIGHT RIFLE.   STEVENS No. 2.

Full-octagon barrel, open sights, nickel-plated frame and butt-plate, oiled walnut stock. In three calibres for the following cartridges:

.22 Long-Rifle R. F., .25 R. F. and .32 Long R. F.

With 24-inch barrel only, weight 7 pounds, ... $17.00

PREMIER RIFLE.   STEVENS No. 7.

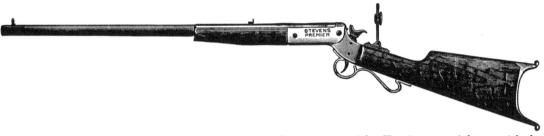

Half-octagon barrel, Beach combination front sight, open rear sight, Vernier peep sight, varnished stock and fore-arm, Swiss butt-plate; frame and butt-plate nickel-plated. In three calibres for the following cartridges:

.22 Long-Rifle R. F., .25 R. F. and .32 Long R. F.

With 24-inch barrel, weight 7¼ pounds, ... $25.00
" 28-inch " " 8¾ " 27.00

LADY'S RIFLE.   STEVENS No. 11 and No. 13.

No. 13. Half-octagon barrel, Beach combination front sight, open rear sight and Vernier peep sight; stock and fore-arm varnished, nickel-plated frame and butt-plate. Splendidly balanced, light weight, especially adapted to ladies' use. In two calibres for the following cartridges:

.22 Long-Rifle R. F. and .25 R. F.

No. 11—Lady's Rifle.

With 24-inch barrel, oiled stock, plain open sights only, weight 5½ pounds, . . . $18.75

DIAMOND MODEL TARGET PISTOL.   STEVENS No. 43.

1898 Catalog

Open Front,	Open Back,
Price, $0.50.	Price, $0.50.

Blued barrel, long plain grip-stock, nickel-plated frame. Cut illustrates pistol, with globe and peep sights.

For the .22 Long-Rifle R. F. Cartridge only.

15

IDEAL ——————— RIFLES
Stevens' New Style Ideal Rifles.
NOTE REDUCTION IN PRICES.

STEVENS "IDEAL" Nº44

No. 44. SPORTING AND GALLERY RIFLE.

Half Octagon Barrel, Rifle Butt Plate, Case-hardened Frame, Oiled Walnut Stock, made for the following cartridges : **22 Long Rifle**, 25 Stevens, 22-7½ Winchester and **32 Long**, rim fire; **22-10**, 25-20 Stevens, 25-25 Stevens, **32 Long**, 32-20 and **38-55 Marlin** and Ballard, center fire.

24 inch,	7¼ lbs.,	with B Sights,	$15.00	24 inch,	with D, E or F. Sights,	$18.00
26 "	7¾ "	"	16.00	26 "	"	"	19.00
28 "	8 "	"	17.00	28 "	"	"	20.00
30 "	8½ "	"	18.00	30 "	"	"	21.00

With E or F Sights, a blank piece will be fitted into rear slot in barrel. For other calibers or special weights not exceeding 9 lbs. an additional charge of $2.00 will be made. Unless otherwise ordered B Sights will be sent.

No.45. RANGE RIFLE.

Half Octagon Barrel, Swiss Butt Plate, Varnished Stock and Fore-end, Case-hardened Frame. Made in three different weights, varying some according to caliber, for the following cartridges: 22 Long Rifle, 25 Stevens, 22-7½ Winchester and 32 Long, rim fire ; 22-10 U. M. C., 25-20 Stevens, 25-25 Stevens, 32 Long, 32-20, 32 Ideal, 32-35 Stevens, 32-40 Marlin and Ballard, and 38-55 Marlin and Ballard, center fire.

	NO. 1.	NO. 2.	NO. 3.	B SIGHTS.	D, E OR F SIGHTS	G SIGHTS
24 inch	6½ lbs.	7¼ lbs.	8¼ lbs.	$18.50	$21.00	$24.00
26 "	6¾ "	7¾ "	8¾ "	19.50	22.00	25.00
28 "	7 "	8 "	9¼ "	20.50	23.00	26.00
30 "	7¼ "	8½ "	9¾ "	21.50	24.00	27.00

For other calibers or special weights not exceeding 9 lbs. an additional charge of $2.00 will be made. Unless otherwise ordered D sights will be sent on these rifles.

Rifles with E, F and G sights will have no rear slot in the barrel.

G sights are without the spirit level. With the level they will list $1.00 higher.

No. 46. RANGE RIFLE.
SAME AS NO. 45 BUT WITH FANCY STOCK. PRICE $5.00 EXTRA.

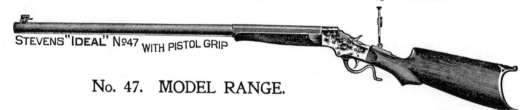

STEVENS "IDEAL" Nº47 WITH PISTOL GRIP

No. 47. MODEL RANGE.

Half Octagon Barrel, Case-hardened Frame, Varnished Pistol-grip Stock, Swiss Butt Plate, made for the same cartridges and in the same weights as No. 45.

	B SIGHTS.	D, E OR F SIGHTS.	G SIGHTS.
24 inch,	$23.50	$26.00	$29.00
26 "	24.50	27.00	30.00
28 "	25.50	28.00	31.00
30 "	26.50	29.00	32.00
Full checked,		$5.00 extra.	

EXTRAS FOR NOS. 44, 45, 46 and 47.

Plain Pistol Grip not checked,	Price, $ 5.00 Extra.	Double Trigger Set Lock,	Price, $4.00 Extra
Fancy Pistol Grip and fore-end, checked,	" 15.00 "	Special Weight Barrel up to 9 lbs.,	" 2.00 "
Plain " " " " "	" 10.00 "	Extra Heavy Barrel up to 12 lbs.,	" 5.00 "
Fancy Stock and fore-end, checked,	" 10.00 "	Cheek Piece,	" 5.00 "

SIGHTS FOR NOS. 44, 45, 46 and 47.

B sights are Rocky Mountain Front, and Sporting Rear.
D " " Beach Front, Open Rear and Vernier.
E " " Lyman Ivory Combination Front, and Lyman Combination Rear, or for Cup Disc on Rear Sight add 50 cts.
F " " Globe Interchangeable Disc Front and Vernier.
G " " Wind Gauge, Front and Mid Range Vernier.

IDEAL ———— RIFLES

No. 48. MODEL RANGE.

Same as No, 47, but with Fancy Stock, $5.co Extra.   With Fancy Stock and full checked, $10.00 Extra.

Double Set Trigger,   -   - $4.00 Extra.

STEVENS "IDEAL WALNUT HILL" No. 49.

No. 49. WALNUT HILL.

Half Octagon Barrel, Case-hardened Frame, Varnished Pistol-grip Stock, with cheek piece, grip and fore-end checked, Swiss Butt Plate, Embossed Frame, made in two weights and for the same cartridges as No. 45.

	NO. 2.	NO. 3.	D, E OR F SIGHTS.	G SIGHTS.
28 inch,	8 lbs.	9¼ lbs.	$39.00	$42.00
30 "	8½ "	9¾ "	40.00	43.00

No. 50. WALNUT HILL.

Same as No. 49, but having Fancy Walnut Stock, $5.co Extra.   Double Set Trigger, $4.00 Extra.

Loop Lever,   -   -   - $1.00 Extra.

STEVENS-IDEAL SCHUETZEN-No. 51

No. 51. SCHUETZEN.

Half Octagon Barrel, Case-hardened, Embossed Frame, extra fancy Swiss pattern Stock, full checked, with cheek piece, large pattern Nickel Plated Swiss Butt, Double Set Trigger.

		G SIGHTS.
30 inch,	13 lbs.	$58.00
32 "	14 "	60.00

No. 52. SCHUETZEN, JR.

SAME STYLE AS NO. 50, BUT HEAVIER AND WITH DOUBLE SET TRIGGER.

		G SIGHTS.
30 inch,	11 lbs.	$54.00
32 "	11⅛ "	56.00

STEVENS-IDEAL SCHUETZEN-No. 53

No. 53. SCHUETZEN RIFLE with PALM REST.

Half Octagon Barrel, Case-hardened Embossed Frame, extra fancy Swiss pattern Stock, full checked, with cheek piece, large pattern Nickel-plated Swiss Butt, Double Set Trigger G Sights, with Adjustable Palm Rest.

THIS RIFLE IS THE SAME AS NO. 51, BUT WITH ADJUSTABLE PALM REST.

		G SIGHTS.
30 inch,	13 lbs.	$63.00
32 "	14 "	65.00

NO DISCOUNT FROM THESE PRICES EXCEPT TO THE TRADE.

J. STEVENS ARMS & TOOL CO., Chicopee Falls, Mass.

OPEN RIFLE SIGHTS AND PISTOL SIGHTS.

Sporting Rear Sight.
Price, $0.80.

STEVENS COMBINATION PISTOL SIGHTS.

Open Front Sight.
Price, $0.50.

Open Rear Sight.
Price, $0.75.

Target Pistol Sights.
Open Front.   Open Back.
Price, $0.50.   Price, $0.50.

Front Sight.
Price, $1.50.

Sporting Leaf Sight, Graduated
to 1000 Yds.   Price, $1.50.

LORD, CONLIN AND GOULD MODEL PISTOL SIGHTS.

STEVENS PISTOL SIGHTS
J. STEVENS ARMS & TOOL Co.,
CHICOPEE FALLS, MASS. U.S.A.

WIND GAUGE REAR
PRICE $1.50

Rear Sight.
Price, $1.75.

Open Front.
Price, $0.75.

Rocky Mountain Front Sight.
Price, $0.50.

Price with Combination Eye-Cup
"   "   plain

IDEAL "SCHUETZEN, JR.," RIFLES.   STEVENS No. 52.

STEVENS-IDEAL SCHUETZEN, JR. No. 52.

Half-octagon barrel, varnished pistol grip-stock of fancy walnut; stock and fore-end nicely checked cheek-piece and special heavy butt-plate, frame and butt-plate case-hardened. Double set triggers.

With G or H sights. H sights are the standard.

Every rifle is carefully tested and a 3¾-inch group of 10 consecutive shots is made at 200 yards with this rifle, using .32–40 or .38–55 cartridges.

For .32–40 and .38–55 cartridges. Extra barrels to order for .22 Short, .22 Long-Rifle and .25 Stevens rim-fire cartridges, also .25-20 Stevens and .25-21 center-fire cartridges.

With 30-inch barrel, weight about 12 pounds, ... $54.00

CONLIN MODEL GALLERY PISTOL.   STEVENS No. 38.

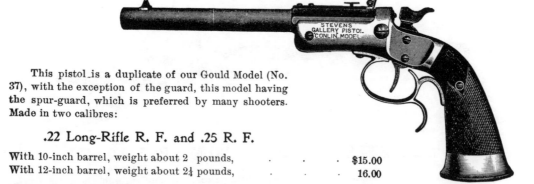

This pistol is a duplicate of our Gould Model (No. 37), with the exception of the guard, this model having the spur-guard, which is preferred by many shooters. Made in two calibres:

.22 Long-Rifle R. F. and .25 R. F.

With 10-inch barrel, weight about 2 pounds,   .   .   . $15.00
With 12-inch barrel, weight about 2¼ pounds,   .   .   .   16.00

LYMAN SIGHTS—FOR HUNTING AND TARGET USE.

No. 6. Leaf Sight. To replace ordinary rear sight.
Price, $1.00.

No. 17.
Target Sight.
With reversible
aperture or pinhead
Price, $1.25.

Showing Aperture.   Showing Globe.
No. 7.
Wind-Gauge Target Sight.
Price, $3.50.

No. 8. Sporting
Wind-Gauge Sight.
Price, $3.00.

Condensed from Stevens Catalog, 1898

STEVENS No. 40.

NEW MODEL POCKET SHOTGUN.

The same as the New Model Pocket Rifle, but bored smooth and choked; uses special Everlasting shells, .38 or .44-calibre (illustrated on page 13), also made for .38-40 and .44-40 cartridges at an extra cost of $2.00.

Price 15-inch, ...	$11.25
Price 18-inch, ...	12.50

STEVENS No. 42.

RELIABLE POCKET RIFLES.

Round barrel, globe and peep sights, with detachable shoulder rest, frame nickeled, weight one pound.

For .22 Long-Rifle R. F.

With 10-inch barrel, plated rest, . . . $8.25

STEVENS No. 41.

DETACHABLE REST

Full nickel-plated, 3½-inch barrel. In two calibres only.

.22 Short R. F., . . .	Price,	$2.50
.30 Short R. F., . . .	Price,	2.50

TIP-UP PISTOL.

Blued barrel, long plain grip-stock, nickel-plated frame. Cut illustrates pistol, with globe and peep sights.

For the .22 Long-Rifle R. F. Cartridge only.

Made in the following styles:

No. 1, 6-inch barrel, with globe front and peep sights (as illustrated), weight 10 ounces,	.	$5.00
No. 2, 6-inch barrel, with open sights (as shown), weight 10 ounces,	.	5.00
No. 3, 6-inch barrel, with both open and peep sights, weight 10 ounces,	.	6.00
No. 4, 10-inch barrel, with globe front and peep sights (as illustrated), weight 12 ounces,	.	7.50
No. 5, 10-inch barrel, with open sights (as shown), weight 12 ounces,	.	7.50
No. 6, 10-inch barrel, with both open and peep sights, weight 12 ounces,	.	8.50

Unless otherwise specified, this pistol will be sent with globe and peep sights, as these are the standard sights.

STEVENS No. 43.

DIAMOND MODEL TARGET PISTOL.

STEVENS–DIAMOND MODEL TARGET PISTOL

OPEN FRONT, PRICE, $0.50.	OPEN BACK, PRICE, $0.50.

STEVENS No. 5.

EXPERT RIFLE.

Half-octagon barrel, Beach combination front sight, open rear sight, and Vernier peep sight, (can be changed in an instant from a globe to a plain open sight rifle), varnished stock, nickel-plated frame and butt-plate. In three calibres, for the following cartridges:

.22 Long-Rifle R. F., .25 R. F. and .32 Long R. F.

With 24-inch barrel only, weight 6¾ pounds, . . . $20.00

STEVENS No. 5.

EXPERT RIFLE.

Half-octagon barrel, Beach combination front sight, open rear sight, and Vernier peep sight, (can be changed in an instant from a globe to a plain open sight rifle), varnished stock, nickel-plated frame and butt-plate. In three calibres, for the following cartridges:

.22 Long-Rifle R. F., .25 R. F. and .32 Long R. F.

With 24-inch barrel only, weight 6¾ pounds, . . . $20.00

STEVENS No. 11 and No. 13.

LADY'S RIFLE.

STEVENS–LADY MODEL

No. 13. Half-octagon barrel, Beach combination front sight, open rear sight and butt-plate. Splendidly balanced, varnished, nickel-plated frame and fore-arm varnished, nickel-plated frame and butt-plate. Splendidly balanced, 1 especially adapted to ladies' use. In two calibres for the following cartridges:

.22 Long-Rifle R. F. and .25 R. F.

19

Catalogue and Buyers' Guide.

FALL AND WINTER 1894—95.

Montgomery Ward & Co.

NEW MODEL STEVENS' RIFLE.—"Sure Shot."

46814 The "Sure Shot" is an entirely new model. The barrel swings to extract the shell instead of "tipping up" as in the old models. Barrels are rifled same as in the higher grades, and is a wonderful shooter. Frame nickel plated, walnut stock, re bounding lock, German silver front sight, finely finished throughout. Stock and barrel easily separated to clean or pack. Barrel 20 inches. entire length 34 inches, weight 3¼ lbs., 22 caliber, rim fire short, long, or long rifle cartridge. Every rifle warranted as long range and as accurate as any 22 caliber rifle in the market. Each.................. ....$6.49

J. Stevens & Co.'s Single Breech Loading Rifles.

Manufactured at Chicopee Falls. Mass. In all styles the barrel "tips up" at the breech the same as a breech loading shotgun. Stock and barrel can be easily separated and packed in a trunk or case. All have nickel-plated frame and mountings, oiled walnut stock, blue barrels and are finely finished throughout. Every rifle is rigidly tested at the factory and warranted perfectly accurate and reliable. There are no better shooting rifles in the market. There are more of these rifles in the shooting galleries than of any other make. There are no better ones.

Stevens' "Expert" Rifles No. 5, Vernier and Open Back Sight and Beach Front Sight.

Weight of Rifles boxed for shipment 15 to 25 pounds. each; 25 caliber rim or center fire same prices as the 22 calibers.

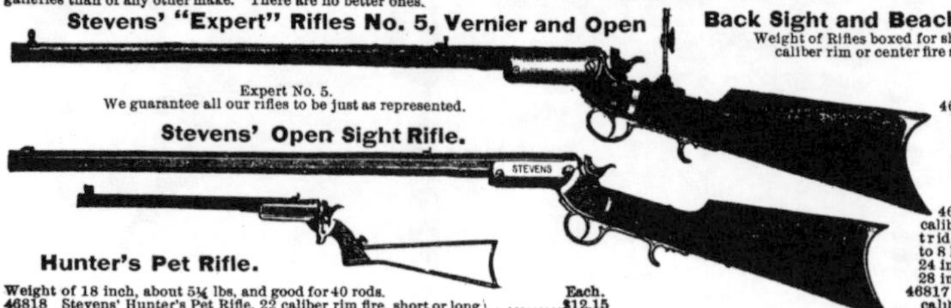

Expert No. 5.
We guarantee all our rifles to be just as represented.

Stevens' Open Sight Rifle.

Hunter's Pet Rifle.

Weight of 18 inch, about 5¼ lbs, and good for 40 rods. Each.
46818 Stevens' Hunter's Pet Rifle, 22 caliber rim fire, short or long.. ....$12.15
46819 Stevens' Hunter's Pet Rifle, 32 caliber, rim fire, 18 in. barrel 12.15
20-inch barrel.................(22 and 32 caliber, same price).................... 13.00

46815 Stevens' Rifle No. 5, 22 caliber, rim fire, weight, 6¼ to 7¼ for 24 in.; 7 to 7¾ lbs. 28 in.
Each.
24 in. barrel.......................$15.00
28 in. barrel.......................... 17.49

46816 Stevens' Open Sight Rifle, 22 caliber, rim fire, short or long cartridges. Weight, 6½ to 7½, 24 in. 7½ to 8 lbs. 28 in.
24 in. barrel.......................$12.00
28 in. barrel.......................... 14.40

46817 Stevens' Open Sight Rifle, 32 caliber, rim fire, short or long cartridges and 25-20 caliber center fire.
24 in. barrel.......................$12.00
28 in. barrel.......................... 13.20

The Stevens' New Model Pocket Rifles.

A fine target or squirrel rifle; good for 100 yards.
46820 Stevens' New Model Pocket Rifle, 22 caliber, rim fire, short or long cartridge, and BB cap cartridges, 22 caliber.

Each.
12 inch barrel, 2¼ lb. weight $8.95
15 inch barrel, 2½ lb. weight 10.13

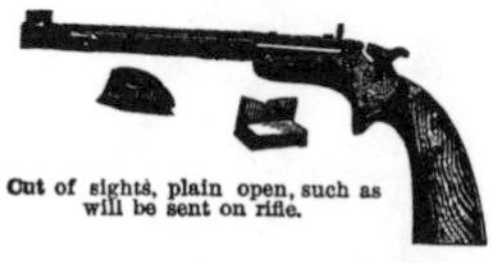

Out of sights, plain open, such as will be sent on rifle.

46821 Stevens' Diamond Model Pistol, single shot, tip-up, blued barrels, long plain grip stock, plated frame, chambered for 22 rim fire short or long rifle cartridges, plain open sights.
Weight, 10 oz. 6 inch barrel, good for 50 yards, each.. ....$4.75
Weight, 12 oz. 10 inch barrel, good for 20 to 100 yards...$6.75
The Stevens' pistols are all made of the very best material, and are all warranted accurate shooters.

46822 Stevens' Single Shot Pistol, tip-up barrel, plated finish, 3½ inch barrel, 22 caliber, rim fire, a fine target pistol...$2.15
30 caliber, rim fire, short............................ 2.10
No better material put in rifles; weight, 8 oz.
Stevens' 25 Caliber Rifles, rim or center fire, can be furnished at same prices as the 22 caliber styles. See "Cartridges" for prices on ammunition. Can furnish any style to order.

Stevens' New Model Favorite Rifle.

As well rifled as the higher cost rifle.

46823 The Favorite is an entirely new model Stevens' rifle. The barrel is held to stock by a set screw, and easily separated or put together. Rifling and quality of barrel same as the higher cost rifle, case-hardened frame, walnut stock, finely finished, warranted accurate, rim fire, 22 caliber; using long or short cartridges. Each
22 in. barrel, about 4½ lbs. weight..... ....$6.95
46823½ Steven's Favorite Rifle, 25 calibre, rim fire, 22 inch barrel. Weight 4½ lbs. Each..$6.95

STEVENS' NEW IDEAL RIFLE—1894 Model.

46838½ Ideal Rifle, No. 109 Half octagon barrel, wind gauge front and mid-range Vernier back sight. no rear barrel sight, fore-end and stock varnished. Frame case hardened and Swiss butt plate, nickel plated. Stock easily separated from barrel when desired.
28-inch, 7 lbs., 25-20 caliber, using No. 47187 cartridge.........................$21.60
30-inch, 8¼ lbs., 32-40 caliber, using No. 47220 cartridge.........................$22.60
Other lengths and weights can be furnished if desired. Prices quoted on application.

THE J. STEVENS ARMS & TOOL CO., CHICOPEE FALLS, MASS.

Malcom's Telescope Sights.

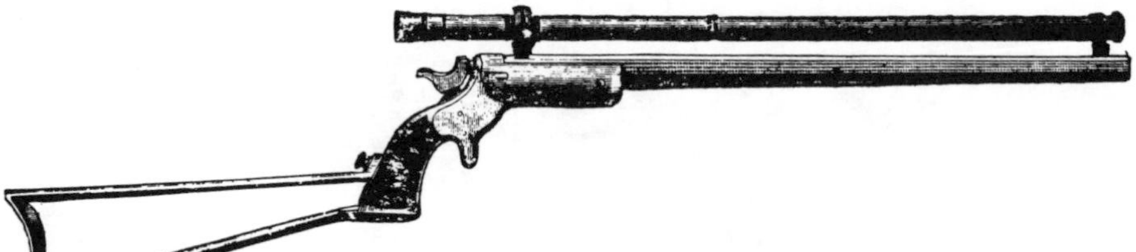

5 shots 5 rods with Hunter's Pet.

Condensed from Stevens Catalog, 1898

10 shots 5 rods, with Premier Rifle.

Malcom's Sights fitted to 10, 12, 15 or 18 inch New Model or Pet Barrel.. $25.00
" " " to 24 or 26 inch Rifle or Pet Barrel.. 30.00

Every rifle is thoroughly tested before it is allowed to leave our factory.

We think you have the most perfect shooting guns made. Blanton, Coffman & Hunt, Cottage Grove, Tenn.

I have always been well pleased with my gun, as it never failed to do excellent work. Refer to me at any time you may see fit. W. N. Ashbaugh, Youngstown, Ohio.

I am more than pleased with the shooting qualities of my Stevens combined rifle and shot gun. G. M. Rowe, Stephentown, N. Y.

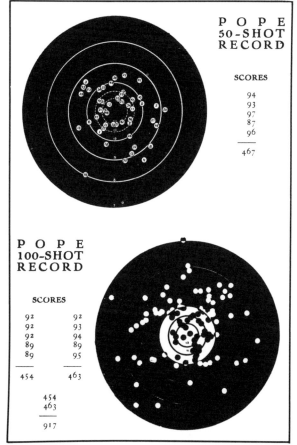

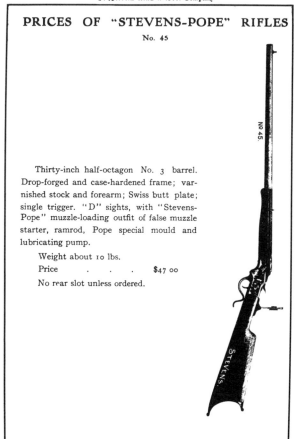

See: Smith, Ray M. THE STORY OF POPE'S BARRELS Harrisburg, PA The Stackpole Co. c. 1960

SPORTSMAN'S MAGAZINE

VOL. I.   OCTOBER, 1896.   NO. I.

POPE MODEL

This model is the same as used by our Mr. Pope in all his 200-yard shooting. It was designed to give a handsome well-made rifle with *all* the finest extras that could help fine shooting, but with no money spent for engraving, etc., that did not help the shooting of the rifle, with the exception of a fine stock.

DESCRIPTION

Thirty-inch or thirty-two-inch No. 4 octagon barrel. Drop-forged action, handsomely case-hardened; double set triggers; fancy pistol grip stock and forearm, Pope model, with cheek piece extra high and full so as to be tight against the face; finely checked and varnished; special deep, snugly-fitting butt plate; special three-finger lever; Pope sights, Pope palm rest and Pope muzzle-loading outfit.

Length of stock 13⅛ in.

Drop of stock 3 in.

Weight 12½ to 13½ lbs.

Price $82 00

The same rifle as above but with plain walnut stock and without checking, $75.00.

Chicopee Falls : Massachusetts : U. S. A.

TELESCOPE SIGHT

Mr. Pope uses in his offhand shooting, where allowed, a special telescope sight, 5 power, about 16 inches long, which is quickly removed and attached without changing the adjustments or necessitating removal of ordinary sights. A telescope is the *only* perfect correction for defective eyesight in shooting (spectacles will not answer), and it enables old men to keep on shooting as well as ever, and also enables one to shoot 10 to 20 shots at close of day *after* others have been obliged to stop by darkness.

Price of Telescope, mounted on barrel, with
    Pope rib and Pope detachable sliding
    mounts $24 00
Same without rib 19 00

To apply these mountings, it is necessary to send rifle to factory, and to give the distance from the eyeball to breech end of barrel (head of shell), when the face is in shooting position.

For other telescopes, of which we make a large variety, send for our telescope catalog.

Prices of STEVENS Ideal Rifles with "Stevens-Pope" Breech Loading Barrels

are $10.00 additional to the list price of the rifle as shown in Catalog No. 51, a copy of which will be sent on application.

J. Stevens Arms & Tool Co.,

Chicopee Falls.

Pope Dept. **Mass.**

No. 47

No. 47

Thirty-inch half-octagon No. 3 barrel. Drop-forged, and case-hardened frame; single trigger, loop lever. Varnished pistol grip stock and forearm; Swiss butt plate, or heavier "Interchangeable" butt plate similar to Schuetzen. "D" sights, with "Stevens-Pope" muzzle-loading outfit.

Weight about 10¼ lbs.

Price . $52 00

No rear slot unless ordered.

No. 49

Thirty-inch half-octagon No. 3 barrel. Drop-forged, engraved and case-hardened action; loop lever; pistol grip stock with cheek piece; stock and forearm varnished and checked. Swiss butt plate. "H" sights, with "Stevens-Pope" muzzle-loading outfit.

Weight about 10¼ lbs.

Price $63 00

No rear slot unless ordered.

No. 49

Chicopee Falls : Massachusetts : U. S. A.

With all Pope muzzle-loading barrels full instructions for loading and handling are sent out with the rifle.

CALIBRES. These barrels are made in calibres shown on page 10.

EXTRAS

Set triggers	$6 00
Extra length barrels, per inch . .	1 00
No. 4 barrels	2 00
No. 5 barrels	5 00
Octagonal barrels	2 00
Engraving to any amount, upward from	5 00
Pope Sights, Rear Wind Gauge and elevating, with interchangeable beveled Disc Globe Front . .	8 75
B Sights, Sporting Rear and Rocky Mountain Front	1 30
D Sights, Beach Combination Front, Open Rear and Vernier Peep .	4 80
E Sights, Lyman Ivory Combination Front, and Lyman Combination Rear, No. 1	4 00
Or for No. 2 Sight with Cup Disc, add 50 cents list . . .	4 50
F Sights, Globe interchangeable Front and Vernier Peep . . .	4 25
G Sights, Wind Gauge Front and Mid-Range Vernier Peep . .	7 00
H Sights, Globe interchangeable Front and Wind Gauge Vernier Peep, with adjustable Eye-cup . .	7 25
Levers, plain	1 50
Loop	2 50
Schuetzen No. 51 . . .	5 50
Schuetzen No. 54 . . .	5 50
3 finger spur	5 00
(This is also made to order for Ballard & Winchester actions)	
Changing dimensions of stock (special hand work)	5 00
Nickel plating frame lever and butt plate	2 50

23

Condensed from Stevens Catalog #50 (1902)

RIFLES—Model—Ideal "Model Range" No. 47

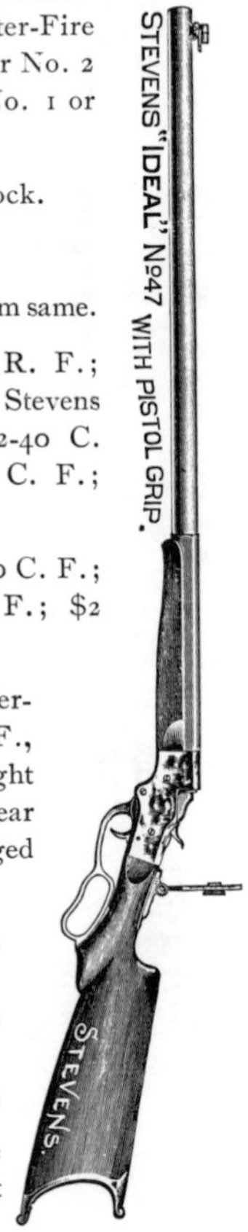

Barrel—Half octagon, standard length for Rim-Fire cartridges 26 inches. Standard length for Center-Fire cartridges 28 inches. The standard barrel is our No. 2 weight, see page 24. We will furnish our No. 1 or No. 3 barrels at regular prices.

Frame—Case hardened, and has a solid breech block.

Trigger—Single. (Double set trigger $6 extra.)

Stock—Varnished Walnut with pistol grip, forearm same.

Ammunition—.22 Short R. F.; .22 Long-Rifle R. F.; .25 Stevens R. F.; .32 Long R. F.; .25-20 Stevens C. F.; .25-21 C. F.; .32-20 C. F.; .32-40 C. F.; .32 Ideal C. F.; .38-40 C. F.; .38-55 C. F.; .44-40 C. F.

Special to order for. 27-7-45 R. F.; .22-15-60 C. F.; .25-25 C. F.; 28-30 C. F.; .32 Long C. F.; $2 extra list.

Sights—Beach combination front, open rear and Vernier peep (D Sights) see page 27. If with F., G and H Sights is furnished without rear-sight slot. If with B, D and E sights, there is a rear slot. Any deviation from this will be charged at $1 extra.

Weight—26-inch, No. 2 barrel for R.F. cartridges, 7¾ pounds.
28-inch, No. 2 barrel for C. F. cartridges, 8¼ pounds. Other lengths proportionately.

Price—Standard length of barrel, $27 00

Component Parts—See pages 34 and 35. The minimum charge for mailing component parts of this rifle is ten cents.

RIFLES—Model—Ideal "Walnut Hill"—No. 49

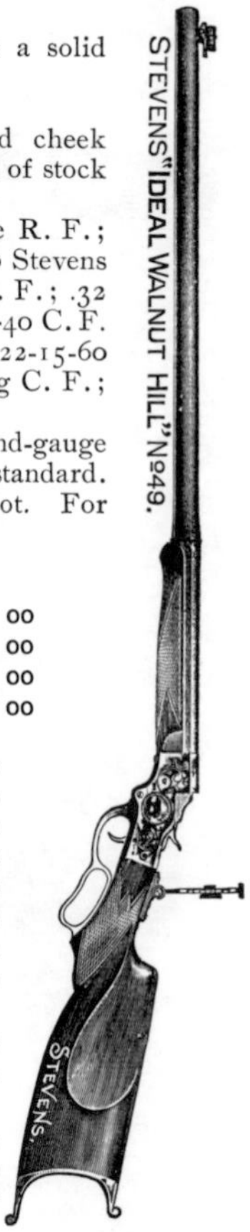

Barrel—Half octagon.
Frame—Case hardened and engraved, and has a solid breech block.
Trigger—Single.
Stock—Varnished walnut with pistol grip and cheek piece. Stock and forearm checked. Length of stock 13 inches, drop 3¼ inches.
Ammunition—.22 Short R. F.; .22 Long-Rifle R. F.; .25 Stevens R. F.; .32 Long R. F.; .25-20 Stevens C. F.; .25-21 C. F.; .32-20 C. F.; .32-40 C. F.; .32 Ideal C. F.; .38-40 C. F.; .38-55 C. F.; .44-40 C. F. Special to order for .27-7-45 R. F.; .22-15-60 C. F.; .25-25 C. F.; .28-30 C. F.; .32 Long C. F.; $2 extra list.
Sights—Globe Interchangeable Front and Wind-gauge Vernier Peep, with adjustable eye-cup are standard. With G and H sights there is no rear sight slot. For sights see page 27.
Weights and Prices—

	No. 2 Barrel	No. 3 Barrel	
28-inch barrel,	8¾ pounds,	10¼ pounds	$42 00
30-inch barrel,	9¼ pounds,	10½ pounds	43 00
With D, E or F sights (28 inch)			39 00
With D, E or F sights (30 inch)			40 00

Extra lengths over 30 and up to 34 inches, per inch $1 00
Double set triggers, extra 6 00
Selected walnut stock, extra . . . 4 00
Extra selected walnut stock, extra . . 7 00
Schuetzen butt plate, extra 2 00
Schuetzen lever, extra 4 00
Palm Rest, extra 5 00
False Muzzle and Bullet Starter, extra 15 00
For further extras see pages 34 and 35.

A 4-inch group of 10 consecutive shots is guaranteed at 200 yards with this rifle, using .28-30. .32-40 or .38-55 cartridges.

Extra interchangeable barrel parts complete, up to 30 inches in length, Nos. 2 or 3 barrels, plain walnut fore-end, checked with H front sight, $14. 32-inch barrel parts, $16.

RIFLES—Model—Ideal "Schuetzen"—No. 51

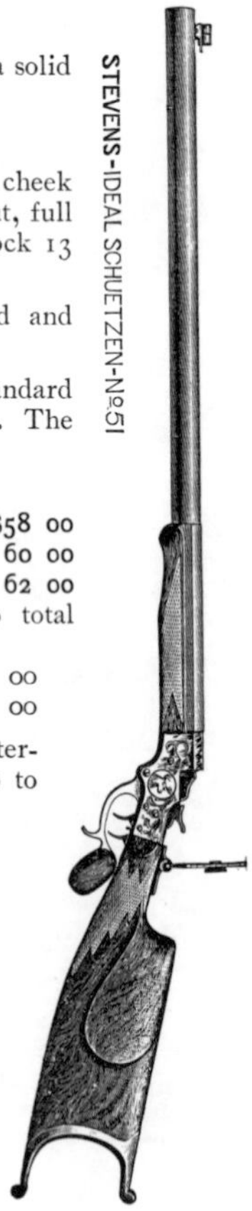

Barrel—Half Octagon.

Frame—Case hardened and engraved, and with a solid breech block.

Trigger—Double Set.

Stock—Extra fancy Swiss pattern stock with cheek piece. Stock and forearm of selected walnut, full checked and highly finished. Length of stock 13 inches, drop 3¼ inches.

Ammunition—Made for cartridges as described and illustrated on pages devoted to ammunition.

Sights—Our "H" Sights (see page 27) are standard and will be so fitted unless otherwise ordered. The barrel is without rear slot.

Weights and Prices—
With 30-in. barrel, wgt. 12 lbs., G or H sights, $58 00
" 32 " " " 12½ " " " 60 00
" 34 " " " 12¾ " " " 62 00
For large Schuetzen frame add ½ pound to total weight of rifle.
Palm Rest, extra $5 00
False Muzzle and Bullet Starter, extra 15 00

Extra interchangeable barrel parts, rim or center-fire complete with forearm and sight, up to 30 inches in length, with
H front sight, fancy fore-end, checked, No 3 barrel . $16 00
H front sight, fancy fore-end, checked, No. 4 barrel 18 00
H front sight, fancy fore-end, checked, No. 5 barrel 21 00
Different front sights at the extra difference in list.
Spirit level in rear slot (extra), . 1 00

RIFLES—Model—Ideal "Schuetzen Jr." No. 52

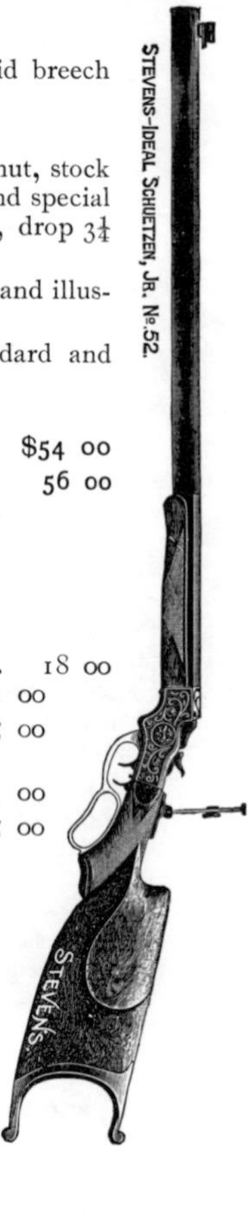

Barrel—Half octagon.

Frame—Case hardened and engraved with a solid breech block.

Trigger—Double Set.

Stock—Varnished pistol grip-stock of fancy walnut, stock and forearm nicely checked, cheek piece and special heavy butt plate. Length of stock 13 inches, drop 3¼ inches.

Ammunition—Made for cartridges as described and illustrated on pages devoted to ammunition.

Sights—Our "H" Sights (see page 27) are standard and will be so fitted unless otherwise ordered.

Weights and Prices—With 30-inch barrel, weight 11 pounds $54 00
With 32-inch barrel, weight 11½ pounds . . 56 00
With large Schuetzen Frame add ½ pound to total weight of Rifle.
Extra interchangeable barrel parts complete up to 30 inches in length. fancy forearm checked, with globe front sight, interchangeable disc 18 00
With wind-gauge front sight . . . $21 00
False Muzzle and Bullet Starter, extra . 15 00
Extra length of barrel over 30 inches, per inch 1 00
Palm Rest, extra 5 00

For further description of sights see page 27.

For further extras see pages 34 and 35.

For "Stevens-Pope" Equipment see pages 36 to 50.

Component Parts—See pages 34 and 35. The minimum charge for mailing component parts of this rifle is ten cents.

Every rifle before being shipped is carefully tested from a machine rest at 200 yards,

THE STEVENS' CRACK SHOT TAKE DOWN RIFLE FOR $2.95.

FOR $2.95 we furnish you the STEVENS' CRACK SHOT RIFLE which is well worth $5.00. This is a strictly American made rifle, smooth, well bored and well rifled, all the working parts are of steel and interchangeable, and if any part breaks we can furnish you another part to replace it. Why buy a hand made Flobert, which no house can guarantee, when you can buy the CRACK SHOT, which is guaranteed and made by one of the best rifle makers in the country. It will pay you in the end to buy a CRACK SHOT RIFLE. This rifle has in addition to its many good features, a safety catch on the frame behind the hammer, so that the rifle can't be accidentally discharged by children, or any one else, until you press the safety catch back with your thumb. This feature has never appeared on any cheap rifle before and is a great point in favor of the STEVENS CRACK SHOT RIFLE.

The CRACK SHOT RIFLE will shoot accurately and is chambered to take a BB cap or 22-caliber short cartridge. We recommend using only 22-caliber short cartridges in it. It has a blued steel barrel, solid breech block, as shown in illustration, and can easily be taken apart by unscrewing the screw in front of the guard. We guarantee the stock to be of the best American walnut. The CRACK SHOT has 20-inch barrel and weighs about 4 lbs.

No. 6R666 Our special price......................................$2.95

Stevens' Favorite Rifle, Detachable Barrel, $5.00

STEVENS' ENTIRE LINE will be found in this catalogue at prices lower than can be had from any other house. OUR PRICES ON STEVENS' RIFLES are for the highest grade tested goods and our prices are based on the actual cost to produce, with but our one small profit added.

THE FAVORITE.   **$5.00**

Is guaranteed as well finished and rifled a barrel as found in the most costly rifles. Entirely new model. The barrel is held to stock by a set screw, and easily separated or put together. Rifling and quality of barrel same as the higher cost rifle. Case hardened frame, walnut stock, finely finished, warranted accurate, all rim fire, the 22-caliber, using long or short, the 25-caliber using 25-caliber Stevens' rim fire and the 32-caliber using 32-caliber long or short rim fire cartridges; 22-inch barrel; weight, 4½ lbs.

No. 6R706 25-caliber rim fire, with open sights. Our price..$5.00
No. 6R707 32-caliber, with open sights. Our special price....... 5.00
No. 6R708 22-caliber rim fire, with open sights. Our price.,.. 5.00
Lyman's Combination Rear and Ivory Bead Front Sights may be fitted to the Favorite at $3.25 extra, to pay for sights and fitting.

Stevens' New Pocket Rifle, $7.50 and $8.44.

A Fine Target or Squirrel Rifle. Good for 100 yards. Latest model, 22-caliber, rim fire, shoots short cartridge or BB caps.

No. 6R716 12-inch barrel, weight, 2¼ lbs. Our special price.....$7.50
No. 6R717 15-inch barrel, weight, 2½ lbs. Our special price.... 8.44

Stevens' Latest Ideal Rifle, 7 to 7¼ Pounds. $8.25

This rifle meets the demand for a reliable and accurate rifle at a moderate price. It is recommended by us and fully guaranteed by the maker. Half octagon barrel, oiled walnut stock and forearm, rifle butt, sporting rear and Rocky Mountain front sights, 7 to 7¼ lbs.

No. 6R718 22-caliber, 24-inch barrel. Weight, 7 pounds. Price.....$8.25
No. 6R719 25-caliber, Stevens rim fire. 24-inch barrel. Price...... 8.25
No. 6R720 25-20-caliber, Stevens center fire, 26-inch barrel. Price.. 8.25
No. 6R721 32-40-caliber, center fire. 26-inch barrel. Price......... 8.25
Extra length of barrel to special order 75 cents per inch. Lyman's Combination Rear Sight, extra $2.20. Lyman's Ivory Bead Front Sight, extra, 70 cents. For fitting sights, extra, 25 cents.

The Stevens' New Model Tip Up Pistol.

22-caliber only. 3½-inch barrel. Stevens' Single Shot Pistol. Tip up barrel, nickel plated finish, 3½-inch barrel, 22-caliber only, rim fire. No better material put in rifles. A fine target pistol. Rifled barrel and well made throughout.

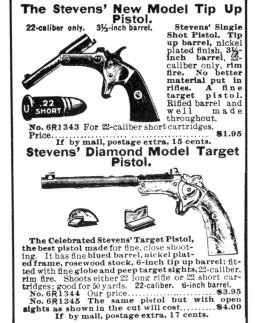

No. 6R1343 For 22-caliber short cartridges. Price.......................$1.95
If by mail, postage extra, 15 cents.

Stevens' Diamond Model Target Pistol.

The Celebrated Stevens' Target Pistol, the best pistol made for fine, close shooting. It has fine blued barrel, nickel plated frame, rosewood stock, 6-inch tip up barrel; fitted with fine globe and peep target sights, 22-caliber, rim fire. Shoots either 22 long rifle or 22 short cartridges; good for 50 yards. 22-caliber. 6-inch barrel.
No. 6R1344 Our price...........................$3.95
No. 6R1345 The same pistol but with open sights as shown in the cut will cost..........$4.00
If by mail, postage extra, 17 cents.

SAVAGE HAMMERLESS REPEATING RIFLES. $21.50

The Savage is a hammerless rifle made on scientific principles and is one of the most powerful shooting rifles yet produced. A steel boiler plate ⅜-inch thick has been perforated by a bullet—caliber .303—fired from a Savage rifle at a distance of thirty feet and it will penetrate 35 pine boards ⅜-inch thick.

No. 6R882 Savage Hammerless Repeating Rifle. Simple in construction, light in weight. Ejects shells from side. Length of barrel, 26 inches; weight, 8 pounds. Magazine holds five cartridges.

VELOCITY 2,000 FEET PER SECOND. Powerful Shooters.

Velocity, 2,000 feet per second. Our special price, with octagon barrel.....................$21.50
No. 6R883 Savage Repeating Rifle, for 30-30 caliber smokeless cartridges. 26-inch octagon barrels. Weight, about 8 pounds. Price............... 21.50

WE CAN FURNISH ALL KINDS OF CARTRIDGES NOT ON THIS LIST AT LOWEST MARKET PRICES.

Cartridges can be shipped with other goods by express or freight, but cartridges cannot be sent by mail, because they are explosive. Prices subject to change without notice. Our ammunition is always fresh. We sell large quantities, consequently have no old stock on hand.

EXPLOSIVES CANNOT BE SENT BY MAIL.   **RIM FIRE CARTRIDGES.**   **EXPLOSIVES CANNOT BE SENT BY MAIL.**

BB	CBC	.22 SHORT	.22 LONG	.22 LONG RIFLE	.22 WINCHESTER RIM FIRE
No. 6R2331	No. 6R2332	No. 6R2336	No. 6R2338	No. 6R2340	No. 6R2344
.22 Ex. LONG	.25 STEVENS	.?0 SHORT	.30 LONG	.32 Ex. SHORT	.32 SHORT	.32 LONG
No. 6R2342	No. 6R2346	No. 6R2348	No. 6R2350	No. 6R2351	No. 6R2352	No. 6R2353

STEVENS-POPE SPECIALTIES

ON APRIL 1, 1901, we purchased the tools and special machinery belonging to Mr. H. M. Pope, then of Hartford, Conn., and engaged his services to continue the manufacture of his barrel, which, from that time, has been known as the "Stevens-Pope."

Mr. Pope has built up a national reputation as a manufacturer of high-grade rifle barrels, and, combining the best features that he was in possession of together with ours, we have been able to produce the most perfect rifle barrels that it is possible to make.

The vast superiority of this barrel was shown on July 11, 1903, at Bisley, England, when the American team won the Palma trophy with a score of 1570, their nearest competitor being the English team with a score of 1555. In cabling with reference to the victory, our representatives abroad sent the following to *Shooting and Fishing*, of New York City:

"The truth of the matter is we owe the victory mainly to the barrels and ammunition used. The former were made by the J. Stevens Arms and Tool Company, of Chicopee Falls, Mass."

(Signed)   Lieut. A. S. Jones,.
Secretary National Rifle Association.

In the United States, the 50-shot record of 467 points out of 500 on the Standard American target, off-hand, at 200 yards, is held by our Mr. H. M. Pope, and was made at Springfield, Mass., on March 21, 1903.

The 100-shot record of 908 points out of 1000, at 200 yards, is also held by Mr. Pope, and was made January 1, 1903, at Springfield, Mass.

Mr. Pope uses in his shooting a .32-40 Stevens rifle fitted with a Stevens-Pope barrel. His best 10-shot scores for one year are as follows:

January	1, 1903,	96	March 21, 1903,		96
January	10, "	97	May	9, "	96
February	6, "	96	May	9, "	97
February	14, "	96	July	25, "	96
February	21, "	96			
March	21, "	97	Total,		963

PISTOLS—Stevens "Gould," No. 37

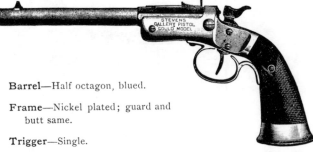

Barrel—Half octagon, blued.

Frame—Nickel plated; guard and butt same.

Trigger—Single.

Stock—Walnut, finely checked.

Ammunition—.22 Long-Rifle R. F.; .25 Stevens R. F. Special to order for .22-7-45 R. F.; .32 Long R. F.; .38 Long Colt C. C. $2.00 extra list.

Sights—Sporting rear and bead front.

Weight—With 10-inch barrel about 1¾ pounds. With 12-inch barrel about 2½ pounds.

Price—With 10-inch barrel **$15** 00
     With 12-inch barrel 16 00
     Pearl Handles, extra 7 50
     Engraving,   " 5 00
     Gold Plating,   " 10 00
     Silver Plating,   " 4 00

Component Parts—See page 46. The minimum charge for mailing component parts of this pistol is ten cents.

PISTOLS—Stevens "Lord," No. 36

STEVENS-LORD MODEL PISTOL.

Barrel—Half octagon, blued. Standard length, 10 inches.

Frame—Nickel plated; spur guard and butt same.

Trigger—Single.

Stock—Walnut, finely checked, with heavy butt.

Ammunition—.22 Long-Rifle R. F.; .25 Stevens R. F. Made to order for .22-7-45 R. F.; .32 Long R. F.; .38 Long Colt C. F. $2.00 extra list.

Sights—Sporting rear and bead front.

Weight—With 10-inch barrel, 2¾ pounds.

Price **$16 50**
     Pearl Handles, extra 10 00
     Engraving,   " 5 00
     Gold Plating,   " 10 00
     Silver Plating,   " 4 00

Component Parts—See page 46. The minimum charge for mailing component parts of this pistol is ten cents.

Stevens Gallery Pistols have done the finest shooting known, and for years have been the standard of accuracy in the leading galleries of the world. Their accuracy with the .22 Long-Rifle cartridge is beyond what experts thought it was possible to secure with a pistol. With the Long-Rifle cartridge they are capable of work at 100 yards almost equal to a rifle.

PISTOLS—Stevens "Conlin," No. 38

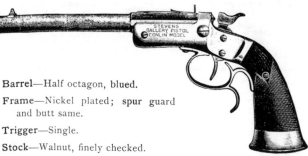

Barrel—Half octagon, blued.

Frame—Nickel plated; spur guard and butt same.

Trigger—Single.

Stock—Walnut, finely checked.

Ammunition—.22 Long-Rifle R. F.; .25 Stevens R. F. Special to order for .22-7-45 R. F.; .32 Long R. F.; .38 Long Colt C. F. $2.00 extra list.

Sights—Sporting rear and bead front.

Weight—With 10-inch barrel about 1¾ pounds. With 12-inch barrel about 2½ pounds.

Price—With 10-inch barrel **$15 00**
     With 12-inch barrel 16 00
     Pearl Handles, extra 7 50
     Engraving,   " 5 00
     Gold Plating,   " 10 00
     Silver Plating,   " 4 00

Component Parts—See page 46. The minimum charge for mailing component parts of this pistol is ten cents.

This pistol is a duplicate of our "Gould Model" (No. 37), with the exception of the guard, this model having the spur guard, which is preferred by many shooters.

Condensed from Stevens Catalog #51 (1904)

STEVENS
RIFLES
THE BULL'S-EYE KIND

This catalog presents
our full line of
Firearms
and Accessories
including

STEVENS
SHOTGUNS
CLOSE SHOOTING
SELF POINTING

REPEATING SHOTGUNS
Double Barrel Hammer and Hammerless Shotguns
Single Barrel Shotguns
HIGH POWER and .22-Caliber REPEATING RIFLES
High Grade Target Rifles
Telescope Sights
SINGLE SHOT RIFLES
Pistols and Pocket Rifles
Accessories

STEVENS Rifles are made to suit the requirements of the most exacting shooter.

Various models are illustrated embodying the most desirable features for field and off-hand or rest target shooting.

Variations from illustrated models may be made in accord with prices given as extras or component parts.

STEVENS Ideal Rifles are universally recognized as the finest type of rifle-making and have for years continued to hold the highest awards for both indoor and outdoor target shooting in all countries.

The WORLD'S RECORD for indoor shooting at 25 yards off-hand was made with a STEVENS rifle.

The rifling of STEVENS barrels has never been equaled.

STEVENS Favorite Rifle continues to hold first place as the most popular and most accurate low-priced rifle that has ever been produced.

The later models have each in their turn established a new standard in the art of small rifle making.

The "Visible Loading" Rifle is the most accurate .22 caliber Repeating Rifle made.

STEVENS "High Power" Rifles are the most accurate that have ever been produced for Big Game Hunting.

Announcement

IN making this catalog our aim has been to produce a book that will concisely show our large line of sporting firearms with illustrations and specifications of each model. Lengthy descriptions and much detailed information are therefore eliminated.

The line of STEVENS Firearms has been largely increased during the last few years. Several new models of great merit have been offered to the trade and have already become popular. The highest grade of mechanical skill and the best materials are used in the manufacture of all STEVENS Firearms.

Our long experience in this business and our policy of guaranteeing our product will assure to the public a continuance of that satisfaction which it has always had from the use of STEVENS Firearms.

Condensed from Stevens Catalog #53 (1911-12)

STEVENS—Single Shot Rifles

"Ideal"

No. 49 "WALNUT HILL" Take-Down List Price **$46.25**

BARREL — No. 3; half octagon; length 28".

FRAME — Drop forged; casehardened; engraved.

ACTION — No. 3 loop lever; AUTOMATIC EJECTOR IN REGULAR .22-CALIBER ONLY; plain extractor in other calibers; drop-down breech block.

STOCK — Walnut, checkered; pistol grip; cheek piece; No. 3 heavy Swiss butt plate; length 13", drop 3¼"; walnut fore-end, checkered.

SIGHTS — No. 210 Globe interchangeable front and No. 104 Wind-Gauge Vernier peep with combination eye cup (H sights).
See page 52 for additional sights.
See page 49 for telescope sights.

WEIGHT — With No. 3, 28" barrel about 10 lbs.

AMMUNITION —
Rim fire — .22 short, .22 long rifle, .22 W. R. F., .25 Stevens, .32 long.
Center fire — .22/15/60, .25/20 Stevens, .25/21, .25/25, .28/30/120, .32 long, .32/20, .32 Ideal, .32/40.

STEVENS—Single Shot Rifles

"Ideal"

No. 51 "SCHUETZEN" Take-Down List Price **$61.00**

BARREL — No. 3; half octagon; length 30".

FRAME — Drop forged; casehardened; engraved.

ACTION — Double set triggers; No. 5 Schuetzen lever; AUTOMATIC EJECTOR IN REGULAR .22-CALIBER ONLY; plain extractor in other calibers; drop-down breech block.

STOCK — Fancy walnut, Swiss pattern, finely checkered; cheek piece; No. 4 Schuetzen butt plate; length 13", drop 3¼"; fancy walnut fore-end, finely checkered.

SIGHTS — No. 210 Globe interchangeable front and No. 104 Wind-Gauge Vernier peep with combination eye cup (H sights).
See page 52 for additional sights.
See page 49 for telescope sights.

WEIGHT — With No. 3, 30" barrel about 11¼ lbs.

AMMUNITION —
Rim fire — .22 short, .22 long rifle, .22 W. R. F., .25 Stevens, .32 long.
Center fire — .22/15/60, .25/20 Stevens, .25/21, .25/25, .28/30/120, .32 long, .32/20, .32 Ideal, .32/40.

27

General Catalog No. 53

J. STEVENS ARMS & TOOL COMPANY
Largest Makers Sporting Firearms in the World
CHICOPEE FALLS, MASSACHUSETTS, U. S. A.
Export Office, 24 State St., New York City, U. S. A.   London Office, 15 Grape St., Shaftesbury Ave., W. C.

Condensed from Stevens Catalog #53 (1911-12)

STEVENS — Single Shot Rifles

"Ideal"

No. 52   **"SCHUETZEN JR."**   Take-Down   List Price **$63.50**

BARREL — No. 3; half octagon; length 30".

FRAME — Drop forged; casehardened; engraved.

ACTION — Double set triggers; No. 7 three finger spur lever; AUTOMATIC EJECTOR IN .22-CALIBER ONLY; plain extractor in other calibers; drop-down breech block.

STOCK — Fancy walnut, checkered; pistol grip; cheek piece; No. 4 Schuetzen butt plate; length 13", drop 3¼"; fancy walnut fore-end, checkered.

SIGHTS — No. 210 Globe interchangeable front and No. 104 Wind-Gauge Vernier peep with combination eye cup (H sights).
See page 52 for additional sights.
See page 49 for telescope sights.

WEIGHT — With No. 3, 30" barrel about 11½ lbs.

AMMUNITION —
Rim fire — .22 short, .22 long rifle, .22 W. R. F., .25 Stevens, .32 long.
Center fire — .22/15/60, .25/20 Stevens, .25/21, .25/25, .28/30/120, .32 long, .32/20, .32 Idea , .32/40.

STEVENS — Single Shot Rifles

"Ideal"

No. 54   **"SCHUETZEN SPECIAL"**   Take-Down   List Price **$77.00**

BARREL — No. 3; half octagon; length 30".

FRAME — Drop forged; casehardened; handsomely engraved.

ACTION — Double set triggers; No. 6 Schuetzen Special lever; AUTOMATIC EJECTOR IN REGULAR .22-CALIBER ONLY; plain extractor in other calibers; drop-down breech block.

STOCK — Extra fancy walnut, finely checkered; cheek piece; No. 5 Schuetzen Special butt plate; length 13", drop 3¼"; extra fancy walnut fore-end, finely checkered; palm rest.

SIGHTS — No. 210 Globe interchangeable front and No. 104 Wind-Gauge Vernier peep with combination eye cup (H sights).
See page 52 for additional sights.
See page 49 for telescope sights.

WEIGHT — With No. 3, 30" barrel about 11 lbs. 9 oz.

AMMUNITION —
Rim fire — .22 short, .22 long rifle, .22 W. R. F., .25 Stevens, .32 long.
Center fire — .22/15/60, .25/20 Stevens, .25/21, .25/25, .28/30/120, .32 long, .32/20, .32 Ideal, .32/40.

J. STEVENS ARMS & TOOL COMPANY
"The Factory of Precision"
CHICOPEE FALLS, MASS., U. S. A.

Export Office: London Office:
24 State St., NEW YORK CITY, U.S.A.   15 Grape St., Shaftesbury Ave., LONDON, W. C.

RIFLE CATALOG

Condensed from Stevens Catalog #54 (1914)

High Power Repeating Rifles
22 Caliber Repeating Rifles
High Grade Target Rifles
Pistols and Pocket Rifles
Single Shot Rifles
Rifle Accessories

STEVENS Single Shot Rifles
"IDEAL"

No. 044½   "ENGLISH" MODEL   Take-Down   Weight about 6½ lbs.   List Price $12.00

Barrel   Half octagon; extreme tapered; length, rim fire 24 inches, center fire 26 inches.   (Not furnished longer than 26 inches or with any other style barrel.)

Frame   Drop forged; casehardened.

Action   No. 1 plain lever; AUTOMATIC EJECTOR IN REGULAR .22-CALIBER ONLY; plain extractor in other calibers; drop-down breech block.

Stock   Walnut; shotgun butt with rubber butt plate; length 13½ inches, drop 2½ inches; walnut fore-end.

Sights   No. 203 Rocky Mountain front and No. 112 sporting rear (B sights).   (No allowance made for regular sights when furnished with special sights.)

Ammunition   Rim fire — .22 short, .22 long rifle, .25 Stevens, .32 long.
Center fire — .25/20 Stevens, .32/20.

Made to order at $2.00 extra list for .22 W. R. F., .22/15/60, .25/21, .25/25, .28/30/120.

STEVENS Single Shot Rifles
"IDEAL"

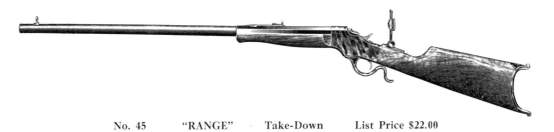

No. 45   "RANGE"   Take-Down   List Price $22.00

Barrel   No. 2; half octagon; length 28 inches.

Frame   Drop forged; casehardened.

Action   No. 1 plain lever; AUTOMATIC EJECTOR IN REGULAR .22-CALIBER ONLY; plain extractor in other calibers; drop-down breech block.

Stock   Walnut; No. 2 Swiss butt plate; length 13 inches, drop 3¼ inches; walnut fore-end.

Sights   No. 205 Beach combination front, No. 112 sporting rear and No. 102 Vernier peep (C sights).

Weight   With No. 2, 28" barrel about 8 lbs. 4 oz.

Ammunition   Rim fire — .22 short, .22 long rifle, .22 W. R. F., .25 Stevens, .32 long.
Center fire — .22/15/60, .25/20 Stevens, .25/21, .25/25, .28/30/120, .32 long, .32/20, .32 Ideal, .32/40.

Condensed from Stevens Catalog #54 (1914)

STEVENS   RIFLES

STEVENS Single Shot Rifles
"IDEAL"

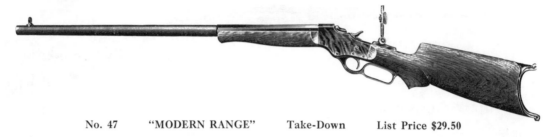

No. 47   "MODERN RANGE"   Take-Down   List Price $29.50

Barrel No. 3; half octagon; length 28 inches.

Frame Drop forged; casehardened.

Action No. 3 loop lever; AUTOMATIC EJECTOR IN REGULAR .22-CALIBER ONLY; plain extractor in other calibers; drop-down breech block.

Stock Walnut; pistol grip; No. 3 Swiss butt plate; length 13 inches, drop 3¼ inches; walnut fore-end.

Sights No. 205 Beach combination front and No. 102 Vernier peep (D sights).

Weight With No. 2, 28" barrel about 8 lbs. 10 oz.

Ammunition Rim fire — .22 short, .22 long rifle, .22 W. R. F., .25 Stevens, .32 long.

    Center fire — .22/15/60, .25/20 Stevens, .25/21, .25/25, .28/30/120, 32 long .32/20, .32 Ideal, .32/40.

STEVENS Single Shot Rifles
"IDEAL"

No. 49   "WALNUT HILL"   Take-Down   List Price $46.25

Barrel No. 3; half octagon; length 28 inches.

Frame Drop forged; casehardened; engraved.

Action No. 3 loop lever; AUTOMATIC EJECTOR IN REGULAR .22-CALIBER ONLY; plain extractor in other calibers; drop-down breech block.

Stock Walnut, checkered; pistol grip; cheek piece; No. 3 heavy Swiss butt plate; length 13 inches, drop 3¼ inches; walnut fore-end, checkered.

Sights No. 210 Globe interchangeable front and No. 104 Wind-Gauge Vernier peep with combination eye cup (H sights).

Weight With No. 3, 28" barrel about 10 lbs.

Ammunition Rim fire — .22 short, .22 long rifle, .22 W. R. F., .25 Stevens, .32 long.

    Center fire — .22/15/60, .25/20 Stevens, .25/21, .25/25, .28/30/120, .32 long, .32/20, .32 Ideal, .32/40.

No. 44 "IDEAL"

Chambered for .22 long rifle, .25 rim-fire and .32 long rim-fire cartridges.

Barrel 26 inch round. Tapered.

Action Single shot. Stevens heavy type drop finger lever, drop breech block, automatic ejector in .22 caliber. Plain extractor in other calibers.

Frame Case hardened, tang tapped for peep sight. Take-down with continuous thread set screw lock.

Stock American Walnut stock and forearm. Stock length 13 inches, drop 3 inches, steel rifle butt plate.

Sights No. 203 German silver knife blade front and No. 112 sporting rear with elevation.

Weight 7 lbs. Length over all 41 inches

For over twenty years Stevens "Ideal" has been used by experts in making world's records. That Stevens rifles are undeniably the most accurate made is proven by the overwhelming number of record targets to their credit and the uniform success that attends their use at competitive matches.

The action of Stevens No. 44 Ideal is operated as follows: The downward and forward movement of the finger lever unlocks breech block and draws it downward below line of bore. Final forward stroke of finger lever operates automatic ejector for .22 caliber cartridges and extractor on large calibers. Closing stroke of finger lever seats loaded cartridge in chamber and places hammer in safe half-cocked position. If desired, barrel can be removed from frame as follows: Take out set screw on under side of frame, open finger lever to withdraw extractor from barrel, unscrew barrel from frame.

The stock and forearm dimensions and special rifle butt plate were designed to make this rifle particularly adapted for extremely accurate off-hand shooting. The long heavy barrel assists in steady holding, the action has a remarkably smooth trigger pull, in fact, every feature of this rifle was carefully worked out through years of expert study to produce an accurate combined hunting and target rifle.

No. 414 "ARMORY"

Chambered for .22 long rifle cartridges. Also chambered and rifled for .22 short cartridges on special order.

Barrel 26 inch round. Tapered.

Action Single shot. Stevens heavy type drop finger lever-drop breech block, automatic ejector.

Frame Case hardened. Take-down with continuous thread set screw lock.

Sights German silver knife blade bead front. Special Stevens receiver peep sight with windage and elevation adjustments.

Stock American Walnut. Shotgun butt with steel butt plate—special long Walnut forearm with large hand hold. Fitted with sling strap loops.

Weight about 8 lbs. Length over all 41 inches.

The Stevens 414 Armory Model was designed for firing from the standard military positions incorporated in matches of the National Rifle Association. The barrel and action are the same as supplied on the No. 44 Ideal rifle and are unexcelled for careful workmanship and accuracy. The stock with shotgun butt and forearm with large hand hold were carefully proportioned for use in firing with sling strap.

Several world's indoor records have been made with this rifle and for the past twenty years it has many times been the choice of experts on American teams in International matches.

STEVENS REPEATING RIFLES

No. 75 "HAMMERLESS"

1929 CATALOGUE No. 57

Barrel   24 inch round tapered.

Action   Sliding forearm, side ejection. Magazine holds fifteen .22 long rifle, seventeen .22 long, or twenty .22 short cartridges.

Frame   Two part take-down with no loose parts.

Sights   Lyman Ivory Bead front and sporting rear with elevation adjustment.

Stock   Selected walnut. Steel butt plate.

Weight 5¼ lbs. Length over all 40½ inches.

Complying with the demands of today, Stevens has produced a new hammerless repeating rifle with a simple two part take-down (no loose parts) unusually rugged, with extremely short movement of breech block, side ejection, convenient safety behind trigger and large capacity tubular magazine.

NEW SAFETY DEVICE

Designed to shoot the modern .22 caliber rim fire ammunition, a special safety feature is an action bar lock of new design which prevents the action from opening by back pressure until forearm is pushed forward after the hammer has fallen. *This device does not function unless back pressure is exerted on forearm when firing.*

Trigger assembly, hammer and lifter assembly, are on floor plate of stock receiver. Barrel receiver, closed at both sides and top, contain bolt assembly in one piece which securely locks in place when rifle is taken down.

The details of finish, special sights, etc., excels other comparative rifles and gives exceptional value at a moderate price.

No. 70 "VISIBLE LOADER"
Chambered for .22 long rifle cartridges

Barrel   22 inch round.

Action   Slide forearm repeater, visible loading. Magazine holds eleven .22 long rifle, or thirteen .22 long or fifteen .22 short R. F. cartridges.

Frame   Solid. Blued.

Sights   Lyman Ivory Bead front and flat top sporting rear with elevation adjustments.

Stock   Walnut stock. Steel butt plate.

Weight 4½ lbs. Length over all 36 inches.

The Stevens "Visible Loader" is a hammer type repeater, so named because the simple, sturdy mechanism which extracts and ejects the fired cartridge case, also raises a loaded cartridge from magazine to barrel while action is open, allowing the shooter to see the loading operation and *know* when rifle is loaded and *know* when it is empty.

This rifle, with recent improvements, is one of the most popular on the market. It is particularly adaptable for hunting purposes because it places a number of shots at the shooter's command without reloading and is one of the safest repeaters made for a man or boy to carry in the field.

No. 26 "CRACK SHOT"

No. 26   Chambered for .22 long rifle and .32 long rim-fire cartridges.

No. 26½   Smooth bore.   Chambered for .22 caliber and .32 caliber *shot* cartridges.

Barrel   20 inch round.   Tapered.

Action   Single shot, lever action drop breech block, positive extractor.

Frame   Take-down.   Blued finish.

Sights   German silver knife blade front.   Flat top open rear.

Stock   Oval shaped Walnut finish stock with steel butt plate.

Weight 3¼ lbs.   Length over all 34 inches.

The Stevens "Crack Shot" provides the popular lever action type of rifle at a low price which makes it particularly desirable to boys. By the forward and downward stroke of finger lever the breech block is drawn downward below line of bore and a positive extractor withdraws the empty shell. Closing of finger lever locks breech block against cartridge and places hammer in safe half-cocked position.

No. 14½ "LITTLE SCOUT"

Chambered for .22 long rifle cartridges.

Barrel   20 inch round.   Tapered.

Action   Single shot, .22 caliber.   Thumb operated drop breech block, positive extractor.

Frame   Take-down.   Case hardened.

Sights   German silver knife blade front.   Flat top open rear.

Stock   Oval shaped Walnut finish stock with steel butt plate.

Weight 2¾ lbs.   Length over all 34 inches.

The Stevens "Little Scout" is the ideal boys' rifle. The simplicity and durability of the action insures safe and positive operation. To load, the hammer is placed in half-cocked position. Breech block is moved downward by thumb lever below line of bore. After cartridge is inserted in chamber, breech block is moved upward by thumb lever, closing action. When hammer falls against firing pin, forward shoulder on hammer has passed under breech block positively locking action.

No. 11 "STEVENS JUNIOR"

Chambered for .22 long rifle cartridges.

Barrel   20 inch round.   Tapered.

Action   Single shot, .22 caliber.   Thumb operated drop breech block, positive extractor.

Frame   Take-down.   Steel frame inserted in one piece stock.

Sights   German silver knife blade front and flat top open rear sight.

Stock   One piece stock and forearm, Walnut finish.

Weight 2¾ lbs.   Length over all 34 inches.

To meet the demand for a rifle with a safe, positive action and accurately rifled barrel the Stevens "Junior" was designed to give those essentials in an extremely low priced arm. The action and barrel are similar to those of the No. 14½ "Little Scout" rifle. The butt stock and forearm are combined in a rigid one piece stock that gives the rifle excellent balance and fine appearance. The arm can be taken down by removing assembly screw.

STEVENS

RIFLES SHOTGUNS PISTOLS
AND
ACCESSORIES

STEVENS SINGLE SHOT RIFLES

"FAVORITE"

No. 27 Full Octagon barrel, chambered for .22 long rifle, .25 rim-fire, or .32 long rim-fire cartridges.

No. 17 Round barrel, chambered for .22 long rifle, .25 rim-fire or .32 long rim-fire cartridges.

No. 20 Smooth bore round barrel, plain extractor only. Chambered for .22 and .32 shot cartridges.

Barrel   24 inches

Action   Single shot—Stevens drop block lever action automatic ejector in .22 caliber—plain extractor in other calibers.

Frame   Blued. Take-down.

Stock   Walnut stock and forearm, shotgun style butt, rubber butt plate.

Sights   Lyman Ivory Bead front and sporting rear sight with elevation. No. 20 fitted with shotgun front sight only.

   Weight 4½ lbs.   Length over all 38 inches.

The action of the Stevens Favorite is a powerful lever type, the downward and forward movement of lever draws the breech block downward below line of bore and operates ejector. After loaded cartridge is placed in chamber of rifle the action is closed and locked by lever and hammer is left in safe half-cocked position. A simple take-down screw allows barrel to be withdrawn from frame for cleaning and transportation.

The stock and forearm are of American walnut and are suitable dimensions for men.   The rifle is regularly equipped with a flat top sporting rear sight with elevation adjustments and German silver knife blade front sight.

"MARKSMAN"

Chambered for .22 long rifle, .25 rim-fire and .32 long rim-fire cartridges.

Barrel   22 inch round.

Action   Single shot. Plain lever barrel tip-up solid frame, positive extractor.

Frame   Take-down.   Blued finish.

Sights   German silver knife blade front and sporting rear sight with elevation.

Stock   American Walnut forearm and stock. Full oval shaped stock with rubber butt plate.

   Weight 4 lbs.   Length over all 36 inches.

The action of the Model 12 "Marksman" is one of the strongest and safest designs. The forward and downward movement of finger lever cams breech of barrel upward to a point where line of bore is above top of receiver. A positive extractor withdraws fired cartridge case. Closing movement of finger lever locks barrel and action and places hammer in safe half-cocked position. The solid breech of frame behind head of cartridge makes the action unusually strong and safe. A simple take-down screw allows withdrawal of barrel from action for cleaning and transportation.

The stock is of full dimensions suitable for adults as well as boys, oval shaped and finely finished.   Forearm well proportioned and carefully fitted.

Stevens "Crack Shot"

No. 26   Made for .22 long rifle and .32 long rim-fire cartridges.

No. 26½   Smooth bore.   Made for .22 caliber and .32 caliber shot cartridges.

Barrel   20 inch round.

Action   Single shot—lever action drop breech block—positive extractor.

Frame   Take-down. Blued finish.

Sights   Bright metal knife blade front. Flat top open rear.

Stock   Oval shaped butt stock with steel butt plate.

Weight 3¼ lbs.   Length over all 34 inches.

The Stevens "Crack Shot" provides the popular lever action type of rifle at a low price which makes it particularly desirable to boys. By the forward and downward stroke of finger lever the breech block is drawn downward below line of bore and a positive extractor withdraws fired cartridge. Closing of finger lever locks breech block against cartridge and places hammer in safe half-cocked position.

A full oval shaped butt stock with steel butt plate and finely polished blued barrel and receiver makes this rifle particularly attractive in appearance. With its sturdy construction and supreme accuracy it will give years of satisfactory service.

One in paper carton.   Parcel post weight 5 lbs.   Twenty-five in a case.   Weight 125 lbs.

When ordering specify model number and caliber.

Stevens Single Shot Rifles

Stevens "Little Scout" No. 14¹⁄₂

Made for .22 long rifle cartridges.

Barrel   20 inch round.

Action   Single shot. Thumb operated drop breech block, positive extractor.

Frame   Take-down—Case hardened.

Sights   Bright metal knife blade front. Flat top open rear.

Stock   Oval shaped butt stock with steel butt plate.

Weight 2¾ lbs.   Length over all 34 inches.

The Stevens "Little Scout" is the ideal boys' rifle. The simplicity and durability of the action insures safe and positive operation. To load, the hammer is placed in half-cocked position. Breech block is moved downward by thumb lever below line of bore. After cartridge is inserted in chamber, breech block is moved upward by thumb lever, closing action. When hammer falls against firing pin, forward shoulder on hammer has passed under breech block positively locking action.

The full oval shaped stock and fine workmanship of all parts makes this rifle one of exceptionally high quality at a very low price.

Its accuracy and fine finish have given it wide spread popularity and have made it the outstanding boys' rifle over the entire world.

One in paper carton.   Parcel post weight 5 lbs.
Twenty-five in a case.   Weight 125 lbs.

Stevens Telescopes

The use of telescopic sights adds much to the pleasure of shooting, particularly on stationary game and in long distance target competitions. With a telescope the object sighted is magnified in proportion to the *power* of the telescope. For hunting conditions a low power telescope 3½ or 6 power, is most satisfactory, while the 8 power lenses are used for fine target shooting.

Stevens telescopes answer every requirement of the marksman and hunter. They are adapted to any sporting rifle and may be fitted by anyone with very slight mechanical skill. If desired they can be easily dismounted to permit the use of the regular sights.

Stevens telescopes are provided with complete adjustments for windage and elevation. The lenses are of the best optical glass, having a sharp definition and brilliant field. These telescopes will give excellent results and yet are moderate in price

No. 8 MOUNTS   No. 1 MOUNTS

Dovetail blocks included with mounts on complete telescopes.   For separate parts see price list.

Stevens Double Barrel Shotguns

The highest perfection of the gun-makers' art has been reached in the manufacture of double barrel shotguns. They are the choice of discriminate sportsmen throughout the World and are made in an elaborate range of styles and grades.

In the Stevens Double Barrel Shotguns will be found the following essential fundamentals that have been carefully developed over years of expert gunmaking. First—positive actions; firing, extracting and cocking with unfailing regularity. Bolting of barrel and frame by compensating levers that insure a tight fit after years of service. Second—The general construction of barrels are similar to those used on the highest priced

double guns. Boring and choking are by the most approved methods that will give patterns equal to any shotguns regardless of price. Third—selected walnut stocks and general finish of complete gun to give a beautiful appearance, durability and balance.

By manufacturing a good selection of standard models in large volume and by using the most modern factory methods of production, Stevens guns are produced equal in every respect to much higher priced guns that are made according to varying requirements of the individual purchaser, involving extravagant cost without increased value.

The barrel and lug are one piece forged from a solid bar of steel. Tension forearm snap prevents forearm from shooting loose by exerting pressure against hinge joint.

The barrels are joined and brazed in a way that provides the strongest breech mechanism that it is possible to make.

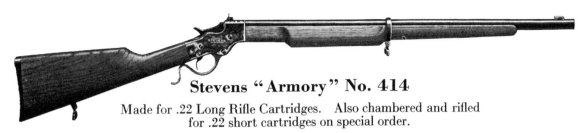

Stevens "Armory" No. 414

Made for .22 Long Rifle Cartridges. Also chambered and rifled
for .22 short cartridges on special order.

Barrel   26 inches round.

Action   Single Shot. Stevens heavy type drop finger lever-drop breech bolt automatic ejector.

Frame   Case hardened. Take-down with continuous thread set screw lock.

Sights   Bright metal knife blade bead front. Special Stevens receiver peep sight with windage and elevator adjustments. Telescope sights fitted to order.

Stock   American Walnut. Shotgun butt with steel butt plate—special long Walnut forearm with large hand hold. Fitted with sling strap loops.

Weight about 8 lbs.   Length over all 41 inches.

The Stevens 414 Armory Model was designed for firing from the standard military positions incorporated in matches of the National Rifle Association. The barrel and action are the same as supplied on the No. 44 Ideal rifle and are unexcelled for careful workmanship and accuracy. The stock with shotgun butt and forearm with large hand hold were carefully proportioned for use in firing with sling strap.

Several world's indoor records have been made with this rifle and for the past twenty years it has many times been the choice of experts on American teams in International matches.

One in paper carton.   Parcel post weight 10 lbs.
Ten in a case.   Weight about 125 lbs.

Stevens Telescopes

No. 8 MOUNTS

No.	Power	Length	Tube Diameter	Mount	Field at 100 yds.
388	8 -diam.	20 inches	¾ inch	No. 8	16 ft.
368	6 -diam.	16 and 19 inches	¾ inch	No. 8	18 ft.
438	3½-diam.	14 and 19 inches	¾ inch	No. 8	23 ft.
468	6 -diam.	13½ inches	¾ inch	No. 8 Special	18 ft

These telescopes are provided with dovetail blocks that screw to the barrel. The base or bottom of the blocks is shaped to fit both round and octagon barrels.

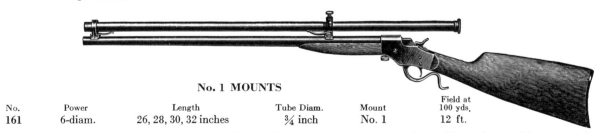

No. 1 MOUNTS

No.	Power	Length	Tube Diam.	Mount	Field at 100 yds.
161	6-diam.	26, 28, 30, 32 inches	¾ inch	No. 1	12 ft.

Telescopes with No. 1 mounts have dovetail bases of the expansion type, and require no filing or fitting. After the regular sights have been removed the front and rear mounts may be pushed into their respective slots and made secure by the two set screws in the base of each mount.

When ordering give make, model, caliber and length of barrel of rifle to be equipped with telescope.

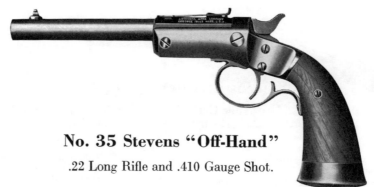

No. 35 Stevens "Off-Hand"

.22 Long Rifle and .410 Gauge Shot.

Barrel Round with octagon breech. Blued.

Length .22 cal. . . . . 6 and 8 inches
.410 gauge . . . . 8 inch and 12¼ inch choke-bored

Action Single shot. Stevens famous Tip-up frame blued, positive extractor.

Sights .22 caliber—adjustable flat top rear and bead front.
.410 gauge—shot gun front.

Stocks Selected black walnut.

Weight .22 caliber—6 inches . . . . 24 ounces
8 inches . . . . 27 ounces
.410 gauge—8 inches . . . . 23 ounces
12¼ inches . . . . 25 ounces

"The Hunters' and Trappers' Friend" is a particularly fitting name given this efficient side arm by those who know its remarkable utility.

It has an excellent "man size" grip, fine clean trigger pull and sufficient weight in frame and barrel for deadly accurate shooting. The tip-up action is quickly operated for re-loading. Its compact size and weight makes it particularly appealing for a trapper or big game hunter to carry—the powerful .22 long rifle cartridge is sufficient to account for all small game and birds. The .410

gauge is ideal for small birds and vermin at short range.

For over sixty years the J. Stevens Arms Company has built single shot pistols that have become world famous for their accuracy, finish, workmanship and durability. The No. 35 pistol is one of the most practical models ever designed for a hunting side arm and has been sold in every part of the World.

Its price is unusually low considering its excellent construction and finish.

One in paper carton. Parcel post weight 3 lbs.

Stevens Single Shot Pistols

No. 10 Stevens "Target"

.22 Long Rifle. Weight 36 ounces.

Barrel Blued, length 8 inches.

Frame Blued finish. Tip-up.

Action Single shot, coil springs, positive extractor.

Sights Open front, open rear with elevation and windage adjustments. Specially designed for target shooting. Distance between sights 10″.

Stock Hard rubber, checkered. Length over all 11½ inches.

The foremost target pistol experts collaborated with the J. Stevens Arms Company in the design of this super-accurate target pistol.

The concensus of opinion required sufficient weight for steady holding, a grip that allowed sighting without cramping the wrist, sights specially adaptable to target shooting and far enough apart to give clear definition of front and rear sights.

In the No. 10 Stevens Pistol will be found all these features worked out to the utmost detail. The location

of the trigger and slanting grip brings the hand in a natural easy position permitting firing without muscular strain. The balanced weight and long sighting base were attained by the projecting frame over the grip. A perfect lock up is secured by tip-up barrel locking against solid receiver.

As for accuracy—Stevens pistols have for sixty years been famous for their fine shooting qualities. The No. 10 Pistol has been used in making record breaking scores and will be found a perfect arm for accurate target shooting.

One in a paper carton. Parcel post weight 4 lbs.

Twenty-five in a case. Weight about 100 lbs.

Stevens "Junior" No. 11

Made for .22 caliber cartridges.

Barrel	20 inch round.	**Sights**	Bright metal knife blade front and flat top, open rear sight.
Action	Single shot. Thumb operated drop breech bolt, positive extractor.	**Stock**	One piece stock and forearm shaped butt and comb.
Frame	Take-down—Steel frame inserted in one piece stock.		

Weight 2¾ lbs.   Length over all 34 inches.

To meet the demand for a rifle with a safe, positive action and accurately rifled barrel the Stevens "Junior" was designed to give those essentials in an extremely low priced arm. The action and barrel are similar to those of the No. 14½ "Little Scout" rifle. The butt stock and forearm are combined in a rigid one piece stock that gives the rifle excellent balance and fine appearance. The arm can be taken down by removing assembly screw.

The all steel construction of metal parts and rigid assembly screw insures lasting service and provides unusual quality to those desiring an accurate, serviceable rifle at lowest price.

One in paper carton.   Parcel post weight 5 lbs.
Twenty-five in a case.   Weight 115 lbs.

Stevens "Marksman" No. 12

Made in .22 long rifle, .25 rim-fire and .32 long rim-fire calibers.

Barrel	22 inch round.	**Sights**	Metal bead front and flat top open rear.
Action	Single shot. Plain lever barrel tip-up solid frame, positive extractor.	**Stock**	American Walnut forearm and butt stock. Full oval shaped butt stock with rubber butt plate.
Frame	Take-down Blued finish.		

Weight 4 lbs.   Length over all 36 inches.

The action of the Model 12 "Marksman" is one of the strongest and safest designs. The forward and downward movement of finger lever cams breech of barrel upward to a point where line of bore is above top of receiver. A positive extractor withdraws fired cartridge case. Closing movement of finger lever locks barrel and action and places hammer in safe half-cocked position. The solid breech of frame behind head of cartridge makes the action unusually strong and safe. A simple take-down screw allows withdrawal of barrel from action for cleaning and transportation.

The butt stock is of full dimensions suitable for adults as well as boys, oval shaped and finely finished. Forearm well proportioned and carefully fitted.

The Model 12 "Marksman" is an ideal rifle for the man or boy desiring a full size extremely accurate single shot rifle at moderate price.

One in paper carton.   Parcel post weight 5 lbs.   Twenty-five in case.   Weight 140 lbs.

Stevens "Ideal" No. 44

Made in .22 long rifle, .25 rim-fire, and .32 long rim-fire calibers.

Barrel 26 inch round.

Action Single Shot. Stevens heavy type drop finger lever—drop breech block, automatic ejector in .22 caliber. Plain extractor in other calibers.

Frame Case hardened. Take-down with continuous thread set screw lock.

Stock American Walnut forearm and butt stock. Stock length 13 inches, drop 3 inches, steel rifle butt plate.

Sights No. 203 bright metal knife blade front and No. 112 sporting rear sight. Tang tapped for peep sight. Special sights or any No. 1 or No. 3 telescope fitted to order. (No allowance made for regular sights when furnished with special sights.)

Weight 7 lbs. Length over all 41 inches.

For over twenty years Stevens "Ideal" has been used by experts in making world's records. That Stevens rifles are undeniably the most accurate made is proven by the overwhelming number of record targets to their credit and the uniform success that attends their use at competitive matches.

The action of Stevens No. 44 Ideal is operated as follows—The downward and forward movement of the finger lever unlocks breech block and draws it downward below line of bore. Fina forward stroke of finger lever operates automatic ejector for .22 caliber cartridges and extractor on large calibers. Closing stroke of finger lever seats loaded cartridge in chamber and places hammer in safe half-cocked position. If desired barrel can be removed from frame as follows—Take out set screw on under side of frame—open finger lever to withdraw extractor from barrel—unscrew barrel from frame.

The stock and forearm dimensions and special rifle butt plate were designed to make this rifle particularly adapted for extremely accurate off-hand shooting. The long heavy barrel assists in steady holding, the action has a remarkably smooth trigger pull, in fact, every feature of this rifle was carefully worked out through years of expert study to produce a deadly accurate combined hunting and target rifle.

Stevens Double Barrel Shotguns

No. 235 Stevens Hammer

Made in 12 and 16 gauge.

Barrels High pressure compressed steel, bored for nitro powder, right barrel modified, left barrel full choked, matted rib.

Length 12 gauge 28–30 and 32 ins. 16 gauge 28 and 30 ins.

Action Top lever and bolt in one piece locking through extension rib, check hook, low circular hammers, rebounding locks, coil mainsprings, large powerful extractors.

Frame Take-down. Case hardened, scroll ornament.

Stock Walnut, checkered pistol grip, rubber butt plate, length 14 inches, drop about 3 inches, fore-end checkered.

Weight 12 gauge 7¾ to 8¼ lbs. 16 gauge 7½ to 8 lbs.

Ammunition Any standard factory loaded shell.

"I like to see the hammers" is often an expression from sportsmen who prefer double guns of this type to the later designed hammerless gun. The No. 235 Stevens hammer gun is one of our best known guns and has been used for years in every part of the world. Its sturdy mechanism and fine appearance is another outstanding achievement of Stevens manufacturing methods.

Many of the characteristic Stevens mechanical features of the 335 Stevens hammerless gun are found in this model. The long frame giving increased leverage to locking bolt, check hook relieving cross bolt of weight of barrels when action is opened, barrel and lug forged in one piece, and the excellent finish of barrel, frame and stock are positive assurances of service and durability.

One in a paper carton. Parcel post weight 12 lbs.
Ten in case. Weight about 120 lbs.

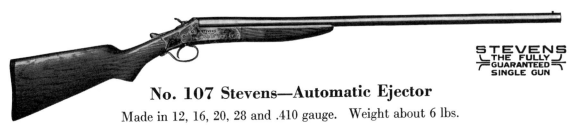

No. 107 Stevens—Automatic Ejector

Made in 12, 16, 20, 28 and .410 gauge.   Weight about 6 lbs.

Barrel   Compressed forged steel, hollow tapered, bored for nitro powder, full choked.

Length
12 gauge............................ 28 to 36 inches
16 gauge............................ 28 to 32 inches
20 gauge............................ 26 to 32 inches
28 gauge............................ 26 to 32 inches
.410 gauge.......................... 26 inches only
Extra charge for 34 inch and 36 inch barrels.

Action   Top snap, low rebounding hammer.   Automatic ejector.

Frame   Take-down.   Case hardened.

Stock   Walnut, full pistol grip, rubber butt plate.   Length 12 and 16 gauge 14 inches, 20, 28 and .410 gauge 13¾ inches, snap fore-end attachment, wide extension forearm.

Ammunition   Any standard factory loaded shell.

No. 105 Stevens—Plain Extractor

Same specifications as above but without automatic ejector.

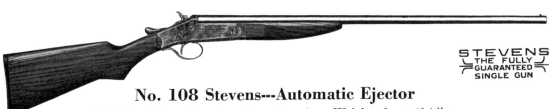

The No. 107 Stevens is the most popular of our single barrel shotguns.   Its medium weight makes it ideal for hunting purposes and the large assortment of gauges and barrel lengths in which it is supplied provides a size for every hunting purpose.

The action is of the top lever type providing a quick and convenient means of opening action for reloading, automatic ejector throws fired shell clear of gun.   Low rebounding hammer leaves gun in safe half-cocked position.   Hammer must be placed in full cock position and trigger pulled before gun can be fired.   This is a desirable safety feature and prevents accidental discharge.   By removing forearm and opening top lever, gun may be taken apart for cleaning and ready transportation.

Special designed American Walnut stock and forearm—polished blued steel barrel and handsome case hardened frame combine in making this gun the most attractive arm procurable at a moderate price.

One in a paper carton.   Parcel post weight 9 lbs.   Ten in a case.   Weight about 95 lbs.

No. 108 Stevens---Automatic Ejector

Made in .410 or 12 m/m, .32 or 14 m/m.   Weight about 4½ lbs.

Barrel   Compressed forged steel, hollow tapered, bored for nitro powder.

Length   .410 or 12 m/m 26 and 30 in.
.32 or 14m/m 30 inch only.

Frame   Case hardened.

Stock   Walnut full pistol grip, rubber butt plate, length 13½ inches, spring fore-end attachment.

Action   Top snap, rebounding hammer.   Automatic ejector.

Ammunition   Any standard 2″ or 2½″ loaded shell.

No. 106 Stevens---Plain Extractor

Same as above but without automatic ejector.

The popularity of the .410 gauge shotgun shells and similar small gauges brought the demand for a special light gun for their use.   The No. 108 Stevens was designed to meet this need and was the first American firearm to use .410 ammunition.   In general design its mechanical construction and general finish is the same as the No. 107 Stevens Single Gun.   A small light frame and light high-pressure steel barrel with proportionately shaped stock and extension fore-arm have been blended into a light, perfectly balanced shotgun.

Guns of these gauges are effective up to 25 yards on small game.   The novice requiring a gun for protection of garden or orchard against small vermin birds and animals will find this arm easier to shoot accurately than a rifle.   Its size and lack of recoil makes it a most suitable gun for ladies and boys.

One in paper carton.   Parcel post weight 8 lbs.
Ten in case.   Weight about 80 lbs.

Field Grade

No. 520 Take-down.　12 Gauge.　Weight about 7¾ lbs.

Barrel	High pressure compressed steel, bored for nitro powder, 28, 30 and 32 inch full choked, 28 and 30 inch modified, 26 and 28 inch cylinder bored.	**Stock**	Checkered walnut, pistol grip, checkered slide handle, rubber butt plate, length 13¾ inches, drop 2⅝ inches.
Action	Hammerless, visible locking bolt, safety firing pin, independent safety, side ejection.	**Ammunition**	Any standard factory loaded shell up to 2¾ inches in length.
Receiver	Drop forged, solid breech.		

Six shots—five in magazine, one in chamber.

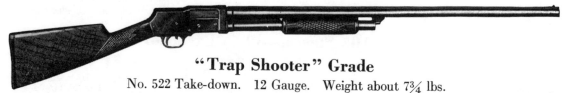

"Trap Shooter" Grade

No. 522 Take-down.　12 Gauge.　Weight about 7¾ lbs.

Barrel	High pressure compressed steel, bored for nitro powder, full choked, hollow matted rib, length 30 and 32 inches. 30″ barrel always furnished unless otherwise specified.	**Stock**	Fancy walnut, checkered, straight grip, rubber butt plate, length 14″, drop at comb 1½″, drop at heel 2¼″, fancy walnut slide handle, checkered. *No deviation.*
Action	Hammerless, visible locking block, safety firing pin, independent safety, side ejection.	**Ammunition**	Any standard factory loaded shell up to 2¾″ in length.
Receiver	Drop forged, solid breech, matted top.		

Six shots—five in magazine, one in chamber.

J. Stevens Arms Company

Stevens Repeating Shotguns

The design of the mechanism of the Stevens Repeating Shotgun is an outstanding example of the wonderful improvement in modern firearms.

Simplicity, Durability and Safety are the outstanding requirements of a firearm and it was these essentials upon which the action was designed.

Simplicity means few parts, making the arm extremely smooth and easy to operate. The Stevens repeating shotgun has the smoothest action of any repeating shotgun. The breech bolt travels backward and forward on a straight line with a minimum of friction.

Durability is secured because with fewer parts they can be made of such ample proportions as to eliminate breakage. A Model 520 Stevens used in testing heavy loads by a leading manufacturer of shotgun shells has been fired over 100,000 times and is still in perfect working order.

Safety is provided throughout. The solid breech presents a thick wall of steel behind the locked breech bolt—defective ammunition cannot endanger the shooter. Breech bolt is locked with large square lug through block and top of frame—the strongest lock on any repeating shotgun and capable of easily withstanding the heaviest loads. It is impossible to discharge a Stevens repeating shotgun before it is closed and locked; takedown device has a screw-down lock insuring barrel being tightly locked on frame. Safety trigger lock is located inside trigger guard at convenient command of shooter allowing firing mechanism to be securely locked until gun is placed at shoulder.

The barrel is carefully bored and reamed by the Stevens slow process method and has brought to this arm the same reputation of fine shooting qualities so well known in Stevens rifles.

The barrel and frame are highly polished and blued; checkered stock and slide handle are carefully proportioned and unusually well finished.

Through Stevens' manufacturing methods this gun is sold at a price considerably below that asked for other repeating shotguns with which it compares equally in appearance, operation, and shooting qualities.

Stevens Single Barrel Shotguns

Stevens Single Barrel Shotguns are particularly adaptable to those desiring an efficient shotgun at a low price. This type of arm is undoubtedly more in use than any other shotgun. Several different styles are shown on the following pages, each made in a large assortment of lengths and gauges—from the light .410 gauge guns for small game to the extra heavy 12 gauge guns for long range shooting with heavy loads.

The J. Stevens Arms Co. is the largest manufacturer of shotguns in the World. The superior excellence of Stevens Single Barrel Shotguns has long been recognized by purchasers in every part of the World and is merited not only because the careful workmanship and selected materials insure long satisfactory service, but for the several outstanding features in general design that are characteristic of Stevens single barrel guns.

The lug and the barrel are one piece forged from a solid bar of steel; this results in a barrel of the greatest strength. The fore-end lug is brazed to the barrel instead of being riveted or set into dovetail slots as is usual in this type of gun. Tension forearm snap prevents forearm from shooting loose by exerting pressure against hinge joint.

Stevens Double Barrel Shotguns

No. 330 Stevens Hammerless

Made in 12, 16, 20 and .410 gauge.

Barrels Blued. High pressure compressed steel, tested with nitro powder, matted rib. 12, 16 and 20 gauge right barrel modified, left barrel full choked. .410 gauge both barrels full choked.

Length
12 gauge	28–30 and 32 inches
16 gauge	28 and 30 inches
20 gauge	26 and 28 inches
.410 gauge	26 inches

Action Hammerless. Top lever and bolt in one piece, coil springs. Large powerful extractors, automatic safety.

Frame Take-down. Beautifully polished and case hardened.

Stock Selected Black Walnut, finely checkered, full pistol grip capped, rubber butt plate. Length 14 in. Drop about 3 inches, walnut fore-end checkered

Weight
12 gauge	7½ to 7¾ lb.
16 gauge	7¼ to 7½ lb.
20 gauge	6¼ to 6¾ lb.
.410 gauge	5¾ to 6¼ lb.

Ammunition Any standard factory loaded shell.

The No. 330 Stevens is our latest model and was designed to supply the popular demand for a serviceable double gun of good appearance to sell at a moderately low price.

The action has many of the exclusive Stevens features that insure a smooth working reliable performance during years of hard usage. Barrels are carefully bored and choked.

Particular attention is given to this gun in securing a handsome finish. Rounded corners of frame, polished barrels and finely checkered stock and forearm are unusual features in comparatively priced arms.

One in a paper carton.   Parcel post weight 12 lbs.
Ten in a case.   Weight about 115 lbs.

STEVENS
THE FULLY
GUARANTEED
SINGLE GUN

No. 115 Stevens---Automatic Ejector
Made in 12, 16, 20 and .410 gauge.   Weight about 6 lbs.

Barrel   Compressed forged steel, hollow tapered, bored for nitro powder, full choked.

Length
12 gauge.......................28–30 and 32 inches
16 gauge.......................28–30 and 32 inches
20 gauge.................26–28–30 and 32 inches
.410 gauge.................................26 inches

Frame   Case hardened.

Stock   Walnut, full pistol grip, checkered and capped rubber butt plate, length 13¾ to 14 inches, wide walnut fore-end, checkered.

Ammunition   Any standard factory loaded shell.

Action   Top snap, low rebounding hammer, automatic ejector.

In the No. 115 Stevens Single Gun are incorporated the refinements of gun finishing so appreciated by most gun users. The barrel and action are similar in design to the popular No. 107 Stevens Single Gun. These parts are carefully fitted and finished in a superior manner.

The stock and forearm are made of selected American Walnut in rubbed finish. Forearm is wide extension type, stock has full pistol grip with hard rubber cap, both finely checkered. The frame is case hardened with highly polished finish.

The sportsman who desires to use a single barrel shotgun will find this gun above the ordinary in general finish and appearance at only slightly increased cost.

One in paper carton.   Parcel post weight 9 lbs.   Ten in case.   Weight about 100 lbs.

Stevens Double Barrel Shotguns

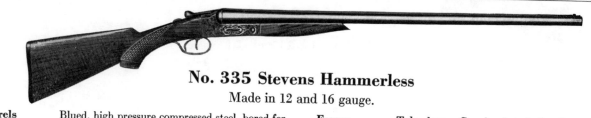

No. 335 Stevens Hammerless
Made in 12 and 16 gauge.

Barrels   Blued, high pressure compressed steel, bored for nitro powder, right barrel modified, left barrel full choked, matted rib.

Length
12 gauge ....28-30 and 32 inch.
16 gauge ....28 and 30 inch.

Action   Hammerless, top lever and bolt in one piece locking through extension rib, spiral main springs, check hook, automatic safety, large powerful extractors.

Frame   Take-down. Case hardened. Scroll ornament.

Stock   Walnut, checkered full pistol grip, capped rubber butt plate, length 14 inches, drop about 3 inches, fore-end checkered. *No deviation.*

Weight   12 gauge 7¾ to 8¼ lbs. 16 gauge 7½ to 8 lbs.

Ammunition   Any standard factory loaded shell.

This model is our best grade double gun and represents a quality considerably beyond other double guns of similar price.

A long frame is used and by bolting the gun at the extreme end of extension rib, the greatest possible distance is secured between hinge-joint and bolting-point, giving unusual leverage to bolt and eliminates tendency of barrels to lift out of frame when fired—in fact, this gun can be fired with top lever bolt removed and holding barrels in frame with the hand alone.

The perfect compensating features in our top lever bolt and extension rib, by means of beveled surfaces, permitting the bolt to enter farther as wear takes place insures a tight fit after years of use.

When action is opened a check hook takes strain from hinge pin. The forearm snaps on the barrel with a strong spring and always exerts a pressure which prevents the barrel becoming loose on the hinge pin and gives a smooth steady action when opening and closing gun.

The compressed steel barrels are bored by an original method and are noted for their long range, and close, hard shooting qualities. Barrel and lug are forged in one piece eliminating possibility of breakage.

The fine finish of this gun combined with its excellent mechanical features and hard shooting qualities makes it one of the most outstanding gun values on the market.

One in a carton.   Parcel post weight 12 lbs.   Ten in a case.   Weight about 120 lbs.

STEVENS
MODERNIZED "IDEAL" MARKSMAN RIFLES
Models 417-417½-418-418½

STEVENS—SCHOOLER OF SHOOTERS

"When I was nine years old, I became the proud owner of a Stevens Favorite .22 caliber rifle, presented to me by my father on Christmas day. Well do I remember the thrill of handling this little rifle, and the profit and pleasure that I derived from the use of it. All my spare time spent in the woods, and tramping over the old Green Mountains with my trusty .22 tucked under my arm gave me a pretty fair start toward the hobby that has come, in later years, to mean so much to me."

So wrote a prominent sportsman in the "American Rifleman" magazine. And how many more hunter-riflemen have said the same thing during the past 68 years since Joshua Stevens staked his reputation on a standard of rifle quality that has never varied to this day. How many marksmen owe their shooting ability, and pleasure to early training with those selfsame Stevens Rifles!

Down through the years Stevens has clung faithfully to the ideals and high standards established by its founder. How much so, is exemplified by these four latest Stevens Models, Nos. 417, 417 1/2, 418, and 418 1/2 . . . developments and modernizations of famous Stevens rifles that made many world records and were the choice of experts in the days of the "Schutzen" rifle clubs and famous shooting matches.

As surely as the famous "Favorite" has been the popular boy's rifle, and the Stevens "Ideal" the choice among marksmen, so surely will these new Stevens models find favor and leadership. For the first time in shooting history, the hunter-rifleman and match marksman have available, at moderate cost, a line of thoroughly modernized, completely equipped rifles.

SPECIFICATIONS

BARREL—28-inch, Heavy, Round, Tested for Accuracy. FRAME—Solid, Hardened and Blued. ACTION—Original Stevens "Ideal" Breech Block, Positive Extractor, Lever Action, Short Fast Hammer Fall, Half Cock Safety Notch. STOCK—American Walnut 13½-inch, Oil Finish, High Comb, Full Pistol Grip Target Model Stock and Forearm, Fitted with 1¼-inch Military Style Sling Strap, Shotgun Butt with Steel Butt Plate. SIGHTS—Lyman No. 17A Front, Telescope Blocks, Lyman No. 48L Receiver sight (Can furnish Lyman No. 103 Tang Peep Sight in place of No. 48L Receiver Sight on request at same price). WEIGHT—About 10½ to 11 pounds. AMMUNITION—.22 Long Rifle, Made to order; .22 Short at no extra charge. PRICE—No. 417-1, fitted with Lyman No. 48L Sight, Retail, $37.50; No. 417-2, fitted with Lyman No. 103 Sight in place of No. 48L, Retail, $37.50; No. 417-3, without front or rear sights, Retail, $26.50; No. 417-4, fitted with Lyman No. 438 Telescope, Retail, $56.75; No. 417-5, fitted with Lyman No. 5A Telescope, Retail, $78.00, plus tax, if and when effective.

Model 417—"IDEAL"
HEAVY TARGET RIFLE

Source: Savage/Stevens brochure, 1932

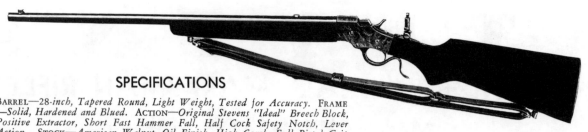

SPECIFICATIONS

BARREL—28-*inch, Tapered Round, Light Weight, Tested for Accuracy.* FRAME —*Solid, Hardened and Blued.* ACTION—*Original Stevens "Ideal" Breech Block, Positive Extractor, Short Fast Hammer Fall, Half Cock Safety Notch, Lever Action.* STOCK—*American Walnut, Oil Finish, High Comb, Full Pistol Grip Stock and Sporting Forearm, Fitted with* 1¼-*inch Military Style Sling Strap, Shotgun Butt with Steel Butt Plate.* SIGHTS—*Lyman No. 28,* 3/32-*inch Gold Bead Front, Single Folding Leaf Middle, and Lyman No. 1A Tang Peep Sight, Barrel Tapped for Telescope Blocks.* WEIGHT—8 *to* 8¼ *Pounds.* AMMUNITION— *Regular and High Speed,* .22 *Long Rifle,* .22 *W.R.F.,* .25 *Stevens R.F.* PRICE —*Retail, $30.00, plus tax, if and when effective.*

Model 417 1/2 "IDEAL" SPORTING RIFLE

ACCURACY

Stevens barrels have always been famous for their accuracy. So widespread ·has been the knowledge of this fact that fine foreign actions are still being sent to Stevens, to be fitted with Stevens barrels.

Not only are Stevens barrels drilled, reamed, rifled and chambered by the most exact methods but these operations are being done by workmen who are specialists in their field—men who in some instances are following in the footsteps of their fathers who were trained in the original precision tool plant of Joshua Stevens.

Every barrel is carefully gauged and inspected after each manufacturing operation. Each arm, when finished is carefully targeted in a machine rest by an expert.

ACTION

The actions of these new Stevens single shot rifles are of the drop lever type, which conforms to the views of expert riflemen. Their design permits ready inspection of the inside of the bar-rel from the breech end, facilitates cleaning, expedites loading and insures maximum safety.

Each model has the original Stevens "Ideal" breech-block, with positive extractor, short, fast, hammer fall, half-cock safety notch and crisp trigger pull.

The operation is simplicity itself; the downward and forward movement of the finger lever unlocks the breech block and draws it downward below the line of bore. Final forward stroke of the lever operates the positive extractor. Closing stroke of lever seats loaded cartridge in the chamber and places the hammer in safe, half-cocked position.

STOCK AND FOREARM

Here is found the most noticeable departure from the earlier models, the result of suggestions in some cases by foremost military authorities and marksmen . . . refinements to meet

SPECIFICATIONS

BARREL—26-*inch, Heavy, Tapered Round, Tested for Accuracy.* FRAME—*New Heavy Junior "Ideal", Take Down, Case Hardened.* ACTION—*Original Stevens "Ideal" Breech Block, Positive Extractor, Lever Action, Fast Hammer Fall, Half Cock Safety Notch.* STOCK—*American Walnut* 13-*inch, Oil Finish, Full Pistol Grip Target Model Stock and Forearm, Fitted with* ⅞-*inch Military Style Sling Strap, Shotgun Butt with Steel Butt Plate.* SIGHTS—*Lyman No. 3,* 1/16-*inch Gold Bead Front, Slot Blank Middle, and Lyman No. 2A Tang Peep Sight.* WEIGHT—6 *to* 7 *Pounds.* AMMUNITION—.22 *Long Rifle (.22 Short to order at no extra charge).* PRICE—*Retail, $15.00, plus tax, if and when effective.*

Model 418—"IDEAL" JUNIOR TARGET RIFLE

Source: Savage/Stevens brochure, 1

46

SPECIFICATIONS

BARREL—*26-inch, Tapered Round, Tested for Accuracy.* FRAME—*New Heavy, Take Down, Case Hardened.* ACTION—*Original Stevens "Ideal" Breech Block, Positive Extractor, Lever Action, Fast Hammer Fall, Half Cock Safety Notch.* STOCK—*American Walnut 13-inch, Oil Finish, Full Pistol Grip Sporting Model Stock and Forearm. Fitted with ⅞-inch Military Style Sling Strap, Shotgun Butt with Steel Butt Plate.* SIGHTS—*Lyman 1/16-inch Gold Bead Front, Slot Blank Middle, and Lyman No. 1A Tang Peep Sight.* WEIGHT—*6 to 7 Pounds.* AMMUNITION—*Regular and High Speed, .22 Long Rifle, .22 W.R.F., .25 Stevens R.F.* PRICE—*Retail, $15.00, plus tax, if and when effective.*

Model 418 1/2—"IDEAL" JUNIOR SPORTING RIFLE

the changed conditions of today's shooting on the range and in the field. A government type sling strap, which has been treated with neats foot oil, has been added as regular equipment. The use of a sling strap enables the shooter to hold steady on the target while in prone, sitting or kneeling position.

Stocks are of American Walnut, with fine oil finish, having high comb, full pistol grip and full size military style butt. The forearm is of modified beavertail design on both target and sporting rifle.

SIGHTING EQUIPMENT

The sighting equipment is of the finest type. Each model is equipped with the most suitable Lyman sights. In addition to the Lyman No. 48 rear and No. 17 front sights, the No. 417 Target model is fitted with telescope blocks. No. 418 model is tapped for telescope blocks.

WEIGHTS

Weights vary from about six pounds on the Jr. 418 and 418 1/2, to ten pounds on the Sr. Ideal 417. Whichever model you select will be perfectly balanced—every ounce of weight is correctly distributed to insure quick, easy sighting, steady holding and smooth, easy operation.

CALIBERS

All four models are chambered for .22 long rifle. In addition, as will be noted in the "Specifications", the 417 and 418 may be made to order at no extra charge for .22 short. Also the sporting models, 417 1/2 and 418 1/2 are chambered for .22 long rifle, .22 W.R.F., .25 Stevens R.F.

Source: Savage/Stevens brochure, 1932

"Gentlemen, we are again about to become a nation of riflemen, and having become that, we shall command peace for ourselves and our posterity. See to it that you use the grandest of weapons properly, as a gentleman and American should—that you never take life—human or animal—needlessly or thoughtlessly, that you never endanger the lives of others, that you conserve the game, that when you kill, you kill painlessly and humanely and with a single shot, that you learn to hold steadily, aim accurately, and squeeze the trigger easily, that you become a nail driving marksman. And then teach your boys to do likewise. Give them an even break. Don't handicap them with cheap, unsuitable, obsolete rifles. Neither you nor they nor our country will get anywhere with such weapons. A good rifle and a good rifleman shoot straight, see straight, think straight, and will run our country straight."

TOWNSEND WHELEN.

POINT BLANK RANGE

For small game shooting point blank range may be defined as that distance up to which the bullet will not rise or fall over 1 inch from the line of aim, and over which no allowance need be made for distance when aiming.

.22 Long Rifle:—Set sights so bullets will strike exact point of aim at 60 yards. Bullets will then strike 1" above line of aim at 30 yards, and drop 1" low at 70 yards.

.22 Long Rifle Hi-speed:—Set sights for 75 yards. Bullet strikes 1" high at 40 yards and 1" low at 85 yards.

.22 W.R.F. Hi-speed:—Set sights for 85 yards. Bullet strikes 1" high at 45 yards and 1" low at 100 yards.

.25 Stevens R.F.:—Set sights for 70 yards. Bullet strikes 1" high at 35 yards and 1" low at 80 yards.

AIMING WITH APERTURE SIGHTS

Align top of front sight in center of aperture of rear sight. Hold front sight just touching bottom edge of bullseye. Never vary from this method of aim.

For target shooting adjust rear sight so bullets group in center of bullseye. For hunting adjust rear sight at point blank range above so bullets group at bottom edge of bullseye (exact point of aim).

SIGHT ADJUSTMENT

Lyman No. 1 and 2 Rear Sights:—A change in elevation of 1 graduation on stem of rear sight moves center of impact of the group 3 inches at 50 yards, 6 inches at 100 yards, etc.

Lyman No. 48 Rear Sight and 5A Telescope Sights:—Smallest reading is half minutes for both elevation and windage. A half minute changes point of impact 1/8 inch at 25 yards, 1/4 inch at 50 yards, 1/2 inch at 100 yards or 1 inch at 200 yards. Remember the rule "1 minute equals 1 inch per hundred yards." Having found the correct elevation for any range, the approximate elevation for all other ranges with the .22 Long Rifle cartridge may be told from the following table of angles of elevation which reads in minutes (not half minutes).

Range—Yards.	22 L.R. Reg. Velocity. Minutes	22 L.R. Hi-Speed Minutes
25	2.0	2.0
50	5.0	5.5
75	8.0	8.5
100	13.0	11.5
150	22.0	18.3
200	32.5	26.0
300	....	43.0

USE OF GUNSLING . . . BASIC PRINCIPLES OF MARKSMANSHIP

For full instructions in the use of the gunsling as an aid to steady holding, for training methods in marksmanship, and for information on the basic principles on which rifle marksmanship is based, send 10c in coin (stamps not accepted) to the Superintendent of Documents, Government Printing Office, Washington, D. C., for "U. S. Army Training Regulations No. 150-5, Marksmanship, Rifle, Individual". Every rifle shooter should have a copy of this pamphlet.

BALLISTICS AND SIGHTING OF STEVENS IDEAL RIFLES, Nos. 417 and 418
TABLE OF VELOCITY AND TRAJECTORY

CARTRIDGE	Weight of Bullet Grains	Muzzle Velocity f.s.	TRAJECTORY Mid Range, Inches 50 Yds.	100 Yds.
.22 Short	30	975	1.3	6.0
.22 Short Hi-speed	29	1100	1.0	4.5
.22 Short, Hi-speed, H.P.	27	1125	1.0	4.5
.22 Long Rifle	40	1090	1.0	4.5
.22 L.R. Hi-speed	40	1300	.7	3.5
.22 L.R. Hi-speed, H.P.	36	1325	.7	3.5
.22 W.R.F.	45	1100	1.0	4.4
.22 W.R.F. Hi-speed	45	1500	.5	2.5
.22 W.R.F. Hi-speed H.P.	40	1525	.5	2.5
.25 Stevens R.F.	67	1180	.9	4.0

NOTE:—The Velocity of each make of ammunition varies slightly. The above are average figures. H.P.—Hollow point.

J. STEVENS ARMS COMPANY
CHICOPEE FALLS, MASS., U. S. A.
Owned and Operated by Savage Arms Corporation, Utica, N. Y.

No. 066
"STEVENS BOLT ACTION REPEATER"
Chambered for .22 long rifle regular and high speed cartridges

Barrel 24 inch round tapered. Take-down. The rifle has a tubular magazine with capacity of fifteen .22 long rifle, seventeen .22 long, or twenty-one .22 short, high speed or regular cartridges.

Action Self cocking, bolt action with independent safety, Chromium plated bolt and trigger.

Stock Turned, Walnut finish. Hard rubber butt plate. Black tip.

Sights Hooded ramp front sight with three interchangeable inserts, receiver rear sight with three aperture sighting discs.

Weight 6 pounds. Length over all 43½ inches.

No. 66 "STEVENS BOLT ACTION REPEATER"
Same specifications as No. 066 shown above except fitted with Gold Bead front and Sporting rear sight with elevation and windage adjustment.

No. 056 "STEVENS BOLT ACTION REPEATER"
Chambered for .22 long rifle regular and high speed cartridges

Barrel Tapered, round 24-inch, with crowned muzzle, for .22 long rifle, .22 long, and .22 short regular or high speed cartridges. Take down, 5-shot detachable clip magazine.

Action Self cocking, bolt action with independent safety, Chromium plated bolt and trigger.

Stock Full size, oval military style, full pistol grip, forearm with black tip, Walnut finish, hard rubber butt plate.

Sights Hooded ramp front sight with three interchangeable inserts and receiver rear with three aperture sighting discs, see illustration above.

Weight About 6 pounds. Length over all 43½ in.

No. 055 SINGLE SHOT BOLT ACTION RIFLE
Chambered for .22 long rifle, .22 W. R. F. or .25 Stevens R. F. cartridges

Barrel 24-inch round, tapered with crowned muzzle for .22 long rifle, .22 long or .22 short, .22 W. R. F., or .25 Stevens R. F., regular or high speed cartridges.

Action Fast large bolt action, self cocking with independent safety. Chromium plated bolt and trigger.

Stock Full size, oval military style, full pistol grip. Forearm with black tip, Walnut finish. Hard rubber butt plate, large take-down screw.

Sights Hooded ramp front sight with three interchangeable inserts and receiver rear with three aperture sighting discs.

Weight About 6 pounds. Take-down. Length over all 43½ in.

No. 55 SINGLE SHOT BOLT ACTION RIFLE

Same specifications as No. 055 shown above except fitted with Gold Bead front and Sporting rear sight with elevation and windage adjustment.

Condensed from Stevens Catalog No. 61 (1935)

No. 053 SINGLE SHOT BOLT ACTION RIFLE

Chambered for .22 long rifle, .22 W.R.F. or .25 Stevens R.F. cartridges

Barrel 24-inch round, tapered with crowned muzzle for .22 long rifle, .22 long or .22 short, .22 W. R. F. or .25 Stevens R. F. regular or high speed cartridges.

Action Fast bolt action, self cocking, with independent safety. Chromium plated bolt and trigger.

Stock Full size, oval military style, full pistol grip. Forearm with black tip, Walnut finish. Hard rubber butt plate, large take-down screw.

Sights Hooded ramp front sight with three interchangeable inserts and receiver rear sight with three apertures. See illustrations.

Weight About 5¼ pounds. Take-down. Length over all 41¼ inches.

No. 53 SINGLE SHOT BOLT ACTION RIFLE

Same specifications as No. 053 shown above except fitted with Gold Bead front and Sporting rear sight.

Nos. 27 and 20 "FAVORITE"

No. 27 Full Octagon barrel, chambered for .22 long rifle, high speed or regular, .25 rim-fire, or .32 long rim-fire cartridges.

No. 20 Smooth bore round barrel, plain extractor only. Chambered for .22 and .32 shot cartridges.

Barrel 24 inches.

Action Single shot—Stevens drop block lever action, automatic ejector in .22 caliber—plain extractor in other calibers.

Frame Blued. Take-down.

Stock Walnut stock and forearm, shotgun style butt.

Sights Gold bead front and sporting rear sight with elevation adjustment. No. 20 fitted with shotgun front sight only.

Weight 4½ pounds. Length over-all 38 inches.

The action of the Stevens Favorite is a powerful lever type. The downward and forward movement of lever draws the breech block downward below line of bore and operates ejector. After cartridge is placed in chamber of rifle the action is closed and locked by lever, and hammer is left in safe half-cocked position. A simple take-down screw allows barrel to be withdrawn from frame for cleaning and transportation.

No. 26 "CRACK SHOT"

No. 26 Chambered for .22 short, .22 long and .22 long rifle, .25 rim-fire and .32 long rim-fire regular cartridges.

No. 26½ Smooth bore. Chambered for .22 caliber and .32 caliber shot cartridges.

Barrel 22 inch round. Tapered.

Action Single shot, lever action drop breech block, positive extractor.

Frame Take-down. Blued finish.

Sights German silver knife blade front. Flat top open rear.

Stock Oval shaped Walnut finish stock with steel butt plate.

Weight 3½ pounds. Length over-all 36 inches.

The Stevens "Crack Shot" provides the popular lever action type of rifle at a low price which makes it particularly desirable to boys.

No. 14½ "LITTLE SCOUT"

No. 14½ Chambered for .22 short, .22 long and .22 long rifle regular cartridges.

Barrel 20 inch round. Tapered.

Action Single shot, .22 caliber regular cartridges. Thumb operated drop breech block, positive extractor.

Frame Take-down. Case hardened.

Sights German silver knife blade front. Flat top open rear.

Stock Oval shaped Walnut finish stock with steel butt plate.

Weight 3 pounds. Length over-all 34 inches.

STEVENS SINGLE SHOT RIFLES

No. 417 "WALNUT HILL"

TESTED FOR ACCURACY

Barrel 28 inch round, heavy tapered.

Action Single shot, original Stevens "Ideal" breech block. .22 L. R., automatic ejector; .22 Hornet, positive extractor. New self-cocking lever action. Short fast hammer fall.

Frame Solid. Case hardened.

Stock American Walnut 13½ inch. Oil finish, high comb, full pistol grip, target model stock and forearm, fitted with 1¼ inch military type leather sling strap, shotgun butt with steel butt plate.

No. 417-1

Sights Lyman No. 17A front, telescope Blocks for Lyman or Fecker telescope sights. No. 48L Lyman receiver sight, see options below.

Chambered for Regular and high speed .22 long rifle and .22 Hornet.

Weight 10½ to 11 pounds.

For additional data, please write for descriptive circular, Form 9132.

No. 417-1 Fitted with Lyman No. 48L sight.
No. 417-2 Fitted with Lyman No. 144 Tang sight in place of 48L.
No. 417-3 Without front or rear sights.

Loop Lever furnished on request. No extra charge

No. 417½ "WALNUT HILL" SPORTING or TARGET RIFLE

Barrel 28 inch round tapered, light weight, tested for accuracy.

Action Single shot, original Stevens "Ideal" breech block. .22 L. R., automatic ejector; other calibers, positive extractor. New self-cocking lever action. Short fast hammer fall.

Frame Solid. Case hardened.

Stock American Walnut, oil finish, high comb, full pistol grip stock and sporting forearm.
Fitted with 1¼ inch Military style leather sling strap. Shotgun butt, with steel butt plate.

Sights Lyman No. 28, 3/32 inch Gold bead front, single folding leaf middle and Lyman No. 144 tang peep sight with click adjustment for elevation and windage. Barrel tapped for telescope blocks.

Chambered for Regular and high speed .22 long rifle, .22 W. R. F., .25 Stevens R. F. and .22 Hornet.

Weight 8 to 8¼ pounds.

Loop Lever furnished on request.
No extra charge

No. 418 "WALNUT HILL" JUNIOR TARGET RIFLE

No. 418½ "WALNUT HILL" JUNIOR SPORTING RIFLE

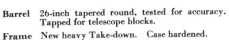

Barrel 26-inch tapered round, tested for accuracy. Tapped for telescope blocks.

Frame New heavy Take-down. Case hardened.

Action Original Stevens "Ideal" breech block.

Sights Lyman Gold bead front and Lyman No. 2A tang peep sight.

No. 416-2 STEVENS—TARGET RIFLE

Fully Equipped—Guaranteed Accuracy

26 inch heavy round tapered barrel, chambered for .22 Long Rifle cartridge. 5-shot machine rest group with each rifle. 5-shot clip magazine. Speed lock, adjustable trigger pull, bolt handle design permits low telescope sight mount. Independent safety with red dot indicator. American walnut stock, oil finish. Adjustable front sling loop. Checkered steel butt plate. Stevens No. 25 hooded front sight with five removable inserts; Stevens No. 106 peep sight with click adjustments. Telescope blocks. Rifle fitted with 1¼ in. leather sling strap. Weight 9½ lbs.

The Model 416-2, complete with sling strap and peep sight equipment, is designed for the rifleman who requires a bolt action .22 caliber repeating rifle of utmost precision. The stock is scientifically proportioned to provide the best possible holding qualities. The barrels are finished to a degree of perfection which enables us to guarantee their accuracy.

No. 416-3 STEVENS .22 CALIBER TARGET RIFLE

Same as No. 416-2 except without front or rear sights.

No. 417 STEVENS WALNUT HILL TARGET RIFLE

28 in. heavy barrel, chambered for .22 Long Rifle, regular or high speed. Lever action. Stevens "Ideal" breech block. Short, fast hammer fall. Automatic ejector. American walnut full pistol grip target model oil finished stock with high comb. Shotgun style butt, with checkered steel butt plate. Broad fore-end. Fitted with military style 1¼ in. leather sling strap treated with Neats-foot oil. Lyman No. 17A front sight. Telescope sight blocks. Weight about 10½ pounds. Length over all, 44 in. Loop style operating lever optional.

Fitted with Lyman rear sights as follows:

No. 417-0—with Lyman No. 52L Extension Sight.   No. 417-2—with Lyman No. 144 Sight.
No. 417-1—with Lyman No. 48L Sight.   No. 417-3—without front or rear Sights.
Any of above furnished with extra-heavy 29-inch barrel at additional charge. See price list.

No. 417½ STEVENS WALNUT HILL SPORTING RIFLE

Same action as No. 417. 28 in. barrel chambered for .22 Long Rifle, .22 W.R.F. or .25 Stevens R.F. Sporting type walnut stock and fore-end, oil finished. 1¼ in. leather sling strap, oil treated. Lyman No. 28 Gold Bead 3-32 in. front sight. Single folding middle sight. Lyman No. 144 tang peep sight. Barrel tapped for telescope sight blocks. Weight 8¼ to 8½ lbs.

No. 418 STEVENS WALNUT HILL TARGET RIFLE

26 in. tapered round barrel, chambered for .22 Long Rifle, regular or high speed cartridges, lever action. Stevens "Ideal" breech block. Short, fast hammer fall. Automatic ejector. American walnut full pistol grip target model oil-finished stock. Broad fore-end. Shotgun style butt, steel butt plate. Fitted with ⅞ in. leather sling strap treated with Neats-foot oil. Partridge type front sight. Lyman No. 144 tang peep sight with click adjustments for elevation and windage. Weight about 6½ lbs. Length over all 41¼ in.

No. 418½ STEVENS WALNUT HILL SPORTING RIFLE

Same action as No. 418. 26 in. barrel chambered for .22 Long Rifle, .22 W.R.F. or .25 Stevens R.F. Automatic ejector in .22 Long Rifle. Positive extractor in other calibers. Sporting type American walnut oil-finished pistol grip stock and fore-end. Shotgun style butt with steel butt plate. Fitted with ⅞ in. leather sling strap treated with Neats-foot oil. Lyman gold bead front sight and Lyman No. 2A tang peep sight. Weight about 6½ lbs. Length over all 41¼ in.

Stevens Walnut Hill Target and Sporting Rifles exemplify the latest advancements in single shot rifle design. They are built for the serious shooter who requires the best obtainable in small bore rifle performance. Each model is fitted with a barrel of guaranteed accuracy and is fully equipped, ready for precision shooting.

No. 35 STEVENS "OFF HAND" SINGLE SHOT PISTOL

Caliber: .22 long rifle regular or high speed. Blued barrel 6, 8 and 12¼ in. lengths, with octagon breech. Single shot with Stevens famous Tip-up action. Positive extractor. Flat top rear sight with elevation adjustment. Bead front sight. Selected black walnut stock. Weight: 6 in., 24 oz.; 8 in., 27 oz.; 12¼ in., 34 oz.

For seventy-five years Stevens has manufactured single shot pistols that have become world famous for their accuracy, finish, workmanship and durability. The No. 35 pistol is one of the most practical models ever designed as a hunting side arm and has been sold in every part of the world.

It has a "man size" grip, clean trigger pull, and sufficient weight in frame and barrel for extremely accurate shooting. The tip-up action is quickly operated for reloading.

No. 066 STEVENS REPEATING RIFLE

Tubular Magazine. For 15 .22 Long Rifle, 17 .22 Long or 21 .22 Short, regular or high speed cartridges

Takedown. 24 in. tapered round barrel with crowned muzzle, chromium plated bolt and trigger. Quick ignition, independent safety. Low lift bolt handle. Red marker indicates cocked action. Full pistol grip stock of American walnut with black tip. Hard rubber butt plate. Equipped with hooded ramp front sight with three interchangeable inserts and removable hood, folding sporting middle sight and rear peep sight with three sizes of aperture openings. Receiver tapped for telescope sight. Weight 5½ lbs.

No. 66 STEVENS REPEATING RIFLE

Same as No. 066 except equipped with gold bead front sight and sporting rear with elevation and windage adjustments.

No. 056 STEVENS REPEATING RIFLE

5-Shot Clip Magazine. For .22 Short, .22 Long and .22 Long Rifle regular or high speed cartridges

Same as No. 066 except equipped with 5-shot clip magazine. Weight 6 lbs. Length over all 43½ in.

No. 56 STEVENS REPEATING RIFLE

Same as No. 056 except equipped with gold bead front sight and sporting rear sight with elevation and windage adjustments.

No. 053 STEVENS SINGLE SHOT RIFLE

For .22 Short, .22 Long and .22 Long Rifle, .22 W.R.F. or .25 Stevens R.F., regular or high speed cartridges

Takedown. 24 in. tapered round barrel with crowned muzzle, chromium plated bolt and trigger, recessed bolt face. Quick ignition, independent safety. Full pistol grip stock of American walnut with black tip. Hard rubber butt plate. Over all length 41¼ in. Equipped with hooded ramp front sight with three interchangeable inserts and removable hood, folding sporting middle sight and rear peep sight with three sizes of aperture openings. Receiver tapped for mounting telescope sight. Weight about 5¼ lbs.

No. 53 STEVENS SINGLE SHOT RIFLE

Same as No. 053 except equipped with gold bead front sight and sporting rear sight, with elevation and windage adjustments.

Patented and Patents Pending

No. 76 STEVENS AUTOMATIC RIFLE — .22 Long Rifle

Adjustable for Automatic Loading, Hand Operated Repeater or Single Shot

Tubular Magazine. 15 .22 Long Rifle, regular or high speed with lubricated bullets for automatic loading. For use as a single shot or bolt action repeater with .22 short, long or long rifle cartridges.

Takedown. 24 in. tapered round barrel with crowned muzzle. Cross bolt locks for use as single shot or repeater. Independent safety. Hammer release mechanism allows the firing of one shot only at each pull of the trigger. Full pistol grip American walnut stock; hard rubber butt plate. Equipped with gold bead front and sporting rear sight with elevation and windage adjustments. Receiver tapped for Weaver telescope sight. Weight about 6 lbs.

No. 076 STEVENS AUTOMATIC RIFLE

Same as No. 76 except equipped with hooded front sight with three interchangeable inserts, rear peep sight with two sighting discs and folding flat top middle sight.

Patented and Patents Pending

No. 57 STEVENS AUTOMATIC RIFLE

Same specifications as No. 76 shown above except equipped with a five shot clip magazine.

No. 057 STEVENS AUTOMATIC RIFLE

Same specifications as No. 57 except equipped with hooded ramp front sight with three interchangeable inserts, removable hood, folding sporting middle sight and receiver peep sight with two sighting discs.

You'll get a brand new shooting thrill the first time you fire shot after shot from a Stevens Automatic rifle, just as fast as you can work your trigger finger. Without shifting either hand, you can hold steadily, concentrate on your aim and place more shots, more accurately, in less time than with any manually operated arm.

The rifle is automatic only in that loading, ejecting and cocking are accomplished by the force of recoil. The trigger must be pulled and released for each shot. If the trigger is pulled and *held back*,

only one shot will be fired.

THREE RIFLES IN ONE
Automatic, Bolt-Action Repeater, Single Shot

As automatic . . . use .22 Long Rifle Cartridges, regular or high speed, with *lubricated bullets*.

As manually operated repeater or single shot rifle . . . use .22 Long Rifle or .22 Long or .22 Short Cartridges.

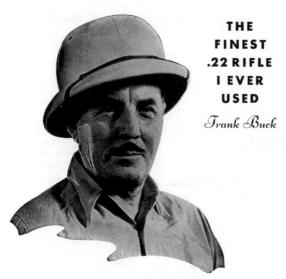

THE FINEST .22 RIFLE I EVER USED

Frank Buck

This is the experience of a man who *knows*. While operating shooting galleries in several cities in Illinois, Mr. Stratman has observed the functioning of .22 caliber rifles under the exacting conditions of range use.

Such remarkable performance is made possible by the use of steel of just the right characteristics for each component of the rifle and by a rigid inspection and gauging routine during the processes of manufacture, followed by a thorough functioning test of the finished rifle. These carefully planned and efficiently executed details of production assure long life and dependability to every Buckhorn Rifle.

★ FAST ACTION

THE Buckhorn Rifle bolt is of heavy construction, with strong extractor and ejector. The bolt stroke is exceptionally short and provides instantaneous ejection of the fired cartridge cases. The bolt of the repeating models is so designed as to insure positive straight-line loading, without the slightest distortion of the bullets.

The quick functioning of the bolt and the speed of the ignition are features of each model which are especially appreciated when shooting at running game or when engaged in rapid-fire target work.

The automatic loading, ejection and cocking of the Nos. 076, 76, 057 and 57 give a speed of fire which adds materially to the effectiveness of the .22 rifle in destroying vermin or in hunting fast-moving game.

★ WELL BALANCED

THE barrel of each Buckhorn Rifle is of sufficient weight for steady aiming and is perfectly balanced by a man-sized stock of correct proportions, with large, well-rounded forestock. This combination of barrel and stock provides holding qualities which enable the shooter to take full advantage of the super-accuracy of the Rifle.

The dimensions of the stock have been carefully worked out to permit the rifle to come up easily into firing position. The corrugated butt plate prevents slipping after the rifle is at the shoulder. This attention to the details of design and balance gives to each of these rifles the superior "holding qualities" which contribute so much to success in either hunting or target practice.

Comfortable to hold and easy to sight, Stevens Buckhorn Rifles never feel "muzzle heavy."

★ ACCURATE

THE FIRST THREE places in the Fifth Annual "Open Road for Boys" National Rifle Match, Light Rifle Division, were won by teams shooting Stevens Buckhorn Rifles. These rifles were purchased by the contestants from their local dealers' regular stocks.

Improved materials and modern equipment have made it possible for the present generation of Stevens experts to attain a degree of precision in barrel production which has established an exceptionally high standard of accuracy. The barrel of *every* Buckhorn Rifle is bored to insure prize-winning performance in *any* company.

★ DEPENDABLE

147,750 shots fired from a Buckhorn Rifle without a malfunction or failure of any kind is the report received from Mr. Dan C. Stratman, Shooting Gallery proprietor, Danville, Illinois.

No. 27 STEVENS FAVORITE—Single Shot Rifle

Barrel: 24 in. tapered crowned muzzle. Full octagon. Chambered for .22 long rifle, .25 rim-fire or .32 long rim-fire, high speed or regular cartridges. Action: Blued, take-down, single shot. Stevens Drop Block Lever action, automatic ejector in .22 caliber—plain extractor in other calibers. Walnut stock and fore-end. Sights: Gold bead front and sporting rear sight with elevation adjustment. Weight 4½ lbs. Length over all 38 in.

The action of the Stevens Favorite is a powerful lever type. The downward and forward movement of lever draws the breech block downward below line of bore and operates ejector. After cartridge is placed in chamber of rifle the action is closed and locked by lever, and hammer is left in safe half-cocked position. A simple take-down screw allows barrel to be withdrawn from frame for cleaning and transportation.

No. 26 STEVENS CRACK SHOT—Single Shot Rifle

Chambered for .22 long rifle or .32 long rim-fire regular cartridges only.

Barrel: 22 in. round, tapered, crowned muzzle. Action: case hardened, take-down, single shot, lever action, drop breech block, positive extractor. Sights: Partridge type front, sporting rear. Stock: Oval shape walnut finish, with steel butt plate. Large fore-end. Weight 3½ lbs. Length over all 36 in.

No. 26½ STEVENS CRACK SHOT

Same as No. 26 except smooth bore full choke. Chambered for .22 shot or .32 shot cartridges.

The Stevens "Crack Shot" provides the popular lever action type of rifle at a low price which makes it particularly desirable for youths.

STEVENS SPORTING ARMS

THE shotguns and rifles illustrated in the following pages represent the latest advancements in sporting arms as developed by an organization which, during the seventy-five years of its growth, has been a recognized leader in pioneering improvements in design and methods of manufacture. *Each model is the perfected product of three-quarters of a century of progress.*

Typical of Stevens achievements have been: 1. The development of the .22 Long Rifle cartridge, now the World's most popular .22 caliber ammunition. 2. The application of precision boring and rifling to .22 caliber barrels. 3. The development of the Stevens "Ideal" breech mechanism for single shot rifles. 4. The invention of an automatic rifle to successfully handle .22 Long Rifle cartridges regardless of variations in breech pressures. These are but a few of the contributions made by Stevens during its seventy-five years of service to sportsmen.

Each shotgun bearing the Stevens or Springfield brand is made from materials carefully selected to best perform the functions required of the several components. All parts are gauged and inspected with infinite care and the assembled guns are subjected to thorough proof and functioning tests. Every barrel is bored, polished and choked according to a precise routine which insures maximum shooting results. Each finished gun represents the highest standard of honest value.

Each rifle in the Stevens and Springfield lines is designed to meet the requirements of hunters and riflemen who are particular about their equipment and who insist upon the best values obtainable. Every part is made from selected materials and is carefully gauged and inspected during the processes of manufacture. Each barrel is bored and rifled with painstaking precision by highly skilled gunsmiths who are trained in the Stevens tradition. Any Stevens or Springfield Rifle you select will be found to possess those qualities of safety, reliability, accuracy and value which have long been associated with the Stevens name.

Large volume production and the use of highly specialized equipment have enabled the Stevens organization to effect economies in manufacture which make it possible to supply sporting rifles and shotguns of advanced design and superior quality at prices which are appreciated by thrifty sportsmen.

Reprinted from Savage/Stevens Catalog 1939

Joshua Stevens built the first Stevens rifle in a little frame building in Chicopee Falls, Mass. It was a good rifle. The barrel had been so precisely bored and rifled that it performed with a degree of accuracy never before attained in a sporting arm. It found a ready market, and Joshua Stevens prospered.

Since that time the demand for accurate Stevens built sporting arms has steadily increased until now the Stevens Plant comprises a large group of modern buildings and each year produces many thousands of sporting rifles and shotguns.

Today, operating highly developed precision machinery, the gun-makers who build Stevens and Springfield rifles and shotguns carry the spirit of fine workmanship and honest value to new and higher levels. The fine craftsmanship for which New England has become famous was never more carefully fostered than among the fathers and sons working side by side in the Stevens plant.

J. STEVENS ARMS COMPANY
Division of SAVAGE ARMS CORPORATION
CHICOPEE FALLS, MASS., U. S. A.

75th
1864-1939
ANNIVERSARY

STEVENS NO. 417 WALNUT HILL TARGET RIFLE

A single shot arm for the .22 Long Rifle rim fire cartridge. It has a 28-inch round, heavy barrel, and weighs 10½ to 11 pounds. The breech action is the falling block, under lever type so popular with many of our older riflemen. The speed lock is extremely fast, the rifle firing from what may be termed the "half cock" position of the hammer. Pulling the hammer all the way back to the "full cock" position sets the hammer at "Safe." Stock, American walnut, oil finished, and of excellent shape and proportions with very wide beavertail forearm. Equipped with 1¼-inch sling swivels, and with Government type 1¼-inch gunsling, which is included in the price. Rifle balances and holds remarkably well, and many shooters think it holds steadier in the standing (offhand) position than any other rifle. Every rifle is tested for accuracy. It is fitted with scope blocks for Fecker and Lyman scopes, and with various sight equipment as follow.

PRICES

No. 417-0, with Lyman No. 17 Front and Lyman No. 52-L
Extension Sight $55.35

No. 417-1, with Lyman No. 17 Front and Lyman 48-L
Rear Sight 53.85

No. 417-2, with Lyman No. 17 Front and Lyman No. 144
Windgauge Tang Sight 48.00

No. 417-3, without front or rear sights, but with scope
blocks 42.65

STEVENS NO. 417½ WALNUT HILL SPORTING RIFLE

Similar to the Stevens No. 417 Rifle except 28-inch barrel is of medium weight, making the rifle weigh about 8 pounds. the beavertail forearm is not so wide, and the barrel is drilled and tapped for scope blocks. Swing swivels and gunsling are included in the price. For the .22 Long Rifle, the .22 W.R.F., and the .25 Stevens rim fire cartridges. In .25 caliber particularly this rifle makes a particularly fine small game rifle as the .25 Stevens cartridge is almost as accurate in it as the target varieties of the .22 Long Rifle cartridge, and the rifle holds remarkably steady in the standing position, making it a fine squirrel rifle. It is regularly fitted with Lyman No. 144 rear tang sight with windage adjustment and with Lyman gold bead front sight, which are excellent hunting sights.

PRICE

Stevens No. 417½ Walnut Hill Sporting Rifle, as above $42.65

STEVENS NO. 418 WALNUT HILL RIFLE

No. 418. 26-inch barrel, takedown, automatic ejector, original Stevens "Ideal" breech block, pistol grip of American walnut, with sling swivels and gunsling. Lyman No. 144 rear sight adjustment for elevation and windage, and black Partridge front sight $21.95

No. 418½ Same as above, but with Lyman No. 2A rear sight and gold bead front sight. .22 Long Rifle, .22 W.R.F. or .25 Stevens R.F., weight 6½ pounds. $19.65

SAVAGE MODEL 23AA SPORTER RIFLE

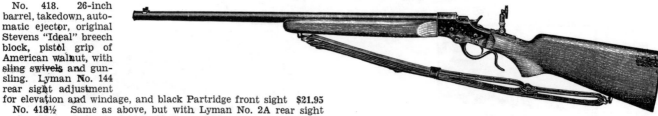

Bolt action, 23-inch barrel for .22 Long Rifle cartridge. Five shot detachable magazine. Pistol grip stock of walnut. Weight 7 pounds. Fitted with bead front and open rear sight.

A very fine weapon for hunting or combined hunting and target shooting when fitted with good sights and a gunsling.
Price $23.75

SAVAGE MODEL 19 TARGET RIFLE

The Savage Model 19 Target Rifle is a bolt action repeating arm for the .22 Long Rifle rim fire cartridge. It has a detachable 5-shot magazine, and can be used either as a single shot or a repeater. The medium weight barrel is 25 inches long, and the sight radius 30½ inches. The rifle weighs about 8 pounds. The barrel is drilled and tapped for Lyman and Fecker scope blocks. The stock is of excellent shape and dimensions, being rather straight for use in the prone position, and the small drop at comb and heel make it suitable for use with telescope sights without alteration. The swivels are for 1¼ inch gunsling. The sight equipment is shown below.

PRICES

Model 19 Rifle with standard extension aperture rear sight with ½ minute click adjustments for elevation and windage, and military blade flat top front sight $29.50

Model 19-L, without sights 24.50

Model 19-H, same as Model 19 above except chambered for the .22 Hornet center fire cartridge 36.00

Model 19-M, same as Model 19, but heavy barrel 36.00

SAVAGE MODELS 29 SLIDE ACTION RIFLE

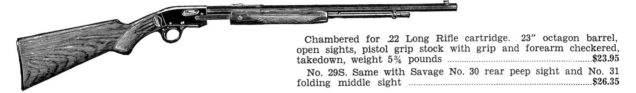

Chambered for .22 Long Rifle cartridge. 23″ octagon barrel, open sights, pistol grip stock with grip and forearm checkered, takedown, weight 5¾ pounds $23.95

No. 29S. Same with Savage No. 30 rear peep sight and No. 31 folding middle sight $26.35

SAVAGE MODEL 99 RS RIFLE

Savage Model 99 RS Lever Action Rifle. Solid frame. Calibers .250-3000 and .303 Savage with 22 inch barrel. .300 Savage with 24 inch barrel. Weight about 7¼ pounds. Barrels specially selected for accuracy. Modern pistol grip stock and forearm of oiled walnut, with high comb and pistol grip and forearm checkered, quick release swivels, and ⅞-inch Government type shooting gunsling. Lyman No. 30½ Windgauge rear sight with cup disc,

folding leaf middle sight, and gold bead front sight. All of these specifications contribute to make this rifle one of the most accurate, dependable, and satisfactory lever action big game rifles ever produced, and we recommend it very highly. Rifle is well suited to a telescope sight.

Savage Model 99-RS Rifle as above, price $64.00

Savage Model 99-R Rifle, same as above, but with open rear sight, no swivels or sling, and barrel not specially selected for accuracy, price 53.50

SAVAGE MODEL 99 HI-POWER REPEATING LEVER ACTION RIFLES

In addition to the Savage Model 99-RS rifle previously described, we are prepared to furnish the following older models of this well known rifle. Made in .22 Hi-power, .250-3000, .30-30, .303 Savage, and .300 Savage calibers unless otherwise stated.

Model 99-H. Carbine, solid frame, 20″ barrel, .250-3000, .30-30, and .303 calibers only. Weight 6¾ pounds $45.00

Model 99-EG. Solid frame, pistol grip, 24″ barrel $47.00

Model 99-G. Takedown, pistol grip, 24″ barrel 54.75

Model 99-T. Solid frame, featherweight model, pistol grip, 20″ barrel, weight 7 pounds (illustrated above) 53.00

Model 99-F. Takedown, straight grip, shotgun butt, 22″ barrel, weight 7½ pounds 53.00

Model 99-K. Takedown, same as Model 99-G but fancy walnut checkering and engraving, and Lyman rear peep sight 85.00

SAVAGE MODEL 23 BOLT ACTION RIFLES

The Savage Model 23 Rifle is a bolt action repeater with 5 shot detachable magazine, 23 inch round barrel, pistol grip stock of very good dimensions, shotgun butt-plate, and is fitted with open sights, as standard. It is furnished in three calibers, the Model 23-B for the .25-30 W.C.F. cartridge, the Model 23-C for the .32-20 W.C.F. cartridge, and the Model 23-D for the .22 Hornet cartridge. The weight is about 7 pounds.

Savage No. 3-A ⅞-inch sling swivels, price 50 cents, and with

the Savage No. 3, ⅞-inch, Govt. type gunsling, price $1.50 extra. Fecker, Lyman, and Unertl small game scopes can also be fitted, and this rifle can also be had with the Weaver scopes with low mounts. See Section IV for scope sights.

PRICES

Savage Model 23-B Rifle, .25-20 W.C.F. Open Sights $32.40

Savage Model 23-C Rifle, .32-20 W.C.F. Open Sights 32.40

Savage Model 23-D Rifle, .22 Hornet. Open Sights 32.40

SAVAGE AUTOMATIC SHOTGUN

MODEL 720: 12 and 16 gauge, 5 shots. Plain round barrel, 26, 28, or 30 inch, full or modified choke or cylinder bore. Full pistol grip and forearm of selected American walnut checkered, 14″ x 1¾″ x 2⅝″. Push button type of safety in rear of trigger guard. Plug furnished to reduce magazine capacity to 2 shots if desired. Receiver channeled and matted in line of sight. Friction ring adjustment for light and heavy loads. Weight: 12 gauge about 8¼ lbs.; 16 gauge about 7¾ lbs.

MODEL 721: Same as Model 720 but with solid raised matted rib.

MODEL 722: Same as Model 720 but with ventilated raised rib.

MODEL 726: "Upland Sporter." Same as Model 720 except magazine capacity is 2 shells, weight 12 gauge about 8 pounds, 16 gauge about 7½ pounds. Receiver artistically decorated with engraving.

MODEL 727: Same as Model 726 but with solid raised rib.

MODEL 728: Same as Model 726 but with ventilated raised rib.

The three "Upland Sporters" above, with 3-shot capacity, are light to carry, fast in action, and easy to point. The receiver is artistically decorated and this, with the special checkering on stock and fore-end combine to make an attractive arm for field use.

MODEL 720-P: Same as Model 720 but with Poly-Choke.

MODEL 726-P: Same as Model 726 except has new Aero-Dyne Super Poly Choke built integral with barrel and equipped with Bev-L-Blok front sight. Furnished only with 28″ overall barrel.

MODEL 740-P: "Skeet Model." Same as Model 726-P, but with fancy American walnut stock, oil finished, with full capped pistol grip, elaborately checkered, with a special beavertail fore-end also elaborately checkered. Weight 8¼ pounds.

MODEL 720-C: Same as Model 720 but with Cutts Compensator.

MODEL 726-C: Same as Model 726 but with special barrel with Cutts Compensator attached, furnished with two choke tubes. Overall barrel length 27 inches.

MODEL 740-C: "Skeet Model." Same as Model 740-P, but with Cutts Compensator. Overall barrel length 27 inches, weight 8¼ lbs.

PRICES

Model 720, 5 shot, plain round barrel	$46.45
Model 721, 5 shot, raised matted rib	54.20
Model 722, 5 shot, raised ventilated rib	60.20
Model 726, "Upland Sporter" 3 shot, plain round barrel	46.45
Model 727, "Upland Sporter" 3 shot, matted rib	54.20
Model 728, "Upland Sporter" 3 shot, ventilated rib	60.20
Model 720-C, 5 shot with Cutts Compensator	64.95
Model 726-C, 3 shot with Cutts Compensator	64.95
Model 740-C, "Skeet Model" 3 shot, with Cutts Compensator	70.45
Model 720-P, 5 shot, with Poly Choke	55.40
Model 726-P, 3 shot, with Poly Choke	55.40
Model 740-P, "Skeet Model" 3 shot, with Poly Choke	58.95

SAVAGE SINGLE BARREL SHOTGUN

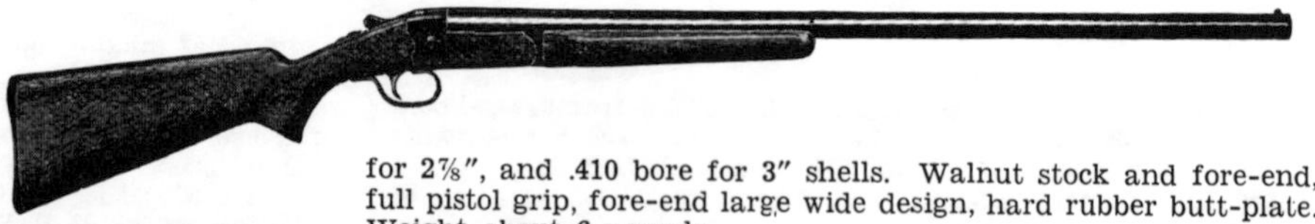

This is the most attractive single barrel shotgun we have seen, and at a most reasonable price. It is hammerless with an automatic top tang safety. All working parts are made of long wearing special alloy steel, and operated by strong coil springs. Automatic ejector is ½-inch wide assuring positive extraction and ejection. Frame polished and blued. Barrel bolted to frame with large beveled locking bolt. Fore-end fastens with tension of heavy steel spring against hinge pin and fore-end barrel lug. Both features designed to automatically take up wear.

MODEL 220 is made in 12, 16, 20, 28, and .410 bore, all full choke. Barrel lengths, 12 and 16 gauge 28 to 32 inches; 20 gauge, 26 to 32 inches; 28 gauge, 28 & 30 inches; .410 bore, 26 & 28 inches. 12, 16 & 20 gauge chambered for 2¾″ shells; 28 gauge for 2⅞″, and .410 bore for 3″ shells. Walnut stock and fore-end, full pistol grip, fore-end large wide design, hard rubber butt-plate. Weight about 6 pounds.

MODEL 220-P is same except it is fitted with a special Poly Choke, built integral with the barrel, which gives the shooter an instant choice of any choke. Special recoil pad. Barrel lengths: 12 ga. 30″; 16 & 20 ga. 28″.

PRICES

Model 220 as above	$11.00
Model 220-P as above	16.00

SAVAGE UTILITY GUN

Provides a .30-30 or .22 Hornet rifle and a sturdy shotgun at less than half the price of a high power repeating rifle. The shotgun is precisely the same as the Savage Model 220 shotgun described above. The instantly interchangeable rifle barrel is built to the same standard as the barrels of the famous Savage high power repeating rifles, and is fitted with open sights. It is regularly furnished in .30-30 and .22 Hornet calibers, but will be furnished to order for the .25-20 or .32-20 cartridges. The gun

with rifle barrel only will also be furnished, and is known as the Model 219. All rifle barrels are 26 inches long.

No. 221.	.30-30	caliber, with	12 gauge	30″	barrel.
No. 222.	.30-30	"	16 "	28″	barrel.
No. 223.	.30-30	"	20 "	28″	barrel.
No. 227.	.22 Hornet	"	12 "	30″	barrel.
No. 228.	.22	" "	16 "	28″	barrel.
No. 229.	.22	" "	20 "	28″	barrel.

PRICES

Utility Gun with rifle and shotgun barrels	$19.35
No. 219 with high power rifle barrel only	14.85

THE POLY CHOKE

The Poly Choke is a device that is screwed to the muzzle of any plain or ribbed single barrelled shotgun which permits of varying the choke at will, by turning the collar on the sleeve of the device, from open cylinder to full choke. The device is 2½ inches long and weighs 2½ ounces for 12 and 16 gauge, and 2 ounces for the 20 gauge. In attaching it the barrel of your gun can be cut off to any length desired, or left at its original length. The weight does not unbalance the gun badly, and by cutting the barrel off about 3 inches the original balance is restored. There is nothing to get out of order, and the device stays set and does not clog from powder dirt or lead.

In all cases the shotgun must be sent to us, or a new gun can have the device installed on it. State the length you wish your barrel to be cut to.

Price, installed on your shotgun $14.75

STEVENS NO. 22-410 OVER AND UNDER RIFLE AND SHOTGUN

This is a weapon which we believe every shooter should own, irrespective of whether he has other guns or not. No gun has ever been made which will be found so universally useful for the sportsman for general use, for the farmer, or for the wilderness hunter who wishes a small game weapon to supplement his high power rifle. On a big game hunt the .22 caliber barrel may be used without danger of the report disturbing big game in the vicinity. Novel features have made it possible to produce a gun weighing only 6 pounds, such weight never before being possible in a combination shotgun and rifle. The slide button barrel selector places either the rifle or shotgun barrel at your immediate command. Both barrels are so rigidly brazed together for their entire length that they become practically one unit.

All the lines and appearance of the gun are exceedingly attractive and the TENITE stock gives it an exceedingly rich and expensive appearance.

Upper barrel for the .22 Long Rifle cartridge, regular or high speed. Lower barrel for .410 bore shot shells, 3 inch case, full choke. Barrels 24″ long, open rifle sights. Low rebounding hammer, single trigger, slide button on right for instant selection of barrel to be fired, separate extractors, top lever operates either to right or left to open action, case hardened frame, takedown.

The full pistol grip stock is made of moulded TENITE (see below), handsomely panelled, with fluted comb and checkered capped grip, and hard rubber butt-plate. Fore-end made of TENITE and equipped with special fastening which prevents gun from shooting loose. Be sure to read the description of TENITE stocks below, and note the unusually low price for this fine and useful gun.

Price, as above $14.95

STEVENS NO. 530-M DOUBLE BARREL SHOTGUN

Made in 12, 16, and 20 gauge and .410 bore. An exceedingly well made shotgun at a very moderate price, and very rich in appearance because the stock and fore-end are made of moulded TENITE (see below), with panelled sides and checkered capped pistol grip. Length 14″, drop 2¾″. Blued forged steel barrels

with matted rib, fitted with two white bead Ivoroid sights. 12 and 16 gauge 26, 28, or 30 inches; 20 gauge 26 & 28 inches; .410 bore 26 inches, all bored right modified and left full choke except .410 bore which is full choke in both barrels. All chambered for 2¾″ shells except .410 bore which is for 3″ shells. Weights, 12 ga. 7½ lbs.; 16 ga. 7 lbs.; 20 ga. 6½ lbs.; .410 bore 5¾ lbs.

No. 530-M as above $22.75
No. 530 MST. As above with non-selective single trigger 26.00

STEVENS TENITE STOCKS

The Stevens Tenite Stocks as fitted to the Stevens No. 22-410 and 530 M guns above only, has the appearance and durability of the finest imported Circassian walnut, London oil finish stocks seen only on the most expensive custom made arms. It is easily the richest appearing stock placed on any standard gun made in America.

Before adopting TENITE as a material for stocks Stevens conducted a most thorough test of it in their Research Department and in the field under actual shooting conditions. It is ideally adapted to withstand the strain and shocks to which gun stocks and fore-ends are subjected in use.

Neither the strength nor the dimensional stability of TENITE is effected by extreme cold or tropic heat, it is impervious to

moisture, and will neither swell, warp, nor crack in any climate or under any weather conditions.

TENITE stocks and fore-ends have a rich, lustrous grained finish, not easily scratched or marred. As the beautiful burled grained pattern runs through and through, should the finish be damaged it can readily be restored by polishing with a fine abrasive.

TENITE has the property of absorbing shock and vibrations, thus making the recoil of the gun less noticeable. The moulding process assures accurate fitting of the stocks to the frames, and the weight of TENITE is uniform making it easier to precisely balance and fit the gun.

STEVENS REPEATING SHOTGUNS

No. 620 Hammerless, slide action, side ejection, takedown. Pistol grip stock of walnut, grip and forearm checkered, rubber butt-plate, length 13¾ inches, drop at heel 2¾ inches. Weight 6 to 7¾ pounds. 12 gauge, 28, 30, or 32 inch, full choke, 28 or 30 inch,

modified, 26 or 28 inch, cylinder bored, 16 gauge, full, modified, or cylinder bore, 26 inch cylinder bore. 20 gauge, 26 or 28 inch, cylinder, modified, or full choke. 5 shots, a plug to reduce the capacity to 3 shots being furnished.

Price $36.25
No. 621 Same with raised matted rib 39.75
No. 620P Same as 620 with Polychoke 41.25

STEVENS BOLT ACTION .410 BORE SHOTGUN

Five shots, one in chamber and four in tubular magazine. 24″ barrel for .410 bore, 3″ shell. Full choke. Takedown. Pistol grip stock. Hard rubber butt-plate, weight about 6 pounds.

Will also handle 2½″ shell. Price No. 59 ....$13.25
No. 58 Same but clip magazine 11.25

STEVENS RETAIL PRICES

EFFECTIVE NOVEMBER 1ST, 1929

RIFLES

No.		Page	Price Each
65	Bolt Action 22 Cal. Repeater......	4	$10.75
75	Hammerless 22 Cal. Repeater......	5	17.50
70	Visible Loader 22 Cal. Repeater.....	5	13.50
27	Favorite Octagon Barrel...........	6	9.80
17	Favorite Round Barrel...........	6	9.25
20	Favorite Smooth Bore.............	6	9.25
12	Marksman......................	6	8.00
26	Crack Shot Rifle Barrel...........	7	6.00
26½	Crackshot Smooth Bore...........	7	6.00
14½	Little Scout...................	7	5.00
11	Stevens Junior..................	7	4.25
44	Ideal.........................	8	19.00
414	Armory.......................	8	21.00
50	Springfield Junior................	9	7.00
49	Challenge.....................	10	6.00
48	Bolt Action....................	10	5.00

SINGLE BARREL SHOTGUNS

No.		Page	Price Each
107	Stevens.......................	11-12	$10.50
105	Stevens.......................	12	10.00
106	Stevens.......................	12	10.00
108	Stevens.......................	12	10.50
89	Dreadnaught....................	13	12.75
116	Stevens.......................	13	13.75
95	Springfield....................	14	10.00
958	Springfield....................	14	10.00
94	Springfield....................	15	8.00
948	Springfield....................	15	8.00

Extra charge for Single Guns with 34-in barrel .50
Extra charge for Single Guns with 36-in. Barrel 1.00
Nos. 105-106-107-108-89 furnished with
checkered stock and fore-end   extra   1.00

DOUBLE BARREL SHOTGUNS

No.		Page	Price Each
330	Stevens Hammerless..............	17	$26.50
335	Stevens Hammerless..............	18	27.50
235	Stevens Hammer.................	18	25.00
311	Springfield Hammerless...........	19	18.50
315	Springfield Hammerless	20	24.00
215	Springfield Hammer	20	20.50

REPEATING SHOTGUNS

No.		Page	Price Each
620	Stevens.........................	22	$39.95
621	Stevens.........................	22	45.00
520	Springfield......................	23	39.95
521	Springfield......................	23	45.00

PISTOLS

No.		Page	Price Each
35	Off-Hand 6″, Tax Included.........	24	$12.50
35	Off-Hand 8″, Tax Included.........	24	13.25
35	Off-Hand, .410 Gauge.............	24	12.00
10	Target, Tax Included..............	25	15.00

STEVENS RIFLE SIGHTS

No.		Page	Price Each
130	Windgauge Vernier................	25	$5.00
120	Windgauge Vernier................	25	4.00
	Combination Eye Cup, Extra.......	25	1.00
203	Rocky Mountain..................	25	.75
210	Globe Interchangeable Disc........	25	2.00
112	Sporting Rear....................	25	1.00
201	Sight Slot Blank.................	25	.50

CLEANING RODS

No.		Page	Price Each
505-506-507-508-518-509-510		26	$ .10
513	....	26	.20
540		26	.50
560-570-605-606-607		26	.15
250	Government.....................	26	.25
95-954	....	26	.50
	Tomlinson Cleaner................	26	.35

SWIVELS, HOOKS AND SLING STRAPS

No.		Page	Per Set
1	Swivels, fitted or loose.............	26	$ .85
2	2D or 2R, Swivels and Hooks, loose..	26	1.00
2	2D or 2R, Swivels and Hooks, fitted..	26	2.00
4	Swivels and Hooks, loose..........	26	1.00
4	Swivels and Hooks, fitted..........	26	2.00

			Each
	Leather Sling Straps.............	27	1.00
	Web Adjustable Sling Strap........	27	1.50
	Stevens Anti-Rust Gun Grease......	27	.15

Parts Price List Sent on Application

J. STEVENS ARMS COMPANY ❦ CHICOPEE FALLS, MASS.

These Prices Effective East of the Rocky Mountains

STEVENS RETAIL PRICE LIST

For 75th Anniversary Catalog
Effective May 12th, 1939

	Price Each	Page
SINGLE BARREL SHOTGUNS		
No. 107 Stevens	$ 9.65	4
No. 105 Stevens	9.15	4
No. 104 Stevens	9.65	5
No. 102 Stevens	9.15	5
No. 116 Stevens	15.00	5
BOLT ACTION SHOTGUNS		
No. 59 Stevens .410 Bore Repeater	11.50	6
No. 58 Stevens .410 Bore Repeater	8.95	6
No. 54 Stevens .410 Bore Single Shot	7.45	7
No. 258 Stevens 20 Gauge Repeater	10.75	7
No. 254 Stevens 20 Gauge Single Shot	7.75	7
DOUBLE BARREL SHOTGUNS		
No. 530 Stevens	22.75	8
No. 530-ST Stevens	25.95	8
REPEATING SHOTGUNS		
No. 620 Stevens	33.65	9
No. 621 Stevens	37.00	9
No. 620-P Stevens	38.65	9
RIFLES		
No. 76 Stevens "Buckhorn" Automatic	15.65	11
No. 076 Stevens "Buckhorn" Automatic	16.40	11
No. 57 Stevens "Buckhorn" Automatic	13.75	11
No. 057 Stevens "Buckhorn" Automatic	14.50	11
No. 66 Stevens "Buckhorn" Repeater	13.25	12
No. 066 Stevens "Buckhorn" Repeater	12.50	12
No. 056 Stevens "Buckhorn" Repeater	9.40	12
No. 56 Stevens "Buckhorn" Repeater	8.95	12
No. 53 Stevens "Buckhorn" Single Shot	5.60	12
No. 053 Stevens "Buckhorn" Single Shot	4.95	12
No. 27 Stevens "Favorite"	9.75	13
No. 26 Stevens "Crack Shot"	4.45	13
No. 26½ Stevens "Crack Shot"	4.45	13
No. 416-2 Stevens Target	27.95	14
No. 416-3 Stevens Target	23.25	14
No. 417-0 Stevens "Walnut Hill"	50.00	14
No. 417-1 Stevens "Walnut Hill"	48.50	14
No. 417-2 Stevens "Walnut Hill"	43.50	14
No. 417-3 Stevens "Walnut Hill"	38.50	14
Nos. 417-0, 417-1, 417-2, 417-3, with extra-heavy 29" barrel, additional charge	25.00	14
No. 417½ Stevens "Walnut Hill"	38.50	14
No. 418 Stevens "Walnut Hill"	19.75	15
No. 418½ Stevens "Walnut Hill"	17.75	15
PISTOLS		
No. 35 Stevens "Off Hand", 6 in.	10.35	15
No. 35 Stevens "Off Hand", 8 in.	10.85	15
No. 35 Stevens "Off Hand", 12¼ in.	11.25	15

	Price Each	Page
SINGLE BARREL SHOTGUNS		
No. 94 Springfield	$ 8.00	16
No. 944 Springfield	8.00	16
DOUBLE BARREL SHOTGUNS		
No. 311 Springfield	20.95	17
No. 311-ST Springfield	24.30	17
BOLT ACTION SHOTGUNS		
No. 39 Springfield .410 Bore Repeater	11.25	18
No. 38 Springfield .410 Bore Repeater	8.50	18
No. 238 Springfield 20 Gauge Repeater	10.35	18
No. 37 Springfield .410 Bore Single Shot	6.85	18
No. 237 Springfield 20 Gauge Single Shot	7.00	18
RIFLES		
No. 87 Springfield Automatic	14.10	19
No. 087 Springfield Automatic	14.75	19
No. 85 Springfield Automatic	12.00	19
No. 085 Springfield Automatic	12.55	19
No. 083 Springfield Single Shot	5.10	20
No. 83 Springfield Single Shot	4.50	20
No. 084 Springfield Repeater	8.95	20
No. 84 Springfield Repeater	8.40	20
No. 086 Springfield Repeater	11.45	20
No. 86 Springfield Repeater	10.80	20
No. 15 Springfield Single Shot	4.00	21

STEVENS RIFLE SIGHTS (Page 21)

	Price Each		Price Each
No. 25	$1.50	No. 19	$ 1.25
No. 100	.80	No. 112	.70
No. 105	4.00	No. 104	.60
No. 106		No. 103	.80

STEVENS CARRYING AND SLING STRAPS (Page 21)

	Price Each		Price Each
No. 3B	$2.40	No. 2	$2.20
No. 2B	3.00	No. 1	.60
No. 3	1.90	No. 0	.60

STEVENS SLING STRAP SWIVEL LOOPS AND HOOKS (Page 21)

	Price Each		Price Each
No. 1	$ .50	No. 4	$ .55
No. 2D	.55	No. 4 Fitted	.75
No. 2R	.55	No. 5	1.00
No. 3	.50	No. 6	1.50

TELESCOPE SIGHTS (Page 22)

No. 10	No. 20	No. 30
$4.75	$8.00	$11.70

CLIP MAGAZINES

	Price Each
5-Shot, for Nos. 056, 56, 057, 57, 084, 84, 085, 85	$ .65
10-Shot, for Nos. 056, 56, 057, 57, 084, 84, 085, 85	.85
3-Shot, for Nos. 58, 38	1.00
2-Shot, for Nos. 258, 238	1.00

Prices Subject to Change Without Notice

PARTS PRICE LIST SENT ON APPLICATION

J. STEVENS ARMS COMPANY
Division of Savage Arms Corporation
CHICOPEE FALLS, MASS., U.S.A.

75th 1864-1939 ANNIVERSARY

Printed in U.S.A.

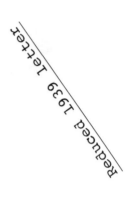

J. STEVENS ARMS COMPANY

DIVISION OF SAVAGE ARMS CORPORATION

RIFLES AND SHOTGUNS

CHICOPEE FALLS, MASS., U.S.A.

June 28, 1939

Mr. Carl D. Spickerman
Route #3 Box #9
The Dalles, Oregon

Dear Sir:

In reply to your letter of June 22nd, would advise we would be unable to furnish any of our rifles equipped with smooth bore barrels except our model #26¢, specifications of which you will note from our catalog.

Yours very truly,

A. B. Woodhall

Sales Department

ABWoodhall/gm

75th 1864-1939 ANNIVERSARY

Reduced 1939 letter

STEVENS RETAIL PRICES

Effective August 15, 1935

RIFLES

No.		Page	Price Each
066	"Buckhorn"	4	$11.95
66	"Buckhorn"	4	10.95
056	"Buckhorn"	4	10.95
56	"Buckhorn"	4	9.95
055	"Buckhorn"	5	7.85
55	"Buckhorn"	5	6.85
053	"Buckhorn"	5	6.50
53	"Buckhorn"	5	5.50
27	"Favorite"	6	8.75
20	"Favorite" Smooth Bore	6	8.00
26	"Crack Shot"	6	4.75
26½	"Crack Shot" Smooth Bore	6	4.75
14½	"Little Scout"	6	4.25
417-1	"Walnut Hill" Target	7	45.00
417-2	"Walnut Hill" Target	7	40.75
417-3	"Walnut Hill" Target	7	35.85
417½	"Walnut Hill" Target	7	35.85
418	"Walnut Hill Jr." Target	8	18.00
418½	"Walnut Hill Jr." Target	8	16.00
419	"Stevens Jr." Target	9	9.95
86	"Springfield"	10	10.50
84	"Springfield"	10	9.35
83	"Springfield"	11	5.40
82	"Springfield"	11	4.90

SINGLE BARREL SHOTGUNS

No.		Page	Price Each
54	"Stevens" .410 S.S.	12	6.85
58	"Stevens" .410 Rep.	12	11.85
	Extra Clip Magazine	12	1.00
37	"Springfield" .410 S.S.	13	6.65
38	"Springfield" .410 Rep.	13	11.50
107	"Stevens"	15	10.50
105	"Stevens"	15	10.00
104	"Stevens"	15	10.50
103	"Stevens"	15	10.00
89	"Dreadnaught"	16	12.75
116	"Stevens"	16	15.00
94	"Stevens"	17	7.75
944	"Springfield"	17	7.75

REPEATING SHOTGUNS

No.		Page	Price Each
620	"Stevens"	18	$40.60
621	"Stevens"	18	44.10

DOUBLE BARREL SHOTGUNS

No.		Page	Price Each
331	"Stevens"	20	29.75
330	"Stevens"	21	25.95
311	"Springfield"	22	21.25
311 S.T.	"Springfield"	22	25.00
3151 S.T.	"Springfield"	23	28.25
3151	"Springfield"	23	24.65

PISTOLS

No.		Page	Price Each
35	Target Pistol, 6 in.	24	10.00
35	Target Pistol, 8 in.	24	10.35
35	Target Pistol, 12¼ in.	24	10.75

SWIVELS, HOOKS AND SLING STRAPS

No.		Page	Per Set
1	Swivels, fitted or loose	24	$0.50
2	2D or 2R, Swivels and Hooks, loose	24	.90
4	Swivels and Hooks, loose	24	.90

No.		Page	Each
3B	⅞" Leather Sling Strap, complete with loops	24	$2.40
2B	1¼" Leather Sling Strap, complete with loops	24	3.00
3	⅞" Leather Sling Strap, only	24	1.95
2	1¼" Leather Sling Strap, only	24	2.40
3A	⅞" Loops only, wood screws	24	.30
2A	1¼" Loops only, wood screws	24	.30
1	⅞" Leather Carrying Strap	24	1.40

See Special Circulars for Stevens and Springfield Bolt Action Rifles

Above Prices include Excise Tax on Guns and Rifles Only and are Subject to Change Without Notice

Parts Price List Sent on Application

J. STEVENS ARMS COMPANY • CHICOPEE FALLS, MASS., U.S.A.

Form 61 PL   Printed in U.S.A.

STEVENS ARMS

Extract reprinted from *The Rifle in America*, Philipe B. Sharpe © 1938, 1947 & 1953

OLD MODEL POCKET RIFLE
Intro. 1869 — Discon. 1917

The old model pocket rifle was one of the first of the Stevens rifle series. They began their firearms business more or less in the pistol game and naturally gravitated into a light rifle with the heavy rifles following later.

This old model pocket rifle was chambered for the .22 short and long rimfires and, when it came out, of course there was no .22 long rifle cartridge. It had a square butt with a sheathed trigger and no trigger guard. A detachable skeleton stock was used. It had a 10-inch barrel, rosewood stock, nickel-plated skeleton shoulder stock and weighed 11 ounces. The same gun was also turned out with a Japanned skeleton stock in place of the nickel-plated number at slightly lower price and the gun was furnished with an 8-inch barrel and with both Japanned and nickel-plated extension stocks. In addition, a model was brought out with 6-inch barrel without the detachable stock and sold at a slightly lower price.

This, like other models, had no forearm and had the usual tip-down Stevens action. To avoid misunderstanding throughout this discourse, "tip-down" and "tip-up" are one and the same thing. Some catalogs list the action one way and some another. This author prefers "tip-up."

NEW MODEL POCKET OR BICYCLE RIFLE
Introduced 1872 — Discon. 1917

The New Model Pocket or Bicycle Rifle was chambered for the .22 long rimfire as was the old model. It was essentially the same gun but was built somewhat heavier. This underwent a few changes. In the old model the firing pin was a part of the hammer and on the new model the firing pin was a separate unit built into the frame. This prevented punctured primers and eliminated more or less the "spit back" of gas into the face.

This new model also had a sheathed trigger with the frame nickel-plated and a nickel-plated detachable skeleton stock. It was made with 10-, 12-, 15- and 18-inch barrels. The later new model brought out several years after the introduction of this gun had a trigger guard in place of the sheathed trigger.

This gun also was manufactured to handle the .25 Stevens and .32 long and short rimfire in addition to the .22 model. The special .22 model was built solely to handle the .22 W.R.F. cartridges. This model, of course, did not handle the short, long and long rifle series.

SPORTING RIFLE
Intro. 1872 — Discon. —

The Stevens Sporting Rifle was manufactured in .22, .32, .38 and .44 calibers. The .22 would handle the short and long as the long rifle was not in existence at the time of its introduction. The .32 model would handle the .32 short and long rimfire numbers and the .38 caliber was built for the .38 short and long rimfires. The .44 caliber was at that time their big bore and was their first attempt at entering the big bore field. This was built to handle the .44 short and the .44 long rimfire cartridges, now obsolete for a great many years.

This had the usual tip-up nickel-plated frame with a latch at the rear of the frame. The latch was in the form of a button projecting about one-quarter of an inch on the left-hand side. It was available in practically any barrel length from 24 to 36 inches. In the .22 caliber the 24-inch barrel model weighed 6½ pounds. Large calibers ran a bit heavier than this.

One model was manufactured in this in a gun-metal frame. All models had a fine cast-steel frame with octagon barrels. The non-adjustable type of sights were used fitting in standard dovetail slots in the barrel, although special sights were available and widely used.

SPORTING RIFLE, CENTRAL FIRE
Intro. 1875 — Discon. —

This model was very similar to the earlier sporting rifle and merely was an adaption to central-fire shells. It had the tip-up barrel and was first produced in the .38/33 Stevens 1⅝-inch shell. Shortly afterwards it came out in the .38/45 Stevens 2⅛-inch shell, the .44/50 Stevens 2-inch shell and the .44/65 Stevens 2½-inch shell. In addition to the special Stevens cartridges, it was manufactured to handle a .38 long or extra long central fire as manufactured by the Union Metallic Cartridge Co. and the UMC .44 long or extra long centerfire.

HUNTER'S PET POCKET RIFLE
Intro. 1865 — Discon. 1897

The Stevens Hunter's Pet Pocket Rifle was one of the popular numbers of its day. It was available in .32 long, .38 long, and .44 long rimfire. All of these models would, of course, handle the short cartridge in their respective cartridge caliber. It was essentially the same as the sporting rifle but had a sheathed trigger and was available in barrel lengths of 18, 20, 22, and 24 inches. Some models were made up to 36 inches long in the barrels. The central-fire calibers were the same as in the sporting rifles central-fire and were first released in 1877.

SPORTING RIFLE NO. 1
Intro. 1872 — Discon. 1897

The Stevens Sporting Rifle No. 1 was made in .32, .38 or .44 long rim or centerfire. The weights in this particular tip-up barrel job ran from 6½ to 8½ pounds. It did not have a wood fore-end, the barrel serving this purpose. Open sights were used and various weights of barrels were available in lengths from 24, 26, 28, and 30 inches. Barrels were full octagon and blued.

The nickel-plated frame and butt plate served as an excellent contrast to the wood stock and these guns were widely used for target purposes. The crude open sights were frequently replaced with the more modern target version in use more than forty years ago. The walnut stock was oil-finished rather than varnished, and reasonably well shaped for ordinary offhand shooting.

SPORTING RIFLE NO. 2
Intro. 1872 + — Discon. 1895

This rifle was one of the early Stevens favorites. It was manufactured in 24-inch barrel length only and weighed 7 pounds. The rifle itself had no forearm but with a heavy octagon barrel offered an entirely satisfactory hand hold. This gun had open sights of the simplest variety, a plain blade front and a tiny V-notch or U-notch rear. There were no adjustments.

The action was of the breakdown type, hinged at the forward part of the frame and with a button on the side of the breech end. Pressing in on the button permitted one to tip the barrel down which operated an extractor withdrawing the shell slightly to the rear so it could be picked loose with the fingers.

Hammer and firing pin were separate units in this particular rifle. The frame was heavily nickel-plated as was the butt plate and a fairly well-shaped oil walnut stock was used. The fancy curved trigger guard formed a pistol grip. The Stevens No. 2 model was manufactured in .22

long rifle rimfire to handle the .22 short, .22 long, and .22 long rifle. A .25 caliber model was produced and handled the .25 Stevens short and long rimfire. The .32 caliber job used the .32 short and .32 long rimfire. All of these guns in 1899 sold for $17.00.

SPORTING RIFLE NO. 3
Intro. 1872 + — Discon. 1895

The Sporting Rifle No. 3 was available in both rim and centerfire models chambered for the .32, .38, and .44 long cartridges. This particular rifle was similar to their gallery type in that it did not have a wood forearm but was available in various lengths of barrels running from 24- to 26-, 28-, and 30-inch lengths. Weight ran 6¼ to 8¼ pounds. This particular model was available either in full-octagon or half-octagon barrel in which the forward half of the barrel was turned down round to just clear the octagon flats. This particular type of octagon barrel was widely used on sporting rifles for appearance and usually cost the same as the standard full-octagon model.

This No. 3 rifle was much better sighted than the Numbers 1 and 2 in that it had a combination front sight of the folding type including a pinhead bead inside of a globe and a blade for hunting. One merely folded this forward or backward to expose the proper sight. The rear sight was of the tang type of peep and thus made an excellent combination. Despite the fact that this was listed as a sporting rifle a great many excellent records were set with it in the old days. The frame and butt plate were, as in other models, full nickel-plated with the barrels blued. This gun had a varnish- rather than oil-finish on the walnut stock.

SPORTING RIFLE NO. 4
Intro. 1872 + — Discon. 1895

The No. 4 rifle was essentially the same as the No. 3 except that it was made in .22 short only and had the special slow twist rifling designed for the short. It was made with half or full octagon barrel and had the Stevens combination sights identically the same as the No. 3. All other specifications were practically the same. Any barrel length from 24 to 30 inches was available.

EXPERT RIFLE NO. 5
Intro. 1883 — Discon. 1895

The Expert Rifle No. 5 was brought out in both rim and centerfire numbers. The .22 long rimfire was first used and later—about 1885 when the long rifle cartridge was developed—this rifle was chambered for it.

It was also made in .32, .38, and .44 long rim-fire and also for the same calibers in centerfire numbers. The half-octagon barrel was standard equipment and the typical Beach folding front sights offering the globe or pinhead bead and a peep on the tang was furnished.

This rifle also had no forearm but had a nickel-plated frame and butt plate. The locking latch on the left side of the breech was altered slightly and improved over that of earlier models. This came in barrel lengths of from 24 to 30 inches but as the large calibers were discontinued in the early 1890's this was then manufactured only for the .22 long rifle, the .25 Stevens rimfire and the .32 long rimfire and with 24-inch barrel only. The gun weighed approximately 6¾ pounds. Varnished stocks were standard on all models.

EXPERT RIFLE NO. 6
Intro. 1883 — Discon. 1895

The No. 6 rifle was essentially the same as the No. 5 with the exception of appointments. The chief change was in an extra fancy stock and in some places a silver-plated trigger guard. The trigger guard was in this model, as in many other Stevens early numbers, also shaped to form a pistol grip on the gun.

The forward part of the guard was attached to the steel frame and the rear part attached to the stock. The No. 6 rifle had a checked stock and was both oil- and varnish-finished.

PREMIER RIFLE NO. 7
Intro. 1884 — Discon. 1895

The Premier was more or less a de luxe version of the previous rifle and was one of the first Stevens numbers to be equipped with a wood forearm.

First brought out in .22 long rimfire, this was later changed to .22 long rifle rimfire and .25 Stevens rimfire and the .32 long rimfire. Earlier models were manufactured in .32, .38, and .44 long rimfire. The gun had a half-octagon barrel wood fore-end, barrel blued with nickel-plated frame and butt plate. The butt plate on this model was of the Swiss type as the rifle was built heavy for offhand shooting.

The gun was well equipped with the folding Beach front sight and a Vernier peep sight on the tang. It was available in both 24- and 28-inch barrels, the 24-inch barrel model weighing 7¾ pounds and the 28-inch model 8¾ pounds. At one time this was supplied in 26- and 30-inch barrels but these were discontinued. The 30-inch barrel job weighed slightly more than 9 pounds.

PREMIER RIFLE NO. 8
Intro. 1884 — Discon. 1895

The No. 8 rifle was essentially the same as the No. 7, but had a fancy stock. This also had the wood forearm, the same sight equipment and a high grade of oil- or varnish-finished stock was supplied, nicely checked for appearance's sake. There was also a certain amount of checking on the wood forearm.

The forearms on these guns were quite short as compared with the modern type of forearms, averaging about 6 inches beyond the forward part of the frame. However, due to the length and design of the frame this actually made forearms from 10 to 11 inches from the center of the trigger to the tip, comparing favorably with some of the more modern types of rifles.

In 1899 the 28-inch barrel job of the No. 7 sold for $27.00.

RANGE MODEL NO. 9
Intro. 1886 — Discon. 1895

The No. 9 was first chambered for the .22 long rimfire and later adapted to the .22 long rifle. It was also made in .32, .38, or .44 long rim or centerfire and some models were chambered for the .32, .38, and .44 Everlasting centerfire. During the later years of its life it was brought out and chambered for the .22/10/45 extra long centerfire number and the .32/35 Stevens. The latter had a tapered shell.

The rifle had the typical half-octagon barrel with wind-gauge front and Vernier rear sights. It had a wood forearm and varnished walnut stock and forearm. The frame and butt plate were nickel-plated as usual. The Schuetzen type of butt plate similar to the Swiss was used.

The rifle weighed from 7 to slightly over 9 pounds depending upon barrel length. It was available in 24-, 26-, and 30-inch barrels as standard. Some of these rifles were made up to 36-inch barrels on a special order.

RANGE RIFLE NO. 10
Intro. 1886 — Discon. 1895

The No. 10 rifle was essentially the same as the No. 9 except for the fancy stock with a certain amount of checking. It was made in practically all of the calibers but its chief popularity was in the .22 long rifle series and in the centerfire types with the Everlasting shells.

LADIES' RIFLE NO. 11
Intro. 1886(?) — Discon. 1895

The Ladies' models of rifles were the same as the Premier and Range types with the exception of a slightly smaller stock, smaller forearm and lighter barrel. It was designed and listed for use of ladies and was extremely popular for this purpose. Many women followed the shooting game.

The Ladies' model was brought out in a half-octagon barrel, 24-inch at first and later at 26 inches. Still later the longer barrel was discontinued in favor of the 24-inch number. Stocks were oil-finished and sights were extremely plain, straight blade fronts and a non-adjustable V-type rear. It had a rifle type of butt plate and nickel-plated frame. The forearm was much smaller and shaped to fit the hand. It was first brought out in the .22 long rifle caliber and later adapted to the .25 Stevens short and long calibers.

In 1899 this rifle sold for $18.75.

LADIES' RIFLE NO. 12
Intro. 1886(?) — Discon. 1895

This No. 12 rifle was essentially No. 11; both specifications and calibers being the same. It was available with an extra fancy oil-finished stock, both the stock and the forearm being checked. The model was discontinued as the standard job proved to be entirely satisfactory.

LADIES' RIFLE NO. 13
Intro. 1886(?) — Discon. 1895

The No. 13 rifle was identical with the No. 11 and made in the same calibers. The only difference in the two models was the Beach combination front sights previously described and the Vernier peep rear sight mounted on the tang, similar to that used on the men's rifles. In 1899 this sold for $21.00, just $2.25 more for the very fine adjustable sights.

LADIES' RIFLE NO. 14
Intro. 1886(?) — Discon. 1895

The No. 14 rifle was the same as the No. 13 with the exception of the stock. This was in the fancy grade in that it had a varnish finish instead of an oil finish. The forearm also was extra fancy and was checked. This particular model, like the other, was only on the market for a short time as it was proven that the extra fancy equipment did not sell as readily as the standard model and before 1898 it had been discontinued.

MAYNARD JUNIOR NO. 15
Intro. 1903 — Discon. 1914

This was a very cheap rifle both in design and in construction. It was built for the .22 long rifle with a blued steel half-octagon 18-inch barrel and an oiled-walnut stock. The stock was made out of a board about ⅝-inch thick, and was merely roughed out to shape with rounded corners.

In later years the stock was improved somewhat along conventional lines with a typical "oval" shape. It had open front and rear sights of the simple type driven into slots in the barrel. This model weighed 2¾ pounds. This rifle bore the same model number as the Crack Shot.

The No. 15 has the same style of breech action as the once famous Maynard rifle, the first successful breech-loading rifle made. It was a tip-up type of action without lock, the trigger guard forming a finger lever and the action being jacked open which slightly ejected the shell to the rear where it could be picked out with the fingers. It was priced in 1901 at $3.00.

MAYNARD JUNIOR NO. 15½
Intro. 1903 — Discon. 1914

This was the same as the standard Maynard Junior rifle but was smoothbored for use with metallic shot cartridges. The .22 long shot and long rifle shot cartridges were widely used for small birds, particularly by taxidermists who wanted to acquire small game of this nature without mutilation.

CRACK SHOT NO. 15
Intro. 1900 — Discon. 1939

The Crack Shot No. 15 rifle was brought out in .22, .25, .32, .38 and .44 long rimfire. In the larger calibers it was also available in centerfire. This particular model was one of the big favorites in the Stevens line and did much to start junior riflemen along the road to marksmanship.

This rifle had a full-octagon barrel available in 24-, 26-, and 28- and 30-inch barrels with longer lengths on special order. The weight was around 6½ to 8¾ pounds. This was the first Stevens rifle to be equipped with the Lyman ivory bead front sight and also the Lyman combination rear sight on the tang. This first Lyman No. 1 folding tang sight designed by William Lyman was first produced in 1879 and, incidentally, although this particular sight has been improved in minor details it is still on the market and it is still a good seller in the Lyman family of sights.

The Crack Shot rifle also had the wood forearm as the rifles without forearms were apparently on the wane in the public popularity.

CRACK SHOT NO. 16
Intro. 1900 — Discon. 1913

The Crack Shot rifle was one of the first in the Stevens line equipped with an automatic ejector. This eliminated the problem of picking empty shells from the chamber and thus getting the fingers soiled with soot. It must be remembered that in those days all ammunition was black powder. Also rifles in use for some time had slightly rough chambers, due to pitting, and this created an extraction problem. Frequently in .22 rifles, until this automatic ejector was designed, it was necessary to pry the fired shell out by means of a knife, screwdriver or some other small tool.

The Crack Shot No. 16 rifle was of breakdown construction. It had a wood forearm attached to the barrel by means of a screw and the frame was much shorter than in previous types. It was of the rolling-block type of construction without a finger lever and the barrel slid into the frame and was clamped by means of a thumb screw at the bottom. The rifle was extremely simple in design and in construction and proved to be extremely popular as a low-priced weapon.

The standard barrel was round in 20-inch length with a case-hardened frame. It was believed one of the first Stevens rifles equipped with a case-hardened frame and proved extremely popular due to the excellent color effects one could get with that system of finishing. Stock was oiled walnut with a forearm of the same material. The butt plate was of hard rubber, also interesting in that most of the early butt plates were metal.

This rifle was chambered for the .22 long rifle or .32 short rimfire. Sights were of the very simple types. A blade sight driven into the barrel (not mounted on a dovetail base) and a simple dovetail non-adjustable rear sight on the barrel formed the sighting equipment. The gun weighed 3¾ pounds. In 1901 this sold for $4.00.

FAVORITE RIFLES
Intro. 1890 — Discon. 1937

Stevens Favorite rifles in several numbers were an attempt to improve upon low-priced rifles on the market including numbers in the Stevens line. This particular gun was thoroughly well made, safe, and more accurate than the other low-priced numbers and fairly well balanced.

When first released on the market it took the public fancy by storm. It soon became the most popular number of the 1900 era in the Stevens family. When it was first brought out it was presented as a light-weight low-priced rifle intended for ladies and small boys, and filled its requirement much better than any of the other rifles including foreign importations.

Soon the rifle had spread beyond its original field and proved an exceptionally fine bicycle or other portable gun as an auxiliary piece of equipment intended chiefly for sport. It could be quickly taken down, being in design along the lines of the Crack Shot model, forearm attached to the barrel, and the barrel sliding into the frame. Instead of the rolling-block action, however, this used a single lever which was far more sturdy and offered a more positive breech lock. The single lever dropped the breech lock out of the way to expose the chamber for easy loading and a groove in the top of the breech block enabled one to readily insert the cartridge even when fingers were cold or with gloves on.

Stevens claimed that "there was nothing cheap about this rifle except the price." The action had a strong frame breech-lever type with the breech lock dropping so low that it could be readily cleaned from the breech end without injury to the cleaning rod. It could be quickly inspected to determine the amount of fouling in the barrel after firing.

Despite the low price the same extreme care was taken in boring and rifling this Favorite model as in higher-priced rifles manufactured by Stevens. They were fitted nicely to the stock and frame so that barrels of different calibers could be used in one breech action, the barrels readily interchanging. The only change necessary to use one breech action and different barrels in more than one caliber was to fit a new breech block to the firing pin and lever. This could readily and speedily be done by removing two screws so the same frame could be used by a rifleman and actually produce two different guns.

All Stevens rifles were take-down design. The standard length of barrel was 22 inches and octagon to the forward end of the forearm and round the remainder of its length. A shotgun type butt was used replacing the long ill-fitting rifle type of butt plate previously used. The complete weight of the rifle was only 4½ pounds.

The Favorite rifle was not supplied to take centerfire cartridges. It was made in .22, .25, .32 rimfire and the .22 was regularly chambered for .22 long-rifle. The entire series of .22 BB, .22 CB, .22 short, .22 long and .22 long-rifle cartridges could be used. A special caliber was the .22/7/45, or .22 W.R.F. This caliber was manufactured at an additional price of $2.00 and of course when this barrel was used the .22 long-rifle and other standard .22 calibers could not be used in the chamber.

An interesting high light of the Favorite line is the development of the .25 Stevens rimfire cartridge. This .25 Stevens was essentially a long shell and to slightly reduce the power, the Peters Cartridge Company, working in conjunction with Stevens, developed a newcomer around 1900 known as the .25 Short Stevens.

In the .32 caliber a special cartridge could be used and the rifle was chambered to handle it. A new cartridge was developed around 1900 known as the .32 long-rifle rimfire. Previous to this practically all of the rimfire cartridges with the exception of the .22/7/45 were outside lubricated. In the bigger calibers these were particularly hard to handle and the .32 long-rifle was a step in the direction of elimination of these others. It was essentially the same as a .32 long but had a slightly undersize bullet.

The bullet was lubricated in grooves inside of the shell similar to centerfire ammunition. A hollow base permitted it to expand to fill the rifling on being discharged. The outside lubricated types had a larger bullet with a case portion fitting inside of the shell slightly smaller in diameter. This is the principle used on the standard .22 long-rifle cartridge today.

The long-rifle cartridge could not be used in those chambers designed to handle regular .32 long rimfire because the shell was somewhat longer. The overall length of the two cartridges was practically the same but with the standard .32 long the case was somewhat shorter with more bullet exposed. In the .32 long rifle the case was built longer and the bullet seated more deeply into the shell to cover the lubricating grooves.

Favorite rifles were also made in several calibers smoothbored for shot intended for small-bird shooting.

FAVORITE RIFLE No. 17
Intro. 1894 — Discon. 1935

This particular number was manufactured and sold in both .22 long rifle, .25 Stevens and .32 long rimfire in the earlier days. Later it was chambered to handle the .32 long rifle as were all guns manufactured after the long rifle came into existence. It had a case-hardened frame, solid breech block, 22-inch half-octagon barrel, oiled walnut stock and forearm and rubber butt plate. Plain open front and rear sights were used.

In 1902 it sold for $6.00. Barrel lengths up to 26 inches could be furnished on special order. The 22-inch barrel was standard and the additional charge was $1.00 per inch up to 26 inches, not furnished longer.

FAVORITE RIFLE NO. 18
Intro. 1895 — Discon. 1917

This rifle was the same as No. 17 except for the equipment. The sights were the typical Beach combination front sight with an open rear on the barrel and a Vernier peep. Weight 4¼ to 4½ pounds. It sold in the standard length of barrel for $8.50 and was furnished, as was the No. 17, in lengths up to 26 inches at $1.00 per inch for anything over standard.

FAVORITE RIFLE NO. 19
Intro. 1895 — Discon. 1917

This was the same as Numbers 17 and 18 rifles in every respect except for sights. In place of the Stevens sights this was usually equipped with a Lyman bead front sight either gold or ivory and Lyman No. 1 folding tang rear peep. It had that useless non-adjustable V-type sight in the rear barrel slot. It seems interesting when one stops to consider that this was a target rifle equipped with peep sights as standard.

In 1902 the price was $9.00. It also was available in extra barrel lengths up to 26 inches at the standard extra price.

FAVORITE SHOTGUN NO. 20
Intro. 1907 — Discon. 1937

While this book does not attempt to discuss shotguns and the majority of shotguns manufactured by different rifle makers has been left out of this book, this is interesting in that it is actually nothing more than the standard barrel *unfinished*. The half-octagon barrel was used with guns exactly the same in Favorite rifle No. 17 in that it had the usual dovetail front sight. Rear sights were missing but the barrel was slotted, indicating that standard barrels were used as *before rifling*. This was a smoothbore gun and was available in .22 and .32 rimfire caliber chambered for the shot cartridges of that day. The price was only $6.00.

FAVORITE BICYCLE RIFLE NO. 21
Intro. 1900+ — Discon. 1916

Early catalogs illustrate this particular rifle inserted in a special take-down case which was supplied by the factory on order only and equipped with straps so that it could be laced to the "diamond" frame of a standard bicycle just below the crossbars. Favorite Rifle No. 21 had a half-octagon barrel with a standard length of 20 inches. The typical breech action was used with a case-hardened frame and single trigger. Oiled walnut stock and forearm with rubber shotgun butt plates similar to other rifles were used.

This gun was available in .22 long rifle, .25 Stevens rimfire and .32 long rimfire. Plain open front and rear sights similar to Favorite No. 17 were used but the rifle was reduced in weight due to the shorter barrel length so that it tipped the scales at about 4¼ pounds.

Instead of changing numbers on this rifle it was available with various sights. The standard job in 1902 sold for $6.00, but with the Beach combination front sight and open rear sight and Vernier peep rear the price was $8.50. With Lyman front and Lyman No. 1 folding rear sight, the price was $9.00. The bicycle case sold for $1.50 and extra lengths of barrels up to 26 inches were available at $1.00 per inch.

All Favorite rifles as previously stated were available with extra barrels. They could be interchanged on the action. The price was unusually low for this change-over.

The 1902 price list shows that the barrel part complete with a specially fitted forearm and an additional breech block and firing pin and other units necessary to make the change-over with the 22-inch barrel in .22, .25, or .32 caliber or .22 or .32 smoothbore was priced at $4.00. For the 24-inch barrel the additional charge was $2.00 and for the 26-inch barrel $4.00 extra. Shot barrels were manufactured only in 22-inch lengths.

Additional charges show that a fancy walnut stock and forearm could be obtained for $4.00 and the same stock and forearm could be nicely checked at the factory for $9.00, an additional charge of $5.00 for labor involved. The pistol grip stock could also be obtained at $5.00 in plain grade and $10.00 in plain grade checked. The fancy pistol grip type was $9.00 with the $5.00 extra for checking. This of course included matching forearms in every instance, and the checking also included work on the forearm.

Another interesting fact about the Favorite rifles was the change in extraction. Early models were made with side extractor. This extractor was located on the left-hand side of the barrel and it was thus necessary to specify the type desired when ordering an additional barrel. By 1901 the entire Favorite line had been changed to a central extractor placed exactly in the center of the barrel beneath the cartridge. This gave more positive extraction and was more simple in construction and more desirable in every way.

CRACK SHOT RIFLE NOS. 26 AND 26½
Intro. 1913+ — Discon. 1939

The Crack Shot rifle is still manufactured in 1938 and is about the lowest-priced number in the Stevens line. This rifle is chambered for the .22 long rifle or for the .32 long rimfire cartridge only. The difference between No. 26 and No. 26½ is purely in the barrel. The latter is a smoothbore full-choke model chambered for the .22 or .32 rimfire shot cartridges.

The barrels on these two guns are tapered with a crowned muzzle. Action is case-hardened of take-down style, single-shot lever action with a solid block. The extractor is geared to a finger lever to withdraw the empty cartridge slightly so it can be removed with the fingers.

Sights are very simple. A German silver knife blade front sight is standard with a flat top open rear sight driven into the slot in the barrel. There are no adjustments.

The stock is beech or birch stained to resemble walnut. Butt plate is of pressed steel. Weight of this rifle is 3½ pounds with an overall length of 36 inches. This was essentially a boy's rifle.

FAVORITE NO. 27
Intro. 1912+ — Discon. 1939

This is another of the Stevens low-priced rifles. It is still manufactured in 1938. It is somewhat heavier than Crack Shot No. 26 and has the typical Favorite action.

The barrel is 24 inches long, well tapered with a crowned muzzle, and is full-octagon, one of the few octagon barrels still left on the market. It is chambered for the .22 long rifle, the .25 Stevens rimfire, or the .32 long rimfire. It is built to handle either high-speed or regular ammunition.

Action includes a take-down style with the Stevens falling-block lever action, plain extractor in the larger calibers, automatic ejector in .22 caliber. Stock is of genuine walnut as is the forearm. Sights include a gold bead front and sporting rear. The latter is adjustable for elevation. Weight of this gun is 4½ pounds, overall length 38 inches.

POCKET RIFLE NO. 40
Intro. (unk) — Discon. 1917

This rifle, also known as the bicycle rifle, is essentially a target pistol equipped with a detachable skeleton extension stock. The stock was made of light-weight steel rod nickel-plated with the bottom tang sliding into a slot in the standard pistol butt. The attachment was made solid by means of a thumb screw attaching to the back tang of the pistol.

The rifle was essentially the same as the old Hunter's Pet but a little bit lighter in weight and was manufactured in .22 long rifle, .25 Stevens rimfire, and .32 long rimfire. At an extra charge of $2.00 it could be supplied chambered for the .22/7/45 Winchester Rimfire. It had the typical half-octagon barrel in 10-, 12-, 15-, and 18-inch lengths and weighed without skeleton stock from 2 to 2¾ pounds depending upon the length of the barrel.

The front sight was the Stevens combination globe and the rear was a folding peep mounted on the barrel about two inches in front of the hammer. It could be used either with or without the detachable stock. In 1899 the 10-inch barrel sold for $9.25, the 12-inch for $10.00, the 15-inch for $11.25 and the 18-inch for $12.50.

VERNIER NEW MODEL POCKET RIFLE NO. 40½
Intro. (unk) — Discon. 1917

This rifle was essentially the same as the No. 40 in that it maintained the same design, same barrel length and weight but had different sights.

The half-octagon barrel had a Beach combination front sight with an open rear sight for pistol use. The open rear was mounted at the forward part of the half-octagon which ended at the front end of the frame. In other words, the dovetail slot was in a different location than the No. 40. On the tang of the pistol grip was mounted a Stevens Vernier peep sight. This also was available at an additional charge of $2.00 chambered for the .22 W.R.F. cartridge. It sold, depending on barrel length of 10, 12, 15, and 18 inches, at prices of $11.50, $12.25, $13.50, and $14.50.

RELIABLE POCKET RIFLE NO. 42
Intro. (unk) — Discon. 1917

This was essentially the Stevens Diamond model target pistol with a 10-inch barrel and skeleton stocks. The skeleton stocks differed from those of the other pocket rifles in its simplicity of design and construction. The usual thumb-screw method of attachment was missing and in its place the very simple skeleton stock was attached by means of sliding it onto the butt of the rifle in a dovetail. This particular model was chambered only for the .22 long rifle rimfire and the frame and skeleton stock were nickel-plated. The barrel was half-octagon to the forward end of the frame and round from that point on. It was listed as a round-barrel job. Open sights were supplied on special order at

the standard price but the regular equipment included a hooded or globed front sight and a simple rear peep sight adjustable for elevation. The gun was very light, weighing 1 pound without the skeleton stock, and in 1899 sold for $8.25. Such rifles were usually "auxiliary" arms.

The Diamond Model was very well constructed for the price and was considered very satisfactory with the .22 long rifle cartridge up to 100 yards.

SURE SHOT RIFLE
Intro. 1891 — Discon. c. 1900

The Sure Shot rifle was another low-priced model chambered only for the .22 short- and long-rifle rimfire. It was of a take-down type of construction with a stock that could be detached. It had a 20-inch barrel and weighed but 3½ pounds. Very little information is available on this model since it appeared on the market for but a short time.

THE IDEAL RIFLE
Intro. 1894 — Discon. 1895

This model was the outgrowth of many years' experience in the manufacturing of rifles. Also the Stevens engineers listened to the advice of riflemen and combined these ideas with their regular designs of actions into a rifle which at the 1894 stage of the shooting game was extremely excellent as a target and miscellaneous shooting weapon.

The Ideal models used high-grade materials and excellent workmanship. They were reasonably light to enable them to be used readily for sporting purposes. Yet they were strong enough to handle any standard loads or handloads adapted to them.

Mechanism of the Ideal rifle was of the then popular type, a lever-action single-shot which permitted of easy inspection and cleaning of the bore from the breech. It was easy to load and so designed that accidents rarely could happen due to mechanism failure.

The take-down system of the Ideal models allowed the barrel to be quickly removed from the action and would thus permit it to be packed into a small case or in a trunk. The objections to take-down actions were overcome with this new design which also permitted interchanging barrels of different calibers into one breech action. One arm could actually be several rifles at reduced expense and the shooter retained the one action, one stock, one trigger pull, and other features so much desired.

One Stevens Ideal action could be fitted with

a .22 caliber barrel for short-range or indoor shooting, a .25 caliber for use on small game, a .32/40 for offhand 200-yard shooting, and a .38/55 for shooting at the same distance either in rest shooting or offhand. This interchangeable barrel plan was quite popular among the experts of the 1900 era.

The barrels were threaded with a sturdy well-shaped coarse thread which screwed into the frame in the customary fashion. A barrel screw passing through the frame from below locked it rigidly in position and prevented any shifting or vibration during firing.

Like the Favorite rifles, the Ideal rifles underwent various changes in evolution. By 1902 all had the new and improved single extractor eliminating the old side extractor also first used in this model as in the "Favorite." This extractor was sufficiently large to grip not only the bottom of the rim but a good portion of the sides thus giving positive extraction as it worked simultaneously with the lever and breech block and overcame the early problems of an extractor slipping by the fired shell in the chamber.

Another improvement in the Ideal rifle was in the action.

In the place of the former breech block, lever and extractor being held in place by large screws that fastened in the frame by threads, a bolt passing through the frame without threads was employed by early 1901. On the outside of this bolt was a V-shaped projection which in turn fitted into a similar depression in the frame thus holding it rigid and making it impossible to turn.

The very excellent Ideal action was available in several frames. In 1894 and 1895 they used the numbers 107, 108, 109, and 110. In 1896 when the firm changed management the old numbers were discontinued and the new numbers still in existence were adopted. In 1902 specifications indicated that the No. 44 Ideal frame weighed 3¼ pounds complete with forearm. No. 45 ran 3½, No. 47, 3¾, No. 49, 4¼, No. 51, 5¾, No. 52, 4¾, and No. 54, 5 pounds. The Ideal rifle No. 44 was generally furnished with No. 2 barrel only, making the total weight of the gun about 7 pounds.

THE IDEAL RIFLE NO. 44
Intro. 1896 — Discon. 1933

In the Model 44 rifle which was the most popular number of the line, the standard barrel was 24 inches long in the rimfire series and 26 inches in the centerfire. A full-octagon barrel was available for $2.00 extra whereas the half-octagon was standard. The frame was case-hardened with a solid breech block and the single trigger was standard. Double set triggers could be furnished for $6.00 extra.

Stocks were walnut with matching forearm and oiled finish. Standard butt plate was the rifle type of metal, nickel-plated.

This Ideal No. 44 Model was available for the .22 long rifle, the .25 Stevens rimfire, the .25/20 Stevens Single Shot centerfire, the .32 long rimfire, the .32/20 centerfire, the .32/40 centerfire, the .38/40 centerfire, the .38/55 and .44/40 centerfires. It was made to special order, bored, rifled and chambered for the .22 short rimfire and also for the .22/7/45 W.R.F. and .22/15/60 Stevens centerfire. Also special Stevens calibers such as the .25/21, .25/25, .28/30/120, .32/20, and .32 Ideal were available at an additional $2.00.

IDEAL ENGLISH MODEL NO. 044½
Intro. 1903 — Discon. 1916

This rifle was very similar to the Model 44½ Ideal except in weight and in stock. It was available in a half-octagon barrel, standard length 24 inches for rimfire and 26 inches for centerfire. A full-octagon barrel was available for $2.00 extra.

Frame was drop-forged and case-hardened with new type action. Single trigger was standard with single set trigger $2.00 extra and double set trigger $6.00 extra. An oiled-walnut stock and forearm were standard equipment with an English shotgun type of butt stock. Length was 13½ inches, drop 2½ inches at heel.

This rifle was chambered for the .22 long rifle rimfire, .22 Stevens-Pope Armory rimfire, .25 Stevens rimfire, and .32 long rimfire. In centerfire numbers it was chambered for the .25/20 Stevens single shot and the .32/20 repeater. On special order it could be obtained for the .22 short rimfire, the .22/7/45 W.R.F. and in centerfire calibers included the .22/15/60 Stevens, .25/21 Stevens, .25/25 Stevens, .28/30/120 Stevens, and others at $2.00 extra.

Sight equipment was of the lowest price type with a "Rocky Mountain" front and open V-type sporting rear. Additional sights at an additional charge could, of course, be obtained.

IDEAL SEMI-MILITARY NO. 404
Intro. 1913 — Discon. 1916

The Semi-Military Model 404 was very similar to the standard Ideal type except that it had a semi-beavertail forearm. It had no "military appearance" except that a sling strap was furnished for prone shooting.

An innovation in this particular gun was that it was take-down with a 28-inch round barrel fitted with a swivel for the forward loop of a sling strap. There was no method of attaching the sling to the butt of the gun and this front swivel was of the detachable type. The swivel was an "eye" mounted on a dovetail base similar to a front sight but upside down beneath the barrel just beyond the forearm. The sling itself was attached by means of a hook type of loop and could be quickly detached and carried separate from the rifle itself.

No choice of barrels was available in this particular model. The frame was drop-forged and case-hardened with a standard No. 44½ action and No. 1 plain lever. It had an automatic ejector and was available only in .22 caliber. Stock was walnut with a shotgun butt and heavy rubber butt plate, length 13 inches, drop 3 inches at the heel. The forearm was 12 inches long, with the swing swivel mounted 14 inches from the front shoulder of the frame. Forearm was checked but the stock was not.

No. 210 globe sights with interchangeable discs were used for the front and No. 42 Lyman receiver with a cup disc mounted on the frame. It was rifled either for the .22 long rifle cartridge or the .22 short and weighed around 8 pounds. The price in 1913 was $27.00.

IDEAL ARMORY MODEL NO. 414
Intro. 1912 — Discon. 1932

This was a military or musket type of single shot target rifle chambered only for the .22 short or .22 long rifle. It was available only in a 26-inch round barrel with case-hardened frame and No. 44 action. No. 1 plain lever was used. An automatic ejector was standard equipment. It was designed for use with a sling strap and had a barrel band at the front portion of the semi-beavertail type of forearm with the sling swivel attached to this band. Another swivel was attached to the butt in the customary fashion. In 1913 the rifle was priced at $12.00 with $1.00 extra for the sling swivel.

The stock was of walnut unchecked. Shotgun butt and heavy rubber butt plate were standard. Length 13 inches, drop 3 inches at the heel. The long forearm extended to within about 8 inches of the muzzle but was not attached to the barrel at the forward end, the one band serving this purpose at about the midway point. Sights included a "Rocky Mountain" front and Lyman Receiver rear sight especially designed for this particular model. It was also tapped for tang sights and weighed around 8 pounds without sling strap.

WALNUT HILL NO. 417
Intro. 1932 — Discon. 1946

This Walnut Hill Model is one of the most popular numbers in the Ideal line today. It is extremely accurate and measures up to the finest .22 target rifle of the day.

Standard barrel is 28 inches long, heavy and round. Each barrel is tested for accuracy. Frame is case-hardened and blued. Action is the original Stevens Ideal with solid breech block, positive extractor, lever action operation with a short type of hammer. Independent half-cock notch on the hammer.

Stock is of American walnut 13½ inches long, oil-finished with a high comb, full pistol grip and full target design of stock. It has a shotgun butt with steel butt plate neatly checked and forearm is of semi-beavertail construction. There is no checking on the standard job.

Standard equipment includes the 1¼-inch military sling strap. Lyman 17A front sights, telescope sight block, Lyman 48L receiver type. The weight of this rifle is about 10½ pounds.

Despite the years, the Model 417 still proves popular among target riflemen. It is carried in the 1946 line of Stevens rifles, with the current versions described in detail at the end of this chapter—a favorite among shooters.

This rifle is chambered for the .22 long rifle regular or high-speed numbers as standard but is bored, rifled, and chambered for the .22 short at no extra charge. Five different models of this are made known as Nos. 417-1, -2, -3, -4, -5. The No. 1 has the sight equipment as specified. No. 2 is fitted with Lyman No. 144 sight in place of the 48L and is somewhat lower in price. No. 3 has telescope sight blocks but no front or rear sight and is intended chiefly for telescope use. No. 4 is the same rifle fitted with Lyman 438 telescope and No. 5 the same gun with no metallic sights but fitted with a Lyman 5A telescope.

TARGET OR SPORTING WALNUT HILL
NO. 417½
Intro. 1932 — Discon. 1940

This is essentially a light-weight version of the standard Walnut Hill rifle slightly lighter in frame and in barrel. The barrel is 28 inches long, tapered, round and light-weight. It is tested for accuracy and will perform nearly as well as the heavy job. Frame is hardened and blued with the typical Ideal falling-block action with the solid breech block, positive extractor speed action with short hammer fall and independent safety notch on the hammer.

Stock is of American walnut, oil-finished with high comb, full pistol grip stock and sporting forearm. Standard equipment includes the 1¼-inch military oil-treated sling strap. Shotgun butt and steel butt plate are standard.

Sights include the Lyman No. 28 gold bead, ³⁄₃₂-inch front sight and folding-leaf barrel or "middle" sight and Lyman No. 144 tang peep sights with click adjustments for elevation and windage. Barrel is tapped for telescope blocks but these are not fitted without an extra charge. Weight of this rifle runs from 8¼ to 8½ pounds and it is made in three calibers, the .22 long rifle, the .22 W.R.F., and .25 Stevens R.F. The price is somewhat lower than the new model No. 417.

TARGET OR SPORTING WALNUT HILL NO. 418
Intro. 1932 — Discon. 1940

This is a single shot take-down type of rifle whereas 417 and 417½ are solid-frame models. It has a 26-inch medium weight tapered round barrel tested for accuracy with case-hardened frame. Action is the same as on the standard model.

Stock is of American walnut 13 inches long, oil-finished, full pistol grip, target model stock, and semi-beavertail forearm fitted with a ⅞-inch military oil-treated sling strap. Shotgun butt and checked steel butt plate are standard.

Regular sights include their blade type front and Lyman No. 144 tang peep sight with click adjustments for elevation and windage. No other sights on the barrel. This rifle weighs but 6½ pounds and is chambered for the .22 long rifle. It is also available for the .22 short at no extra charge. This is a much lower-priced model and differs in appearance chiefly in size and in the finger lever. The old-style finger lever is used instead of the improved type closely hugging the pistol grip as in the 417 and 417½.

TARGET OR SPORTING WALNUT HILL NO. 418½
Intro. 1932 — Discon. 1940

This particular model is a sporting version of 418 with the same 26-inch tapered round barrel tested for accuracy, case-hardened frame, same action and same stock. It is equipped with a ⅞-inch military sling, shot gun butt and steel butt plate. Sights include the Lyman gold bead front,

Lyman 2A tang, peep rear sight. This rifle also weighs 6½ pounds and is chambered for the .22 long rifle and available also in .22 W.R.F. or the .25 Stevens R.F. calibers.

JUNIOR TARGET RIFLE NO. 419
Intro. 1932+ — Discon. 1936

The 419 Model is a bolt-action type of rifle and is completely equipped to satisfy the junior rifleman.

This particular rifle is chambered for the .22 long rifle but can also be used with the shorts and longs. It is designed for use with high-speed ammunition. Barrel is a 26-inch tapered type and has a crowned muzzle.

The action is of bolt type with a safety firing pin. The bolt is case-hardened to eliminate wear. Hammer or cocking piece has a knurled rim for easy gripping. Also the face is fluted to prevent light reflection in the eyes. This gun was designed for use with high speed ammunition and has a safety. The rifle can be unloaded with the safety on.

Stock is of one-piece construction, straight grain American walnut of a target model. The typical finger grooves are on the side to mar the appearance of this which was customary at the time the rifle was introduced. Stock is oil-finished with a full pistol grip. Standard equipment includes a ⅞-inch military type sling strap oil-treated and the butt is fairly full of shotgun type and has a steel butt plate.

Sights include a blade-type front sight with a Lyman No. 55 receiver rear sight adjustable for both elevation and windage. This particular sight was designed especially for use on this rifle. The complete job, including sling strap, was about 5½ pounds in weight.

This was, of course, a take-down arm with a thumb screw in the middle of the forearm. Bolt handle was fairly large and reasonably well-shaped.

IDEAL RANGE NO. 45
Intro. 1896 — Discon. 1916

The Model 45 was essentially the same as the Model 44 except in its appointments. It was built but slightly heavier in the barrel and equipped with target sights as standard. The barrel was half-octagon with 26 inches as the standard length in the rimfire series and 28 inches for the centerfires. Standard barrel was the No. 2 but No. 1 and No. 3 barrels (lighter and heavier) could be furnished at the same price.

Single trigger was standard with double set

triggers for $6.00 extra. Stock was of varnished walnut with matching forearm. No checking. Swiss butt plate was standard but this was also available with a rifle butt plate in metal or a shotgun butt plate in rubber. No extra charge. The rifle was designed chiefly for offhand shooting with the standard stock, as the length was 13 inches and 3¼-inch drop at the heel.

Calibers available included the same numbers as the Model 44 with the same special to order numbers at $2.00 extra. Standard sights included the Beach combination front with open rear and Vernier peep on the tang. This was known as their "D" combination. With the 26-inch barrel for rimfire cartridges the weight ran about 7½ pounds. With the 28-inch No. 2 barrel for centerfire cartridges, the weight was about 8 pounds. Longer barrel lengths were available up to 34 inches to increase their weight considerably.

Lists in 1902 showed the different combination of sights indicated by letters. "B" sights included the sporting rear and the "Rocky Mountain" front. "D" sights included the Beach combination front and open rear and Vernier peep on the tang. "E" sights consisted of the Lyman ivory combination front sight and a Lyman combination No. 1 tang peep rear or their No. 2 sight with a cupped disc. The cupped disc added fifty cents to the cost. Their "F" sight combination included the globe interchangeable front and the Vernier peep rear. Their "G" sights included the wind gauge adjustable front sight and midrange Vernier peep tang sight. Their "H" sights consisted of a globe interchangeable front, wind gauge Vernier peep sight on the tang and adjustable eye cup.

IDEAL RANGE NO. 46
Intro. 1896+ — Discon. 1916

This Model 46 rifle was the same as the Model 45 in every respect but the additional number was given to designate their fancy stock. This Model number was discontinued fairly early to eliminate the confusion of an additional number. The Model 45 was then made available in this fancy grade as an "extra."

IDEAL "MODEL RANGE" NO. 47
Intro. 1896 — Discon. 1916

This particular model is very similar to the standard job except in stock and finger lever.

On this model a pistol grip was used and a loop-type finger lever similar to that used in repeating rifles then on the market.

For standard equipment is included a half-octagon barrel 26 inches long in the rimfire series

and 28 in the centerfires. Their Standard No. 2 barrel was furnished unless otherwise ordered. No. 1 and No. 3 barrels were available at no additional cost. Specifications concerning frame and trigger were the same as on the Model 44. Stock was of varnished walnut with pistol grip and matching walnut forearm. It was available in the same calibers as the Models 44, 45, and 46 including the special calibers indicated for the Model 45 at the same extra charge. Standard equipment included the "D" sights.

When the "F," "G," and "H" sight combinations were furnished the barrels were sent through without the customary rear sight slots. When furnished with "B," "D," and "E" sights the barrel was slotted for a rear sight. To leave this out with that sight combination cost $1.00 extra.

The Model 47 rifle with the 26-inch No. 2 barrel for rimfire cartridges weighed 7¾ pounds and with the No. 2 28-inch barrel for centerfires about 8¼ pounds. With the standard barrel the price was $27.00.

On this and other heavy target models the No. 3 barrel 28 inches long or longer and heavier barrels including No. 4 could be furnished, and when so ordered an interchangeable butt plate, heavier than the regular "Swiss" type and on similar lines to the famous "Schuetzen," was included at no extra charge. This added half a pound to the weight of the rifle.

IDEAL "MODEL RANGE" NO. 48
Intro. 1896 — Discon. 1916

This model was the same as the No. 47 except that the stock and the forearm were fancy and were available with checking. It was a de luxe number and was discontinued early to avoid confusion.

IDEAL WALNUT HILL NO. 49
Intro. 1896 — Discon. c. 1916

This rifle has probably done as much to contribute to the reputation of Stevens rifles for accuracy as any model ever placed on the market. The famous Walnut Hill is still manufactured and still popular among target shooters. As in other models the barrel was half-octagon, frame was case-hardened and engraved. The breech block was solid, single trigger was standard. The stock was varnished walnut with a pistol grip and well-shaped cheek piece. Both stock and forearm were checked. Length of stock 14 inches, drop 3¼ inches at heel.

This rifle was regularly available in a wide range of calibers, including the .22 short rimfire, and .22 long rifle rimfire, the .25 Stevens rimfire, the .32 long rimfire, the .25/20 Single-Shot centerfire, the .25/21, .32/20, .32/40, .32 Ideal centerfire, .38/40, .38/55 and .44/40. On special order it was available for the .22/7/45 W.R.F., .22/15/60 centerfire, the .25/25, .28/30, .32 long and .32 long centerfire at $2.00 extra.

Sights offered almost anything one could desire at that time. Standard equipment was the "H" type and therefore no rear-sight slot marred the barrel.

In 1902 specifications show that with the 28-inch barrel in No. 2 size the rifle weighed 8¾ pounds and 10¼ pounds with No. 3. With the 30-inch barrel it weighed 9¼ and 10½. Prices on these two guns were $42.00 and $43.00 with "G" and "H" sights. With "G," "E," or "F" sights the cost was $39.00 in 28-inch length and $40.00 in 30-inch length. Extra lengths over 30 and up to 34 inches were $1.00 per inch extra. Double set-triggers were $6.00 additional. Walnut stock extra $4.00, and extra selected walnut stock $7.00. Schuetzen butt plate extra $2.00 and Schuetzen finger lever extra $4.00. Palm rest could be fitted for $5.00 and for muzzle-loading types of shooting a false muzzle and "bullet starter" cost an additional $15.00. A wide variety of extras in sights and miscellaneous equipment up to and including gold-plating of the frame were available. A gold-plated frame, lever and butt plate cost $15.00 extra. A silver-plated lever, butt plate and frame cost but $4.00 and a nickel-plated frame, lever, and butt plate was $2.50 extra.

One thing the manufacturers used to do some forty years ago was guarantee accuracy. With this particular rifle a guaranteed accuracy with a ten-consecutive-shot group was 4 inches at 200 yards using the .28/30, the .32/40 or the .38/55 cartridge. Extra interchangeable barrel parts complete up to 30 inches in length including numbers 2, 3, or 4 barrels, plain walnut forearm checked with "H" front sight, was $14.00, and $16.00 for the 32-inch length. The fancy forearm was $2.00 extra. Different combinations of front sights altered the price according to the difference in list price of the sights themselves.

IDEAL WALNUT HILL NO. 50
Intro. 1897 — Discon. 1932

The Walnut Hill No. 50 rifle was the same as the No. 49 except that it included a fancy stock. It was discontinued in 1916 and revived again in 1927, being finally dropped from the line in 1932.

IDEAL SCHUETZEN RIFLE NO. 51
Intro. 1896 — Discon. 1916

This particular model was similar to the Walnut Hill with a few extra adornments and cost considerably more. The barrel was half-octagon in various weights, case-hardened and engraved frame, and with solid breech block. Double set-triggers were standard. Extra fancy Swiss pattern stock with cheek piece of selected walnut, full checked and highly finished. No pistol grip. Length of stock 13 inches, drop 3¼ inches at heel. The butt plate was a standard Schuetzen with prongs at both heel and toe.

"H" sights were used unless otherwise ordered.

With the 30-inch barrel this rifle weighed 12 pounds and with the 32-inch 12½. The 34-inch job weighed 12¾. Prices ran with the standard "G" and "H" sights $58, $60 and $62.

A large Schuetzen frame was also available which added a half-pound to the weight of the rifle.

A number of extras were also available for this particular model including the palm rest, extra charge $5.00; false muzzle and bullet starter, extra $15.00; and interchangeable barrel parts rim or centerfire, complete with forearm and sights up to 30 inches in length ran from $16.00 to $21.00 depending upon the sight equipment and weight of the barrel. The regular "H" front sight with fancy forearm checked and No. 5-grade barrel was $21.00 completely fitted with forearm to match the standard rifle stock. This gun was available for the calibers mentioned for the Walnut Hill model. The prices were those in effect in 1901.

IDEAL SCHUETZEN JUNIOR NO. 52
Intro. 1897 — Discon. 1916

The No. 52 was very similar to the standard Schuetzen rifle in many respects. The original Schuetzen No. 51 had a single lever with a Walnut Hill type pistol grip on the end whereas the No. 52 rifle used the plain loop lever. There was slightly different engraving on the frame but essentially this was about the same as the No. 51. The No. 52 did, however, have a pistol grip stock of the straight type. Stock was in varnished walnut, fancy grade, both stock and forearm nicely checked, with cheek piece, special Schuetzen butt plate similar to but not identical with that of the No. 51 rifle.

This model was available both with the standard and heavy Schuetzen frames. In the standard frame with 30-inch barrel, the weight was 11 pounds, or about a pound less than the No. 51.

IDEAL SCHUETZEN SPECIAL NO. 54
Intro. 1897 — Discon. 1916

This rifle was another of the special Schuetzen numbers of somewhat lighter weight similar to the Schuetzen Junior. Barrel was half-octagon, frame was case-hardened and highly engraved with a heavy Swiss type butt plate in place of the Schuetzen form. A special lever, different from any of the others, was used for operation.

The stock was of the straight type rather than pistol grip and the operating lever had a walnut handle to form a pistol grip. A prong at the lower end served as a finger rest. Double-set triggers were standard. Extra fancy walnut stocks with a well-shaped cheek piece, checked pistol grip and forearm were standard. Length of stock was 13 inches, drop 3¼ inches at the heel. It was built to handle the same ammunition as the other numbers.

IDEAL LADIES' MODEL NO. 55
Intro. 1897 — Discon. 1916

The Ladies' Model was a lighter and lower-priced gun using the Ideal action. The barrel was half-octagon, 24 inches long and the frame was case-hardened. The typical Ideal solid breech block was used. Single trigger was standard and a pistol grip stock and forearm of fancy selected walnut highly finished and nicely checked with a Swiss butt plate was standard equipment. On special order at no extra charge this also could be furnished with an English shotgun rubber butt plate at the same price.

Being a light-weight rifle this was slightly different from others then on the market. It was chambered and rifled for the .22 short rimfire and also for the .22 long rifle rimfire. It could be obtained as standard equipment chambered only for the .22/7/45 W.R.F., the .25 Stevens R.F., and .32 long R.F. In the centerfire calibers it was chambered only for the .22/15/60 Stevens.

"D" sights were standard but the rifle could also be obtained equipped with Lyman No. 1 peep sights on the tang, open rear sight on the barrel, and Lyman combination No. 5 front sight without extra charge. With the standard barrel and Swiss butt plate this rifle only weighed 5¼ pounds but was exceptionally accurate for a light rifle. The 1902 prices on this gun for the 24-inch barrel were $25.00 and with the 26-inch barrel $27.00.

The No. 55 was one of the most desirable models for use by ladies and boys in the entire Ideal line. Despite its light weight it was well balanced and nicely finished and graceful in appearance.

IDEAL LADIES' MODEL NO. 56
Intro. 1906 — Discon. 1916

This gun was very similar to the No. 55 except in certain refinements. It was a slightly more expensive gun and was brought out several years after the No. 55 made its appearance. The barrel was half-octagon, 24 inches long in rimfire numbers and 26 in centerfire. Full-octagon barrels could be supplied for $2.00 additional.

The frame was a drop-forged number, case-hardened, and the action was new and improved somewhat over the older type. Single trigger was standard, with a single set-trigger for $2.00 extra and double set-trigger for $6.00 extra. Pistol grip stocks and forearm of fancy selected walnut was used, highly finished and nicely checked. Swiss type butt plate was standard and was case-hardened instead of nickel-plated. It could also be furnished with the standard Stevens shotgun rubber butt at the same price.

Their No. 56 model was available in .22 long rifle rimfire, the .22 Stevens-Pope Armory rimfire, the .25 Stevens rimfire, .32 long rimfire and in the centerfire numbers the .25/20 Stevens Single Shot and .32/20 repeater.

STEVENS LITTLE KRAG RIFLE NO. 65
Intro. 1906 — Discon. 1911

The Stevens Little Krag rifle was offered to meet an increasingly popular demand for a small rifle having a military double-pull bolt action. It was designed along the pattern of the then popular Krag-Jorgensen rifle used during the Spanish-American War period by the Army.

The Little Krag rifle was a model of simplicity possessing but very few components. It could be easily taken apart for cleaning purposes or to replace any units. It was a take-down type of rifle, of course, and somewhat light in weight. It was designed as a boy's rifle at a time when the Krag military rifle was still popular.

One special feature of this particular model not found in other bolt action guns of that era was that the barrel was removable and could be replaced. Other low-priced rifles had the barrel and receiver made as one unit. The barrel could be fairly easily removed by unscrewing and a new barrel could be inserted without the use of tools.

In construction the bolt had many features for that period. The bolt head was removable so in case of damage a new firing pin could be inserted and the cost was only twenty cents.

The rifle was cocked by drawing back the hammer or cocking piece as it is usually called in a bolt action arm. This was made with a large knurled head for easy cocking. When the rifle is cocked it is locked so that the action could not be accidentally opened until the hammer was lowered.

This particular rifle was bored to take the celebrated .22 long rifle or the then popular .22 Stevens-Pope Armory cartridges. It had excellent low-priced peep sights and many other unique features.

The round barrel was standard equipment in 20-inch length. The frame was blued steel with single trigger. This particular action could not be fitted with a set trigger. Oiled-walnut stock and forearm were used with a rubber butt plate. This particular gun was also able to handle the .22 shorts or the .22 long cartridges. Standard sights included the Beach front, open rear or "B" front and peep rear. The peep was very simple in construction, non-adjustable and consisted of a single block of metal knurled to fit the regular slot in the barrel just in front of the receiver. The rifle was a boy-size number and weighed but 3¼ pounds. In 1907 when it was first listed it sold for $5.00.

STEVENS BUCKHORN NOS. 53 AND 053
Intro. 1935 + — Discon. 1947

The Buckhorn rifle was a low-priced single shot designed to appeal to youngsters.

These models are single shots with a well-shaped bolt lever, extremely fast in action, self-cocking and with independent safety. Bolt and trigger are chromium-plated. A full sized oval military stock is used with a full pistol grip. Stock is of American walnut with a black forearm tip obtained by dipping in black lacquer to simulate buffalo horn used in expensive rifles. Butt plate is of hard rubber.

This rifle weighs about 5¼ pounds and has an overall length of 41¼ inches. It differs in the Models 53 and 053 only in sights. Model 53 has gold bead front and sporting rear, the latter adjustable for both elevation and windage. In addition, the Model 053 has a hooded sight with a ramp and interchangeable inserts, including a blade, peep and round bead. Rear sight is of the receiver type and has an adjustable peep disc with three sizes of peep holes obtained merely by sliding a plate in the back of the sight from side to side. This plate is self-centering.

VISIBLE LOADING REPEATING RIFLES
NOS. 70, 70½, 71, 71½, 72, 72½
Intro. 1907 to 1913 — Discon. 1930 to 1934

The Stevens Visible Loading rifles were designed for .22 caliber cartridges only. No. 70 was listed as No. 70LR as was No. 71 and No. 72. All of these rifles were the same except for sight combinations.

The Visible Loading Model was a repeater with tubular magazine beneath the barrel and a pump or slide action. The 20-inch barrel was standard with a case-hardened frame which appeared very much like the standard Walnut Hill or Ideal frames except in its weight. The stock was varnished as was the slide handle. Rubber butt plates were standard equipment. The same length of the rifle overall was 35 inches and weight about 4½ pounds. The magazine held eleven .22 long rifles, thirteen .22 longs or fifteen .22 short rimfire cartridges.

On the Model 70LR rifle bead front and a simple rear sight adjustable for elevation was standard equipment. In 1911 this gun sold for $12.00. No. 70½ was the same as No. 70LR except for the barrel. This was intended for gallery use and was rifled and chambered especially for the .22 short rimfire. The price is the same.

No. 71LR was the same as No. 70LR except that it was fitted with No. 2 Beach combination front sights, No. 106 Stevens Leaf sight in the barrel slot and No. 102 Vernier peep sight on the tang. The price was $10.50. No. 71½ was the same gun with a barrel especially rifled and chambered for the .22 short.

No. 72LR was the same as No. 70LR except that it was fitted with No. 5 Lyman front sights, with No. 106 Stevens Leaf sights and Lyman 18 combination tang rear sight. The price was $11.00. The leaf sight was in the way of the peep.

No. 72½ was the same as No. 72 gun except that it was built for the .22 short only.

REPEATING GALLERY RIFLE NO. 80
Intro. 1906 + — Discon. 1910

This was a rather unique repeating rifle in that the action was entirely different from anything which had appeared on the market previously. It was a take-down arm and yet was excellently designed. It had a few features that might well have been retained in guns of later design.

This gun first made its appearance about 1906 and contained many then new and novel features. The mechanism was attached to the receiver in connection with a sliding forearm and the stock with trigger guard was attached by means of a take-down screw at the forward portions.

The action in principle was of the bolt type operated by pump or slide lever. It was a repeater with a tubular magazine beneath the barrel. An interesting feature of the action was that when the slide handle was operated it merely traveled rearward 1¼ inches. The breech bolt in the action operated the block lever first in an upward direction and then to the rear, extracting and ejecting the empty cartridge case. The forward motion forced a fresh cartridge from the carrier as it fed from the magazine tube into the chamber.

The construction of the breech bolt was very simple and was such that when the action was closed, it presented a solid top preventing dirt or any obstruction from entering into the action to clog it.

Manipulation of this bolt made it impossible to discharge a cartridge until the action was thoroughly closed and locked.

Cartridges were fed from the magazine into the carrier which placed them into the barrel horizontally, giving an excellent feed for the repeating type of action, particularly with the delicate little .22 rimfire.

The main and sear springs in this particular action were also a new departure in that they were of the coil type rather than the flat spring previously used in other actions. It was not even necessary to take the mechanism apart to clean it as with the action jacked open the cleaning rod could be pushed clear through from the breech.

When the action was taken down, it exposed the entire working mechanism, which could be readily cleaned and oiled without disassembling.

The Stevens repeating rifle was designed to handle four different cartridges, the .22 short, long, long-rifle, and .22 Stevens-Pope Armory. Cartridge stop or adjuster for the different sizes was attached to the carrier and it was necessary to make this slight adjustment by hand in changing from one cartridge to another.

The rifle was manufactured as standard equipment with a 24-inch round barrel fitted with a bead front sight and sporting rear. Overall length was 41½ inches. The trigger guard formed a pistol grip but could be obtained with a plain guard, not forming a pistol grip on special order at no additional charge. This rifle weighed 5¼ pounds complete.

Shortly after its introduction and even before this particular rifle had made its first appearance on the market but after illustrations had been made up for the 1907 catalog, a number of important changes were made in the gun. The short forearm had previously been sawed off and slightly fluted but when the arm was released a steel tip was used to give a more finished appearance. It was originally announced that the butt plate would be of aluminum, but only a few were so manufactured and a rubber butt plate was standard equipment. A new style trigger guard was also adopted not having the imitation pistol grip design.

For gallery purposes this rifle was chambered to shoot .22 shorts only at no extra charge. The magazine held 16 shorts, 14 longs, 12 long rifles or Stevens-Pope Armory. In 1907 the price was $12.00.

REPEATING HIGH-POWER NO. 425
Intro 1910 — Discon. 1918

In the little-known guns of the Stevens line was their special repeating high-power lever action rifle. This had much the same appearance as the Marlin lever with side ejection and a solid top.

It was made in the .25, .30, .32, or .35 Remington rimless calibers and was a typical loop lever type of action. The nickel steel barrel 22 inches long was standard with a solid steel receiver. The action included a coil main spring in place of the flat type used in other rifles of that day. Stock was walnut with checked steel butt plate, rifle style. The walnut forearm had a blued steel metal tip or cap.

Standard sights included the German silver blade front and a sporting or adjustable V-type rear. It was tapped for tang peeps and also for regular barrel telescope sights, screw holes being filled with the customary dummy screws. The magazine had a capacity of five cartridges with one in the chamber, making this arm a six-shot weapon.

HIGH-POWER REPEATING NOS. 430, 435 AND 440
Intro. 1910 — Discon. 1918

This rifle was the same gun as the No. 425, except for the stock, which was fancy. The No. 425 had a plain stock and the No. 430 was selected wood and fairly well checked in the grip and forearm.

An additional number was the 435 which was the same gun with a fancy stock and a certain amount of simple engraving on the receiver. The entire top of the receiver was matted. The breech block was frosted and the finger lever had engraving.

STEVEN'S BOLT ACTION REPEATER
NOS. 56 & 056
Intro. 1935 — Discon. 1948

This particular rifle was another confusing number in that it bore the same number as the Stevens Ladies' Model No. 56. The rifle was entirely different in every respect. It was a repeating type of rifle but instead of the tubular magazine had a clip type of magazine similar to Model 66 described later. The barrel was 24 inches long, tapered with a crowned muzzle. It was chambered for the .22 long and long rifle, either in high-speed or standard cartridges. The clip magazine was detachable and held five shots. Action was the typical bolt action type with thumb-operated independent safety.

The stock had an excellent well-shaped forearm and was made of American walnut with a black forearm tip. This tip was essentially a black lacquered job on the same wood but was made to simulate the famous buffalo horn type of forearm tip, as used on expensive high-power rifles. Hard rubber butt plate is standard.

Sights include a gold bead front, sporting rear type adjustable for both elevation and windage. The Model 056 has a ramp front sight, hooded, with three removable inserts and a receiver peep rear sight.

STEVENS REPEATER NO. 66
Intro. 1930 — Discon. 1948

This was Stevens first attempt at bolt-action repeating rifles and had a tubular magazine design of action. It was announced as the lowest priced all steel repeater on the market when it first came out and sold for $11.75.

It had a 22-inch round barrel as standard equipment and the gun was the typical takedown type with tubular magazine. The magazine held thirteen .22 long rifles, fifteen .22 long or nineteen .22 short cartridges. Standard sights included the Lyman ivory bead front and sporting rear type adjustable for elevation. The stock was of beech or birch, walnut-stained and oil-finished, of the typical so-called "military" type. Butt plate was of steel. The rifle weighed 5 pounds and had an overall length of 39½ inches.

This particular type of rifle did not have the safety cocking feature and the operation of the bolt handle left the rifle cocked and ready for firing. It was designed as a boys' rifle but was widely used as a general all-around "plinking" rifle for men. The forearm was fairly large and well shaped to give a good grip. Bolt-action mechanism was easily operated with a short stroke. A convenient thumb-operated safety was located near the rear of the bolt. Later this rifle became known as the Buckhorn Model with the slightly improved stock, improved bolt handle, and other features mentioned on the Model 066 described below. Sights were changed to a gold bead front and sporting rear sights. The black forearm tip was added.

BUCKHORN REPEATER NO. 066
Intro. 1931 — Discon. 1948

Essentially this was a revised model of the No. 66 and was better designed in every way. It was a bolt-action repeater with a 24-inch round barrel, well tapered and take-down mechanism. The rifle had a tubular magazine having a capacity of fifteen .22 long rifle, seventeen .22 long, and twenty-one .22 short cartridges. The action was designed to handle either regular or high-speed numbers. It was self-cocking with independent thumb operation of safety. The bolt and trigger were chromium-plated.

The stock on this rifle was much better than the old Model 66, being full size, military type, full pistol grip, and built of American walnut. The forearm had a black tip which was obtained by painting or enameling and appeared like an expensive buffalo horn tip installation used on special custom-built high-power rifles. Hard rubber butt plate was used.

Special sights were used on this particular rifle. A hooded ramp front sight came equipped with three interchangeable inserts and a removable hood. It was necessary to replace the hood to use the special inserts. The regular inserts included a blade or square post type, a special peep, and a round bead. The rear sight was of the typical folding sporting type on the barrel and should have been omitted.

BUCKHORN AUTOMATIC NOS. 76 and 076
Intro. 1938 — Discon. 1947

These two rifles, Models 76 and 076, are the latest developments of the Stevens factory. Announced in March 1938 they are also the first attempt by Stevens to build an automatic rifle and in this they have incorporated some unique and interesting features.

Models 76 and 076 differ only in the matter of sights, the better grade sights appearing on the rifle with the "0" preceding the model number as in other Buckhorn rifles.

Each of these new arms has a 24-inch round tapered barrel. The gun is take-down in construction with a knurled thumb nut at a point in the middle of the forearm just in front of the receiver. These rifles have a tubular magazine with a capacity of fifteen .22 long rifle regular or high-speed numbers and is built to be used only with lubricated ammunition where used as an automatic rifle. Special arrangement of the mechanism permits this gun to be used as a standard repeater and when used in this manner, both the shorts and longs can be handled in both regular and high-speed numbers. When used as a repeater of bolt-action type, the magazine has a capacity of fifteen .22 long rifle, seventeen long, and twenty-one .22 shorts.

Action is automatic with an independent safety. Chrome-molybdenum steel is used in all action parts subjected to high shock from the recoil of the repeating mechanism.

Pressing the thumb bolt to the left locks the action for use as a single-shot rifle or repeater and the action is very simple in design and can be disassembled for cleaning without the use of tools. Hammer release mechanism allows the firing of one shot only with each pull of the trigger.

BUCKHORN TELESCOPE RIFLES NOS. 53T, 56 AND 66T
Intro. 1936 — Discon. 1940

These models are the standard Buckhorn rifles having the same model numbers but are equipped with the Stevens-Weaver telescope sights made by W. R. Weaver of El Paso, Texas. The typical open sights are on the barrel where they can be used. No 53 has a low-priced Weaver telescope sight which Stevens lists as their No. 10, whereas Nos. 56T and 66T are equipped with the Stevens-Weaver No. 20 telescope sight which Weaver calls his 29S.

Model 53T is the single-shot number; No. 56T is the repeater with the clip magazine, and No. 66T the repeater with the tubular magazine.

BOLT ACTION TARGET RIFLE NO. 416
Intro. 1937 — Discon. 1948

The Model 416 rifle is Stevens' attempt at a medium-priced heavy-weight target rifle completely equipped. This came out in three types known as 416-1, 416-2, and 416-3, the variation in these types being purely a matter of sights.

The barrel is 26 inches long, heavy tapered and chambered for the .22 long rifle cartridge. A five-shot machine rest target accompanies each rifle to show exactly what the barrel will do.

Action is of the bolt type with a five clip magazine, speed lock with short firing pin fall, adjustable trigger pull. Bolt handle is placed in a low position which permits of a telescope sight mounted close to the barrel for sporting purposes if desired thus giving the same sighting plane with a telescope as with the regular sights.

Independent safety with a red dot indicator is operated by the thumb and is located on the right hand side of the action.

Stock is of American walnut, oil-finished, built large and heavy for target use. The rifle comes equipped with sling strap with an adjustable position for the front sling swivel in keeping with the current 1937-1938 trend in heavy target rifles. A 1¼-inch oil-treated military sling strap is standard equipment as is a checked steel butt plate.

Sights include the new Stevens No. 25 hooded front sight with five removable inserts and a Lyman 57 rear sight designed to fit the rifle. Telescope blocks are also standard. The arm complete with sling strap weighs about 9½ pounds.

BOLT ACTION REPEATER NOS. 84 and 084
Intro. 1935 — Discon. —

The two rifles are the same with the exception of sight equipment. They are both clip magazines of bolt-action type, chambered for the short, long and long rifle and are take-down in construction. The clip is detachable and holds five cartridges.

The barrel is a tapered 24-inch round type with crowned muzzle separate from the receiver. Action is of self-cocking design, bolt type with independent safety and a chrome-plated bolt and trigger. Stock is the full-sized military type with a short forearm, full pistol grip and made of beech or birch stained to resemble walnut. The rifle weighs about six pounds and has an overall length of 43½ inches.

On Model 84 a gold-bead front and sporting type rear sight adjustable for both elevation and windage is standard equipment. These rifles are drilled and tapped for Weaver telescope sights. On the Model 084 a hooded ramp front sight with 3 removable inserts is standard. Hood is removable in accordance with the system of interchanging the blade, peep and bead inserts. The standard middle sight is left on the Model 084 for no reason at all. This is adjustable for elevation and windage. A receiver peep sight with the typical Stevens three-aperture sighting disc is standard.

BOLT-ACTION REPEATER NOS. 86 and 086
Intro. 1935 — Discon. —

Here again we have two, the only difference in which is the sighting equipment. These rifles are almost identical with the Models 84 and 084 with the exception of the magazine type. In this model a tubular magazine is used instead of the clip type. ◆━━━━━━━━━━━━━━━━━

AUTOMATIC REPEATER NOS. 87 and 087
Intro. 1938 — Discon. —

Here again we have Stevens' latest attempt at an automatic rifle, this gun being very similar to their Nos. 76 and 076 except that it does not have the Buckhorn type of forearm tip. The discussion of the Models 76 and 076 automatics applies to this. The only difference noticeable is that a steel butt plate is used in place of hard rubber and the comb is not fluted. Also it is a somewhat lower-priced number using beech and birch in the stock stained to resemble walnut. Action and sighting equipment is identical.

SINGLE-SHOT BOLT-ACTION NOS. 83 and 083
Intro. 1935 — Discon. 1939

Once again we have two rifles identical with the exception of sights. These two new rifles introduced in 1938 have 24-inch round tapered barrels with crowned muzzle and are available in 3 calibers chambered for the .22 long rifle, long and short, and also for the .22 W.R.F. or .25 Stevens R.F. The bolt action has a chrome-plated bolt handle and the action is the typical take-down type. Beech or birch is used for the stock stained to resemble walnut finish. Steel butt plate is standard. The rifles weigh about 5 pounds, with an overall length of 41¼ inches.

Sights in Model 83 include the gold-bead front and sporting rear, the latter adjustable for both elevation and windage. Model 083 typical hooded ramp front sights with three interchangeable inserts is standard, a folding sporting middle sight and a receiver rear sight. The latter is of Stevens design and typical with that used on the Buckhorn models, having a three-aperture sighting disc.

SINGLE SHOT NO. 15
Intro. 1936 — Discon. —

This No. 15 single shot bolt-action rifle is a comparatively new development more or less in a form of a revival of their old-time rifle. It has a 22-inch tapered barrel, take-down style, with a barrel and receiver made in one piece. It is designed for the .22 short, long or long rifle either high-speed or regular cartridges. The bolt action has a rebounding safety lock and prevents accidental discharge. A positive ejector and double strength extractor is used. Beech or birch is used in the stock of stained walnut finish with a full pistol grip. Steel butt plate is standard. Sights include a white metal bead front and a sporting rear sight, the latter adjustable for elevation. This rifle weighs 4 pounds and has an overall length of 37 inches.

BUCKHORN AUTOMATIC NOS. 57 AND 057
Intro. 1939 — Discon. 1947

These Models 57 and 057 are clip-loaded .22 automatic or more accurately *semi-automatic* repeaters, and are essentially modifications of previous numbers with slight refinements. They will handle either the regular or high speed cartridges in .22 long rifle only, as a semi-automatic rifle, but they may also be used with shorts or longs as a bolt-action repeater. This interesting feature is added to the rifle since the lesser-powered cartridges would not properly function the rifle as a self-loader.

The semi-automatic action locks closed by pressing the bolt handle inward, thus necessitating that it be pulled outward to free the lock, and to the rear to eject the fired cartridge case and feed a new cartridge into the chamber. It may be used in this fashion with all ammunition. The 5-shot clip magazine may be detached by pressure on an easily reached latch to the rear of the bottom of the magazine. The stock is of the one-piece sporter type with pistol grip and black forearm tip. A take-down screw permits quick removal of the barrel and action from the stock for easy transportation. The butt plate is of black composition.

The Model 57 is equipped with a gold bead front sight and an open sporting rear sight. The latter is adjustable for elevation. The Model 057 is identical with the Model 57 except in the matter of sight equipment. This model has a hooded ramp front sight with three interchangeable inserts. The hood may be removed.

SPRINGFIELD JUNIOR NO. 53
Introduced 1931

This was the best of the Springfield series and was supposed to be made by the "Springfield Arms Co.," which was merely a brand of rifles manufactured by Stevens in their own factory.

Despite the fact that this was made by the so-called "Springfield Arms Co." Stevens always listed in their catalogs that the Springfield Arms Co. was their own firm and stated, "This brand of firearms is manufactured in the same factory as our famous Stevens brands of rifles and therefore has the same care and precision machining and fitting of the parts—the barrels are bored and rifled by the famous Stevens method and are consequently extremely accurate and safe."

An interesting feature of the entire Springfield line of rifles is the design of the firing mechanism. When the bolt was closed on a loaded cartridge the firing pin was left at a half-cocked position and was held away from the cartridge rim by a new design of lock and kept the rifle from being fired by striking the end of the bolt. When one was ready to fire the bolt must be cocked by drawing back the cocking piece to the full notch.

This rifle, of course, was designed for use by small boys and the safety feature was carefully engineered. In the No. 53 rifle every effort was made to build a semi-man-size gun. Rear sight was a flat top elevating type and a Lyman ivory bead front sight. Barrel length was 24 inches. The stock was of beech or birch, walnut finished in military style with a steel butt plate.

SPRINGFIELD AUTOMATIC MODEL 872

Introduced 1940

This Model 872 is essentially the same as the earlier Models 87 and 087 except that it is built *only* for the .22 Short cartridge. This is a slightly less expensive version of the Buckhorn models but the description of the Model 87 previously given covers this except for the cartridge. It will use regular or high speed .22 shorts. The tubular magazine handles 21 cartridges, and lubricated ammunition is recommended.

SPRINGFIELD AUTOMATIC MODELS 85 AND 085

Introduced 1939

Here again we have a slightly lower priced version of a Buckhorn added to the Springfield line. The Models 85 and 085 are essentially the same as the Buckhorn Models 57 and 057. They are clip loaded, clips having a capacity of five shots. They may be functioned as semi-automatic or self-loading rifles, or as locked breech bolt action repeaters. As semi-automatics they use only the .22 long rifle cartridge in regular or high speed; as repeaters of the bolt action family, they will handle shorts or longs.

THE WALNUT HILL MODEL 417S

Although previously described in this chapter, the revival of this popular favorite in 1945, when returning to commercial production after a long session of producing military rifles, shows that the single shot target rifle for serious business has not lost favor among good riflemen.

As produced in the 1946 line, most of the old versions are again available. Stevens now lists these as the Models 417, 417-0, 417-1, 417-2 and 417-3. The Models -4 and -5 have been dropped. The Model 417 has a heavy 28-inch barrel, but because of the short falling block breech action, the long barrel is no more clumsy than any 26-inch barrel in a bolt action. The short, fast hammer fall insures good ignition and precision shooting. The lever-operated action is equipped with an automatic ejector to discard the fired case. Stock is of the pistol grip variety, two piece, with high comfortably thick comb, and shotgun-type butt. Butt plate is of checked steel to prevent slipping. The large thick forearm makes a comfortable grip for target shooting and the rifle is regularly equipped with a 1¼-inch military sling strap, oil finished. Standard sights include a Lyman 17-A front and telescope sight blocks. Overall length is 44 inches, and weight about 10½ pounds.

The 417-0 is identical with the above except that it is fitted with a Lyman 52L rear sight. The 417-1 substitutes the Lyman 48L rear sight. The 417-2 substitutes the Lyman 144 rear sight. The 417-3 is fitted with scope blocks, but has neither front nor rear sights. The above data on the Walnut Hill Model 417S appeared in earlier editions. It will be understood that the year 1946 was hectic and transitional. The Savage-Stevens boys were transferring from military to sporting production and in contemplation of revival of the Walnut Hill, they included it in the price list for that year. It was never returned to production.

The Rifle in America   Corrections: Courtesy E. F. Mason

Old Model Pocket Rifle 1869 *to 1915*, New Model Pocket or Bicycle Rifle 1872 *to 1915*, Sporting Rifle *1871 to 1875*, Sporting Rifle, Central Fire *Feb. 1, 1877* to unknown, Sporting Rifle No. 1 *1889* to 1897, Sportring Rifle No. 2 (*.22 cal. only)* 1889 to 1895, Sporting Rifle No. 3 *1889* to 1895, Sporting Rifle No. 4 *1889* to 1895, Range Model 9 & 10 were *Schuetzen Rifles*, Ladies Rifles No. 11 & 12 *had open sights*, No. 13 *had Vernier sights* and No. 14 *was custom made (top of the line)*, Crackshot No. 15 1888 *to 1898 (a heavy tip-up rifle)*, Crack Shot No. 16 had *a thumb safety,* Favorite Rifles *1896* to 1939, Favorite Ladies Model No. 21 *1911 to 1916 were custom made for $25.00*, Pocket Rifle No. 39 *(shot)*1898 *to unknown*, Pocket Rifle No. 40 *1907 to 1912*, Vernier New Model Pocket Rifle No. 40 1/2 *1902 to 1906*, Reliable Pocket Rifle No. 42 *1898 to 1902*, Sure Shot Rifle (*J. Stevens' last design, named for Annie Oakley and was too expensive to manufacture)*, The Ideal Rifle *had a side plate, two frame sizes and untreaded barrels.*, The Ideal Rifle in 1896 for Models 107, 108, 109 & 110 *were the first to have threaded barrel shanks*, Stevens Junior No. 11 *1926 to 1939 was the lowest priced rifle at $4.00 retail*, Walnut Hill 417 & 417 1/2 *were also available in Hornet*, Ideal Walnut Hill No. 50 1897 to *1916*, Ideal Schuetzen No. 51 *was the heavy model*, Ideal Ladies' Model No. 56 *used the 44 1/2 action*, Repeating High-Power No. 425 1910 *to 1916*, High Power Repeating Nos. 430, 435 & 440 1910 to 1916 SOURCE: *THE RIFLE IN AMERICA* by Philip B. Sharpe NY: Funk and Wagnalls Company (Harper & Row) c. 1938, 1947 & 1953. 800 pp. (1st Ed. © 1938 by Wm. Morrow and Co.). Reprinted with acknowledgement of Harper & Row.

83

Reprinted from THE SPORTING GOODS DEALER.   October, 1904.

MAKING PARTS OF GUNS.

The Machines that Are Necessary in the Manufacture of Frames, Hammers, Triggers and Springs--A Few Processes Explained and Illustrated.

Perhaps the average person who owns a good shotgun and takes pride in the work it performs, its perfection of parts and the finish of the whole regards it merely as a means toward the attainment of an end—that of shooting quail in the uplands, or ducks in the marshes —giving little thought to the fact that it is a machine in which there are many parts, all working harmoniously together, some performing at high tension and withstanding the relatively tremendous shock of the discharge, others lying dormant until called upon to assist in a minor way in the perfect functions of the gun. Perhaps he purchased the gun because of the quality of its barrels or the simplicity of its mechanism, giving little or no heed to the minor parts, which he may never have seen at all if the gun worked properly and to his satisfaction. But if anything goes wrong with the gun while he is afield, and it will not perform its functions properly, investigation may prove to the owner that a very small and apparently insignificant part has become broken and that the gun is inoperative in consequence and will remain so until a gunsmith can be consulted or the part sent back to the factory.

This is an awkward situation to be placed in, for when one is far afield or in the backwoods and the number of his vacation days is limited, sending the gun to the makers is not to be thought of, and the only alternative will very often be to lay the gun aside and borrow another one, or failing in this, hunt up the nearest gunsmith or mechanic and prevail upon him to make a new part and replace it. Then, and not until then, will the sportsman begin to realize the importance

AUTOMATIC SCREW MACHINES.

of the machine in the making of modern gun parts, and the skill, patience and experience necessary on the part of machine operators and inspectors in the great gun plants. But while the broken part may have been defective and escaped detection, if it is a spring or some part subject to the effects of changes in temperature, it may snap without warning at any time and the most expert mechanic will concede that no matter how perfect the part, it may break or it may last for years—you can take your choice.

We can recall several occasions on which the springs of first-class firearms snapped during the night while in camp and neither in use nor under tension. Watchmakers often receive complaints from customers that the mainsprings of their watches have snapped without any apparent reason, and investigation will sometimes show that a spring has broken into several pieces while yet new. But do not ask the watchmaker to replace the spring free of charge. And so it is with minor parts in firearms. We took a high-grade firearm on one occasion to a gunsmith in a backwoods village and asked him to replace the mainspring, which had broken in the night, with a new one. This he could not do, as he had never before seen a gun just like this one. Could he make a new spring? Oh, yes, he could make a new one; a much better spring than the broken one. And the time

taken and the cost? Merely a half hour or so and a nominal fee. So he went to work at eleven o'clock on a day that was glorious for shooting but intolerable to pass in his stuffy shop. He took the broken spring and made one like it, finishing it up with infinite care and not a little skill of a rough-and-ready sort, and at noon tried to place it in the gun, only to find it too long by an eighth of an inch and no possible way to alter it, because of its peculiar form. With more care than ever he made another spring, and this one was of proper length and form, but when it came to fitting it in place the gunsmith perspired and fumed and fretted but failed, and at last we took the gun from him and relying solely on main strength and perhaps a bit of horse sense, with an implement we have not the temerity to name, seated the spring in its place, adjusted the tension and replaced the other parts in the frame. The spring was honestly made but so strong it required a great effort to raise the hammer, although we did not dare remove it to reduce its power, fearing further complica-

tions. At three o'clock, then, we asked the amount and our friend counted the hours it had taken him to make the two springs and acknowledged that while the accepted spring was cheap at $1.75, he was willing to take a little less for the other one, or $3.25 for both. This because he had kept us waiting longer than at first expected. We convinced him of the error of that train of reasoning, paid him his price for one spring and left him sitting outside his shop, where we had found him, but wiser than before. The spring he made is still in use in that gun after the lapsing of ten years. The expert workman who subsequently reduced its power said it was a good one and paid a compliment to the skill of the cross-roads gunsmith who made it but marveled greatly when informed that it was merely a second-attempt copy and represented almost a whole day of perspiring, hammering and filing on the part of two men when the makers of the gun could replace it for 35 cents and it could be duplicated hundreds of times any day in their factory.

We count it among our privileges to have watched a gunmaker of the old school take a section of English walnut, three bits of Indian buffalo horn, a pair of imported fluid steel barrels, a chunk of forged steel and sundry small pieces and make from them as handsome a gun without a single exception as any we have ever seen, but during the long weeks he worked on this gun when other work did not press him, with two exceptions, it was touched by no tools save those on his little workbench and his footpower lathe. The milling of the frame was also done by him, but in the shop of a machinist, and when the gun was ready for it, the jeweler took it in hand and added a simple monogram and a few ornaments. Almost daily we watched the parts assume form and beauty, and when informed that almost $1,000 changed hands when the gunsmith admitted he could do no more toward its perfection, we could but think the gun was worth the price asked, although many persons might glance at it carelessly and say they would by preference choose a gun of a $75 grade and more ornamentation.

Despite the fact that no gun could possibly be made with greater care and precision than this one, whose locks were original in design and as perfect as the smallest part of a high grade fishing reel, it was not within his power for the maker to guarantee that its minor parts

PROFILING DEPARTMENT.

would not break, which would entail the making of a new part by hand, something not every gunsmith could be trusted to do.

Granted, then, that the barrels are first-class and the workmanship on good material above reproach, in the hands of the average field or marsh shooter the machine-made gun will give as much satisfaction as could be expected of the hand-made weapon, although its life must of necessity be shorter. This counts for little with the great army of shooters, however, for not many of them can claim more than a fortnight annually in which to burn powder, and the gun which might be shot to pieces in a few years of frequent shooting of heavy loads at the traps will last a lifetime on game and is within the reach of slim pocketbooks.

Just as hand-made guns showed improvement from time to time as workmen became more skilled and could command better tools, so have the parts of machine-made guns been improved in every way. Today it is possible to secure new parts by mail with the assurance that they can be put in place, if not by the owner then by a gunsmith at less expense of time and money than would be required in sending the gun to the factory for repairs. But while we have said that parts may break in any gun through no fault of the maker or anyone else, it is very seldom that they do break, and as we have pointed out,

those in the high grade gun are no more immune than others. The machine-made gun, on the other hand, possesses advantages peculiar to it alone, for the owner of one may at an insignificant additional cost provide himself with duplicate mainsprings or any other small parts, and the dealer who keeps guns of certain makes in stock can and should if he does not keep a few parts for which he may receive hurry calls due to minor mishaps.

How small parts of guns are made in the modern factory may not be known to every dealer in these splendid offsprings of combined hand and machine labor, hence we hope the following brief description of a few processes, and the illustrations accompanying them, may be read with profit. For the pictures we are indebted to the J. Stevens Arms & Tool Company of Chicopee Falls, Mass., in whose plant they were made.

One of our illustrations shows the case-hardening kilns at the Stevens plant. The work performed in this department will interest any visitor who has a fondness for gun frames or minor parts that have been treated by this process until the original color of the steel disappears and in its place there is to be seen a variegated pattern impossible to describe or to imitate with brush or steel, and which we once heard an old-time cowpuncher call "pinto," which seemed good enough to remember, as the spots and variations in the color of the pony's coat were in his mind when he thus referred to the finish of the frame of a peculiarly handsome rifle treated in this manner.

These kilns are the furnaces where the work known as kiln case-hardening is performed, and case-hardening. in turn, is the effect produced on receivers, frames, levers, hammers, triggers, top snaps, guards and other steel parts after these have been drop forged. It is a surface hardening, but the depth of its influence varies with the process and if it is desired to engrave any part that is also to be case-hardened, the engraving must be done first, else the steel will be rendered too hard for the cutting of delicate lines and tracery. As a general thing, however, case-hardening is considered sufficient in itself, for it greatly enhances the beauty of the various parts while at the same time serving the useful purpose of preventing exposed portions from rusting.

In the common case-hardening bone and leather are the materials used, but for the high color effects burnt or charred bone is employed, and as this latter process is that which has been adopted for its work by the Stevens company, we will refer to it first.

These kilns are always kept at extremely high temperatures. The frames, levers and other parts to be treated are brought from their respective departments in the great plant and placed in small boxes or pots which are then put in the ovens. There they remain for three to four hours before the proper color is assured and the process complete. The pots are then removed from the ovens and the parts immersed in water, the greatest possible care being taken that the air is excluded.

Cyanid case-hardening differs from kiln case-hardening, the latter being the better process. The cyanid imparts only a surface finish, while the bone penetrates deeper and has much more lasting strength.

The cyanid process is used only where the effect of the color from the kiln action is desired, but in which hardening is not an object. The method is similar to that of the kilns. The parts are placed in

giving the Stevens way. The parts, therefore, are first suspended on wires and submerged in potash with the object of removing from the pores and surface all oil, grease or other substances which would prevent the even and smooth deposit of copper on the parts. Taken from this bath in due time, they are rinsed thoroughly in water, care being exercised to avoid touching them with the hands. A bath in mercuric acid follows, then several washings in clear water and a thorough rubbing with pumice stone. Copper plating is the next step, after which the parts are ready for their final bath in the nickel. In this they remain on the wires for about three hours, and after being taken out have a metallic white finish. As a general thing it requires about five hours to nickel a part, after which it is taken to the buffing room. As in case-hardening, the polishing of a part has a great deal to do with the grade of nickeling. It need not be buffed, however, but generally is. This imparts the mirror-like polish which is so much admired by some sportsmen.

NICKEL-PLATING BATHS.

red-hot furnaces, as illustrated, but instead of remaining there several hours are taken out after about twenty minutes' time and are finished in the same manner as those undergoing the bone process.

Frames and other parts that have passed through these fiery furnaces are practically in a finished state after they have been oiled to prevent rusting, and are ready to be sent to the assembling rooms and fitted to the barrels or other parts. It is very important, however, that the parts be polished carefully before they go into the case-hardening kilns, for the finish imparted there depends entirely on the grade of polishing which has been imparted. Every scratch or flaw or mark will be brought to notice most prominently after the case-hardening, and there is then no way in which the error may be corrected.

One of our illustrations shows the nickel-plating baths in which numerous small parts are treated, including the frames of pocket rifles and target pistols, palm-rests, loading implements, etc. The process is almost entirely a chemical action, but as there are more ways than one of doing the work, and various manufacturers employ different methods in minor particulars, it is worth while

The punch press is an important machine in the modern gun factory, for with it one man can do as much work as several could do by hand under old methods. Its principal work is punching out hammers and triggers from bars of steel, while similar but smaller ma-

CASE-HARDENING KILNS.

chines are used to punch out all kinds of flat springs and top-snap levers. Upon pressing down a foot lever, a die punches out the hammer, or whatever part the machine is adjusted for, from the bar of steel. The parts are then drop forged, finished by other machines, and blued. The blued finish, particularly for receivers and some smaller parts, is seen oftener today than formerly, and this finish is very handsome on plain guns, but of course far less durable than case-hardening, as it will wear off and rust if not oiled now and then.

Profiling machines are employed in the finishing of parts that cannot be worked to advantage on the milling machines. Frames and parts that require milling are taken from the milling machines after having reached the end of that stage of the work and turned over to the profilers. There the sides are shaved off, so to speak, following the form of patterns on the left, these latter being guided by pieces known as guide pins or formers. This work requires great care and of course the operators of the profiling machines are men of experience and known skill in this special branch of modern gunmaking.

The screw machines shown in another illustration are known as the Hartford, Cleveland and Acme automatic screw machines. They are better than the hand machines because one man can operate from two to eight of them, but in the quantity of work turned out the hand machine keeps pace with its rival, the automatic. In this work long bars of steel are inserted in one end of the machine and finished screws are turned out at the other end, the work of milling, threading and cutting being all performed by one of these machines, and its capacity ranges from 400 to 2,500 finished screws in a day. It can almost be said that in this branch of the work there is no waste, and indeed there is very little aside from the depreciation in the value of steel that comes in bars and is returned in part as shavings. These when gathered up are saturated with oil. The oil is extracted and saved for further use. The shavings are then baled and shipped to the steel companies, to whom they are sold.

One of the reasons why this great industry has become a success is the economy practiced in the matter of material and small parts. Given a model, patterns and a few tools and any expert gunmaker can turn out finished guns, but he cannot sell them at popular prices because, after paying for all the parts he does not himself make,

ment of machine tools to obtain so many of the parts necessary in making up a gun that the work he does on them may only be superficial: in fact little more than assembling. The barrels he can obtain

PRESS FOR PUNCHING TRIGGERS, ETC.

in whatever shape he desires, and any grade. Complete forearms can be purchased in quantities. Buttstocks come in a semi-finished state, ready for the necessary hand finishing and fitting. If he adapts the receiver to standard parts, he may purchase his top snaps, firing-pins, locks and metal screws in quantities and obtain the pistol grip, caps, butt-plates and wood screws in the same manner. But while this is true there is still a great deal of hand and machine work to be done. So that he is compelled to obtain a higher price for his gun than the large companies, in order to come out even

In the Stevens plant, for example, where raw material is purchased in immense quantities and every part of the gun taken from this raw material, the cost of each finished part, however small or large it was, represents only a fraction of its cost if purchased in a finished state Furthermore, the company can guarantee its finished guns when it has a thorough knowledge of the quality of each part. And when one workman becomes expert in the fabrication of a certain part—say a spring or a sear—and complaints come in from the inspectors regarding that one part, the company can locate the fault instantly and correct it. There is no guess-work in the system of a great plant like this one.

Many of the machines are employed in other work beside that of part making for the Stevens shotguns, for some of these are capable of adjustment for work on parts of rifles, telescopes, mountings, pistols, etc., both time and

CYANID CASE-HARDENING KILNS.

there would be no profit for him if the guns were sold at a moderate price. It is possible for a workman supplied with an ordinary equip-

money are saved in the cost of every firearm, and as prices are restricted, the dealer obtains a living profit when he sells a gun.

Reprinted from **THE SPORTING GOODS DEALER**   January, 1915.

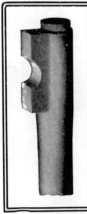

Gun Barrels Bored from Bar Steel in America

Entertaining and Instructive Article on an Industry that Is yet in its Infancy in this Country, with Pictures from Factory of J. Stevens Arms & Tool Company.

A T THIS time when the European war is causing havoc among the manufacturers on the Continent, the future gun barrel suply for such American firearms makers as have been accustomed to depend on Belgium is problematical. It is needless to say that the Liege barrel manufacturers, who have had the bulk of this trade, are for the present and probably for some time to come entirely out of the running. While English gun makers are in position to supply a limited number of barrels at very high prices, their attention is now largely occupied elsewhere. It looks very much as if American gun makers who haven't the equipment to make their own barrels will be put to some inconvenience to keep supplied, and that prices must necessarily be higher.

Extensive Machinery Needed.

Probably some folks will wonder why progressive American manufacturers have allowed themselves to remain dependent on a foreign source of supply for so important a portion of their product. The truth is that the machinery necessary to equip a barrel manufacturing plant is so expensive that it is beyond the means of most of the smaller gun makers. Gun barrel making is really a business in itself, requiring a large investment and a considerable amount of special knowledge. In several foreign countries, notably Belgium, barrel making has been conducted as a separate business for many years.

Methods Used Are a Mystery.

The methods used in making gun barrels, particularly barrels for shot guns are a mystery to the uninitiated, and a source of wonder to many skilled mechanics. How it is possible to bore a hole of extreme accuracy and almost absolute straightness through a solid bar of high-grade steel, possessing great strength and toughness for a distance varying from 26 to 36 inches, is beyond most people. The belief seems to be quite general that shot gun barrels are made of steel tubing. That is not the case, but gun makers have at times fervently wished for an easier and quicker way of making what is, without doubt, the most difficult to manufacture as well as the most vital part of their product.

In the plant of the J. Stevens Arms & Tool Company, of Chicopee Falls, Mass., shot gun barrels are made along the lines set forth in this article, which are those dictated by the best practice, although varying in certain details from the methods used by other makers. In this space it is impossible to do more than to mention briefly some of the more important operations.

In the beginning the raw material in the form of bar steel is purchased from the steel makers in the correct diameter and in lengths that will cut up to the best advantage. This steel is made of special analysis and must pass severe tests before the gun maker will accept it. It is tested for breaking strain in machines designed for that purpose and is analyzed by expert metallurgists both in process and after it is finished. It is handled as carefully as is humanly possible from the mixture that goes into the furnace to the final rolling and shipment. The gun maker's reputation depends on the quality of his barrels and consequently the utmost pains are taken to get the very best steel and to have it free from imperfections of every kind. Failure to pass any single inspection or test, either chemical or physical, is sufficient reason to cause its rejection.

Cut Into Barrel Lengths.

When the steel is received by the gun maker and accepted as satisfactory, it is cut into barrel lengths in a machine adapted for that work. This machine is not of particular interest except that it is very rapid, cutting through a good sized bar in a very few seconds. The short barrel lengths are then sent to the forge shop where they are placed in furnaces and brought to forging heat. They are then put, one at a time, into a large and powerful swaging or upsetting machine, which displaces the metal,

CUTTING BAR STEEL INTO BARREL LENGTHS—SLOW BORING SHOTGUN BARRELS IN STEVENS FACTORY.

TURNING THE BARRELS AFTER THEY HAVE BEEN BORED AND JOINING THE BARRELS OF DOUBLE GUNS.

enlarging the diameter of the bar for a space of several inches, but shortening its over-all length somewhat. They are then allowed to cool slowly to relieve forging strains and to refine the metal, when they are again brought to a forging heat and placed under a heavy drop hammer, which forces out part of the metal, forming a projection or lug. This is the forged lug method as practiced by the manufacturer mentioned. The majority of gun makers do not attempt to produce a one-piece barrel and lug, contenting themselves with a brazed-on lug. The illustrations show this lug very clearly, both in single and double barrel types.

The forged bars with projecting lugs are next placed in an acid bath where they are "pickled" to remove the scale caused by heating. They are then washed to remove all traces of acid and are straightened. The ends are machined so that they will fit the special holders in the boring machines. The boring or "driling" machines, as they are called, are most ingenious and complicated pieces of mechanism and represent a high type of the machine tool builders' art. They are so constructed that the bar which is to be bored is revolved at a high rate of speed. The drill, or cutting tool does not revolve, but advances toward the work almost imperceptibly as the hole gradually increases in depth.

Machine that Does the Work.

It is necessary here to say a few words regarding the drill itself. It is a peculiar tool, like no drill made for any other purpose. It is hollow, and the part which does the cutting, that is, the portion from the point back about six inches is made of the best grade of tool steel, properly tempered and ground to size within the thousandth part of an inch. The shank, or part beginning at the rear end of the cutting portion and extending back about 40 inches, is usually made from a piece of special steel tubing and has a straight groove running from one end to the other. The drill, or cutting part, also has this groove,

the groove in the drill matching the one in the shank, so that it is continuous from end to end. The purpose will be explained.

The Drill Does Not Revolve.

When the forged bar is placed in the machine and the power started, the bar begins to revolve with great rapidity. Immediately the drill pushes forward against the work, and the operator opens a valve which allows a lubricating fluid to flow under high pressure through the hollow shank and drill to the cutting nt. This lubricating fluid is usually a good grade of lard oil, which seems to be the best thing for the purpose. When the drill begins to cut, it starts a chip of metal from the work. This chip is only a very few thousandths of an inch thick, not thicker than the paper on which this is printed; consequently when several cubic inches of steel have been converted into chips, curled and twisted, they occupy a much greater space than in the original solid state.

The boring operation is a very delicate and sensitive one, because it is not possible to put a great amount of strain on the drill. It is to be remembered that the drill and shank combined are over 40 inches long, that the point of the drill can not be held rigid, and that the shank is only attached to the machine at its rear end, which is the sole support. Hence, it is not possible to put any strong twisting strains on the drill by trying to force it too much. This explains why only a very thin chip is possible. It also shows in part why good steel is so essential, steel that is of exactly the same degree of hardness throughout, without soft spots or extra hard ones.

After boring, the barrels are straight-

DOUBLE BARRELS BEFORE JOINING.

ened by experts who have had long training in this work. It is done in part by special machines and in some cases with ordinary hammers. A barrel straightener can instantly detect the slightest deviation from true straightness.

Following comes the reaming or second boring operation. This is to enlarge the hole, bringing it nearer to the finished size. This work is important, but much easier to accomplish than the drilling. Next comes another straightening operation which is immediately followed by what is called "rough turning." Rough turning is done on machines similar to lathes, but which are built especially for the purpose, as is nearly all the machinery used in barrel making. The purpose of turning is to remove the surplus metal from the outer surface of the barrel, bringing it down to the proper shape and thickness. The cutting tool travels along the barrel, following a form to give the required outline.

Final Finishing of Barrels.

After rough turning, the barrels are again straightened, as there is a slight possibility of their becoming bent in turning. They are then subjected to a final or finish turning operation and are straightened once more. Following this comes a closely supervised and detailed inspection for defects of every kind. The barrels are most carefully gauged to ascertain the exact thickness of the walls in all parts.

This completes some of the most difficult and perhaps the most interesting parts of the barrel work, although many operations follow. Among these are the choke boring, grinding outer surface, polishing inside, joining together double barrels, chambering, blueing, etc. When the barrel is finally completed and has passed many inspections for every kind of a defect, it is given the proof test to determine whether or not it possesses an inherent weakness which would make it unsafe. If the barrel successfully withstands this test, it is pronounced satisfactory. Later, when fitted to the action it is tested for pattern.

STEVENS

NEW VISIBLE LOADING

Repeating Rifle
No. 70

The most accurate .22 Calibre Rifle made

Barrel rifled with slow twist, one turn in 25 inches

Weight 4½ pounds. Extra strong double extractors
Handles 15 .22 Short Cartridges, which are always in sight while
being fed into chamber

The Stevens No. 70 Repeater is absolutely guaranteed and bound to give universal satisfaction

No. 70. Fitted with bead front and sporting rear sights, price **$9.00**

No. 71. Fitted with Beach combination front, Stevens leaf and vernier peep sights, **11.50**

No. 72. Fitted with Lyman front No. 5, Stevens leaf and Lyman No. 1 sights . . **12.00**

If you cannot obtain STEVENS from your dealer, we ship direct, express prepaid, upon receipt of Catalog price. Send 8c in stamps for complete Firearm and Telescope Catalogs. Valuable books of reference for present and prospective shooters

J. STEVENS ARMS & TOOL CO.
P. O. BOX 132
CHICOPEE FALLS, MASS.

Source: OUTDOOR LIFE August, 1909

STEVENS

WITHERING HOT WEATHER makes you think of vacation time and all of its attendant pleasures. Days spent in the cool woods, with its tonic atmosphere, will brace you up for another year. A STEVENS ARM you must have to make your outing a complete success.

OUR LINE:

Rifles - - - - from $2.25 to $150.00
Pistols - - - - " 2.50 " 50.00
Shotguns - - - - " 7.50 " 35.00
Rifle Telescopes - - - " 8.00 " 42.00

"Stevens-Pope" Rifle Barrels, Shotgun Cleaners, Cleaning Rods, Gun Greases, Sights, Etc., Etc.

WHERE NOT SOLD BY DEALERS, WE SHIP DIRECT EXPRESS PREPAID, UPON RECEIPT OF CATALOG PRICE.

Send for 140-page illustrated catalogue. If interested in SHOOTING, you ought to have it. Mailed for four cents in stamps to cover postage.

Our attractive Lithographed Hanger will be sent anywhere for 6 cents in stamps.

J. STEVENS ARMS & TOOL COMPANY,
POST OFFICE BOX 132,
CHICOPEE FALLS, MASS., U. S. A.

Source: OUTDOOR LIFE August, 1906

STEVENS

FAVORITE RIFLE

No. 17

A Beautiful Example of Careful, Accurate Workmanship.

LIST PRICE $6.00. Ask Your Dealer.

The Only Boys' Rifle Used by Men

Favorite barrels are rifled more accurately than many rifles selling as high as $50.00. **For this one reason alone more Stevens Favorites are sold than any other rifle model in this country.** This is because Stevens careful, accurate rifling combines straighter shooting with long range and power.

Points for the Sharpshooter and Hunter

If you want expert information on Sharpshooting, Hunting or Trap Shooting, write us a postal telling which subject interests you most. By return mail comes our letter giving you this valuable information, besides the big Stevens Gun Book—209 illustrations and 160 pages about Rifles, Shotguns, Pistols and Rifle Telescopes. **Write Today.**

J. Stevens Arms & Tool Company

P. O. Box 132

Chicopee Falls, Mass.

Makers of **Rifles, Shotguns, Pistols** and **Rifle Telescopes** having an accuracy unparalleled in the world

Source: OUTDOOR LIFE May, 1910

STEVENS

Indoor Target Shooting With a "Off Hand" Target Pistol No. 35

A Great Winters' Sport

Coolness—Deliberation—Self-Control—and Better Vision are all promoted by this admirable recreation, to say nothing of the pleasures of friendly rivalry with congenial associates.

The Stevens Off Hand Target Pistol No. 35—

a wonder for Accuracy. "Hang" and balance just right, too. Adapted for .22 short, .22 long Rifle or .25 Stevens Rim Fire Cartridges.

With 6 in. barrel, weight 1 lb. 6 oz. LIST PRICE **$7.50**
With 8 in. barrel, weight 1 lb. 8 oz. LIST PRICE   **8.50**
With 10 in. barrel, weight 1 lb. 10 oz. LIST PRICE   **9.50**

Ask your Dealer to show you a STEVENS PISTOL No. 35. INSIST ON STEVENS. THERE ARE NO SUBSTITUTES.

Our General Catalog No. 53 illustrates and describes all our Pistol Models, as well as our varied line 𝒐𝒇 Rifles and Shotguns.

Stevens Pistols, Rifles and Telescopes hold more Records for Accuracy **than all other makes combined.**

NEED WE SAY MORE IN THEIR FAVOR?

J. STEVENS ARMS & TOOL COMPANY

P. O. BOX 132

CHICOPEE FALLS, MASS.

LARGEST MAKERS SPORTING FIREARMS IN THE WORLD

Source: OUTDOOR LIFE January, 1913

The sign of a good Sportsman—A STEVENS EQUIPMENT.

The sign of a good Merchant—A STEVENS DISPLAY.

Our RIFLES—SHOTGUNS—PISTOLS represent the largest line in the World.
There's a STEVENS for every need—for every conceivable purpose.
Known for two generations as the BEST at POPULAR PRICES.

Go to your Dealer and examine a STEVENS.
Throw it to your shoulder.
Then let us know what you think of it.

J. STEVENS ARMS & TOOL COMPANY

P. O. Box 132

CHICOPEE FALLS, MASS.

Source: OUTDOOR LIFE March, 1913

To Shoot or Not to Shoot
That is the Question.
❧ ? ? ? ❧

There is a tremendous difference between HIT-
TING AND MISSING---as all shooters know.
Get a Stevens and have the assurance that
our reliable arms shoot where
you hold them. UNERRING ACCURACY has been the
predominant characteristic of the STEVENS for
almost fifty years.

We Manufacture:

RIFLES, PISTOLS, SHOTGUNS, RIFLE TELESCOPES

Where not sold by local merchants, we ship direct, EX-
PRESS PREPAID, upon receipt
of price.

Send 4 cts. in stamps for 140-page
illustrated catalog. A handy book
of ready reference for all who
shoot, or are going to.

Our attractive 3-color Aluminum Hanger will be mailed anywhere on receipt
of 10 cents in stamps.

J. STEVENS ARMS & TOOL COMPANY

Post Office Box 132

CHICOPEE FALLS, MASS., U. S. A.

Source: OUTDOOR LIFE April, 1906

STEVENS

IDEAL RIFLE No. 44½

"BULL'S EYE KIND"--

The finest men's single shot rifle in the world

LIST PRICE $12.00

Made in standard lengths—weights and calibers. Fitted with Rocky Mountain Front and Sporting Rear Sights.

STEVENS IDEAL RIFLES are the international standard by which all others are judged. Hold first honors for Accuracy in United States—Great Britain —South Australia and Western Australia.

STEVENS SHOTGUNS— RIFLES—PISTOLS—TELE-SCOPES—made in the factory of precision with an Accuracy Unparalleled in the World.

SEND FOR LATEST 160 PAGE CATALOG
YOUR DEALER HANDLES STEVENS

J. STEVENS ARMS & TOOL CO.

P. O. BOX 132

CHICOPEE FALLS, MASS.. U. S. A.

Source: OUTDOOR LIFE February, 1910

PENETRATION

THROUGH 17 ⅞-INCH BOARDS WITH A

STEVENS

"HIGH POWER" RIFLE

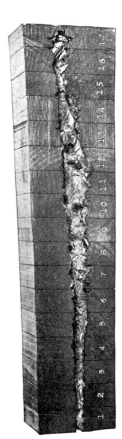

The ammunition makers only claim a .35 Caliber Auto-loading Cartridge bullet will penetrate 13 such boards, but if used with a STEVENS "HIGH POWER" RIFLE you

INCREASE THE KILLING FORCE 30%
TRY IT and PROVE IT FOR YOUSELF

BIG ENOUGH FOR THE BIGGEST GAME OF NORTH AMERICA

Our No. 11 Rifle Catalogue (Free). Contains Considerable Interesting Information. Illustrates the Mechanism and all Varieties of STEVENS "HIGH POWER" MODELS

J. STEVENS ARMS & TOOL COMPANY

P. O. Box 132

CHICOPEE FALLS, MASS.

Largest Makers Sporting Firearms in the World

Source: OUTDOOR LIFE November, 1912

93

STEVENS

Shoot a Stevens. Get all the pleasure and service out of a firearm that is possible to obtain. **Stevens Rifles, Shotguns, Pistols,** have "proved good" for thousands of Sportsmen—they will meet your wants in every way.

Ask your dealer and insist on our popular make. If you cannot obtain, we ship direct, *carriage charges prepaid,* upon receipt of catalog price.	Send for 140-page illustrated catalog. If interested in *shooting*, you ought to have it. Mailed for four cents in stamps to cover postage.

Our attractive three-color Aluminum Hanger will be sent anywhere for 10 cents in stamps.

J. STEVENS ARMS & TOOL COMPANY,
Post Office Box 132
CHICOPEE FALLS, MASS., U. S. A.

Source: **OUTDOOR LIFE March, 1906**

Big Enough for the Biggest Game of North America
Big Game Hunters' First Choice—

STEVENS

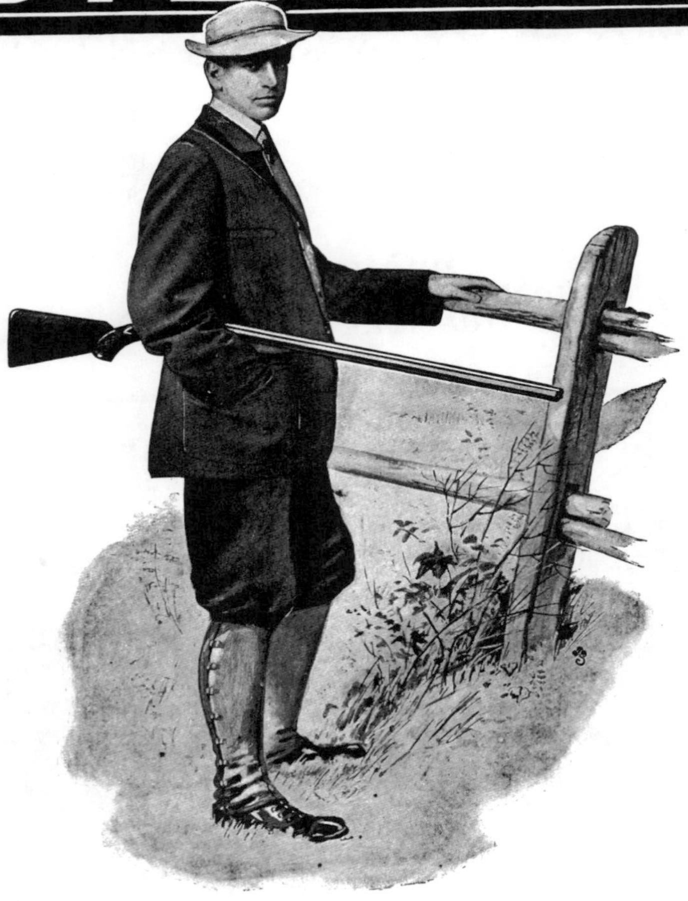

"HIGH POWER" REPEATING RIFLES Nos. 425 to 440

List Prices range from $20 to $90.
Compact Design—Symmetrical Lines—Safe and Efficient Mechanism.
Made in .25, .30-30, .32 and .35 Calibers.
Use Remington Auto-Loading cartridges.
SURE FIRE—NO BALKS—NO JAMS.

STEVENS RIFLES—
The Most Accurate in the World.

¶ Send for "High Power" Repeating Rifle Catalog and "How to Shoot Well."
Have your Dealer show you a

STEVENS
High Power

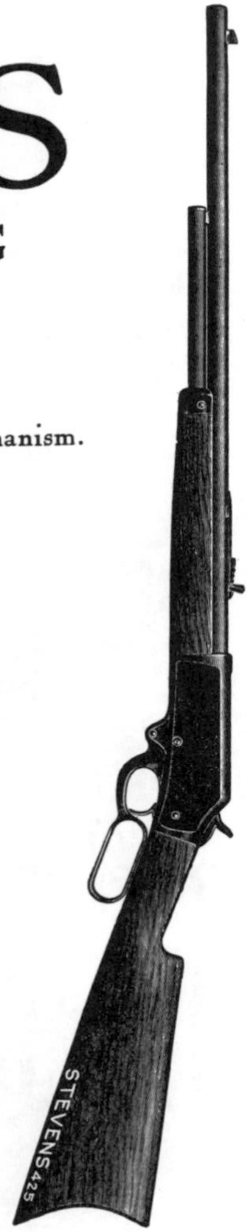

No. 425
LIST PRICE $20

J. Stevens Arms & Tool Company
P. O. Box 132
CHICOPEE FALLS, MASS.

Source: **OUTDOOR LIFE February, 1913**

IN SEARCH OF THE 'IDEAL' RIFLE

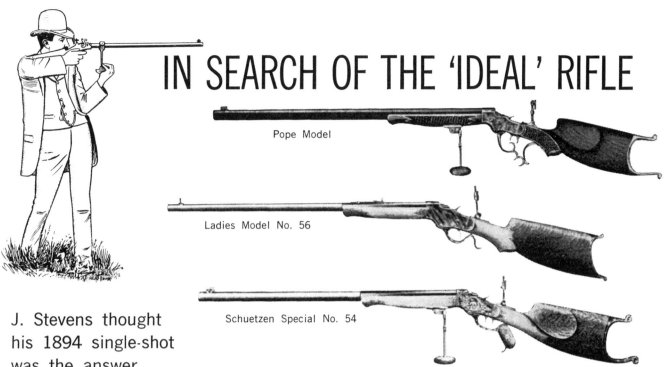

Pope Model

Ladies Model No. 56

Schuetzen Special No. 54

J. Stevens thought his 1894 single-shot was the answer

By JAMES E. SERVEN

Single-shot rifles by Joshua Stevens were popular among turn-of-the-century sportsmen. The guns on these pages are all models of the "Ideal" series.

WHAT is an ideal rifle? The J. Stevens Arms & Tool Co. of Chicopee Falls, Mass., thought they had the answer in 1894. Many shooters agreed and purchased hundreds of rifles in the line that Stevens christened "Ideal." In 1901 America's premier barrel-maker, Harry M. Pope, became associated with the company and added new lustre to the Stevens reputation.

During the period from 1894 to 1916, Stevens produced its most beautiful and widely acclaimed single-shot rifles. These were built on either the No. 44 or No. 44½ action, and were all grouped under the "Ideal" heading.

Stevens used names such as Ideal, Hunter's Pet, Expert, Premier, Crack Shot, Sure Shot, Favorite, Marksman, and Little Scout to identify a type of firearm. For type variations he used numbers.

Stevens also made repeaters with bolt, pump, lever, and automatic actions, a wide variety of shotguns, and also machinist's tools such as calipers, dividers, gauges, scribers, nippers, and cutters. The firm also manufactured Stevens-Duryea automobiles.

The Stevens story began near the close of the Civil War in 1864 when Joshua Stevens decided he could capitalize on the demand for small pistols using the new metallic cartridges. So in a small 2-story wooden building at Chicopee Falls, adjoining Springfield, the first .22 single-shot pocket pistols were produced by Joshua Stevens and partners W. B. Fay and A. Bartlett under the trade name J. Stevens & Co.

At first, progress was slow. By 1869, however, they found that a single-shot pistol with a long barrel and an attachable shoulder stock would sell. Soon, along with Frank Wesson, Stevens became the leading maker of such arms. Its single-shot pistols in the Lord, Gould, and Conlin models eventually became popular with both serious marksmen and plinkers. They also did not neglect rifles and shotguns, producing several models with tip-up barrels. The emphasis in all cases was in producing low cost arms.

In 1886 the business was incorporated as the J. Stevens Arms & Tool Co. When the Ideal dropping-block rifles were introduced in 1894, the Stevens firm occupied about 17,000 sq. ft. of floor space and employed 44 people. During 1894 and 1895 the various grades of Ideal rifles then manufactured were given numbers 107, 108, 109, 110, but the new management discarded these for a new numbering system.

Exit Joshua Stevens

Having accumulated a substantial fortune, Joshua Stevens withdrew in 1896. The company under the new management of Irving H. Page progressed rapidly. By 1898 the number of employees had increased to 150, and by 1901 the work force had been increased to 900. In 1902 the floor space of the 2 Stevens river plants and its "hill" plant across the street totaled over 10¼ acres. It was during that period Stevens claimed to be the world's largest producer of sporting firearms.

In Stevens's Aug. 1, 1900, catalog, Ideal rifles were made in a basic Ideal Sporting and Hunting Rifle No. 44 which sold with standard equipment for $10. Next was the Ideal Range Rifle No. 45 priced from $18 to $30 depending on barrel length (26" to 34") and a wide range of sights classified as B, D, E, F, G or H, to indicate by letter the types available from plain hunting to adjustable target sights.

The Ideal Model Range No. 47 (changed later to Ideal Modern Range No. 47) was more elaborate with pistol grip, stock and loop lever. It cost $5 more than a corresponding No. 45 rifle which had no engraving on the frame or checkering on the stock.

The Ideal Walnut Hill Rifle No. 49 was an extremely popular and ornamented rifle. It had a Swiss buttplate, straight grip stock with cheekpiece and checkered grip, finely checkered forearm, and an engraved receiver. The No. 2 and No. 3 barrels used for this model (and in fact the various weight barrels for all models) were a standard half-octagon in shape. A 28" No. 3 barrel brought the weight to 10¼ lbs. and the base price was $39. Special sights, double set triggers, decorative wood, Schuetzen buttplate and lever, palm rest, false muzzle, and bullet starter were all extras, totaling $4-more than the base cost of the rifle.

Further along in the line was the Ideal Schuetzen Rifle No. 51. This was

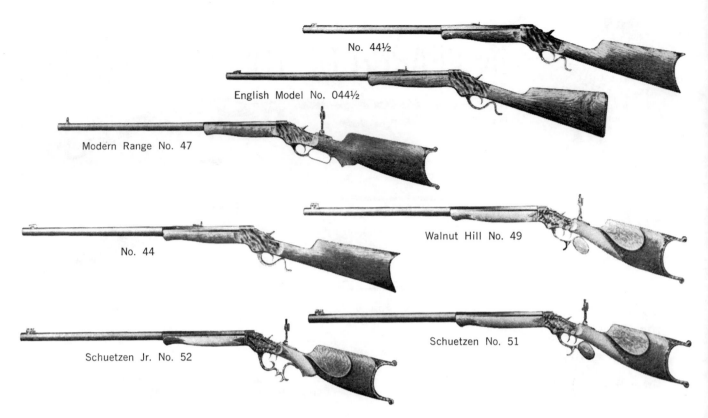

No. 44½

English Model No. 044½

Modern Range No. 47

No. 44

Walnut Hill No. 49

Schuetzen Jr. No. 52

Schuetzen No. 51

a heavier rifle with 30"-34" barrels available in No. 3, 4, or 5 weights. The stock had a Swiss pattern without pistol grip, and the frame was engraved. A complete gun weighed from 13 to 15 lbs., and the base price was $58. The palm rest, false muzzle, and bullet starter added $20 to the cost. Interchangeable barrels in any of the 3 above weights, complete with adorned forearms, cost $16, $18, and $21 respectively. The barrels on all Stevens models were easily removed, and the company described its models as "takedown."

Similar to the No. 51, but slightly lighter and with a pistol grip stock and loop lever, was the Ideal Schuetzen, Jr. No. 52. The base price was $54.

Coming close to the end of the line in 1900 was the Ideal Schuetzen Special Rifle No. 54. It was a fine rifle with Swiss stock, specially designed lever, engraved frame, and elaborate sights. With 30" barrel the gun weighed 11 lbs., and the base price was $58. With palm rest, false muzzle, and bullet starter the cost was $88.

The Ideal Lady Model No. 55 completed the line in 1900. It was a lightweight rifle weighing only 5¼ lbs. with 24" barrel. It had a walnut stock with checkered pistol grip and a checkered forearm; the frame was not engraved; base price was $25.

All these rifles were built on the No. 44 action and designed for a great variety of blackpowder cartridges from .22 rimfire to .38-55 center-fire.

The Stevens Catalog No. 50 contained this announcement concerning the recent association of Harry M. Pope with the firm:

"You will note by the announcement below of Mr. H. M. Pope, that we have made arrangements to manufacture and sell his celebrated rifle barrels. Mr. Pope has built up a national reputation as a manufacturer of high-grade rifle barrels, and combining the best features of the 2 companies, will be able to produce one of the most perfect rifle barrels it is possible to make. There will be no reduction in the price of this special work. Mr. Pope will personally supervise all fine rifle and pistol work and fit barrels to any standard action. The new barrel will be known as the 'STEVENS-POPE'."

Harry Pope's letter dated April 1, 1901, and addressed "To My Friends and Patrons," read:

"My business having increased beyond my capacity, and being anxious to fill my orders more promptly, I have sold all my tools and special machinery to the J. Stevens Arms & Tool Co. The business will be conducted by them, but I am to remain in full charge of all the work on the high-class rifles and tools on which I have been working in the past, and no such work will leave the factory without my personal inspection and approval."

Associated with Pope was F. C. Ross, a marksman of international reputation. After construction, inspection, and fitting, the barrels were shot for accuracy by Ross who it was claimed could demonstrate the perfection of the barrels in a way to satisfy the most exacting marksman.

Soon after Pope joined the Stevens company they issued a "Catalog of the Stevens-Pope Specialties." This special catalog contained a description of the Stevens-Pope rifling with its 8 wide grooves and narrow lands with gently rounded corners, cut to a depth of about .004". In addition to material concerning calibers, loads, and a list of some of the records made with Pope barrels, there was also information on Pope-type false muzzles, bullet starters, molds, bullet lubricating pumps, loading flasks, palm rests, and re- and de-cappers, with details of the Pope system of loading bullets from the muzzle.

This special catalog illustrated, described, and priced Ideal rifles fitted with Stevens-Pope barrels including the grades bearing Nos. 45, 47, 49, 51, 52, and 54.

Additionally a "Pope Model" was shown. This rifle had one of the few full octagon barrels ever seen on a Stevens Ideal rifle. It was claimed to be the same model used by Pope in all his 200-yd. shooting and "designed to give a handsome well-made rifle all the finest extras that could help fine shooting, but with no money spent for engraving, . . . that did not help the shooting of the rifle, with the exception of a fine stock."

There was an option of a 30" or 32" No. 4 octagon barrel. The action was drop-forged and case-hardened, double set triggers; special 3-finger lever; Pope style pistol-grip stock 13⅝″ long with 3″ drop and with an extra high cheek-piece; deep Swiss buttplate; Pope muzzle-loading outfit, palm rest and special sights. The weight was from 12½ to 13½ lbs., and the price was $82.

Exit Harry Pope

Pope was a genius, and as with most specially gifted persons he was temperamental and restless. With the Stevens-Pope system of barrelmaking well established, Pope turned his thoughts to other horizons, and on the last day of 1905, terminated his association with the Stevens firm. He later said that he personally made all the Stevens-Pope barrels numbered under about 1250.

San Francisco was Harry Pope's new destination and on Apr. 17, 1906, the first day he opened his new shop, the earthquake and fire struck San Francisco, practically wiping him out. Following 2 years of temporary jobs, Harry Pope established, in 1908, a shop at Jersey City, N.J., where he continued to make fine barrels for many years.

The Stevens firm also produced a variety of telescope sights. It acquired the telescope business of the Cataract Tool & Optical Co. of Buffalo, N.Y., in 1901, along with the services of F. L. Smith who had been the manager and expert in manufacturing the Cataract sights. Stevens Co. proceeded to make telescope sights not only for its own rifles but models designed for mounting on Winchester, Remington, Savage, Marlin, and Colt rifles.

Transition to smokeless powder

At the turn of the century, there was a rapid transition from blackpowder to smokeless powder cartridges. The greater pressures of the smokeless powders presented major problems to armsmakers whose rifle actions were not constructed to handle high-pressure loads with complete safety.

It may have been purely a coincidence, but shortly after Pope joined the Stevens organization, its No. 51 (1904) catalog announced the improved Stevens Ideal No. 44½ Model adapted to smokeless powder cartridges. Stevens declared that the takedown system applied to its regular Ideal rifles in the past would be retained in the new model, and that all rifles, from No. 44½ to No. 54, would have the new action.

In this action style Stevens also made the No. 044½ English model. This was made with a light-weight tapered barrel,

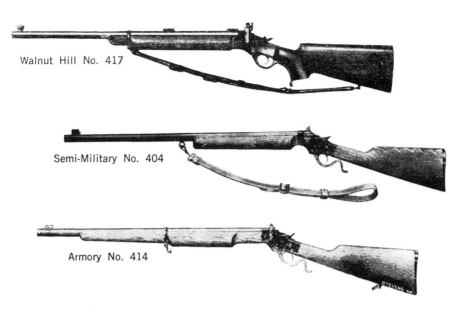

Walnut Hill No. 417

Semi-Military No. 404

Armory No. 414

and English shotgun stock.

The Ideal rifles with the No. 44½ high-wall action were sometimes referred to as "The New Action Rifles Model 1903." The new No. 44½ action was a great improvement over the No. 44 and helped to increase the popularity for the Stevens Ideal line. Prospering, Stevens opened branches in New York and London, and agencies were established in Germany, Norway, Sweden, Denmark, Australia, Mexico, Cuba, and various parts of South America.

There were minor changes in the Ideal rifle listings in Stevens' Catalog No. 52 (1907-1909) and its 1911 Catalog No. 53. The No. 44 action rifles continued to be listed for low-power cartridges and still had a base price of $12 in the plainest model as had the new No. 044½ action light English model with tapered barrel and shotgun-type butt. The 1907-1909 Catalog listed for the first time an "Ideal Ladies Model No. 56" which varied in some important respects from the No. 55. It was 1¼ lbs. heavier than the No. 55. A full octagon barrel was available for $2 extra. Probably the major reason for this separate listing was that the No. 55 used the old No. 44 action, while the No. 56 employed the new No. 44½ action. Also a 26″ barrel was required for the center-fire cartridges, and a 24″ barrel was the standard in the No. 55 designed for the light rimfire cartridges. However, the Ideal Ladies Model No. 55 was soon discontinued.

In the No. 53 catalog of 1911 an attractive rifle described as the "Semi-Military Model No. 404" appears. Unlike the majority of other "Ideal" rifles after 1903, it employed the No. 44 low-wall type of receiver for it was made only in cal. .22 long rifle. A shotgun butt with rubber buttplate was em-

ployed along with an extra wide nicely checkered forearm. A No. 210 globe interchangeable front sight was coupled with a No. 42 Lyman receiver sight with cup disc. This gun weighed about 8 lbs. and was the fore-runner of Stevens Ideal Armory Model No. 414, also made in .22 caliber and built on the No. 44 action.

The Armory Model, introduced in 1912 appeared first in Catalog No. 54 (1912-1914), was designed for indoor and short range firing, offering competition to Winchester's .22 caliber "Winder Musket" of somewhat similar design. A forestock, held by one barrel band, extended under the 26″ round barrel to within a short distance of the muzzle. It was shaped with a bulging hand hold. A Rocky Mountain front sight was matched with a receiver sight designed for this rifle.

Gathering war clouds

The Armory rifle was the last of the Ideal rifle models to be introduced before World War I cast its shadow over the manufacture of all rifles for civilian use. As war threatened, Stevens realized how seriously it would affect its activities. Stevens took a first step in preparing for wartime conditions by transferring its telescope business to the Lyman Gun Sight Corp. Lyman had acquired the business of the Ideal Manufacturing Co. of New Haven, which was the Nation's foremost producer of loading tools. The old Ideal handbooks were great favorites with shooters and the J. Stevens Arms and Tool Co. advertised in these handbooks. Perhaps Stevens decided to capitalize on the popularity of the old Ideal name when it introduced its Ideal rifles. Data on the rifling in Stevens barrels contained in Ideal handbooks and Stevens catalogs is listed below:

CALIBER	ONE TURN IN
.22 Short rimfire	25"
.22 Long rifle rimfire	16"
.25 Stevens rimfire	17"
.22-15-60 Stevens center-fire	12"
.25-20 Stevens	13"
.25-21 Stevens	13"
.25-25 Stevens	13"
.28-30-120 Stevens	14"
.32 Rimfire	25"
.32 Ideal	18"
.32-40	16"
.38-55	18"

Stevens claimed their vernier rifle sight was the "neatest, safest, most convenient sight made." Wind and elevating movements are independent of each other; one whole movement of either screw equals one inch on a 200-yd. target.

Stevens barrels were manufactured for most of the standard calibers of its time, some of which were originated by the company with the object of obtaining the highest possible accuracy. Prominent among these Stevens originals were the famous .22 long rifle and the .25 Stevens rimfire; their original center-fire cartridges were in calibers .22-15, .25-20, .25-21, .25-25, .28-30. Except for the slightly necked .25-20 these Stevens center-fire cartridges all had long, slim straight cases. Others of special interest were the .32 Ideal and the .32-35-165 Stevens.

The golden era of the single-shot breech-loading rifle began in the early 1870's when American marksmen, using Sharps and Remington breech-loading "Creedmoor" rifles, wrested the world championship in rifle shooting from Irish and English marksmen; an end to the era of fine single-shot rifle manufacture was in sight when war broke out in Europe in 1914.

As American involvement in World War I approached, the trend in cartridge design had turned to such calibers as the cal. .30 bottleneck cartridges with smokeless powders that provided high velocity and low trajectory. Few single-shot actions were strong enough for these high pressure loads. The bolt action became the favorite and single-shot match rifles were fast losing ground.

Thus by 1916 the curtain was falling on most all fine single-shot rifles. Wartime demands and other problems laid a heavy hand on the Stevens management at Chicopee Falls, and the plant was turned over to the Westinghouse Electric Co. to meet the demands of war production.

Company reorganized

In 1916, the Stevens firm was reorganized, and the name changed to J. Stevens Arms Co. In 1920 the J. Stevens Arms Co. merged with the Savage Arms Corp., then with headquarters at Utica, N.Y. The premises in Chicopee Falls were taken back from Westinghouse and manufacturing of

Stevens rifles resumed.

The Savage Arms Corp. continued building a few of the pre-war Stevens Ideal models after 1920. They were the No. 44 in .22, .25 and .32 rimfire calibers and also the No. 414 Armory Model in .22 caliber. By 1932, however, both of these rifles were discontinued. In that year they were replaced by 2 excellent smallbore single-shot rifles classified as the No. 417 Stevens Walnut Hill Target Rifle and the No. 418 Stevens Walnut Hill Target Rifle. The No. 417 was heavier, more expensive, and had a 28" round barrel and a lever that conformed to the contour of the pistol grip; it weighed 10½ lbs. The No. 418 had a tapered 26" barrel with plainer lever and other component parts and weighed only 6½ lbs. Sporting models in either gun were available and designated as No. 417½ and No. 418½. Target models were available in cal. .22 long rifle only, whereas the sporting models might be had in .22 long rifle, .22 WRF, or .25 Stevens rimfire. The No. 418 was discontinued in 1941 and the No. 417 went out of production 2 years later.

Phil Sharpe, author of *The Rifle In America*, was sentimental toward the Stevens rifles, stating that none of his other .22 rifles could top the accuracy of his Stevens Walnut Hill No. 417½. Other experts of the day have emphasized the quality of Stevens barrels. On this point Col. Townsend Whelen wrote in his *The American Rifle:* "The barrels were almost always superbly accurate, and many fine scores have been made with Stevens rifles." Stevens made the barrels for the American team which won the Palma Trophy at Bisley, England, on July 11, 1903. Lt. A. S. Jones, Secretary of the National Rifle Association, wrote: "The truth of the matter is we owe the victory mainly to the barrels and ammunition used. The former were made by the J. Stevens Arms and Tool Co. of Chicopee Falls, Mass."

Although as a separate and distinctive name in arms manufacture the Stevens firm ceased to exist in 1920, Stevens rifles have continued to make history as part of the expanded Savage Arms Corp. Like all other giants in the arms industry—Winchester, Colt's, Remington—Savage Arms, although operating as a separate company, has become a division of a larger diversified corporation.

Today a final chapter is being written in the Stevens story at Chicopee Falls. Following 2 disastrous fires within a year, the old factory buildings are now being torn down under an urban renewal demolition grant.

Chicopee Falls, however, will long be remembered as one of the great arms-making centers. Among the many arms manufacturers who have turned out guns was the Ames Manufacturing Co., established in the early 1800's. It became well known for the production of swords, bayonets, rifles, and cannons. The Massachusetts Arms Co. was also organized there in 1849 and turned out many revolvers and rifles, including the Maynard. Joshua Stevens started arms manufacture in 1864. The Savage Arms Corp. into which Stevens was absorbed in 1920 then continued arms activity in Chicopee Falls, moving its headquarters from Utica, N.Y. in 1956.

In 1960 demands for better manufacturing facilities prompted the Savage Arms Corp. to move its operations to a modern plant at Westfield, a few miles west of Chicopee Falls. The old multi-story Chicopee Falls buildings were sold.

The modern machinery of the Savage Arms Corp. is humming today at Westfield, turning out a great variety of modern sporting arms. The know-how gained from Arthur Savage, Joshua Stevens, and A. H. Fox, along with the skills of their associates and successors is applied, and some of these guns still bear the Stevens name. ∎

Arthur Savage & Joshua Stevens

By Walter Wolk

Suppose you're a newcomer in the arms-making industry—an upstart battling giants that have devoured small competitors. Suppose you've invented an amazing rifle—but no one knows about it. And suppose the rugged men of the American frontier won't even try your rifle because they figure the caliber is too small to slap down a grizzly or an elk. What do you do? You prove that your gun can stop a whale! It's as simple as that . . . *if* the year is 1900 and *if* you're as brilliant as Arthur Savage.

Let's do some more supposing. You're a fairly successful gunsmith, but you've had some failures, too. Years ago you invented a revolver that might have become famous, but an old friend of yours named Sam Colt sued you over patent rights, and he won, and you were out of business. You sweated and scraped and in '64 you opened a one-room gun plant. You scraped some more and built up a good business, but nothing world-shaking. And you want to shake the world. What do you do? You develop the .22 Long Rifle cartridge—the world's best-selling shell. That's what you do if you're Joshua Stevens.

These two men both attained seemingly impossible goals, and in the process they laid the foundations for the Savage Arms Corporation, today one of the largest producers of sporting arms in the world. Ever since the turn of the century the company's products—which now include Savage, Stevens and Fox arms—have appealed to gun lovers who appreciate quality and reliability.

Arthur William Savage was born in the West Indies on May 13, 1857. His father was England's Special Commissioner to the West Indies, residing in Kingston, Jamaica, where his job was to set up an educational system for newly freed slaves. Arthur received an excellent education, but not of a kind calculated to mold a great gun inventor; his studies in college included such subjects as classical languages. His schooling was a far cry from the rudimentary education of the early Yankee gunsmiths who pioneered in firearms development. And yet he had a great deal in common with those men. He was anything but the sheltered, bookish type.

As soon as he finished college he took off for Australia and spent the next 11 years managing a cattle ranch. While there, he married a girl named Annie Bryant and they began raising a family that eventually included four sons and four daughters.

Not very much is known of those early years, but this is certain: Savage was fascinated by firearms and he had plenty of chance to use them. Seeking new wildernesses to conquer, he returned to the West Indies to manage a coffee plantation and there he handled firearms of every type. He also had a deep interest in machinery of all kinds and was continually experimenting on improvements. Among his inventions was a military missile which he developed with the help of another man; known as the Savage-Halpine torpedo, it was bought by the government of Brazil. But by this time his main interest was, without a doubt, small arms. He knew that big things were happening in the United States, and it was here that he decided to enter the field.

The giants—Winchester, Remington and Colt—dominated the industry, and many smaller companies had been swallowed up during their development. The only hope for the survival of a new enterprise was to offer something new.

In 1894 Savage organized such an enterprise in Utica, N. Y. The purpose of the Savage Arms Company was to produce a hammerless lever-action rifle designed by the inventor. Smokeless powder was already beginning to revolutionize the industry, and this rifle fired high-power smokeless loads. Conventional big-bore, low-pressure, black-powder ammunition was already becoming obsolete.

The new rifle was the famous Model 99, and it was so good that today, after half a century, it still bears the same designation and the same basic design. The new cartridge, also Arthur Savage's invention, was in .303 caliber (not to be confused with the .303 British, a military load of later vintage that was used a great deal in World War II). Soon after its introduction in .303, the gun was offered in a variety of calibers, including .30/30.

The 99 is a hammerless lever-action rifle utilizing a short lever throw. It has a rotary magazine rather than the familiar tubular type. In this magazine sharp-pointed bullets could be used; such bullets, if used in the tubular type of magazine, presented the danger of accidental detonation during recoil when the point of one struck the primer of the next. The rotary design also eliminated the marring of the bullets themselves. No lugs or bolts were used in the arm. The breech was closed and the action was so strong that high-power, high-pressure ammo could be used safely. Side ejection made possible the mounting of a scope directly over the barrel. More important to most riflemen of that day, the short lever throw made the rifle a lightning-fast repeater.

As fine as the new arm was, it did not mean immediate easy sledding for Savage. Many of the old mountaineers and frontiersmen were reluctant to

GUNS AND HUNTING/JANUARY, 1962

continued

try a new—and relatively small—caliber. The .303 was competing with such loads as the old .45/70, but Savage was by no means stumped. In his company's catalog for 1900, he saw to it that there were several testimonials extolling the cartridge as a big-game stopper that had proved itself with one-shot kills on moose, deer, caribou, mountain sheep and grizzly bear. And the real clincher in that catalog was a letter from Mr. E. T. Ezekiel of Wood Island, Alaska, telling how he had actually killed a whale with an expanding .303.

The Model 99 very quickly made a name for itself as a noteworthy deer killer—a reputation it has rightly kept to this day. The company was a growing success, and it began to bring out additional cartridges, calibers and arms. In 1916 Savage merged with the Driggs-Seabury Ordnance Company of Pennsylvania. Then, during World War I, the firm gave up making sporting arms to produce Lewis machine guns for the Allies. When peace came the company was reorganized under the name Savage Arms Corporation, civilian production was resumed and, in 1920, Savage purchased the famous J. Stevens Arms and Tool Company of Chicopee Falls, Mass.

While Savage had been building up his arms business, a gunsmith named Joshua Stevens had also made a name for himself. Stevens was born in Chelsea, Mass., in 1814. He originally made his living as a machinist, but his interest in guns soon led him to investigate the technique of their manufacture. As early as 1838, when he was 24 years old, he was working for Cyrus B. Allen, a noted armsmaker of Springfield, Mass. While in Allen's employ he became a master gunsmith. A few years later he met Sam Colt, who was greatly impressed with Stevens' skill and knowledge; in fact, Colt asked him to go along on a tour of the countryside, looking for a likely site on which to build an arms factory. Colt finally opened his plant in Hartford, Conn., and the two men parted good friends.

It is therefore ironic that a short while later Colt sued Stevens. The incident occurred when Stevens invented a revolver—strictly on his own—and Colt claimed the gun was an infringement on his patent rights. Colt won the case, and Stevens quickly found himself out of the revolver business.

Far from discouraged, he went right on designing and making guns, slowly but steadily gaining renown. Finally, in 1864, he opened the plant that was to become the J. Stevens Arms and Tool Company. It began as a one-room shop, adjacent to a Chicopee Falls sawmill, but by 1875 Stevens managed to remodel and double the plant, and by 1896 it took up eight acres of floor space.

Will power and sheer drudgery had a great deal to do with this accomplishment—but so did Yankee ingenuity, new methods and advanced machinery. First he became known as an excellent maker of single-shot rifles and of "tip-up" pistols (whose actions were similar to those of modern shotguns). Then he did some experimenting, with the aid of a man who had worked for the old Union Metallic Cartridge Company—which later was to become Remington. Stevens and this man, whose last name was Thomas and whose first name seems to have been lost in a jumble of company records, made arms history. They developed the .22 Long Rifle cartridge—the world's best seller.

A variety of arms and new loads followed. Stevens brought out the first single-barrel shotguns of modern design, and he had a whole line of them in both hammer and hammerless versions. He originated the method of forging a shotgun barrel and lug in one piece—a construction which is still regarded as the safest and strongest. And he introduced a great rifle called the Ideal, a single-shot falling-block model, together with the famous rimfire .25 cartridge.

Stevens, who was too shrewd to rely only on his

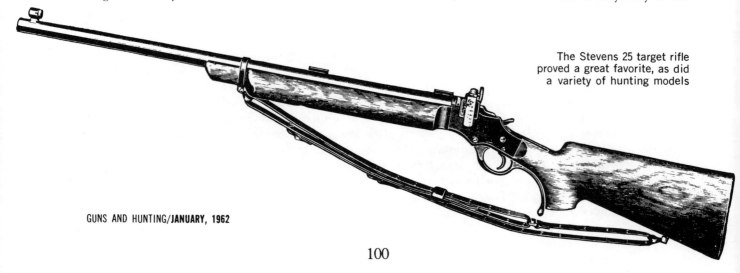

The Stevens 25 target rifle proved a great favorite, as did a variety of hunting models

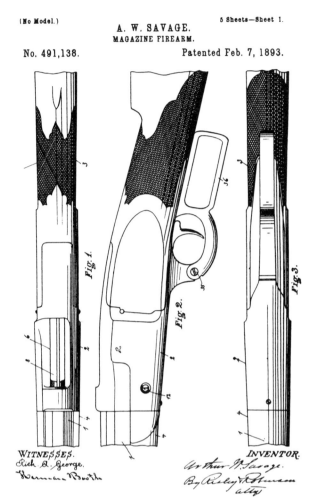

(No Model.)   5 Sheets—Sheet 1.

A. W. SAVAGE.
MAGAZINE FIREARM.

No. 491,138.   Patented Feb. 7, 1893.

WITNESSES.   INVENTOR.
Rich. A. George.   Arthur W. Savage.
Herman Booth   By Reily & Robinson
                                                atty

These are original design drawings for the
99, signed by the inventor and patented in 1893,
a year before he organized Savage Arms

(No Model.)   5 Sheets—Sheet 3.

A. W. SAVAGE.
MAGAZINE FIREARM.

No. 491,138.   Patented Feb. 7, 1893.

WITNESSES   INVENTOR.
Rich. A. George.   Arthur W. Savage
Herman Booth   By Reily & Robinson
                                                atty

This cutaway view, one of the patent diagrams,
shows some of the details of the
99's magazine, chamber, lever and trigger mechanism

own ingenuity, obtained the services of the noted Harry Pope, one of the world's best rifle-barrel makers. It was Pope who redesigned the Ideal to handle high-pressure smokeless ammo. The Stevens-Pope combination was so successful that the firm was able to sell hundreds of thousands of rifles to sportsmen all over the continent. When Stevens died in 1907, at the age of 92, he left a solid company and a corps of fine gunsmiths who were able to go right on introducing new designs.

Only two years later the firm delighted shotgunners by giving them their first modern 12-gauge repeater, manufactured under a patent agreement with the legendary John M. Browning. In 1913 another first was scored—the first .410 ever made in the United States. Before the first world war, J. Stevens Arms could claim the position of world's largest producer of sporting arms.

Like all arms manufacturers, Stevens turned to

the production of combat weapons with the opening of hostilities. Unfortunately, the wartime development of repeating arms soon made the fine Stevens single-shot rolling-block rifles obsolete, but when Savage and Stevens merged after the war, the new corporation could boast of marketing the country's most complete line of sporting arms. Savage-Stevens later purchased the A. H. Fox Company, famed for the beautiful design and workmanship of its shotguns.

The story of most major American arms companies is one of merger, of several fine firms eventually combining to form one great one. But in the case of Savage-Stevens the story is also one of extremely clever invention and dogged determination and the courage of an inventor's convictions; perhaps that explains why so many outdoorsmen still swear by the .22 LR for small game, and for big game the good old Model 99.   ∎

Hitting the Bullseye Since 1864
Stevens

Outdoor Life: March, 1921

Save Your Allowance and Buy a Stevens

DID you ever shoot? Not an air rifle or some make-believe weapon—but a regular rifle that will hit the mark—that is built to last —that will make anybody proud to own—A Stevens.

Winter or summer, indoors or out, the boy with a Stevens' Rifle always has fun.

And it doesn't cost much either, because Stevens' Rifles are priced so that every fellow can buy one. Just save part of your allowance every week for a while. Then go to your father. Show him your savings and he'll probably be glad to make up the difference, and you'll have a rifle of your own in a short time.

That's why "Stevens for boys" has long been a tradition, and fathers prefer to start their sons with a Stevens.

J. STEVENS ARMS COMPANY
CHICOPEE FALLS, MASS.
Executive and Export Offices: 50 CHURCH ST., NEW YORK
Owned and Operated by
SAVAGE ARMS CORPORATION, NEW YORK

TRADE MARK
-STEVENS-
REG. U·S·PAT OFF.& FGN.

Rifles - Shotguns - Pistols

STEVENS 22's

No Greater Value the World Over

No matter whether you use a ".22" for sport, trapping, or for destroying destructive vermin, you'll find the greatest values— greater accuracy, reliability, ease of operations and safety in a Stevens! And of all the popular 67-year old line of Stevens rifles, this new No. 66 gives you value that cannot be found in ".22's" at *twice the price!*

New Model 66

A sturdy accurate takedown, bolt-action repeater-tubular magazine (twice the capacity of clip magazine rifles)—Stevens superior bored barrel —short stroke bolt action, exceptionally safe, genuine Lyman Ivory Bead Front Sight—British Military type stock (pistol grip). Shoots .22 Short, Long or Long Rifle Cartridges.

Price $10.75

Don't fail to see the Stevens—and particularly the new "66" at your dealer's.

J. STEVENS ARMS COMPANY

CHICOPEE FALLS, MASS.
Owned and operated by
Savage Arms Corporation,
Utica, N. Y.

SVG

STEVENS

J. Stevens
And His Pistols

By Herschel C. Logan

AMERICAN shooters owe a debt of gratitude to A. C. Gould, the noted shooter and arms authority of his day. Gould did as much as any man to stimulate interest in guns and shooting, by founding the magazine known today as THE AMERICAN RIFLEMAN and by authoring two important books on firearms developments. He wrote in his book *Modern Pistols and Revolvers* (1888): "The Stevens pistols have made some of the most wonderful scores known. The barrels, upon which so much depends, seem to be perfect, and probably at the present time there are more Stevens pistols in the hands of famous marksmen throughout the world than any other make." This is enough to arouse an interest in these guns of other days and the man who made them.

Joshua Stevens was born in Chester, Hampden County, Massachusetts, on September 10, 1814. At the age of 20 he became an apprentice to a Chester toolmaker.

For some years following 1837 Stevens was engaged, with Edwin Wesson (an elder brother of Daniel Wesson)

HERSCHEL C. LOGAN, *Salina, Kans., has written and illustrated many articles on collector arms and ammunition. He is author-illustrator of books entitled* Cartridges *and* From Handcannon to Automatic.

and S. C. Miller, in the manufacture of hand-turned-cylinder percussion revolvers. These arms were produced under patent No. 182 (April 29, 1837) issued to Daniel Leavitt. The business was located at Hartford, Connecticut.

Stevens was employed for a time by Cyrus B. Allen, a gunmaker of Springfield, Massachusetts, later known as the maker of Elgin cutlass pistols and Cochran turret revolvers.

Worked briefly for Colt

During the late 1840's Stevens is reported to have worked for Samuel Colt, and to have helped establish Colt's Hartford factory.

In 1850 upon establishment of the Massachusetts Arms Company at Chicopee Falls, to produce revolvers under the Edwin Wesson patent No. 6669 (August 28, 1849), young Stevens became associated with this new company. It was during this period that Stevens applied for, and received, four patents on percussion revolvers. They were:

(1) No. 7802 (November 26, 1850) —Six-shot hammerless tip-up revolver hinged in the rear of cylinder, double-action, powder and ball, no loading lever. (The .28 caliber Massachusetts Arms Company, Maynard primer revolver carries this patent date on the barrel release.)

(2) No. 8412 (October 7, 1851)—

Side hammer tip-up revolver with frame hinged at rear of cylinder, powder and ball, loading lever.

(3) No. 9929 (August 9, 1853)— Hammer (side) and hammerless types of powder and ball revolvers, frame hinged at rear.

(4) No. 12189 (January 2, 1855)— Six-shot double-action, powder and ball, solid-frame, solid-top revolver with (right) side hammer and a single nipple which must be capped with each shot.

Even though the Massachusetts Arms Company was prevented by court action brought on by Colt from producing a revolver based on Edwin Wesson's patent, they did continue to produce a few small arms under other patents, including those of Joshua Stevens.

Formed own company

Late in 1864, following receipt of patent No. 44123 (September 6, 1864) for a single-shot pistol, Stevens made the decision to start out on his own. His first shop was in a small room adjoining a sawmill on the north side of the Chicopee River.

Organized on a modest scale, and not subjected to the rapid expansion as beset other companies of that war-time era, the firm of J. Stevens & Company was able to establish itself on a solid foundation. Stevens, being a resourceful individual, supplemented his armsmaking with other items.

From a reference source in Chicopee comes this bit of interesting data on the early firm:

"In 1867, 20 men were employed in

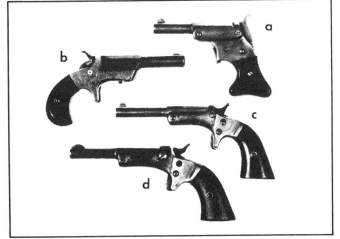

Fig. 1: Early Stevens pistols: a) Original tip-up model, .30 caliber; b) Gem side-swing-barrel pistol, .22 caliber; c) First model tip-up with split breech and circular side-plate; d) Model No. 41 tip-up pistol

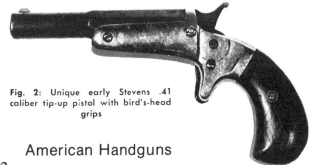

Fig. 2: Unique early Stevens .41 caliber tip-up pistol with bird's-head grips

American Handguns

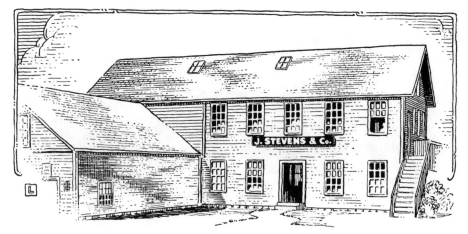

From this building on the banks of the Chicopee River came the first Stevens pistols and rifles

the manufacture of pistols, calipers, dividers, and pruning shears. The half-time service of a traveling salesman was secured and in 1868 the plant was enlarged somewhat. In 1872 the plant started the manufacture of a breech-loading shotgun and 40 men found employment in the shop. This was just before the panic of 1873, but in 1877-78 orders were plentiful and it was necessary to start night work in order to keep up with the demand for sporting rifles. With the general improvement in business in 1880-81 it was planned to double the existing production capacity."

In 1885 the company was incorporated with a capital of $40,000 as the J. Stevens Arms & Tool Company. Joshua Stevens and W. B. Fay each subscribed 120 shares of stock in the new corporation. Fay had been a gunsmith. George S. Taylor took ten shares; his brother James subscribed 110 shares and was appointed treasurer. I. H. Page, the bookkeeper, took 40 shares.

In January 1896 Page bought the stock held by Stevens and Taylor and assumed entire control, acting as president and treasurer.

Stevens lived nearly 11 years more, even to seeing the firm he had organized engage in the manufacture of one of the country's early horseless carriages, the Stevens-Duryea automobile. He passed away in 1907 at the age of 92.

Now subsidiary of Savage

Savage Arms Corporation secured an interest in the firm in 1920, at which time the name was changed to J. Stevens Arms Company. Later, in 1936, Savage assumed full control of the company. Operating today as a subsidiary of Savage Arms Corporation, the Stevens firm still produces rifles and shotguns.

So much for the historical background of this American arms company.

Let us now turn to the handguns produced by them. It should be pointed out that this study is not an effort to list every type and model produced by Stevens, if such were possible; rather, it is to present a general picture of the pistols produced by Stevens during their period of handgun production.

Generally conceded to be the first of the Stevens line is their Vest Pocket Pistol (Fig. 1a), a uniquely-shaped single-shot of .30 caliber. Even though it has the familiar barrel catch found on all Stevens tip-up pistols, it does not have the extractor, which was a part of his first patent on these arms. Since this model seldom shows up on dealer lists, it is logical to assume production was not large. It is a well-built, compact little piece and a worthy progenitor of the Stevens line.

Hardly had the little Vest Pocket been placed on the market than it was succeeded by a new single-shot. This new pistol, produced under Stevens' patent of September 6, 1864, provided these features as outlined in his patent application. "The nature of my invention consists in an arrangement and combination of a breech-elevating spring and a cartridge-shell discharger or starter in such a manner that the said spring, while performing its function of elevating the barrel at its breech, shall retract the cartridge-shell discharger or starter for the purpose of either wholly or partially expelling from the barrel the shell or case of the exploded cartridge."

Known at the time as a 'tip-up' pistol, due to the action of the spring in tipping up the breech of the barrel when pressure was exerted on the barrel release button, this pistol (Fig. 1c) was the first of the popular Stevens tip-up series. This early type is easily distinguished by its split breech and the distinctive circular side-plate on the left side of the frame. Made in both .22 and

.30 calibers, they could be purchased with either brass frame and blued barrel or fully nickel-plated. The round-and-octagonal barrel was 3½ inches in length. This little pocket and target pistol must have been quite popular because it was still listed in firearms catalogs of the late 1880's, more than 20 years after its advent. Perhaps the price of $2.50 had something to do with it. For taxidermists' use the pistol could be supplied with an eight-inch smooth-bore barrel, for dust shot, at a price of only $5. Before it was removed from the line, this first model with ejector was made for a time without the circular side-plate. In other respects it was the same.

Model with bird's-head grips

Unusual among the early Stevens products, and believed to be most unique, is the .41 caliber tip-up (Fig. 2) with bird's-head grips, which was a feature unknown to any other Stevens tip-up pistol. The one illustrated has all the features of the early model, including the split breech, the spring tip-up, and the circular side-plate. The four-inch round-and-octagonal barrel is rifled with five lands and grooves, left-hand twist. The serial number is 82. Could this have been a bid by Stevens to enter the derringer market, which at that time was so active? If so, despite its sturdy construction and its free-and-easy feel in the hand, it had two strikes against it in the competitive derringer field. Its overall length of 6½ inches, as compared with the mere 4½ to five inches of the usual pocket derringers then on the market, soon took it out of competition, and by so doing relegated it to

Joshua Stevens

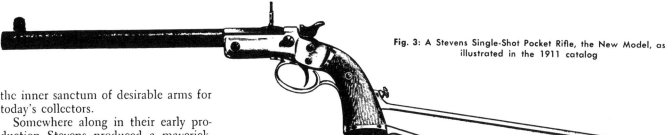

the inner sanctum of desirable arms for today's collectors.

Somewhere along in their early production Stevens produced a maverick, insofar as their tip-up line was concerned. Listed in their catalogs of the 1880's was an inexpensive, single-shot, side-swing-barrel pistol without extractor (Fig. 1b). It could be supplied in either .22 or .30 caliber. Unmarked except for the serial number and the name 'Gem' stamped on the top of the three-inch round-and-octagonal barrel, it has often been erroneously ascribed to Marlin. True there is enough similarity—at first glance—between it and the Marlin 'OK' single-shot to warrant such an assumption. However, upon careful examination there are enough distinguishing features to place it in the Stevens camp, where it rightfully belongs. The slope of the frame away from the split breech; the placing of the trigger pin in the spur trigger housing; the inside projecting arm from the frame to hold the grip screws, and the fastening of each grip separately, all lend credence to its being a genuine Stevens even if its being in the Stevens catalog is not sufficient reason for designating it a Stevens 'Gem'.

Here the Stevens line of pistols widens and becomes quite prolific, and it is a bit difficult, in the absence of actual factory records, to place the proper sequence to this or that model.

Popularized pocket rifles

Even though other manufacturers had produced pistols with extension stocks, it remained for Stevens to popularize this combination with their line of 'Pocket Rifles'. It is regrettable that today, through an interpretation of the National Firearms Act of 1934, the combination is considered a 'firearm' as defined by the Act. The pistol without stock is legal, but with stock attached it is considered as a sawed-off shotgun or rifle which may be concealed upon the person and therefore illegal.

Charles Folsom of New York, an agent for 'J. Stevens & Co.'s Celebrated Arms', in the 1883 issue of his catalog has this to say: "Among the first small arms made by J. Stevens & Co. was what is called the 'Old Model Pocket Rifle' (circa 1869) with barrels from 6 to 10 inches long and very light in all its parts, the whole weight being 10 ounces only. These have a very large

sale, and in the hands of skilled marksmen did some remarkable shooting at short ranges. There is a limited demand for them still, but they have mostly given way to the New Model which, while it occupies but little more space, is heavier and stronger in every part, and will throw a ball much farther with accuracy. The 15- or 18-inch will really shoot almost as well as a rifle."

One of the popular pistols, and one which enjoyed a lengthy sale, was the graceful Diamond Model No. 43 (Fig. 4a). Equipped with either open or peep sights, it was available in .22 long rifle caliber in either six- or ten-inch barrel length. (The .22 long rifle cartridge was introduced about 1889 in Stevens pistols. It was originated by Union Metallic Cartridge Company at the request of Stevens.) The Diamond was listed at $5 to $8.50 in the 1898 Stevens catalog. The split breech of the earlier types had given way to a solid breech with firing pin on this and subsequent models. Many men today have fond memories of using one of these light guns in their youth.

The Diamond Model with ten-inch barrel and extension stock was designated as the Reliable Pocket No. 42. It was chambered for the .22 long rifle and .22 Stevens-Pope Armory rimfires. Though it would shoot the short and long rimfires, the factory did not recommend them for accuracy.

Produced simultaneously with the Diamond Model was a single-shot pocket pistol known as the Tip-up No. 41 (Fig. 1d). It was identical with the Diamond Model but with shorter grips and a shorter barrel. Removal of grips from a Diamond pistol will show how relatively simple it was to adapt the frame to the Pocket Model. Made in both .22 rimfire short and .30 rimfire calibers, this popular pocket gun was in the line for many years.

Variety of models made

With the advent of the New Model Pocket or Bicycle No. 40 (Fig. 3) (circa 1872) barrel length and calibers were varied. Calibers listed in a later catalog were .22 long rifle, .22 Stevens-Pope Armory, .25 rimfire, and .32 long

rimfire. Barrel lengths were ten, 12, 15, and 18 inches. An identical model equipped with special sights was called Stevens Vernier New Model No. 40½. The same guns were also produced with a smoothbore choked barrel to use .38-40 Everlasting shells. It was listed as Shotgun No. 39. The 1906 catalog contained a note that this model had been discontinued.

Not only were Stevens pistols made for target shooting but they were also designed for hunting. This is evident from the designation of Hunter's Pet No. 34 for another tip-up pocket rifle. In addition to the .22 rimfire, .32, .38, and .44 center-fire, barrels could be chambered for the .38 or .44 caliber Everlasting cases, and also for the 20-gauge shotshell. The octagonal barrel lengths were 18, 20, 22, and 24 inches. Prices ranged from $11 to $14.75, with a $1 increase for each two-inch addition to the barrel length. The 1898 catalog also listed the following calibers for the Hunter's Pet: .22 long rifle rimfire, .25 rimfire, and .32 long rimfire. A 'Vernier' Hunter's Pet was available at the same time. In addition to special sights, it was equipped with a round-and-octagonal barrel. Price in 1898 for this special model was $16. At least one specimen of this later model is known to have been made into a .38 caliber handgun with a much shorter barrel. It is believed to have been a factory job due to the shorter version of the octagonal part of the barrel. If such was the case then it may be expected that other specimens will show up in the future.

Produced outstanding target pistols

Comes now what are perhaps the most distinguished models of the Stevens line, certainly insofar as their target models are concerned. They are the noted Lord Model Gallery Pistol No. 36, Conlin Model No. 38, Gould Model No. 37 (Fig. 5 a, b, c), and the

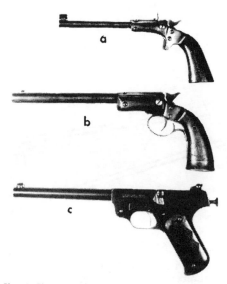

Fig. 4: Three popular Stevens target pistols of other days: a) Diamond Model No. 43, .22 caliber; b) Off-Hand Target No. 35, .22 caliber; c) The No. 10 Stevens Target, .22 caliber

Off-Hand Model No. 35 (Fig. 4b).

It was Frank Lord, a celebrated New York pistol shot, who suggested the model which bears his name. Physically large and endowed with large hands, he desired a heavy pistol with a long grip. The Lord Model, weighing three pounds in .22 caliber with ten-inch barrel, was the result. Ira Paine, one-time champion pistol shot of the world, commented thus on this addition to the Stevens line: "Your Lord Model is certainly a *wonderful* pistol. I have taken a life in my hands with it some thousands of times, and it has never failed me." Paine preferred, and used, this model in exhibitions throughout his distinguished career.

Named for James S. Conlin of Conlin's Shooting Gallery in New York City, the Conlin Model while retaining the spur on the trigger guard from the Lord Model was nevertheless the beginning of the popular Off-Hand Model. It was made in .22 long rifle and .25 rimfire, and upon special order could be supplied in .32 long, .38 long, .32-44 S&W, and .38 S&W at extra cost. Barrel lengths were ten and 12 inches; weight two to 2¼ pounds.

A. C. Gould, in an attempt to adapt a pistol more to his liking, reworked one of the Conlin Models and sent it to the factory. The result became the Gould Model. Fitted with an open wind-gauge rear sight and bead front sight, it was one of the truly great target pistols of its time. Lighter and smaller than the big Lord Model, the Gould Model appealed to noted shooters of that day. W. W. Bennett, famous holder of the 50-shot record at 50 yards on Standard American Targets, wrote, "I consider my Gould Model far superior to any other pistol or revolver made".

Popular over long period

Following its illustrious predecessors came the Stevens Off-Hand Target Pistol No. 35 (Fig. 4b), a model which was to enjoy many, many years of popularity in the Stevens line, and in fact only disappeared from their catalogs in recent years. First made with a heavy cast trigger guard, the later models employed a lighter strap iron guard. Otherwise the pistol still retained the features of the first adaptation from the Gould Model. It was made in both .22 and .25 calibers, and could be procured with either six-, eight-, ten-, or 12¼-inch barrel lengths.

The Off-Hand Model No. 35 Autoshot could at one time be had in .410-bore for rodents, roadside hunting, and general shooting where a shotshell was desired, but under present interpretation of the National Firearms Act such arms are subject to registration.

Still employing their 'tip-up' action, Stevens early in this century brought out their Single-Shot Target Pistol No. 10 (Fig. 4c). Totally unlike any of its predecessors it is designed along the lines of an automatic. Sights were open at the front, while the rear had elevation and windage adjustments. It is said that many target pistol experts collaborated with the Stevens company in the designing of this latest model in their famous line. It seems to have been produced for only a short period of time, and although not particularly scarce, specimens in good condition are met with rather infrequently today.

Recent years have seen the disappearance from the market of all models of this once-illustrious line of Stevens single-shot pistols—a line which had its birth in 1864 in a small frame building on the banks of the Chicopee River.————————■

My personal thanks to the Public Library of Chicopee, Mass., G. Robert Lawrence, Richard Short, Maj. Hugh Smiley, Frank Wheeler, Art Tucker, Col. L. C. Jackson, Charles T. Waller, Howard Scott, A. W. Rowe, Bob McReynolds, and others who so kindly assisted with this study.—H. C. L.

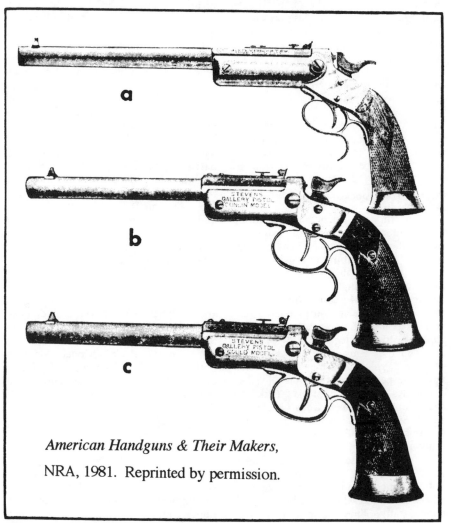

American Handguns & Their Makers,

NRA, 1981. Reprinted by permission.

Fig. 5: The three noted Stevens target pistols: a) Lord Model No. 36; b) Conlin Model No. 38; c) Gould Model No. 37

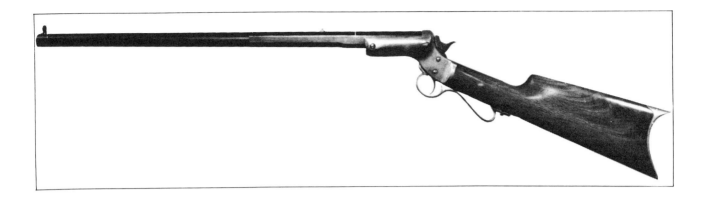

THE FIRST STEVENS RIFLE, THE TIP-UP

Period: Circa 1870-1900

Pages 107-116 reprinted by permission from *Single Shot Rifles and Actions*, 1969 Ed., by Frank de Hass.

Joshua Stevens was born on September 10, 1814, in Chester, Hampden county, Massachusetts. It is known that at the age of about 20 he worked for a toolmaker in Chester. A few years after this it is known that he worked for a small arms manufacturing firm in Hartford, Connecticut, headed by Edwin Wesson and S. C. Miller, which firm made percussion revolvers. He gained further skill and knowledge in the arms making business by also working for a gunmaker in Springfield, Massachusetts, by the name of Cyrus B. Allen. It is also thought that he worked for Samuel Colt sometime in the late 1840s. From this job Stevens moved to Chicopee Falls, Massachusetts, and began working for a new firm, the Massachusetts Arms Company.

It was while Joshua Stevens was employed by this firm that he first displayed his inventive talents.

In short order in 1850, 1851, 1853 and 1855 he applied for and obtained four patents on percussion revolvers. A few of the Stevens patented revolvers were produced by the Mass. Arms Company.

In 1864, at the age of 50, after receiving a patent (#44123, dated September 6, 1864) on a simple breech loading single shot pistol, Stevens decided to start his own arms making business. The firm was named J. Stevens & Company, and on this single and simple patent, and beginning in a very small shop, he slowly and surely built a sizable arms industry. By 1870, when it is believed the first real full sized Stevens rifle was made, the firm had expanded and was em-

ploying about 40 men. With the introduction of the full sized rifle and similar shotguns, the Stevens firm continued to grow. In about 1885 the Stevens firm was incorporated as the J. Stevens Arms & Tool Company. Joshua Stevens stayed with the growing firm until about 1896 when he sold his interests. He died in 1907 at the age of 92.

The patent Stevens obtained in 1864 was for a simple break-open breech loading firearms mechanism. The patent drawing shows a pistol, with the barrel hinged to the front part of the frame. A sliding extractor under the breech end of the barrel was connected to the frame by a link, and on opening the action, in which the breech end of the barrel tipped up, the extractor would be activated. A most simple locking device through the frame locked the barrel in firing position. The firing mechanism was composed of a hammer, flat main spring and a spur trigger. The firing pin was made integral with the hammer.

The inventive and industrious Stevens, while making pistols on the original design, changed, improved and transformed it and introduced literally dozens of variations and models. Within a short time he was making the pistols in various small rim-fire calibers. Then he turned to pistols with longer barrels and different grip shapes. After this he began furnishing some of the pistols with a detachable shoulder stock and called these arms "pocket rifles." Then longer barreled pocket rifles were made, fitted with various sights, but still with the metal

skeleton stock.

To expand his marketing possibilities Stevens decided to produce regular styled rifles and shotguns, along with the take-down pocket rifles.

The result was the first true Stevens rifle, believed to have been first made shortly after 1870. Two improvements were made on the rifle action: the spur trigger was eliminated and a regular trigger and trigger guard was used, and a separate firing pin fitted in the standing breech was used instead of the integral firing pin tip on the hammer. Because the breech tipped up on opening the action, these rifles were then commonly called the Stevens Tip-up, and they are still known by this name today.

There can hardly be a simpler rifle and action than the Stevens Tip-up. Parts and manufacturing operations were held to the minimum so the guns could be made easily and cheaply. In spite of this, these guns were unusually well made and finished, and specimens of these guns in excellent condition are quite striking with their polished and blued barrels, nickel plated receiver and richly colored and varnished wood.

The action is constructed very simply, the receiver (2) is a one-piece steel casting with integral upper and lower tangs. Evidently the casting is so made that very few machine operations were required to finish it except for drilling some holes for the

Illustrated above: A typical example of a Stevens Tip-up rifle. This one is the Stevens Expert No. 5 chambered for the .22 Short rimfire cartridge. From the George Lorenz collection.

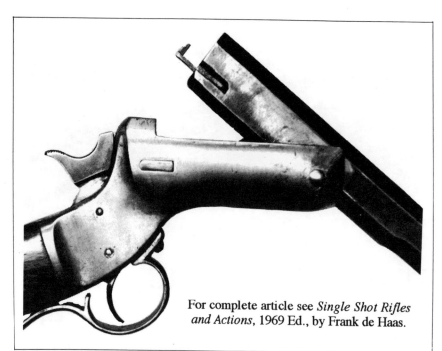

For complete article see *Single Shot Rifles and Actions*, 1969 Ed., by Frank de Haas.

Action area of Stevens Tip-up rifle. Note groove at side of barrel for receiving barrel lock, thinned or rebated middle section of receiver and protruding extractor.

action screws, some milling on the inside for it to accept the hammer, trigger and lock parts, and polishing the outside for its final finish.

The receiver has a very odd shape with a sharp drop from the standing breech to the upper tang. It is also quite thin in its center section. This odd appearance can best be seen in the close-up photos of this action. Odd as it may look, the action does not feel that way when holding the rifle in the firing position.

The butt stock is held to the receiver via the two tangs and the tang screw (21) connecting the two tangs, and by the wood screw in the end of the lower tang. The trigger guard (17) which was made in various shapes for the different models of this rifle, is attached to the lower front of the receiver by a screw (14) and to the lower tang by a screw (22). In most cases the trigger guard forms some sort of pistol grip.

The firing mechanism in the Stevens Tip-up guns was made extremely simple and most of the Stevens single shot rifles which were to follow it in later years, including the No. 44½ Stevens, had firing mechanisms patterned after it. The hammer (1) is fitted in a recess in the receiver and held there, and pivots on a screw (8) through the receiver. The trigger (16) is likewise held in the receiver and pivots on a screw (15) through the receiver. The upper part of the hammer, or the part which is exposed, is made quite wide, with the spur well shaped and checkered for easy manual cocking. The part of the hammer which extends into the receiver is made thinner. It is made with a deep safety notch in which position the

trigger holds the hammer nose off of the firing pin, and from which position the trigger is not easily pulled. A shallow sear notch to the rear of the "safe" notch into which the sear tip of the trigger engages holds the hammer in full cock position when hammer is drawn back. The trigger is given tension by the flat trigger spring (18) which is held to the lower tang by a screw (20).

The curved flat main spring (19) fits between a notch in the rear of the hammer and a small stud on the lower tang to provide power to the hammer. The bearing point of the end of the main spring against the hammer is located at a point so that the hammer is under much more tension when it is against the firing pin than it is when the hammer is in the full cock position. That this is so is very commendable, as this greatly lessens the pressure on the sear when the hammer is cocked with the result that a lighter and shorter trigger pull can be had and maintained. The same leverage principle was also employed in most of the Stevens single shot rifles which followed. If a reverse leverage principle was used, where the main

spring tension against the hammer is increased the further it is pulled back, with a resulting heavier sear pressure, then the sear notch must be made correspondingly deeper and the result is a heavy and long trigger pull if the rifle is to be safe.

The firing pin (4) is positioned in the standing breech part of the receiver and is held in place by a threaded bushing (3) turned into the receiver. This is a very good arrangement. Although not shown in the sectional view drawing, in practically all of the Stevens Tip-up rifles the firing pin was made with a spring retractor, a small coil spring around the tip of the firing pin to retract the tip of the pin out of the receiver face after hammer is placed in the half-cock position.

The barrels of all of the Stevens Tip-up guns were made having considerable extra metal under the breech end to provide enough metal for the hinged screw hole and for milling of the dovetail extractor groove in which the extractor (6) is fitted.

The front extension of the receiver is hollowed out deep enough to accept the extra metal of the barrel at this point. The long extractor groove is wide enough to fit over the extractor pull stem (11) and the extractor stud (13). Each end of the extractor pull stem is fastened to, and hinged to, the extractor stud and end of extractor by pins (10 & 12). In many cases the extractor pull stem is made in two pieces threaded together as shown. The extractor stud is threaded into the bottom of the receiver extension. The barrel hinge screw (9) is positioned through the walls at the front end of the receiver extension, and threaded into the right wall.

Not shown in the drawing, but shown in the parts photo, is the simple Stevens locking system. The L-shaped lock (23) fits through the receiver in a hole as indicated by number 5 in the drawing, going in from right to left. The right side of the receiver has a square recess made into it so the widened end of the lock fits snugly in place. The hole for the lock in the left side of the receiver is recessed a short ways for the lock spring (24). The end of the lock stem is threaded to accept the push-button

STEVENS TIP-UP ACTION SPECIFICATIONS

Type	Single shot, tip-up barrel.
Receiver	Machined steel casting, with integral upper and lower tangs.
Receiver finish	Nickel plated. Optional — blued.
Take-down	Barrel removable from action by removing hinge screw.
Stock fastening	Via the two tangs, tang screw and wood screw.
Ignition	Manually cocked exposed hammer, powered by flat main spring. Separate firing pin in receiver.
Trigger	Plain, with trigger in direct contact with hammer.
Safety	Hammer has "safe" or half cock notch.
Extractor	Automatic, non-ejection.

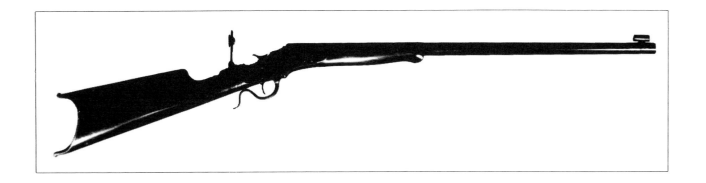

THE STEVENS "SIDE PLATE"
Period: Circa 1888

Perhaps the most sought after rifles bearing the J. Stevens name are those having an action made with a side plate. Most collectors of Stevens rifles have heard about this Side Plate Stevens single shot rifle, but not very many of them have ever seen one, and fewer yet are the ones who own one. There is a shroud of mystery around these rifles making them all the more interesting. To the Stevens collector and firearms student I will herewith present all the information I have gathered on these rifles.

As described in the previous chapter, in the period a few years before and after the 1870s the entire line of Stevens firearms, including pistols, rifles and shotguns were based on the tip-up type of action. Although this type of action was good, it was fast becoming out-dated and a number of other firms had already developed single shot actions far superior to it. Joshua Stevens was an easy going man and he was not to be rushed, but during the early 1880s he evidently began working on a single shot action to eventually replace the tip-up type. There is little question but that the Side Plate action was the result, with it becoming the first Stevens action with a swinging breech block to be operated by an under finger lever.

Here the real mystery begins, for it is not known when the Side Plate rifles were first introduced, how long they were made, or how many were made. That they were manufactured

is certain, as there are enough of these rifles still in existence to prove this, even though the number is very small.

Of the specimens of the Stevens Side Plate rifles which I have seen or know about, most of them had the following barrel marking, in one line:
J. STEVENS A & T CO, CHICOPEE FALLS, MASS. PAT'D. AUG.11,1885
One of these rifles, however, had a different barrel marking as follows, in one line:
J. STEVENS & CO. CHICOPEE FALLS, MASS. PAT. SEPT.8,1884
It is believed that the firm name of J. Stevens & Co. was changed to the J. Stevens Arms & Tool (A & T) Co. in 1888.

There is little question but that the Side Plate was developed in the years indicated by the patent dates, and therefore must have preceded the introduction of the Stevens Favorite and No. 44 rifles with the one-piece receiver, which rifles generally bear the 1894 patent date. Some of the Favorite rifles with one-piece receivers have an 1889 patent dating, and it is thought the "true" Stevens Favorite rifles were introduced in about 1890 or shortly thereafter. Therefore, based on this information I would judge the Side Plate rifles were made for only a very short time—perhaps not more than a year—and sometime during the period between 1888 and 1893.

The only marking on the Side

Plate actions is the serial number stamping on the lower tang, with the same number also often stamped on the front face of the receiver. The lowest numbered Side Plate I have seen was 57, and the highest one was 1184. However, others have observed these rifles with a serial number slightly above 2000, but every indication is that very few were made.

As the name implies, the actions of these rifles were made with a side plate, and this is the main identification feature. The plate is on the right side and includes practically all of the side of the receiver except for the upper part which accepts the barrel shank. At this point there is a line where the side plate and the receiver join. The side plate is removable, but this requires removing the main screws on which the action parts pivot. Thus the plate is not quickly removable and in the illustration of the action with the side plate removed, the screws were replaced in the action to correctly position the various action parts.

There were two distinct sizes of the

Illustrated above: A fine example of a Stevens "Side Plate" target rifle. This rifle is in near original condition and it would be a prize for any serious Stevens collector. The 26" part octagonal barrel is chambered for the 25-20 Single Shot cartridge. The sights consist of a globe front and a wind-gauge tang sight. This rifle is owned by Eugene Beving, Dickens, Iowa.

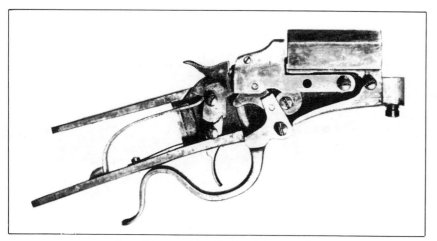

Large Stevens action with side plate removed.

Side Plate actions and rifles, as can be seen in the illustrations and noted on the specification chart. The main difference in the size was that the small action is thinner, and with all the action parts thinner and comparatively smaller.

As can be noted in the illustrations there are other minor differences in the construction of these actions. In the small action shown there is a small set screw in the bottom of the receiver which projects inside and contacts the bottom of the breech block when the action is opened. If the screw were turned in quite far it would prevent the action from opening as far as if the screw were turned out. I can see no valid purpose for this screw.

Another difference is the anchor screw in the large action. The side plate of the small action is held in place by the four action screws, on which the hammer, trigger, finger lever and breech block pivots. The larger Stevens Side-Plate action has an additional screw which I call the anchor screw, located at the front of the plate and it serves only to hold the plate in place against the main receiver. This screw turned in very tightly strengthens the action considerable by preventing the side plate from shifting back when rifle is fired. This lessens the strain on the four other action screws.

Still another difference is in the position and type of take-down screw employed. The smaller action is provided with a ringed take-down screw so it can be loosened and tightened with the fingers in taking the rifle apart. This screw is located in the underside of the front part of the frame, just like in the standard Favorite actions. In the larger Side Plate action the take-down screw has a screw driver slot, its head is flush with the bottom of the receiver, and it fits into a projection extending from the front of the receiver. This was evidently done to make room for the anchor screw. The end of this

take-down screw fits in a recess in the shoulder of the barrel as it is positioned ahead of the barrel shank.

The small side-plate action shown has a rounded receiver top, while all of the larger side-plate actions I have seen had half octagonal receiver tops.

As compared to most other Stevens actions made before or afterwards, the Side Plate action was extremely well made. In most respects I would rate it a better action than the No. 44 Ideal—even without the side plate feature. I can see no advantage in this feature, it serves no real purpose.

The main part of the receiver (10) is a steel casting, with the upper and lower tang made integral with it. The receiver is bored out in front to accept the barrel shank and the inside machined to accept the various action parts. This machining was made easier by one side of the receiver being open, but this was off-set be-

cause extra precision machining was required to accept the side plate to cover this opening.

The side plate (25) is also a casting and it is machined, and hand fitted, to fit closely the open side of the receiver.

The inside of the receiver and the side plate are machined to form shoulders to support the rear of the breech block when it is in the closed position. The plate is held in place entirely by the four main action screws, with each screw going through the plate, through the individual action part, and then threading into the left wall of the main receiver. An additional anchor screw (13) is used in the larger actions.

The breech block (8) is L shaped and is held in place in the receiver and pivots on the breech block screw (14). The breech block contains the firing pin (5), held in place by the retainer pin (6). A small coil spring (26) around the tip of the firing pin retracts it so the tip will not hang up in a fired case on opening the action. The left side of the breech block is milled out to fit over the extractor (9), which is held in place against the left receiver wall, and pivots on screw (15) threaded into the wall. On the large action a pin (7) through the breech block activates the extractor on opening the action when it comes into contact with the extractor. On the small action the left side of the breech block is so milled as to form a shoulder to activate the extractor.

The finger lever (22), which also acts as the trigger guard, is of the standard hook type and is held in the receiver by, and pivots on, the finger lever screw (16).

Parts Legend

1. Tang sight plug screws (2)
2. Main spring
3. Hammer screw
4. Hammer
5. Firing pin
6. Firing pin retainer pin
7. Extractor knock-off pin*
8. Breech block
9. Extractor
10. Receiver
11. Barrel
12. Take-down screw
13. Side plate (anchor) screw*
14. Breech block screw
15. Extractor screw
16. Finger lever screw
17. Lower link pin
18. Upper link pin
19. Link
20. Trigger
21. Trigger screw
22. Finger lever
23. Trigger spring screw
24. Trigger spring
Not shown in drawing:
25. Side plate
26. Firing pin retractor spring
27. Stop screw**
* This part in large action only
** This part in small action only

STEVENS "SIDE PLATE" ACTION SPECIFICATIONS

Type	Single shot, swinging block, operated by under finger lever.
Receiver	Machined steel forging with integral upper and lower tangs. Right side (plate) of receiver made separate.
Receiver finish	Color case hardened. Optional-blued.
Take-down	Barrel is slip-fit into receiver and removable by loosening set screw in bottom of receiver.
Stock fastening	Via the 2 tangs and 2 wood screws.
Ignition	Manually cocked exposed hammer, powered by flat main spring. Separate firing pin in breech block.
Trigger	Plain, with trigger in direct contact wth hammer.
Safety	Hammer has "safe" or half cock notch.
Extractor	Automatic, non-ejecting.

	Large Action	Small Action
Weight	1 lb. 12 oz.	1 lb. 4 oz.
Thickness	1.00"	.810"

THE STEVENS "FAVORITE"

Period: Circa 1889-1935

There is little question but that the most popular boy's rifle ever made was the Stevens Favorite. In the 45 or so years that these lever action swinging block rifles were manufactured, countless thousands of these fine little rifles were sold the world over. Today, gun editors probably receive more inquiries about the Stevens Favorite than they do of any other obsolete single shot rifle. This indicates a great interest in this rifle as well as the fact that there are a great number of these rifles around the country.

Questions most often asked about the Stevens Favorite rifle and action are: Who invented the Favorite action? When was the Favorite rifle first introduced? Is there any way to tell the approximate date of manufacture of a given rifle? How many variations and models are there of the Favorite rifle? How strong is the Favorite action? Can the Favorite rifle be rechambered to another caliber or can the action be rebarreled to another caliber? How can the action be tightened up? Therefore, in this chapter I will try to answer these and other questions about this once very popular single shot rifle.

The Stevens Favorite action was the invention of Joshua Stevens and manufactured by the firm of J. Stevens Arms & Tool Co., Chicopee Falls, Mass. Originally this firm, which was established in 1864, was known as the J. Stevens & Co. and the name was changed to J. Stevens A & T Co. in about 1888. Later, in about 1916, the firm name was changed to the J. Stevens Arms Co. To my knowledge, the Favorite rifles were only made under the last two firm names and not under the firm's original name.

The forerunner of the Stevens Favorite action and rifle was a Stevens rifle known as the "Side Plate," as described in the previous chapter. This was the first under lever operated swinging block action developed by Stevens and it was patented in 1884. It is called the "Side Plate" action because the receiver is made with a removable side plate. This particular action and rifle was made in two sizes, and minus the side plate feature and other slight modifications; the smaller one became the Stevens Favorite, and a few years later the larger one became the No. 44 Stevens. Although the smaller "Side Plate" rifle may once have been named the Favorite, I will—for the sake of better identification—call the "Side Plate" actions and rifles as such, and classify the Favorite actions and rifles as the ones developed afterwards having the one-piece receiver.

The original, or "first" Stevens Favorite rifle, based on my studies of this rifle, bears the patent date of October 29, 1889. I would assume from this that it was introduced on that date or very shortly afterwards. Specimens of this early Favorite rifle which I have observed are marked as follows, on the top flat of the barrel between rear sight and breech, in three lines:

J. STEVENS A & T CO.
CHICOPEE FALLS, MASS
PAT. OCT 29. 89

There were no caliber markings anywhere on the rifle. One specimen had no serial number, while others had this number stamped on the lower tang. The only other markings were on the hard rubber butt plate which had the words "Stevens Favorite" imprinted across it. To simplify matters,

I will call this rifle the M-1889 Favorite.

The M-1889 Favorites were made with a 22" part octagonal, part round tapered barrel, with the octagonal part ending at the forearm tip. Of the octagonal part only the top and sides are milled with flats as the part of the barrel covered by the forearm is rounded. The slim tapered forearm and the straight gripped stock are made of walnut. As shown in the photograph of the M-1889 action, it has a ringed take-down screw and a flat main spring which is held in place by a stud on the lower tang, in the very same manner as employed in the "Side Plate" actions.

At this point the many variations of the Favorite begin, for even in this early version changes were made. This particular M-1889 Favorite action as shown has a centrally located extractor. Another M-1889 action which I observed had the extractor to the left of the breech block, and instead of the integral lug on the lower tang to hold the main spring, it had a stud screw like the early No. 44 Stevens actions. This particular action also had very short tangs. The M-1889 action as shown also has slightly shorter tangs than the later Favorite actions. However, except for these differences in the action the M-1889 Favorite rifles were almost identical to the Stevens No. 17 Favorite to be described later. Specimens of the early Stevens Fa-

Illustrated above: The No. 27 Stevens Favorite rifle with a 24" octagon barrel. This is the version made just prior to its discontinuance in 1934. It is based on the "heavy" Model 1915 Favorite action which has a squarish breech block and a knurled headed take-down screw. The same rifle with a round barrel was the No. 17.

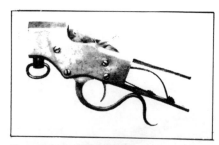

The original Model 1889 Stevens Favorite action. Note the "bow" type main spring held in place by lug on lower tang.

vorite rifles are quite rare, and although I have not seen one in the .32 rimfire caliber I would assume they were also made in this caliber.

In a very short time the original short tanged M-1889 Favorite action was modified by lengthening the tangs and changing the main spring design, plus other minor changes. The barrel of this new rifle bore the patent date markings of April 17, 1894, which I will refer to as the Model 1894. It is this Stevens Favorite rifle which became highly popular, and it is the one most commonly encountered today. At the same time the M-1894 Favorite was introduced, the Stevens firm also introduced the No. 44 Ideal rifle. The Favorite and No. 44 Stevens actions are basically alike in most respects except the No. 44 is larger, heavier, stronger and more refined, and intended for the larger center-fire cartridges, while the Favorite action was intended for the smaller rimfire cartridges.

There were several versions of the Favorite rifle introduced at this time. The first one, and it can be considered the basic model, is the No. 17 Favorite. This model remained in the Favorite line-up—with minor modifications—until the Favorite rifles were discontinued in about 1935. It started out in 1894 closely resembling the earlier 1889 version, with a 22" half octagonal barrel and selling for about $5.00, and finished up selling for $8.95, but with a round barrel. Introduced originally, or shortly thereafter, with the No. 17, were the No. 18, No. 19, No. 20, and 21. The Nos. 18 and 19 were the same as the No. 17, but fitted with different sights, including tang rear sights. All were available in three standard calibers: .22 Long Rifle, .25 Long and .32 Long Rimfire. For a short time, on special order only, the Favorite was available in the .22 W.R.F. caliber.

During the early years these Favorites could be special ordered with barrels up to 26" in length and with a pistol grip stock. The No. 18 and No. 19 rifles, as well as the special order rifles were generally discontinued by 1915. The No. 20 Favorite was a smooth bored shotgun chambered for either .22 or .32 rimfire shotshells. The top of the receiver on this model

was usually rounded with a shallow sighting "U" groove cut in the top and with a shotgun bead sight on the muzzle of the round barrel. This model remained in production until about 1935 with the only noticeable variation being in the action, when a change was made to the heavier Favorite in 1915, as will be described later.

The No. 21 Stevens rifle is supposed to have been a "bicycle rifle." It was merely a short barreled version of the No. 17 and could be had with a canvas carrying case so the rifle could be carried on a bicycle. This rifle could also be ordered in different barrel lengths (and cases to match), and with different sights. This rifle was also generally discontinued by 1915.

During most of these early years, a special and fancy Favorite sporting rifle was made available. This one was regularly furnished with a pistol grip, with the stock and forearm made of figured walnut, and with the grip and forearm checkered. It was available in the different rimfire calibers, with different shapes and lengths of barrels, with special sights, etc. These Favorite rifles are very scarce today.

Variations in the barrel marking exist in the M-1894 Favorite rifle, but most of them were stamped as follows, in two lines:

J. STEVENS A & T CO.
CHICOPEE FALLS, MASS, U.S.A. PAT. APR. 17, 94

The caliber marking is usually on the left side of the barrel.

In about 1915 the Stevens firm introduced a major change in the Favorite action. The No. 17 Favorite was retained, but now made with a round barrel, and built on a new action. Also retained were the No. 20 smooth bored rifles having round barrels. A new number was introduced at about this time, namely the No. 27, furnished with a full octagonal barrel. For a few years there were also the No. 28 and No. 29, which were the same as the No. 27 but furnished with different sights, as in the case of the earlier No. 18 and 19 rifles. When the Stevens Favorite rifle was finally discontinued only the No. 17, No. 20 and No. 27 were left.

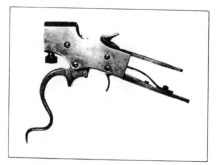

The Stevens Favorite action open.

Early Stevens Favorite with later-style knurled take-down screw.

The Model 1915 Favorite action was made slightly heavier than the previous Favorite action, and it is often referred to as the "heavy" Favorite action. Other changes are evident in the shape of the breech block, often referred to as the "flat top" breech block, and inside the action it had a coil main spring rather than a flat main spring as in the original No. 17. The main spring detail of the Model 1915 Favorite is shown in drawing A. The main spring assembly consists of: yoke and main spring guide (3), main spring (4) and sleeve (5). Pin (2) in the end of the yoke bears against the rear of the hammer (1) while the sleeve is positioned against the grooved screw (6) turned into the lower tang. This system was a great improvement over the flat main spring system, as the flat springs were prone to break.

The Model 1915 Favorite rifles were usually marked on the barrel thus;

J. STEVENS ARMS COMPANY
CHICOPEE FALLS, MASS, U.S.A.

The top tang of the M-1915 is marked "MODEL 1915." Most all of the M-1894 and M-1915 Favorites were also marked on top flat of the receiver as thus:

TRADE MARK
FAVORITE
REG. US PAT OFF & FGN

In about 1920 when Savage gained control over the Stevens arms plant, the Savage trademark—the letters SVG within a circle—also was generally stamped on the side of the frame.

At this point the reader will likely have noticed the frequent use of words like 'generally,' 'usually' and 'about.' These general terms are necessary because the history of the Favorite rifle is extremely hazy and jumbled. Factory records of the serial numbers are non-existent so it is impossible to pinpoint dates or know how many were made or when action modifications took place. From my own records of the many Favorite rifles I have examined and from published sources of information on this rifle, I'll attempt to piece together as many additional facts as possible, other than those already given.

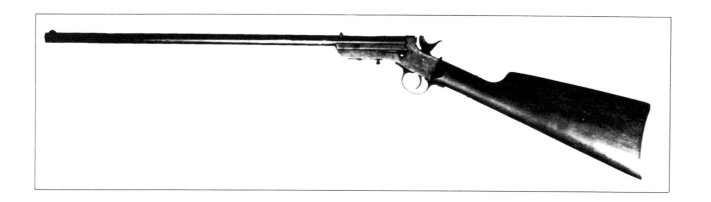

THE STEVENS "SURE SHOT"
Period: Circa 1895

Of all the different makes of single shot rifles the Stevens line is perhaps the best known. It was also the most diversified line in the number of different types of actions used. Because they were so common and because there were so many models, the Stevens line of single shots are of special interest to both beginner and advanced collectors. Stevens rifles with the name of "Little Scout," "Favorite" and "Crackshot" are very well known, and while the name "Sure Shot" would fit right in with these names the Stevens rifle bearing this name is little known and quite rare. Therefore, information on the Stevens Sure Shot rifle and action will be of special interest to the advanced Stevens collector and firearms student.

My research on the Stevens Sure Shot rifle did not uncover much about its history. Philip B. Sharpe's *The Rifle In America* lists it, but it is not illustrated, and the entire description of the rifle is contained in one short paragraph. Sharpe indicates this rifle was introduced in 1891 and discontinued in about 1900. I failed to find any mention of this rifle in any other gun book in my rather extensive library, including books which have given a great deal of space to most of the other Stevens single shot rifles.

To get first hand information on the Stevens Sure Shot rifle the Savage Arms Company was contacted, but they too were unable to give any definite information on it. They did say, however, that this rifle appeared in the 1895 Stevens catalog, but that it was not listed in the 1898 catalog,

and concluded that production must have been very limited.

Prior to about 1894 the principal type of action used by Stevens for building single shot rifles and pistols was the tip-up, or break-open action. By 1890 Stevens had designed and introduced an entirely different type of single shot action, one having a lever operated swinging breech block housed in a solid frame, to become known as the "Favorite" and "Ideal" rifles. The Sure Shot rifle was developed in this same "change-over" period, probably as an experimental venture on the part of Stevens in case the swinging block rifles didn't pan out.

In another chapter in this book another side-swing rifle is discussed, namely the Lee Side-swing rifle. James Paris Lee obtained a patent on this design in 1862 and he later failed in his venture to manufacture these rifles. However, Lee continued to work in the firearms design field and later on patented some very successful ideas. It is believed—although I have nothing to substantiate this—that Lee might have contributed to the Stevens Sure Shot design. At any rate, although the Stevens side-swing action was a great improvement over the original Lee design, it too was destined to early obsolescence.

Unlike the original Lee design—which was a full sized man's rifle—the Stevens Sure Shot was intended to be a boy's or beginner's rifle, and was made very light and small. It was chambered for the .22 rimfire caliber with a 20″ round tapered and rifled barrel with the rifle weighing only 3½

pounds. It was available with either a nickel plated or color case hardened receiver, and with the remainder of the parts blued. It was made with a walnut butt stock fitted with a curved steel butt plate. Like the original Lee rifle, the Stevens Sure Shot had no separate wood forearm as such; rather the front extension of the receiver acted as the forearm.

It is the side-swing feature that sets this Stevens rifle apart from all the other Stevens single shot rifles. One might say the action was a copy— with numerous improvements, of course — of the type action used on some of the single shot derringer cartridge pistols that were once popular. Except for the side-swing feature the Sure Shot mechanism was of the same general principle as the Stevens Tip-up. The receiver of the Sure Shot did not have the drop and odd appearance of the Tip-up and it was a lot thinner. The side view photo shows the Sure Shot action very clearly and the top view of the open action shows the very narrow frame and how the action opens.

Essentially the Sure Shot is a break-open type of action, but with the breech end of the barrel swinging to the side rather than tipping up. The barrel is hinged to the front end of the receiver and locked closed by a push button plunger arrangement. It is a slightly more complicated action than the original Stevens Tip-up, but more unhandy to operate and use.

Illustrated above: Stevens Sure Shot rifle from the Otto Wolhowe collection.

The Stevens Sure Shot action.

The Stevens Sure Shot rifle and action is well constructed. The bore in the round barrel (1) appears to be slightly off-center at the breech end, this to leave some additional metal at the breech end, and into which a groove is milled to accept the extractor (4). To the barrel is attached a base plate (22). This plate is grooved to fit the round barrel and is attached by two screws (2) and (11). In addition, this plate appears to also be sweated in place with soft solder. The front of the plate extends beyond the end of the breech and forms a tongue which will fit in a groove cut below the standing breech in the receiver. The plate holds the extractor in place, with the stud on the front of the extractor fitting through an oblong hole in the plate so the extractor cannot fall out. The bottom of this plate is also milled to accept the end of the locking bolt and is made with a lug to form the hinge stud.

The receiver (17) is entirely machined from a steel forging or casting, with the upper and lower tangs made integral with it. The front extension of the receiver is milled flat and then the front end milled out to accept the hinge stud, and drilled to accept the take-down stud (3). The upper end of the take-down stud is made with a wide lip which fits a groove in the hinge stud, thereby holding the base plate and attached barrel against the receiver and allowing it to pivot. A flat spring (23) attached to the bottom of the take-down stud holds the stud in place and forms a take-down lever by which the stud can be turned to release the barrel. A small knob (24) screwed into the end of the spring lever provides a means to turn the take down stud and at the same time acts as a plunger to hold the lever and stud from turning.

The rear end of the receiver extension is also milled out to accept the extractor bar (19), which is held in place and pivots on screw (20). The stud on the end of the extractor fits in a hole in this bar and when the action is swung open the bar pulls the extractor back to extract the case.

The locking parts consist of the locking bolt (5), locking bolt release plunger (21) and the locking bolt spring (25). These parts are fitted in two holes drilled in the receiver extension. The release plunger is also fitted with an enlarged nut on one end so it can be easily depressed, and with a large headed screw on the other end to hold it in place. Beveled surfaces on both locking bolt and release plunger provide means to pull the locking bolt down out of the recess in the base plate when the plunger is depressed. The coil spring under the locking bolt supplies upward tension to the bolt to keep it in the locked position unless pulled down by the plunger. The locking system is simple yet very reliable.

Unlike most of the later Stevens boy's rifles which usually were made with very small and weak firing pins, the Sure Shot is made having a large headed firing pin (8) that is not easily battered or damaged by snapping the hammer on it. It is held in the standing breech part of the receiver by the retainer pin (7). The firing pin is held back at all times except during actual firing by the retractor spring (6). The retractor spring keeps the firing pin back so the tip will not interfere with opening or closing the action.

The firing mechanism consists of the hammer (9), hammer screw (10), trigger (28), trigger screw (27), main spring (14), trigger spring (13), and the spring screws (15) and (31). Provision is made for the hammer to rebound by a tension screw (12) which is adjustable to halt the tension of the main spring on the hammer when it is in the down position. This allows the hammer to rebound slightly after firing to allow the firing pin to retract, which in turn allows the breech to be opened and closed without interference from the firing pin tip.

The separate trigger guard (29) is attached to the receiver by two screws (26) and (30). The stock is held to the receiver by the tang screw (16).

All in all, the Stevens Sure Shot shows much better construction throughout than any of the Stevens single shot boy's rifles that were introduced later on. All the parts are well made and fitted and the few moving parts work smoothly.

To operate this Stevens rifle the projecting large end of the release plunger is depressed with the thumb which unlocks the barrel and it can be swung open, with the breech end moving to the right. A cartridge can then be inserted into the chamber, and while pressing lightly on the cartridge the breech can be closed. The base plate has a slight bevel where it first contacts the locking bolt, and as the barrel is closed the locking bolt is automatically pushed down, and snaps into the locking recess when barrel is fully closed.

To take the rifle down the knob on the take-down lever is grasped and the lever turned one half circle.

For complete article see *Single Shot Rifles and Actions*, 1969 Ed., by Frank de Haas.

The Stevens Sure Shot action.

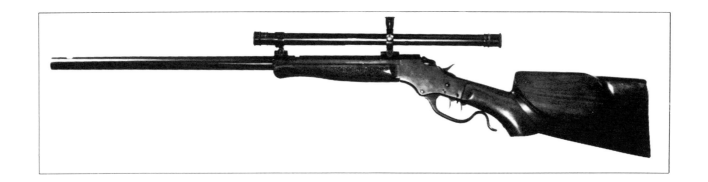

THE STEVENS NO. 44½

Period: 1904-1916

The No. 44½ Stevens action is unquestionably the finest and strongest single shot action ever made by the former J. Stevens Arms & Tool Company of Chicopee Falls, Mass.

There were many and varied Stevens single shot rifles in the early history of the company, such as the "Hunter's Pet" on the original tip-up action, the "Favorite," the "Ideal 44," the "Crack Shot," the "Walnut Hill," the "Little Scout" and others, but none wore the Stevens name as proudly as the No. 44½ Ideal. Odd as it may seem, although it was the "ultimate" action in the Stevens line, it possibly is the least known, and probably was made in the fewest numbers and for the shortest period of years of any of the more popular Stevens single shots.

Prior to the introduction of the 44½ action, the old Stevens tip-up rifle and later the Ideal No. 44 Stevens rifles had served their owners for both hunting and target shooting. At about the turn of the century cartridges loaded with smokeless powders were being introduced, necessitating a stronger action than the No. 44. About 1904 the Stevens company introduced an "improved" single shot action, one that would safely hold the pressures of the cartridges then being loaded with the smokeless powders. This action was called the No. 44½ Ideal.

As will be shown later, the No. 44½ action was a vast improvement over the older No. 44 in practically every way. When the No. 44½ action was first introduced it was the stated intention of the Stevens company to replace all models of their rifles having the No. 44 action with those having the new stronger and improved No. 44½ action. This change-over was

partially successful, but although the No. 44½ action was hailed as one of the best actions available at that time, and as being far superior to the No. 44, we note that it was discontinued by 1916. It was never to be made again. Meanwhile, the No. 44 action was never fully discontinued, and such Stevens rifles as the Favorite, Model 414 Armory and the Walnut Hill series—all having No. 44 design actions, remained popular for many years after the death of the No. 44½.

One reason for the short life span of the No. 44½ Stevens action may have been due to its having started life near the end of the single shot rifle era. By 1900 the single shot rifle was being cast aside in favor of the many fancy repeating rifles and only the specialized target shooter stuck by the single shot. Had the No. 44½ action been introduced in the 1870s and '80s like the Remington, Winchester, Sharps and Ballard, the story would certainly have been different. As it was, even though the No. 44½ action was everything it was claimed to be, it never really got a good chance in life. However, there must have been a lot of these actions made in its 12 years of existence for it is not too difficult to obtain one today.

I would like to think that the No. 44½ Stevens action could have made a grand comeback. In the early 1930s

The Stevens No. 44½ Action.

the .22 Hornet was introduced commercially, and a lot of wildcat cartridge designing was going on—as witness the .22 R-2 Lovell. At this time there was a great demand for single shot actions. Stevens was still making the Walnut Hill No. 417 Target Rifle in .22 Long Rifle caliber and they hastily adapted it to the .22 Hornet, but good as the No. 417 action was, it was not quite up to the task of safely holding Hornet pressures. Had Stevens re-introduced the No. 44½ action with the debut of the Hornet cartridge, I believe it would have found wide acceptance.

The Stevens No. 44½ is a single shot true falling block action, operated by an under finger lever which also acts as a trigger guard. It is fired by a manually operated exposed hammer. As shown in the photograph, the No. 44½ action has a smooth flat sided receiver with a case hardened finish. The receiver and top tang are made in one piece, the lower tang is separate and is attached to the receiver with three screws. The stock is attached to the receiver tangs by a wood screw at the end of each tang.

The action can best be compared with its older brother the No. 44 action, as described in a preceding chapter. These two actions have the same general over-all appearance—in size, shape, weight and finish. The tangs on both actions are similar, as well as the semi-takedown feature employing a set screw. The firing mechanism is also similar on both actions, both having about the same hammers and

Illustrated above: A custom varmint rifle in the .22 R-2 Lovell caliber made up on the Stevens No. 44½ single shot action. Rifle is fitted with Lyman 5A scope.

115

triggers with flat trigger and main springs. The similarity extends further, as the finger lever, extractor and link are also nearly alike in both actions.

However, to the firearms student and gunsmith the difference between the No. 44½ and No. 44 Stevens actions is like day and night. The basic difference between the two actions is in the design of the breeching system and in the material of the receiver. The No. 44½ is made from a piece of drop forged steel whereas the No. 44 receiver is a casting. The No. 44½ is a true falling block action with the breech block fitted in milled recesses in the receiver, while the No. 44 has a breech block that hinges on a pin. To the casual observer this difference may appear minor in nature, but it is actually of major importance. This difference allows the No. 44½ to be safely used for cartridges that develop more than twice the breech pressures that would be considered safe for the No. 44 action.

How does the No. 44½ Stevens action compare in design and strength with some of the other single shot falling block actions? As far as strength is concerned the No. 44½ action—with a properly altered firing pin—will safely handle many cartridges that normally develop up to 50,000 pounds per square inch breech pressures. Its only limiting factor is that its barrel shank is quite small in diameter so it should not be used for cartridges having a large diameter case like the .45-70 or .30-40. The No. 44½ action has been widely used to build many fine custom varmint rifles in many calibers, such as the .22 Hornet, .218 Bee, .219 Zipper and to their improved or K versions and to such popular wildcats as the R-2 Lovell, .22 Niedner, .219 Wasp and others.

As for the design of the falling breech block, the No. 44½ is not unlike most of the other falling block actions —in that the block slides in milled recesses in the receiver. The difference is that in most of these actions the breech block moves straight up and down at right angles to the barrel and the cartridge must be completely chambered before the breech block can be closed. The Stevens No. 44½ action has a breech block that lies at an 8 degree angle to the barrel so that when it is lowered it moves slightly back. But much more important is the feature which allows the breech block to "rock" backwards and forwards as it is lowered and raised in the receiver. In the No. 44½ action the cartridge need not be fully seated into the chamber, because both the angle in which the block moves and the "rocking" action enable the breech block to slip behind the head of the partially chambered cartridge and then seat it fully as the breech is closed.

To understand this action better and to show how the breech block "rocks," the operation cycle will be explained in slow motion. During this explanation you should refer to the sectional drawing of this action and also study the photograph of the opened action.

The drawing shows the action closed with the hammer resting on the half-cock position.

To operate the action the end of the finger lever (21) is grasped and pushed downward. The finger lever is held in the receiver (6) and hinges on the lever pin (25), and is held in the closed position by the tension of the spring and plunger assembly (23) & (24) located in the base of the finger lever. This plunger presses against the lower part of the link (22). As the finger lever is pressed down the link is rotated backwards on the two link pins (26) & (27). Initial movement causes the projection on the link to depress the lever plunger and spring, and also causes the rear of the link to come into contact with the hammer (11). Had the hammer been resting on the firing pin (9) it would also have been touching the link, in which case the initial movement of the finger lever would also have pushed the hammer back off the firing pin and into the safe position. As the lever is opened further the link continues to push the hammer back and at the same time begins to pull the breech block (7) down within the receiver to open the breech. As the action is being opened the link slides off the hump on the hammer, allowing the hammer to return to the safe position.

At this point, when the breech block is nearly all the way down and the action almost completely opened, the rocking motion becomes evident. In the front left part of the receiver is a spring and plunger assembly (3) & (4) which bears against the face of the breech block. In the photograph of the opened action, and in the blacked out and dotted line portion of the drawing, the lower extensions of the breech block can be seen showing how the front of the extensions have been milled out. As the breech block

is lowered the cutaway in the extension allows the bottom of the breech block to go forward. As the finger lever is completely opened, drawing the breech block all the way down, it also tends to pull the bottom of the block forward—rocking it about ¼". Meanwhile, the plunger assembly pushes and holds the top of the breech block back against the rear raceways in the receiver and helps hold it in the rocked position. At the same time, when the finger lever is completely swung open, it activates the extractor (5) which is also pivoted on the finger lever pin.

A great number of articles have been written about the No. 44½ Stevens action and almost all of the writers praise the rocking breech block as having been so designed to function as a "cartridge seater." This may be true in a sense but I believe the original purpose was to make room for the centrally located extractor (the same as in the No. 44 action) to work properly. Thus for Stevens to retain this simple extractor and make room for it to extract a cartridge from the chamber there was nothing else to do but make the breech block "rock." I believe this was the original purpose of this design and that the rocking motion happened to function as a cartridge seater. This latter may be a useful function as will become evident when the action is loaded, or it may be a curse as will be noted later on.

To load, the cartridge is dropped into the chamber. It need not be pushed clear into the chamber, it can be stopped by the extended extractor or by the bullet touching the throat. The cartridge head can be as much as 3/16" out from the face of the breech. Grasping the finger lever and pulling it back causes the rocked breech block to rise, allowing the top edge of the block to slip easily behind the cartridge head. As the block is raised the cut-away extensions come into contact with the receiver, and as it lifts farther causes the block to "right" itself or to rock back into its normal position.

STEVENS NO. 44½ ACTION SPECIFICATIONS

Type	Single shot, falling block, operated by under finger lever.
Receiver	Machined steel, with integral upper tang.
Receiver finish	Color case hardened.
Take-down	Semi-take-down, by loosening take-down screw and unscrewing barrel.
Stock fastening	Via the two tangs and two wood screws.
Ignition	Manually cocked exposed hammer, powered by flat main spring. Separate firing pin in breech block.
Trigger	Plain, with trigger in direct contact with hammer (Optional double-set).
Safety	Hammer has "safe" or half cock notch. Hammer automatically placed in safe position when action is opened or closed.
Extractor	Automatic, semi-ejection. (Automatic ejector optional in .22 LR.)
Weight	2 lbs. 1 oz.
Thickness	1.100"
Side wall thickness	.115"

Pages 107-116 reprinted by permission from *Single Shot Rifles and Actions*, 1969 Ed., by Frank de Hass.

STEVENS NOTES

Some Stevens notes derived from single-shot books by James J. Grant, a very important writer for all early American arms collectors.

• Stevens Side Plate Rifles. Examples exist of early, pre-1894 models, e.g., one is the size of later Favorites and another is almost as large as the Ideal No. 44. Essentially, these were limited production prototypes created to work out necessary design features without the full cost of major tooling before market worthiness was demonstrated.

Relatively few Tip-up rifles had pistol-grip stocks and are therefore quite rare. Ladies models were also quite scarce and were made on three different action frames: the Favorite No. 21, Favorite No. 55 and the Model .044 1/2 (No. 56). All were deluxe, light weight models of limited production. They typically had select wood, pistol-grip stocks and small Swiss butt plates. Variations were to be found in part because they were built on two different Favorite frames. Calibers available included .22 rim-fire, .22 W.R.F., .25 rim-fire, .32 rim-fire & special order .22/15/60. The commonly produced light boy's rifles included the Stevens Maynard Junior, Little Scout, Crack-Shot, Marksman, and ,of course, the Favorite. Actually the Favorite became so numerous (over 1,000,000 made) that the serial numbers were dropped in favor of a system of code identification. The Favorites start with the Model No. 17 and continue through No. 21. The No. 20 is a Favorite shotgun. In Catalog No. 52 the Model No. 21 was dropped. The Model No. 56 Ladies rifle made its first appearance in Cat. No. 52. Ultimately the Model No. 21 became a plain Favorite with a 20 inch barrel.

• Stevens Hunter's Pet (heavy frame) was the first pocket rifle model and is pictured on the cover of the first Stevens catalog of 1875. This heavy pistol/rifle was nickle plated and came with a detachable shoulder stock. It was available in .22 short rim-fire, .32, .38 & .44 calibers (rim or center-fire). Weight 5 to 5 3/4 pounds. Priced $18 to $21.00. The Hunter's Pet shotgun had essentially the same style. It was chambered for Stevens Everlasting center-fire shells. The Hunter's Pet was also available as a combination gun with rifle barrel and interchangeable shot barrel. The Stevens Vernier Hunter's Pet rifle was identical except for a rear tang sight.

• Reliable Pocket Rifle. A small pistol frame with 10" part octagon barrel that was chambered for the .22 short only. It was offered with globe and peep sights. It had a detachable shoulder rest made from a single rod. Price was $10.50 to $11.00.

• New Model Pocket Rifle (Bicycle model) This model had a heavier pistol frame and was nickle plated. The detachable shoulder stock came with the more customary two-rod design. Weight was 2 to 2 3/4 pounds. Barrels were 10, 12, 15 & 18" in length. Available in .22 & .32 rim-fire. Price was $12,25 to $16.00..

• STEVENS FAVORITE First version introduced about 1894 (see side plates). The first models with rolling blocks were designated Model 107, 108, 109 & 110. However, after reorganization of the company in 1896 model numbers 44, 45, 47, 49, 51, 52, 54 & 55 were adopted.
• Stevens Ideal No. 44 Rifle. Introduced in 1894. By 1895 all tip-up rifles were discontinued.

• Ideal 44 Rifle. A plain, basic model with a wide range of calibers available. This model was priced near $10 with plain sights. Many options were also available. The Ideal Range Model No. 45 was the same as the Model No. 44 except for refinements such as Swiss butt plate and higher quality.

• Ideal Range Model 46. Same as the No. 45 but with fancy walnut stock.

• Ideal Range Model 47. Also the same as the No. 45 but included pistol grip and a loop lever. The Ideal Range Model 48 was the same as the No. 47 but included select walnut stock, checkered pistol grip and fore end.

STEVENS TIP-UP SERIES AS OFFERED IN 1888:

• Model 1 Tip-up Rifle. Made in .32, .38 & .44 rim & center-fire calibers.

• Model 2 Gallery Rifle. Made in .22 short, rim-fire caliber only and usually had plain, open sights.

• Model 3 Tip-up Rifle. Same as the Model 1 except was offered in either full or half octagon barrel and had Stevens combination open and peep sights.

• Model 4 Gallery Rifle. Same as Model 2 except had combination sights.

• Model 5 Expert Rifle. Offered with half octagon barrel and Vernier peep sight on the tang. Nickle plated and available in .22

short, .32, .38, or .44 long in rim-fire or center-fire. Initial price range $25 to $31.

- Model 6 Expert Rifle. Same as the Model 5 except for fancy walnut stock and slightly higher price range of $28 to $34.

- Model 7 Premier Rifle. Included half octagon barrel, Vernier peep sight, Swiss butt plate & nickle plating. Available in .22 short rim-fire plus .32, .38 & .44 rim-fire or center-fire. Price range was $29 to $32.

- Model 8 Premier Rifle. Same as the Model 7 but with fancy walnut stock and fore end. Price was $32-38 in .22 & $32-35 in larger calibers.

- Model 9 New Model Range Rifle. Offered half octagon barrel, wind gauge front sight and Vernier rear sight, varnished stock and fore end & nickle plating. This was considered the most accurate of the Tip-up rifles. Available in .22, .32, .38, .44 & Stevens .32/35/165. Price $31.50-37.50.

- Model 10 Range Rifle. Same as Model 9 with extra fancy stock. Price: $34-40. Chambered for .22 Long rim-fire rather than .22 short. The .22 extra long center-fire Maynard cartridge was also offered.

- Stevens Ladies Rifles Models 11, 12, 13 & 14. These were always special models. They had lighter frames and barrels, special tip-up design, nickle plating, walnut stock and fore end. Calibers offered were .22 rim-fire & .22 center-fire (not interchangeable).

• Stevens Arms (excluding the New England Westinghouse WWI years) never made a military rifle. The Stevens focus was mostly on target and small game firearms. The earliest years of meeting the big demand for self-protection pocket pistols were later transformed to heavy barrel rifles of small caliber and on essentially the same actions. The Model 1894 44 action with sharp, cut away side walls was distinctly inferior to the strong falling blocks of Models 49-52 with 44 1/2 actions. These premier, single-shot rifles were forever discontinued by 1916 as lucrative war contracts and world-wide demand for repeating actions crushed the market for excellence in single-shot target rifles. The doldrums for Stevens original arms would continue until 1920 when Savage Arms acquired the mammoth facilities to focus on shotgun production Also, Stevens did introduce a lever action in high-power calibers as an exception to the long established image of "boys rifles." The Model 425 was produced in .25, .30, .32 & .35 Remington rimless calibers and has always been a very good mechanism.

• Stevens Walnut Hill 49-44 1/2 & Schuetzen Jr. 52-44 1/2 were certainly among the finest single-shots ever made. The Schuetzen Special Model 54 was the highest grade regularly made in 44 1/2 type action.

• Ideal Walnut Hill No. 49. This was the lowest grade Stevens that was regularly engraved. This model offered many design variations with respect to engraving, etching, checkering, select walnut stocks and fore ends, Swiss butt plates and sight options. Base price was $42.

• Ideal Walnut Hill No. 50. Same as the No. 49 with select, fancy walnut stock (No. 46, 48 & 50 were illustrated in early catalog series of Ideal rifles but did not have much longevity.

• Ideal Schuetzen No. 51. Differences included a heavier action, straight grip tang, cheekpiece, Schuetzen butt plate #4, fancy checkering, engraved frames & a wide range of calibers. Weight range was approximately 12 to 12 1/2 pounds Base price: $58.

• Ideal Schuetzen Junior No. 52. Similar to the No. 51 except in a higher grade. Distinctions include a pistol-grip frame and stock with loop lever. Visually very appealing. Base price: $54.

• Ideal Schuetzen Special No. 54. This was the highest grade regularly made by Stevens. Features included an engraved and case-hardened frame, straight tang and grip model with double set triggers, special Schuetzen lever #6 & Schuetzen butt plate #5. Weight with a 30" barrel was approximately 11 1/2 pounds. Base price: $68.

• Ideal Ladies Model No. 55. A fancy model with lighter weight, single trigger and plain #1 lever. Also had pistol grip stock with light #2 Swiss butt plate. Weight: 5 1/4 pounds.

Other Early Stevens Models Notes

• Stevens Favorite. These exceptionally popular small rifles were made during the same period that the 44 action was at its peak. A special, fancy model Favorite was also produced with a pistol-grip stock, fancy walnut stock and checkering. The base price for that version was $18.00. The base price for the common, plain Favorite was $6.00.

• Stevens Pocket (Bicycle) Rifle was very similar to Stevens Tip-up rifle series. One common distinction, however, was the addition of a trigger guard to all later models.

• New Model Pocket Shotgun No. 39. This model had 15" to 18" barrels, smooth bore and choke. The removable nickle stock was standard. Base price: $11.25 to 12.50.

118

• New Model Pocket (Bicycle) Rifle No. 40. Prices offered on this model were as follows: 10" barrel $9.25, 12" barrel $10.00, 15" barrel $11.25 & 18" barrel $12.50. Features included a detachable shoulder stock, combination Stevens sights both front and rear.

• For further detail about Stevens early pistols see Stevens Pocket Rifles by Canadian writer, Kenneth Cope.

• Guns Magazine, Feb. 1969, reports that only 10 Bisley model Stevens were ever made. There was a distinct European license to produce Stevens rifles and pistols that is not commonly known. Slightly modified versions were produced in both England and Germany. Consider the Stevens Ideal No. 700 as advertised in the 1911 book titled Rifle and Carton (i.e., "target") by Ernest H. Robinson, Published by Edmund Seale, London.

• Mr. Grant reports that all Stevens factory records were mysteriously destroyed shortly after WWI when Congress threatened to investigate the company's alleged illegal profiteering on WWI contracts. It should be remembered that "Stevens" management throughout World War One was strictly a Westinghouse Electric matter.

Stevens By Another Name

Springfield Arms Co., Chicopee Falls, Mass. was strictly an assumed business name of Stevens Arms (Savage era). Some additional exceptions include: Model 16 Crackshots listed as "The 22 Spencer, Pat. App'l for" & Model 16 Crackshot listed as "Rogers Arms Company Pat. Appl. for .22 Long Rifle." Such exceptions add diversity and depth to the collector's quest. The quest never ends.

INDISPENSIBLE COLLECTOR REFERENCE BOOKS BY JAMES J. GRANT

Single-Shot Rifles, Gun Room Press, Highland Park, NJ © 1947, 385 pp.

More Single-Shot Rifles, Gun Room Press, Highland Park, NJ, © 1959, 322 pp.

Boy's Single-Shot Rifles, Wm. Morrow & Co., NY, © 1967, 597 pp.

Still More Single-Shot Rifles, Pioneer Press, Union City, TN, © 1979, 211 pp.

Single-Shot Rifles Finale, Wolf Publishing Co., Prescott, AZ, © 1991, 133 pp.

FOX GUN COMPANY

Probably no arms manufacturing company in this country has climbed so rapidly to the front in so few years of existence as the A. H. Fox Gun Co. of Philadelphia, makers of the A. H. Fox gun. Mr. Fox, inventor of this arm, has given the best years of his life to a study of the firearms business, and therefore, aside from his being an active sportsman, he is naturally well qualified to put out something especially fine in a shotgun. "The finest gun in the world," is what he calls the product of his factory, and thousands of American sportsmen, into whose hands the arm has already fallen, believe it was properly named.

The Fox gun was first introduced about 1905, and the success it met with has been truly phenomenal. The present company employs over a hundred men, turns out about five hundred dollars' worth of finished guns a day, and is capitalized at four hundred thousand dollars, with about one-half of this amount paid in cash. The factory is located in the northern suburbs of Philadelphia, and was recently built expressly for the manufacture of shotguns.

Source: <u>Outdoor Life</u>, August 1909.

The A. H. Fox gun.

The A. H. Fox Gun Co. factory.

See: *A. H. Fox: "The Finest Gun in the World,"* by Michael McIntosh

Stevens Repeating Gallery Rifles

Made to take .22 Short, .22 Long, .22 Long-Rifle and .25 Stevens R. F. cartridges. Shoot 16 Short, 14 Long, 12 Long-Rifle; twelve .22 Winchester R. F. and twelve .25 Stevens R. F. cartridges; 24-inch Round Barrel; extreme length 41½ inches. Fitted with Bead Front and Sporting Rear Sights; Varnished Black Walnut Stock; Blued Trigger Guard; Rubber Butt Plate.

Manufactured by

J. STEVENS ARMS & TOOL COMPANY
CHICOPEE FALLS, MASS.

STEVENS IDEAL
No. 700.

THE LATEST PATTERN RIFLE FOR TARGET OR SPORTING WORK.

Can be used with or without Telescope.

Price (as illustrated) - - 168/-
Price (without Telescope) - 95/-

Illustrated Price Lists of Rifles, Pistols, Shotguns, Telescopes, Sights, Etc., on application.

J. STEVENS ARMS & TOOL Co.,
15, GRAPE STREET, SHAFTESBURY AVENUE, LONDON, W.C.

Telephone   Telegrams
9199 GERRARD.   "STEVARMAIN, LONDON."

Stevens Ideal No. 700 as advertised in the 1911 book titled *Rifle and Carton* (i.e., "target") by Ernest H. Robinson, Publisher: Edmund Seale, London. This is one example of the European license to produce Stevens Arms in both England and Germany.

J. Stevens stamped the caliber on both pistols and rifles if other than .22. Most arms were .22 caliber rimfires. The Crack Shot #16 had serial numbers from 1 to 2,000, the No. 15 Little Maynard, the No. 65 Little Krag, and the No.'s 14 and 14½ Little Scouts all sold for $3.00 or less originally. They were the only guns without serial numbers. In 1898 J. Stevens started new serial numbers on the No. 41 pistols. All guns manufactured had company name and serial numbers on the gun and often the major parts. The only gun not stamped with the company name was the Gem (their lowest priced gun), but even on the Gem serial numbers appear on the frame and barrel. All tip-up rifles and shotguns carry serial numbers on the important parts. The Hunter's Pet had two different casting patterns and both were different from the Lord pistol. The Favorite was the first American sporter to exceed one million units. — *Ed Mason*

J. STEVENS ARMS COMPANY

DIVISION OF SAVAGE ARMS CORPORATION

RIFLES AND SHOTGUNS

CHICOPEE FALLS, MASS., U.S.A.

Form letter, 1939

We take pleasure in enclosing the catalog which you recently requested.

The Stevens and Springfield rifles and shotguns described in this catalog were designed by experts and each represents an outstanding value in its particular field of use. Stevens target rifles have long enjoyed an international reputation for accuracy.

Any of the leading hardware or sporting goods dealers in your locality will be pleased to supply you with the particular Stevens or Springfield sporting arm you desire whether it be a rifle for small game, or target practice, or a shotgun for upland game, wild-fowl, trap or skeet shooting.

If, after reviewing the catalog, there is any doubt in your mind as to which shotgun or rifle you should buy, do not hesitate to write us and we shall be glad to have one of our shooting experts advise you concerning the arm he thinks is best adapted to your requirements. If your dealer does not have in stock the particular model you want or for any reason cannot secure it promptly, please advise us.

We assure you that your consideration of Stevens products is very much appreciated.

Yours very truly,

T. L. Hopkins.

Sales Manager

T.L.Hopkins:GH

J. Stevens Arms Company

OWNED AND OPERATED BY
SAVAGE ARMS CORPORATION
UTICA N.Y.

MANUFACTURER OF

SHOTGUNS, RIFLES, PISTOLS

CHICOPEE FALLS, MASS. U.S.A.

Form letter, 1935

We take pleasure in enclosing the Stevens catalog which you recently requested.

The Stevens rifles and shotguns described in this catalog were designed by experts and each represents an outstanding value in its particular field of use. Stevens target rifles have long enjoyed an international reputation for accuracy.

Any of the leading hardware or sporting goods dealers in your locality will be pleased to supply you with the particular Stevens arm you desire whether it be a rifle for small game, or target practice, or a shotgun for upland game, wild-fowl, trap or skeet shooting.

If, after reviewing the catalog, there is any doubt in your mind as to which shotgun or rifle you should buy, do not hesitate to write us and we shall be glad to have one of our shooting experts advise you concerning the arm he thinks is best adapted to your requirements. If your dealer does not have in stock the particular model you want or for any reason cannot secure it promptly, please advise us.

We assure you that your consideration of Stevens products is very much appreciated.

Very truly yours,

J. STEVENS ARMS COMPANY

T. L. Hopkins

Sales Manager

T.L.Hopkins:KM

A STEVENS COLLECTOR POINT OF VIEW

Stevens firearms were a gentleman's gun to be used in competitive shooting. Yet they were also the workingman's (and boy's) gun to be used in the field for target shooting and hunting some game. Countless boys and, no doubt, uncountable girls, grew up with a Stevens as their first rifle. Possession and use would have been one of the early rights of passage into adulthood.

Stevens Arms produced more shotguns in more varieties than any other gun manufacturer. The range was from a .410 shot pistol to a World War One trench shotgun complete with a bayonet. The latter was produced during the war years by New England Westinghouse, since the original company (1864-1915) never produced a military arm.

The finest achievements of Stevens Arms Company were in the area of competitive, high quality, single-shot target rifles. This was especially true after the addition of refinements added by Harry Pope who was associated with Stevens Arms from 1901-1903. Stevens-Pope rifles are cherished to this day for both accuracy and aesthetic beauty.

As an individual collector of firearms you're certain to find unlimited possibilities for pride and curiosity with Stevens firearms. Personally, I've never found any two Stevens that were exactly alike.

Bill Purington, Collector/Exhibitor, August, 1991

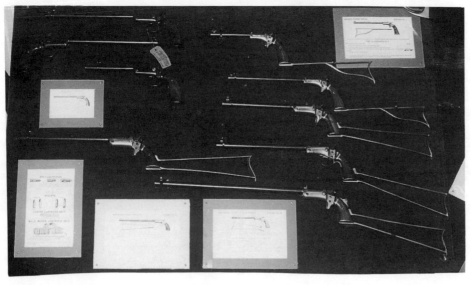

Sample of Bill Purington's Stevens Firearm Exhibit   122

Brief History of the Massachusetts Arms Company

by Ted M. Szetela, Chairman, Chicopee Historical Commission

The Massachusetts Arms Company was formed in 1850 upon permission of the State Legislature on March 5th of that year to incorporate with capital not to exceed $100,000.

The capital for the new arms-making company was set at $70,000 by such men as Timothy W. Carter, then agent for the Chicopee Manufacturing Company; James T. Ames, president of the Ames Manufacturing Company; John Chase, manager of the Springfield Canal Company; Chester W. Chapin, president of the Connecticut River Railroad, who later became president of the Boston & Maine Railroad; Roy A. Chapman, paymaster at Chicopee Manufacturing Company; Benjamin F. Warner and others.

The new company first purchased property consisting of land, power site, machine shops and tools owned by the Ames Manufacturing Company on the south bank of the Chicopee River in Chicopee Falls.

Production of firearms and machinery commenced under the agency of Mr. Carter in the manufacture of a revolving pistol under the Leavitt and Wesson patents. The Wesson revolver, the first "tip-up" breech-loading pistol, an invention attributed to Joshua Stevens, a young gunsmith then in the employ of Colonel Samuel Colt of Hartford, Connecticut.

Mr. Stevens, who worked for Colt in 1848 and 1849, came to Chicopee Falls in 1850 to join the Massachusetts Arms Company to engage in the extensive manufacture of the Wesson revolver he invented.

After the manufacture and sale of the Wesson revolver had assumed considerable proportion, Mr. Colt, who had watched with much interest and consternation the development of this particular weapon, filed a claim of patent infringement.

Following drawn-out litigation in the United States federal court, Colt succeeded in obtaining a verdict favorable to him and a perpetual injunction against the Massachusetts Arms Company. The loss was costly to the budding Chicopee arms concern and it was reported that $25,000 had to be paid to Colt as a means of settlement of the case.

Following the court injunction the Massachusetts Arms Company turned to the manufacture of other patent firearms under license [*Note: primarily the production of the Maynard rifle to avoid almost certain bankruptcy due to the spurious lawsuit by Samuel Colt*]. During the Civil War the company prospered as 200 men were employed in manufacturing breech-loading arms, chiefly of the Maynard patent, for the United States Union Army cavalry.

At the close of the Civil War there was a sharp decrease in production as the need for firearms lagged. Pending a movement on the part of stockholders the business was closed and the entire stock and franchise was purchased by Mr. Carter, who continued the business until February 1, 1876, when the Carter property was sold to the Lamb Knitting Machine Company.

The Lamb Company, organized in 1866 for the manufacture of domestic knitting machines was, at the time of the purchase of the Carter property, manufacturing the celebrated hunting, sporting & Creedmoor rifles known as the "Maynard."

In 1864 Joshua Stevens, the inventive genius who made the first model of Colt's revolver and devised various improvements, left the Massachusetts Arms Company and formed the J. Stevens Company in partnership with Asher Bartlett and William B. Fay, for the manufacture of a single-barrel pistol of a new type.•

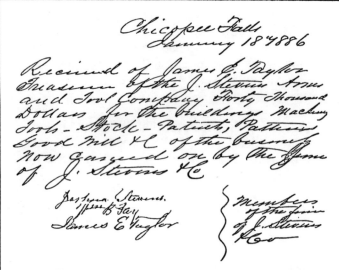

The incorporation of the J. Stevens Arms and Tool Co. in 1886 took over the assets of J. Stevens & Co.

An Announcement

THE Savage Arms Corporation has purchased the entire capital stock of the J. Stevens Arms Company of Chicopee Falls, Mass.

The success which the two companies have met individually in the past is, we are sure, sufficient guarantee of the ability and efficiency of the respective organizations at Utica and Chicopee Falls to serve you in the very highest degree both in product and service.

As heretofore, correspondence and orders for our Savage products are to be addressed to Utica, N. Y., and correspondence and orders for our Stevens products are to be addressed to the J. Stevens Arms Company, Chicopee Falls, Mass. The export offices for both Savage and Stevens will be situated at 50 Church St., New York City, after July 1st, 1920.

We are proud to rely, as in the past, upon the full cooperation of our established distributors and now, with our greatly augmented line, we trust that this relationship will become the most important one in the small-arms field.

SAVAGE ARMS CORPORATION, Utica, N.Y.

Executive and Export Offices
50 Church Street, New York

Catalogue of Stevens product will be mailed on application.

In January, 1920 The Savage Arms Corp of Utica, N.Y. purchased the entire capital stock of the J. Stevens Arms Co. This announcement appeared in the 1920 Savage catalog.

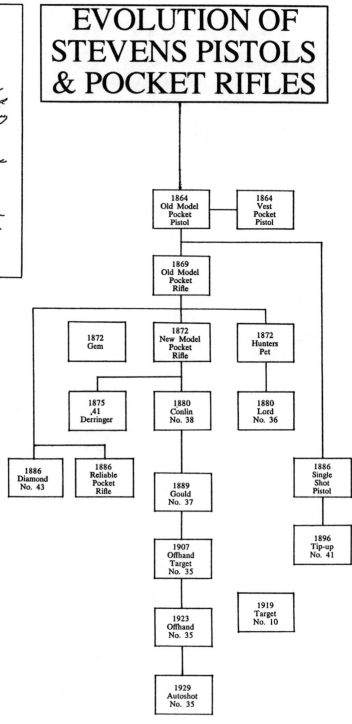

EVOLUTION OF STEVENS PISTOLS & POCKET RIFLES

Source: Kenneth L. Cope's book titled *Stevens Pistols and Pocket Rifles* © 1971 [recently reprinted]. Reprint courtesy of Museum Restoration Service, Box 70, Alexandria Bay, NY 13607. To order Mr. Cope's book call Museum (613) 393-2980.

Stevens Single-Shot Pistols

By KENNETH L. COPE

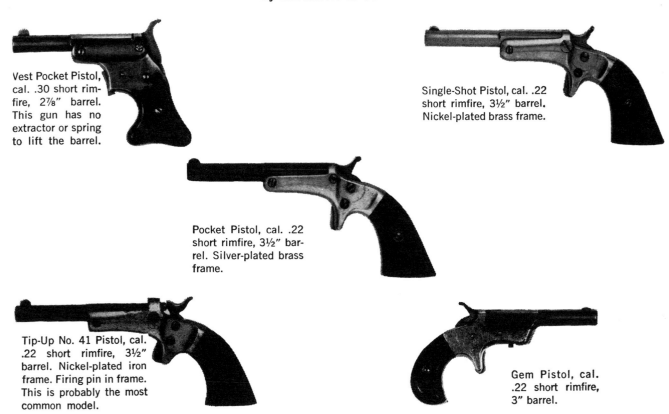

Vest Pocket Pistol, cal. .30 short rimfire, 2⅞" barrel. This gun has no extractor or spring to lift the barrel.

Single-Shot Pistol, cal. .22 short rimfire, 3½" barrel. Nickel-plated brass frame.

Pocket Pistol, cal. .22 short rimfire, 3½" barrel. Silver-plated brass frame.

Tip-Up No. 41 Pistol, cal. .22 short rimfire, 3½" barrel. Nickel-plated iron frame. Firing pin in frame. This is probably the most common model.

Gem Pistol, cal. .22 short rimfire, 3" barrel.

ONCE the most popular single-shot target pistols in America, Stevens pistols have faded into obscurity. There were 14 distinct models made over a span of 78 years, but except for common models they are now little known.

Joshua Stevens, founder of the Stevens firm, died in 1907 at the age of 92. He was born in 1814 at Chelsea,* Mass., where he received his early training as a machinist. In 1838 he was employed by Cyrus B. Allen in Springfield, Mass. He left Allen in the early 1840's to join Samuel Colt.

After working for Colt for some years, Stevens invented a revolver which he began to manufacture under his own name. A patent infringement suit by Colt terminated its production.

U. S. Patent No. 44123 for a single-shot pistol was granted to Stevens on Sept. 6, 1864, and J. Stevens & Co. was founded that same year. This patent became the basis for all except 2 of the 14 Stevens pistol models. The identical tip-up action principle was used from 1869 to 1894 for Stevens rifles and shotguns also.

Early Stevens pocket pistols were only moderately successful. The rise of the Stevens pistol, especially the target models, began after 1886 when Stevens developed the .22 long rifle cartridge. First manufactured by the Union Metallic Cartridge Co., the .22 long rifle proved to be, as it remains today, an ideal target cartridge.

During the 1880's and 1890's, the single-shot target pistol achieved its peak of popularity, and was considered superior to the revolver for target shooting. Stevens single-shot target pistols were recognized as the best at that time.

A. C. Gould, author and firearms authority of the 1880's and 1890's, made a test of .22 target pistols at the Walnut Hill Range, Woburn, Mass., in September 1888. He found that a Stevens target pistol, using the then new .22 long rifle cartridge, would ". . . shoot finer than any target in use among pistol shooters would measure." During this particular test, Gould shot a 1⅝" group at 50 yds.

The year 1888 also saw the introduction of competitive 50-yd. pistol shooting in America. At a match held during the fall meeting of the Massachusetts Rifle Ass'n, Stevens pistols were used by the first prize winner, W. W. Ben-

nett, and by J. B. Fellows, who shot a perfect score of 5 tens, the only perfect score made that year. This domination of the target pistol field was not to last, however. By 1904, the last year a Stevens pistol won the United States Revolver Association Championship, 2 of the 4 Stevens target models had been discontinued and full-adjustable sights were no longer supplied on the others. Introduced during the decline of the target models, the small-frame Tip-up No. 41 pocket pistol and the heavier frame Offhand No. 35 sporting pistol were produced in large quantities. These are the models most commonly encountered today.

In January 1920 the Savage Arms Corp. gained control of Stevens. Only the Offhand No. 35 model was continued. It was first made in pre-World War I form; later it was made in slightly modified form, and in the .410-bore Autoshot No. 35 model.

The only new model to be introduced after Savage assumed control was the Target No. 10, patented Apr. 17, 1920. Externally similar to an automatic pistol, it was the only departure from the 1864 styling since the discontinuance

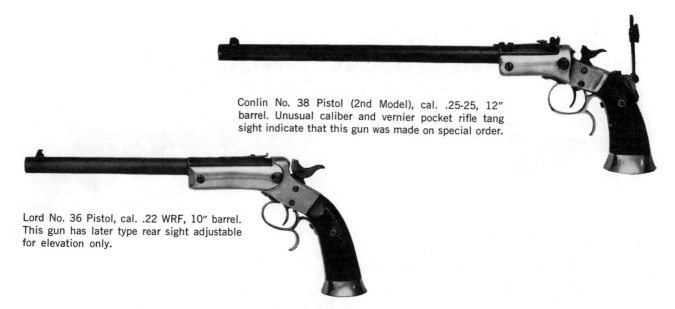

Conlin No. 38 Pistol (2nd Model), cal. .25-25, 12" barrel. Unusual caliber and vernier pocket rifle tang sight indicate that this gun was made on special order.

Lord No. 36 Pistol, cal. .22 WRF, 10" barrel. This gun has later type rear sight adjustable for elevation only.

of the Stevens derringer model in 1890.

Although the Target No. 10 never achieved the popularity of the earlier target models, this model is a very interesting one. It was the first production single-shot target pistol to use the better pointing automatic-style frame and to have the striker blow in direct line with the barrel.

Depending on date of manufacture, Stevens pistols were marked as follows:

1864-1888—"J. Stevens & Co. Chicopee Falls, Mass."
1888-1919—"J. Stevens Arms & Tool Co. Chicopee Falls, Mass. USA"
or
"J. Stevens A&T Co. Chicopee Falls, Mass. USA"
1919-1942—"J. Stevens Arms Co. Chicopee Falls, Mass. USA"

The marking is on the barrel in 2 lines and, on early models, includes the patent date, Sept. 6, 1864. The serial number is usually found on the left side of the barrel and under the left grip. A star may precede the serial number, but its meaning is unknown to this author.

The caliber marking, if present, is stamped above the serial number or on the barrel flat. Most were not marked to indicate caliber. Even on those pistols so marked, often only the bore size is shown. A pistol marked .25, for example, can be a .25 rimfire, .25-20 center-fire, or chambered for some other cal. .25 cartridge. My 2nd Model Conlin pistol, marked only with a .25 under the serial number, is chambered for the .25-25 cartridge.

One model conforms to none of the usual rules for marking. The Target No. 10 model has the caliber plainly marked under the barrel with all other markings on the side of the frame.

Stevens pistols with English proof marks are known. Many were sold in England prior to World War I and some have come back to the United States. A Diamond model in my collection bears a Birmingham view mark in use prior to 1904 and proof marks used only after 1954. The proving of export firearms is required under the British Gun Barrel Proof Acts of 1868 and 1950. The later marks include the caliber (.22 long rifle) and the chamber length (.610").

The following list of standard models cites their features. The Stevens firm was accommodating to special orders. Thus deviations in barrel length, caliber, sights, and finish will be encountered.

Production records of all Stevens pistols have been lost and the quantities produced or the serial number ranges of the various models are not known.

Many Stevens target pistols offered for sale today are actually Hunter's Pet or Pocket Rifles with the detachable shoulder stock missing. These are recognizable by the dovetail cut in the butt and, in most models, by the folding rear sight. Now loosely classified as pistols, they were regarded by the manufacturer as light rifles. They are a separate class of firearm, and are not covered here.

Except as noted, all models listed are of the same basic design in which the rear of the barrel tips up when a release stud on the side of the frame is depressed.

THE POCKET MODELS

Vest Pocket Pistol—Flat-sided iron frame; fish-tail grip. Cals. .22 short and .30 short rimfire, 2⅞" barrel. Sheath trigger; no extractor on some specimens; hammer has integral firing pin. Marked "Stevens & Co. Vest Pocket Pistol, Chicopee Falls, Mass." Only Stevens pistol to be marked with model name. Externally similar to Remington vest pocket derringer, but has typical Stevens tip-up barrel. Usual finish is full nickel.

One of the original models introduced when company was founded in 1864, it was discontinued in 1875. Also known as "Kickup" model.

Pocket Pistol—Small, rounded brass frame; oval grip. Cals. .22 short and .30 short rimfire, 3½" barrel. Sheath trigger; small stud on barrel release. Hammer has integral firing pin. Notch in hammer is rear sight. The spring under the barrel forces the barrel up and operates the extractor when the release stud is depressed. Automatic extraction is sole feature claimed by Stevens in his 1864 patent. Listed in Stevens catalogs as Old Model Pocket Pistol following introduction of Gem Model. Usual finishes are full nickel or nickel frame with blue barrel.

This model was introduced in 1864 and shown in patent description. It was discontinued in 1888 when replaced by Single-Shot Pistol.

Single-Shot Pistol — Identical to Pocket Pistol model except that barrel spring was replaced by a linkage which operates extractor when the barrel is manually tipped up. Barrel elevating spring design patented by Stevens proved weak in use and few pistols are found with spring intact.

Introduced in 1888 as improved version of the Pocket Pistol, the Single-Shot Pistol was discontinued in 1898 when replaced by Tip-Up No. 41.

Tip-Up No. 41—The only tip-up model so designated by Stevens. Similar to Single-Shot Pistol model, but with firing pin mounted in frame; flat hammer nose; larger mushroom-shaped stud on the barrel release, and a frame groove for use as rear sight. This model was first made in cals. .22 short and .30 short rimfire. After 1903 it was avail-

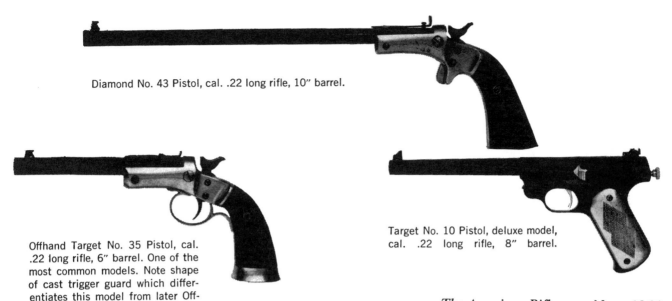

Diamond No. 43 Pistol, cal. .22 long rifle, 10″ barrel.

Offhand Target No. 35 Pistol, cal. .22 long rifle, 6″ barrel. One of the most common models. Note shape of cast trigger guard which differentiates this model from later Offhand No. 35 model.

Target No. 10 Pistol, deluxe model, cal. .22 long rifle, 8″ barrel.

The American Rifleman, Nov., 1966

able in cal. .22 short only. The last Stevens pocket model, it was introduced in 1898 and discontinued in 1916.

Later production of the Single-Shot Pistol also had larger stud on the barrel release.

Gem Pistol—Small birdshead grip derringer similar to Marlin OK model. Cals. .22 short and .30 short rimfire. Three-inch barrel swings to side to load. Usual finish is full nickel.

Introduced about 1872, it was only model to depart from tip-up barrel design, and was discontinued in 1890.

THE TARGET MODELS

Lord No. 36—Only Stevens pistol made on heavy Hunter's Pet frame, it was first offered in cal. .22 short rimfire only, later in .22 long rifle, .22 Stevens-Pope Armory, .22 WRF, .25 Stevens, .32 long rimfire, and .38 long Colt center-fire. Ten or 12″ barrel; spur on trigger guard for second finger; very long, heavy butt with checkered grips. Rear sight adjustable for windage and elevation until 1903, when replaced by sporting sight adjustable for elevation only. Also available with open, non-adjustable sights. Usual finish is nickel frame with blue barrel. Named for Frank Lord, who was a well-known pistol shot.

Introduced in 1880, Lord model was longest lived and most famous Stevens target pistol. Discontinued in 1911.

Conlin (1st Model)—Made on medium-weight pocket rifle frame. Cals. .22 short, .22 long, and .32 long rimfire. Spur trigger; checkered grips; 10″ and 12″ barrel lengths. Usually supplied with combination sights adjustable for elevation only, but also available with open, non-adjustable sights. Usual finish is nickel frame with blue barrel.

Introduced in 1872, this model was at first a pocket rifle, without provision

for detachable shoulder stock. Later listed as a gallery pistol, it was named about 1885 for James S. Conlin, owner of a New York shooting gallery. Discontinued in 1888 when it was replaced by Conlin No. 38 (2nd Model).

Conlin No. 38 (2nd Model)—Similar to 1st Model, but has regular trigger and trigger guard with outside finger spur. Full-adjustable target sights. Made in cals. .22 long rifle, .22 Stevens-Pope Armory, .22 WRF, .25 Stevens, .32 long rimfire, and .38 long Colt center-fire. Usual finish is nickel frame and blue barrel. Introduced in 1888 to incorporate features suggested by A. C. Gould as improvements on 1st model, it was discontinued in 1903.

Gould No. 37—Identical to Conlin 2nd Model, but without trigger guard spur. Named for A. C. Gould, author of *Modern American Pistols and Revolvers* and editor of *The Rifle,* predecessor to THE AMERICAN RIFLEMAN.

Introduced in 1890 after Gould refused to allow Conlin 2nd Model to be named for him. He objected to trigger guard spur. Discontinued in 1903.

Diamond No. 43—Made on the light pocket pistol frame. Cals. .22 short, .22 Stevens-Pope Armory, and .22 long rifle rimfire. Sheath trigger; some have checkered grips; 6″ or 10″ barrels. Available with globe front and peep rear, open front and rear, or with both types of sights. Usual finish is nickel frame and blue barrel.

Introduced in 1888, Diamond model was only Stevens target pistol made on light frame. At first considered too light for accurate shooting, it proved to be an excellent target pistol, and was discontinued in 1916.

Offhand Target No. 35—Lower priced revival of Gould model, with rear sight adjustable for elevation only; plain uncheckered grips; 6″, 8″, or 10″ barrel.

Cals. .22 short, .22 long rifle, .22 WRF, and .25 Stevens rimfire. Usual finish is nickel frame and blue barrel.

Introduced in 1907, this model was called a target pistol by Stevens, but was not meant for competitive target shooting. Discontinued in 1916.

A replica of this model has been imported in recent years.

Target No. 10—Made on a frame externally similar to an automatic pistol; 8″ barrel tips up to load when released by catch on left side of frame; cocking knob on rear of frame; full-adjustable rear sight. Cal. .22 long rifle only. Deluxe model available with blued barrel, browned frame, nickel plated trigger and barrel catch, and checkered aluminum grips. The standard model had hard rubber grips, and trigger and barrel catch were blued.

Introduced in 1920, this attempt to reenter target pistol field was not overly successful. Discontinued in 1933.

THE SPORTING MODELS

Offhand No. 35—Identical to Offhand Target No. 35 pistol except for stamped, sheet metal trigger guard used after 1929, instead of earlier cast guard. Available with 6″ or 8″ barrel in cal. .22 long rifle and, from 1923 to 1929, in .410-bore smoothbore. Usual finish is full blue. Introduced in 1923, it was postwar revival of Offhand Target No. 35 model, without the claim to target pistol status. Discontinued in 1942, this was the last Stevens pistol.

Autoshot No. 35—Offhand No. 35 model .410-bore smoothbore. Available with 8″ or 12¼″ barrel; checkered grips; shotgun bead front sight, and a groove rear sight in top of frame. Usual finish is full blue.

Introduced in 1929, and discontinued in 1934 when passage of National Firearms Act imposed $5 transfer tax. ■

J. Stevens Arms History Written 1942

In a little two-story mill at Chicopee Falls, Massachusetts, with about twenty hand-picked workers, one horse, and one wagon, Joshua Stevens (in 1864) founded the sporting arms business that bears his name.

The business was incorporated in 1886. The floor space in 1895 was 17,000 square feet with about 44 employees.

January 1, 1896, the Company came under new Man-agement and new methods; the floor space being increased to 34,000 square feet, with about 150 employees.

In 1901 it was increased to 271,000 square feet and to about 900 employees. In December, 1901, another factory of 180,000 square feet was added which increased the floor space to over ten and one-quarter acres. This plant was purchased from the Overman Wheel Company, and for a short period of time, Stevens continued to complete the assembly of bicycles in process.

Since then a new building with additional space of 85,000 square feet has been added. The Plant covered over twelve and one half acres.

In 1914, the Hill Plant of the J. Stevens Arms & Tool Company, and the Stevens-Duryea Plant, now a portion of the River Plant, were acquired by Westinghouse, who during the first world war made the Russian Rifle, producing 1,800,000 rifles during the period of 1915 to the date of the Armistice. [*Author's Note: New England Westinghouse "mysteriously" acquired the largest sporting arms company in the world for apparent political and/or profiteering motives just as Europe was about to enter a worldwide war. Many of the Russian "Nagant" 7.62mm rifles were never delivered because of distrust following the assassination of Czar Nicholas II, his family, and the fanatical Bolshevik Revolution in 1917. The World War eventually ended and military arms glutted the market. Irving Page, however, died of a heart attack while persistently trying (without success) to buy back his Stevens sporting arms company. A major fire destroyed most of the Stevens records immediately following Congressional inquiries about war-time profiteering. Draw your own conclusions*].

In 1920, Savage Arms Corporation purchased the Hill Plant from [New England] Westinghouse, and operated it as a separate company until 1936, and from that time on, it has been operated as a Division of Savage Arms Corporation.

During the years of 1926 to 1931 inclusive several small competitive firearm companies were purchased, including Page-Lewis Company, Davies-Warner Arms Corporation and the Crescent Firearms Company, such consolidation of interests representing the most complete line of firearms offered by any one manufacturer.

On February 21, 1941 Savage purchased from the Westinghouse Company buildings on the Chicopee River with a floor space of 159,451 square feet; and later in the year on August 1, 1941 [*exactly one month before the invasion of Poland*] purchased the Lamb Knitting Machine Company plant with an additional floor space of 105,000 square feet.

Both of these plants which were acquired in 1941 are used exclusively for the manufacture of the British Lee Enfield Rifle.

Stevens have been the pioneers in the development of new rifles, shotguns, and cartridges; the outstanding developments being the development of the .22 Long Rifle cartridge, .25 Stevens Rim Fire cartridge. Stevens have also been noted for the superior accuracy of their rifle barrels, having manufactured some of the finest target rifles in the world.

Stevens in its long history have manufactured various caliber small bore rifles, high power rifles, .22 caliber pistols, single barrel, double barrel shotguns, repeating shotguns, bolt action shotguns and Over and Under rifle and shotgun combination.

At the present time J. Stevens Arms Company, Division of Savage Arms Corporation have 264,451 square feet of floor space at the River Plant, and 267,104 square feet at the Hill Plant devoted practically 100% to the manufacture of small arms for military purposes. Source: **Anonymous**. Dated 11/30/42. Provided courtesy of Springfield Armory National Historic Site Archives.

Savage's calender of 1904 when the firm also sold ammunition.

THE SAVAGE HAMMERLESS RIFLE—MODEL 1895.

The illustration represents a six shot repeater rifle of light weight, having all the latest improvements, the highest type of the modern gun, after every test has been applied, both to the mechanism and ammunition. It is the production of the Savage Repeating Arms Company, manufacturers of military and sporting rifles and carbines, metallic ammunition, smokeless powder, etc., Utica, N. Y. The sectional view shows the action closed, with reference letters referring to the following parts: A, the guard lever; B, the catch on the automatic cut-off; C, the automatic cut-off; E, the breech bolt; F, the extractor; G, the automatic carrier; H, the shoulder in the receiver for engaging the end of the guard lever for locking the guard lever when the gun is fired; K, the sear; N, the hammer or firing pin; O, the main spring; P, the sear screw; R, the trigger; S, the trigger safety; U, the breeching up shoulder; V, the bolt for locking the action; Y, the indicator hole for showing the position of the firing mechanism, to show whether the rifle is cocked or uncocked.

The projecting hammer has been entirely eliminated from the gun, in which either black or smokeless powder can be used, although the gun is specially designed to use smokeless powder without dilution. Four different kinds of ammunition are provided, ranging from the expanding bullet, for large game, to the miniature lead bullet cartridge. The action is easily dismounted and assembled, a new feature being the concentric arm of the finger lever, which at all times protects the trigger from being accidentally operated. The movement of this lever is short and requires but little power. The arm is a rapid firing magazine and single loading rifle, an automatic cut-off retaining the magazine cartridge in reserve when the arm is used as a single loader, and allowing a cartridge to be fed up into the chamber when one has not been placed in the breech opening. The change from a single loader to a magazine gun is always automatic.

The Savage smokeless powder is manufactured without the use of nitroglycerine in any form, and with this powder and the small caliber metal jacketed bullet an initial velocity of over 2,000 feet a second is obtained, giving a flat trajectory and affording a point blank range up to 250 yards. The barrel is also non-fouling, and hundreds of shots may be fired without it being necessary to clear the bore.

The Savage hammerless safety guard lever repeating military rifle has been selected and recommended after exhaustive competitive tests at Creedmoor by the New York State Board of Examiners appointed by the Governor of the State to select and recommend the best type of magazine breech loading rifle for re-arming the National Guard of the State. The board, in making its report to the Governor, says: "We have also very critically examined a number of military magazine rifles in use in this country and in Europe of foreign invention, and are free to say that, in our opinion, all points considered, the Savage magazine rifle herein recommended is far superior in simplicity of construc-

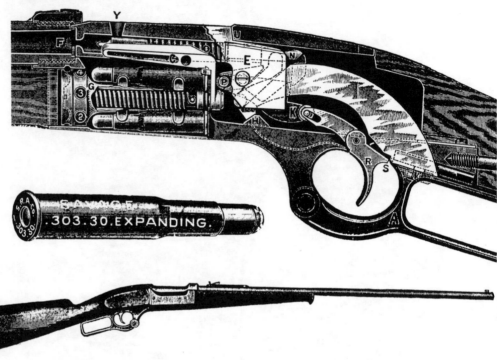

THE SAVAGE HAMMERLESS MAGAZINE RIFLE MODEL 1895.

tion, safety, durability, effectiveness, accuracy, beauty of outline, ease and certainty of manipulation, and for the double and ready use as a single loader or as a magazine gun, to any foreign magazine gun we have inspected."

SAVAGE
ARMS
Model 1895
𝔖𝔠𝔦𝔢𝔫𝔱𝔦𝔣𝔦𝔠 𝔄𝔪𝔢𝔯𝔦𝔠𝔞𝔫.

SEPTEMBER 5, 1896.

SAVAGE ARMS COMPANY,

High-Grade,		
Hammerless	Manufacturers	Metallic
Military	....of....	Ammunition,
Sporting Rifles,		Reloading
Carbines.		Tools,
		Sights, &c.

UTICA, NEW YORK, U. S. AMERICA.
...1903...

SAVAGE RIFLE, Model 1899.

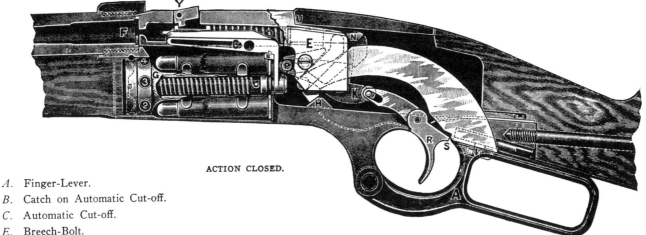

ACTION CLOSED.

A. Finger-Lever.
B. Catch on Automatic Cut-off.
C. Automatic Cut-off.
E. Breech-Bolt.
F. Extractor.
G. Magazine Carrier.
H. Projection on Receiver for Finger-Lever.
K. Sear.
N. Hammer.
O. Main Spring.

P. Sear Screw.
R. Trigger.
S. Trigger Safety Projection.
U. Recoil Shoulder.
V. Trigger and Lever Lock.
Y. Indicator.

Model Rifle 1899 is manufactured with the new hammer indicator.
When the hammer is at full cock the Indicator *Y* projects above the breech-bolt; when the rifle is fired or the hammer is down, the indicator is flush with the top of the breech-bolt.

CATALOGUE NO. 15

SAVAGE ARMS COMPANY

MANUFACTURERS OF HIGH GRADE
HAMMERLESS FIRE-ARMS

Ammunition, Reloading Tools, Sights, Etc.

Factories and Home Office: UTICA, NEW YORK, U.S.A.

London Office and Warehouse:
13-15 WILSON ST., LONDON, E. C.

Continental Warehouse:
6 PICKHUBEN, HAMBURG, GERMANY.

SPECIAL NOTICE — Terms and Instructions

All prices in this catalogue are net cash. We do not quote discounts, except to dealers in actual trade.

Goods never sent on approval.

Prices subject to change without notice.

All goods sent to us must be pre-paid to Utica, N. Y., and plainly marked with sender's name and address.

All goods shipped by us will be securely packed ; but our responsibility ceases when shipment is receipted for by transportation company.

When no specific shipping instructions are given, we reserve the right to ship by the quickest or cheapest method for our patrons.

Cash in full must accompany all orders for parts or repairs, otherwise same will be sent C. O. D., in which case there will be additional charges for return of money.

Sights, parts, and all small accessories not exceeding forty-eight ounces in weight, may be sent by mail, pre-paid, at the rate of one cent per ounce, to any address in the United States, Mexico, Canada and all U. S. Possessions.

Loaded cartridges, primed shells, powder, oils, primers and all explosives are prohibited from the mails.

SAVAGE ARMS CO., UTICA, N.Y. U.S.A.

Savage Hammerless Sporting Rifle

There is a particular excellence of workmanship, material and finish on all Savage rifles and the 303 is this same "Savage Quality" all through. Remember these facts when the hunting fever comes.

For shooting in the Rockies, the Northwest, Canada, Newfoundland, Maine, etc., and wherever big game abounds, the 303 Savage is the gun to pin your faith to. Ask the most successful big game hunters. It is sold by the makers under an honest guarantee.

Model 1899 — Six Shot Repeater — 303 Caliber

SPECIFICATIONS	Price	Caliber	Weight	Code
26 inch Octagon Barrel Rifle, six shots	$21.50	303	8 lbs.	Bait
26 " Round Barrel Rifle, six shots	20.00	303	7½ lbs.	Abate
26 " Half Octagon Barrel Rifle, six shots	21.50	303	7 lbs. 12 oz.	Cub

Furnished with any of the extras on page 35

THE rifle illustrated above is, without doubt, the best and most popular big game arm ever built. In fact, this 303 repeater has been used with the greatest success in nearly every country of the world on all kinds of dangerous game and under the hardest sort of shooting conditions. Preeminently it stands in a class by itself. The tight fit of the metal-cased bullets gives increased velocity and accuracy and, at the same time, the soft-nosed load mushrooms in the most perfect manner. The bullets instantly expand on striking flesh alone. When you consider the fact that the 303 Savage has greater killing power at 150 yards than the 45-90, some idea of its deadly hitting force is unmistakably evident. Moreover, the arm itself is light in weight, has slight recoil, and is capable of grouping shots in a five-inch circle at 200 yards. Its accurate range is 1000 yards. Furnished with steel or rubber shot gun butt plate without extra charge. Pistol grip, $2.50 additional.

SAVAGE ARMS CO., UTICA, N.Y. U.S.A.

Savage Rifle (MODEL 1899)

ACTION CLOSED

ACTION OPEN

A Finger-Lever
B Catch on Automatic Cut-off
C Automatic Cut-off
E Breech-Bolt
F Extractor
G Magazine Carrier
H Projection on Receiver for Finger-Lever
K Sear
N Hammer
O Main Spring
P Sear Screw
R Trigger
S Trigger Safety Projection
U Recoil Shoulder
V Trigger and Lever Lock
Y Indicator

A Finger-Lever
B Catch on Automatic Cut-off
C Automatic Cut-off
D Breech-Opening
E Breech-Bolt
G Magazine Carrier
H Projection on Receiver for Finger-Lever
K Sear
L Retractor
N Hammer
P Sear Screw
R Trigger
S Trigger Safety Projection
U Recoil Shoulder
V Trigger and Lever Lock

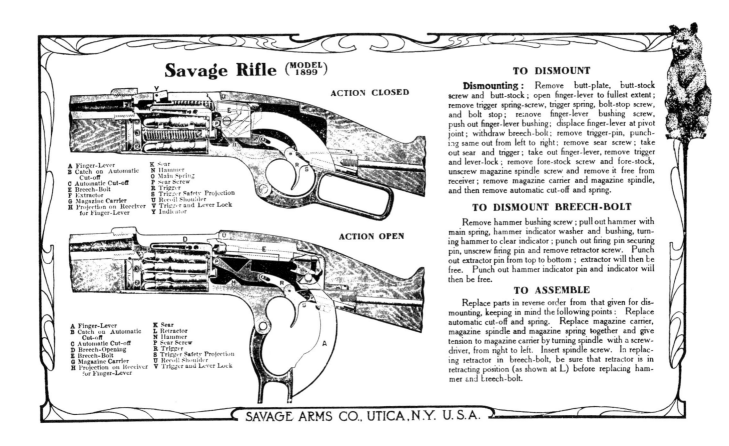

TO DISMOUNT

Dismounting : Remove butt-plate, butt-stock screw and butt-stock ; open finger-lever to fullest extent ; remove trigger spring-screw, trigger spring, bolt-stop screw, and bolt stop ; remove finger-lever bushing screw, push out finger-lever bushing ; displace finger-lever at pivot joint ; withdraw breech-bolt ; remove trigger-pin, punching same out from left to right ; remove sear screw ; take out sear and trigger ; take out finger-lever, remove trigger and lever-lock ; remove fore-stock screw and fore-stock, unscrew magazine spindle screw and remove it free from receiver ; remove magazine carrier and magazine spindle, and then remove automatic cut-off and spring.

TO DISMOUNT BREECH-BOLT

Remove hammer bushing screw ; pull out hammer with main spring, hammer indicator washer and bushing, turning hammer to clear indicator ; punch out firing pin securing pin, unscrew firing pin and remove retractor screw. Punch out extractor pin from top to bottom ; extractor will then be free. Punch out hammer indicator pin and indicator will then be free.

TO ASSEMBLE

Replace parts in reverse order from that given for dismounting, keeping in mind the following points : Replace automatic cut-off and spring. Replace magazine carrier, magazine spindle and magazine spring together and give tension to magazine carrier by turning spindle with a screw-driver, from right to left. Insert spindle screw. In replacing retractor in breech-bolt, be sure that retractor is in retracting position (as shown at L) before replacing hammer and breech-bolt.

SAVAGE ARMS CO., UTICA, N.Y. U.S.A.

Savage Hammerless Sporting Rifle (MODEL 1899)

TO load the magazine throw down Finger-Lever and insert cartridges into the magazine by pushing them (heads to rear) down and under the Catch B on Automatic Cut-off C. The capacity of the magazine is five cartridges. A sixth cartridge can be placed in the Breech-Opening above the Catch B. On closing the Finger-Lever the cartridge in the Breech-Opening will be carried forward by the Breech-Bolt into the chamber of the barrel. The rifle is then ready to fire. If it is desired to have the cartridges in the magazine and none in the chamber of the barrel, load one or more cartridges into the magazine, press with the finger of the left hand the Automatic Cut-off back into its recess, keeping it back while the Finger-Lever operates the Breech-Bolt forward and beyond the point of engagement with the cartridge head in the magazine.

THE RIFLE AS A SINGLE-LOADER

The act of placing a cartridge into the Breech-Opening forces the Automatic Cut-off back into its recess in the Receiver, retiring the uppermost cartridge in the magazine below the line of movement of the Breech-Bolt, so that only the cartridge in the breech-opening will be engaged by the breech-bolt on its forward travel. If the operator does not place a cartridge in the Breech-Opening, and there are one or more cartridges in the magazine, the Breech-Bolt on its forward travel will engage and carry forward into the barrel chamber the uppermost cartridge in the magazine. The firing mechanism can be placed in an uncocked position by holding back the Trigger R while closing the Finger-Lever A. The Hammer N will in that case pass over and not engage with the face of the Sear K. This should always be done when laying the rifle aside, and the trigger should not be snapped when the chamber of the barrel is empty. If the rifle is cocked and a cartridge is in the barrel chamber, open the lever about two inches (until a sharp click is heard), hold back trigger, as described above, and the mechanism is uncocked. In this case it is not necessary to throw out the cartridge of the chamber. The action can be locked by pushing forward the Lock V, which locks the trigger and lever. The Indicator Y shows the position of the firing mechanism.

SAVAGE ARMS CO., UTICA, N.Y. U.S.A.

WHEN Arthur W. Savage came west it was not to grow up with the country. He had already achieved fame and fortune through a capacity for the grinding sort of work upon which the average captain of industry thrives. He had earned the right to retreat from the ranks of Tired Business Men; to settle down and play with his two hobby-horses in a pleasant pasture. These hobbies were the harmless ones of oil-painting and gardening. Why not a San Diego pasture? Having roamed the world around and sampled every brand of climate, it was Savage's conviction that San Diego, though not the site of the original Garden of Eden, was its modern prototype; the very spot in which to train eight younger Savages of assorted ages in the paths in which a double-quartet family should go. So he established a San Diego home, acquired the garden of his dreams, laid in a supply of canvases for hours of ease at an easel—and then what happened?

He reënlisted in the ranks of Tired Business Men, literally; for did he not make a big dent in the San Diego scenery by erecting therein and thereupon a factory—the biggest of its kind in California—for the tired vehicles upon which the business man daily depends? What Westerner has not met, face to face, the Indian trade-mark of tire familiarity smiling from billboard pillar to post? The Savage Tire Company of San Diego has been so much of a commercial success that its founder has "started something" else to keep it company in the industrial development of San Diego, and a plant will soon be built for the A. J. Savage Munitions Company, recently incorporated. More attractive offers for the location of this factory were made in the East than could be offered here, but it is Savage's belief that "a man's business should be where he lives." The story of this interesting adopted-Westerner's life is forged in the foundry of fiery endeavor, hammered in the school of hard knocks, riveted and bolted by the forces of a persistent will. The arms and the man have had a co-related success. It is not of record that the infant Arthur, sixty years ago the newest arrival on the island of Jamaica in the West Indies, tossed away his first rattle with intuitive contempt and wailed, not for a slice of the West Indies moon but for a Johnny-get-your-gun type of toy; neither do we know that his first lisp was for a mechanically-perfect miniature railroad train or that his first tooth was sharpened upon a cartridge, but here are a few Savage facts:

Born on the other side of the globe in 1857, young Arthur was educated in England and in the public schools of Baltimore, Maryland. For more than thirty years he has been a regular American in legal citizenship. Before declaring allegiance to Uncle Sam he traveled extensively, a soldier of fortune, ever in quest of business adventure and ever making good. In the West Indies he was a coffee planter. In Australia he became a cattleman. While at the antipodes he helped organize cavalry during the trouble then pending between France and England over New Caledonia. This task completed, he came to the United States to live permanently.

He managed the railroad that ran from Rome to Schenectady, now a part of the New York Central system, and he built the Saratoga Electric roads. Later he established the Savage Arms Company in Utica and built up one of the greatest firearms enterprises in the country. Where is there a Westerner who does not know and respect the Savage rifle? Over twenty different types of guns have been marketed by this company. The first hammerless repeating rifle and the first sporting smokeless cartridges came from the fertile brain of this man.

Nor has Arthur W. Savage's ingenuity stopped with guns. He invented the Savage Dirigible Torpedo which was used with telling effect by Brazil in its war of rebellion. The present widely used method of drying wool, and machines for the decortication of fiber, were devised by him. The Savage Steel Pneumatic Tire and the process of making the Grafinite inner tubes are among his contributions to the rubber industry.

Yet in his diversions Arthur Savage went as far from bullets and gun powder as he could get, and it was the opportunity to ride his twin hobbies three hundred and sixty-five days in the year that induced him to select San Diego as his home. The famous San Diego brand of tempered sunshine enabled him to try out new varieties of flowers and shrubs regardless of the seasons, and the Italian scenery surrounding his new home constantly tempted him into the open air with brush and palette. Like many others he came to San Diego to rest and retire; having rested, the climate and his boundless energy led him once more to resume his career as a builder. But those who know him best declare that he would rather discover a new flower than invent a new type of gun.   F. W. P.

In the West Indies a coffee planter; in Australia a cattleman; in California he is the A. W. Savage of tire and munitions fame

SAVAGE ARMS COMPANY

Historical Summary

Savage Repeating Arms Co.	1893-1897
Savage Arms Company *	1897-1917
* Driggs-Seabury Corporation	1915-1917
Savage Arms Corporation **	1917-1981
**A Division of Emhart Corp.	1945-1981
Savage Industries, Inc.	1981-1988
Savage Arms, Inc. (See Appendix A)	1988 +

First Savage Rifle

The Savage Model 1895 Lever Action Repeating Rifle was made from 1895 to 1899. A total of approximately five thousand rifles were manufactured for Arthur Savage by the Marlin Firearms Company of New Haven, Connecticut. The contour and basic action of the Model 1895 was very similar to its modified successor, the classic Model 1899.

Arthur W. Savage

In contrast to Joshua Stevens, a pioneer in breech-loading firearms as well as caustic black gunpowders, Arthur Savage pioneered the more powerful and less caustic smokeless gunpowders. He was able to start manufacturing firearms without all of the "old tooling" of the earlier firearms technology. Also, in contrast to specialized single-shots, Arthur Savage was able to focus his attention on hammerless repeating arms with the intent of producing a desirable and powerful, large game weapon.

On April 5, 1894, Arthur Savage founded the Savage Repeating Arms Company in Utica, New York, with the intent of manufacturing and marketing the lever action Model 1895. In time the new company offered single-shots, repeaters and auto

loading .22 calibers. Eventually, Savage Arms offered repeating shotguns such as the Model 21 and automatic pistols manufactured in .32 and .380 caliber in the semi-hammerless style. Faced with a challenge, the company introduced a .45 caliber auto pistol and attempted to win acceptance by the U.S. Army. However, after failing the cement mixer test (long hours of tumbling in wet cement) the .45 auto failed because of the quality of its precision design. It was simply machined too tight for such improbable abuse. The long and cruel tests favored the loosely machined and therefore much less accurate Colt .45. A few of these high quality, prototype autos remain in existence and are highly prized by Savage auto collectors.

Arthur Savage, firearms enthusiast and inventor, conceived of a distinctly different type of high powered repeating rifle. He had already accumulated enough working capital through the sale of Australia's largest cattle ranch to launch both the manufacture and marketing of his technically sound ideas on a broad scale. Starting out in Utica, New York and incorporated under West Virginia laws, the company remained in that location until 1946. Effective December 16, 1897, before the production of a prototype firearm could be accomplished, the business was re-incorporated under the New York state laws as the Savage Arms Company. The company prospered under this arrangement until being sold during the European war year of 1915.

War Years

In August, 1915, the Driggs-Seabury Ordnance Company of Sharon, Pennsylvania bought the business outright and formed a war material company known as the Driggs-Seabury Corporation. By June 1, 1917, the corporate name was changed to Savage Arms Corporation. The war years had done much to familiarize shooters with bolt actions. Savage Arms was in a position to take advantage of this trend among small, medium and high caliber rifles. The Model 20 therefore became one of the most popular bolt action rifles within this category.

Post-war Growth

Early in 1920 Savage Arms acquired all of the outstanding capital stock of the J. Stevens Arms Company and became the sole owners and operators of that large, famous and then 56 year old company. For the next sixteen years Stevens Arms was operated as a wholly owned subsidiary of Savage Arms. On January 2, 1936, Stevens Arms was entirely absorbed and made a division of Savage Arms Corporation.

In 1926 Savage Arms acquired the Page-Lewis Company of Chicopee Falls, Massachusetts (manufacturers of .22 caliber rifles) and transported all of their activities to the nearby Stevens' facilities. By 1930 Savage Arms was able to acquire the A. H. Fox Gun Company of Philadelphia. All equipment for the manufacture of premium grade shotguns was moved to Utica, New York. Likewise, in May, 1930, Savage Arms acquired the assets of Davis-Warner Arms Corporation of Norwich, Connecticut. About seven months later in January, 1931, all

assets of another Norwich, Connecticut manufacturer, Crescent Firearms Company, was acquired. These two companies were organized as the Crescent-Davis Arms Corporation and was handled as a wholly owned subsidiary of the J. Stevens Arms Company but still located in Norwich, Connecticut. This composite company was dissolved during the depths of the Great Depression, November, 1935. All equipment was relocated to the Stevens' facilities and manufacture essentially continued under Stevens' established procedures and guidelines.

In addition to rifles, shotguns and automatic pistols, the Savage Arms Corporation has periodically produced other related products including sights, metallic ammunition, smokeless gunpowder (believed actually produced by DuPont, 1907), reloading tools, etc. The dominant and most successful product for most of its continuing history has been the Model 99 (the original name of Model 1899 was shortened to the popular Model 99 in 1922). This distinctive, lever action, high power rifle remains in demand and production to this date.

History of Arthur William Savage

by
James R. Carr, *Savage Automatic Pistols*
St. Charles, IL c. 1950

Arthur William Savage, the founder of the Savage Arms Company, was born in Kingston, Jamaica in 1857. He received his education in England and became an artist on the staff of the *London Graphic*.

However, the yearn for adventure brought him to Australia in search of black opals. Captured by the natives, he lived an extraordinary two years with them before returning to civilization. While in Australia he raised cattle and started a family. At 34 he returned to Jamaica to become a coffee planter. It was here that he first became interested in firearm design. His first venture, to improve the British service rifle, was a success and while in New York, he sold his invention. Shortly afterward he was hired to manage the Rome to Schenectady railroad. His interest in firearms remained.

In 1894 the Savage Arms Company was formed to manufacture a hammerless lever-action-repeating-high-power rifle invented by Arthur W. Savage.

He managed the firm until 1911 and in 1912 moved to San Diego *[to start a tire factory]*. The Driggs-Seabury Ordnance Company was merged with the Savage Arms Company in 1915 and after WWI the company was reorganized as The Savage Arms Corporation.

His industrial genius was put to use in San Diego where he became the first manufacturer of tires west of the Mississippi. He continued with his inventions but his love for art and paintings occupied most of his time in his later years.

On Sept. 22, 1938, Arthur W. Savage took his life after a long and painful illness.

Like many of the great American men, his industrial and inventive ability gave this country impetus to become the industrial giant of the world.

Birth of the Savage Auto Pistol
by James R. Carr

Shortly after the turn of the century, Elbert Hamilton Searle began experimenting with the development of automatic pistols. Application for his first patent No. 804984 was filed November 25, 1903 and granted November 21, 1905. This was to be the forerunner of the Savage Automatic Pistol.

William Condit, who was in the investment business in Philadelphia, Pennsylvania was assigned three-quarters of the rights to the patent. He evidently was Searle's financial backer and probably was responsible for selling Searle's pistol to the Savage people. (The exact relationship between Searle, Condit and Savage has not been clearly established at this writing).

A specimen of this first pistol is not known to this author [Carr] but is believed to be in a .45 caliber.

What spurred Mr. Searle to work on designs of automatic pistols is not known but it is likely that Colt's work in this field was certainly a factor.

Several months after Searle's patent was granted the Unites States Government asked various manufacturers to submit pistols for test trials for adoption by the military.

It was about this time that Savage became interested in Searle's pistol or vice-versa as Searle needed a manufacturer to produce his gun. In any event after several delays the tests finally were held in January of 1907. The Savage .45's had evolved to patent No. 936369 applied for on April 25, 1907 and granted October 12, 1909. It will be further noted that this pistol, except for minor changes, closely resembles the pocket pistol which was introduced in 1908.

Some of the objections of the board were that both pistols had defective side ejection, no chamber load indicator and no automatic safety. Both Savage and Colt were requested to produce, with the noted changes, 200 pistols to be issued to the Cavalry. Savage did not agree to produce the pistols until the later part of that year. These 200 plus, pistols were tested by the Cavalry in 1908 and 1909. This pistol has been called by many names and this author will designate the pistol—the .45 Savage Automatic Pistol 1907 Military Contract.

Further modifications were made in the pistols after their failure in 1908 and 1909.

On March 3, 1911, the Board Officers convened for the testing of Colt's and Savage's improved pistols.

The greatest moment in American Automatic Pistol History had arrived—Colt won; Savage lost. The Savage .45 automatic never appeared again in either the Military or Commercial model. Most of the Savage .45's that exist today are the ones tested by the Cavalry. There were probably 300 Savage .45 Caliber automatics made—this included all of the prototypes that were not serialized.

James R. Carr

Note: The **A.J. Savage Munitions Company** in 1919 was located in a four-story structure at 326 West Market (corner of State & Market Streets) San Diego, Calif. Also, for a description of Model 99 variations from 1899 to 1970 see the following article: **"Savage 99**: Neglected Historical Notes" by Richard Hummel, *The Rifle Magazine*, May-June, 1971.

Savage Innovations

Savage Arms was quick to utilize technical advances in both smokeless gunpowders and cartridge design. The company introduced the .22 High Power (now obsolete), the .250/3000 cartridge (at one time boasted the astonishing velocity of 3,000 feet per second), the famous .300 Savage and .303 Savage. Much of the ballistic development and promotion was forced on Savage Arms to counter fierce competition from the .30 caliber Winchesters. Almost simultaneously Savage Arms began diversifying their lines of high power and .22 caliber rifles, auto pistols and eventually introduced repeating and auto shotguns.

After acquiring the J. Stevens Arms Company and others, Savage Arms could rightfully claim to be manufacturers of the widest variety of sporting arms in the world. Also, in addition to firearms, Savage also produced ammunition but soon discontinued the practice in favor of subcontracting ammo which carried the Savage brand name.

The Savage Arms Corporation has consistently maintained an active and experimental ballistics testing program. Mammoth size and creative management has allowed Savage Arms to remain actively experimental in product design, innovation and safety. Each gun is always subjected to rigid inspection and testing before leaving the plant. Savage Arms have an excellent history for being nearly trouble-free, well constructed, balanced, reliable and reasonably priced. The legacy of good design and fine craftsmanship (on a much reduced scale) continues to this date. Officially, Savage Arms will acknowledge its one hundredth anniversary beginning in 1994 (See: *Savage Reaches for Its Centennial*).

Special thanks are offered to the corporate officers within the company today and retired company historian, Mr. Roe S. Clark for assistance in providing factual, historical information and of consenting to review this book for technical accuracy prior to distinctly revised third printing. •

By David O. Moreton

The Savage Story

"To most hunters, Savage means the Model 99, but
Arthur Savage was also a remarkable man."

Historically, the United States has either spawned or attracted the truly great geniuses of firearms invention and design throughout the years. Most of these individuals were usually adventuresome extroverts with a flamboyancy typical of their era.

In many instances their early lives were in themselves adventures of the first magnitude. For example, Arthur William Savage was born on May 13, 1857 in Kingston, Jamaica, British West Indies. His father, a native of Wales, was Special Commissioner from England to the West Indies, whose duty it was to organize and set up an educational system for newly freed slaves. Arthur Savage received the classic education which his family's social station dictated. He showed an inquisitive intelligent, practical approach to problems without a reliance on books. After attending and completing his education in public schools in Baltimore, Md. and in England, his curious nature asserted itself by extensive travel and exploration.

He led a very nomadic life, the high point reached when, in his thirties, he went to Australia, exploring the interior in a covered wagon. He was married in Australia in 1878 to Annie Bryant. This union produced eight children—four boys and four girls. Arthur John Savage was born in the covered wagon. At one time the senior Savage was captured and held prisoner for nearly a year by Australian aborigines before escaping. Sources report that he eventually became owner or manager of Australia's largest cattle ranch.

After eleven years 'down under' he sold the ranch and returned to Jamaica where he purchased and managed a coffee plantation. It was at this time that he developed a remarkable talent and genius for invention. It was in the field of inven-

Arthur William Savage in his heyday as a prolific inventor and producer of guns.

tion that he and his son Arthur John were to become famous.

One of the Savages' better known inventions was the Savage-Halpine torpedo, designed and developed in collaboration with Halpine. The torpedo was very successful in its day and was eventually adopted by the Brazilian Navy. Prior to this, the U.S. Navy tested it and was profoundly impressed, seriously considering its adoption. But as the story goes, political considerations got in the way of naval authorities. Later in his career, Savage pioneered in the development of another military weapon for which he has never received recognition—the recoiless rifle.

Eventually Arthur W. Savage moved his family to Utica, New York where for a time he was manager/superintendent of the Utica Belt Line Railroad, and was also connected with the Utica Magazine Hammer Company. It was during this period that he became convinced that there was a prosperous future for someone who could establish a progressive sporting arms

company to compete with the already well established Colt, Remington and Winchester companies.

To this end the design of a revolutionary new rifle took precedence over the various machines and appliances which were advancing his reputation as an inventor. Savage was sure the new rifle would have to be designed around a cartridge loaded with what was then the new smokeless powder. Development work was carried out in his home workshop during spare time.

It was in 1893 that Arthur W. Savage at age 36 patented his lever action rifle and during that year and the one following he organized the Savage Arms Company in Utica. The new gun was named the Model 1895 for the year the fledgling company went into production. Initial production took place in rented quarters on Hubbell St. in Utica. The rifle was very different from other lever actions of the day. It was "streamlined", truly a hammerless design; the entire mechanism was enclosed within the steel receiver. The Savage was the first to use a coil mainspring and employed a firing mechanism similar in some respects to a conventional bolt action.

Probably the most important innovation introduced with the Model 1895 was the rotary magazine which permitted the use of pointed bullets for the first time in a lever action. Logically, the use of pointed bullets was unsafe in the tubular magazine because the point rests on the primer of the cartridge in front of it. Recoil could cause accidental firing under certain conditions. Additional advantages of the rotary or spool magazine were elemination of the magazine tube under the barrel which affects accuracy, and a cartridge counter to tell the shooter how many cartridges remained in the five shot magazine.

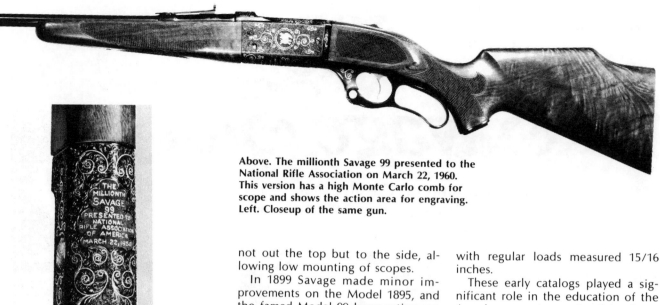

Above. The millionth Savage 99 presented to the National Rifle Association on March 22, 1960. This version has a high Monte Carlo comb for scope and shows the action area for engraving. Left. Closeup of the same gun.

not out the top but to the side, allowing low mounting of scopes.

In 1899 Savage made minor improvements on the Model 1895, and the famed Model 99 lever action we know today came into being and has remained much the same since then.

As was the vogue in the late 1800's and early 1900's, the struggling Savage Arms Company made considerable use of testimonial letters in their catalogs of the early twentieth century—all expounding the virtues of the Savage .303 cartridge. Included were reproductions of targets: one showed a ten shot group fired with a lead bullet miniature—a cartridge designed for short ranges and places where it would be unsafe to fire full charges. These loads used 6 grains of powder and a 100 grain bullet, compared to 22 grain powder charge and 180 or 185 grain bullet of standard load. The group fired with the so-called miniature load measured 1-5/8 inches while a ten shot group at 100 yards

with regular loads measured 15/16 inches.

These early catalogs played a significant role in the education of the American sportsman to the advantages of smokeless powder sighting such as a reduction in recoil, high velocity, and less fouling of the rifle bore. The targets mentioned attested to the accuracy potential of smokeless powder loads.

The testimonial letters further solidified the Savage Model 99's position with reports of single shot kills using the Savage .303 cartridge, on every species of game from coyote to whale. By the year 1903 the Model 99 was available in .25-35, .32-40, .83-55, .30-30 and .303 calibers. The Model 99 was produced with a full octagon, half octagon or round barrel, as a take down rifle, a full rifle, a carbine and full length stocked military rifle.

In 1902 the company's first buildings were erected in the eastern part of Utica on Turner Street and extended east into the town of Frankfort. The property consisted of 35 acres and eventually had floor space of approximately 700,000 square feet.

In 1904 A. W. Savage sold out his interests in the Savage Arms Company to a group of Utica businessmen and moved to San Diego, California where he and his son Arthur John established the Savage Tire Company, which was relatively successful, employing at one time 2000 people. At the same time, Arthur John set up a small gun factory which later failed due to problems in the issuing of capital stock.

The two Savages then bought large citrus groves in California, to fair success. In the early thirties, the elder Savage sold his groves and turned to drilling two oil wells which ran dry. Apparently both Savages suffered large financial setbacks, but, undaunted, took up gold

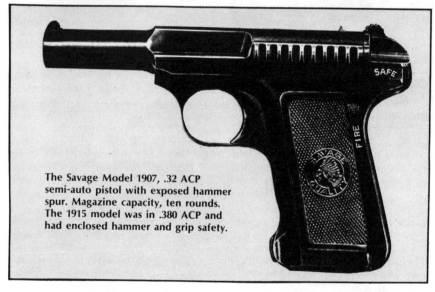

The Savage Model 1907, .32 ACP semi-auto pistol with exposed hammer spur. Magazine capacity, ten rounds. The 1915 model was in .380 ACP and had enclosed hammer and grip safety.

Other innovations included a through-bolt mounting of the stock to the action, a far superior method which was more rigid than designs using the tang mounting means. Also, the rifle could be fired as a single shot with either a full or empty magazine. Empty, the shooter drops a round into the loading port and closes the action. With the magazine full the shooter repeats the aforementioned procedure but holds the cartridge down against an automatic cutoff and closes the action.

Another feature to influence future purchasers when the use of scopes became popular was side ejection. Fired shells were ejected

The Savage Story

mining in Northern California. Although the gold was in the mine, so was water, rising faster than any pump could handle. This was also abondoned after substantial loss. By this time Arthur W. was in his early 80's, failing in health. He turned to writing his memoirs. He died soon after starting, at the age of 84.

His son Arthur J. Savage continued his efforts in design and development of firearms. While A.J. was not the extrovert his father had been, he

last of which was a 15 shot .22 autoloading rifle. At the time it had a profitable estimated retail price of $15, due to minimal machine operations. Failing health prevented pursuit of this last Savage design, and on his death in 1953 the project died with him.

With the introduction of the improved version of the Model 1895 in 1899 the Savage Arms Company proceeded to expand its line of sporting arms and introduced its slide action and single shot bolt action .22's in 1903. These were followed in 1907 by the Savage Automatic pistol in .380 and .32 calibers in both military and civilian models.

While Arthur J Savage was reput-

By 1914 made in .32 and .380 calibers. Available with spur cocking lever.

In 1915 made in .32 only.

Discontinued in 1916.

Model 1915—Similar to M/1907 but hammerless and had a grip safety., .32 or .380 calibers.

Model 1917—Return to cocking spur. No grip safety.

Discontinued about 1925.

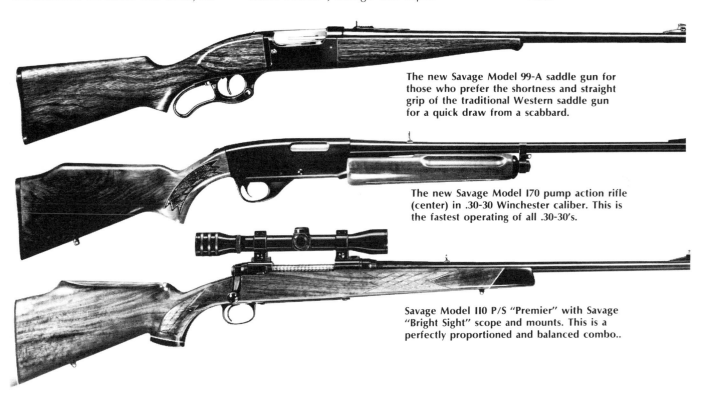

The new Savage Model 99-A saddle gun for those who prefer the shortness and straight grip of the traditional Western saddle gun for a quick draw from a scabbard.

The new Savage Model 170 pump action rifle (center) in .30-30 Winchester caliber. This is the fastest operating of all .30-30's.

Savage Model 110 P/S "Premier" with Savage "Bright Sight" scope and mounts. This is a perfectly proportioned and balanced combo..

was considered one of the really expert technicians behind the scenes. He is judged to be responsible for devlopment of the first Savage slide action .22, forerunner of the Model 29. He apparently also worked on the original bolt action single shot, and made modifications on it and the slide action. He was reputedly the principal designer of the Savage automatic pistol, and did other work on the early Savage pump shotguns.

After his father's death A.J. Savage retired to working in his own laboratory, which was completely equipped: full size barrel drilling machine, stock shaper, a rifling machine, three conventional lathes of varying sizes, and a milling machine. Following in his father's footsteps, A.J. developed a number of .22's, the

edly the principal designer of the Savage Automatic, the credit for the design as given and the patent issued went to Major Elbert Hamilton Searle, a former ordnance officer of the Springfield armory. Three models were produced, the Model 07, 15, and 17 with a number of minor variations. According to early Savage literature, the Savage automatic was adopted as the official service pistol of the Army of Portugal.

Serial number data on the Savage automatic is as follows, with some pertinent model modification information:

Model 1907—Introduced about 1907. .32 caliber only. Had exposed cocking spur. 10 shot clip.

MODEL 07–15–17 .32 caliber pistol		
1908-1909	1 to	10,000
1909-1910	10,000	20,000
1910	20,000	30,000
1910-1911	30,000	40,000
1911-1912	40,000	50,000
1912	50,000	60,000
1912	60,000	70,000
1912-1913	70,000	80,000
1913	80,000	90,000
1913-1914	90,000	100,000
1914	100,000	110,000
1914-1915	110,000	120,000
1915	120,000	125,000
1915	125,000	130,000
1915-1916	130,000	136,520
	136,520	150,000(omitted)
1915-1916	150,000	160,000
1916-1917	160,000	170,000
1917	170,000	180,000

1917-1919	180,000	190,000
1919	190,000	200,000
1919	200,000	220,000
1919-1920	220,000	230,000
1920	230,000	240,000
1920-1922	240,000	246,020
	246,020	246,620(omitted)
1922-1926	246,621	256,000

MODEL 07—15—17
.380 Caliber Pistol

1913	2000 to	4000
1913-1914	4000	6000
1913-1914		
1915	6000	8000
1914-1915	8000	10,000
1915-1916	10,000	12,000
1915-1916		
1917-1919	12,000	14,000
1919-1920	14,000	16,000
1920	16,000	20,000
1920-1921	20,000	22,000
1920-1921		
1922-1923	22,000	24,000
1923-1924		
1925	24,000	25,242
	25,243	26,000(omitted)
1925-1926		
1927	26,000	28,000
1927-1928	28,000	29,699
	29,670	29,861(omitted)

With the advent of World War I in 1914, the arms companies of the United States expanded their facilities and in 1915 the stock of the Savage Arms Company was purchased by Driggs—Seabury Ordnance Company and the name was changed to Savage Arms Corporation in 1919. Plant facilities and equipment were greatly expanded during the first world war as a result of large orders for gas-operated drum-magazine type air-cooled, Lewis Machineguns placed with Savage by the United States, British and Canadian governments. Savage manufactured over 70,000 such guns and established a training school for the U.S. Marine Corps., giving instructions in the use of Lewis Machineguns. A plant in Pennsylvania produced large quantities of 6 inch shells, 3 inch and 6 pounder guns, gun mounts, truck frames and other military equipment.

In 1920, the J. Stevens Arms and Tool Company of Chicopee Falls, Mass. was bought from the Westinghouse Electric and Manufacturing Company. This well known sporting arms company was founded in 1864 by Joshua S. Stevens and had developed a splendid reputation for the quality of its rifles and shotguns. During World War I its facilities had been used for the manufacture of Browning Machineguns under Westinghouse ownership. Incidentally, it was in the Stevens plant that one of the first automobiles was made in America. Called the Stevens-Duryea (Duryea for the designer), it was another first in the history of Savage—Stevens. The business was a wholly owned subsidiary later merged with Savage Arms Corporation, with brands still produced under the Stevens name.

The assets of several other firearms manufacturing companies were also acquired in the intervening years. These included the Page-Lewis Company, the Davis-Warner Company, The Crescent Firearms Company and the A.H. Fox Gun Company in 1929. The acquisition of these companies greatly strengthened the corporation position in domestic and foreign markets, making the Savage Arms Corporation one of the leaders in the sporting arms industry. Its line included all popular models used in this country and in the export markets.

When the world war I ended, Savage had resumed manufacture of sporting arms and high power rifle and pistol cartridges, and also engaged in the manufacture of a broad scope of machines and appliances. However, by the beginning of World War II, Savage manufacturing activities were principally reduced to sporting arms and ice cream cabinets.

In 1939, Savage was approached by the Auto-Ordnance Corporation regarding the manufacture of

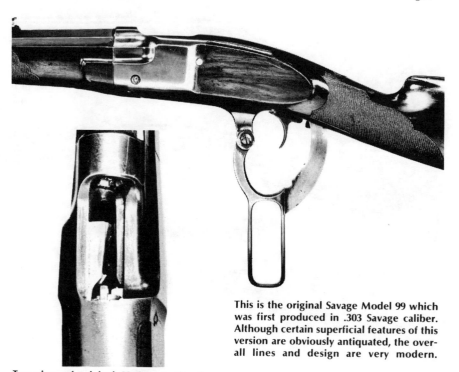

This is the original Savage Model 99 which was first produced in .303 Savage caliber. Although certain superficial features of this version are obviously antiquated, the overall lines and design are very modern.

Top view of original 99 Savage showing follower of rotary magazine and ejector.

Thompson .45 caliber submachine guns. An initial order for 10,000 guns was signed on December 15, 1939. Auto-Ordnance made its tools available to Savage and preparations were quickly made for production. The first submachine guns were completed in four months and large additional orders were placed. A maximum monthly production of 55,000 guns with numerous spare parts was attained. The manufacture of Thompson submachine guns was terminated in early 1944, after approximately 1,250,000 submachine guns and tremendous quantities of spare parts had been made.

On September 6, 1940 Savage entered a contract with the U.S. government for the manufacture of 10,000 .30 caliber and 25,000 .50 caliber Browning aircraft machine guns and large quantities of spare parts. Under the contract terms, Savage acquired, for the government's account, a large quantity of machinery and purchased or made a wide variety of tools and gauges to be used in the production of the said Browning guns. The first .50 caliber machine gun was completed in July, 1941, four months ahead of schedule. The production of guns was quickly and constantly increased to a monthly level of 8500 and the company was honored in July, 1942 by being one of the first 47 companies in the entire United States to receive the Army-Navy "E" Award for high efficiency in the

The Savage Story

production of military equipment. Additional Army-Navy "E" Awards were given to the Utica plant in 1943, 1944 and 1945 in further recognition of their efficiency in the war effort. By June, 1945 over 300,000 .50 caliber Browning machine guns, large quantities of Browning spare parts and large quantities of special type stellite-lined aircraft barrels for Browning machine guns had been manufactured.

speed .50 caliber Browning machine gun and to tool for their production at a level of 8500 guns per month. This work was discontinued before completion, because the capitulation of Japan in the middle of August, 1945 brought with it the immediate cancellation of all uncompleted military contracts.

During World War II Savage produced more than 2,500,000 aircraft type machine guns, submachine guns, and infantry rifles. To accomplish this, the corporation greatly expanded both its employment and its manufacturing facilities. Between 1920 and 1939, total employment at

The very popular Savage Model 24 combination gun which is perfect as a pest or meat gun. Available in .22 LR/20 ga. .22 LR/.410 also .22 mag r.f. & same shot gauges, .222 Rem., .30-30/20.

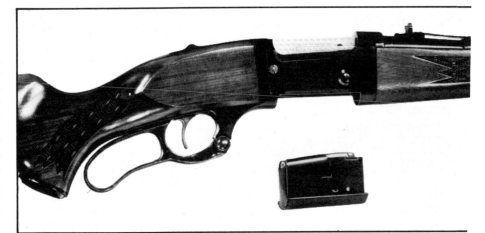

The new version of the Savage 99, the 99-C which features a detachable box magazine for those who like to or must carry rifle unloaded but quickly ready for hunting.

During the early part of 1941, the British government was desperately in English Lee-Enfield rifles. Savage agreed to manufacture a large portion of their requirements and two plants in Chicopee Falls were purchased and specially equipped for the purpose. The corporation's Stevens plant was also converted for use on the contract. The order was signed in March, 1941, and specified 333,000 such rifles. The first rifle was finished three months ahead of schedule and was presented in July of 1941 to Sir Clive Ballieu, the British representative. After the enactment of the Lend-Lease Act, the British contract was cancelled and replaced by a contract with the United States government, which specified a larger quantity of Lee-Enfield rifles, requiring doubling of the production schedules. The maximum schedule of 60,000 guns per month required by the new contract was quickly reached. The one millionth Lee-Enfield rifle was presented by Savage to Brigadier General Guy H. Drewry of the United States Army, on May 18, 1944. The United States terminated the manufacture of the rifles by Savage as of June 30, 1944.

In 1944 Savage began the manufacture of large quantities of nose and tail bomb fuses, rocket nozzle assemblies, booster adapters and Springfield rifle barrels, all at the

Stevens Hill plant. These attained a high level of production during the early part of 1945.

As the European phase of the war drew to a close, the government began to limit the production of Browning machine guns by Savage and other makers. On June 1, 1945, all unfilled orders for M2 machine guns were cancelled with the exception of a small number, to be completed before July 1, 1945. Only production of stellite-lined aircraft type barrels was continued at a high level for use in the war against Japan. Savage had achieved outstanding quality results with this type of barrel.

Savage Arms Corporation was also requested at this time to re-tool with all possible speed for the production of the new type M3 high-

its plants in Utica and Chicopee Falls had fluctuated between 800 and 2000. During World War II, employment quickly expanded to more than 13,000 employees in all of its plants. At the outbreak of the war the floor space of the Savage plants approximated 930,000 square feet. The purchase of two plants in Chicopee Falls brought the total to 1,175,000 square feet.

Savage applied its sound knowledge of arms manufacture to the production of military arms, with its costs and selling prices to the government being reduced from time to time. Countless problems were met and overcome in getting the necessary machinery, and in the buying and manufacturing of the large number and variety of jigs, fixtures and cutters needed. Exceedingly dif-

(top) A remarkable Savage pistol, the .45 ACP. Savage semi-auto submitted for test to the Army Ordnance Test Board which finally adopted the Colt Model 1911 auto. This pistol shows the clean, functional lines Savage guns are known for. A very rare pistol. An experimental cal. .25 ACP semi-auto Savage pistol (bottom). At this period, almost all pistol manufacturers rushed to produce a version of the .25 ACP. This vogue is now at low ebb but round persists in autos.

ficult problems in obtaining and training workmen and supervisors were also solved.

Prior to the conclusion of hostilities and the completion of the corporation's military program, Savage management considered the changes that peace would bring. New products, the improvement of old products and new techniques were given consideration. As a result, Savage went into the lawn mower business in 1944, by purchasing the capital stock of the Worcester Lawn Mower Company, manufacturers for nearly fifty years of a complete line of fine lawn mowers. As a division of Savage, a line of mowers bearing the Savage name were marketed with the Worcester line.

In 1946 sporting arms production in Utica was consolidated with the entire division and made the move from Utica, New York to Chicopee Falls, Massachusetts in 1947, where the Sporting Arms Division was integrated with the affiliated Stevens Arms Company.

In 1957, ten years after the consolidation of the Sporting Arms production, a major interest in the Savage Arms Corporation was acquired by the American Hardware Corpora-

tion of New Britain, Connecticut. In 1960 the Chicopee Falls operation was discontinued and Savage Arms transfered its manufacturing operations and offices to a modern single level plant at Westfield, Massachusetts. American Hardware Corporation's holdings were increased in 1963, and by merger, Savage Arms became a division of that corporation. American Hardware is best known to the consumer as manufacturers of such brands as Corbin, Russwin and Kwikset.

In 1964, another merger involving Savage took place between American Hardware and Emhart Manufacturing of Bloomfield, Connecticut, a leading producer of equipment for making glass containers and packaging machiner. As a result, Savage Arms is today a division of the Emhart Corporation.

At the present time, Savage Arms produces what is considered the world's most complete line of sporting firearms under the Savage, Stevens and Fox names as well as private brand names. Savage is the importer of German made Anschutz and Savage/Anschutz target rifles as well as Imperial Metal Industries Eley .22 rim fire ammunition for rifle and pistol.

The Model 99 rifles were not completed or shipped in numerical sequence, therefore we find that the serial numbers, by year, while being close to the following list, are not absolutely correct. Individual numbers may vary in shipping date by several years in certain instances.
the lowest number is 3156 shipped 8/3/97; 8200 last number in first series shipped 4/2/97

New series starts

10,000 -		Nov. 98 & early 99
10,000 -	13,400	1900
13,400 -	19,500	1901
19,500 -	25,000	1902
25,000 -	35,000	1903
35,000 -	45,000	1904
45,000 -	53,000	1905
53,000 -	67,500	1906
67,500 -	73,500	1907
73,500 -	81,000	1908
81,000 -	95,000	1909
95,000 -	110,000	1910
110,000 -	119,000	1911
119,000 -	131,000	1912
131,000 -	146,500	1913
146,500 -	162,000	1914
162,000 -	175,500	1915
175,000 -	187,500	1916
187,500 -	193,000	1917
VERY FEW SHIPPED THIS YEAR		1918
193,000 -	212,500	1919
212,500 -	229,000	1920
229,000 -	237,500	1921
237,500 -	244,500	1922
244,500 -	256,000	1923
256,000 -	270,000	1924
270,000 -	280,000	1925
280,000 -	292,500	1926
292,500 -	305,000	1927
305,000 -	317,000	1928
317,000 -	324,500	1929
324,500 -	334,500	1930
334,500 -	338,500	1931
338,500 -	341,000	1932
341,000 -	344,500	1933
344,500 -	345,800	1934
345,800 -	350,800	1935
350,800 -	359,800	1936
359,800 -—	Book 63	1937
	381,351	1938
381,351 -	388,640	1939
388,651 -	398,400 Book 64	1940
398,401 -	409,980	1941
409,981 -	421,190	1942
421,191 -	423,040	1943
423,041 -	425,700	1944
425,701 -	427,700	1945

Savage Model 99 serial numbers which are considered as current are now logged in a computer so that if there is a question of date of manufacture after 1945, the serial number is fed into the machine and the data on that particular number is read out, date, caliber, purchaser, etc. 🐾

SAVAGE ARMS CORPORATION

Largest Manufacturer of Sporting Arms in the World

1929

GUARANTEE

SAVAGE Arms Corporation guarantees its rifles and shotguns against defects in material and workmanship, and warrants them to be accurate, reliable and durable when properly used and cared for and when proper ammunition is used.

Savage Arms are made of the best material in the market. The parts after each process of manufacture are gauged and inspected with care, and the complete guns are subjected to a severe and thorough system of proof, inspection and test.

We will gladly repair or replace free of charge Savage Arms claimed to be defective, if our investigation shows that a defect or imperfection exists.

SPECIAL NOTICE

SAVAGE arms and ammunition are on sale in most retail hardware and sporting goods stores. If your local dealer does not have in stock the particular model or caliber of firearm and ammunition you desire, they can be secured within a few days from his nearest jobbing distributor.

All the standard arms and ammunition illustrated and described in this catalogue are carried in stock by jobbing distributors in every large city in the United States and Canada.

We will gladly give any further information desired on our product, or advise regarding the selection of a firearm and ammunition.

Catalog No. 65

SAVAGE
RETAIL PRICE LIST

Effective January 2, 1929

	Price Each
Model 99 Lever Action Hi-Power Rifles	
Model 99-A, Solid Frame	$ 41.00
Model 99-B, Takedown	46.00
Model 99-E, Solid Frame	41.00
Model 99-F, Takedown	46.00
Model 99-G, Takedown	49.50
Model 99-K, Takedown	80.00
Model 99-H, Carbine—Solid Frame	37.50
Savage Combination Kit Case (Only)	15.00
.410 Gauge Shotgun Barrel for Model 99 Takedown Rifles	10.00
Combination Kit Case—Complete with Style G Rifle and .410 Barrel	74.50
Model 20—Bolt Action Hi-Power Rifle	45.00
Model 40—Super Sporter (Standard Grade)	35.00
Model 45—Super-Sporter (Special Grade)	44.50
Model 23-A .22 Caliber Sporter Rifle	18.50
Model 23-B .25-20 Caliber Sporter Rifle	22.50
Model 23-C .32-20 Caliber Sporter Rifle	22.50
Model 19 N. R. A. Match Rifle	23.75
Model 29 Slide Action Repeating Rifle	19.50
Model 04 Single Shot Rifle	8.00
Model 28 Repeating Shotgun	
Model 28-A Standard Grade	44.50
Model 28-B Standard Grade with Raised Matted Rib	53.00
Model 28-C Riot Gun	44.50
Model 28-D Trap Grade	60.00
Model 28-S Special Grade	49.00

Savage Metallic Center-Fire Cartridges

	Retail Price per 100
.30-'06 Springfield 180 Grain Soft Point Bullet	$ 10.45
.30-'06 Springfield 220 Grain Soft Point Bullet	10.45
.300 Savage 180 Grain Soft Point Bullet	9.00
.300 Savage 150 Grain, either Soft Point or Metal Cased Bullet	9.00
.303 Savage 190 Grain, either Soft Point or Metal Cased Bullet	7.25
.30-30 Savage 165 Grain, either Soft Point or Metal Cased Bullet	7.25
.250-3000 Savage 87 Grain, either Soft Point or Metal Cased Bullet	8.00
.22 Savage Hi-Power 70 Grain, either Soft Point or Metal Cased Bullet Packed 20 in a box.	7.25
.25-20 Savage 60 Grain, either Soft Point or Metal Cased Bullet	3.50
.32-20 Savage 80 Grain, either Soft Point or Metal Cased Bullet Packed 50 in a box.	3.50

SAVAGE MODEL 99 CARBINE

MODEL 99-H CARBINE. Solid Frame. 20 inch special medium weight barrel. Walnut carbine stock and forearm. Steel butt plate. Weight 6½ pounds.

CALIBERS: .30-30 and .303.

The Savage Carbine has been designed for men who want a compact, sturdy, well balanced rifle to be carried on the saddle or in thick timbered country, that is light and fast in action, but packs a blow powerful enough for any big game.

Note its clean cut line, not an extra ounce of weight anywhere, yet it holds firm and steady. Its barrel is made of the same "Hi-Pressure" steel as all other Savage Model 99 barrels and is rifled in the exacting Savage way. These features combine in making this rifle admirably adapted for guides, trappers and others desiring a sturdy, solid frame rifle for rough service at a low price.

99-H Carbine

SAVAGE MODEL 99
Styles A-B and E-F

MODEL 99-A. Solid Frame. 24 in. tapered round barrel. Raised ramp front sight base. Rifle butt plate. Weight about 7¼ pounds.

MODEL 99-B. Takedown. Same specifications as above with takedown feature. Weight about 7½ pounds.

CALIBERS: Models A-B. .30-30, .303 and .300.

The Model 99-A Solid Frame Rifle is the original design through which the fame of the Savage Model 99 was developed. The 24 inch barrel in all calibers, the rifle butt plate and straight stock appeals to the sportsman who prefers the longer barrels for assistance in steady, accurate aim, improved cartridge ballistics and reduced recoil.

Model 99-B Takedown is the same rifle as Model 99-A with takedown feature added.

MODEL 99-E. Solid Frame. Tapered round barrel. Raised ramp front sight base. Shotgun butt. Weight about 7 pounds.

MODEL 99-F. Takedown. Same specifications as above with takedown feature. Weight about 7¼ pounds.

CALIBERS: Models E-F, .22 Hi-Power, .30-30, .303 and .250-3000 with 22 in. barrel. .300 with 24 in. barrel.

Model 99-E Solid Frame and 99-F Takedown are the featherweight designs, so called, because the shorter barrel and straight stock with shotgun butt plate makes a quick handling, easy to carry rifle chambered for the most powerful cartridges.

Model 99-E

Model 99-A

SAVAGE MODEL 99
Styles G and K

MODEL 99-G. Takedown. Tapered round barrel. Raised ramp front sight base. Shotgun butt, full pistol grip, checkered stock and forearm, checkered trigger and corrugated steel butt plate. Weight about 7¼ pounds.

CALIBERS: .22 Hi-Power, .30-30, .303 and .250-3000 with 22 inch barrel. .300 with 24 inch barrel.

MODEL 99-K. Takedown. Same specifications as Model 99-G with following refinements: Selected American Walnut stock and forearm—special fancy hand checkering on forearm, panels and grip. Receiver and barrel artistically engraved. Action carefully fitted and stoned. Lyman rear peep sight, folding middle sight and white metal bead front sight.

CALIBERS: Same as the Model 99-G.

The outstanding high power rifle of today is the Savage Model 99, style G. It is our most popular rifle and is selected by sportsmen who want a moderate weight rifle uniting fine finish with extreme efficiency. Especially adapted to high concentration cartridges because of the exceptional strength and safety of the action, this rifle is ideal for any American game shooting.

The Model 99-K is our finest finished rifle and is a beautiful specimen of high class rifle making. The checkering and engraving are unusually rich and makes the rifle an appealing possession to the discriminating sportsman.

Model 99-G

Model 99-K

THE MODEL 99 SAVAGE
Hi-Power Rifles

This is the famous repeating rifle that first introduced the hammerless, solid breech design and rotary type of magazine. Its popularity in every hunting field is immense—for it embodies all the technical superiority and mechanical perfection of tested Savage methods.

Extra safety is built into the Model 99 mechanism. The breech bolt has an unusually large locking area, wedging solidly against the receiver. The cycle of operation is quick and positive—permitting easy firing from the shoulder. All Savage Model 99 rifles are made with barrels of "Hi-Pressure" steel, especially adapted to modern smokeless powder cartridges. And sportsmen around the world know the Savage reputation for careful, accurate rifling and chambering.

The present models now more fully meet the needs of the sportsman than ever before; for a new barrel with raised ramp front sight base has been designed to give maximum ballistic efficiency of cartridges and improved balance. Larger forearms, new finish of metal parts, and many other refinements have been added.

GENERAL SPECIFICATIONS

Hammerless, solid breech, lever action. Hi-Pressure steel barrel, polished breech bolt, case hardened lever, blued receiver. Varnished American Walnut stock and forearm. Steel butt plate. White metal bead front sight on raised ramp base and adjustable flat top sporting rear sight. Six shots, magazine capacity five cartridges. Magazine rotary box type with numeral indicator. Hammer indicator showing automatically cocked or fired position of hammer. *Made in seven styles and five calibers.*

SAVAGE
Center-Fire Metallic Cartridges

AVERAGE BALLISTICS

Rifle Cartridges Smokeless Powder	Weight of Bullet Grains	Muzzle Velocity Ft. Seconds	Muzzle Energy Ft. Pounds	Velocity 100 Yards	Energy 100 Yards	Mid Range Trajectory 100 Yards	200 Yards
.25-20 Hi-Power	60	2300	705	1857	459	1.03	4.92
.32-20 Hi-Power	80	2100	782	1620	466	1.22	6.41
.22 Savage Hi-Power	70	2800	1218	2431	917	.63	2.95
.250-3000	87	3000	1737	2643	1349	.54	2.49
.30-30	165	2150	1692	1876	1288	1.07	4.9
.303	190	2000	1686	1763	1311	1.23	5.6
.300 Savage, 150 Grain	150	2700	2426	2465	2034	.66	2.9
.300 Savage, 180 Grain	180	2400	2300	2160	1863	.99	3.6
.30-'06, 180 Grain	180	2700	2910	2510	2515	.06	2.8
.30-'06, 220 Grain	220	2450	2940	2210	2385	.08	3.5

.30-'06 SPRINGFIELD. *Smokeless Powder.*
180 grain, soft lead point, sharp nose bullet.
220 grain, soft lead point, blunt nose bullet.
Adapted to Savage Models 40 and 45 Super-Sporter Rifles, also Remington, Winchester, Springfield and Mauser Rifles.

.300 SAVAGE. *Smokeless Powder.*
150 grain, soft lead point or full metal jacket, sharp nose bullet.
180 grain, soft lead point only, blunt nose bullet.
Adapted to Savage Model 99 Lever Action, Model 20 Bolt Action and Models 40 and 45 Super-Sporter Rifles.

SAVAGE MODEL 20
Hi-Power Rifle

The manufacture of the Model 20 Rifle has been discontinued. This model is now superseded by the Models 40 and 45 Super-Sporters.

MODEL 20. Bolt Action, Solid Frame, Repeating Rifle. 24 inch medium weight tapered barrel. White metal bead front sight. Lyman No. 54 rear peep sight with micrometer windgauge and elevation adjustments, mounted on tail block. Full shaped, one piece pistol grip stock of selected American Walnut, rubbed varnish finish, checkered on forearm and grip, corrugated trigger, corrugated steel butt plate. Sling strap screw eyes. Six shots, magazine capacity five cartridges. Weight 7 pounds.

CALIBERS: .250-3000 and .300 Savage with 24 inch barrel.

For the many sportsmen desiring the simple, positive bolt action in a sporting rifle the Model 20 Rifle is appealing because the entire arm was designed for hunting requirements.

The bolt with locking lugs behind chamber is the conventional design of most military rifles, but has been modified to eliminate unnecessary weight. The stock has the required high comb for use with peep sights, a large forearm for better grip and balance and medium weight barrel. A new highly polished finish adds to the arm's attractive appearance. Many experts proclaim the Savage Model 20 as the finest bolt action rifle made for American big game fields.

Model 20

149

SAVAGE SPORTER RIFLE

Model 23-A

MODEL 23-A. .22 Caliber Repeating Bolt Action Rifle. 23 inch round barrel. One piece stock and forearm of American Walnut, full curve pistol grip, finished in rubbed varnish. Sights are Rocky Mountain knife blade front and flat top elevator adjustment rear, of sturdy construction. Safety at rear of receiver can be operated by hand in firing position. Five shot detachable box type magazine. Chambered for .22 long rifle cartridge. Weight 6 pounds.

The Savage Model 23-A Sporter has the same barrel and action as the famous Savage Model 19 N. R. A. Match rifle. This exceptionally accurate barrel and mechanism so appealed to the small bore rifle experts that a special Sporter stock was designed for hunting purposes.

Those sportsmen who desire to use the .22 caliber cartridge for shooting squirrels, woodchucks, rabbits, coons, muskrats, and other small game valued for fur, or to be exterminated as pests, will find the Model 23-A Sporter to be an ideal small game rifle.

Model 23-A

SAVAGE SUPER-SPORTER RIFLES

A BIG game rifle that American sportsmen have craved for years—embodying many features heretofore found only in expensive imported rifles. Chambered for such outstanding cartridges as the famous .30·'06 Springfield and .30·30, .250·3000 and .300 Savage, the Sporter Rifle is a quality arm at a remarkably low price.

Locking lugs are set in the walls of the heavy receiver behind magazine. This absence of lugs back of the chamber allows the magazine to feed cartridges directly into the chamber, and consequently the bolt handle has about one inch less backward travel than with lugs on forward end of bolt locking behind chamber. For this reason, the Super-Sporter is easily operated without removing from the shoulder.

The bolt is completely housed in against dirt, snow, etc. The ignition is exceptionally rapid, the firing pin having a ⅜ inch stroke. Another feature is the hunter's ability to insert a fresh magazine while the bolt is closed and a loaded cartridge is in the chamber.

Note the influence of military experts in the grip and butt stock with high comb. The popular British type forestock makes for finer balance and ease in sighting. The barrel is a new design with raised ramp front sight base — the steel of standard grade Government specifications. Model 45 follows the specifications of Model 40, having in addition a new No. 40 Lyman peep sight and folding middle sight, made especially for this rifle.

SAVAGE MODEL 19
N. R. A. Match Rifle

MODEL 19. .22 Caliber Repeating Bolt Action Rifle. 25 in. barrel. Action obtains half cock on opening stroke, full cock on closing stroke. Both operations by caming movements reduce cocking effort to minimum. Caming action of bolt on opening stroke gives strong primary extraction. Full military stock, oil finished, pistol grip, bands and swivel for sling straps. Aperture rear sight, with windage and elevation adjustments and Marine Corps Type front sight. Five shot detachable box magazine. Chambered for .22 long rifle cartridges. Weight 7 pounds.

Marksmen will find this model particularly adaptable to firing from the various standard positions incorporated in matches of the National Rifle Association. It is a carefully designed instrument of precision, representing as far as practicable a consensus of opinion of the world's finest small bore rifle experts. It is the rifle used by sharpshooters as an understudy to a military rifle and cannot be excelled for accurate shooting qualities by any other small bore rifle.

Model 19

SAVAGE SPORTER
RIFLES
Models 23-B and 23-C

MODEL 23-B. .25-20 Caliber Repeating Solid Frame Bolt Action Rifle. 25 inch round barrel, one piece walnut stock, full pistol grip. Five shot detachable box type magazine. Weight 6 pounds.

MODEL 23-C. .32-20 (.32 Winchester) Repeating Bolt Action Rifle. Same specifications as above.

In the introduction of the Models 23-B and 23-C Sporter rifles, sportsmen were given a Bolt Action rifle for small and medium game designed to handle the efficient .25-20 and .32-20 cartridges at an extraordinary low price.

The action and general design is similar to the Model 23-A Sporter except that all parts are larger and bolt has a heavy locking lug on rear of bolt turning in the heavy wall of the receiver. This design allows cartridges to feed directly from magazine into chamber and makes the bolt throw short and easy to operate.

The barrels are made of the same Hi-Pressure steel as is used in Savage Model 99 Hi-Power rifles and are carefully rifled to give extreme accuracy. The pistol grip stock was carefully designed to give perfect balance and attains the fine outlines and easy handling characteristic of Savage rifles. The loading is quick and positive — detachable box magazines are interchangeable, allowing loaded magazines to be carried and quickly changed. Safety in rear of receiver can be operated by the hand in firing position.

These points of excellence, combined with the superior ballistics of the new Hi-Power cartridges for which it is chambered, makes this rifle particularly desirable to the sportsman needing a light, strong, deadly accurate medium-caliber rifle for all-round shooting.

Model 23-B-C

SAVAGE MODEL 25
.22 CALIBER RIFLE

MODEL 25. .22 Caliber, Takedown, Repeating, Hammerless, Slide Forearm Action. 24 in. octagonal barrel with white metal bead front sight and adjustable flat top sporting rear sight. Full pistol grip, American Walnut stock, with steel butt plate. Chambered to shoot without adjustment .22 caliber short, long, or long rifle, rim-fire cartridges. Magazine capacity 20 short, 17 long or 15 long rifle cartridges. Weight about 5½ pounds.

Extremely smooth, the action of the Model 25 rifle is easy to operate. The solid breech, solid top and side ejection encloses all the moving parts within the receiver. The graceful outlines characteristic of Savage arms is increased in the Model 25 rifle by the introduction of an action slide handle as long and well shaped as a regular forearm.

The combination of many unusual features in the design of this rifle, such as the long forearm, full pistol grip stock and long barrel, have been blended with a simple, sturdy action in producing a rifle acclaimed by firearm experts.

SAVAGE MODEL 04
.22 CALIBER RIFLE

MODEL 04. .22 Caliber, Takedown, Bolt Action, Single Shot. 18 in. round barrel with bead front sight, adjustable flat top rear sight. Varnished American Walnut Stock, shotgun butt with steel butt plate. Chambered for .22 caliber long rifle rim-fire cartridges, although .22 short or .22 long cartridges may be used. Weight about 3 pounds.

Big game hunters, timber cruisers, trappers and woodsmen favor this model as an auxiliary to their big game rifles because of its accuracy, simplicity, reliability and light weight.

It is a combination representing the greatest durability in the smallest bulk and light weight. The rifle may be taken down for convenience in carrying by unscrewing the takedown screw which attaches the stock to the barrel.

The parts are few, large and strong, the coil springs are used throughout. The stock is in one piece, made of selected American Walnut and so designed to give the rifle a perfect balance. The rifle is manufactured throughout from the very finest materials and is offered as a high grade single shot arm to those desiring the best possible materials and workmanship.

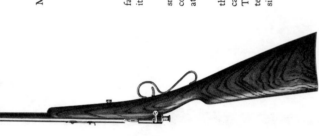

Model 04

Model 25

SAVAGE ARMS

Source: *The Rifle in America*   by Philip B. Sharpe

SAVAGE ARMS

Savage has had an interesting history, as their development occurred about the time of the introduction of smokeless powder which revolutionized rifle cartridges. The history of the company indicates that the original Model 99 Lever Action High Power Rifle, invented by Arthur Savage, continues to be the dominant product in the arms production of the Utica plant.

The company was quick to take advantage of advances in powder making and cartridge design, and introduced successively the .22 High Power, the .250/3000 and the .300 Savage. During the time these developments were taking place in high-power rifle cartridges, the company began extending their line of firearms by the production of .22 rifles, automatic pistols and, later, repeating and automatic shotguns.

Through the acquisition of the Stevens Arms Company and other subsidiaries, the company are now manufacturers of the widest variety of sporting arms in the world. Their line embraces all types of .22 caliber, medium-power and high-power rifles, and all styles of shotguns.

During the period of the development of the .22 High Power, .250/3000 and .300 Savage Cartridges, the company operated their own loading plant but several years ago the manufacture of cartridges was discontinued. The ammunition sold today under the Savage brand is manufactured under contract for them, but Savage continues to maintain an extensive experimental ballistic department.

Savage has experimented with a great many interesting and novel ideas. Nothing of a ballistic nature has been too novel or too revolutionary for the Savage engineering personnel to consider and to experiment with. As is customary, many of these new ideas failed to work out, but the research was well worth the effort, and in any form of research an organization learns a great deal which can be applied to routine manufacture.

Savage arms have always undergone rigid inspection of each gun, and each unit is given a very definite proof test, invariably comparing favorably with the proof test required by foreign nations. It is interesting to note that in the United States there is no requirement and no standards for the proof-testing of firearms, as every modern manufacturer so tests his equipment as a safety precaution and for the most part lives up to the English proof-test requirements. In many cases these requirements are exceeded in standard proof tests.

Savage introduced a great many interesting calibers of cartridges bearing their own name, among them being the .303 Savage, the .22 Savage high-power, and the .250/3000 Savage. Recent years since the World War have seen the introduction of the .300 Savage. All Savage rifles, it is interesting to note, were manufactured definitely with smokeless powder in view as the firm was founded at the beginning of the smokeless powder era of American rifle manufacture.

Accordingly, they were not handicapped as were some other manufacturers with equipment and tools designed for the manufacture of black-powder rifles and they began from scratch.

Among the many things originated by Savage were the solid-breech hammerless principle in repeating rifle construction. This eliminated protruding action parts during the operation of the repeating mechanism. All of this was self-contained within the receiver. In addition, with this mechanism they were able to develop not only a solid breech and top action but the side-ejection principle, and the complete enclosure of all mechanism insured the rifle from a jamming due to foreign material dropping into the action while in the woods.

Another feature introduced by Savage according to their claims was the general use of helical or coiled wire springs in American sporting rifle and pistol construction. Today this is almost universally used and the flat spring is rapidly falling into the discard. Coil springs are less inclined to give trouble through breakage and loss of tension than the older style flat spring. Savage rifles have generally been conceded to be as trouble free as any sporting arm can be made.

The design of the Savage rifle, due to its hammerless construction and balance, left little to be desired. In general appearance it was neat, balanced well and stood the acid test of shooting. These original lever-action repeaters in their revised form are extremely popular among lever-action fans today.

The famous .303 Savage rifle made its original reputation in the hands of those who lived by and with the rifle—professional hunters. The startling success of their original smallbore rifle, the famous .22 Savage known as the "Imp," commenced with its astonishing work on big bear in Alaska and grew with its appreciative reception by members of forest crews. Developments today indicate that the .22 Hi-Power is an obsolete number and it is far from equal to smallbore calibers recently appearing on the market. It was, however, a pioneer cartridge and this must be conceded today.

And thus we review Savage arms.

THE SAVAGE RIFLES

Savage Repeating Military Rifle
Intro 1895 Disc 1899

The Savage Repeating Military Rifle was Arthur Savage's first attempt at building firearms. Who made these rifles is not definitely recorded but it is believed that they were made in small quantities for him by Marlin.

These early guns were essentially the same mechanism as the present Savage commercial rifle known as the Model 1899. Without a question of doubt the commercial arm showed a number of improvements but the military board convened at New York December 16, 1890, and continued until July 1, 1892, studying in detail various trial tests for magazine guns at Governors Island, N. Y., July 1891. Among the items submitted were two .30-caliber guns bearing the Ordnance Department numbers of 35 and 42 and listed as "revolving cylinder" weapons with a nine-shot capacity magazine. Weight was 10 pounds, 4 ounces and was submitted by Arthur Savage from the address 1 Adams St., Brooklyn, N. Y. In this trial the Krag-Jorgensen No. 5 bearing the Ordnance Department test No. 28 was finally adopted; and thus was born the Model 1892 Krag. All other arms were rejected and this included the military rifles of various foreign nations tested at the same time.

In addition to this number Savage introduced the .303 Savage caliber in a special repeating

military rifle submitted to and tested by the New York State Board in 1895 and also by the U. S. Navy Board. This rifle was a six-shot number with a 30-inch barrel and weighed 8¾ pounds. Very little data are available on it at the present time and there are no records as to whether it was accepted and given any production trial.

Savage Repeating Sporting Rifle Model 1895

This Model 1895 rifle was believed to have been made by the Marlin Firearms Company, and was a sporting version of the military type submitted to the New York State Board but was marked Savage Repeating Arms Co., Utica, N. Y., and introduced only in .303 Savage caliber.

In 1895 the newly formed Savage Repeating Arms Co. issued a catalog on this model, the forerunner of the later 1899 type. This catalog bore the date of June 1895 and indicated that the rifle had a 26-inch round barrel, six-shot magazine capacity of the rotary type used in the Model 1899 and weighed 7 pounds. A half-octagon barrel job weighing 7½ pounds was also manufactured and a full-octagon barrel tipping the scales at 7¾ pounds was listed. All in all Savage manufactured about 5000 of these rifles, the majority of them being produced during the first year or two.

In addition to the Model 1895 rifle Savage had a carbine type which was practically the same rifle with a 22-inch barrel. It had the typical band around the forearm in the conventional carbine style and was intended for saddle use or for the hunter who preferred a short gun. This was made in .303 caliber only. The Model 1895 rifles were discontinued at the time the Model 1899 with the improved action of the same general design was introduced.

Savage Repeating Rifle Model 1899
Intro 1899 Disc 1908

This rifle introduced in January 1899 is the first new number produced by the Savage Arms

Co. after its incorporation in 1897. The action was unique as compared with other actions and except for minor refinements has still been retained for nearly sixty years. Arthur Savage designed this action well.

Essentially, this was a hammerless type of gun of lever-action variety, sleek, and with a closed solid breech receiver and side ejection. According to original Savage specifications this was a solid top. Actually, the top is open to approximately the length of the breech bolt. This bolt drops down when being operated; hence the bolt is enclosed.

The entire rear of the receiver is solidly constructed to completely enclose the mechanism so no gas can leak back through the action and reach the shooter's face in case of defective ammunition. The magazine is of the rotary type, magazine capacity being five cartridges in any of the standard calibers in which it has been made. This gives a six-shot gun with one cartridge inserted in the chamber. To load the magazine it is necessary to open the breech by throwing the finger lever downward and forward. The cartridges are then dropped into the opening and pressed downward and to the left, whereupon they automatically fall into proper position in the rotary magazine carrier and are revolved underneath out of sight still enclosed within the receiver itself. On the left-hand side of the receiver is a small opening through which a brass magazine indicator bearing numbers is exposed showing exactly how many cartridges are in the magazine at any time. This indicator can be read even in very poor light.

To use the rifle as a single-loader, the act of placing a cartridge into the breech opening forced the automatic cut-off back into its recess in the receiver retiring the uppermost cartridge in the magazine below the line of opening at the breech bolt. If the operator does not place a cartridge in the breech opening when there are one or more cartridges in the magazine, one of these is rotated into position by the spring-driven carrier, the forward motion of the bolt pushing it out of its holder into the chamber.

Instructions in an early book concerning the lowering of the hammer (all hammerless actions actually have a "hammer" but this is concealed within the receiver) state:

"If the rifle is cocked and the cartridge is in the barrel chamber, open the lever about two inches until a sharp click is heard. Hold back the trigger as described above and the mechanism is uncocked. In this case it is not necessary to draw out the cartridge in the chamber. The action can be locked by pushing forward the safety which locks the trigger and finger lever."

An interesting feature of this action was designed into the original Model 99 and has been continued to date. It is the hammer indicator. Today this is a button or pin located at the rear of the receiver and when projecting beyond the top of the receiver indicates that the hammer is cocked. If this is flush with the surface, the hammer is down.

In the earliest Model 1899 rifles which were made for more than ten years, instead of a round button, this consisted of a small bar located at the forward end of the breech bolt just in back of the chamber. When this projected up, the hammer was cocked. It was actuated by the firing-pin mechanism. In later years this projection on the forward part of the breech bolt was omitted and in place of it, a round pin was located at the back of the breech bolt in the receiver portion itself. This has been continued to date. When this pin sticks up the hammer is cocked and when it is down the action is uncocked or discharged. Thus the operator always has a visible safety which can be seen or felt regardless of illumination.

With the Model 1899 action the cocking of the hammer does not occur until the latter portion of the closing motion of the finger lever. This greatly reduces the effort of cocking the gun and in the opening movement all energy is expended in extracting the cartridge instead of cocking the hammer as in other lever-action guns on the market. This cocking action takes place in the last two inches of return travel of the finger lever. At that time the hammer engages the sear and the finger lever commences to travel down in the cam slot in the bolt and consequently cams the rear end of the bolt upward to lock it rigidly in the recoil shoulders in the receiver.

This camming movement and the compression of the mainspring are both in use during the last part of the closing movement of the finger lever. When the rear end of the breech bolt is cammed upward, the locking surface at the rear engages against the lockup face of the receiver, as Savage calls it, and the face of the hammer is drawn up towards the point of the sear. By means of this mechanism the action is cammed rigidly closed and many experts claim that this Savage action as made today on the original design and with improved materials such as heat-treated steels is the strongest lever-action rifle on the market. One thing is certain, it takes in the .308 Winchester cartridge, the highest-pressure lever-action cartridge available.

This action has a rebounding firing pin. A special retractor spring after discharge causes the firing pin to withdraw from the primer. This permits of easy ejection. What is more important, the cartridge can be carried in the chamber with the hammer down with perfect safety. Instructions for releasing this hammer are given above. To recock, it is not necessary to jack the action completely open but merely to a point where that same audible click is heard—about two inches' movement of the finger lever. Then by closing it, the indicator pin will signify that the action is cocked and ready for discharge.

After discharging a cartridge the forward or downward movement of the finger lever first draws the blade of the finger lever out of engagement with the lever-bite in the receiver. At the same time the travel of the finger-lever hub in the cam slot of the bolt commences to draw the rear end of the bolt down and to draw its locking faces out of engagement with the corresponding faces milled into the rear of the receiver. This also has a slight camming effect to the rear of the entire bolt thus loosening the fired shell in the chamber. The grip of the extractor then starts the fired shell to the rear. This gives a primary extraction. Savage claims that this primary extraction is about ten times the pressure on the finger lever.

The continued forward travel of the finger lever results in drawing the breech bolt to the rear. This ejects the fired shell and releases the automatic magazine cut-off. The shell is ejected to the right and the action can be immediately closed thus scooping another cartridge out of the magazine and riding it into the chamber.

The Model 1899 was first introduced in .303 caliber, a cartridge essentially the same as the .30/30 but apparently designed with very minor differences in dimensions in an effort to have a "distinctive" cartridge. This .303 Savage cartridge has never been adapted to any other make of gun. When the rifle first made its appearance in January 1899, it was available in this caliber only, in octagon, half-octagon, or round barrels 26 inches long and with either a shotgun or rifle style of butt plate. The rifle style of butt-plate is today obsolete on practically everything and was deeply curved with metal toe and heel. It was supposed to fit the shoulder but rarely did.

Savage Repeating Military Rifle Model 1899
Intro 1899 Disc 1908

The Savage military rifle was manufactured for various National Guard units and may account for the misunderstanding among many soldiers today who still insist that the .30/06 cartridge is a ".30/30." Brought out in 1899 in .303 Savage only, this was released in 1902 in the standard .30/30 Winchester cartridge which was added at that time to the sporting rifle line by popular demand, hence there actually *was* a .30/30 military rifle although it never was the official arm of the United States Army or Navy.

This military rifle was available either with a triangular or sword type bayonet. No data are available on the numbers of this manufacture.

Savage Repeating Military Carbine
Intro 1899 Disc 1908

The military carbine was essentially the carbine version of the rifle. Data on barrel lengths are not available but it is believed that this military carbine had a 22-inch barrel as against 30 inches for the rifle. Carbine was not equipped for bayonet use and had the typical carbine stock.

Savage Repeating Rifle Model 1899
Intro 1899 to date

This was the refined version of the same old 1895 sporting rifle with several new calibers added. By 1907 Savage had introduced this rifle in take-down style available in other calibers than the original .303. It was listed in the 1907 catalog as available with a round, octagon, or half-octagon barrel, the round barrel listing for $20.00 and the octagons for $21.50. This was in the solid-frame style. The take-down was available with the round barrel only and cost $25.00. The standard stock was the straight type without pistol grip but pistol grip was available for $2.50 extra. This necessitated a slightly different shape to the finger lever and to the lower receiver tang to fit the curve of the pistol grip.

By 1907 Savage was also claiming many interesting things for the accuracy of this rifle. Their catalog No. 16 states that the .303 cartridge would group its shots in a five-inch circle at 200 yards and had an accuracy range of 1,000 yards. This is possible, but the author would like to see this latter stunt performed.

The 1907 catalog also shows this model 1899 as available in .38/55 caliber and all calibers could be obtained with either steel-rifle style butt-plate or rubber shotgun forms at no extra charge. The indicator was continued on the breech bolt at that time.

Another caliber introduced in 1902 and still manufactured according to the 1907 catalog was the .30/30 caliber and also the .32/40 high-power as well as the Winchester .25/35. This .25/35 developed by Winchester for use in their own arm was successfully copied by Marlin in their .25/36 Marlin number and Savage at that time began to handle it.

The carbine type of Model 1899 listed in the 1907 catalog shows the 20-inch round barrel stepping down from the earlier 22-inch numbers. This was available in .25/35, .30/30, .303, .32/40 and .38/55 calibers. All rifles by that year were using slender forearms equipped with the then popular "knob" tip. The butt-plate on the carbine was of steel but of the typical carbine style more along shotgun lines than the so-called "rifle" butt-plate.

Sights on the standard rifle were of the so-called buckhorn variety adjustable for elevation and windage plus a simple blade front sight. On the carbine type Savage included their open barrel sight but this was of special Savage design, micrometer screw adjustable for elevation. For an open sight this was an excellent feature. The

carbine was available with and without the pistol grip selling for $20.00 with a straight stock and $22.50 for the pistol-grip style. They listed this as having an accuracy range of 600 yards. All carbines were quoted as weighing 7¼ pounds.

Another Model 99 rifle available in 1907 was known as their "Saddle Gun." This was a slightly different version of the carbine type. The carbine had a ring in the left side of the receiver but the Saddle Gun omitted this ring. Barrel length of all Saddle Guns was 22 inches—just 2 inches longer than the carbine. Weight was the same. This apparently was made possible by the reduction of the wood in the stock somewhat and possibly a more slender barrel. The forearm tip was extremely slender on this and had a semi-knob forearm tip. A peculiar shape of butt-plate giving no pitch to the stock was used. This was of semi-rifle style, neither being the customary rifle nor the better shaped shotgun type. It sold for $20.00 with the straight grip and $22.50 with pistol grip.

Model 1899 Featherweight
Intro 1901   Disc 1940

The Featherweight rifle was available in 1907 in only 3 calibers—.25/35, .30/30, and .303. Every effort was made to reduce the weight of this to the absolute minimum. This was actually brought down to 6 pounds. It was made in that year only in solid-frame style. Later the take-down feature was added, and still later the weight was slightly increased. It had the 20-inch round barrel and was priced at $25.00. Stock was of shotgun style fitted with a rubber butt-plate. The metal bead front sight was brazed to the barrel rather than inserted in a dovetail slot. Accordingly, it could not be removed. The rear sight was of the open barrel type but was the Savage micrometer style which could be adjusted to $\frac{1}{1000}$th of an inch. An odd type of forearm was supplied and the stock was of the straight-grip type, no pistol grip being available at this time.

SPECIAL TYPES

In 1907 this take-down rifle was available in .25/35, .30/30, .303, .32/40 and .38/55 calibers with 22- and 26-inch barrels only. The 26-inch barrel weighed about 7¾ pounds and the 22-inch barrel 7½. Only round barrels were available on this particular model.

Also by 1907 Savage introduced a number of specially engraved models with de luxe carving, checking, and what have you. The highlight of the line was the Savage Monarch and the catalog illustration shows that the forearm had a combination of flower carving and checking, the carving being raised in relief. The same general design was carried out on the receiver engraving continuing down onto the finger lever. Standard sights included a folding non-adjustable barrel sight in the standard dovetail slot and a Lyman peep sight on the tang. The entire inside mechanism was also hand-finished, and this was the finest stock number Savage ever turned out. The price was $250.00.

Second grade in the de luxe numbers was the "Rival" which had unique checking on the stock and a game panel carved in the receiver. Scroll engravings surrounded the game panel and decorated a portion of the finger lever. Stock and forearm on both of these rifles were of high grade Circassian walnut. The price of the Rival was $100.00.

The "Victor" grade bore these same neat fancy checking designs on the pistol grip and forearm with a game panel on the receiver and an elaborate scroll engraving surrounding it. The price was $75.00. All three of these grades were available with octagon or half-octagon barrels.

The lowest de luxe grade was the Savage Crescent, available with round, octagon or half-octagon barrels, either 22 or 26 inches long. This had neat fine checking on the grip and forearm, the game panel on the sides of the receiver with fine engraving covering the remainder of the receiver. The price was $63.50 for the round barrel and $65.00 for the octagon or half-octagon, and $68.50 for the round barrel in take-down, regardless of length.

Still stepping down was the Savage Leader, a rifle with neat checking on the stock and forearm and scroll engraving on the receiver. It was available with a round barrel at $45.50 and an octagon or half-octagon at $47.00. Fancy English walnut stocks were $5.00 additional.

The next number in the specially finished series was the grade AB supplied with round barrel at $37.50 and octagon at $39.00 plus $5.00 for extra fancy English walnut stocks. This had a neat checking design on the stock, although it was of the more simple type, and a scroll panel on the sides of the receiver.

The grade BC was still lower in price and had scroll engraving on the receiver, the same general checking design on the stock, and sold for $34.00 with octagon barrel and $32.50 for the round barrel. With the exception of the American walnut stocks this arm corresponded with the general specifications as grade AB. A catalog states: "It has the same beautiful scroll design, pistol grip and checking." Despite that the illustration shows an entirely different design of scroll engraving although the checking is identical.

The lowest-price special number was the grade CD supplied in octagon or half-octagon barrels for $27.00 and round barrels for $25.50. This had a simple plain walnut stock with checking. Other than the simple outline engraving on the receiver there were no other decorations. The A2 Special and A2 Regular were two straight-grip rifles priced slightly lower. The A2 Special had an octagon or half-octagon barrel priced at $26.50 and a round barrel at $25.00. A very simple checking was used on the grip and on the forearm, not as expensive or as elaborate as on the better grades. Both sides of the receiver had simple yet neat and artistic scroll designs. American walnut was used for these stocks.

The A2 Standard Model 1899 had the same design of checking used on the A2 Special. There was, however, no engraving on the receiver. Price was $22.00 for the solid frame and $27.00 take-down and $23.50 for the octagon or half-octagon solid frame. The price therefore was but $2.00 over the regular price.

By 1925 this Model 99 rifle had been improved slightly and made available in various other grades known as A, B, C, D, E, F, and G.

The front sight on the Model 99A, B, and C and carbine style was dovetailed in a barrel slot and regularly equipped with a German silver knife-blade front sight. The raised front-sight base of the Model 99E, F, and G types was made integral with the barrel and was regularly equipped with a white metal bead sight. The rear sight on all styles was a flat-top sporting sight of Savage design. All receivers were drilled and tapped for a tang type of Lyman peep. The take-down type was continued.

The Models A and B were the same guns except that the A was solid frame with 26-inch round standard barrel and rifle butt-plate weighing 8 pounds. The Model B was a take-down rifle of the same specifications. Model C was the same gun with a shotgun butt-plate and 22-inch round barrel. The weight ran 7 pounds, 10 ounces. The Model D was the same short barrel job in take-down. These were made available in .30/30, .303 and .300 Savage calibers. The .300 caliber was not available with a barrel shorter than 24 inches.

The Model 99 carbine was a solid-frame job only with a 20-inch special medium-weight barrel, and special design of carbine stock. The weight was 7 pounds and this was available at that time only in .30/30 and .303 calibers.

Model E was the light-weight tapered barrel shotgun butt, weight 6¼ pounds and the Model F a take-down of the same version. These two models were supplied in .22 high-power, .30/30 and .303 with a 20-inch barrel and .250/3000 with a 22-inch barrel. The .300 caliber was available in 24-inch barrel.

The Model 99G was a take-down light-weight job except that it had a full pistol grip, shotgun butt, checkered stock and forearm, checked trigger and corrugated steel butt-plate. This was essentially a de luxe version of the Model F.

Jumping ahead to 1933, we find that the Models A and B, solid frame and take-down, were available with a 24-inch barrel, rifle butt-plate, raised ramp front sight base, open sporting rear, weight 7¼ pounds, and available in .30/30, .300, .303 calibers only. The Model 99B or take-down version weighed 7½ pounds and had the same specifications as the Model A. The Model 99E had the same raised ramp front sight base, shotgun butt, weighed 7 pounds and was available with a 22-inch barrel in .22 Hi-Power, .30/30, .303 and .250/3000 calibers. The .300 caliber was available only in 24-inch barrels.

The Model 99F weighing 7¼ pounds was the same gun in take-down style.

The Model 99G was also their de luxe version with a ramp front sight base, gold-bead front sight, open rear sight with shotgun butt, pistol-style grip with checked forearm, checked trigger and corrugated steel shotgun style butt-plate.

Weight ran about 7¼ pounds and with the 22-inch barrel the calibers available were the .22 high-power, .30/30, .303 and .250/3000. The .300 caliber was available only in 24-inch barrels.

The new model introduced was the Model 99K, a take-down version still more de luxe than the G grade. It was available in .22 high-power, .30/30 and .303 and .250/3000 in 22-inch barrels and .300 Savage with 24-inch barrel. Specifications were the same as the Model 99G with additional refinements including the selected American walnut stock and forearm with hand-rubbed, oil-finished, special fancy hand checking on the forearm, side panels of stock, and pistol grip. The receiver and barrel were artistically engraved. The action was carefully hand-fitted and lapped for smoothness. Rear sight was the Lyman folding peep with a folding middle sight, and gold bead front. Also in 1933 they listed the Model 99 carbine as their 99-8. This was a solid-frame number only available with 20-inch special medium weight barrel available in .30/30, .303 and .250/3000 caliber. Stock was of fancy grain walnut and the forearm was fitted to the barrel with the customary band. A varnish finish was used with the carbine style steel butt-plate. Rear sight was an adjustable semi-buckhorn and a bead front sight without the ramp was used.

Two newcomers were the Models 99R and 99RS. Both of these were solid-frame units and showed the first attempt of Savage to modernize the shape of the forearm in keeping with the current style of large rather than flat slender forearms. The Model R was available in .250/3000 Savage and .303 Savage calibers with a 22-inch barrel and the .300 Savage with 24-inch barrel. Weight ran around 7½ pounds. Rubbed oil finish was used and an adjustable semi-buckhorn rear sight with gold bead front sight mounted on a ramp was standard equipment. A much neater shape of pistol grip with a diagonal design of checking was used.

The RS model was the same as to specifications except for a few minor refinements. It was regularly equipped with detachable sling swivels and a leather sling strap. A folding middle sight was used, a gold bead front sight mounted on a neat ramp and a Lyman folding peep sight adjustable for both elevation and windage was standard equipment.

Any of the take-down models of the 1899 rifles

can be equipped with a .410 bore auxiliary shotgun barrel interchangeable with all caliber rifles. Savage however requests that the rifle be sent to the factory for the necessary adjusting.

This barrel weighs about two pounds and has a length of 22 or 24 inches.

In 1938 the Savage line of Model 1899 rifles still shows eight styles of stock and barrel dimensions and in five calibers. All triggers are now matted for smooth, easy control. Operating levers are case-hardened or blued and receiver is blued. Still remaining in the line is the 99F take-down. A tapered neat round barrel with raised ramp front sight base, 22-inch barrels in .250/3000, .303, .30/30 and .22 Hi-Power caliber, and 24-inch barrels in .300 Savage caliber. A light-weight, straight-grip stock and very slender forearm, slightly checked on both grip and forearm are used. Rubbed oil finish is standard. Stock dimensions for the standard job are 1⅞ inch drop at comb, 2⅝ at heel and 13 inches length of pull. Butt plate is 1½ by 4⅞ inches. Weight about 7½ pounds. The rear sight is a flat-top buckhorn type mounted on the barrel and adjustable for elevation only.

The Model 99G is available in the same barrel lengths but it has a pistol-grip stock in the same slender knob-tip type of forearm. Stock dimensions are the same. Weight runs about 7¾ pounds. Model 99H is the Featherweight model with a tapered light-weight round barrel, raised ramp front sight base and 20-inch barrel in .250/3000, .303, .30/30 and .22 high-power and 22-inch length only in the .300 Savage caliber. Stock dimensions are the same. Weigh about 6¾ pounds. There is no checking on this job and a carbine type of butt-plate is used. The carbine forestock is much thicker than on the rifle and is held to the barrel at the forward end by a band. Weight of this carbine type with a straight stock and no decorations or checking is about 6¾ pounds.

The Model 99G take-down model is similar to the F but in slightly better grade. A large full-sized forearm has an ample amount of checking and the pistol-grip stock has a cap and neat checking. It has the same short barrel but sights include a new red bead front with new semi-buckhorn rear sight mounted on the barrel. This semi-buckhorn has no sighting notch but a white line in the back. Forearm dimensions are 10½

inches long, 1½ wide and 2 inches deep. Stock dimensions are the same as the standard on all models. Weight of this rifle is about 7 pounds.

The Model 99EG, also a solid-frame model, is available in the same calibers but has a 22-inch barrel for the .250/3000, .303, .30/30 and .22 high-power and 24-inch barrel for the .300 Savage. It has no checking but has a pistol-grip stock. Stock is not as well shaped as on the Model 99T and has that slender old-fashioned forearm with a knob tip. Weight is about 7¼ pounds.

The Model 99K take-down is also one of the slender forearm knob-tip affairs but is elaborately decorated. It has the same specifications as the Model 99B except that the stock is of American walnut, highly selected for finish, and with a hand-rubbed oil finish. Elaborate checking on the forearm, panels and grip is used. Receiver and barrel are artistically engraved. The action is carefully hand-fitted and stoned. Sights include the Lyman rear peep, folding middle sight, and gold bead front. Weight runs around 7¾ pounds.

The Model 99R solid-frame rifle is one of the neatest and best-shaped rifles in the line. This is available only in .250/3000 Savage, .300 Savage and .303 Savage calibers. It has a tapered medium-weight round barrel with a raised ramp front sight base and is made in two barrel lengths, the .250/3000 and .303 Savage being in 22-inch lengths and the .300 Savage in 24-inch length. Stock specifications on this show a large well-shaped neatly formed pistol grip highly checked, full forearm, also neatly checked, and a 1⅝-inch drop at comb, 2⅞ drop at heel, and 13½-inch length from trigger to center of butt-plate. The butt-plate is 1⅝ inches wide and 5⅛ long. The pistol grip has a neat rubber cap. Weight of this rifle runs about 7¼ pounds.

The Model 99RS solid-frame job is made only in .250/3000 and .300 Savage calibers. It is essentially the same as the Model R except in refinements. To the author's way of thinking this is the finest specimen in the standard Savage line. The open buckhorn rear sight on the barrel is omitted and replaced with a folding-leaf barrel sight and gold bead front sight on a ramp and a Lyman folding-tang peep sight with micrometer adjustments for windage and elevation. It has quick detachable sling swivels and comes fully equipped with a ⅞-inch leather sling strap. This rifle is neat, well-shaped, well-balanced and a fine performer for accuracy.

Savage still continues the .410 bore shotgun barrel for any Model 99 take-down rifle.

SPECIAL SAVAGE CARTRIDGES
The Savage .22 Hi-Power

This particular cartridge was the product of the inventive genius of Charles Newton and first made its appearance about 1912. Essentially it was the .25/35 Winchester cartridge necked down to .22 caliber and was one of the first successful attempts at creating a truly smallbore high-pressure cartridge. This particular caliber used the 70-grain full metal jacket or soft-point pointed bullet at a muzzle velocity of 2800 f.s. giving a muzzle energy of 1218 foot-pounds. The remaining velocity at 100 yards drops to 2431 and the energy to 917 foot-pounds.

At 100 yards the mid-range trajectory is .63 inches and at 200 yards this climbs to 2.95 inches. At 300 yards the mid-range trajectory is 7.75 inches and at 500 yards 30.34 inches. The cartridge is quite successful as a deer number for short-range shooting up to about 100 yards. Savage claims that this downed some of the biggest and toughest game, not only in North America but throughout the civilized world, even listing that it had taken lions, tigers and, on occasion, elephants. This author would feel very uncomfortable equipped with this caliber tackling an angry grizzly.

The .250/3000 Savage

This cartridge was introduced in 1913. This was also a product of the inventive brain of Charles Newton. He designed it as a better balanced, more accurate and more satisfactory job than the .22 Hi-Power and sold his ideas to Savage.

Early in 1932 the author was discussing this particular cartridge with Newton down in New Haven, Connecticut.

"I designed the .250 with a 100-grain bullet," Newton explained. "It was my intention to make this number a good, accurate, heavy-bullet job at a velocity of 2800 f.s. When Savage took over the rights they wanted a higher velocity than

they were getting from the little 'Imp' and strove to reach the 3000 f.s. figure. With the powders available at that time the only way to do this was through the reduction of bullet weight and over my hearty objections they cut this bullet down to 87 grains. They achieved the 3000 f.s. velocity figure by doing this but they greatly handicapped the possibilities of this excellent little cartridge. Since that time, what with improved powders now on the market, I have been trying to get every ammunition manufacturer in the country to experiment with 100-grain bullets, all without success. I think that if the 100-grain bullet were driven 2800 f.s. velocity, you would see the .250 made into a real killing cartridge."

Charles Newton died two months after that chat. He never lived to see the 100-grain bullet. Less than three months after his death the Peters Cartridge Co. announced a new number—the .250 Savage with a 100-grain bullet with a muzzle velocity of 2850 f.s. Within a year every ammunition manufacturer was loading this caliber but the others still had the muzzle velocity of around 2700 f.s. Today I believe the majority of them are loading this particular caliber at the full 2850 figure. The bullet has a much better chance of arriving in good condition. It penetrates through brush better, upsets more uniformly on game and does not create the surface wounds frequently attributed to the little light-weight 87-grain bullet. It is unfortunate that Newton could not see his ambition realized.

The .300 Savage

The .300 Savage was an attempt of the Savage Arms Co. to produce a high-power, rimless .30-caliber cartridge adapted to the rather short Model 99 lever-action rifle. In developing this they attempted to duplicate the ballistics of the popular .30/06 cartridge then having a 150-grain bullet at a muzzle velocity of 2700 f.s. The cartridge was quite successful despite the unique shape of its very sharp shoulder created by a powder space as large as possible in a cartridge of that length.

The .300 Savage cartridge is not an ideal type but gives satisfactory results for the man who desires a .30 caliber high-power rifle and since its introduction in 1920 has enjoyed a reasonable popularity, particularly among the lever action fans.

OTHER SAVAGE RIFLES
Savage Hammerless Repeater Model 1903
1903-1916 (1,000 made 1922)

The Model 1903 rifle was a .22-caliber repeater of rather unique design entirely different in appearance from other rifles on the market before and since. It was a pump-action type but therein the general similarity with other guns ended.

It used the clip-type magazine in place of the tubular form so widely used by other slide-action rifles and would handle the .22 short, .22 long and .22 long-rifle cartridges without any change in the mechanism. There was no outside exposed hammer to bother the aim or catch in clothing, thus causing accidents. A shotgun type of safety on the tang was in perfect control of the mechanism at all times and an entirely closed-in breech with a small ejection port at the right side of the receiver prevented dirt from entering the mechanism and creating trouble.

This Model 1903 was an odd-appearing gun with a knob-ended pistol grip frequently called a "half-pistol grip." A slender slide handle and long octagon barrel looked strangely out of place in comparison with each other and the general impression the author has of this gun is that "something is missing." Nevertheless, it performed excellently and had a reasonably long life on the market. A clip-type magazine slid into position at the forward end of the trigger guard and each one had an automatic stop so when the magazine was emptied the bolt remained open thus indicating the necessity for replacing the magazine. Spare clips could be carried properly charged with either of the three .22 rimfire numbers.

The gun was of take-down style very conveniently designed for ease of operation. To take it down it was necessary to remove a large knurled-head take-down screw on the right side of the receiver after the magazine was removed. This exposed the entire barrel from the breech end, making for easy cleaning.

The standard model of this rifle had a 24-inch octagon barrel, pistol grip and rifle butt-plate weighing 5¼ pounds and the price was $14.00 in 1907.

The 1903 repeater was also available in what was generally classified as the "English Model" stock. This essentially was the same as the standard model except that the shotgun style butt was used with a rubber butt-plate. Weight ran 5½ pounds and with the same octagon barrel the price was $15.00.

Another model of this rifle was equipped with a gallery register and one of these was used at the St. Louis World's Fair and met considerable success there. This gallery-register type had an automatic counter located beneath the barrel just in front of the slide handle where it registered the number of times the rifle was fired through the action of the slide handle itself. This St. Louis World's Fair model was shot in the gallery there, according to the counter, 42,-351 times. The demand for this counter-type from shooting galleries caused Savage to place it on the market. In 1907 this type sold for $25.00 complete with counter. Specifications were the same as for the standard model in every respect.

An addition to the standard grade of Model 1903 repeaters Savage had four fancy grades known as "Grade EF," "The Expert," "Grade GH" and "The Gold Medal." In these the "EF" grade was the most expensive. It was the standard job dressed up with a very excellent grade of English walnut, half-pistol-grip style, selected for figure and neatly checked. Sights were the Rocky Mountain blade type front and the Savage micrometer rear mounted on the barrel. The receiver was elaborately engraved with a beautiful game panel surrounded by scroll work. In 1907 this model listed for $40.00. Their "Expert" grade was, as Savage put it, "A very beautiful number which has probably had a larger sale than any fancy .22-caliber rifle ever made." A highly figured half-pistol-grip stock of fancy American walnut was used and a unique form of scroll engraving on both sides of the receiver. It was priced at only $29.00.

The "GH" grade and "The Gold Medal" were the two lower-priced fancy numbers. The "GH" had a Savage micrometer rear sight and Rocky Mountain front, no engraving, but a very neat checking job on the plain, half-pistol-grip American walnut stock. It sold for $17.75. The "Gold Medal" grade had a less elaborate form of checking on the same type of stock with an ornamentation in the form of engraving of animal design on the receiver. This was priced at only $17.00.

In addition to the regular 1903 rifles a wide variety of extras and fancy woods were listed in the early catalogs. All kinds and grades of stocks in fancy and extra fancy type were supplied, various grades of checking, nickel plating and nickel-plated trims, silver-plated trimmings, gold plating and gold-plated trimmings, standard barrels with special stock finishes, swivels and sling straps, special stock measurements and miscellaneous engraving running up to their grade "G" at $130.00 over the list price of the gun and other accessories and all kinds of special sights. The Savage catalog bears one interesting and cryptic comment:

"Set triggers cannot be furnished on any Savage rifles. All trigger-pulls are short and crisp without any creep."

Savage Junior Rifle
Model 1904
Intro 1904   Disc 1915

The Savage Junior was one of the early attempts at producing a bolt-action single-shot rifle in the low-price class. When it first came out it sold for $5.00 and enjoyed a great deal of popularity throughout its life.

For a low-priced gun this was built with an exceptionally sharp eye towards quality and good workmanship. It was a little bolt-action type, simple in design and in appearance and yet properly constructed for strength and performance. Savage advertised this particular rifle not only as a good gun for a boy but as an auxiliary rifle for the adult to have around camp. It was, of course, a single-shot rifle adapted to the .22 short, long, and long-rifle cartridges. To load, one merely dropped a cartridge into the receiver and closed the bolt. This action cocked the piece. The rearward motion of the bolt handle merely had to extract and eject the fired shell.

In 1907 Savage pointed out in their catalog: "The stock is American walnut and not stained maple or inferior wood." It was furnished only as a standard number with no variations from the original specifications. It had a little 18-inch round barrel, weighed 3 pounds and had a shotgun type of butt stock. It was, of course, a take-down arm and when taken down would pack into a space equal to the length of the barrel.

Model 1905 Target Rifle
Intro 1905   Disc 1915

This little .22-caliber arm was designed to give a somewhat larger and better rifle for adults and large boys than the Model 1904. It was, of course, chambered for the .22 short, long, and long-rifle cartridge only and was somewhat heavier, tipping the scales at 4¾ pounds.

The barrel length was 22 inches and the rifle was regularly equipped with a Swiss butt-plate, something unusual in a low-priced arm. For a short .22 barrel, this particular rifle had one fairly heavy.

A very interesting development of this rifle was an adjustable trigger-pull. At the bottom of the trigger was a special screw which regulated the depth of engagement of the sear and thus would permit of a reasonable range of adjustment. To get at this it was necessary to remove the stock. This was a rather simple problem since it was a take-down arm. Sights included an ivory bead front with the famous Savage micrometer rear of open type located on the barrel in front of the receiver port.

Both the Models 1904 and 1905 Savage rifles had the receiver made as a continuation of the barrel. This simplified manufacturing and at the same time added sleekness to the line of the arm itself. The Model 1905 rifle sold for $7.50.

Another variation of the Model 1905 single-shot was the so-called English pattern. This had the same features as the regular target rifle in every respect with the exception of the stock which had a butt of the shotgun type. Length of this stock was 14 inches. This English number listed as "Style C." The price was only $6.50. The difference in price was made possible by slightly cheaper grades of sights using a plain metal bead front and standard adjustable rear.

This same English-pattern rifle was also available in a number they called "Style B." It was the exact specifications of "Style C" except that it was equipped with the regular target sights the same as on the 21 Savage micrometer open rear sight on the barrel and an ivory bead front. This was priced at $7.50, the same as the regular target grade.

In addition a special grade of Model 1905 rifle was furnished, a special target model with a fancy figured American walnut stock, nicely checked, Swiss butt-plate, and ivory bead front. It sold for $15.00.

All of these Savage single-shot rifles, both Models 1904 and 1905, used the double folded trigger guard attached with screws to the stock. This guard not only formed a protection over the trigger but curved downward at the grip to form a semi-pistol-grip style of stock.

Savage Hammerless Repeater Model 1909
Intro 1909   Disc 1915

The Model 1909 Hammerless Repeater was the identical same action as the Model 1903 but was built with slightly different stock and barrel. A new model number would suggest a new rifle but this was not the case. The comments on the Model 1903 will apply equally well to the Model 1909.

The major differences in the Model 1909 was a 20-inch round barrel, straight stock, without pistol grip and a shotgun style of butt. It was, of course, a take-down and of the slide-action variety. This ran 4 pounds, 10 ounces, and the price in 1910 was $10.00. Extra magazines of the clip type were listed at 25 cents each. The major difference in the slide handle was that this was plain and did not have the customary flutes used in the Model 1903.

Model 1911 Repeater
Intro 1911   Disc 1915

The Model 1911 Repeater was a unique bolt-action repeating rifle patterned after the modern military service arm. The chief claim to unique design lay in the magazine type. It was chambered for .22 shorts only and the magazine was located in the butt stock loaded through the butt-plate. The capacity of this tubular magazine was 20 cartridges.

The rifle was short and light, weighing but 4 pounds and having a 20-inch round barrel. Its price in 1911 was $6.50. The action was strong, simple and durable, easy to operate and capable of standing rough service and poor weather.

Stock was of American walnut with a shotgun-style steel butt-plate. A metal bead front sight was standard and the rear sight was of adjustable flat-top open type located on the barrel. No choice of specifications was available in any variation from the standard.

Automatic Rifle Model 1912
Intro 1912   Disc 1916

The Savage automatic rifle Model 1912 was the first successful automatic rifle chambered for standard .22 long-rifle cartridges. It was built in this caliber only and would take no other. Savage specifications indicate that this self-loading hammerless type of take-down rifle was designed to handle only the Lesmok or semi-smokeless variety of cartridges with crimped bullets and a caution in large type appearing on the instruction sheet states: "Owing to the variation in .22 caliber ammunition, under no circumstances attempt to use other than these cartridges." Please notice the specification for "crimped" ammunition. Many of the early match grades of cartridges did not have their bullets crimped in. These of course were designed for use in single-shot target rifles.

This Model 1912 rifle was produced to meet the great demand for an accurate and serviceable .22 caliber automatic rifle to handle standard ammunition. The mechanism was, of course, semi-automatic or self-loading. The recoil, each time the rifle was fired, threw out the empty shell, cocked the arm, and scooped a loaded cartridge from the magazine into the barrel leaving the rifle ready for the next shot. Only one shot could be discharged at each pull of the trigger.

The rifle was of take-down construction and when taken down the barrel, forearm, and right top of the receiver together with the breech bolt and certain mechanical parts remained together as a unit. The left half of the receiver remained attached to the butt stock.

The probable reason for the discontinuance of this rifle was its size. It was an extremely small, light-weight arm, with a 20-inch round barrel, American walnut stock and forearm, shotgun butt with steel butt-plate, metal bead front sight dovetailed into the barrel and a special Savage design of micrometer rear sight of the open variety located on the barrel just in front of the receiver. The take-down length was 23½ inches and the weight only 4½ pounds. An interesting fact is that this Model 1912 rifle appeared in that year and sold for but $12.00. Considering competitors' self-loading .22 rifles this was a unique feature in price alone.

The magazine system was very quick and convenient. It followed the customary Savage design of a detachable box-type magazine located in front of the trigger guard and when in place formed a continuation of the bottom of the guard. It came regularly equipped with two magazines. Each magazine held 7 cartridges. When the last shot was fired and the clip was empty the action remained open. Savage claimed rapidity of fire enabled the shooter to release six shots in one second.

The short barrel was bored, rifled, and finished with typical Savage accuracy and care. The rifling was deep enough to rotate the bullet properly but not so deep as to deform the bullet and affect accuracy. Savage claimed that the smoothness of interior finish was that of the finest handmade target barrel. The repeating mechanism was particularly designed with the accuracy of the rifle as the first consideration. As a result it was thus possible to prevent any irregularity or lack of uniformity of velocity due to the automatic operation. Careful chronograph tests show that their automatic action develops exactly as high and uniform velocity as the hand-operated arm having the same length of barrel.

In any autoloading or automatic rifle safety is a very necessary requirement, perhaps more so than in manually controlled repeating arms. Savage claimed that this little rifle was well adapted for the use of feminine shooters and thus required special attention to the important feature of safety. The strong positive safety was, as Savage stated, "not located down in the trigger guard as in other rifles where it is not seen unless hunted for and is liable from excitement or inexperience to be forgotten, but is put in the proper place on the upper tang in front of the grip as on hammerless shotguns. The shooter cannot help seeing it and feeling it. It is quickly and easily operated by a touch of the thumb. This safety is also provided with an indicator showing at a glance in daylight or a touch in the dark whether the hammer is cocked or not, an additional and important safety feature."

Durability or length of life is of extreme importance and unusual in any autoloading rifle, particularly during the period in which this Model 1912 was brought out. Savage claims that this autoloading arm was fully as durable as the hand-operated type. The mechanism was strong and simple. The principal springs were all spiral and tested with the greatest care for resilience. The design of the moving parts prevented their receiving any excessive strain or shock of recoil under automatic operation. The take-down device was especially convenient as the breech bolt could readily be removed with the fingers, and the barrel cleaned from the breech—the only proper way if accuracy is to be preserved in a rimfire arm.

One of the best features of this little automatic rifle was the design of the stock and forearm. It was not a pistol-grip type of weapon, bore no fancy checking or other decorations. On the other hand, the forearm was large and full-shaped, all in keeping with the current ideas along those lines.

This, together with the short barrel, made the gun extremely neat both in appearance and balance, being neither butt- nor muzzle-heavy. If revived today, that little rifle should be an excellent success but it went the way of all arms making their appearance ahead of the times. Savage designed and built it well. Throughout the duration of its life it proved extremely popular and many an exhibition or trick shot used this extensively for fast or fancy shooting.

Model 1914 Hammerless Repeater
Intro 1914   Disc 1924

Here was another Savage slide-action hammerless repeater. In this case the arm was equipped with a tubular magazine and had a much neater appearance than the earlier Models 1903 and 1909.

This slide- or trombone-action type of repeater had a much longer slide handle than the earlier types and was constructed to handle .22 short, long, and long-rifle cartridges indiscriminately, without any change in mechanism. The

ACTION OF ORIGINAL SAVAGE MODEL 1899
(Note cocking indicator on front end of bolt)

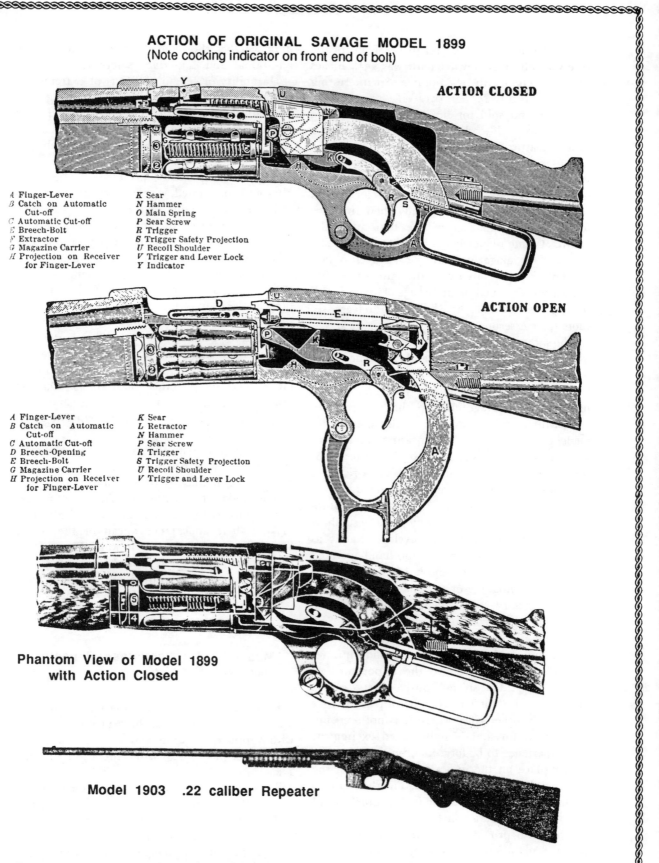

ACTION CLOSED

A Finger-Lever
B Catch on Automatic
  Cut-off
C Automatic Cut-off
E Breech-Bolt
F Extractor
G Magazine Carrier
H Projection on Receiver
  for Finger-Lever

K Sear
N Hammer
O Main Spring
P Sear Screw
R Trigger
S Trigger Safety Projection
U Recoil Shoulder
V Trigger and Lever Lock
Y Indicator

ACTION OPEN

A Finger-Lever
B Catch on Automatic
  Cut-off
C Automatic Cut-off
D Breech-Opening
E Breech-Bolt
G Magazine Carrier
H Projection on Receiver
  for Finger-Lever

K Sear
L Retractor
N Hammer
P Sear Screw
R Trigger
S Trigger Safety Projection
U Recoil Shoulder
V Trigger and Lever Lock

Phantom View of Model 1899 with Action Closed

Model 1903 .22 caliber Repeater

SAVAGE .22 CALIBER RIFLES

1. MODEL 3 BOLT ACTION. 2. MODEL 4 BOLT ACTION REPEATER. 3. MODEL 5 BOLT ACTION REPEATER. 4. MODEL 19-33 BOLT ACTION TARGET REPEATER. 5. MODEL 23AA SPORTER REPEATER. 6. MODEL 6 AUTOMATIC

SAVAGE RIFLES

7. MODEL 29 CALIBER .22 REPEATER

SAVAGE HIGH POWER

8. MODEL 99T LEVER ACTION REPEATER. 9. MODEL 45 BOLT ACTION SPORTER. 10. MODEL 219
.30-30 SINGLE SHOT HAMMERLESS

magazine held 20 .22 shorts, 17 .22 longs, and 15 .22 long-rifles.

The arm was hammerless with a solid breech, solid top and side ejection similar to the Model 1903. The stock on the new Model 1914 was far better shaped than the early type of rifles. It was full-pistol-grip type, well curved, and with a fairly large shotgun-style butt. This model was one of the finest slide-action repeaters on the market and in design was many years ahead of its day. In this respect, Savage listened to the ideas of noted firearms authorities before designing the rifle and followed their suggestions as closely as possible.

The Model 1914 retained the time-tried and approved features of the mechanism of the old Model 1903. The breech bolt and action were very similar in design and locked in exactly the same way. The firing mechanism, ejector, and safety were identical. The take-down device owing to its long bearings operating almost the entire length of the receiver was especially strong and rigid. A simple but ingenious design of carrier and action slide made it impossible for more than one cartridge at a time to be released from the magazine, regardless of whether short- or long-rifles were mixed indiscriminately.

The magazine was completely closed and locked preventing another cartridge from entering the receiver until the action had been opened to extract and eject the fired shell. Therefore, in case of any accident to the cartridge in the chamber it could in no way discharge another cartridge lying loosely in the bottom of the receiver. All of the early Savage barrels for the Model 1914 were rifled with six lands and grooves. In 1919 Savage introduced their famous Model 1919 N. R. A. rifle with a four-groove barrel. This produced excellent accuracy and Savage was so well pleased with it that they adapted the 1914 barrels to the four-groove system and all made after the date of 1919 showed this type of Savage N. R. A. rifling.

The Model 1914 repeater was regularly equipped with a 24-inch octagon barrel, tubular magazine, extra long slide handle, extra full pistol grip, corrugated steel butt-plate, and 24-inch octagon barrel. Sights included a bead front and open sporting rear. Apparently, this was also made with a 22-inch octagon barrel as it is so listed in some earlier catalogs. Weight of this

rifle ran about 5¾ pounds. It was also available with various extras in accordance with the Savage policy of fancy work, special stock, engraving, and so forth.

Savage NRA Match Rifle Model 1919
Intro 1919   Disc 1933

The design of the Model 1919 rifle was undertaken at the request of a number of the most prominent and most skillful smallbore riflemen of the country. A good bolt-action repeater was not available—a repeating target rifle of sufficient size, weight, and accuracy for truly serious target shooting. Accordingly, Savage went to work to fill this particular demand.

The Model 1919, frequently called the Model 19, is a five-shot bolt-action repeater, having a full-length military type of pistol-grip stock, with a forward band at the end of the stock attaching to the barrel and a midway band also attaching to the barrel. While it has been obsolete for a great many years, it made rifle history for Savage.

The stock was of pistol-grip style with a large thick butt-plate of steel, a 25-inch round barrel and a post or blade front sight along the accepted military lines. The rear sight was an innovation. Savage introduced their own make of receiver peep rear sight of micrometer adjustment for both elevation and windage, with a half-minute click. The rifle was built rather heavy, tipping the scales at 7 pounds—better than any .22 repeating rifle then on the market.

Barrels were rifled with the new system, experimentally developed by the Savage Company, and having four grooves with the lands and grooves of equal width. This was the result of extensive tests of all available types of rifling then in use and it proved to be highly satisfactory.

Numerous factory tests of all kinds of rifling in .22 barrels were run with this new action and in machine-rest tests up to 300 yards the 1919 system proved to be superior. Factory barrels ran equal in accuracy to a great many of the fancy-named handmade barrels then being supplied to target riflemen to order.

Each Model 1919 rifle was individually targeted and accuracy verified at the factory before shipment. They performed beautifully, even in the days when .22 ammunition was not up to the present standard. The 1920 catalog on ammunition for .22 target shoots has an interesting comment well worth quoting.

"AMMUNITION—Accurate shooting requires not only an accurate barrel but also accurate ammunition. Inaccurate ammunition will not shoot well even in an accurate barrel. Sometimes it may injure the barrel. Smokeless powder, although wonderfully satisfactory in centerfire cartridges, is not well adapted to rimfire varieties, being less accurate, less powerful, and less uniform than black powder, and much less accurate, uniform, and powerful than Lesmok and semi-smokeless powders. Besides this, rimfire smokeless cartridges leave a residue that is practically certain to rust and ruin barrels in which they are used, no matter how carefully they are cleaned." A bit of further explanation of this is in order.

The author's interest in match rifle shooting began back around 1917 and when the Model 1919 rifle came out he was among the first to acquire it. This particular job was highly satisfactory but in the early 1920's there was but a single cartridge available suitable for real match shooting. I refer to the cartridge which made rimfire history and established all of the match records of that era—the U. S. N. R. A., manufactured by the United States Cartridge Company, of Lowell, Massachusetts.

Incidentally, this cartridge was manufactured in a division of the Winchester Repeating Arms Co. when the United States Cartridge Company discontinued their big Lowell plant. Immediately, upon the close of the World War, they made arrangements with Winchester to use part of their manufacturing facilities for the construction of United States ammunition. It was all marketed by the United States Cartridge Company of New York City and the older riflemen will recall with keen pleasure that famous red and blue box of .22 long rifle ammunition. All other ammunition makers, of course, loaded Lesmok and semi-smokeless powder. Some of them had some very good ammunition but in this author's opinion the U. S. N. R. A. had no competition for a great many years in the early 1920's. The combination of Lesmok powder and their particular development of a primer was

ideal. Ignition was perfect, accuracy was practically equal to the best of today's ammunition.

Some further comment on .22's may explain the objection to the smokeless variety in early days. Early smokeless powders adapted to rimfire cartridges were extremely difficult to ignite and accordingly an extra strong, highly corrosive primer, containing a large quantity of powdered glass, was used. This powdered glass contributed greatly to the erosion and the residue added to the corrosion of the barrel. Rifles used with smokeless powder, particularly if in rimfire calibers, soon went to pieces, sometimes within 1000 to 1500 rounds of ammunition. Lesmok powder in a properly cleaned barrel failed to create serious damage even after 50,000 to 75,000 rounds.

Even today Lesmok powder, despite its many disadvantages, still holds the top place among the rimfire match shooters. Development of modern smokeless powders and modern non-corrosive primers has greatly eliminated the destructive effect and inaccuracies of the early smokeless .22's so that today one need never fear about using smokeless ammunition. As a matter of fact, it is to be recommended, and match grades of smokeless cartridges are available which will equal or outshoot the Lesmok variety.

It is a little-known fact today that the early 1919 rifles were available chambered for .22 short rimfire cartridge, always a popular number for indoor gallery shooting. Up to 25 yards, the .22 short was equal to the .22 long-rifle from an accuracy standpoint, particularly in the earlier days. Today it is falling into the discard for match shooting and therefore its development by ammunition makers has been sadly neglected. Model 1919 rifles designed for using the .22 short had special magazines which would handle the short perfectly and the rifles were not only chambered but rifled with a slow twist to handle this particular cartridge. This special caliber was available only on individual order at the factory although no extra charge was made for it.

The Savage receiver micrometer sights are well worthy of discussion. This sight had two knurled thumb screws, one on top and one on the left side controlling elevation and windage. The top screw handled the elevation, and by turning it clockwise or from left to right the sight was lowered, thus making the rifle shoot lower. Turning the screw in the opposite direction the position of the shot on the target was raised. The windage screw on the left side of the sight when turned clockwise moved the sights to the left, thus making the rifle shoot in that direction. These windage and elevation screws had little click indicators for accurate adjustment. Each click of the elevation or windage screws represented one minute of angle, or one inch change of impact at 100 yards.

The clicks were not only audible but sufficiently snappy so that they could be felt under the fingers, enabling accurate adjustment for re-locating shots even when shooting from a dark firing point. This was of particular value in indoor range shooting.

A good example of the correction value of this sight which will not be news to the modern advanced rifleman but of interest to some of the younger generation is the ease of correction with these micrometer click sights.

Suppose one is shooting on a 75-foot range. One carefully aimed "sighting shot" shows an 8 o'clock bullet hole in the target one-half inch low and an inch to the left of the center of the bullseye. To correct for this and bring the succeeding shot into the center of the bullseye, the elevation screw is given two clicks to the left so as to raise the sights two minutes of angle and the windage screw is given four clicks to the left for four minutes of angle. The next shot is centered.

This minute of angle stuff is very simple to recall. Bear in mind that one minute of angle is merely one inch at 100 yards. One minute of angle at 50 yards is one-half inch and at 25 yards one-quarter inch. At 200 yards it is 2 inches. Accurately adjustable sights of this nature are a necessity for serious target shooting, as different makes of ammunition and frequently different lots of the same make will show a different elevation in your particular rifle. The sights make it easy for you to correct it instantly and without excessive shooting in through the trial and error system.

Savage mentioned the importance of fouling a barrel before shooting when they brought out the Model 1919. This is today a religion with all target riflemen. A serious shooter would never start a string using a clean bore. The point of impact is frequently much higher for the first shot than for succeeding shots. The first bullet wipes out all traces of oil or cleaning solution left in the barrel and deposits a thin film of bullet lubricant and powder fouling for the entire length of the bore. Succeeding shots do not change a great deal. Each bullet wipes out a good deal of debris of the first cartridge. Therefore, the good target man always throws his first shot, and sometimes three or four shots, into the target butts or otherwise discharges one in a safe manner, to be sure that the rifle is properly settled.

The Model 1919 Savage used the detachable box magazine, each with a capacity of five cartridges. To fill the magazine it was removed from the rifle by pushing forward a small knob on the bottom of the magazine to release the magazine from its catch. This tilted the magazine somewhat, releasing a spring affair which locked it into position. It could then be drawn out through the bottom of the magazine well.

The magazines were charged outside of the rifle and any desired number of extra magazines could be carried in the pocket or shooting kit. The system of charging these magazines with a wide variety of clip magazines on the market today is so well known that it does not warrant repeating here. It will suffice to say that the Savage magazine was not as highly refined as the present type of Savage, Winchester, Stevens, Remington, and other clip-type magazines. This, of course, is to be expected.

The magazine was quickly snapped into position by pushing it up into the magazine well to the full length of its travel whereupon a charged magazine was slipped into position and held securely. To load, it was merely necessary to raise the bolt handle, draw it rearward to the full extent of its scope, push it forward again and turn down the bolt handle. The rifle was then loaded and cocked. This particular action was designed to cock on the closing stroke of the bolt.

The safety was located on the right side of the bolt housing in back of the bolt handle and directly above the trigger. When the safety was raised the firing mechanism was securely locked and the rifle could not be fired. When the safety was down, the arm was ready to be discharged.

Match riflemen rarely used their magazines in slow-fire shooting, and this Model 1919 was designed so that it was a simple matter for the shooter to start his cartridges in the chamber with his fingers through the ample receiver opening. The closing of the bolt completed the operation.

The Model 1919 had one minor fault in common with most of the low-priced .22's on the market—the sear acted as a bolt stop. To remove the bolt from the receiver it was necessary to open the action by drawing the bolt to the rear until it struck its stop at the rear end of its travel. Then the trigger was pressed and the bolt withdrawn from the receiver. To reinsert the bolt it was necessary to hold down the trigger until the sear had cleared the bolt stop. This type of mechanism is satisfactory if handled correctly but if abused is inclined to change the smooth operation of the trigger pull.

This particular rifle had the barrel and receiver made in one piece, which has both advantages and disadvantages. It is necessary to replace the entire receiver whenever a barrel requires attention. On the other hand, the one-piece construction insures rigidity.

NRA Target Rifle Model 1933
Intro 1933 Disc 1941

When this rifle was first brought out it was called the "New Savage Model 19 N. R. A. .22-caliber target rifle 1933 design." The Savage designation is self-explanatory.

The Model 1919 rifle had rapidly become obsolete due to improved .22 match rifles then available on the market. The Model 1919 had a great many weak points including a rather ugly-looking stock with crude finger grooves in the forearm, and stock shape which is today considered ill-fitting and crude in its type of sights. The original micrometer rear peep sight did not use a target disc so the rifleman had to be content with a simple peep-hole in an elevating micrometer-controlled slide. Riflemen demanded something better and Savage undertook to fill this demand.

In co-operation with the National Rifle Association this 19-33 design was completed. It is frequently called today the Model 19-33 and in

some cases the 1933. Regardless of the designation, it is today one of Savage's best target rifles.

The Model 19-33 was chambered only for the .22 long-rifle cartridge and adapted to either high-speed or standard numbers. Stock was of excellent shape, thick in the butt, full in the forearm and, with the accepted target rifleman's idea of a forearm, extending approximately one-half the length of the barrel. This stock was of a good grade selected straight-grain American walnut with an excellent full-pistol grip. Stock measurements show a drop at the heel of $1\frac{7}{8}$ inches, at comb of $1\frac{5}{8}$ inches, a length of $13\frac{1}{2}$ inches, from trigger to center of butt-plate, and an overall stock length of 32 inches. The butt-plate was $1\frac{5}{8}$ inches wide and $5\frac{1}{8}$ inches long, ample for any shooting position.

In this model, as in the early 1919 types, the barrel and receiver were in one piece, the barrel itself being 25 inches long and the barrel and receiver assembly about 32 inches long. An improved target sight of new design was used giving a sighting radius of $30\frac{1}{2}$ inches between front and rear units. This was of the peep or aperture type with elevation and windage adjustments provided with positive clicks graduated to one-half minutes of angles—one-half of those of the Model 1919 types. Front sight was of the straight-blade military type slightly under-cut to eliminate glare and mounted on a dovetail base inserted into the barrel.

The barrel itself was drilled for telescope sight blocks for the lad who preferred glass-sight shooting. Weight of the rifle was also increased, due to the large and much better-shaped stock, to about 8 pounds and it came regularly equipped with sling swivels for a standard $1\frac{1}{4}$-inch military sling strap. The forward swivel was attached to a barrel band at the front of the forearm and was located $16\frac{1}{2}$ inches forward of the trigger. The action itself was greatly improved and is entirely different from the Model 1919. The loading port was greatly increased in size to make for easier single-shot loading. A somewhat improved five-shot rigid detachable magazine was used and in recent years this has been still further improved.

The action is, of course, of bolt design but in the 33 model was of the "speed" type, with a very strong firing spring which greatly shortened the

 The Rifle in America © 1938, 1947, 1953 by Philip B. Sharpe

SAVAGE ARMS

hammer fall. Savage claims that the lock time is less than ²⁄₁₀₀₀ of a second. The mechanism cocks on the opening stroke of the bolt whereas the earlier model cocked on the closing stroke. The bolt head is recessed to completely inclose the rim of the .22 cartridge. It is equipped with two locking lugs as against one on the earlier types. Firing pin and bolt face are built of high-grade alloy steel scientifically heat-treated.

Since this rifle made its appearance some five years ago the author has heard but one objection to it and that is the Savage design of rear sight. While this is a highly accurate rear sight enabling ultra-fine adjustments, the top of the elevating screw is approximately three-quarters of an inch above the top of the sight disc when the standard ⅝-inch diameter disc is used. This creates a major problem of entering the rifle into a gun case.

In 1936 Savage brought out an improved version of this sight—an extension type of rear sight which lowered the top of the elevation to approximately one-quarter of an inch. This had the windage control screw and scale located on the right rather than the left side and brought the sight approximately 1⅜ inches closer to the eye.

This improved sight is now standard.

In addition, in recent years Savage has adapted this same Model 1919 to the requirements of riflemen who prefer the Lyman 48 rear sight and lists this particular job as their Model 19-L. It is the same as the standard rifle in every respect except that the Savage rear sight is omitted and a Lyman 48-Y is used with a Lyman No. 17A hooded front sight with removable inserts.

In addition those riflemen who demanded a truly heavy rifle succeeded in getting this in 1934 when Savage introduced their Model 19-M heavy barrel job. This was the same as the standard rifle except for an extra heavy barrel, 28 inches long and 1³⁄₁₆ inches in diameter at the muzzle. The longer barrel gave a 34-inch overall sighting radius and this barrel is, of course, fitted with telescope sight blocks. Standard sights include the improved Savage No. 15 extension type rear sight described above, a hooded globe-post front sight with removable hood and an adjustable trigger pull. Weight of this model is around 9¼ pounds—an ideal target rifle weight.

Savage Model 19H Hornet Rifle
Intro 1933 Disc 1940

The Model 19H rifle is the answer of the Savage factory to a request for a suitable medium-priced super-accurate rifle chambered for the .22 Hornet and of target design and weight. Handling this little high-speed centerfire cartridge it delivers excellent accuracy although we have yet to see the accuracy of the same cartridge in a good single-shot duplicated in this Savage bolt-action repeater. Specifications for the Hornet model were the same as for the Standard Model 19-33.

Barrel, of course, is of high-pressure smokeless steel. The loading port, bolt mechanism and magazine were the same as that used in the rifle to be described later—their Model 23D.

Savage Model 1920 Hi-Power Bolt Action
Intro 1920 Disc 1928

This Model 1920 Savage Hi-Power rifle was the first attempt of the Savage Arms Company to turn out a bolt-action high-power rifle. As in most high-power bolt actions it was a solid-frame job and was excellent in its design. It had a very short life, which is to be regretted as it had many features the later types of Savage rifles do not include.

The Model 20 had a light-weight tapered barrel with a lug integral with the barrel on which was mounted the white metal bead front sight. Rear sight was of the typical open adjustable sporting type with adjustments for elevation only. It was of flat-top rather than buckhorn variety and the stock was of walnut given a varnish finish. It had a very neat-shaped pistol grip, rather slender and weak through the grip, corrugated trigger and corrugated steel shotgun butt-plate. A certain amount of checking covered the grip and parts of the very slender knob-tip forearm. Weight of this rifle was only 5 pounds, 14 ounces. It was available when first brought out in .250/3000 caliber with a 22-inch barrel and .300 Savage caliber with a 24-inch barrel. A few in .30/06 caliber were made with 24-inch barrels and proved satisfactory in service.

173

This Model 20 represented the latest and highest development of the American hunting rifle at the time of its introduction. It was the first of a long line of Savage improvements in modernizing their line.

When this rifle made its appearance it was considered the acme of perfection. Today with our standards of thicker and heavier stocks and larger forearm it would not be considered a satisfactory number. The rifle as a whole shows extreme attention to detail in turning out a master sporting rifle. In this particular model the barrel and receiver were separate units, the barrel fitting into the receiver in the conventional fashion. The top of the receiver ring and receiver bridge were carefully matted to prevent the reflection of light while sighting. A large locking lug at the forward end of the bolt insured extreme strength of the action and this rifle was capable of standing the maximum pressures in use during its era.

In accordance with the improved designs of rifles of military types the action was cocked by a camming operation on the opening of the bolt handle. This camming operation not only cocked the firing pin but at the same time exerted tremendous primary extraction power, starting even the tightest shells. The firing pin and the knob on the cocking piece were built as one unit and the rifle could readily be cocked by hand if it was not desired to carry it in that condition.

An additional safety feature was the locking of the root or base of the bolt handle in a special slot at the rear of the receiver. This gave an additional safety-lug feature although all of the strain was taken by the two locking lugs in the receiver ring.

The magazine was of the non-detachable type loaded through the opening in the top of the receiver when the bolt was withdrawn in conventional Springfield style. It had a capacity of five cartridges staggered in two columns. With this magazine filled and one in the chamber a six-shot rifle was had. High-pressure steel was used in the rifle barrel and simple sights as described. Special rear peep sights could also be supplied by the factory or tapped in styles manufactured by rear sights builders.

It is interesting to note that this receiver was designed for clip loading if desired although neither of the two special cartridges—the .250/3000 or the .300 Savage—were ever supplied by a factory packed in clips. The conventional method is to single-load these in the magazine by dropping one into the receiver opening and pressing it down until it catches and then feeding in another in the same manner.

A very interesting feature of this rifle—and to this author's way of thinking an important improvement—was the shotgun-type safety located on the upper tang of the receiver. The safety locked the sear against disengagement with the cocking piece and also locked the bolt against opening. The shotgun-type safety is the quickest of all safeties to handle and, due to the design of this particular type, locking the sear rather than blocking the trigger insured the piece against accidental discharge. This feature is today being used on some of the high-priced imported Mauser bolt-action rifles as an extra feature for which a very substantial charge is made.

The butt-plate on the Model 20 is of corrugated steel to insure against slipping on the shoulder. As in other rifles of that particular period, the bolt could be withdrawn by holding back the trigger, allowing easy access to the barrel from the breech end for cleaning. This method of withdrawing the bolt is extremely simple but creates the problem of using the sear as a bolt stop. Continued rough use is inclined to change the trigger pull somewhat.

Around 1925 Savage released the job they called the improved Model 20. This was essentially the same rifle with a slightly different type of stock having minor improvements in dimensions, and different style of checking and sling eyes located in the butt, permitting the use of quick detachable swivels and of sling straps. The forearm was increased somewhat in size although it was still slender as compared with the modern specifications for bolt-action arms. The open barrel sight was omitted and in accordance with this the barrel was not slotted. A Lyman 54 receiver peep sight was located just in back of the bolt handle where it gave greatly improved performance over the older type of crude open sights. A white metal bead front sight mounted on a base made integral with the barrel was retained. The re-designed barrel was also increased somewhat in weight thus providing a more rigid barrel capable of higher accuracy and velocity.

It will be recalled that the original .300 Savage

had a bullet weight of 150 grains at a muzzle velocity of 2700 f.s. About this time ammunition companies introduced a 180-grain .300 Savage bullet at a muzzle velocity of 2400 f.s. This heavier bullet did not perform very well in the light-weight barrel and may have in some way prompted the decision of Savage to increase the weight of the gun. Whereas the early weight was only 5 pounds, 14 ounces, the 1925 version tipped the scales at 6¾ pounds, some 14 ounces extra weight, about half of which was in the stock and the remainder in the barrel. No other major changes were made in this rifle until its discontinuance. It was a beautifully shaped little arm with a well-curved bolt handle sloping gracefully to the rear where the large operating knob was just slightly in front of the trigger showing ease of operation. In the minds of many rifle owners this discontinued model was the most graceful arm that Savage ever turned out.

Savage Sporter Model 1922
Intro 1922   Disc 1922

The Savage Model 1922 was on the market but a short time. Essentially, this was an experimental model, and this author has never seen one of them and has very little information on it in his files. He cannot find it listed in any catalog. It was made only in .22 long-rifle and was a sporting version of the Model 1919, with a sporting type of stock, slightly lighter barrel and similar specifications. It had a five-shot magazine of box type with a 23-inch round barrel and weighed in the vicinity of six pounds. It had a very short life on the market occasioned by the introduction of the Model 23A, which corrected the weak points of the Model 1922.

Model 1923 Bolt Action Sporter
Intro 1923   Disc 1946

The Model 23 line of rifles covers a wide variety of low- and medium-power calibers running to .22 long-rifle and various centerfire numbers such as .25/20, .32/20 and .22 Hornet.

The first of these new Model 1923 rifles to be

released was the 23A in .22 long-rifle caliber. All of these are bolt-action repeaters with box or detachable clip magazines and with the barrel and receiver made in one piece. All were manufactured with full-pistol-grip stocks, well shaped through the butt, with a shotgun type of butt. The forearm of the original model was the typical slender type with the knob tip but this was discontinued in favor of a plain full type of forearm much better adapted to the ideas of modern riflemen.

A large loading port located on the left side of the receiver permitted single-shot loading if desired. It had a swift, easy bolt action which has been improved upon since its introduction so that today these make excellent medium-priced rifles for their particular field.

The Models 23B and C were chambered for the .25/20 and .32/20 cartridge respectively and were adapted for miscellaneous medium-size game. The Model 23D was designed for the Hornet. All magazines had a five-shot capacity and the sights included a blade-type front sight and an open sporting rear type of the flat V-notch variety adjustable for elevation only. All stocks on the original rifles were given a varnish finish and all models weighed about 6 pounds with the exception of the Hornet which tipped the scales at 6½ pounds. The Model A rifle chambered for the .22 long-rifle cartridge had a 23-inch round barrel. All others ran 25 inches.

By 1933 these rifles had been stepped up greatly in quality and appearance and workmanship. They had established a name for themselves as the first efficient bolt-action repeating rifle designed to handle the .25/20 and .32/20 numbers. The Hornet was available at that time just in Winchester's Model 54 and Savage was the first to bring out this caliber in the medium priced field. All Savage Hornets this author has seen were chambered somewhat oversize.

The action remained practically unchanged on the improved model. It obtained half-cock on the opening stroke and full-cock on the closing stroke. Both operations used a camming movement to reduce the cocking effort to a minimum. A large square locking lug was located on the left-hand rear of the bolt, which together with the root of the bolt handle fitting into a recess in the receiver gave double locking lugs at the rear end of the breech bolt. The rifle was always fully locked before the firing pin could be released.

Barrels were all made of the same high-power smokeless steel used in the famous Model 1899 and the shape of the pistol grip was altered somewhat at this time and the stock was made reasonably full. The butt itself was built slightly heavier and the varnish finish continued. The forearm showed the major improvement, being left large and knobless to add grace and a good handful to this particular little rifle. The same crude sights with the exception of a gold bead front were continued but the receiver was tapped for the Lyman 48Y micrometer receiver peep.

Extras in 1933 included an oil finish on the stock at $5.50 additional and checking on grip and forearm another $5.00, and ⅞- or 1¼-inch leather sling straps and non-detachable or quick-detachable type sling swivels either in ⅞- or 1¼-inch types could be had. Incidentally, the earlier type could be used with the Special Savage Model 1919 N. R. A. micrometer rear peep sight if desired. These receivers were tapped for them. The same rotary type of safety blocking the sear was used on all of these models throughout the duration of their life, and consisted of a thumb-operated safety just behind the bolt handle where it could readily be moved upward or down. The down position made it practically flat with the surface of the stock at that point. In that position the safety was off. Raising it upward placed it "on" so it could be snapped off quickly while the shooter was throwing the arm to his shoulder.

In 1938 Savage lists these three rifles with the exception of the Model A which is called the Model 23AA. This particular number is a .22 long-rifle with 23-inch barrel and the old style knob-tipped forearm. The varnish finish has been abandoned in favor of the almost universal oil finish. Stock specifications this year show a drop in comb of 1⅝ inches and at heel 2¾ inches. Length of stock is 13½ inches. This is equipped with a white metal bead front sight and flat-top open sporting rear sight. The receiver is tapped for the improved No. 15 Savage extension receiver peep sight and weighs around six pounds.

Their Model 23B has a high-pressure smokeless-steel barrel, same stock specifications, but the forearm is the improved type 1½ inches wide and minus the knob tip. It has a much neater general appearance. This Model 23B is chambered only for the .25/20 and the receiver is tapped for the new No. 15 Savage extension peep rear sight or the Lyman 48 micrometer receiver sight. The magazine in this caliber is of four-shot capacity.

The Model 23C is available only in .32/20 caliber and is identical with the Model 23B in all specifications except caliber, while the Model 23D is the .22 Hornet with the same specifications.

Savage Repeating Rifle Model 25
Intro 1925   Disc 1929

The Model 25 was a slide-action repeater essentially a revised version of the Model 1914. This may have been the identical same gun revised although it does show slightly more modern specifications than the early type. It was of course a hammerless, slide- or trombone-action type of .22 caliber rifle. A very long fluted slide handle was used as in the Model 1909 and the magazine was similarly of the tubular type. The ejection port was located on the right side of the receiver so that no fired shells could be thrown into the shooter's face. In addition an indicator was located on the top tang right where it could be quickly located by the thumb and show the cocked or fired position of the hammer. When cocked the indicator pin projected slightly as in the Model 1899 hammerless high-power. The take-down screw was located just above the forward part of the trigger guard and was heavily knurled with a deep coin slot. The locking mechanism was similar to the Model 1909 and extremely rigid.

The barrel was 24 inches long, full octagon and an excellent shotgun-type pistol-grip butt stock. Stocks were of American walnut. Butt-plate was of corrugated steel for the proper action on the shoulder. The tubular magazine held 20 short, 17 long, or 15 long-rifle cartridges and would handle cartridges mixed indiscriminately. The weight ran 5¾ pounds. Sights were the crude open type, flat-top hunting style adjustable for elevation only and a bright metal blade front sight. The receiver tang was tapped for a good micrometer or otherwise adjustable peep sight if desired, but this was not regularly furnished.

Slide Action Repeater Model 29
Intro 1929   Disc

The Model 29 is the final revised version of the famous tubular magazine 1914 and a revised version of the 1925 model. It is a take-down .22 long rifle caliber with 24-inch octagon barrel, gold bead front sight and flat-top open rear sight located on the barrel, the rear sight being adjustable for elevation. A full pistol grip is used, neatly checked. The forearm is of the long, smooth type rather than fluted and has a simple diamond style checking. It weighs around 5½ pounds.

When this first came out Savage listed it as their de luxe rifle. With the exception of stock and forearm specifications this remained the same as the Model 1925 except for the elimination of a rather useful feature—the indicator pin which projected above the top rear of the receiver to indicate whether the hammer was cocked or not, rather important in a hammerless gun. An improved safety of the push-button type was used, located in the rear of the trigger guard just in back of the trigger. Pushed in flush with the edge of the trigger guard on the right side the safety was off. In the reverse direction, it was on. A Lyman gold bead front sight was used and an open rear. Butt-plate was of hard rubber.

The 1938 specifications show that this rifle is retained about as first introduced except that the top tang of the receiver is drilled and tapped for the No. 30 Savage rear peep sight.

In addition this same rifle is fitted in the Model 29S which has the same specifications as the Model 29 except that it is regularly equipped with a Savage No. 30 rear peep sight and a Savage No. 31 folding middle sight. The price for this Model 29S is but $2.50 over the Model 29 price.

Super Sporter Models 40 & 45
Intro 1928   Disc 1940

These two rifles are identical except for appointments. The Model 40 is listed as the standard grade and the Model 45 as the special grade.

They are bolt-action, high-power rifles in .250/3000 Savage, .30/30 in 22-inch barrels and in .300 Savage and .30/06 Government in 24-inch barrels. The Model 40 has an adjustable flat-top open rear sight located on the barrel just in front of the receiver with a white metal bead front sight mounted in a base integral with the barrel.

The Model 45 is the same as the Model 40 as to caliber and specifications, except that a certain amount of checking is used and a receiver peep rear sight is located on the left side of the receiver just above the cocking piece. For some peculiar reason the rear sight was originally included. This rear sight was of No. 40 Lyman receiver rear peep with adjustments for both elevation and windage. Rear sight was of the folding-leaf type. Practically no change has been made in this rifle since its introduction to date of 1938.

Both the Model 40 and Model 45 rifles have a four-shot detachable box magazine removed to the bottom of the magazine well. They are today the only truly high-power bolt-action rifles having a removable magazine.

Models 4 & 4S Repeaters
Intro 1933   Disc

Models 4 and 4S are entirely different models from the Models 04 and 1904 previously manufactured and long since discontinued. The Model 4 is a .22 caliber bolt-action repeater of excellent size, shape, and general appearance. It is a take-down arm fitted with a 24-inch take-down barrel with crowned muzzle. It is chambered for the short, long, and long-rifle cartridges, both regular and high-speed. A five-shot detachable clip magazine is used. As in other repeaters the bolt-action mechanism is self-cocking. Stock is one-piece American walnut, well shaped with a good pistol grip, fluted comb and large well-shaped forearm.

In this particular model, the barrel and tubular receiver are separate units. The bolt handle is angled backwards for graceful appearance and easy manipulation. In addition the entire bolt and bolt handle are chrome-plated as is the trigger, and all operating parts are neatly polished. The magazine is of the five-shot detachable-clip type using the same locking system which may be found in the Model 19-33. The weight of the gun runs around 5½ pounds. On the Model 4 a gold bead front sight is used with an open sporting rear sight of flat top variety adjustable for elevation. The pistol grip only is checked; no checking on the forearm.

The Model 4S is the same as the Model 4 rifle except for sighting equipment. The open rear sight on the barrel is omitted and the barrel slot filled with a dovetail blank base. Front sight is a hooded peep of Savage design with three interchangeable inserts—flat top post, bead, and peep. This is neatly mounted on a ramp base dovetailed into the barrel. The detachable hood must be used with this sight as the hood holds the inserts in place.

The rear sight is a receiver peep of Savage design using a large eye disc with a special plate on the face of the disc having three sizes of apertures which may be moved to expose the desired size instantly.

The only change in the 1938 line is to eliminate the blank sight base used on the barrel and substitute a folding middle sight of Savage design. All other specifications remain the same. Hard-rubber butt-plates are used on these models.

Models 3, 3S & 3T Single Shots
Intro 1931   Disc 1952

The Model 3 rifle is a low-priced single-shot of the same general outline as the Model 4.

This rifle is, of course, a take-down number fitted with a 26-inch round barrel and a tubular receiver. As in the Model 4 this single-shot has its barrel fitted into an receiver rather than made as one combined unit. The stock bears no ornamentation but is of genuine walnut of more or less the outline of the Model 4 except that the fluted comb has been omitted. A hard-rubber butt-plate 1⅜ by 4½ inches is used and the forearm is 1⅞ inches wide at the take-down screw. Overall stock length is 28¼ inches and overall length of the rifle 43 inches. This little rifle is a light-weight number tipping about 4½ pounds on the author's scales. The action is designed

for either standard or high-speed cartridges of .22 short, long, or long-rifle varieties and the action mechanism is almost identical with the Model 4 with the exception of the elimination of the repeating magazine. A rotary cocking-piece type of safety is used. Bolt face is recessed to enclose the cartridge head. The action cocks on the opening stroke of the bolt and full-cocks on the closing stroke.

On the Model 3 or standard grade the sight equipment is a gold bead front and a flat-top open rear sight located on the barrel adjustable for elevation only. On the Model 3S there are no changes in the rifle itself but the sight equipment is identical with the equipment used on the Model 4S previously described. As in the Model 4S when this was first introduced, a blank sight base was used in the barrel slot replacing the open rear sight. In recent years and to date a folding flat-top barrel sight is used in this position.

When this first came out they also introduced a special rifle known as the Model 3ST or target grade. This was identically the same rifle as the Model 3S with the addition of a ⅞-inch sling strap, sling studs and swivels. The Model 3ST has been discontinued, but the 3 and 3S appear in the 1946 line without change.

Models 5 & 5S Bolt Action Repeater
Intro 1936   Disc

The Model 5 is very similar to the Model 4 rifle except that a tubular magazine is used instead of the detachable box type. The barrel is 24 inches long, round, neatly tapered and with a crowned muzzle. It is chambered for the .22 long-rifle cartridge but will handle the long and short numbers either in regular or high-speed varieties without adjustment of mechanism. Magazine capacity is 15 long-rifle cartridges, longs, or 21 shorts.

The action is similar to other Savage bolt types but cocks on the opening stroke. It has a short hammer fall giving speed ignition and a convenient independent safety located where it can be operated by the right thumb just at the right-hand side of the rear of the receiver. The bolt is chromium-plated as is the trigger but the bolt handle is not angled as in other models.

Stock is a one-piece number with a full pistol grip, fluted comb and of walnut, oil-finished. The grip is checked. There is no checking on the forearm. Butt-plate is of hard rubber. Sights include a gold bead front and sporting type open rear, adjustable for both elevation and windage. Receiver is also tapped for mounting telescope sights of Weaver design. This rifle weighs about 6 pounds and has an overall length of 43½ inches. It is of take-down construction in the conventional manner, using a large knurled thumb nut beneath the forearm.

The Model 5S is the same as the Model 5 except for special Savage sights previously described for the Models 3S and 4S.

Models 6 & 6S Automatic Repeaters
Intro 1938 Disc

Two new numbers in the Savage line for 1938 are the Models 6 and 6S. These automatic repeaters are unique in that they combine in one rifle a bolt-action single-shot, a bolt-action tubular magazine repeater, and an autoloading repeater.

As a bolt-action gun this rifle is extremely fast, and while announced early this year it did not make its appearance until around May 1.

As a bolt-action repeater, operation of the bolt knob differed from the conventional .22 types in that it was a straight pull, backward and forward. The shift from the automatic action to the repeating bolt-action type was accomplished through the bolt handle itself. When pulled out as far as it would go to the right, the action performs as an autoloading type and on discharge of the cartridge in the chamber, this bolt handle together with the breech bolt is blown backward to the full extent of its travel and returned by means of recoil springs, scooping a cartridge from the tubular magazine carrier mechanism into the chamber for another shot. It does not discharge automatically but requires a separate pull of the trigger for each shot. The tubular magazine capacity is very similar to the Model 5 holding 15 long rifles, 17 longs, and 21 shorts.

The barrel is 24 inches long, round, neatly tapered and with a crowned muzzle. To lock the breech so that the gun can be operated as a repeater or as a single-shot, the bolt or operating handle is closed with a cartridge in the chamber and then pushed inward. This rides through an opening in the left-hand side of the receiver, locking the breech bolt rigidly in place so that it cannot blow open. To then operate as a single-shot one discharges the piece, draws the end of the bolt handle out of this locking port and draws the bolt to the rear to extract and eject the fired shell.

The action is of chrome-molybdenum alloy steel and a tubular receiver, the barrel being fitted into the receiver. It is thoroughly heat-treated for maximum strength and the action can be readily disassembled without tools for cleaning. It is probably the simplest form of autoloading action on the market today. A typical thumb-operated safety is located above the trigger on the right side of the stock and can be reached by the thumb. This is believed to be the lowest-priced automatic rifle ever placed on the market and bears the retail price of $15.50 on the Model 6 and $16.25 on the 6S.

Sights for the standard and the "S" special number are the same as on the Models 3, 4, and 5, and a description of them will not be repeated here.

TELESCOPE-EQUIPPED RIFLES

The Models 3, 4, 5, and 6 are available in 1938 equipped with Savage-Weaver telescope sights manufactured for Savage by Weaver complete with Weaver mounts. The peep and special ramp front sights are not used on these models as they are not necessary but the lower grade of bead front and open rear are mounted. The rifle comes factory-equipped with these telescope sights.

The Model 3 uses the Savage No. 10 telescope which is a Weaver No. 329. Magnification is 3-power, micrometer focus at eyepiece, length 10 inches, weight 8 ounces complete with mounts. Adjustment for elevation and windage of the click type internal in the telescope. Fine cross-hair reticule is used. The open sight on the rifle can be used without removing the telescope from the arm but this scope is detachable complete with its mount as in all other Weaver types.

The Models 4T, 5T and 6T use the Savage No. 20 telescope sight—the Weaver No. 344.

Magnification is 4-power and specifications similar to the 329 Weaver with a single exception. The Model 329 has the internal adjustments for the reticules at the eyepiece end of the scope. The Model 344 is 12 inches long and weighs 10 ounces complete with the mount but has internal adjustments located two-thirds of the way towards the objective end through the telescope and situated between the mount arms. Crosshair reticule is used.

In addition Savage included in their 1938 line their No. 30 telescope sight designed for use on any of the high-power bolt-action or lever-action types of repeaters. This can, of course, be used on any .22 caliber. This No. 30 Savage telescope is the Weaver No. 29S with double internal adjustments for elevation and windage with half-minute clicks. The lens system is fully achromatic, micrometer focus at the eyepiece, length 10 inches, weight with mount about 9 ounces and magnification is 3✕. The field of view on this particular scope is 29 feet at 100 yards. As in other Weaver scopes, tube diameter is ¾ of an inch and eye relief is 3 inches, slightly greater than on the Weaver 344.

The Models 23AA and 23D were also supplied factory-equipped with the No. 20 telescope (the Weaver 344) and the Model 99 lever-action and Models 40 and 45 bolt-action can be equipped with the Savage 30 (Weaver No. 29S) or the 330S Weaver telescope.

The 1946 line fails to include any telescope sights, and while most of their rifles can readily be equipped with telescopes, the current line must be accepted without optical sights.

Model 219 Hammerless Single Shot High Power

Intro 1938   Disc 1949

Early in 1938 Savage brought out a very neat single-barrel, hammerless low-priced shotgun which they listed as their Model 220. Shortly thereafter they announced that they were bringing out a Model 219 hammerless single-shot rifle. These two arms are identical except that a rifle barrel is fitted to the hammerless shotgun frame.

The barrel is tapered, medium weight, round, of course, and with a raised ramp front sight

base. Length 26 inches. The barrel and its breech lug are forged in one piece.

This model 219 was produced first for the .25/20 Repeater and .30/30 Winchester cartridges. On resuming production in 1945, Savage added the .22 Hornet and the .32/20 to the line. The Hornet was produced in small quantities in 1939, and this author tried one with a telescope sight fitted and found it unusually excellent in performance. For the man who is content with a single shot hunting rifle, this is the answer, as it is one of the lowest priced numbers in the field of centerfire weapons.

The rear sight on these rifles is adjustable for elevation only, and is of the open or barrel type. The front sight is a gold bead mounted on a ramp. Ejection is automatic when the shotgun-type breech is opened. A walnut stock with matching forearm is plain, although a pistol grip is standard. There is no checking. The forearm fastens to the barrel against the tension of a heavy steel spring bearing against the frame and the forearm barrel lug. Both of these features are designed to automatically take up wear. Weight is about 6½ pounds.

Utility Guns
Intro 1938   Disc 1947

The Utility rifles, or, more properly, *Utility Combinations,* are actually two guns in one. The owner has a single barrel shotgun and a rifle barrel, quickly interchanged. Originally introduced in 1938 as the Model 22Y, they are called in 1946 as a consecutive series running from Models 221 to 231, inclusive. The two separate barrels with individual forearms come fitted to a single frame. The rifle barrel has a thin rifle type forearm, the shotgun barrel a thicker shotgun type. Action is hammerless with the thumb-operated shotgun-style of safety and the breakdown shotgun-type lever.

All rifle barrels are 26 inches long, round, and tapered, and are similar to those used on the Model 219. The Model 220 is the same weapon with a shotgun barrel—no rifle barrel—while the Model 221 has a .30/30 rifle barrel and a 30-inch 12 gauge shotgun barrel. The Model 222 has the same rifle barrel with a 28-inch 16 gauge shotgun barrel. The Model 223 has the same rifle barrel with a 28-inch 20 gauge barrel. The Model 224 has a .25/20 rifle barrel with the 30-inch 12 gauge barrel. The Model 225 has the same caliber rifle barrel with the 28-inch 16 gauge barrel and the Model 226 has the same rifle barrel with a 28-inch 20 gauge barrel.

Models 227, 228 and 229 have 26-inch .22 Hornet barrels with respective 12 gauge 30-inch, 16 gauge 28-inch, and 20 gauge 28-inch shotgun barrels. The Model 230 has a 26-inch .32/20 rifle barrel with a 30-inch 12 gauge barrel and the Model 231 has the same rifle barrel with a 16 gauge 28-inch barrel. No 20 gauge barrel is made in this combination.

Models 7 & 7S Automatic Rifles
Intro 1939 Disc 1947

Latest numbers in the Savage line include the Models 7 and 7S .22 rimfire semi-automatic rifles. These are essentially the same rifles as the Models 6 and 6S with clip magazine feed instead of the tubular type used on the earlier models.

The Model 7 has a 24-inch tapered round barrel with a crowned muzzle. It is of the conventional "takedown" design with a forearm screw holding the barrel and action to the stock. It operates as a self-loader with regular or high speed lubricated .22 long rifle cartridges, but may be used as a bolt action repeater with .22 short, long and long rifle cartridges.

Used as a locked-breech repeater, the bolt or operating handle is pushed inward, locking sidewise through the left side of the receiver. To function after firing, it is necessary to pull the bolt outward and then straight to the rear. It should be remembered that this locking is *not a safety!* An independent safety is used. This little 6-pound rifle is well stocked with checkering on the pistol grip. Standard sights include a gold bead front and an open barrel rear, the latter adjustable for elevation.

The Model 7S is the same rifle with the Savage peep sight equipment. This includes the hooded ramp front sight with removable hood and three inserts—a bead, a blade, and an open or hollow bead. A receiver peep rear sight with two discs has adjustments for elevation and windage.

Model 602 Automatic
Intro 1940 Disc 1946

This model needs little discussion. Essentially it is the Model 6 rifle previously described, but this semi-automatic is chambered and rifled only for the .22 *Short* cartridge. It has a tubular magazine with a capacity of 21 cartridges.

Model 99 Rifles for 1946

This line of rifles has been well discussed earlier in this chapter. Many of the variations of the action brought out 47 years ago have fallen by the wayside, but three types remain. The featherweights have gone. Savage has standardized on the popular models and calibers.

The 1946 line includes the Models 99-EG, the 99-R and the 99-RS, all in solid frame. Improved steels, the alloys developed during World War II, are being used. Only two calibers remain— the .250 and .300 Savage. Gone are the old .303 and .30/30. The .300 Savage cartridge is available in the Savage line with a 150 grain soft point bullet at a velocity of 2660 f.s. The 180 grain soft point is loaded at 2380 f.s. In the .250 Savage caliber only the Model 99-EG or standard grade is available. Savage still supplies the 87-grain bullet cartridge loaded at 3000 f.s. muzzle velocity, and the 100-grain bullet at 2810 f.s.

The Model 99-EG still retains the slender knob-tip forearm considered obsolete by most sportsmen today. The 99-R is the thick modern forearm with a better grade of checkering, while the Model 99-RS is the deluxe version with a Redfield No. 70 peep rear sight and a gold bead front sight. A ⅞-inch sling and quick-detachable swivels are standard on this model.

SAVAGE IN WORLD WAR II

In common with all other commercial firearms manufacturers, Savage entered the Second World War early, discontinuing most of its production of commercial sporting weapons about 1940. And since the J. Stevens Arms Company of Chicopee Falls, Mass., is a part of the Savage organization, its history cannot well be discussed separately.

Early in 1940 Savage began to convert much

of its facilities to the manufacture of the .45 Thompson sub-machine gun for the British. Soon the Stevens plant was producing some of the components for the famous Model 1928 "Tommy Gun." The Thompson was produced up to about the middle of the war, first for the British, and later for the United States Government. When the M3 sub-machine gun—the stamped-metal product variously named by the public as the "Buck Rogers Gun" and by the GI simply as the "Grease Gun"—was adopted, production of the Thompson was discontinued. Savage manufactured a total of 1,501,000 Thompson guns.

At Stevens a military rifle was manufactured, first on British contracts, and later for the British under Lend-Lease. Stevens produced the famous Short Lee-Enfield in modified version. This firm apparently did something the British were unable to do—standardize the rifle so that parts were interchangeable. Their latest version of this—there were slight model changes—was the British "No. 4 Mk. 1*" and all models were produced for the .303 British service cartridge.

Early in the war Stevens experimented with barrels having two wide grooves instead of the conventional 4- or 5-groove barrel. These proved as accurate and as long-lived as the other barrels and became standard in the line.

Although these Short Lee rifles were never issued to U. S. troops, all manufactured under Lend-Lease were stamped on the receiver, "U. S. Property." The only Stevens identification was a large "S" in front of the model number on the receiver. Stevens acquired two additional facilities in Chicopee Falls to expand their production, and by the time manufacturing was stopped in August 1945, had produced well over 1,000,000 of these modified Enfields.

The cessation of sub-machine gun manufacture at the Savage plant at Utica, however, did not mean the end of war work for the parent Savage plant. Immediately they converted to the production of United States Caliber .50 M2 Basic aircraft machine guns. In a routine inspection visit to the Savage plant in 1944 while on duty with the Ordnance Department of the Army, this author watched with amazement the precision methods of manufacture Savage was using to produce this heavy weapon. Rejections were lower than most facilities making this weapon, yet manufacturing costs were being reduced, and production was at a faster rate than even the firm had hoped for. Contracts were terminated in August 1945, and show that this one plant delivered 295,361 Caliber .50 guns. In addition, during the early stages of manufacture, they produced 14,800 Caliber .30 Browning Aircraft machine guns, but this program was discontinued when the Air Corps decided that American fighter craft should all be equipped with the much heavier and more powerful .50 caliber to replace the old .30.

By the time that Savage went into the production of machine guns, all plant facilities were converted and machinery for the manufacture of sporting weapons, long unused, had to be moved out and stored to make room for the machine gun program.

The end of the war and the problems of reconversion made a major change in Savage plans. During the Summer of 1946, Savage decided to close their Utica arms plant and move all machinery to Chicopee Falls. The Stevens line will be manufactured in the old Stevens works, while the new Chicopee plant, utilized for the manufacture of the British rifle, will be the new home of Savage rifles and Fox shotguns. During the late summer and Fall, Savage trucked all machinery to the Massachusetts plant and started production as rapidly as batteries of machines could be set up.

At press time it appears that full production on Savage rifles will be under way by January 1, 1947. In the future, correspondence concerning Savage rifles should be addressed to the firm at Chicopee Falls, Mass.

Source: *The Rifle in America* by Philip B. Sharpe NY: Funks & Wagnalls
© 1938, 1947 & 1953. 800 pp. First Edition © 1938 by Wm. Morrow & Co.

SAVAGE MODEL 99 HIGH POWER RIFLES

Source: STOEGER ARMS CORP. Cat. #31 © 1939 Reprinted by permission

This is the famous repeating rifle that first introduced the hammerless, solid breech design and rotary type magazine. Its popularity in every hunting field is tremendous—for it embodies all the technical superiority and mechanical perfection of tested Savage methods.

An extra margin of safety is built into the Model 99 mechanism. The breech bolt has an unusually large locking area, wedging solidly against the receiver. The cycle of operation is quick and positive—permitting easy firing from the shoulder. All Savage Model 99 rifles are made with barrels of "Hi-Pressure" steel, especially adapted to modern smokeless powder high power cartridges. Sportsmen around the world know the Savage reputation for barrel accuracy.

GENERAL SPECIFICATIONS

Hammerless, solid breech, lever action. Hi-Pressure steel barrel, polished breech bolt, case hardened lever, blued receiver. Varnished American Walnut stock and forearm. Steel butt plate. White metal bead front sight on raised ramp base and adjustable flat top sporting rear sight. Six shots, magazine capacity five cartridges. Magazine rotary box type with numerical indicator. Hammer indicator showing automatically cocked or fired position of hammer. Made in 9 styles and 5 calibers.

CALIBERS OF THE 99 MODELS

.22 Savage Hi-Power—Accurate at long ranges. The ideal cartridge for use on small and medium game, from woodchucks to wolves. For use in Savage Rifles: Models 99-E, 99-F, 99-G and 99-K.

.30-30 Savage Hi-Power—Extremely popular throughout the country, this cartridge is standard for deer and similar game at moderate ranges. Possesses splendid accuracy. For use in Savage Rifles: Models 99-A, 99-B, 99-E, 99-F, 99-G, 99-K, 99-H Carbine.

.303 Savage Hi-Power—Famous for over twenty-five years for its deadly accuracy and hard hitting. Dependable for deer, caribou and black bear. A fine cartridge in timbered country. For use in Savage Rifles: Models 99-A, 99-E, 99-F, 99-G, 99-K, 99-R and Model 99-H Carbine.

.250-3000 Savage Hi-Power—Noted for its high speed and accuracy, this cartridge is powerful enough for any animal in North America. Excellent for mountain sheep, goats, deer, etc. For use in Savage Rifles: Models 99-E, 99-F, 99-G, 99-K, 99-R, 99-S.

.300 Savage Hi-Power—For biggest American game, this is a super-modern cartridge, similar in ballistics to the .30 Springfield-Government Cartridge. Ideal for Alaskan bear, moose, and elk. For use in Savage Rifles: Models 99-A, 99-E, 99-F, 99-G, 99-K, 99-R, 99-RS.

MODEL 99-F

FOR BIG GAME   **CALIBERS:** Model F, .22 Hi-Power, .30-30, .303 and .250-3000 with 22 in. barrel. .300 with 24 in. barrel.

Model 99-F. Takedown. Tapered round barrel. Raised ramp front sight base. Shotgun butt. Weight about 7 pounds.

Model 99-F Takedown is the featherweight design, so called, because the shorter barrel and straight stock with shotgun butt plate makes this rifle, which is chambered for the most powerful cartridges, quick handling and easy to carry. Stock dimensions, 1⅞ x 2¾ x 13⅛ inches. Butt plate 1½ x 4⅞ inches. Matted trigger.

Model 99-F, Takedown $53.00

MODELS 99-G & EG

FOR BIG GAME   **CALIBERS:** .22 Hi-Power, .30-30, .303 and .250-3000 with 22 inch barrel. .300 with 24 inch barrel.

Model 99-G. Takedown. Tapered round barrel. Raised ramp front sight base. Shotgun butt, full pistol grip, checkered stock and forearm, checkered trigger and corrugated steel butt plate. Matted trigger. Weight about 7¼ pounds.

The Savage Model 99, Style G is our most popular rifle and is selected by sportsmen who desire a rifle of moderate weight, fine finish and extreme efficiency. Especially adapted to high concentration cartridges because of the exceptional strength and safety of the action. Ideal for all American game.

Model 99-EG is same as the Model 99-G, but solid frame and without checkering.

Model 99-G, Takedown $54.75
Model 99-EG, Solid Frame—No Checkering 47.00

MODEL 99-T—FEATHERWEIGHT

FOR BIG GAME   **CALIBERS:** .22 Hi-Power, .30-30, .303 and .250-3000 with 20 inch barrel. .300 with 22 inch barrel.

Model 99-T. Solid Frame. Featherweight. Tapered, light weight, round barrel with raised ramp front sight base. Barrel length 20 inches for .250/3000, .303, .30/30 and .22 Hi-Power cartridges; 22 inch barrel for .300 Savage cartridges. Sights: red bead front, new semi-buckhorn rear, without sighting notch. Light weight full pistol grip stock and large wide forearm of selected walnut, oil finished. Forearm dimensions: 15 inches long, 1½ inches wide and 2 inches deep. Stock dimensions 1⅞ inches drop at comb, 2¾ inches drop at heel, 13⅛ inches long. Butt plate 1½ x 4⅞ inches. Matted trigger. Weight 6¾ pounds.

Model 99-T, Solid Frame $53.00

.410 BORE SHOTGUN BARREL FOR MODEL 99 TAKEDOWN RIFLE

.410 Bore Auxiliary Shotgun Barrel—Interchangeable with all caliber rifle barrels on Savage Model 99 Takedown Rifles. Rifle should be sent to factory for necessary fitting or adjusting to the receiver. For 2½" .410 gauge shells only. Shells do not function through magazine. In ordering, specify style, caliber and serial number of rifle. Weight about 2 pounds. Length 22 or 24 inches.

Price $7.00

SAVAGE MODEL 99 HIGH POWER RIFLES

MODEL 99-H CARBINE

THE FAVORITE SADDLE RIFLE

CALIBERS: .30-30, .303 and .250-3000

Model 99-H Carbine—Solid Frame. 20-inch special medium weight barrel. Walnut carbine stock and forearm. Steel butt plate. Adjustable semi-buckhorn rear sight and bead front sight. Weight 6½ pounds. Matted trigger.

The Savage Carbine has been designed for men who require a compact, sturdy, well-balanced rifle, for use in the saddle or in thickly timbered country. A rifle that is light and fast in action, but which packs a blow with sufficient power for big game.

Note its clean-cut lines, not an extra ounce of weight anywhere, and it holds firm and steady. Its barrel is made of the same "Hi-Pressure" steel that goes into all other Savage Model 99 barrels and is rifled and chambered in accordance with the exact Savage standards. These features combine to make this rifle admirably suited for guides, trappers and sportsmen desiring a sturdy rifle for rough, exacting service at a low price.

Model 99-H Carbine—solid frame..........................$45.00

MODEL 99-R

THE IDEAL DEER RIFLE

CALIBERS: .250-3000 and .303 with 22 in. barrel. .300 with 24 in. barrel.

Model 99-R—Solid Frame. Tapered medium weight round barrel. Raised ramp front sight base. Special large stock and forearm of selected walnut, oil finish, corrugated steel butt plate of shotgun design. Full pistol grip stock. Fine checkering on grip and forearm. Adjustable Semi-Buckhorn rear sight and gold bead front sight. Matted trigger. Weight about 7¼ pounds.

The Model 99-R has been designed to meet the demands of expert riflemen requiring a solid frame rifle of extreme accuracy. An ideal deer rifle.

Model 99-R, solid frame..................................$53.50

MODEL 99-RS

FOR BIG GAME

CALIBERS: .250-3000 with 22 in. barrel. .300 with 24 in. barrel.

Model 99-RS. Solid Frame. Same specifications as Model 99-R with following refinements: Lyman windgauge and elevation adjustment rear peep sight, Lyman folding leaf middle and gold bead front sight. Also equipped with ⅞ inch combined adjustable leather sling and carrying strap with quick release swivels and screw studs. Weight about 7½ pounds.

The Model 99-RS is the same rifle as the Model 99-R, with additional equipment consisting of special sights, with accurate windage and elevation adjustments and a sling strap, which is provided for ease in carrying and as an aid to steady holding.

Model 99-RS, solid frame. $64.00

MODEL 99-K

FOR BIG GAME

CALIBERS: .22 Hi-Power, .30-30, .303 and .250-3000 with 22 inch barrel. .300 with 24 inch barrel.

Model 99-K—Take-down. Same specifications as Model 99-G with following refinements: Selected American walnut stock and forearm—special fancy hand checkering on forearm, panels and grip. Receiver and barrel artistically engraved. Action carefully fitted and stoned. Lyman rear peep sight, folding middle sight and gold bead front sight. Matted trigger.

The Model 99-K is our finest grade rifle and is a beautiful specimen of the gunmaker's art. The checkering and engraving are unusually attractive.

Model 99-K, Takedown $85.00

 STOEGER ARMS CORPORATION © 1939

STEVENS WALNUT HILL TARGET AND SPORTING RIFLES

Down through the past 70 years STEVENS has clung faithfully to the ideals and high standard established by its founder. How much so, is exemplified by these four latest Stevens Models Nos. 417, 417½, 418 and 418½ . . . developments and modernization of famous Stevens rifles that made many world records and were the choice of experts in the days of the "Schutzen" rifle clubs and famous shooting matches.

NO. 417

FOR TARGET SHOOTING

NO. 417 STEVENS "WALNUT HILL" HEAVY TARGET RIFLE—For HiSpeed or regular cartridges. BARREL—28 inch heavy, round, tested for accuracy. FRAME — Casehardened. ACTION — Original Stevens "Ideal" Breech Block, Automatic Ejector, Lever Action, Short, Fast Hammer Fall. STOCK—American Walnut 13½-inch, Oil Finish, High Comb, Full Pistol Grip Target Model Stock and Forearm, Fitted with 1¼-inch military Style, Neatsfoot Oil Treated Sling Strap, Shotgun Butt with Steel Butt Plate. SIGHTS—Standard Equipment Lyman No. 17A Front, Telescope Blocks, Lyman No. 48L Receiver Sight. WEIGHT—about 10½ pounds. AMMUNITION—.22 Long Rifle Regular or

High Speed—made to order .22 Short at no extra charge.

	Prices
No. 417-0, fitted with Lyman No. 52L Extension Sight	$50.00
No. 417-1, fitted with Lyman No. 48L Sight	48.50
No. 417-2, fitted with Lyman No. 144 Sight in place of No. 48L	43.50
No. 417-3, without front or rear sights	38.50

Extra heavy 29 inch barrel add to above prices $25.00

LOOP LEVER FURNISHED ON REQUEST, NO EXTRA CHARGE

NO. 417½

FOR SMALL GAME

NO. 417½ STEVENS "WALNUT HILL" HEAVY "WALNUT HILL" RIFLE—For HiSpeed or regular cartridges. BARREL—28 inch, Tapered Round, Light Weight, Tested for accuracy. FRAME — Casehardened. ACTION—Original Stevens "Ideal" Breech Block, Positive Extractor, Short, Fast Hammer Fall, Independent Safety Notch on Hammer, Lever Action. STOCK—American Walnut, Oil Finish, High Comb, Full Pistol Grip Stock and Sporting Forearm, Fitted with 1¼ inch Military Style, Neatsfoot Oil Treated Sling Strap, Shotgun Butt with Steel Butt plate. SIGHTS—Lyman No. 28

Gold Bead 3/32 inch Front, Single Folding Leaf Middle, and Lyman No. 144 Tang Peep Sight with Click Adjustment for Elevation and Windage Barrel Tapped for Telescope Blocks. WEIGHT—About 8¼ to 8½ pounds. AMMUNITION—.22 Long Rifle, Regular or High Speed. .22 W.R.F. Regular or High Speed. .25 Stevens R.F.

No. 417½ .... Price **$38.50**

LOOP LEVER FURNISHED ON REQUEST, NO EXTRA CHARGE

NO. 418

FOR SMALL GAME

NO. 418—STEVENS "WALNUT HILL" TARGET RIFLE—For HiSpeed or Regular Cartridges. BARREL—26-inch, Tapered Round, Tested for Accuracy. FRAME—Case Hardened. ACTION—Original Stevens "Ideal" Breech Block, Automatic Ejector, Lever Action, Short, Fast Hammer Fall, Half Cock Safety Notch. STOCK—American Walnut 13-inch, Oil Finish, Full Pistol Grip Target Model Stock and Forearm, Fitted with ⅞-inch Military Style, Neatsfoot

Oil Treated Sling Strap, Shotgun Butt with Steel Butt Plate. SIGHTS—Patridge Type Front, and Lyman No. 144 Tang Peep Sight with Click Adjustment for Elevation and Windage. WEIGHT—About 6½ pounds. AMMUNITION—.22 Long Rifle Regular or High Speed (.22 Short to order at no extra charge). No. 418 .... Price **$19.75**

NO. 418½

FOR SMALL GAME

NO. 418½—STEVENS "WALNUT HILL" Sporting Rifle—For HiSpeed or Regular Cartridges. BARREL —26 inch, Tapered Round, Tested for accuracy. FRAME—Case Hardened. ACTION—Original Stevens "Ideal" Breech Block. Positive Extractor, Lever Action, Short, Fast Hammer Fall, Half Cock Safety Notch. STOCK—American Walnut 13-inch Oil Finish, Full Pistol Grip Sporting Model Stock and Forearm, Fitted with ⅞ inch Military Style, Neatsfoot Oil Treated Sling

Strap, Shotgun Butt with Steel Butt Plate. SIGHTS—Lyman Gold Bead Front, and Lyman No. 2A Tang Peep Sight. WEIGHT —About 6½ pounds. AMMUNITION—.22 Long Rifle, Regular or High Speed, .22 W.R.F., Regular or High Speed, .25 Stevens R.F.

No. 418½ .... Price **$17.75**

STOEGER ARMS CORPORATION © 1939

SAVAGE SMALL BORE .22 CALIBER RIFLES

MODEL 19
TARGET RIFLE

Model 19—.22 caliber repeating bolt action rifle (new design). Caliber—.22 long rifle, rimfire, suitable for use with all "high-speed" and "regular" cartridges. Stock—one-piece, oil finished, walnut, pistol grip with beaver-tail forearm full 2 inches wide, checkered steel butt plate. Drop at heel 1⅞ inches, drop at comb 1⅝ inches, length 13½ inches, butt plate 1⅝ inches wide, 5⅛ inches long, over all length stock 32 inches. Barrel—heavy 25-inch barrel, 30½ inches over all sighting radius. Magazine—5-shot, curved, detachable; positive loading; a spring snap lock at rear functions easily and locks securely. Bolt action—2 locking lugs. New high-speed lock—the speed of the new lock is less than 2/1000 of a second. Open loading port—the large loading port will be appreciated whenever rifle is used in single shot firing. Sights—New design, No. 15 Savage aperture extension rear sight with click adjustments for elevation and windage. Drilled for telescope sight blocks. Weight—about 8 pounds. Swivels—for 1¼-inch sling strap; front swivel 16½ in., forward of trigger.

Model 19-L—.22 long rifle. Standard rifle as above except with Lyman No. 48-Y micrometer rear sight and No. 17-A hooded front sight.

Model 19-M—Heavy Barrel Target Rifle, cal. .22 Long Rifle, weight 9¼ lbs. Barrel: Extra heavy (13/16" diameter at muzzle) 28" long, 34" overall Sighting radius. Fitted with Telescope sight blocks. Sights: No. 15 Savage extension rear above. Hooded front sight with removable hood. Adjustable trigger pull.

Model 19-H—.22 Hornet. Same sights, stock and barrel specifications as standard Model 19. Barrel is high-pressure smokeless steel. Loading port, magazine and bolt mechanism same as Model 23-D. Chambered for the sensational Hornet Cartridge. Barrel drilled for telescope sight blocks. The straight stock makes this the ideal arm to equip with telescope for target practice or precise small game and vermin shooting.

Model 19—target rifle, .22 long rifle $36.00
Model 19-L—target rifle, .22 long rifle 48.25
Model 19-M—heavy barrel target rifle, cal. .22 long rifle........ 41.85
Model 19-H—target rifle, .22 Hornet 42.50

MODEL 23AA
GAME RIFLE

FOR SMALL GAME   **CALIBER: .22 Long Rifle**

Model 23AA—.22 caliber repeating bolt action rifle. Barrel—23-inch round, tapered. Chambered for .22 short, .22 long and .22 long rifle, regular and high speed cartridges. Action—polished bolt, double locking lugs. New high-speed lock—the speed of the new lock is less than 2-1000

of a second. This speed eliminates shift in aim between release of trigger and ignition. Lever type safety. Magazine—5-shot, detachable, curved design. Spring catch lock. Stock—One-piece stock and forearm of selected American walnut, full curve pistol grip, rubbed varnish finish. Sights—white metal bead front and flat top elevator adjustment rear sight. Receiver tapped for new No. 10 Savage aperture rear sight. Weight—about 6 pounds.

Model 23-AA—.22 caliber Sporter Rifle.....................$21.50

MODEL 3
GAME RIFLE

FOR SMALL GAME   CALIBER: .22 Long Rifle

Model 3—.22 caliber bolt action single shot rifle, take-down. Barrel—26-inch round, tapered. Chambered for .22 short, long and .22 long rifle, regular or high-speed cartridges. Action—chromium plated bolt and trigger. Stock—one-piece full pistol grip stock and large forearm of selected walnut, finger grooves in forearm, steel butt plate 1⅜ x 4½ inches. Forearm 1⅜ inches wide at take-down screw, stock length 28¼ inches. Overall length 43½ inches. Sights—gold bead front sight and adjustable flat

top rear sight. Receiver drilled and tapped for No. 55 Lyman rear peep sight. Weight—about 4½ pounds.
Model 3—single shot bolt action rifle $5.65

Model 3-S—Specifications—Same as Model 3 Rifle shown above, except equipped with hooded front sight with 3 interchangeable inserts and receiver rear peep sight; with elevation and windage adjustments and sighting disc with three sizes of aperture openings—large, medium and small.
Price $6.40

Model 3-ST—Target—Same as 3-S, equipped with ⅞ inch sling strap and sling loops and studs.
Price $8.40

MODEL 4
GAME RIFLE

FOR SMALL GAME   CALIBER: .22 Long Rifle

Model 4—.22 caliber bolt action repeating rifle, take-down. Barrel—tapered, round, 24-inch, with crowned muzzle, for .22 long rifle, .22 long or .22 short, regular or high-speed cartridges, 5-shot detachable clip magazine. Action—all parts finely polished, self-cocking, bolt action with independent safety, chromium plated bolt and trigger. Stock—one-piece full pistol grip stock and large forearm of selected walnut, finger grooves in

forearm, steel butt plate. Sights—gold bead front and sporting rear with elevation adjustment. Receiver drilled and tapped for No. 55 Lyman receiver sight. Weight—about 5½ pounds.
Model 4—bolt action repeating rifle $11.00
Model 5—Same as Model 4, but with tubular magazine. Price.... 13.35
Model 4-S—Specifications—Same as Model 4 Rifle shown above, except equipped with hooded front sight with 3 interchangeable inserts and receiver rear peep sight; with elevation and windage adjustments and sighting disc with three sizes of aperture openings—large, medium and small.
Price $11.75
Extra Magazine .... .65
Model 5S—Same as Model 4S, but with tubular magazine. Price.. 14.10

MODEL 6-S
AUTOMATIC RIFLE

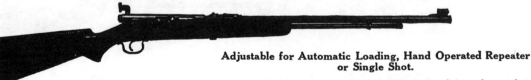

Adjustable for Automatic Loading, Hand Operated Repeater or Single Shot.

Tubular Magazine—15 .22 Long Rifle, regular or high speed with lubricated bullets for automatic loading. For use as a single shot or bolt action repeater with .22 short, long or long rifle cartridges.
TAKEDOWN—24 in. tapered round barrel with crowned muzzle. Cross bolt locks for use as single shot or repeater. Independent

safety. Striker release mechanism allows the firing of one shot only at each pull of the trigger. Stock: Full pistol grip, checkered. American walnut, hard rubber butt plate. Sight equipment same as Model 3-S. Weight about 6 lbs.
Model 6-S $16.25
Model 6—Same as above except equipped with goldbead front and open rear sights....................................... 15.50

SAVAGE & STEVENS .22 CAL. RIFLES WITH 'SCOPES

The Savage and Stevens Arms Company have taken the lead in offering their most popular .22 Cal. rifles completely factory fitted and equipped with telescope mounts and sights. The telescopes used are of the well known Weaver design. The 3 power No. 10 'scope corresponding to the Weaver No. 329, while the 4 power No. 20 'scope with internal windage and elevation corresponds with the Weaver No. 344. The popular and well proven type "M" mounts are used thruout. Since full details of both the rifles and scopes will be found elsewhere in this catalog, we are presenting herewith only illustrations of the guns in question with a brief description together with price which includes complete outfit exactly as illustrated.

Price $10.40
Model 3-T Bolt Action Single Shot
With No. 10 Telescope Sight

.22 caliber short, long or long rifle; regular or high speed, 26 in. barrel; walnut stock; take-down. Length over all 43 inches. Gold bead front sight and adjustable flat top rear sight.

.22 caliber, short, long or long rifle, regular or high speed. 24 inch barrel, 5-shot clip magazine, walnut stock. Take-down. Gold bead front sight and sporting rear sight with elevation adjustment.

Price $19.00
Model 4-T Bolt Action Repeating Rifle
With No. 20 Telescope Sight

Price $21.35
Model 5-T Bolt Action Repeating Rifle
With No. 20 Telescope Sight

.22 caliber, short, long or long rifle, regular or high speed. 24 inch barrel. Tubular magazine. Capacity: 15 .22 long rifle, 17 .22 long or 21 .22 short cartridges. Oil finished walnut stock. Gold bead front and sporting rear sight with elevation and windage adjustments.

.22 long rifle, regular and high speed. 23 inch tapered barrel. 5-shot clip magazine. Bolt action, two locking lugs. Quick ignition, convenient safety, polished bolt. Oil finished walnut stock. White metal bead front and flat top elevation adjustment rear sight.

Price $29.50
Model 23-AA Sporter
With No. 20 Telescope Sight

.22 caliber short, long or long rifle, regular or high speed. 24 inch barrel, bolt action, single shot. Pistol grip stock, forend with black tip, walnut finish. Gold bead front and sporting rear sight with elevation and windage adjustment.

Price $44.00
Model 23-D (.22 Hornet)
With No. 20 Telescope Sight

.22 Hornet caliber. 25 inch high-pressure smokeless steel barrel, 5-shot clip magazine. Bolt action, two locking lugs. Quick ignition, convenient safety, polished bolt. Oil finished walnut stock. White metal bead front and flat top elevation adjustment rear sight.

Price $10.45
Stevens No. 53T Buckhorn Rifle
With No. 10 Telescope Sight

.22 caliber short, long or long rifle, regular or high-speed. 24 inch barrel, 5-shot detachable clip magazine. Bolt action. Pistol rip stock, forend with black tip, walnut finish. Gold bead front and sporting rear sight with elevation and windage adjustment.

Price $18.50
Stevens No. 56T Buckhorn Rifle
With No. 20 Telescope Sight

.22 caliber short, long or long rifle, regular or high speed. 24 inch barrel. Tubular magazine, capacity 15 .22 long rifle, 17 .22 long or 21 .22 short cartridges. Bolt action. Gold bead front and sporting rear sight with elevation and windage adjustments.

Price $20.50
Stevens No. 66T Buckhorn Rifle
With No. 20 Telescope Sight

STEVENS-SPRINGFIELD BOLT ACTION .22 CALIBER RIFLES

MODEL 416-1 STEVENS TARGET RIFLE

For .22 R. F. Long
Rifle Cartridges

A NEW MATCH RIFLE
Fully Equipped——Guaranteed Accuracy

This new rifle represents the most recent offering in the .22 target line and is a genuine contribution by the Stevens factory to the small bore shooter. For the first time a really substantial, well proportioned match rifle with proper weight, balance, trigger pull, target sights and great accuracy is available at a price within reach of many who formerly had to content themselves with inferior rifles.

No. 416-1 Specifications:
Barrel—26-inch. Heavy Tapered Round, .22 Long Rifle. A five shot machine rest group with each rifle guarantees extreme accuracy.
Action—Bolt Action, Five Shot Clip Magazine, Speed Lock,

Adjustable Trigger Pull, Bolt Handle of design to permit telescope sight in low position giving same sighting plane as regular sights, Independent Safety with Red Dot Indicator.
Stock—American Walnut, Oil Finish, Adjustable Front Sling Loop, Fitted with 1¼-inch Neats-foot Oil Treated Leather Sling, Checkered Steel Butt Plate.
Sights—New Stevens No. 25 Hooded Front Sight with Three Removable Inserts, Lyman 57 Rear Sight, Telescope Blocks.
Weight—With Sling Strap about 9½ pounds.
Ammunition—.22 Long Rifle Regular or High Speed.

No. 416-1, As shown above $29.75
No. 416-2, Post Front and Receiver Peep Rear Sight.......... 24.75

MODEL 083

FOR SMALL GAME AND TARGET

Caliber .22 Long Rifle, .22 Long, .22 Short, .22 W. R. F., or .25 Stevens R. F.

Barrel—24-inch Round, Tapered with Crowned Muzzle for .22 L. R., .22 L. or .22 S. and .22 W. R. F., Regular or High Speed Cartridges.
Action—Fast Bolt Action, Self Cocking with Safety Firing

Pin prevents accidental discharge. Chromium plated bolt and trigger.
Stock—Full size, Oval Military Style, Full Pistol Grip, Walnut Finish, Steel Butt Plate, Large Take-down Screw.
Sights—Hooded Ramp, Removable Hood, Front Sight with three interchangeable inserts and receiver rear with three sighting discs. Also folding sporting middle sight.
Weight—About 5 pounds. Take-down. Length over all 41¼ inches.

Price $5.75

MODEL 084

FOR TARGET SHOOTING AND SMALL GAME

Caliber .22 Long Rifle, .22 Long and .22 Short

Barrel—Tapered, Round, 24-inch, with Crowned Muzzle for .22 L. R., .22 L. or .22 S., Regular or High Speed Cartridges, Take-down, 5 shot Detachable Clip Magazine. Action—Self Cocking, Bolt Action with Independent Safety, Chromium Plated Bolt

and Trigger. Stock—Full size, Oval Military Style, Full Pistol Grip, Walnut Finish, Steel Butt Plate.
Sights—Hooded Ramp Front sight with removable hood and three interchangeable inserts. Receiver rear with three sighting discs, also folding sporting middle sight. Ammunition—Any .22 L. R., .22 L., or .22 S., High Speed or Regular Cartridge.
Weight—About 6 pounds. Length over all, 43½ inches.
Price $10.25

MODEL 086

FOR TARGET SHOOTING AND SMALL GAME

Caliber .22 Long Rifle, .22 Long and .22 Short

Action—Self Cocking, Bolt Action, with Independent Safety, Chromium Plated Bolt and Trigger.
Stock—Turned, Walnut Finish. Steel Butt Plate.
Sights—Hooded Ramp Front Sight with three interchangeable inserts, Receiver rear sight with sighting disc, also folding sporting middle sight. Weight—5½ pounds. Length over all, 41½ inches.

Barrels—24-inch, Round, Tapered. Take-down. The rifle has a tubular magazine with capacity of thirteen .22 long rifle, fifteen .22 long, or nineteen .22 short, High Speed or Regular Cartridges.

Price $11.25

STOEGER ARMS CORPORATION © 1939

SAVAGE OVER AND UNDER SHOTGUNS

MODEL 420
MODEL 430

The Savage Over-and-Under Double has filled the long felt demand for such a gun. It is beautifully designed, of safe construction and has fine balance, especially recommended for Field and Skeet shooting. Once you use one of these new Over-and-Under guns you will find a different reaction of the recoil; no side whip, therefore much faster to fire your second shot. For the hunter used to shooting a rifle it will appeal instantly, doing away with the side by side vision always found to interfere with the sighting of a double barrel shotgun.

Model 420—Hammerless, Takedown made in 12, 16 and 20 Gauge. Stock of selected oil finished walnut with full pistol grip. (No checkering.)

Barrels to be had 12 and 16 Gauge in 26 inch, 28 inch and 30 inch length and in 20 Gauge, 26 inch and 28 inch.

Chokes: Modified and Full or Open cylinder and Improved cylinder for skeet shooting.

Action with automatic top tang safety, hammerless with unbreakable coil springs, all working parts are made to give long wearing service. The front trigger fires the lower barrel and the rear trigger the upper barrel.

Stock dimensions on all guns are 14 inch length, drop at heel 2¾ inch, at comb 1⅝ inch.

Weight—12 Ga./28 inch about 7 lbs. 12 oz.
Weight—16 Ga./28 inch about 7 lbs. 6 oz.
Weight—20 Ga./28 inch about 6 lbs. 13 oz.

Price $35.00

Model 430—Hammerless, Takedown made in 12 16 and 20 Gauge. Same specifications as Model 420 with following extras:

Barrel with matted side line on top barrel.

Stock of selected Fancy Crotch Walnut with full pistol grip beautifully checkered and fitted with Jostam Anti-Flinch Recoil Pad.

Price $39.50

Extras for Models 420 and 430:
Non-selective Single Trigger.........................Price 7.50
Extra set of barrels for Model 420..................... 17.50
Extra set of barrels for Model 430..................... 20.00

STEVENS REPEATING SHOTGUNS

MODEL 620

This gun has many features well liked by those who have used it. The take-down is one of the simplest ever constructed and is based on the Browning patents. This gun will stand heavy loads when used for Field shooting or in the Duck blind, and when given proper care it will last a life time. As a Riot gun it is used for guard duty and stands rough handling. In price it is the cheapest, but in quality it counts among the best.

Model 620 Repeating Shotgun to be had in 12 Ga. 28, 30 and 32 inch full choked, 28 and 30 inch modified, 26 and 28 inch cylinder bored;

16 Ga. 28 inch full, modified or cylinder bored, 26 inch cylinder bored; 20 Ga. 26 and 28 inch cylinder, modified or full choke.

Action Hammerless, visible locking bolt, safety firing pin, independent safety side ejection, take down and solid breech drop forged.

Stock of American walnut with checkered full pistol grip and checkered slide handle, rubber buttplate. Length 13¾ inches. Drop at heel 2¾ inches.

Weight: 12 Ga., about 7¾ lbs., 16 Ga. 7¼ lbs., 20 Ga. about 6 lbs.

Magazine capacity—Six Shots. A plug is furnished to cut down magazine capacity to 3 shots to conform with Government regulations on migratory birds.

Price $33.65

Model 620 Riot Gun comes only with 20 inch cylinder barrel. 33.65
Model 621 the same as Model 620 with raised matted solid rib. 37.00

STEVENS DOUBLE BARREL HAMMERLESS SHOTGUNS

MODEL 530

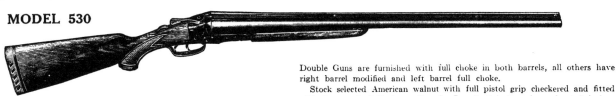

The Stevens factory has been making shotguns for a good many years and knows how to make them to stand up under any and all conditions. Here is a model designed according to the most modern ideas, nothing forgotten to make these guns as wanted by the shooter for field and skeet.

Model 530 comes with blued compressed forged steel barrels tested with Nitro Powder. Length: 12 Ga. 26, 28, 30 and 32 inches; 16 Ga. 26, 28 and 30 inches; 20 Ga. 26 and 28 inches; 410 Ga. 26 inches with matted rib and 2 Lyman ivory bead sights. All 12 Ga. 32 inch and 410 Ga.

Double Guns are furnished with full choke in both barrels, all others have right barrel modified and left barrel full choke.

Stock selected American walnut with full pistol grip checkered and fitted with Jostam Anti-flinch recoil pad. Length 4 inches, drop about 3 inches. Frame is polished and case hardened. Action is hammerless with coil springs of new design.

Weight: 12 Ga. 7½ to 8 lbs., 16 Ga. 7 to 7½ lbs., 20 Ga. 6½ to 6¾ lbs., 410 Ga. 5¾ to 6 lbs.

Price $27.50

Model 530ST Same specifications as Model 530 except fitted with non-selective single trigger.

Price $36.95

SAVAGE AUTOMATIC SHOTGUNS

SAVAGE "UPLAND SPORTER"
12 and 16 Gauge—3 Shots

MODEL 726

FOR SKEET AND FIELD SHOOTING
FOR TRAPS AND DUCK SHOOTING

The Upland Sporter is a new three-shot automatic especially designed for field shooting. It is light to carry, fast in action and easy to point. The receiver is artistically decorated and this with the special checkering on stock and forearm combine to make an attractive arm for field use. It excels in ease of operation, shooting qualities and all-around dependability.

MODEL 726

Plain round barrel.

BARRELS—12 gauge, 28, 30 and 32-inch lengths; 16 gauge, 26, 28 and 30-inch lengths. Full, modified or cylinder bore.

STOCK—Selected American walnut. Full pistol grip checkered on grip and forestock. Push-button type safety in rear of triggger guard. Magazine capacity two shells, with one in chamber, giving three shots. Receiver channeled and matted in line of sight. Friction ring adjustment for light and heavy loads. Receiver artistically decorated. Weight, 16 gauge, about 7 pounds; 12 gauge, about 7¼ pounds.

Price $43.50

(Model 720, similar to Model 726 but 5 shot capacity available at same price.)

MODEL 727

With solid raised matted rib. Same specifications as Model 726. Raised rib on barrel gives a flat line of sight from receiver to end of barrel.
Price $51.25

(Model 721, similar to Model 727 but 5 shot capacity, available at same price.)

MODEL 728

With ventilated raised rib. Same specifications as Model 726.
Price $57.25

(Model 722, similar to Model 728 but 5 shot capacity, available at same price.)

EXTRA BARRELS FOR AUTOMATIC SHOTGUNS

Plain round barrel..$18.50
With raised matted rib...................................... 26.25
With ventilated raised rib.................................. 32.25

SAVAGE AUTOMATIC SHOTGUN WITH CUTTS COMPENSATOR

MODEL 720-C—5 shot
MODEL 726-C—3 shot

Model 720-C..$57.75
Model 726-C.. 57.75

Same specifications as Models 720 and 726 as described above except as follows: 20-inch Special Barrel with Cutts Compensator

attached furnished with two choke tubes. Spreader tube making barrel length overall 24⅝ inches. No. 705 Full Choke Tube making barrel length overall 26¼ inches. Modified choke tube will be substituted if specified.

MODEL 740-C—3 shot Skeet Model

With Cutts Compensator and two tubes as above. With special large Beavertail forearm and selected American walnut stock both elaborately checkered and oil finished. Receiver artistically

decorated on sides, channeled and matted in line of sight. Friction ring adjustment for light and heavy loads. Weight about 8½ pounds.

Price $63.50

FOX SHOTGUNS

12, 16 AND 20 GAUGE

A GRADE

SPECIFICATIONS

Barrels, high quality alloy forged steel, adapted to smokeless or black powders. Dark walnut stock; checkered and engraved; half pistol grip; 12, 16 and 20 gauge: 26, 28, 30 and 32 inch barrels. Full pistol or straight grip to order at no extra charge. Weight, 12 gauge, 6¾ to 8 pounds; 16 gauge, 5¾ to 7 pounds; 20 gauge, 5¾ to 6¾ pounds; various drops and lengths of stocks.

Grade A...$49.00
A. E. with Automatic Shell Ejector.......................... 59.50

STOEGER ARMS CORPORATION © 1939

The 1907 Savage Automatic Pistol

During the development of the .45 caliber pistol for military use Savage came up with the idea of bringing out a pocket model. This was the era of the pocket pistol for home and self protection. The .32 ACP had already proved itself as a popular cartridge thus the first Savage pocket automatic was developed in this caliber. The man undoubtedly responsible for its development within the Savage factory was C.A. Nelson.

Savage started work on the .32 in 1907 although none were produced until 1908. It was also at this time that many changes were being made on the .45 by Mr. Searle. These new modifications were also incorporated into the .32. The Savage pocket automatic was ready for production in late 1907 and Savage so designated its first pistol as Model 1907.

The first pocket .32 was delivered to Benjamin Adriance, President of Savage on March 22, 1908. It was Serial No. 2. There is no record of Serial No. 1. The other early pistols went to the officers and other gun manufacturers. William D. Condit also received some of the early pistols. Whether he was technically interested in them or whether he used them for promotion is not known. The Marshall Wells Co., The Simmons Hardware Co., and the E.K. Tryon Co. were the first commercial establishments to purchase Savage autos. In later years they were large purchasers and outlets for these pistols.

Total production for the year 1908 was rather meager, approximately 2,000 were made, however many of these were listed as spoiled.

The first use of a Savage in other than commercial use was a sale to the City of Fitchburg in 1908. Later many of Savage's customers included Police Departments, Banks, and even the Military.

Although articles had appeared as early as 1907, a large advertising campaign was not begun until 1909. Ads then appeared in many of the nationally known periodicals.

Their main theme centered around Savage's quick shooting and natural pointing ability. Testimonials by noted people in the firearms world added color to many of the advertisements. Savage also put out two booklets; "The Tenderfoot's Turns" and later "It Banishes Fear." Both are excellent examples of the art of advertising of this era.

Some articles from gun magazines of the day go as follows:

"Outdoor Life" — November 1910, "Experience with Savage Automatic Pistol by Ashley A. Haines — "Before proceeding further it might be proper to state that from the several hundred shots fired from this Savage not a single misfire occurred nor did the arm in a single instance fail to function perfectly — Furthermore I might add that the arm is very finely finished, fits the hand nicely being brought onto the target with little effort on the shooter's part, and that as the mechanism is very simple and every part made from best material . . . and for those who can shoot it accurately it is a vicious shooter . . . The strange part of it lies in the fact that I could not possibly do any better when firing deliberately and doing my very best to keep the shots in the center."

Reprinted from SAVAGE AUTOMATIC PISTOLS by James R. Carr; St. Charles, IL ca. 1950.

Savage .32 Caliber

The easiest way to follow the development of the Savage automatic pistol is to study the .32 caliber.

The bulk of automatic pistols that Savage manufactured were produced in this caliber.

There are three basic models: Model 1907, Model 1915, Model 1917.

The model number indicates the year in which the pistol was introduced or developed. These are the model numbers given by the Savage Arms Company.

A great deal of confusion has been created particularly with reference to Model 1907 in that it has often been called Model 1905; or Model 1910.

The confusion is understandable because:

1. Every model is stamped Pat. - November 21, 1905. Thus it is often referred to as Model 1905.
2. Although the first Model was introduced in 1907 a limited number were manufactured. It was not until 1910 that the pistol began to gain prominence. The pistol manufactured in 1910 also varied in many respects to the one introduced in 1907. This 1910 issue was then produced in great quantities. So here again it is easy to understand why and how it became known as the Model 1910.

Model 1915 is often referred to as the "grip safety model" or "hammerless" model. The Model 1915 is hammerless and fitted with a grip safety.

Model 1917 is the only model so designated on the pistol, "Savage 1917 Model" is stamped on the left side of most Model 1917's. It is also known as the "wide gripped model."

Number of 32 Caliber Savages made by year!

MODEL 1907 .32 Caliber

Production probably started in early 1908. The first .32 pistol recorded was shipped to Benjamin Adriance on April 22, 1908; serial number 2. There is no record of what happened to serial number 1.

Year	Number Manufactured	Approximate S. N. at the end of year
1908 -	2,000	2,000
1909 -	13,000	15,000
1910 -	15,500	30,500
1911 -	20,000	50,500
1912 -	30,000	80,500
1913 -	19,500	100,000
1914 -	15,750	115,750
1915 -	14,250	130,000

MODEL 1915 .32 Caliber Hammerless Grip Safety

1915 -	6,379	136,379
1916 -	123	136,502

MODEL 1907 .32 Caliber

1916 -	16,752	150,000 - 166,752
1917 -	17,748	184,500
1918 -	1,346	185,846
1919 -	38,004	223,850
1920 -	5,951	229,801

MODEL 1917 (New Grip)

1920 -	11,199	241,000
1921 -	4,750	245,750

1922 through 1926 - the recorded serial numbers in the Savage ledgers end with 246,020. They start again at 246,620 to 259,472, but there is no mention of to whom they were sold.

The total number produced during this period from 1922 - 1926 was 13,122.

TOTAL NUMBER .32 Caliber

1907 -	209,791
1915 -	6,502
1917 -	29,071
Total -	245,364

SAVAGE .32 CALIBER PISTOLS

Models - Issues - Modifications with approximate Serial Range Quantities

Early Model 1907

	Serial Range	Quantity
1907-08	2 - 3000	3000
1907-09 Modif. #1	3000 - 7100/8400	4100 - 5400
1907-09 Modif. #2	7100/8400 - 10980	2600 - 3980

Common 1907 Models

	Serial Range	Quantity
1907-10 Modif. #1	10,980 - 19,500	8400
1907-10 Modif. #2	19,500 - 65,000	45,500
1907-12 Transitional	65,000 - 80,500	15,500
1907-13 Modif. #1	80,500 - 87,900	7,400
1907-13 Modif. #2	87,900 - 124,000	30 - 40,000
	150,000 - 167,000	
1907-13 Modif. #3	105,000 - 130,000	30 - 45,000
	136,000 - 167,000	
1907-17 Modif. #1	167,000 - 176,300	9,300
1907-17 Modif. #2	176,300 - 184,600	7,700

Late Model 1907

	Serial Range	Quantity
1907-19 Modif. #1	184,600 - 203,400	18,800
1907-19 Modif. #2	203,400 - 229,800	26,400

Total Model 1907 - 202,000 - 233,000

Model 1915

	Serial Range	Quantity
1915	103,000 - 136,500	6,500

Model 1917

	Serial Range	Quantity
1917-20	229,800 - 245,000	15,200
1917-22	245,000 - 259,472	12,000 - 14,472

Total Model 1917 - 27,200 - 29,670

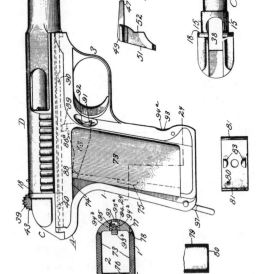

.45 Cal. Savage 1906 Prototype

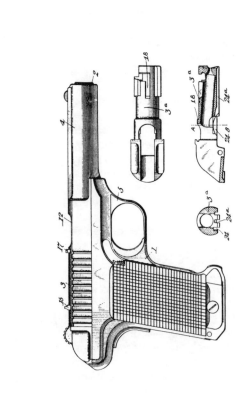

.45 Cal. Savage 1907 Prototype

Source: *SAVAGE AUTOMATIC PISTOLS,* by James R. Carr

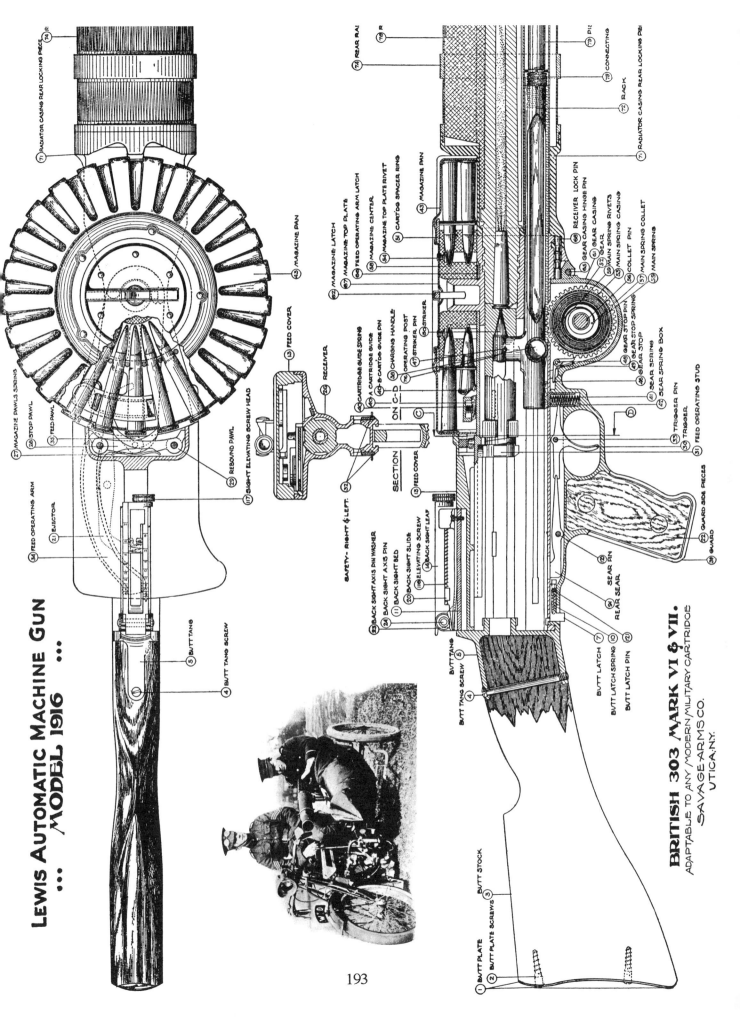

LEWIS AUTOMATIC MACHINE GUN
... MODEL 1916 ...

74(R) RADIATOR CASING REAR LOCKING PIECE

71 RADIATOR CASING

43 MAGAZINE PAN

27 MAGAZINE PAWLS SPRING
28 STOP PAWL
35 FEED PAWL
29 REBOUND PAWL
117 SIGHT ELEVATING SCREW HEAD

84 FEED OPERATING ARM
21 EJECTOR

5 BUTT TANG
4 BUTT TANG SCREW

12 FEED COVER
26 RECEIVER

40-A CARTRIDGE GUIDE
40-B CARTRIDGE GUIDE PIN

82 MAGAZINE LATCH
67 MAGAZINE TOP PLATE
66 FEED OPERATING ARM LATCH
65 MAGAZINE CENTER
64 MAGAZINE TOP PLATE RIVET

ON C-D

SECTION ON C-D
13 FEED COVER

SAFETY - RIGHT & LEFT

23 BACK SIGHT AXIS PIN WASHER
24 BACK SIGHT AXIS PIN
11 BACK SIGHT BED
20 BACK SIGHT SLIDE
19 ELEVATING SCREW
14 BACK SIGHT LEAF

6 BUTT TANG
5 BUTT TANG SCREW
4 BUTT TANG SCREW

1 BUTT PLATE
2 BUTT PLATE SCREWS
3 BUTT STOCK

79(R) REAR RAI
79 REAR RAI

74 RADIATOR CASING

50 STRIKER
47 STRIKER PIN
76 OPERATING POST
78 CHARGING HANDLE

44 CARTRIDGE SPACER RING
54 MAGAZINE PAN

68 RECEIVER LOCK PIN
63 GEAR CASING HINGE PIN
61 GEAR
60 MAIN SPRING RIVETS
59 MAIN SPRING CASING
56 COLLET PIN
57 MAIN SPRING COLLET
58 MAIN SPRING
62 SEAR CASING
55 SEAR
48 GEAR STOP PIN
52 GEAR STOP SPRING
49 GEAR STOP
46 SEAR SPRING
42 SEAR SPRING BOX
41 GEAR SPRING
45 TRIGGER PIN
33 TRIGGER
39 FEED OPERATING STUD
31 FEED OPERATING STUD

22 GUARD SIDE PIECES
30 GUARD

15 SEAR PIN
34 REAR SEAR

9 BUTT LATCH
7
10 BUTT LATCH SPRING
8 BUTT LATCH PIN

79(R) R
79 PI
73 CONNECTING
72 RACK
71 RADIATOR CASING REAR LOCKING PIE

BRITISH 303 MARK VI & VII.

ADAPTABLE TO ANY MODERN MILITARY CARTRIDGE

SAVAGE ARMS CO.
UTICA. N.Y.

WHOLESALE & RETAIL PRICES ON SAVAGE SPORTING ARMS, 1942

WHOLESALE AND RETAIL PRICES
ON SAVAGE SPORTING ARMS

WHOLESALE PRICE LIST
Effective January 2, 1942

The Wholesale and Retail Prices listed herein on Savage Brand Sporting Arms have been established as minimum Fair Trade Prices in all States having Fair Trade Laws.

(All prices include U. S. Excise Tax except on those items indicated as not subject to U. S. Excise Tax)

MODEL			Wholesale Price	Retail Price
Applies to Price List No. 28-42				
SAVAGE UTILITY GUN—Rifle and Shotgun				
Model 221	.30-30 Cal.	12 Ga. 30"		
Model 222	.30-30 Cal.	16 Ga. 28"		
Model 223	.30-30 Cal.	20 Ga. 28"		
Model 224	.25-20 Cal.	12 Ga. 30"		
Model 225	.25-20 Cal.	16 Ga. 28"	$18.60	$24.85
Model 226	.25-20 Cal.	20 Ga. 28"		
Model 227	.22 Hornet	12 Ga. 30"		
Model 228	.22 Hornet	16 Ga. 28"		
Model 229	.22 Hornet	20 Ga. 28"		
Model 230	.32-20 Cal.	12 Ga. 30"		
Model 231	.32-20 Cal.	16 Ga. 28"		
MODEL 219 SINGLE SHOT RIFLE			14.35	19.10
SINGLE BARREL SHOTGUN				
Model 220			10.65	14.20
Model 220-P			15.40	20.45
AUTOMATIC SHOTGUN—5 Shot—Standard Design				
Model 720			45.70	60.90
Raised solid matted rib, extra			7.65	10.20
AUTOMATIC SHOTGUN—3 Shot Upland Sporter				
Model 720			45.70	60.90
Raised solid matted rib, extra			7.65	10.20
AUTOMATIC SHOTGUNS—Guard and Riot Gun				
Model 720 Guard and Riot			45.70	60.90
Fitted with 1¼" loops and studs			1.15	1.35
1¼" Leather strap			2.20*	2.65*
AUTOMATIC SHOTGUNS WITH AERO-DYNE SUPER POLY CHOKE				
Model 720-P—5 Shot or 3 Shot			53.85	71.85
Model 720-P—3 Shot—Skeet Model			57.15	76.25

* Not Subject to U. S. Excise Tax.

MODEL	Wholesale Price	Retail Price
AUTOMATIC SHOTGUNS WITH CUTTS COMPENSATOR		
Model 720-C—5 Shot or 3 Shot	66.65	83.25
Model 720-C—3 Shot—Skeet Model	71.95	89.90
EXTRA BARRELS FOR AUTOMATIC SHOTGUNS		
Plain Round Barrel	18.25	24.30
Barrel with Raised Solid Matted Rib	25.85	34.45
HI-POWER REPEATING LEVER ACTION RIFLE		
Model 99-EG	46.30	61.75
Model 99-R	52.75	70.00
Model 99-RS	63.10	83.95
MODEL 23 "SPORTER" RIFLES		
Model 23-C	31.85	42.50
Model 23-D	31.85	42.50
Extra Magazines for Model 23-C and 23-D	1.10*	1.45*
MODEL 29 SLIDE ACTION REPEATING RIFLE		
Model 29	23.15	30.75
AUTOMATIC REPEATING RIFLE—.22 LONG RIFLE		
Model 7 Clip Magazine	15.20	18.95
Model 7-S Clip Magazine	15.85	19.75
Extra Magazines for Model 7 and Model 7-S 5 Shot	.70*	.90*
10 Shot	.90*	1.25*
Model 6 Tubular Magazine	17.10	21.35
Model 6-S Tubular Magazine	17.75	22.15
Model 602 Tubular Magazine—.22 Short	17.10	21.35
REPEATING RIFLE—.22 CALIBER		
Model 5 Tubular Magazine	13.95	17.50
Model 5-S Tubular Magazine	14.65	18.30
Model 4 Clip Magazine	10.50	13.10
Model 4-S Clip Magazine	11.15	13.95
Extra Magazines for Model 4 and Model 4-S 5 Shot	.70*	.90*
10 Shot	.90*	1.25*
SINGLE SHOT .22 CALIBER RIFLE		
Model 3	5.70	7.10
Model 3-S	6.35	7.90

* Not subject to U. S. Excise Tax.

1945

"I'LL PICK A SAVAGE RIFLE EVERY TIME"

"Those Savage rifles in the rack are the same ones I'm showing you in these action pictures. I'll pick a Savage every time... you can't beat 'em for accuracy, dependability and value.

"Take a look at this Savage .22 automatic rifle. It's great for speed shooting at small running game, informal target shooting or 'plinking'. It's one of a complete line of Savage .22's and medium power rifles. Then, here's the famous Savage Model 99 Hi-Power Rifle. It's always been my first choice for big game hunting because of its perfect balance, lightning-fast lever action and pulverizing power."

 WAR PRODUCTION COMES FIRST . . .
Savage has produced over 2,000,000 military arms, including Browning Caliber .50 aircraft machine guns, Thompson submachine guns, and rifles. Of course, the requirements of our armed forces will continue to come first .. but YOUR Savage will be worth waiting for.

For Speed Shooting . . .
Savage Model 6—.22 Caliber Automatic. Three rifles in one . . . automatic . . . bolt action repeater . . . single shot.

For Big Game Hunting . . .
Savage Model 99 Hi-Power Rifle. A variety of calibers, including the famous Savage .300 and Savage .250-2000.

Savage Arms Corporation, Utica, N.Y.
Plants in Utica, N.Y. and Chicopee Falls, Mass.

SAVAGE
WORLD FAMOUS FOR DEPENDABILITY AND ACCURACY

THE AMERICAN RIFLEMAN
MAY, NINETEEN FORTY-FIVE
Reprinted by permission

SAVAGE RETAIL PRICE LIST

For Catalog No. 76

Effective October 15, 1946

RIFLES

	Price Each	Page
Model 99 Lever Action Hi-Power Rifles		
*Model 99-EG, Solid Frame	$88.80 92.95	4-5
*Model 99-R, Solid Frame	101.10 105.25	4-5
Model 99-RS, Solid Frame	120.90 126.55	4-5
*Model 23-D .22 Hornet Sporter Rifle	57.95 60.65	6
Model 23-C .32-20 Caliber Sporter Rifle	57.95	6
Extra Magazines for Models 23-D and 23-C	1.90 2	6
Model 7 Automatic Rifle	25.90	8-9
Model 7-S Automatic Rifle (Peep Sights)	26.95	8-9
Extra Magazines for Models 7 and 7-S, 5 Shot	1.30	8-9
Extra Magazines for Models 7 and 7-S, 10 Shot	1.55	8-9
*Model 6 Automatic Rifle .22 Long Rifle	28.45 30.25	8-9
Model 6-S Automatic Rifle (Peep Sights)	31.70 33.30	8-9
Model 5 Bolt Action Repeating Rifle (Tubular Magazine)	23.90 24.50	10-11
Model 5-S Bolt Action Repeating Rifle (Tubular Mag., Peep Sights)	24.95 25.72	10-11
*Model 4 Bolt Action Repeating Rifle (Clip Magazine)	19.60 21.50	10-11
Model 4-S Bolt Action Repeating Rifle (Clip Mag., and Peep Sights)	20.75 22.55	10-11
Extra Magazines for Models 4 and 4-S, 5 Shot	1.55 1.70	10-11
Extra Magazines for Models 4 and 4-S, 10 Shot	1.60 1.75	10-11
*Model 3 Single Shot Bolt Action Rifle	12.90 15.50	10-11
*Model 3-S Single Shot Bolt Action Rifle (Peep Sights)	16.90	10-11
*Model 29 Slide Action Repeating Rifle	42.20	12

AUTOMATIC SHOTGUNS

	Price Each	Page
*Model 720—3 or 5 Shot	87.95	14-15
Model 720-P—3 or 5 Shot	103.80	14-15
Model 720-C—3 or 5 Shot	108.10	14-15
*Model 745—3 or 5 Shot, 12 Gauge	93.25	14-15

SINGLE BARREL SHOTGUNS

	Price Each	Page
Model 220 Hammerless, 12, 16, 20 and .410 Gauge	21.50	16
Model 220-P Single Barrel Shotgun with Polychoke	30.95	16

SAVAGE SINGLE SHOT HI-POWER RIFLE

	Price Each	Page
Model 219, .30-30, .32-20, .25-20 and .22 Hornet Calibers	26.20	17

SAVAGE UTILITY GUN (Shotgun and Rifle)

	Price Each	Page
Model 221, .30-30 Cal. with Interchangeable 12 Ga. Barrel	37.00	17
Model 222, .30-30 Cal. with Interchangeable 16 Ga. Barrel	37.00	17
Model 223, .30-30 Cal. with Interchangeable 20 Ga. Barrel	37.00	17
Model 224, .25-20 Cal. with Interchangeable 16 Ga. Barrel	37.00	17
Model 225, .25-20 Cal. with Interchangeable 16 Ga. Barrel	37.00	17
Model 226, .25-20 Cal. with Interchangeable 20 Ga. Barrel	37.00	17

*Indicates models which will be available during 1946.
New production of models not so marked subject to indefinite delay.

SAVAGE UTILITY GUN (Shotgun and Rifle) Continued

	Price Each	Page
Model 227, .22 Hornet Cal. with Interchangeable 12 Ga. Barrel	$37.00	17
Model 228, .22 Hornet Cal. with Interchangeable 16 Ga. Barrel	37.00	17
Model 229, .22 Hornet Cal. with Interchangeable 20 Ga. Barrel	37.00	17
Model 230, .32-20 Cal. with Interchangeable 12 Ga. Barrel	37.00	17
Model 231, .32-20 Cal. with Interchangeable 16 Ga. Barrel	37.00	17

*SAVAGE CLEANING PREPARATIONS

	Price Each	Page
Savage Solvent	.35	18
Savage Gun Oil	.25	18
Savage "Rustveto" Gun Grease	.30	18
Savage Gun Cleaning Kit	.80	18

*ACCESSORIES

	Price Each		Page
No. 1—Carrying Strap	2.00		18
No. 1-A—Carrying Strap	1.00		18
No. 1-B—1 in. Wide Leather Carrying Strap	1.90		18
No. 2—1¼ in. Leather Sling Strap	3.00		18
No. 3—⅞ in. Leather Sling Strap	2.65		18
No. 4—⅞ in. Wide, Light Web Sling Strap	.35		18
No. 2-A—1¼ in. Sling Loops and Studs	.80	Per set of two	18
No. 3-A—⅞ in. Sling Loops and Studs	.80	Per set of two	18
No. 4-A—Detachable Sling Loops and Studs	4.00	Per set of two	18

*SAVAGE CENTER-FIRE METALLIC CARTRIDGES

	List Price per 1000	Page
Packed 50 in a box		
.22 Hornet, 45 Grain, Hollow Point Bullet	$41.88	19-20
.25-20 Savage, 60 Grain, either Soft Point or Metal Cased Bullet	47.77	19-20
.25-20 Savage, 60 Grain, Hollow Point Bullet	49.77	19-20
.32-20 Savage, 90 Grain, either Soft Point or Metal Cased Bullet	48.64	19-20
.32-20 Savage, 80 Grain, Hollow Point Bullet	51.76	19-20
Packed 20 in a box		
.22 Hi-Power, 70 Grain, Soft Point Bullet	84.82	19-20
.250-3000 Savage, 87 Grain, Soft Point Bullet	101.09	19-20
.250-3000 Savage, 100 Grain, Soft Point Bullet	101.09	19-20
.30-30 Savage, 170 Grain, Soft Point Bullet	90.26	19-21
.303 Savage, 180 Grain, Soft Point Bullet	90.26	19-21
.300 Savage, 150 Grain, Soft Point Bullet	114.08	19-21
.300 Savage, 180 Grain, Soft Point Bullet	114.08	19-21
.30 Springfield '06, 180 Grain, Soft Point Bullet	129.96	19-21
.30 Springfield '06, 220 Grain, Soft Point Bullet	129.96	19-21
.30-40 Krag (.30 Army) 180 Grain, Soft Lead Point Bullet	119.15	19-21
.30-40 Krag (.30 Army) 220 Grain, Soft Lead Point Bullet	119.15	19-21
.32 Winchester Special, 170 Grain, Soft Lead Point Bullet	90.26	19-21
.35 Remington, 220 Grain, Soft Lead Point Bullet	101.09	19-21

*Indicates models which will be available during 1946.
New production of models not so marked subject to indefinite delay.

Form 76C   10-46-5M

.22 CALIBER RIFLES

★ **MODEL 4**

24 inch round tapered barrel. Proof tested. Crowned muzzle. Bolt action repeater. 5-shot detachable clip magazine; extra 10-shot magazines can be furnished. Chambered for .22 Long Rifle, .22 Long or .22 Short cartridges, both regular or high-speed. Bolt head encased. Recessed bolt face. Self-cocking action on open-ing stroke. Independent safety. High luster finish on bolt and trigger. Gold bead front sight and sporting rear sight with elevation adjustments.

One-piece stock and forestock of selected walnut with checkered full pistol grip and fluted comb. Oil finished. Hard composition butt plate. Weight about 5½ lbs.

★ **MODEL 4-S**   Same as Model 4 except with Savage Peep Sight Equipment.

★ **MODEL 3**

Bolt action single shot. 24 inch round tapered barrel. Proof tested. Takedown. Crowned muzzle. Chambered for .22 Long Rifle, .22 Long and .22 Short cartridges, both regular or high-speed. Self-cocking action on opening stroke. High luster finish on bolt and trigger. Bolt head encased. Recessed bolt face. Independent safety.

One piece genuine American walnut stock. Full pistol grip. Fluted comb. Oil finish. Hard composition butt plate. Large broad forestock. Adjustable flat top rear sight and gold bead front sight. Weight about 5 lbs.

★ **MODEL 3-S**   Same as Model 3 except with Savage Peep Sight Equipment.

★ **MODEL 5**

Bolt action repeater. Takedown. Tubular magazine. Capacity: 15 .22 Long Rifle, 17 .22 Long or 21 .22 Short cartridges, high-speed or regular. 24 inch round tapered barrel with crowned muzzle. Proof tested. Recessed bolt face. Bolt head encased. Self-cocking action on opening stroke. Quick ignition. Independent safety. High luster finish on bolt and trigger. All parts finely polished.

Sporting rear sight with elevation adjustments. Gold bead front sight. Tapped for Weaver telescope sights. Weight about 6 lbs.

One-piece stock and forestock of selected walnut with checkered full pistol grip and fluted comb. Oil finished. Hard composition butt plate.

★ **MODEL 5-S**

Same as Model 5 except with Savage Peep Sight Equipment.

★ MODEL 99-EG SOLID FRAME

REPEATING RIFLES

CALIBERS: .250/3000 and .300 SAVAGE

24 inch tapered, medium weight round barrel. Proof tested. Matted trigger. Rotary box-type magazine with numeral indicator. Capacity 5 cartridges plus one in chamber making rifle a 6-shot repeater. Light weight capped full pistol grip stock and tapered fore-end of selected walnut. Rubbed oil finish, checkered grip and fore-end. Corrugated steel butt plate of shotgun design. Stock dimensions 13″ x 1⅞″ x 2⅝″. Butt plate 1½″ x 4⅞″. Adjustable semi-buckhorn sporting rear sight and white metal bead front sight on raised ramp base. Case hardened lever. Polished breech bolt. Blued receiver. Receiver tang tapped and drilled for all standard aperture sights. Weight about 7¼ lbs.

★ MODEL 99-R SOLID FRAME

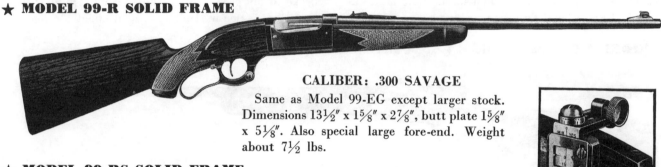

No. 70-LH Redfield Micrometer Sight

CALIBER: .300 SAVAGE

Same as Model 99-EG except larger stock. Dimensions 13½″ x 1⅝″ x 2⅞″, butt plate 1⅝″ x 5⅛″. Also special large fore-end. Weight about 7½ lbs.

★ MODEL 99-RS SOLID FRAME

Same specifications as Model 99-R with following refinements: Redfield No. 70 windage and elevation adjustment rear peep sight (illustrated) and gold bead front sight; ⅞″ leather sling strap with quick-release swivels and screw studs.

★ MODEL 7

24 inch round tapered barrel. Proof tested. Crowned muzzle. Takedown. Chambered for .22 Long Rifle, regular or high speed cartridges with lubricated bullets. When hand operated as Bolt Action Repeater or Single Shot, .22 Long and .22 Short cartridges may also be used. Independent safety. High luster finish bolt and trigger. 5-shot clip magazine. Extra 10-shot clip magazine available. One-piece walnut stock and forestock, oil finished. Full pistol grip, checkered. Fluted comb. Hard composition butt plate. Gold bead front sight and sporting rear sight with elevation adjustments. Weight about 6 lbs.

★ SAVAGE UTILITY GUN

Here is the most economical way to own a fine high power rifle and a shotgun. The Savage Utility Gun consists of a stock and single shot action and a choice of a combination of interchangeable rifle and shotgun proof tested barrels. With either you have a light, trim, fast-handling arm with the shooting qualities of guns costing many times as much.

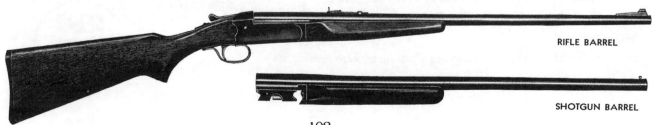

RIFLE BARREL

SHOTGUN BARREL

Hi-Power Metallic Cartridges

Savage

Effective: January 28, 1959

Index	Description	Bullet Wt. Grains	Case Quan. M	Case Weight (lbs.)	Retail Per Box	List Per 1000	Wholesale Price Per Thousand				
							Zone 1	Zone 2	Zone 3	Zone 4	Zone 5
*S-222	.222 Remington	50	1	29	2.80	140.00	105.18	105.36	105.54	105.72	105.90
#S-22	.22 Hornet	45	2	33	6.00	120.00	90.11	90.22	90.33	90.44	90.55
#S-25-S	.25-20	86	2	51	5.10	102.00	76.66	76.82	76.98	77.14	77.30
#S-32-S	.32-20	100	2	53	6.30	126.00	94.69	94.88	95.07	95.26	95.45
*S-243-8	.243 Winchester	80	1	53	4.10	205.00	154.09	154.43	154.77	155.11	155.45
*S-243-10	.243 Winchester	100	1	55	4.10	205.00	154.09	154.43	154.77	155.11	155.45
*S-250-L	.250/3000 Sav.	87	1	48	3.85	192.50	144.69	145.00	145.31	145.62	145.93
*S-250-L	.250/3000 Sav.	100	1	49	3.85	192.50	144.69	145.00	145.31	145.62	145.93
*S-270-10	.270 Winchester	100	1	59	4.55	227.50	171.06	171.49	171.92	172.35	172.78
*S-270-13	.270 Winchester	130	1	65	4.55	227.50	171.06	171.49	171.92	172.35	172.78
*S-270-15	.270 Winchester	150	1	67	4.55	227.50	171.06	171.49	171.92	172.35	172.78
*S-30	.30-30 Win. & Sav.	170	1	55	3.60	180.00	135.36	135.72	136.08	136.44	136.80
*S-303	.303 Savage	180	1	58	3.70	185.00	139.12	139.49	139.86	140.23	140.60
*S-300-HP	.300 Savage	150	1	58	4.40	220.00	165.40	165.80	166.20	166.60	167.00
*S-300-P	.300 Savage	180	1	60	4.40	220.00	165.40	165.80	166.20	166.60	167.00
*S-308-P	.308 Winchester	110	1	55	4.55	227.50	171.11	171.59	172.07	172.55	173.03
*S-308-P	.308 Winchester	150	1	60	4.55	227.50	171.11	171.59	172.07	172.55	173.03
*S-308-P	.308 Winchester	180	1	65	4.55	227.50	171.11	171.59	172.07	172.55	173.03
*S-306-PS	.30-06 Spfd.	180	1	71	4.55	227.50	171.11	171.59	172.07	172.55	173.03
*S-306-H	.30-06 Spfd.	220	1	76	4.55	227.50	171.11	171.59	172.07	172.55	173.03
*S-304-L	.30-40 Krag	180	1	65	4.55	227.50	171.10	171.57	172.04	172.51	172.98
*S-32-W	.32 Win. Spec.	170	1	55	3.70	185.00	139.10	139.45	139.80	140.15	140.50
*S-35-R	.35 Remington	200	1	62	4.10	205.00	154.15	154.55	154.95	155.35	155.75

Prices include Federal Excise Tax of 11%

#Packed 50 in a box   *Packed 20 in a box

FAIR TRADE

The wholesale and retail prices for all Savage Center Fire Metallic Cartridges have been established in all states having Fair Trade Laws. This price list constitutes the notice of amendment provided for in paragraph 2 of the original Savage Center Fire Metallic Cartridges Fair Trade Agreement and the prices set forth herein supersede and are to be substituted for the prices set forth in the notice of amendment dated January 3, 1955.

Savage Arms Corporation
Chicopee Falls, Massachusetts

914-C

Savage

DEALER PRICE LIST

EFFECTIVE JANUARY 7, 1959

HI-POWER RIFLES

Model Number		Wholesale Price**	Retail Price**
Lever Action Repeating Rifles			
99-EG	Calibers: .300 and .250-3000 Savage;	$85.25	$113.65
99-F	.243, .308 and .358 Winchester	89.80	119.75
99-R		87.55	116.75
Bolt Action Repeating Rifles			
110	Calibers: .30-'06 Sp.fld., .243, .270 and .308 Win.	84.40	112.50
110-MC		84.40	112.50
110-MCL		91.85	122.50
340	Calibers: .222 Remington, .22 Hornet and .30-30	43.90	58.50
	Extra clip magazine: 4 shot for .222 Rem. and .22 Hornet; 3 shot for .30-30. State caliber (not taxed)	1.50	2.00
Single Shot Rifle			
219	Calibers: .30-30 and .22 Hornet	28.15	37.50

AUTOMATIC SHOTGUNS

Featherweight			
775	12-16 gauge — plain barrel	87.75	117.00
775-SC	12-16 gauge — with Savage Super-Choke	95.25	127.00

SLIDE ACTION REPEATING SHOTGUNS

30	12 gauge — Ventilated rib	61.90	82.50
30-AC	12 gauge — Savage Adjustable Choke, vent. rib	65.65	87.50

SINGLE BARREL SHOTGUNS

Hammerless			
220	12-16-20-28-.410 gauge (except 12 ga. — 36")	26.00	32.50
220	12 gauge — 36" barrel	27.60	34.50

OVER AND UNDER RIFLE AND SHOTGUN

24	.22 caliber over barrel and .410 gauge under barrel	34.00	42.50

.22 CALIBER RIFLES

Bolt Action Repeating Rifles			
4 Deluxe	clip magazine	25.20	31.50
	Extra clip magazine for Model 4 — 5 shot (not taxed)	1.25	1.65
	10 shot	1.50	2.00
5 Deluxe	tubular magazine	28.60	35.75
Automatic Repeating Rifles			
6 Deluxe	tubular magazine	32.05	42.75
Slide Action Repeating Rifle			
29-G	hammerless	37.15	49.50

**U. S. Excise Tax included

FOX

DOUBLE BARREL SHOTGUNS

Model Number		Wholesale Price**	Retail Price**
B	12-16-20-.410 gauge — ventilated rib	$75.60	$94.50
B-ST	12-16-20-.410 gauge — ventilated rib, gold plated single trigger	83.60	104.50

STEVENS

SLIDE ACTION REPEATING SHOTGUNS

77	12-16-20 gauge	52.15	69.50
77-SC	12-16-20 gauge — with recoil pad and Savage Super-Choke	61.15	81.50
77-M	Magnum — 12 and 20 gauge — with recoil pad	61.15	81.50

BOLT ACTION REPEATING SHOTGUNS

58	12 gauge	29.20	38.95
58-AC	12 gauge — with Savage Adjustable Choke	31.45	41.95
58	16 gauge	28.45	37.95
58-AC	16 gauge — with Savage Adjustable Choke	30.70	40.95
58	20 gauge	25.45	33.95
58-AC	20 gauge — with Savage Adjustable Choke	28.45	37.95
	Extra clip magazine for Model 58 and 58-AC 12-16-20 gauge, state gauge (not taxed)	1.50	2.00
59	.410 gauge, tubular magazine	29.40	36.75
58	.410 gauge, clip magazine	23.95	31.95
	Extra clip magazine for Model 58-.410 ga.	1.50	2.00

SINGLE BARREL SHOTGUNS

94	12-16-20-28-.410 gauge (except 12-16 ga. — 36")	23.60	29.50
94	12-16 gauge — 36" barrel	25.20	31.50
94-Y	20-.410 gauge — with recoil pad — youth's model	25.20	31.50

DOUBLE BARREL SHOTGUN

311	12-16-20-.410 gauge	54.80	68.50

.22 CALIBER RIFLES

Single Shot Rifle			
15	24" barrel	13.20	16.50
15-Y	Short stock — 21" barrel — youth's model	13.20	16.50
Bolt Action Repeating Rifles			
84	clip magazine	23.60	29.50
	Extra clip magazine for Model 84 — 5 shot (not taxed)	1.25	1.65
	10 shot	1.50	2.00
86	tubular magazine	27.15	33.95
Automatic Repeating Rifles			
85-K	"Scout" carbine — 20" barrel with 5 and 10 shot clip magazines	28.95	38.50
	Extra clip magazine for Model 85-K — 5 shot (not taxed)	1.25	1.65
	10 shot	1.50	2.00
87	tubular magazine	29.60	39.50
87-K	"Scout" carbine — 20" barrel, tubular magazine	30.40	40.50

**U. S. Excise Tax included

Savage Arms Corporation

Sporting Arms Division **1959** Chicopee Falls, Mass., U. S. A.

SAVAGE STEVENS FOX RIFLES AND SHOTGUNS 1959

Savage hi-power bolt action rifle

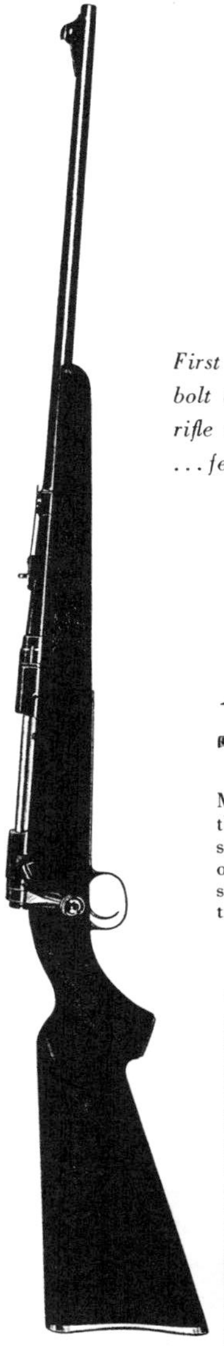

110

Calibers
long action—.30-06 and .270
short action—.243 and .308

First new bolt action rifle in years ... featherweight

A completely new bolt action rifle developed and manufactured entirely in America. Brilliant simplicity of design and precision engineering have produced a rifle that combines beautiful lines and perfect balance with rugged strength, velvet-smooth action and exceptional accuracy. Chambered for four favorite calibers, .243, .270, .30-06 and .308.

Barrel—Tapered, medium weight, chrome-molybdenum steel, proof-tested. Full-floating for utmost accuracy. Length, 22″. **Action**—Cocks on opening. Double front locking lugs for maximum strength. Recessed bolt head fully enclosed in receiver when firing. Receiver has twin gas ports for added safety. Indicator shows by sight or touch when action is cocked. Bolt easily removed and disassembled without tools. Top tang safety locks bolt, sear and trigger. Crisp trigger pull is readily adjusted by screw located directly in front of safety. **Magazine**—Staggered box type; built-in buffer protects bullet tips. Holds 4 cartridges; one in chamber makes 5 shots available. **Stock**—Gracefully contoured stock of selected walnut with checkered pistol grip and fore-end. Non-slip anodized aluminum butt plate. Capped pistol grip. Medium high fluted comb. Dimensions: trigger pull 13½″; drop at comb 1½″, at heel 2½″. **Sights**—Gold bead front sight on removable ramp. Semi-buckhorn rear sight has step elevator, folds flat for scope use, returns to same elevation setting. Receiver tapped for aperture sights and top-mount scopes. Bolt design permits low scope mounting. **Weight**—About 6¾ pounds. Length over-all 42½″-43″.

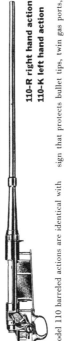

MODEL 110 BARRELED ACTIONS

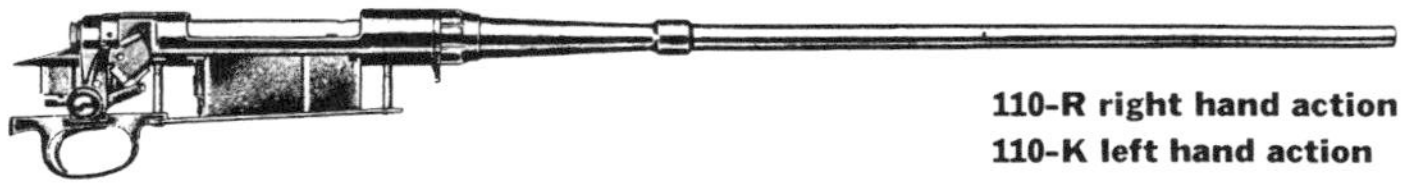

110-R right hand action
110-K left hand action

Model 110 barreled actions are identical with the regular Model 110 rifle except that the stock, front and rear sights and sight slots are omitted. It has the same unique features: superb accuracy, top tang safety, adjustable trigger pull, cocking indicator, magazine design that protects bullet tips, twin gas ports, double front bolt locking lugs, low scope mounting; all the attributes that have given the Savage One-Ten immediate acceptance by gun experts and sportsmen alike.

SOME OF THE FEATURES OF THE GREAT NEW MODEL ONE-TEN

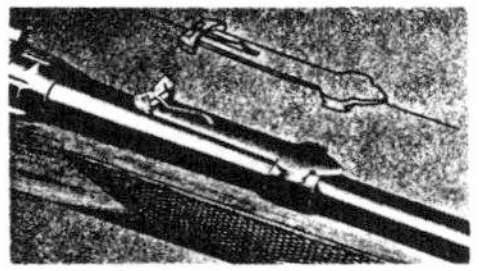

Folding Rear Sight . . . The new Savage rear sight folds for use with low mount scopes.

Telescope and Aperture Sights . . . Receiver tapped for popular scope top mounts and aperture sights.

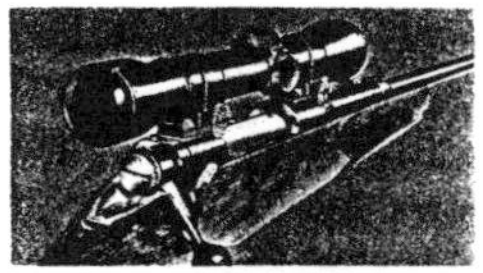

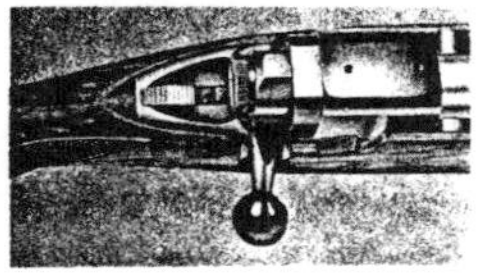

Top Tang Safety . . . Locks trigger, sear and bolt. Easily accessible for right or left-handed shooter.

New Design Bolt—Double Front Locking Lugs . . . Lugs cam into front of receiver for a strong lockup, added safety.

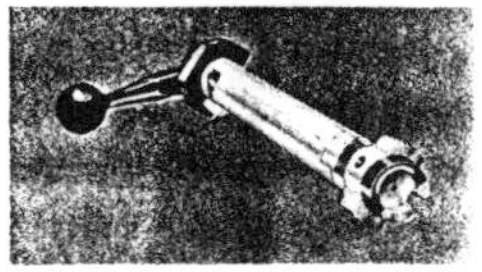

Savage hi-power cartridges

.25-20 WINCHESTER *86 grain soft point bullet*
A splendid medium power cartridge for small game. Box of 50.

.32-20 WINCHESTER *100 grain soft point bullet*
An excellent medium power cartridge. Box of 50.

.22 HORNET *45 grain soft point bullet*
One of the most accurate small bore, high speed cartridges. Ideal for target shooting or for small and medium game. Box of 50.

.222 REMINGTON *50 grain soft point bullet*
A modern, high speed, flat trajectory cartridge of extreme accuracy. Ideal for long range small game and varmint shooting. Box of 20.

.243 WINCHESTER *80 and 100 grain pointed soft point Top Notch bullets*
This recently developed 6 mm. cartridge produces very high velocity and fine accuracy and energy at extreme ranges. Two practical bullet weights make it an excellent choice for varmints and for medium game such as deer, antelope, etc. Box of 20.

.250-3000 SAVAGE *87 and 100 grain soft point Top Notch bullets*
Noted for high speed and accuracy; powerful enough for any animal in North America. Box of 20.

.270 WINCHESTER *100 and 130 grain pointed soft point; 150 grain soft point Top Notch bullets*
One of America's most popular and effective cartridges. Three bullet weights for everything from varmints to the largest North American game. Box of 20.

.30-30 WIN. & SAVAGE *170 grain soft point Top Notch bullet*
Extremely popular; standard for deer and similar game at moderate ranges. Possesses splendid accuracy. Box of 20.

.300 SAVAGE *150 and 180 grain pointed soft point Top Notch bullets*
A newly designed pointed soft point bullet extends accuracy and power of the .300 cartridge to extremely long ranges. Box of 20.

.308 WINCHESTER *110, 150 and 180 grain pointed soft point Top Notch bullets*
Latest development in .30 caliber sporting ammunition. Similar to the military 7.62 mm. NATO cartridge. Three bullet weights for everything from varmints to largest American game. Box of 20.

.32 WINCHESTER SPECIAL *170 grain soft point Top Notch bullet*
For deer, black bear and similar game at moderate ranges. Box of 20.

.35 REMINGTON *200 grain soft point Top Notch bullet*
Ideal for all large game at moderate ranges. Box of 20.

.303 SAVAGE *180 grain soft point Top Notch bullet*
Famous over 50 years for deadly, hard hitting accuracy. Dependable for deer, caribou and black beer. Fine in timbered country. Box of 20.

.30-40 KRAG (.30 KRAG) (.30 ARMY) *180 grain soft point Top Notch bullet*
For Krag and other military and sporting rifles. Box of 20.

.30-06 SPRINGFIELD *180 grain pointed soft point, 220 grain Soft point Top Notch bullets*
An outstanding all-round cartridge for every type of American big game. Box of 20.

Savage cleaning preparations

SAVAGE SOLVENT

Savage Solvent was developed in the Savage laboratories for the purpose of removing powder and primer residue, metal fouling and leading from the barrels of rifles, shotguns, pistols and revolvers. Each 2 oz. bottle in individual carton. Packed one dozen in display carton.

SAVAGE GUN OIL

A colorless, refined oil of high viscosity, which is free of acid. Compounded especially for use in the actions of fine sporting arms. 3 fluid ounces. Packed one dozen in display carton.

SAVAGE "RUST VETO" GUN GREASE

For the preservation of the barrels of fine sporting arms. Also an ideal rust preventive for skates, fine tools, etc. 1¾-oz. tubes in individual cartons. Packed one dozen in display carton.

SAVAGE GUN CLEANING KIT

The Savage Cleaning Kit includes a bottle of Savage Solvent, a can of Gun Oil and a tube of Gun Grease.
This combination includes the materials necessary for the care and preservation of all sporting arms and should be in the gun case of every sportsman. Packed one dozen in carton.

sights and accessories

NO. 150 Savage micro peep sight (includes hooded metal bead front sight and special rear sight elevator). For all Savage and Stevens .22 caliber rifles except Models 29 and 15.

NO. 175 Savage micro peep sight (includes hooded ramp front sight). For Models 322-342; 325-340.

SLING STRAP SWIVEL LOOPS AND STUDS

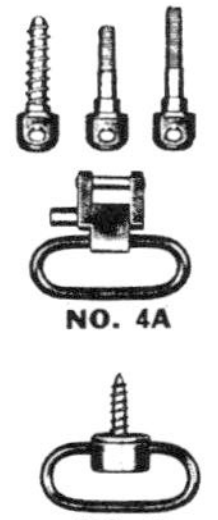

NO. 4A

NO. 7

NO. 1 ⅞″ loops and band for single barrel shotguns (specify gauge).

NO. 2D ⅞″ or 1¼″ carrying swivel hooks and screw eyes. Swivel hooks only. Screw eyes only.

NO. 4A ⅞″ or 1¼″ detachable loops and studs. Studs only. (When ordering No. 4A, state model of gun and if fore-end is regular or beavertail).

NO. 7 ⅞″ or 1¼″ swivel loops with wood screws.

CARRYING AND SLING STRAPS

NO. 1B ⅞″ carrying strap with swivel hooks.

NO. 2 1¼″ adjustable leather sling strap.

NO. 3 ¾″ adjustable leather sling strap.

SAVAGE STEVENS FOX RIFLES AND SHOTGUNS

THESE NEW MODELS WILL BE FEATURED IN SAVAGE NATIONAL ADVERTISING

SEND THIS ORDER TO YOUR JOBBER TODAY

TO:

Jobber's Name _____
Street Address _____
City, Zone, State _____
When Ship _____

SHIP TO:

Store Name _____
Street Address _____
City, State _____
Ship Via _____

SHIP THE GUNS INDICATED BELOW

quantity	model	cal./ga	description	retail price	wholesale price
			SAVAGE HIGH POWER RIFLES		
	110-MCL	.243	Left hand, featherweight bolt action rifle	$122.50	$91.85
		.308	with Monte Carlo Stock	122.50	91.85
		.270		122.50	91.85
		.30-'06		122.50	91.85
	110-MC	.243	Featherweight bolt action rifle	112.50	84.40
		.308	with Monte Carlo Stock	112.50	84.40
		.270		112.50	84.40
		.30-'06		112.50	84.40
	110	.243	Featherweight bolt action rifle	112.50	84.40
		.308	with sporter stock	112.50	84.40
		.270		112.50	84.40
		.30-'06		112.50	84.40
	219	.30-30	Single shot, hammerless, take-down rifle	37.50	28.15
		.22 Hornet		37.50	28.15
			SAVAGE SLIDE ACTION SHOTGUNS		
	30	12	Lightweight, ventilated rib, slide action shotgun		
			26" IC , 28" M , 28" F , 30" F	82.50	61.90
	30-AC	12	Lightweight, ventilated rib—Savage Adjustable Choke	87.50	65.65
			STEVENS SLIDE ACTION MAGNUM SHOTGUNS		
	77-M	12	3" Magnum Shotgun 30" Full	81.50	61.15
		20	3" Magnum Shotgun 28" Full	81.50	61.15
			FOX DOUBLE BARREL SHOTGUNS		
	B-ST		Gold plated single trigger, raised ventilated rib		
		12	26" IC-M , 28" IC-M , 28" M-F , 30" M-F	104.50	83.60
		16	26" IC-M , 28" M-F	104.50	83.60
		20	26" IC-M , 28" M-F	104.50	83.60
		.410	26" F-F	104.50	83.60
	B		Chrome plated double triggers, raised ventilated rib		
		12	26" IC-M , 28" IC-M , 28" M-F , 30" M-F	94.50	75.60
		16	26" IC-M , 28" M-F	94.50	75.60
		20	26" IC-M , 28" M-F	94.50	75.60
		.410	26" F-F	94.50	75.60
			STEVENS AUTOMATIC RIFLES		
	85-K	.22	"Scout" carbine, autoloader, clip magazine	38.50	28.95
	87-K	.22	"Scout" carbine, autoloader, tubular magazine	40.50	30.40

Buyer's Signature _____   Date _____

963-1A

Savage MODEL 110 RIFLE

BARRELED ACTIONS

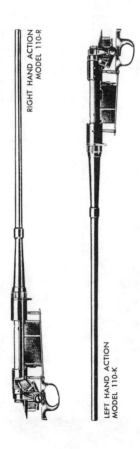

LEFT HAND ACTION
MODEL 110-K

RIGHT HAND ACTION
MODEL 110-R

CALIBERS: .243, .270 and .308 Winchester; .30-06 Springfield

Since the introduction of the Savage Model 110, shooting enthusiasts have asked for a barreled action of this outstanding rifle so they could "custom make" the One-Ten to their own specifications.

Model 110 barreled actions are identical with the regular Model 110 rifle except that the stock, front and rear sights and sight slots are omitted. It has the same unique features: superb accuracy, top tang safety, adjustable trigger pull, cocking indicator, magazine design that protects bullet tips, twin gas ports, double front bolt locking lugs, low scope mounting; all the attributes that have given the Savage One-Ten immediate acceptance by gun experts and sportsmen alike.

SPECIFICATIONS. Barrel: Tapered, medium weight, chrome-molybdenum steel, proof tested. Full floating for utmost accuracy. Length 22". **Action:** Cocks on opening. Double front locking lugs for maximum strength. Recessed bolt head fully enclosed in receiver when firing. Receiver has twin gas ports for added safety. Indicator shows when action is cocked. Bolt easily removed and disassembled without tools. Top tang safety locks bolt, sear and trigger. Crisp trigger pull is readily adjusted by screw located directly in front of safety. Receiver tapped for aperture sights and top mount scopes. **Magazine:** Staggered box type. Buffers protect bullet tips. 4 cartridges; one in chamber makes 5 shots. **Weight:** Approx. 4½ lbs. Length overall, 30" - 30½".

PRICES

(Subject to change, F.O.B. Chicopee Falls)

	Suggested Wholesale Price Incl. Tax	Suggested Retail Price Incl. Tax
Right Hand	$65.65	$87.50
Left Hand	$73.15	$97.50

Savage Arms Corporation

Chicopee Falls, Massachusetts

Sporting Arms Division

BA-914

A SAVAGE PARTS DISTRIBUTOR'S POINT OF VIEW
by Walter H. Lodewick

You can't make money by selling a part twice. That is, if a wrong part is shipped because of customer misidentification (at times the manufacturer contributes to the potential problem with extensive model variations, subtle name changes and non-interchangeable parts), sorting out the problem and shipping the correct part quickly eats up any profit margin. In one extreme case, a man sent 25¢ for a part he had seen listed somewhere for that amount. No amount was included for the cost of maintaining scarce parts inventory, for searching, order filling, packaging, invoicing, or postage. Result: When the same man was informed there would be a $2.00 minimum charge on small part orders, he complained at length in writing to the manufacturer. The company's response was essentially, "You're lucky, most parts ordered direct from the factory have *at least* a $2.00 minimum order price."

It continues to amaze some collectors that a vintage firearm does not appear to be 100% factory made because of the addition of accessories obviously produced by a different company. The truth is, factories have often accommodated customer requests for different sights, scopes, slings, butt plates, engraving, checkering, etc. for "special orders." On one occasion a factory visit turned up a number of bardels and actions that had been drilled and tapped for scope mounts and appeared "out of production." When questioned the factory representative said, "You know how hard it is to drill and tap a firearm after it's been heat treated? Well, we always do some ahead of specal orders and have them heat treated afterwards."

Factual records about company history and changing policies have often been as elusive as the changes in management. Under the long-standing Emhart Hardware ownership there were often times when a chief operating officer would be brought in for a year at a time to give them top management experience. It didn't necessarily matter that the person had little knowledge or interest in manufacture of firearms and related subjects. The levels of high quality firearms manufacture — down to the smallest parts — have varied over the years along with the apparent dedication and professionalism that make up the total company. At one time, for example, it required an entire wall for model 110 gun stocks to attempt to keep up with right hand, left hand, all the different caliber variations and other features. Contract policies with parts distributors also had a way of continuing to change with the rotating top management and apparent search for profitability. Customer loyalty appears strongest for the earlier models that were produced in what was probably a more appreciative and demanding time. It's the love of quality firearms and the desire to know more that appear to keep serious collectors enthused.

Model 340
.222 Rem. .22 Hornet
.30/30 Calibers

The Standard Model 340 gives the sportsman, *at amazingly low cost*, a fine, high quality rifle in a choice of three popular calibers — .222 Rem., a modern, hi-speed, flat trajectory medium game cartridge; .22 Hornet, for years the favorite cartridge of the varmint shooter; .30 30, the most widely known and used hi-power cartridge in America.

You'll find Model 340 an unusually accurate rifle — the result of a unique assembly method which assures exact head space control, allowing the full ballistics potential of each cartridge to be realized.

Just a look at its modern design and styling will convince you of Model 340's stand-out value. Its handsome walnut stock is well proportioned at pistol grip and forend for comfortable, natural holding. Trigger pull is clean and crisp; the safety is under your thumb; the bolt handle just where you want it — in direct line with trigger. The action is smooth, lightning-fast in loading and ejecting. Bolt head and breech are encased in solid housing with a bolt shield for protection against dirt, weather, and rough handling. All these features, together with its exceptionally fine sighting equipment make Model 340 the outstanding value in its field.

Model 340-S De Luxe

Model 340-S De Luxe is the same as Model 340 above except fitted with the following special equipment: Savage No. 175 Micro Peep Sight, disc elevator rear sight, Hooded Ramp Front Sight, fine checkering on grip and forearm, fitted with sling screw eyes for a carrying strap.

**CONSUMER CATALOG
NO. 1-53**

SPECIFICATIONS

MODEL 340: Round, tapered barrel. Length: .222 Rem. cal., 24"; .22 Hornet, .30 30 cals., 22". Self cocking bolt action. Design of bolt, sear, and trigger mechanism assures lightning fast ignition, positive operation, clean, crisp trigger pull. Exact head space control assures extreme accuracy. Thumb operated safety locks sear and bolt. Detachable clip magazine. Capacity: .222 Rem., .22 Hornet cals., 4 cartridges; .30 30 cal., 3 cartridges. One piece walnut stock with semi-beavertail forearm, full pistol grip, corrugated butt plate. Ramp front sight with gold insert and disc elevator rear sight with click adjustments. Receiver tapped for Savage No. 175 Micro Peep Sight and (except .30 30 cal.) for Weaver Telescope Detachable Side Mount. Weight, about 6¾ lbs. Length, overall: .222 Rem. cal., 42"; .22 Hornet, .30 30 cals., 40".

MODEL 340-S DE LUXE: Same specifications as Model 340 except fitted in addition with Savage No. 175 Micro Peep Sight, and hooded ramp front sight with gold insert. Checkered grip and forearm. Sling screw eyes for a carrying strap.

set your
sights on
the
Savage 340
superb accuracy, year-'round use

It's always "open season" with the Savage 340 ... chambered for 2 great varmint cartridges and America's most popular deer caliber. Stock has medium-high comb and trim lines for steady handling, fine balance and streamlined appearance.

This rugged bolt action repeating rifle has a ramp front sight and rear sight with elevation adjustment ... drilled and tapped for popular receiver sights and 'scope mounts. Available in 3 great calibers:

.222 Remington 50 grain bullet—A flat-shooting extremely accurate cartridge. The advanced design of the 340 brings out the ballistic potential of this high velocity cartridge.

.22 Hornet 45 grain bullet—High velocity and fine accuracy make the .22 Hornet a favorite varmint cartridge. An economical cartridge that delivers peak accuracy in the Savage 340.

.30-30, 150 and 170 grain bullets—The most widely known and used high power cartridge in America. For more than 50 years it has proved its effectiveness on deer and medium-sized game.

The 340's exclusive head space control and specialized Savage manufacturing methods give you extreme accuracy at a price so low you can buy the 340 complete with 'scope for less than you might expect to pay for the rifle alone. See it at your dealer's now.

There is a complete line of Savage, Stevens and Fox shotguns and rifles for every shooter and every kind of shooting. *Write for free rifle or shotgun catalog. Savage Arms Corporation, Chicopee Falls 7, Mass.*

$57.50

SAVAGE · STEVENS · FOX FIREARMS

Maybe we should call it the Super Matchless 54.

The Anschutz Super Match 54. Used by all winners in the 1964 Tokyo Olympics, and five out of six in the 1968 Olympics in Mexico. That's 11 out of 12. Well, you can't win 'em all, all the time. (But no other rifle even comes close.)

You can have the matchless 54 action in three models. All have the same satin-smooth action, fully adjustable trigger, and hand-lapped barrels. Stock design is the chief difference.

1413 (shown): Free-style International Super Match 54. Features butt plate with lateral, horizontal, vertical, and cant adjustments. Yoke-style palm rest. R.H. $325. L.H. $335. Sights extra.

1411: Prone stock model, designed especially for American matches. R.H. $155. L.H. $167. Sights extra.

1408: Meets all International Shooting Union requirements. Stock suitable for all match events. R.H. $155. L.H. $167. Sights extra. Other Anschutz target rifles from $67.50. Free 36 page color catalog. Write Savage Arms, Westfield 238, Massachusetts 01085.

Please include zip code.

the most versatile gun you can own . . . a

Savage 24

The only gun of its kind in America . . . combines precision .22 cal. rifle and .410 gauge shotgun barrels. With the famous all-purpose Savage 24, you're set for anything . . . fun, fur or feathers—all year 'round.

Use the .22 upper barrel for plinking, target shooting or small furred game. Flick the selector and the .410 gauge lower barrel is set for flying pests, game or targets.

Perfect for use around the farm or camp, the Savage 24 is also ideal for the beginner. Lightweight (about 6¾ lbs.), compact and streamlined. Upper barrel shoots all .22 rimfire cartridges, lower barrel chambered for .410 gauge 2½" or 3" shells. Single trigger . . . single sighting plane . . . selector button permits instant choice of either barrel. Ramp-type front and adjustable rear sights . . . walnut stock . . . take-down. See it at your dealer's now.

There is a complete line of Savage, Stevens and Fox shotguns and rifles for every shooter and every kind of shooting. *Write for free rifle or shotgun catalog.* *Savage Arms Corporation, Chicopee Falls 37, Mass.*

$41.50

Savage
TRADEMARK

SAVAGE • STEVENS • FOX FIREARMS

ALL PRICES SUBJECT TO CHANGE SLIGHTLY HIGHER IN CANADA

This unique firearm was a famous and familiar gun during World War II. Because of its versatility, it was used as standard equipment by the U. S. Air Force in their "Survival Kits". The Savage 24 enabled crews of downed aircraft to survive indefinitely by shooting small game for food.

SAVAGE MODEL 99 SERIAL NUMBERS

(Starting number: 10,000)

Year	Serial Number	Quantity
1898	10000-10300	300
1899	10301-11500	1200
1900	11501-13400	1900
1901	13401-19500	6100
1902	19501-25000	5500
1903	25001-35000	10000
1904	35001-45000	10000
1905	45001-53000	8000
1906	53001-67500	14500
1907	67501-73500	6500
1908	73501-81000	7500
1909	81001-95000	14000
1910	95001-110000	15000
1911	110001-119000	8000
1912	119000-131000	22000
1913	131001-146500	15500
1914	146501-162000	15500
1915	162001-175500	13500
1916	175501-187500	10500
1917	187501-193000	5500
1918	Production suspended - WWI	
1919	193001-212500	19500
1920	212501-229000	16500
1921	229001-237500	8500
1922	237501-244500	7000
1923	244501-256000	11500
1924	256001-270000	14000
1925	270001-280000	10000
1926	280001-292500	12500
1927	292501-305000	12500
1928	305001-317000	12000
1929	317001-324500	7500
1930	324501-334500	10000
1931	334501-338500	4000
1932	338501-341000	2500
1933	331001-344500	3500
1934	344501-345800	1300
1935	345801-350800	5000
1936	350801-359800	9000
1937	359801-370000	10200
1938	370001-381350	11350
1939	381351-388650	7300
1940	388651-398400	9750

"The records of Model 99's with numbers above 500,000 are on microfilm, and the numbers 514740 to 514975 are missing, which indicates that several whole pages were skipped when they were filmed. Model 99 rifles were made and shipped, although in small numbers, all during the war [WWII].... The last rifle made in Utica was numbered 447601 and it was shipped Oct. 11, 1945. Production started at Chicopee Falls with number 500000." —Roe S. Clark, Arms Historian (Stevens • Savage • Fox) *Courtesy of Charles F. Snell, Savage Arms collector, Grants Pass, Oregon.*

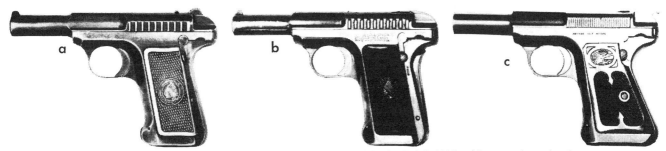

The 3 basic Savage pocket pistol models: **(a)** The original Model 1907 with pressed steel grips and small safety lever but without words "Safe" and "Fire"; **(b)** Model 1915 hammerless with grip safety and large word "Savage" on frame (this also appears on many 1907 models); **(c)** Model 1917

SAVAGE POCKET PISTOLS

Models and variations of a once popular pocket automatic

By DANIEL K. STERN

A NUMBER of years have passed since the last Savage pistol was made in 1928. Although they are not antiques, they do have an interesting history, novel operating features, considerable accuracy, excellent balance, grips which point naturally, good sights, and unusually fine trigger pull.

Many variations made

The Savage pocket pistols were produced in cals. .32 and .380, each made in 3 models, plus a number of variations due to changes in design not warranting re-designation. Through these changes can be traced the evolution of a firearm from introduction to obsolescence—in the case of the Savage pocket pistols, a span of 21 years during which more than 270,000 were sold.

More than a dozen Savage pistols are needed to cover the 3 calibers, various models, and major variations.

There has been a general lack of knowledge concerning Savage pistols. For example, the original cal. .32 model, officially designated Model 1907, is usually referred to as the Model 1910, less often as the Model 1909, and, by some, as the Model 1905, probably because it bears that patent date.

The scarce grip-safety, concealed-hammer Savage is almost always labeled a variation of the original gun, although Savage issued it as the Model 1915. Late variations of the Model 1907 are at times confused with the Model 1917.

There are obscure areas which even the company cannot clear up, due to the long period which has elapsed since production ceased and the fact that the factory moved twice in those years.

Thus, this account is constructed from available information and production records of Savage Arms Corp., their specimen pistols, those of the author and other guns examined and checked by him—all told, these were nearly 40.

Savage pocket pistols were beautifully made and finished. Their designer was Maj. Elbert Hamilton Searle, an Ordnance officer formerly stationed at Springfield Armory. The guns were produced under 2 basic patents granted to him in 1905. His locked-breech design utilized bullet thrust to delay opening of the breech.

An early Savage folder says, "The opening of its breech and the rearward escape of gas is mechanically prevented until the bullet has left the barrel".

Unsupportable conclusions

From this Savage drew rather unsupportable conclusions—that "superior accuracy and penetration are obtained" and that their gun was the only one to get "full accuracy and power out of every cartridge fired".

Nor was the advertising department content to let things rest there:

"Woodsmen . . . have on a number of occasions killed bear, mountain lion and elk. It (the Savage) has proved its accuracy at Sea Girt and Camp Perry in the hottest competition with the big military and target revolvers".

Although the big game part might well have occurred in isolated instances, the target-pistol accuracy claim is stretching things and, actually, was not needed. As noted earlier, the Savage had enough legitimate good points not to need such dubious puffing.

Another claim—and a true one—was that the Savage could fire 11 shots faster than any other pistol, to be exact in 2⅖ seconds. What was not said, of course, was that no other pistol had the magazine capacity of the Savage. All of this in a gun weighing only about 19 ozs. empty with a 6½″ over-all length. Even the 21-oz. cal. .380, which measures 7″ over-all, holds 10 rounds counting the chambered round. The Savage magazine is one of the strongest and best ever made.

Of the 5 comparable American pocket automatics, the Savage is the lightest

Cal. .25 Savage automatic pistol, commercial sale of which the company considers doubtful. Note grip safety and later versions of rear sight and slide serrations

in weight by up to 4 ozs., yet holds as many as 3 more cartridges.

Savage was the first American arms company to provide a challenge to Colt in the automatic pocket pistol field.

Indicative of their efforts to improve these pistols are the more than 30 changes made in the cal. .32 Model 1907 pistol alone, a gun which appears in no fewer than 12 variations.

Although the slide legend lists only one patent date, Searle received, in addition to the original pair, 2 later patents for minor improvements. Three more were issued to Charles A. Nelson, who invented the grip safety and other changes in the Model 1915.

Production of the first gun, the cal. .32, began on Apr. 22, 1907. It is finished in bright blue, and trigger and magazine release are case-hardened.

Serial numbers started at "1" and progressed upward. These pistols were made with a slide, or 'bolt' as Savage called it, with both front and rear sights pressed in place. Ribs and slide serrations are rounded and wider-spaced than in succeeding issues. The slide is bored to take a barrel of about .417″ outside diameter with a corresponding counter-recoil spring encircling it.

On top of the slide is the 2-line legend in capital letters: "MANUFACTURED BY SAVAGE ARMS CO. UTICA, N. Y., U.S.A. PAT.-NOV. 21, 1905".

In larger letters at the end of the 2 lines is a bold: "CAL. 32".

The serial number is on underside of the frame in front of the trigger guard. Magazine release is in leading edge of grip frame and works from the top rather than customary bottom position. The idea, and a good one, is that it can be easily released by the third finger of the right, or firing hand, without having to change grip on the gun. However, this release was too ingenious and simple for people accustomed to a release operated by the left hand, a practice difficult with the Savage. Moreover, the release has to be pressed down again to allow entry of a fresh magazine.

Unconventional mainspring

The trigger is attached to a trip-lever which forces the sear up and out of its notch, allowing the cocking lever to drop as the burr-type hammer and firing-pin spring drives the striker into the cartridge. In this action there is no conventional mainspring. The firing pin is surrounded by a coil spring and joined to the rounded hammer, lower portion of which is the cocking lever.

When the pistol recoils during firing, the cocking lever is returned to position as it hits the back of the frame, readying the weapon for a second shot.

A manual safety is on left side of the frame. When turned up to 'safe' position, the safety lever brings an eccentric into play inside the frame, blocking fall of the cocking lever. Unless this lever drops, the firing pin cannot move forward to fire the cartridge.

The lever originally provided differs from the one usually seen in that it has a smaller head, is somewhat dished out, or concave, and has no knurling as do the later ones. Moreover, the words 'Safe' and 'Fire' do not appear on the frame.

The breechblock is retained by a single shoulder engaging a matching shoulder in the slide. Extractor is mounted on the right and is highly efficient, tossing empties 15 to 20 ft. to the side.

Although the trigger mechanism utilizes several pieces, it works in a straight line and is usually beautifully polished and fitted, to give a trigger pull far better than average.

Simply disassembled

One of the assets of the Savage is its extremely quick and simple takedown. With clip out, pull slide back and lock it with safety. Squeeze hammer and cocking lever, give them a quarter turn right, and out comes the whole breechblock. Barrel and slide can be pulled off by releasing safety while pulling trigger. Everything is then exposed. No screws are present in this model.

Grips, originally of steel, snap into place. Removal is not necessary or recommended. Later, hard rubber grips were standardized. These are easily broken if removed improperly.

In the original pistol, the magazine recess walls are thinner than in later models and lack the square corners commonly seen.

This, then, is the original Savage Model of 1907, a gun rarely seen today. Considerable detail has been supplied to permit explanation of later design changes.

Production of the original model was limited; probably not more than a few thousand, perhaps less. Highest serial noted is No. 867.

First to go were the steel grips, the small safety latch, and the thin-walled magazine recess. The steel grips are slippery and not as attractive as the hard rubber, which is undoubtedly why they were discarded.

The safety release was found to be too small, and the larger knurled one substituted. Also, the words "Fire" and "Safe" were added.

The thicker walls and squared ends of the magazine recess provide better protection for the magazine.

With these changes came the widely

seen second variation of the Model of 1907. These were the first of many changes during the next decade, making possible even more variations than indicated here. However, the guns were all Model 1907's to Savage.

Production was brisk

Production moved at a fairly brisk pace, although it was mid-1909 before the first 10,000 pistols were finished. Production then started to pick up with

Original (l.) and later systems of marking serial number on gun. Change is believed to have been made at about #50,000

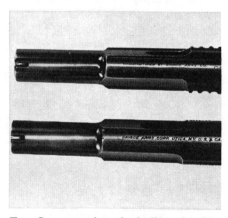

Two Savage pocket pistol slides showing variation in stamping. Early slide (at top) has original legend

serials reaching the mid-30,000's by the end of 1910. The pistol cost $15 then.

Output took a big jump in 1912 with 30,000 made that year.

At or about gun No. 50,000 Savage moved the serial number from the underside to the leading edge of the frame.

Sometime in 1912, and before gun No. 72221 left the production line, the breechblock was strengthened by addition of a rib which locked between corresponding frame ribs.

Savage meanwhile had been experimenting with a cal. .380 pistol, a caliber

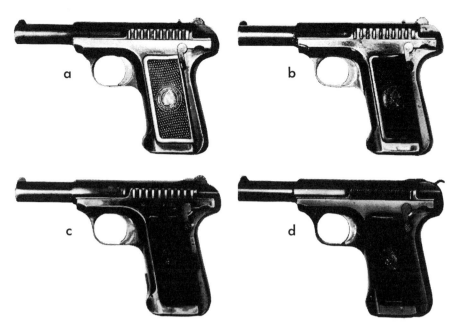

Four issues of the Savage Model 1907; **(a)** First Issue; **(b)** Second Issue with different grips, safety, and safety markings; **(c)** Eighth Issue with numbered breechblock, larger barrel, forged rear sight, and new magazine latch; **(d)** Final Issue, similar to Model 1917 except for the old type frame and grips

American Handguns

already produced by Colt for about 5 years. The year 1913 saw the introduction of the Savage cal. .380, and many additional changes in the cal. .32 pistol as well.

One change, quite likely made before the cal. .380 was introduced, involved the diameter of the barrels. Up to gun No. 75,000 finished barrel outside diameter is about .417″. Possibly Savage at this point decided to turn cals. .32 and .380 barrels from the same diameter stock. In any event, cal. .32 barrels were increased to an outside diameter of around .448″. Later parts lists noted: "When new barrels are required for pistols whose serial number is below 75,000, it is necessary to return pistol to factory."

But this was but one of many modifications made around the same time, or by early 1914 at the latest.

The rear sight, formerly separate, is now forged on the slide. Operation of magazine release latch is reversed to work from bottom. Fresh magazines can also be inserted without having to depress the catch. The revamped latch can still be worked by the little finger of right hand, but not as well as before.

The change does permit easier magazine removal using the left hand.

Magazine latch reversed

Originally the magazine had a single latching notch in the front side above the floorplate. A second hole is cut ¾″ above the first, permitting use of the new magazine in either old or new pistols. The original magazines do not lock when inserted in the later guns

because this second hole is lacking. Eliminated from the frame at the same time is an elliptical depression on either side of the original latch.

Other changes were also made. A trigger locking bar was added, a slim strip of steel engaging the sear trip lever at one end and safety lug at the other. With the safety on, the locking bar prevents the sear trip lever from moving back to engage the sear while the eccentric blocks fall of the cocking lever.

The sear was made stronger and given a greater bearing surface where it engages the sear trip lever.

Less important are 2 slide changes. A bigger ejection port is provided and given more slope at the rear. Slide serrations, while still rounded, were altered by widening the ribs and narrowing the grooves.

At about the same time, a device known as a chamber indicator appeared. This is a strip of metal yoked around the rear of the barrel with a long arm running parallel to the barrel. At the breech end it has an inward pointing tip. Thus, with a cartridge in the chamber, running the finger over the ejection port area of the barrel indicates if the gun is loaded because the chamber indicator projects slightly.

This idea, borrowed from the Luger, was not too successful, the indicator being easily broken, and was later dropped. Late production Model 1907's do not have it. It is not a part of the extraction apparatus.

Serial numbers do not start with zero for the cal. .380. Instead they begin with No. 2000 and carry the letter B.

The cal. .380 pistol weighs a couple of ounces more, has a ½″ longer barrel and proportionally greater over-all length, but is otherwise almost identical to the cal. .32. One surface difference is the groove that runs down the slide from rear to front sight.

In early 1914 still more changes were occurring. Serials in the cal. .32's had passed 100,000, while the slower-moving cal. .380 was at about No. 6000B or a little higher. Savage cal. .380 figures are a bit confusing at this point. At any rate, more than 4000 of the cal. .380's had been made.

Now, for the first time, the word Savage begins to appear on the left side of the frame. Earliest cal. .32 seen so marked is No. 101737 while the earliest cal. .380 is 7245B. This does not mean, particularly in the latter caliber, that it could not have occurred several hundred numbers earlier.

Within a matter of days, judging by serial numbers, Savage started to number breechblocks as well as frames. Hardly had they started, when they stopped. My cal. .32 No. 102404 has such a breechblock number, but No. 101737 does not. Neither does gun No. 103384. Savage, however, has a cal. .380, No. 6332B, which has the breechblock serial, but not the word Savage, while my cal. .32 has both. It is not known by the company today just why they started or stopped these.

Not more than a week or two could have passed before Savage changed the legend stamped on the slides of both calibers from start of production.

New slide legend

The new slide legend reads: "Savage Arms Co. Utica, N.Y. U.S.A. Cal. .32/Patented November 21, 1905— 7.65 m.m." All of this, including caliber, is in identically sized small capital letters but set in italic sloped type rather than Roman upright letters. Change came somewhere between No. 103384 which carries the old legend and No. 108602 which has the new one. In cal. .380, pistol No. 8573B still carries the old legend, but doubtless some made later were changed.

The rounded burr-type hammer of the Savage is difficult to cock with the thumb of the firing hand.

Recognizing this, the catalog for the summer of 1914 noted that new pistols would be supplied with rounded hammer or new spur-type cocking lever.

Savage eventually offered to install spur-type hammers on all previously issued pistols for $1.50. Thus you may see spur-type hammers on pistols with low serials, and you may see round cocking levers on guns as high—or higher—than 179,350. In neither case does it mean you have a Savage rarity. About all that can be said is that pistols with the new slide legend, spur hammers, and serial number above 110,000 are likely to be genuine. Too few cal. .380's have been seen to set a number point of reference for this caliber.

Meanwhile, Savage had been contemplating the concealed hammer, grip-safety products of Colt and Smith & Wesson and decided to offer a similar weapon. This was the Model 1915. The grip safety, based on patents of Nelson, operates off the trigger locking bar, already a part of the revamped pistol. Until the grip is squeezed, the bar prevents the sear trip from moving back and engaging the sear. The regular safety also operates as before.

Made hammerless

Rear end of the striker is made smaller and covered with a shroud, making it a hammerless weapon. Also added to the Model 1915 is a hold-open device to retain the slide back when the last shot is fired. A lever on the right side of the frame above the trigger guard can be depressed to release the slide manually when the user does not wish to reload.

Savage's 1915 Summer catalog says, "Magazines for the 1907 Model are different from those for the 1915 Hammerless". Unfortunately, this was true. The 1907 magazine is not cut away for the hold-open lever and will not seat by a good ⅛".

An additional change was made in the rear sight of the Model 1915 in which the raised portion of the slide was lengthened from about 7/32" to 9/32" and the sight groove lengthened from 3/8" to 9/16". This change will be found also in some slides of regular Model 1907's, as both were produced concurrently in cals. .32 and .380.

Savage engineers at this time were working on a cal. .25 model to complete their pocket pistol series.

Roe S. Clark, Jr., of the Savage Research and Development Div., says, "I doubt very much if the cal. .25 pistol was ever offered to the public. I have heard that less than 12 were produced."

There is no question that the cal. .25 is an extremely scarce item. The picture of the factory specimen pistol supplied by Mr. Clark shows the 1917-type slide serrations, while another pictured in W. H. B. Smith's *Book of Pistols and Revolvers* has the slide serrations of the earlier 1907-1915 models.

I believe that experimentation with the cal. .25 extended over a period of at least 2 years and that some guns got out of the factory as possible samples, perhaps to check public reaction.

The Model 1915 had only a brief

life of about 2 years, being dropped on introduction of the Model 1917.

Shortly before the Model 1915 bowed out, 2 changes were made in the Model 1907. The word "Savage" was dropped from the frame as was the unsatisfactory chamber indicator.

For some reason, today obscure but possibly due to the advent of World War I, the Model 1907 continued in production with the new Model 1917.

The new pistol has the familiar flared grip to give it a bit more slope and a little racier appearance. Grips are shaped to match and are screw fastened. All hammers are spur type. On the slide legend, "CO" becomes "CORP". Finally, the bright blue of the earlier Model 1907's and 1915's is replaced by a dull blue-black and the wide-spaced, round slide serrations yielded to closely-spaced flat ones. On the left side of the frame were the words: "SAVAGE 1917 MODEL".

The final Model 1907 cal. .32 and the sixth variation of the cal. .380 matched their successors in all respects except that the old-style, straighter frame was retained along with the older type grips. In finish, hammer, legend, and slide serrations they fol-

The cal. .380's were made until 1928, but production from the end of 1920 totaled barely over 9000. Total cal. .380 production from 1913 was only 28,104, making the cal. .380 by far the scarcer of the 2 production calibers.

The Model 1915 is the scarcest in either caliber. Savage thinks a total of about 35,000 were made in both calibers, although this writer believes it to be far fewer, possibly less than 11,000, and no more than 15,000.

Model 1907 .32's

Of the cal. .32's, the Model 1907 is the most common but some of the variations, particularly the steel-gripped original and those with numbered blocks and frames, are rare.

While there are about 8 cal. .32's to every cal. .380, the former offer many more variations and tell a more complete story than do the bigger guns. Nearly new specimens also seem to be more common.

The Model 1907 cal. .380's are the most plentiful, with the Model 1917, although more were made, seemingly harder to come by. This model was once used by the Portuguese military, so some may be in Europe.

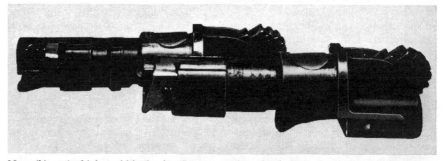

New (l.) and old breechblocks for Savage pocket pistol. Note lack of rib and smaller sear on old. New sear is better positioned and has greater bearing surface. This alteration, as can be seen, necessitated many changes in the machining of the breechblock

lowed the Model 1917 pattern. The Model 1907's were finally discontinued late in 1919 or early in 1920. Gun No. 226825 is the highest numbered Model 1907 I've seen. There are a great many of these cal. .32 pistols in the 200,000-210,000 range, however. Cal. .380's that were noted were in the 15,000B series. In both calibers, figures include Model 1907 pistols.

After 1920, production slowed rapidly. Anti-pistol laws were being widely enacted, and people seemed to have lost interest for firearms in general and pocket pistols in particular.

From late 1920 until production of cal. .32's ceased in 1926, only about 15,600 were made. Savage lists its last cal. .32 serial as No. 256,000 although over 14,000 of these numbers were never made, leaving total cal. .32 production at 241,920.

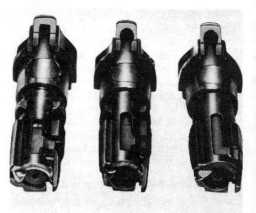

Another view of breechblocks. Old L-type sear (r.) is shown with newer types. Left front corner of final block (l.) has been altered from the center type. Constant change and improvement was characteristic of Savage pistols

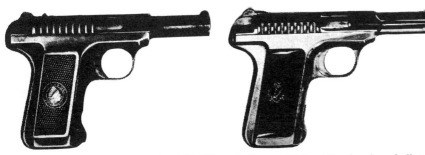

Right side of original Model 1907 (l.) and later pistol with chamber indicator shows how frame was altered and magazine latch reversed. Changes in ejection port and slide serrations can also be seen

During its existence the Savage was subjected to a number of criticisms, some relatively unfounded.

It was said to recoil more heavily than comparable guns. I have not found this to be noticeable. True, it is lighter, so a bit more recoil could be expected.

More serious is the charge that the guns would, on occasion, fire full automatic. A dirty weapon can cause this as can a weak sear spring.

However, out of the nearly 40 guns checked, some of which were fired a total of several hundred times, only one gave this trouble.

The Savage pistol cannot be carried with hammer down and chamber loaded. The striker, when uncocked, bears against the primer and a sharp blow or fall can easily fire the pistol.

Finally, Savage never got around to providing a 'magazine safety' for blocking discharge of a cartridge in the chamber when the magazine is out.

To trained shooters this is no handicap, but it may be dangerous should the gun fall into the hands of careless or inexperienced persons.

Nonetheless, the many good qualities of the Savage outweigh its shortcomings. Beautifully built, pointing naturally, and most specimens having superb trigger pulls, it has surprising accuracy.

Production of this article would not have been possible without the help of the Savage Arms Corp., and specifically O. M. Knode and Roe S. Clark, Jr., who dug through old records and checked factory samples to confirm much of the information herein.—D.K.S.

American Handguns

TABLE 1
MODELS 07, 15, 17
CAL. .32 PISTOL

1908-1909	1	to 10000
1909-1910	10000	20000
1910	20000	30000
1910-1911	30000	40000
1911-1912	40000	50000
1912	50000	60000
1912	60000	70000
1912-1913	70000	80000
1913	80000	90000
1913-1914	90000	100000
1914	100000	110000
1914-1915	110000	120000
1915	120000	125000
1915	125000	130000
1915-1916	130000	136520
	136520	150000 (omitted)
1915-1916	150000	160000
1916-1917	160000	170000
1917	170000	180000
1917-1919	180000	190000
1919	190000	200000
1919	200000	220000
1919-1920	220000	230000
1920	230000	240000
1920-1922	240000	246020
	246020	246620 (omitted)
1922 thru 1926	246621	256000

Tables 1 and 2 were supplied by Savage Arms Corp. and give serial numbers and years of production by caliber. Table 3 is an attempt by this writer to recreate production volume by model and caliber. It is based on Tables 1 and 2 and on specimens known to exist.

TABLE 2
MODELS 07, 15, 17
CAL. .380 PISTOL

1913	2000	to	4000
1913-1914	4000		6000
1913-1914-1915	6000		8000
1914-1915	8000		10000
1915-1916	10000		12000
1915-1916-1917-1919	12000		14000
1919-1920	14000		16000
1920	16000		20000
1920-1921	20000		22000
1920-1921-1922-1923	22000		24000
1923-1924-1925		24000	25242
		25243	26000 (omitted)
1925-1926-1927		26000	28000
1927-1928		28000	29669
		29670	29861

TABLE 3

ESTIMATES OF MODEL PRODUCTION

(This table is based on production dates correlated as far as possible to known specimens. Some variation should be expected.)

Cal. .32

Model 1907 (all variations)	180,000
Model 1915	11,500
Model 1917	49,500

Cal. .380

Model 1907 (all variations)	10,000
Model of 1915	3,000
Model of 1917	14,100 ∎

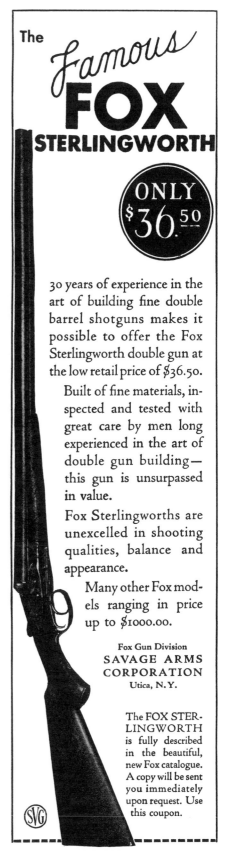
Source: American Handguns & Their Makers (NRA), 1981. Reprinted in the memory of Daniel K. Stern who has been described as a great, former newspaper writer and researcher. Special thanks also to National Rifle Association.

was Savage's better mousetrap, but nobody

THE Savage Model 1915 Pocket Auto-loading Pistol endures as proof positive that more sophisticated is not always more saleable. An attempt to improve Savage's already popular Model 1907 autoloader, the 1915 pistol failed in the marketplace, and, instead of a commercial success, has become an elusive and desirable collectors' item.

What became the M1915 began to exist about 1912, with experimental attempts to add a grip safety to M1907 pistols. The grip safety itself derives from three U.S. patents requested by Savage designer Charles A. Nelson on Oct. 15, 1912, each of which describes a grip safety for incorporation in the M1907 design.

Each of these safeties was very complicated and, although patented, none was used in production. They received U.S. patent numbers 1,080,364 on Dec. 2, 1913, 1,082,969 on Dec. 30, 1913, and 1,085,698 on Feb. 3, 1914. In June of 1914, Nelson applied for a patent on a fourth type of

Purchasers of Savage's Pocket Automatics also often got a book, *It Banishes Fear*, touting the gun's value for self-defense.

grip safety. This patent, No. 1,168,024, granted Jan. 11, 1916, also covered a slide hold-open device, a simplified magazine catch (which was, in fact, used on Savage M1907s made in and after 1912) and a new, simplified sear trip. Finally, two of Nelson's fellow employees, Charles Lang and William Swartz, piggy-backing on Nelson's idea, came up with a fifth type of grip safety, which actually was used.

What led to this desire to modify the M1907? The answer usually given is Savage's competition, but those who say this overlook two facts. The first is that until 1913 Savage had only Colt as a domestic competitor. The flood of autos from overseas was more than a decade away. Second, during those years Savage pistols were selling as well as Colts did. This fact is brought out by a comparison of pre-World War I Savage and Colt production rates.

If we allow for the fact that Savage's autos sold slowly in their first year of

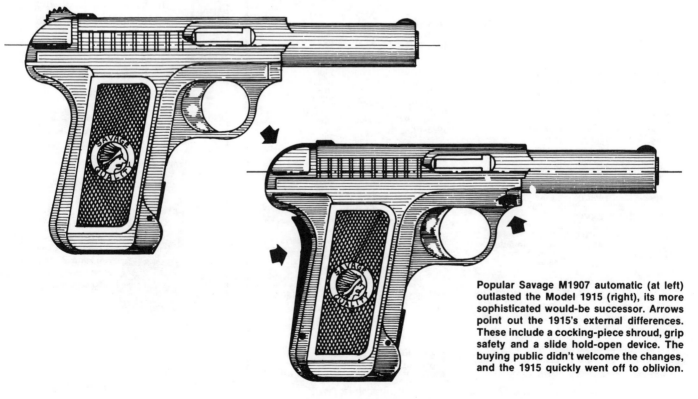

Popular Savage M1907 automatic (at left) outlasted the Model 1915 (right), its more sophisticated would-be successor. Arrows point out the 1915's external differences. These include a cocking-piece shroud, grip safety and a slide hold-open device. The buying public didn't welcome the changes, and the 1915 quickly went off to oblivion.

POCKET AUTO...

beat a path to their door.

BY DONALD M. SIMMONS

production (1908), and for their having no .380 until 1913, we can see that Colt and Savage were neck and neck in the production of pocket autos up until 1915. In early 1915 Savage, responding not only to Colt's offering of a hammerless, grip safety-equipped pocket auto but also to the introduction of a similar auto by S&W, announced their Model 1915 pistol. The M1915 Savage featured Nelson's

patented sear trip and slide hold open device, the Lang and Swartz grip safety and a concealed cocking piece.

Though the changes made in the 1915 Savage appear cosmetic, they actually amounted to a major redesign of the pistol, requiring extensive changes in both production and tooling.

The concealed cocking piece for example required that the M1907's burr-headed

cocking piece be removed and a shroud added to the end of the breech block and pinned in place at the bottom of the shroud.

The grip safety required milling the rear of the frame and drilling a hole at the base. The grip safety sliding lock entailed delicate machining in the area of the manual safety which had an additional cut made in its barrel. The trigger locking bar had to have its rear end machined to a flat locking surface, and, in some cases, a clearance cut had to be added to the top rearward edge of the left grip.

The addition of the hold-open device called for a notch on the right slide guide rails and extensive machining on the right trigger well in the frame. This desirable device also demanded a special magazine that had a small lip added to its follower and a notch in the magazine lips. The M1907 magazine will not operate the slide hold-open or lock in the magazine well of the M1915 without being forced.

APPROXIMATE NUMBER POCKET PISTOLS PRODUCED						
	SAVAGE			COLT		
Year	.32's	.380's	Total	.32's	.380's	Total
1908	2000	—	2000	13000	2000	15000
1909	13000	—	13000	12000	2000	14000
1910	16000	—	16000	14000	3000	17000
1911	20000	—	20000	19000	3000	22000
1912	30000	—	30000	18000	3000	21000
1913	20000	4000	24000	17000	4000	21000
1914	16000	3000	19000	14000	5000	19000
1915	14000	1000	15000	21000	6000	27000

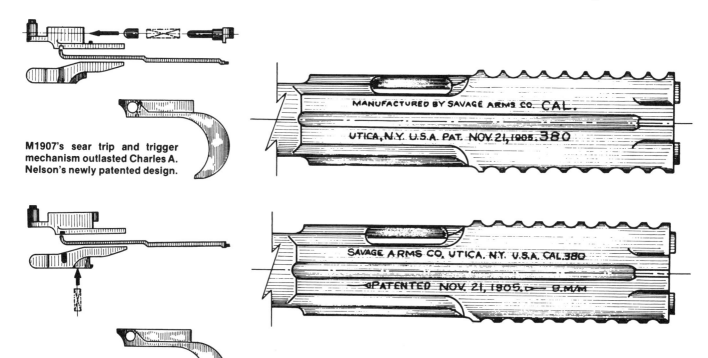

M1907's sear trip and trigger mechanism outlasted Charles A. Nelson's newly patented design.

MANUFACTURED BY SAVAGE ARMS CO. CAL.
UTICA, N.Y. U.S.A. PAT. NOV. 21, 1905. .380

Nelson's simplified M. 1915 sear trip was dropped quickly, maybe because of accidental firings.

SAVAGE ARMS CO. UTICA, N.Y. U.S.A. CAL. 380
PATENTED NOV. 21, 1905. 9. M/M

Logo variations exist on M1915 .380 cal. Savage automatics. Logo at top is rarely found on M1915s, while the lower one is the common variety. The mark appearing before the word "Patented" and after "1905" is referred to as the trumpet by collectors of Savage pistols.

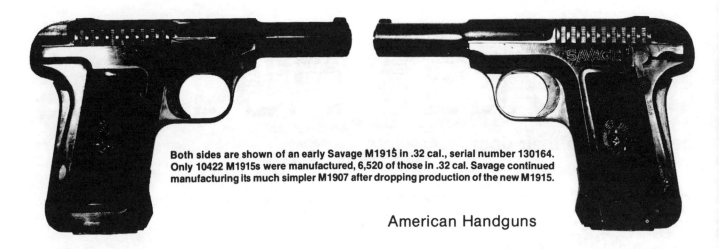

Both sides are shown of an early Savage M1915 in .32 cal., serial number 130164. Only 10422 M1915s were manufactured, 6,520 of those in .32 cal. Savage continued manufacturing its much simpler M1907 after dropping production of the new M1915.

American Handguns

The new type sear trip did away with a small locking toe and its spring and plunger used in M1907 pistols. During disassembly these parts had a way of flying across the room and were easily lost. The new sear trip was locked in by the forward end of the trigger bar and had no tendency to fly like its predecessor. In Nelson's patent, he describes the new sear trip's action as follows:

"For preventing double-firing in the present case the sear trip has a rigid toe which, when a pull on the trigger brings it against the vertical face of a fixed shoulder on the gun frame and this results in the discharge of the arm and is followed by the depression of the sear-trip under the wiping action of the rearward sliding breech bolt (actually the slide), snaps under the shoulder and locks down the sear-trip out of the path of the cocked sear in the ensuing return of the (slide) under pressure of the (recoil spring). This construction simplifies the sear-trip, insures much greater reliability of the action thereof and makes it better adapted to withstand wear and tear, it being noted that the elasticity of the flesh of the user's

finger affords the necessary impetus to the sear-trip to cause it to catch under the shoulder."

All this sounds great and, as a disconnector during intentional firing of the pistol, it works fine. But as Daniel K. Stern, author of *Ten Shots Quick,* points out, Savage was quick to get rid of Nelson's sear trip and return almost instantly to the older 1907 type. Why? The answer lies in the possibility of an accidental firing of the pistol equipped with Nelson's sear trip. The accident requires a lot of unusual actions on the part of the shooter, but it could and possibly did happen. The stage is set when the last round of the magazine is fired. In this case the slide travels to the rear, cocks the firing pin (Savage M1915 pistols, unlike most striker-fired pistols, cock during the opening motion of the slide, not upon closing), and locks open on the empty magazine.

Now, suppose the shooter is left-handed and has his finger on the trigger, depressing it a little but not enough to lock the toe under the shoulder. If he inserts a loaded magazine and raises the hold-open arm

with his right forefinger to drop the slide, the pistol might discharge. In this case, the "elasticity of the flesh of the user's finger" doesn't come into play; the sear trip engages the sear as the slide slams forward, and the gun fires. So, one of the M1915's improvements turns out to be an accident looking for a place to happen.

Potentially dangerous sear trip and all, the M1915 pistol had 10 parts not found on M1907 pistols, used seven modified M1907 parts and 15 parts that were interchangeable between models. Three parts, used in M1907 guns, were deleted from the M1915 design.

The higher production cost of the M1915, plus the fact that Savage sold it at the same price as their M1907 pistols — $15 for a .32 and $16 for a .380 — doomed the "improved" pistol to early retirement. The M1915 only lasted for three years and through a total production of 6520 in .32 and 3902 in .380.

Because the Model 1915 was only assembled for three years, and because real production occurred only in 1915, one would suspect that there were no variations in this model. This is not true.

M1915 with serial number 13004B was made in October, 1915. This doesn't equate with other guns.

This .380 was made in May, 1916, but carries lower serial number than does gun at left, 12256B.

Though not made until January, 1917, this .380 carries a serial number near gun at left, 12605B.

214

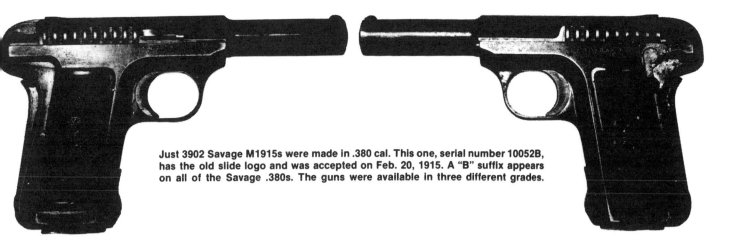

Just 3902 Savage M1915s were made in .380 cal. This one, serial number 10052B, has the old slide logo and was accepted on Feb. 20, 1915. A "B" suffix appears on all of the Savage .380s. The guns were available in three different grades.

The M1915 .380s were the first to be manufactured, and the serial number for the first pistol was 10,000B. The letter B is always added as a suffix to M1915 serial numbers on .380 cal. guns. Production of .380s began in February, 1915. The M1915 in .32 cal. was first produced in April, 1915, beginning with serial number 130,000. The slide legend on an M1907 .380 was:

MANUFACTURED BY SAVAGE ARMS CO. CAL. .380 UTICA, N.Y. U.S.A. PAT-NOV. 21, 1905

This marking will also be found on the first few hundred .380 M1915s, making a very rare variation. I have seen two M1915 .380s, Nos. 10052B and 10111B, with these old slide markings. The legend was then changed to:

SAVAGE ARMS CO. UTICA, N.Y. U.S.A. CAL.380 ◁ PATENTED NOV. 21, 1905 ▷ 9. M/M

This marking is called the trumpet type by collectors because of the little figures in the second line which spaced it to match the upper line. This legend is found on most M1915 .380s and came into use around serial number 10400B.

The legend on the M1915 .32 was always the same:

SAVAGE ARMS CO. UTICA, N.Y. U.S.A. CAL. 32 PATENTED NOVEMBER 21, 1905 — 7.65 M-M

Most Model 1915s in either caliber will have the large stamped SAVAGE on the left hand side of the frame just above the grip piece. They will also have the words SAFE and FIRE around the manual safety. At least one M1915 .32, serial No. 134452, was made without the SAVAGE mark on the frame.

The trigger of the late M1907 Savage pistols had a small pin driven into its upper face. This pin kept the sear trip from slipping up during assembly and disassembly. The Nelson patent sear trip had no need for the pin and therefore most M1915s will be found without it. Probably because Savage had some M1907 triggers in stock, these will also be found on about one pistol in three.

Another variation found in either caliber is the installation of the 1907-type sear trip in some M1915 pistols. This has been observed on M1915 .32s, numbered 130699 and 136297 and .380s numbered 12256B and 12768B.

Still another variation which has been encountered is a Model 1915 without the loaded chamber indicator and no cuts for it on the barrel. This variation is undoubtedly due to Savage equipping the pistol with a new barrel some time after they had dropped the loaded chamber indicator.

M1915 .380 number 11655B is an example of this variation.

Another variation rarely seen but worth mentioning is that some breechblocks were given a serial number to match that of the frame. This double numbering occurs on M1915 .32 number 133854 and on .380 number 22904B.

Jim Carr, author of *Savage Automatic*

Savage made ammunition for its .32 and .380 pocket pistols, as this full box of .380 ammo illustrates. Savage actually out-produced Colt in this field during two years, 1912-13. Logic dictates that the much-improved Savage M1915 would have captured the marketplace.

Savage 1915

American Handguns

Pistols, had a M1915 with a lanyard loop attached to its magazine somewhat like that on early Colt M1911s. Jim's pistol was a .32 number 135988. It is the only M1915 I know of so equipped and could indicate the interest of some country's military forces in these pistols.

That Savage autos were used overseas is well known. M1907s were used by both the French and the Portuguese; the French just before the introduction of the M1915, and the Portuguese just after. While no military purchase of the M1915 is known to have been made, they will occasionally be found with foreign proof marks. Three such M1915 .380s, numbers 10052B, 10390B and 11785B, are known. These three pistols were purchased from Savage by a John Rollins and Son in 1915. These are British proofed but have no military markings. The typical "crown" over "V" proof marks are found on the frame near the manual safety; on the slide over the left slide pulls near the rear sight; on the left side of the rear of the breech block; and on the barrel visible through the ejection slot above the loaded chamber indicator. On the barrel is a "crown" over "P".

Savage Arms Co. always offered various grades of their autos. The regular finish was a high-luster blue. The barrel and the loaded chamber indicator are polished and left bright. The trigger and the magazine catch are a mottled, case-hardened finish. The special grades came with pearl grips with the Savage, Indian-head medallion, and various grades of engraving were also available. These grades were called "Protector," "Monitor," and "Special." I have only seen one M1915 "Monitor" grade with pearl medallion grips. In preparing for this article, I found three M1915s in .32 cal. (132350, 134452 and 136247) which had pearl medallion grips, and one .380 (22904B). These are all rare factory variations. Savage also offered, as a "special," nickel plating. While I have seen M1907s with this finish, I have never seen an original factory nickeled M1915, but such pistols may exist.

As production of the M1915 .32s ground to a halt in 1916, there had been 6250 made. Although the serial numbers ran from 130000 to 137690, there were many blanks in the higher numbers of Savage's books. The production of the .380s lasted a year longer, but only about 400 pistols were assembled during 1916 and 1917. The total production of M1915, .380s was 3902, with the serial numbers running from 10000B to 13900B and a few before 10000B and a few after, like Jim Carr's .380 22904B, with pearl medallion grips, which was made up much later than 1917. As previously stated, the M1907 was not discontinued with the introduction of the M1915, and Savage made about 49000, M1907 .32s during the years in which the M1915 pistols were being produced. In any one of these years, M1907 .32 production exceeds the entire production of the M1915.

The M1915 should have been a successful arm, but it wasn't; and the only real reason must have been that the public didn't like it. It couldn't have been Nelson's sear trip alone. I think that the loss of the cocking piece which gave the shooter and indication of whether the pistol was cocked had a lot to do with the M1915's lack of acceptance. The public wasn't ready for a slide hold-open device in a pocket pistol and didn't appreciate this feature as we do today. The grip safety has always had its supporters and its opponents, but I for one don't feel comfortable carrying a loaded cocked pistol with its manual safety off and relying on its grip safety only.

As late as 1925-1926, we find that Von Lengerke and Detmold of New York was selling, of all things, M1915s. These must have come from some wholesaler's overstock but as an epitaph to the Model 1915, here is their description:

SAVAGE AUTOMATIC PISTOLS
THE .32 and .380 SAVAGE AUTO-
MATIC PISTOLS
.32 Calibre Pocket Model

"The Savage Automatic is a powerful, accurate and rapid fire pistol, which carries ten cartridges in the magazine. An extra one may be placed in the chamber, giving the arm a capacity of eleven shots. The mechanism is semi-automatic or self-loading, in which the recoil or firing the cartridge extracts and ejects the empty shell, cocks the pistol, reloading it in readiness for the next shot, to fire each of which the trigger must be pulled.

"The pistol in its new form is entirely hammerless, with the upper end of the cocking lever covered and the entire top of the breech plug enclosed, which prevents the necessity or possibility of cocking or uncocking the pistol without retracting the bolt. No. G251 — .32 Calibre Automatic — hammerless — grip safety and magazine capacity of 10 shots. Barrel 3¾ inches — weight 20¼ ounces — length overall 6½ inches. Price $19.00.

Extra Magazines each $1.00
.380 Calibre Pocket Model

"The .380 has the same mechanism as the .32 and is operated in exactly the same way. It differs only in calibre, length of pistol, length of barrel, weight, and magazine capacity. Weight 21 ounces; length overall 7 inches; length of barrel 4¼ inches. Price No. G252 $19.00. Extra magazines, each $1.00."

So ends the story of the Savage autoloading pistol Model 1915. While not a success in the market, it is a very rare and under-appreciated collector's item. ∎

1915 Pocket Auto **BY DONALD M. SIMMONS** *Reprinted by permission.)*

Savage Automatic Pistol

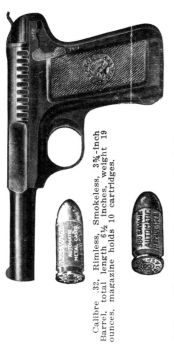

Model 1907

Calibre .32, Rimless, Smokeless, 3¾-inch Barrel, total length 6½ inches, weight 19 ounces, magazine holds 10 cartridges.

Calibre .380, Rimless, Smokeless, 4¼-inch Barrel, total length 7 inches, weight 21 ounces, magazine holds 9 cartridges.

NOTE — Special rimless, smokeless automatic pistol cartridges must be used. .32 calibre takes .32 Automatic Savage or .32 Automatic Colt or 7.65 mm. Browning — all different names for the same cartridge. .380 calibre takes .380 Automatic Savage or .380 Colt Hammerless, or 9 mm. Browning Short — all different names for the same cartridge. These cartridges, under one of their names, may be obtained all over the world.

HE SAVAGE AUTOMATIC PISTOL, Model 1907, is a ten-shot self-loading arm which combines in the size and weight of a small pocket gun the desirable features and qualities of the best military pistols.

The action of the pistol is semi-automatic, or self-loading. The recoil from firing each cartridge automatically extracts and ejects the empty shell, cocks the firing-pin, and puts a loaded cartridge into the barrel, leaving the pistol ready to be fired again. **Only one shot is fired at one pull of the trigger,** but the eleven shots the .32 pistol contains may be fired in 2⅖ seconds. More shots may be fired from the Savage pistol in a given time than from any other pistol of the calibre, because its magazine holds more cartridges, and because the empty magazine may be expelled by one finger of the hand holding the pistol, and another loaded magazine instantly inserted with the other hand.

Superior accuracy and penetration are obtained from the Savage because its barrel is as long as or longer than those of other pistols using the same ammunition, and because the opening of its breech and the rearward escape of gas is mechanically prevented until the bullet has left the barrel. The Savage will be found the only pistol of the calibre that gets the full accuracy and power out of every cartridge fired.

The details of design are most modern, and ensure the utmost reliability and durability. There are no screws, and every spring is spiral and unbreakable. The pistol may be completely dismounted and assembled without tools. The barrels are made of the same grade of steel used for the barrels of the U. S. Army rifle, and every part and point in the mechanism subject to wear or strain is properly tempered.

In use the Savage has distinguished itself in every direction. Inexperienced women have used it successfully in defense of themselves, their homes and their children. Woodsmen, hunters, trappers, forest rangers, etc., who require the most gun in the least bulk, select it, and not only get small game regularly with it, but have on a number of occasions killed bear, mountain lion and elk. It has proved its accuracy at Sea Girt and Camp Perry in the hottest competition with the big military and target revolvers.

It is the standard equipment of many police departments, especially where the severe requirements of the work demand the greatest efficiency. It is used and endorsed by the highest and most respected police and detective authorities of the country, and by the best known and ablest amateur firearms experts and critics. And it has been adopted as the service pistol of the Army and Navy of Portugal.

Savage Automatic Pistol

MODEL 1917

Calibre, .32 Rimless, Smokeless; 3¾-inch barrel, total length 6½ inches, weight 19-ounces. Calibre, .380, Rimless, Smokeless; 4¼-inch barrel, total length 7 inches, weight about 22 ozs. Magazine holds 9 cartridges.

NOTE — Special rimless, smokeless automatic pistol cartridges must be used. .32 calibre takes .32 Automatic Savage or .32 Automatic Colt or 7.65 mm. Browning — all different names for the same cartridge. .380 calibre takes .380 Automatic Savage or .380 Colt Hammerless, or 9 mm. Browning Short — all different names for the same cartridge. These cartridges, under one of their names, may be obtained all over the world.

HE SAVAGE AUTOMATIC PISTOL, Model 1917, is a ten-shot, self-loading arm which combines in the size and weight of a small pocket gun the desirable features and qualities of the best military pistols.

The action of the pistol is semi-automatic, or self-loading. The recoil from firing each cartridge automatically extracts and ejects the empty shell, and puts a loaded cartridge into the barrel, leaving the pistol ready to be fired again. **Only one shot is fired at one pull of the trigger,** but the eleven shots the .32 pistol contains may be fired in 2⅖ seconds. More shots may be fired from the Savage pistol in a given time than from any other pistol of the calibre, because its magazine holds more cartridges, and because its magazine holds more cartridges, and because the empty magazine may be expelled by one finger of the hand holding the pistol, and another loaded magazine instantly inserted with the other hand.

Superior accuracy and penetration are obtained from the Savage because its barrel is as long as or longer than those of other pistols using the same ammunition, and because the opening of its breech and the rearward escape of gas is mechanically prevented until the bullet has left the barrel. The Savage will be found the only pistol of the calibre that gets the full accuracy and power out of every cartridge fired.

The details of design are most modern, and ensure the utmost reliability and durability. There are no screws, and every spring is spiral and unbreakable. The pistol may be completely dismounted and assembled without tools. The barrels are made of the same grade of steel used for the barrels of the U. S. Army rifle, and every part and point in the mechanism subject to wear or strain is properly tempered.

In use the Savage has distinguished itself in every direction. Inexperienced women have used it successfully in defense of themselves, their homes and their children. Woodsmen, hunters, trappers, forest rangers, etc., who require the most gun in the least bulk, select it, and not only get small game regularly with it, but have on a number of occasions killed bear, mountain lion and elk. It has proved its accuracy at Sea Girt and Camp Perry in the hottest competition with the big military and target revolvers.

It is the standard equipment of many police departments, especially where the severe requirements of the work demand the greatest efficiency. It is used and endorsed by the highest and most respected police and detective authorities of the country, and by the best known and ablest amateur firearms experts and critics. And it has been adopted as the service pistol of the Army and Navy of Portugal.

by DANIEL K. STERN

SAVAGE
.32 Caliber Automatic Pistol

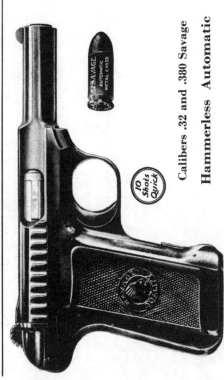

Calibers .32 and .380 Savage
Hammerless Automatic

.32 STANDARD GRADE—The .32 SAVAGE Automatic is a powerful, accurate and rapid-fire pistol, which carries 10 shots in the magazine. An extra one may be placed in the chamber, giving the arm a capacity of 11 shots.

The mechanism is semi-automatic or self-loading, in which the recoil of firing the cartridge extracts and ejects the empty shell, cocks the pistol and reloads it in readiness for the next shot, to fire each of which the trigger must be pulled.

Capacity of Magazine, 10 shots. Four-inch barrel. Weight 19 oz. Length over all, 6½ in. Full Blued.

.32 STANDARD GRADE	$15.00
.32 PROTECTOR GRADE	27.50
.32 MONITOR GRADE	35.00
.32 SPECIAL GRADE	45.00
.32 Extra Magazines, each	.50

Important Features of the .32 and .380 Pistols

Aim easily as pointing your finger; entire arms can be quickly taken completely apart and put together without tools; safety is positive and can be operated with thumb of firing hand. The only automatic that has an indicator which tells at all times whether pistol is loaded. Weight from three to four ounces less than other automatics. Operation is always positive.

PLATE 31 — "10 SHOTS QUICK"

This page from a 1914 catalog shows the "10 Shots Quick" slogan in use. Note reference to ordinary Model 1907 as a "Hammerless Automatic." Well, in a sense it was, but perhaps page had been originally planned for Model 1915 pistol.

SAVAGE
.380 Caliber Automatic Pistol

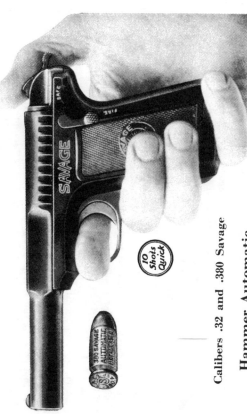

Calibers .32 and .380 Savage
Hammer Automatic

.380 STANDARD GRADE—The .380 has the same mechanism as the .32 and is operated in exactly the same way. It differs only in caliber, length of pistol, length of barrel, weight and magazine capacity. In the .380 there are combined accuracy, available stopping power, magazine capacity, reliability and durability of a military pistol, in the size and weight of a pocket arm.

Weight 21 ounces. Length over all 7 inches. Length of barrel 4½ inches.

.380 STANDARD GRADE	$16.00
.380 PROTECTOR GRADE	28.50
.380 MONITOR GRADE	36.00
.380 SPECIAL GRADE	46.00
.380 Extra Magazines, each	.50

PLATE 37 — 1914 CATALOG PAGE WITH SPUR .380

Spur cocking piece along with the word SAVAGE on frame mark this as one of later guns. Try to release clip holding pistol as shown. Photo courtesy Savage Arms.

The Savage 45 Auto

The author of "10 Shots Quick," the first complete book on the Savage automatics, reveals some interesting facts about this elusive and desirable pistol. Savage may have lost the bid to make our service sidearm but in doing so they forced the Colt to become a highly refined and reliable shootin' iron.

SHOOTING TIMES

by DANIEL K. STERN

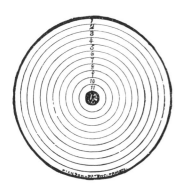

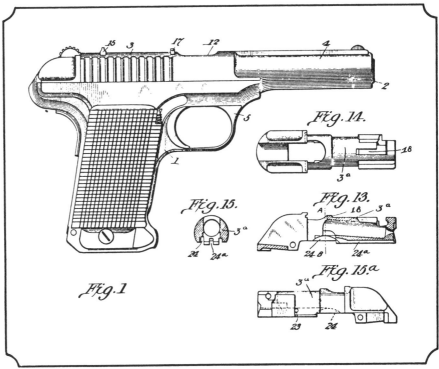

Fig. 14.

Fig. 15.

Fig. 13.

Fig. 1

Fig. 15.ª

DURING THE EARLY winter of 1907, most of the world's best-known self-loading pistols were on hand to show the United States Army what they could do.

The favored American representative was from the venerable Colt Company whose military handgun experience covered 70 years and which had been experimenting with automatic pistols for a decade or more. Colt arms had served the nation well in three major wars as well as in countless Indian skirmishes, and the company expected their 45 auto pistol would be the self-loading pistol which would carry on the tradition.

From Germany the Deutsche Waffen and Munitions-fabriken of Berlin sent a potent contender—its already famed Luger, revamped to handle the bigger American cartridge. A second German pistol in the competition was the Bergmann.

Webley & Scott, Great Britain's outstanding arms maker, was represented by the Webley-Fosbery automatic revolver, considered by many the ultimate in the revolver field. Since it was known that some of the services still strongly preferred revolvers, both Colt and its great American rival, Smith & Wesson, had their finest conventional revolvers on hand to

219

keep the Webley-Fosbery from feeling lonesome.

And, of course, there were several little-known entries, obvious long-shots, including one from Savage Arms, a relative newcomer to the ranks of the arms manufacturers and definitely a tyro as far as making handguns of any kind was concerned.

The Savage 45 fully met the dictionary definition of unique. It was the only one the company had, a condition fairly typical of most of the minor contenders. The Savage pistol was the brain child of Elbert Hamilton Searle of Philadelphia who had been trying to develop a self-loading pistol for several years and had made his first patent application in 1903, later had a brainstorm and came up with the idea of using the bullet's thrust down the rifling as a means of slowing the opening of the breech.

No doubt Sarle and his supporters from the Savage Company had hopes for their gun, but there were probably few others. Yet when the last shot was fired and the silence of early spring descended on the test ranges at the Springfield Armory, the Savage 45 had done the impossible—it had held the mighty Colt to a draw.

In the words of the Army board: "The Savage and Colt pistols possess sufficient merit to warrant their being given a further test under service conditions." In short, field tests in the hands of troops.

How had Savage accomplished the impossible?

In several ways. First, by its simplicity of construction. The Savage had just 34 parts, including four in the magazine; nine fewer than the Colt total and 14 less than the Luger. Moreover, there wasn't a V-spring in the Savage—all springs were tough, resilient coils. The Colt had a couple of the V-type, the Luger had four.

The board's report had other good things to say about the Savage, noting that "among the most desirable features of the Savage pistol are...the number of cartridges (eight) held by the magazine; the way the pistol lies in the hand, the expulsion of the magazine by the pistol hand and the ease with which the mechanism may be retracted."

Moreover the Savage had won the grueling dust test hands down. This test involved corking the muzzle and placing the gun, action closed, in a box and then blasting it with fine sand for one minute. Magazines, both loaded and empty, were similarly exposed to the dust. After the test, the shooter could blow on his piece and dust it off with his hand, but that was all.

This test didn't appear to faze the Savage, with or without its clip loaded. In one case it emptied its magazine in 51.6 seconds, and in the other in 53. The best the Colt could do was one minute, 53 seconds, less than half as fast as the slowest Savage time. The Luger was even worse with a best of two minutes, 32 seconds.

If anything, the rust test was even nastier. Here the gun barrels were corked at both ends, then the weapons were dunked into a saturated solution of sal-ammoniac for five minutes, then hung up indoors for 22 hours. Each gun then had the task of firing five shots. Here the Colt was an easy first, doing its job in one minute, eight seconds. Savage came in a slow second with exactly two minutes. Both guns did it under their own power. The Luger, which had to be operated by hand, took more time than both American guns combined, three minutes, 20 seconds.

On the velocity test, Savage squeezed in first with an average of 819 fps with the Luger doing 809 (but less with German ammo) and Colt bringing up the rear with 775 fps.

On accuracy, the Colt had it, possibly because the Savage had a tremendous kick. In his book "Pistols and Revolvers", the late Major General Julian S. Hatcher, then a major, (1927) wrote:

"The author (Hatcher) has one of these Savage 45s (a later pattern than the 1907 gun)...and it is in excellent condition, but it is almost painful to shoot it. It has a much worse recoil than that of any hand firearm in common use." This, he said, was because "the opening action...is not delayed so much as it is in...the Browning (Colt), and as a result, the moving parts take up a very high velocity, giving an excessive recoil."

One of the ordnance people whose job it was to fire the guns during the four-year battle for supremacy is reputed to have said that firing 2,000 rounds with the Colt was easier than firing 500 with the Savage.

In the final reckoning, it was a fatal weakness. At the end of the tests in 1907 the Army wanted 200 Colts and the same number of Savages for a field test and made suggestions to both companies as to changes they deemed necessary before either pistol could be adopted by the services. Both were advised of the need for a grip safety and a preference for side ejection. Savage was also ordered to move its front sight back from its exposed position at the front of the slide, fasten it more securely, and to junk the metal grips originally provided. In those days they were called "side plates."

Colt promptly offered to supply its 200 for $25 each. Savage, possibly chagrined by not winning a big contract or because the depression of 1907 was further cramping its rather limited resources, declined at first to supply the guns. But by mid-August, after Luger had agreed to replace Savage and then backed out, Savage reconsidered and agreed to produce the 200 for $65 each, along with extra clips and spare parts. The formal contract was signed Oct. 21, 1907. In March of 1908 Colt delivered its guns to Springfield, months before even the first of the Savages was ready. It wasn't, in fact, until the end of August, 1908, that Savage really got moving, proba-

SHOOTING TIMES

SAVAGE AUTOMATIC PISTOL, CAL. 45

bly because they were occupied with the birth pains of their pocket 32.

Three more months slipped by before the 200 Savages were put on the train from Utica to Springfield. According to Lt. Col. R. C. Kuhn, USAFR (Ret.), eminent authority on 45 automatics, only 195 of the 200 finished the somewhat more than 200 mile trip to the Armory. Two weeks later, on Dec. 15, Savage shipped five replacements for the pilfered guns.

But, Col. Kuhn says, the Savages were "all in unsatisfactory condition, so they were sent back to be put in usable or serviceable condition." The return trip was even more disastrous than the original one. When Savage counted the returns, there were 128 guns. A package containing 72 autos disappeared enroute, as Savage somewhat indignantly wired the Armory.

The reworked guns, plus presumed replacements for the missing 72, were returned to Springfield on March 16. Elected by the Army to try both automatics, the Colts and the Savages, was the Cavalry, which was not overly enthusiastic about its role. Test or no test, progress or no progress, the Cavalry still preferred the revolver, and its opinion didn't change.

Despite the Cavalry's adverse view, another Army board re-tested the top contenders at Springfield from Nov. 10-18, 1910. Colt had revamped its entry extensively, and it now closely resembled the still-in-the-future Model of 1911. It was a vastly improved gun over the one entered in the 1907 tests. Savage, too, had come a long way, but the smaller company not only lacked the resources, but the overall experience of Colt, both in R&D and production.

Nonetheless, the Savage gave a strong account of itself. It had the fastest time for complete disassem-

bly, outscored the Colt in penetration of solid oak blocks, but again lost out on speed of fire and accuracy, quite likely because of the heavier recoil. Also, this time Colt edged Savage on average velocity, 858 fps to 846 fps, but an improvement by both over their earlier velocity performances. On the endurance test, after the first 1,000 rounds, Colt had a clear edge in performance although neither gun could claim anything like perfection.

The upshot was a report by the board that it "Believed the (Colt) to be much the more satisfactory," but neither, as presented, was considered good enough "for adoption into the service."

Undeterred, Savage reworked its representative for what both companies must have known would be the final round, the tests of March, 1911. This time Savage regained the velocity laurels, 849 fps to Colt's 828, and it still had fewer parts, but these advantages were not nearly enough. The Colt had the better accuracy and endurance. Actually, both guns ran through the first 1,000 rounds of the 6,000 round endurance test without a hitch of any kind. Although the Savage did far better than before, this time it was up against an unbeatable performance. The Colt ran through all 6,000 rounds without a miss while the Savage virtually went to pieces in the final 1,000 rounds with 31 malfunctions and five parts developing defects.

Not only did the heavier recoil pound the shooter, but it pounded the working parts of the gun as well, and in the final analysis this is what beat the Savage. The Colt was the new Service automatic.

Much, however, can be said for the Savage and its gallant stand. Without the stiff competition it offered Colt, the armed services would not have had as fine a gun as they eventually got, and this is a fact that is

This 1907 45-cal. pistol is in the Savage museum. The gun has a long grip safety, checkered wood grip panels and integral front sight. Note differences in frame at the bottom of the grip, slide design from ejection port forward, and different hammer.

Reprinted by permission of *SHOOTING TIMES*

often overlooked.

The question of how many Savages were made and in what models is open to doubt. The number 200 is often used because this was the original government order. The losses by thefts in 1908 and 1909, and the subsequent replacement of at least 77 pistols, would indicate the government got no fewer than 277. General Hatcher in "Pistols and Revolvers" writes that the Army's 45s were sold after the tests, which was when he got his, and should account for the survivors of the test batch.

Savage's production records, however, list 290 serials. It is this writer's opinion that some, at least, of these guns were made in *addition* to the U.S. order and were for sale to the general public. It may well be that the military series and this possible commercial group both started with #1. Since the Savage record is incomplete, no one can say for sure, but on April 14, 1922, some 47 Savage 45s were sold to the E. K. Tryon Company. This sale was followed on Aug. 31 by another to the same firm of 58 more pistols for a total of 105. Four others in the 290 are accounted for by sales made between Feb. 3 and Sept. 11, 1922. An additional 11 show storeroom acceptance on Aug. 31, 1922, some 47 Savage 45s were sold to the E. K. Tryon Company. This sale was followed on Aug. 31 by nine which came in for repairs between Oct. 28, 1922 and June 10, 1933. The gun repaired on the final date, #193, is listed as belonging to Lt. Col. Calvin Goddard, noted ballistics expert of years past. Admittedly, some of the nine may be from the Army test batch.

Since the 45-cal. listings of Savage referred to are part of the pocket pistol sales records, actually inserted at the end of the volume begun in 1911 and covering 380 sales, it is my belief that it was made at a later date, and that the blank numbers refer to pistols sold before the close-out to Tryon. Incidentally, the highest numbered gun sold to that firm was #278.

Adding substance to this belief is a note on the flyleaf of another volume of Savage records which says that #214 was sold on Nov. 4, 1913. In the complete record, the line behind #214 is blank. This reinforces the theory that the 170 blanks were for guns sold before the later listing was made to take care of the close-out.

Certainly the 170 blank numbers are fewer than the total received by the government for their tests, and far fewer than the number needed because of the transportation losses between Utica and Springfield.

Thus, there must have been at least 378 pistols made and possibly as many as 550. And it is equally conclusive by the record that from 1913 through 1922, and possibly earlier, Savage, like Colt, sold its 45 to civilian customers.

Since the Savage 45 was worked over a number of times—probably nine—and although some of these variations were extremely limited, as few as a single pistol in at least one instance, it is highly possible that the version sold to the public could well be different than those in the final Army tests. W. H. B. Smith in his *Book of Pistols and Revolvers* calls one such gun a "special." Such a gun, owned by Savage, is illustrated here.

But public response may well have been the same as the Army's. The pistol kicked too much, and besides being unpleasant to shoot, hastened its own destruction through excessive breakage.

And that was a failing Savage could not conquer because to do so would mean a much stronger counter recoil spring to absorb the shock which, in turn, only meant the shock was transmitted to the forward motion of the slide, and also eliminated one of the points the Army liked, "the ease with which the mechanism may be retracted."

Neither of the other two alternatives was feasible. Reducing the powder charge would not have given the velocity desired, and apparently increasing the weight of the slide wasn't enough, although factory specimens of slides indicate some efforts were made to achieve this.

Time mellows and casts a halo over men and their machines. Today the Savage 45, the midget who battled the colossus for four years, is one of the most prized—and expensive—of modern collector hand guns. ●

Savage's Classic

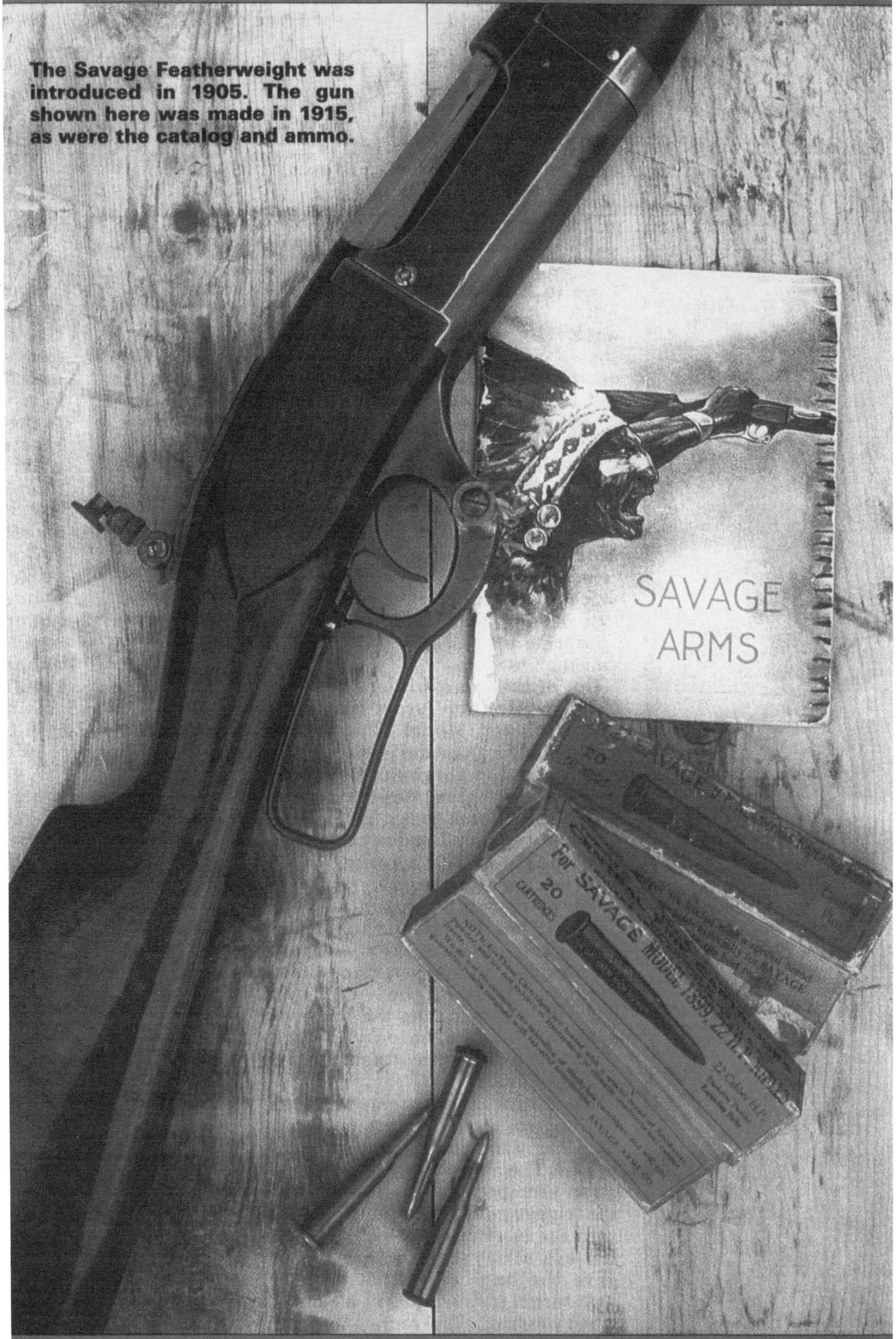

The Savage Featherweight was introduced in 1905. The gun shown here was made in 1915, as were the catalog and ammo.

SAVAGE
ARMS

SAVAGE

Featherweights

By Mike Nesbitt

The term "featherweight" might not have been coined by Savage for their very light versions of the Model 1899 rifle, but they must have been one of the first. Regardless of who said it first, the Savage 99 featherweights made the term a standard phrase and they started the trend for shorter and lighter big game rifles. Those trends are still being followed today

For 69 years, the Savage 99 Featherweight was the top choice

for hunters who wanted a light, fast-handling lever-action rifle.

by other rifle makers, even though the last Savage 99 version called the Featherweight was made in 1973.

Savage brought their first Featherweight to the market in, perhaps, early 1905. This rifle was featured in the 1904 catalog and listed at $25, while all other round-barreled Model 1899s were priced at $20. The glowing words in that catalog stated that the "Savage Model 1899 Feather Weight" was the lightest big game repeating rifle in existence and they gave the weight of this model as only six pounds. That is light, even by today's standards, and from its introduction, Savage made sure that their featherweights were kept in the eye of the rifle buyer.

Several things were done to reduce weight on those old Featherweights. The stocks were made slimmer and trimmer, shaving them down to remove every available ounce. When they couldn't remove any more from the outside they went to the inside of the stock. Underneath the buttplates on these Featherweights the stocks were hollowed out. Many old timers discovered this cavity under the hard rubber buttplates and made use of it by filling it with some items needed for survival; matches, extra cartridges, and anything else which might fit in that fairly generous hole. The forearms were also hollowed out, which kept the weight down by another ounce or two. Later, a smooth steel buttplate became optional.

Barrels were cut to 20 inches and tapered as thin as they could practically be. These Featherweights were the first Savage 99s to have their front sights mounted to a raised lug on top of the barrel. The very early versions, according to the catalog, had a sight which was brazed to the barrel and could not be removed. Later models had an integral lug with a carbine-type blade front sight secured with a cross

screw. The Featherweight barrels were too thin to cut a dovetail in.

RIFLE OF THE FUTURE

Of the early Savage 1899s, the Featherweights were the only ones which were not available in the

Butt plate styles changed over the years. They covered hollow recesses cut in the stocks of early rifles to cut down weight.

black powder .32-40 or .38-55 calibers. They were made only in .25-35, .30-30, or .303 Savage until some more modern cartridges were introduced. Why the .32-40 and .38-55 were excluded from the Featherweights is not really clear to me. Those two famous cartridges were included in all other models at that time, even the saddle ring carbine. Perhaps it was because the Featherweight was a rifle of the future and the black powder cartridges were things of the past.

In 1907 another feature was added to the Featherweights as well as every other version of the round-barreled 99 except the carbines: the take-down feature was made available. Savage is known for having one of the most successful take-downs ever made, and they had a special offering that could be ordered only for the Featherweights.

The little rifle could be ordered with two barrels to increase the versatility of the gun. A .303 or .30-30 would be fitted with an extra .25-35 barrel. The idea was to use either of the two .30 calibers when after big game and then use the .25-35 while hunting nothing bigger than deer. Appar-

This .303 Savage Featherweight was made in 1911 and shows the pre-1920 "perch-belly" stock.

ently the two-barrel offering was not popular, for it was only cataloged for a short time.

Five years later, Savage introduced a high-velocity cartridge which caused quite a stir. This was the .22 Savage High Power which fired a 70-grain bullet at the fantastic velocity of 2,800 feet per second. The new catalog was made available only in the take-down Featherweight, and Savage people were so proud of this velocity cartridge that they listed its mid-range trajectory to 1/1,000 of an inch. That's real important to a man who is more than likely firing the rifle with open sights.

The catalog of 1917 shows the Featherweight available in all of the special fancy grades as well as the standard-length rifles. These included the A-2, the CD, AB, and the named grades such as the Leader, the Victor, and the Premier. Those names or letter designations were all titles which indicated the amount of extras that were put on the rifles such as grade and finish of the wood, style of checkering and style of engraving. One version, called the Excelsior Grade, was available in the Featherweight only, while the others were available either as a take-down Featherweight or as a take-down round-barreled 22 or 26-inch rifle. The Premier Grade was the most expensive with a price of $129.99 for the Featherweight version, and that had elaborate engraving featuring game scenes surrounded with scroll and included the owner's name on the bottom of the receiver.

In 1920, the whole line of Savage 99 rifles and carbines was renamed and the Featherweights became the 99E in solid frame and the 99F in take-down. Previous to this time none of the standard Savage 99s were given letter designations; all were known by titles such as Featherweight, Carbine, Standard Rifle, or Saddle Gun. Now the model letter described the version of the rifle

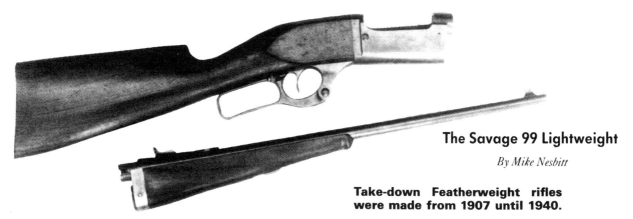

The Savage 99 Lightweight

By Mike Nesbitt

Take-down Featherweight rifles were made from 1907 until 1940.

such as 99A, a 26-inch barreled solid frame, or 99B, 26-inch take-down. Those versions had heavy barrels with rather little taper. The 99E and 99F had varying barrel lengths depending on the caliber but regardless of which cartridge they were chambered for, they were true featherweights.

In .22 H.P., .30-30, and .303 Savage these E's and F's were made with 20-inch barrels. The .250-3000 was added to these two models with a 22-inch barrel and the new .300 Savage was available with a 24-inch tube. Other changes were also apparent. The perch-belly stock was gone and the new stocks were so straight along the bottom line that they were almost unattractive. The buttstocks and forearms were no longer hollowed out, and the hard rubber buttplate was replaced with a plate made of steel with deep grooves to keep it from slipping on the shoulder.

The front sight was still the carbine type until 1927 when the E and F models, along with the checkered pistol-gripped Model G, received ramps which accepted a dovetail sight. At that time, the barrel length for the .22 H.P., .30-30, and .303 became 22 inches along with the .250-3000. The barrel length for the .300 Savage remained at 24 inches.

These changes all contributed to add weight to the featherweights and the 1932 catalog lists the average weight for the 99E at seven pounds. The 99F take-downs weighed a quarter-pound more because of the receiver extension and take-down latch. The 99 models A and B were only a quarter-pound heavier at that time because in 1927 they also received 24-inch lightweight barrels but retained the crescent rifle buttplate. Prices had also changed, and the 1932 list shows the E model at $45 and the take-down F at $50.60.

The E model was discontinued in the next year, which left the F model as the only featherweight in the line

of 99s. Replacing the E was a new model which was a cross of characteristics of both the E and the G models. Like the E, the new model was solid frame and un-checkered with a 22-inch barrel in .22 H.P., .250-3000, .30-30, and .303 Savage. The .300 Savage was also included in the new model with a 24-inch barrel. Like the G model, the new rifle had a pistol grip and the stock and forearm were made in the same profile as the G. Logically enough, the new rifle was called the 99EG, one of the most popular 99s ever introduced.

The F model stayed in the line unchanged until 1938. At that time checkering was added to the take-down featherweight, making it the only straight-grip 99 to receive checkering in its standard grade. In 1940 the F model was discontinued. After World War II the F model did not re-appear, nor did any of the Savage 99 take-downs. The last listed price for the F model was $53.50.

In 1935 another rifle was introduced which was also called a featherweight. This was the compact 99T. The T was actually a 99H carbine given a nicely proportioned pistol-grip stock and a hand-filling forearm. Both pieces of wood were checkered, and the barrel length was 20 inches for the .22 H.P., .250-3000, .30-30, and .303 Savage. The .300 Savage was made in the T model with a 22-inch barrel. Weight for the 99T averaged 6¾ pounds.

The T was Jack O'Connor's favorite model 99, and he often wrote about the performance of his own 99T in .250-3000. When Savage discontinued this model, he recommended that it be re-introduced. Savage told O'Connor that the T would be made again. It never was, but it would still be a grand idea.

LAST OF THE FEATHERWEIGHTS

Instead of re-introducing the T after World War II, Savage waited until 1955 to put another Feather-

weight into the 99 line. This was the 99F (new series), a rather special rifle with a number of unique features. The barrels were sharply tapered and the rear sight was dovetailed into a raised base similar to that on the standard-weight Model 70 Winchester. This also was the first 99 to have the complete model designation stamped on the barrel. A recontoured lever, a little thinner in the web, was used to help reduce weight and the new 99F weighed about 6½ pounds.

The 99F (n.s.) had a 22-inch barrel in all calibers. At first it was chambered only for the .250/3000 and .300 Savage, but a short time later the .243, .308, and .358 Winchester cartridges were added. The .284 Winchester, with the magazine capacity reduced by one round, was added in 1964. Not all cartridges retained their popularity, however. The famous .250/3000 was dropped in 1961, the misunderstood .358 was discontinued in 1969, and the .284 was dropped in 1971.

Over these years the 99F (n.s.) remained primarily unchanged. The biggest modification came in 1961 when the top tang safety was added and the 99F (n.s.) was the only 99 to survive the transition to the new safety. In 1965 the 99F (n.s.) received the impressed checkering, a feature which impresses no one, and this model was dropped from the production eight years later in 1973.

Over the span of 69 years, minus the war years and the decade after World War II, the Savage featherweights were made in many styles and chambered in at least nine different calibers. These lightweight rifles carved their own notch in history and their triumphs over the game trails around the world will be discussed in hunting camps for years to come. The Savage 99 is one of the all-time great lever action rifles which has stood the test of time, and for a great part of that time the Featherweight was the most favored 99 of all.

GUNS • FEBRUARY 1987

"AN EXPANDED AND FULL PRODUCT LINE" may have one meaning to the merchandising experts. To a shooter it simply means that whatever his need...

Savage
HAS IT IN '71

By Dave Moreton

GUNS & AMMO / AUGUST 1971

Reprinted by permission

Savage Arms is located just off the Massachusetts Turnpike in Westfield, Mass. Upon my arrival, public relations director John Marsman, led the way to his office where he had a number of rifles and shotguns displayed on the conference table.

A light-brown styrofoam box with the words Stevens Favorite in late 1800s-style type on the cover caught my eye at once. For an older gun buff like myself this struck a responsive chord. Sure enough, when I removed the cover I recognized the "Spit'n image" of the rifle described in Colonel Townsend Whelen's definitive work, The American Rifle, published way back in 1918. The "Favorite" was to the firearms industry what Henry Ford's Model T was to the auto industry. The original Favorites were chambered for the improved .22 Long Rifle, the Long and Short cartridges and the .25-caliber Stevens rimfire. Later a .32-caliber rimfire was added and a few rifles were even chambered for some of the smaller centerfire cartridges such as the 22-7-45 and the .25-20.

Joshua Stevens' little rifles originally sold for six dollars in the plain version. Other grades were available and some were equipped with special target sights which priced the rifle as high as $8.50. While the Savage company's publicity releases do not mention the fact, it should be pointed out that a direct descendant of the "Favorite" was the fabled Walnut Hill rifle which for nearly a half century was considered the world's finest .22 target rifle.

The modernday version of the Stevens Favorite is an authentic reproduction of the original and it seems quite logical for Savage, which acquired the Stevens firm in 1920, to reintroduce the Favorite. The recreation of the original model is being done in a limited collector's edition and priced at $75.

Specifications of the Favorite are as follows: The octagonal barrel is 22 inches in length. The stock is select, oil-finished walnut replete with Schnabel forend and crescent-shaped brass butt plate. Its dimensions are: Length 13¼ inches, drop 1½ inches at the comb and 2½ inches at the heel. The over-

all length is 37 inches and weight averages 4½ pounds. The lever, rear sight ramp and hammer are gold plated. The front sight blade is cartridge brass, as is the butt plate. Only two structural changes have been made in the original "Favorite" design; there is a wider hammer face and a release mechanism which prevents damage to the firing mechanism if the lever is opened with the hammer at cock.

The words "Stevens Favorite" are inscribed on both sides of the case-hardened receiver and a brass medallion inletted into the stock bears a portrait of Joshua Stevens, his name, and "father of .22 hunting."

This editor has fired his replica "Favorite" with over 10 different brands of .22 Long Rifle ammunition. To say the Model 71, as the Savage replica is known today, is accurate would be a classic understatement.

Marsman's conference table held other new products for 1971. It is hard to recall which of the other new Savage models for this year caught my eye next. It was either the Model 24 Combination gun or the 99A Lever gun. In the latter case, we have a historical new lever gun — the Model 99A — a saddle gun with a touch of western Americana in its features. The new saddle gun sports a straight western-style stock and Schnabel forend.

However, before you say "ho-hum so what's so new about it?" the 99A has been chambered for that long-time favorite the .250 Savage or .250-3000. In spite of the fact that the .250-3000 was first introduced in about 1914 by the late Charles Newton of Newton Cartridge fame, its popularity has held through the years as an excellent combination varmint and deer cartridge at ranges up to 200 yards.

The last Savage rifle chambered in .250-3000 was produced about ten years ago and since then there has been a steady flow of testimonial letters requesting its return to the line. These requests increased until the Savage management could no longer ignore them, so by popular demand the .250-3000 is back. (A full field test report on the 99A will appear in a later issue. ed.)

As mentioned above, the Model 24 combination gun had also caught my attention. This line of combination rifle/shotgun now has a third version, the 24D priced at $77.95. This model has redesigned breech and separated barrels. The stock of the 24D is walnut with

The Savage Model 330 is available in 12 or 20 gauge at $199.95; or, a 12-gauge gun with a set of 20-gauge barrels can be had, with soft case, for only $287.50.

The Savage shotgun line for 1971 includes the Model 550 (top) double barrel, available in 12 or 20 gauge, with single trigger and raised, ventilated rib. It is priced at $172.95. The Model 444 over and under (second from top) features auto safety, ejectors, ventilated rib and single selective trigger. List price, 12 or 20 gauge, $289.95. The Savage Model 30 (second from bottom) slide action is available in 12, 20 or .410 gauge with ventilated rib barrel in several lengths and chokes at $116.95. Another version of the Model 30 is the slug gun (bottom), which is fitted with a 22-inch barrel and rifle sights. In 12 or 20 gauge it is priced at $99.95. Interchangeable barrels are priced from $21.75 (plain) to $43.25 (with ventilated rib) for the M 30s.

The popular Savage Model 110-C (top) features a detachable clip magazine and can be had in a left-hand version (110-CL) for those who need it. It is priced at $146.95 (right-hand), left-hand and magnum calibers are slightly higher. The Model 99 (above) is available in a choice of five models and four calibers with prices starting at $135.95.

impressed checkering while the frame has a decorated satin black finish. The new version is chambered in either .22 Long Rifle with a .410 or 20-gauge shot barrel below or a .22 Magnum and 20-gauge combo. In the appropriate combination, it'll make an excellent turkey gun.

Incidentally the frame of the new 24 is not of monoblock construction and the barrel spacing allows better barrel alignment.

The Savage management is continuing to expand its shotgun line, with a new double gun in 12 and 20 gauge priced at $172.95, called the Model 550. What strikes you first about the new double is a wide, ventilated rib and the case-hardened finish of the frame.

The 550 has automatic selective ejectors and top-tang safety. This new double is available in a variety of barrel lengths in the following combinations: 12 and 20-gauge 26-inch cylinder and improved — modified and full; 12-gauge only, 30-inch modified and full; 16-gauge, 28-inch modified and full and in .410-gauge, 26-inch modified and full.

From my practice swings in Marsman's office the 550 seems to be nicely balanced and points easily and naturally. Final proof will be found in the field.

This year, Savage is offering three new field-grade Model 30 slide-action shotguns in a selection of popular barrel lengths and chokes, plus a slug gun and another version with an adjustable choke. The pump will be available in 12 and 20 gauge in the following barrel/choke combinations: 26-inch, improved-cylinder; 28-inch modified and full and a 30-inch full in 12 gauge. The slug barrel with rifle sights is 22 inches and in 12 and 20 gauge.

The above barrel/choke combinations are available with plain or ventilated rib with the exception of the slug barrel which is ribless. The Model 30AC is a 26-inch version in 12 and 20 gauge with an adjustable choke.

Prices for the Model 30s start at $96.95 in 12, 20 and .410 and go up

A combination (M24) rifle/shotgun, is to be had in various configurations of .22 LR, .22 Magnum, .222 Remington and 20 or .410 gauges. Prices start at $63.95.

In addition to a full line of .22 rifles, Savage also offers Anschutz pellet rifles. The Model 335 in .177 caliber is a single-shot break action and is priced at $58.95. The Model 250 (not shown) is made for competition. It is a single shot with fixed barrel and movable compression cylinder; price $155, without sights.

to $124.95 for the Model 30-T, a 12-gauge trap version. Interchangeable barrels are priced at $21.75 for the plain barrel and $43.25 for the vent rib; slug barrels go for $28.25.

In the Savage over/under line there are three new changes in the 444 and 330 series. Of most importance to this editor is the availability of interchangeable barrels in 20 and 12 gauge for the Model 330.

If you presently own a 12-gauge Model 330 it is possible to have fitted a new set of 28-inch, 20-gauge barrels choked modified and full, for $110. However, the gun must be returned to the factory for precise fitting. The basic price of the 330 in 12 or 20 gauge is $199.95; buying the set boosts the price to $289.95. As mentioned above, the 20-gauge barrel also sells separately.

The Model 440, which is the more refined over/under Savage import, will be available in three new 20-gauge borings. A 26-inch barrel is available choked for skeet in both tubes and also a 26-inch barrel bored improved cylinder and modified and finally a 28-inch barrel choked modified and full. These combinations should make a lot of 20-gauge upland game hunters happy, to say nothing of the skeet fans.

This year, Savage's 110C and 110CL (left-hand action) bolt rifle will be chambered for the .25-06 Remington, the .300 Winchester Magnum and the 7mm Remington Magnum. This brings the number of calibers in the 110 series to seven of the newest and most popular available.

The last offering on the conference table was the Anschutz 335 air rifle which comes supplied with or without match-grade sights. The 335 is .177 caliber and has a 12-groove, 18½-inch barrel of high-grade steel fitted to a monobloc receiver.

This precision rifle is a single-shot break action which locks at the bottom of the breech, interlocking with the receiver. The trigger of the 335 is an adjustable two-stage of match quality. Stock-wise the 335 is plain hardwood with checkered pistol grip, walnut finish, Monte Carlo style with a cheekpiece and rubber butt plate with white-line spacer. The open-sight version of the 335 retails at $58.95 while the version with 6706 Anschutz target sight retails at $81. The target sight features 1/6-minute click adjustments for windage and elevation. It is available separately at $23.

As with any company that expands its line there are some deletions; most startling is the elimination of the .308 chambering in the 110 bolt-action rifle. Also missing this year are the Savage Model 630 and 730 reloading presses.

The Savage line-up for '71 contains some impressive changes and additions, not the least of which is the "Favorite," for it marks the Savage entry into the commemorative field.

When introduced in 1920, the .300 Savage cartridge offered unprecedented power in a light deer rifle. Today, it is still remarkably modern in both concept and performance.

By John Wootters

THE TIMELESS .300 SAVAGE

GUNS & AMMO/MAY 1983

■ When I reached the ripe old age of 16 years, and had seven or eight years of deer hunting and about a dozen whitetail bucks under my belt, my father announced that my Christmas present that year would be a deer rifle of my choice. Until then, all my hunting had been with family-owned or borrowed guns; none of them were my very own. What followed that announcement was a month-long seizure of agony and ecstasy; with the entire array of sporting rifles then on the market to choose from, I suffered and sweated over the selection.

All this took place at the tail end of World War II, before the post-war production of civilian firearms got cranked up, and the "array" was not exactly staggering. I ruled out the bolt actions with hardly a second thought, as did most whitetail hunters in those days, and that left the Winchester, Marlin, and Savage lever actions, and the Remington Model 141 pump

and Model 81 long-recoil semi-automatic, and not much else. Even so, a 16-year-old gun buff in that dilemma was like a kid in a candy store; I changed my mind at least once a day for weeks on end!

The one element that never changed, however, was my conviction that I wanted my new rifle to be chambered to the .300 Savage cartridge. I'd collected deer with it, as well as with the .30-30 WCF, .30 and .35 Remington, and one or two older rounds, and the Savage cartridge impressed me with its positive killing power.

It still does. My final choice was a Savage Model 99EG in .300, fitted with a Redfield receiver peep sight, and it remained my standard whitetail armament for a decade, during which time I walloped a couple of dozen or so deer with it. Then, in 1956, I swapped the old Savage for a brand-new, scope-sighted Winchester Model 88 chambered for the brand-new .308 WCF car-

tridge. I loved the new rifle (and still do) but after a few seasons it dawned on me that the .308 was doing nothing that the .300 Savage hadn't. We don't hear much about the .300 Savage these days, and I'm not aware of any rifles of current manufacture being chambered for it except the original, Savage's M-99, but the round is just as good as it ever was and there are thousands of used guns so chambered on the market at good prices. Perhaps it will not be amiss to take a quick second look at this "obsolescent" cartridge.

Not many of today's generation of shooters realize just how far ahead of its time the .300 Savage was when it was first introduced in 1920, or how "modern" it was in both concept and performance. This cartridge arose from exactly the same thinking that produced the .308 WCF (as a sporting round) 35 years later.

Both of them were, in their respective

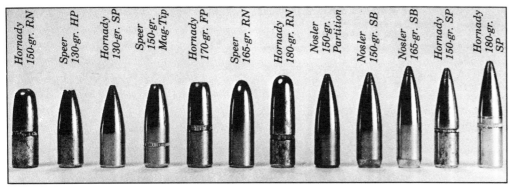

Hornady 150-gr. RN | *Speer 130-gr. HP* | *Hornady 130-gr. SP* | *Speer 150-gr. Mag-Tip* | *Hornady 170-gr. FP* | *Speer 165-gr. RN* | *Hornady 180-gr. RN* | *Nosler 150-gr. Partition* | *Nosler 150-gr. SB* | *Nosler 165-gr. SB* | *Hornady 150-gr. SP* | *Hornady 180-gr. SP*

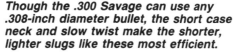

Though the .300 Savage can use any .308-inch diameter bullet, the short case neck and slow twist make the shorter, lighter slugs like these most efficient.

GUNS & AMMO/MAY 1983

Because the .300 Savage case has little body taper and a short neck, heavy bullets like this 200-gr. Nosler RN must be deeply seated, which reduces case capacity.

130-gr. Hornady Spire Point | *150-gr. Speer Mag-Tip* | *165-gr. Nosler Solid Base* | *180-gr. Hornady RN*

The reloader enjoys best results with the .300 Savage if he carefully selects bullets that are the shortest available in their weights, like these shown above.

IMR 4064 is the classic powder recommended for use in the .300 Savage cartridge, but the author experimented with these others and found them interesting and useful, though not revolutionary.

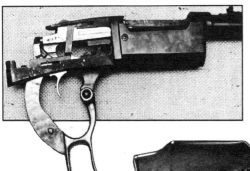

The Savage Model 99 was used to introduce the .300 Savage in 1920, and today is the only rifle in this chambering still manufactured.

Because the Savage Model 99 uses stack loading rather than a tubular system, it handles spitzer bullets.

eras, intended to be a short-cased .30-06, so to speak, cartridges which would work in short, lightweight repeating actions and deliver ballistics approaching those of the old 'ought-six. In both cases, the approach was the same—a short, fat case with minimum body taper and a very short neck to maximize powder space within a limited overall case length. In one way, the Savage round was even more "modern" than the .308, in the sharpness of its shoulder angle, which was 30 degrees. It was not until the introduction of the .284 WCF in 1963 that any standard factory cartridge sported a sharper one, and, even today, only the .284 exceeds the .300 Savage in that department.

HANDLOADING THE .300 SAVAGE

BULLET	POWDER	CHARGE WT. (GRAINS)	VELOCITY (FPS)	REMARKS
130-gr. Speer HP or FN	H322	41	2,705	Varmint, predators
130-gr. Hornady SP	IMR 3031	41.5	2,855	Small deer
150-gr. Speer RN or Mag-Tip	H322	40	2,520	Good deer load
150-gr. Nosler Solid Base	IMR 4064	41	2,535	
165-gr. Speer RN	WW748	41	2,400	Excellent brush load
165-gr. Nosler Solid Base	IMR 4895	38	2,485	
170-gr. Hornady FN	IMR 4064	38	2,390	Good accuracy, hits hard
180-gr. Hornady RN	WW760	44	2,350	Bear, deer at medium ranges
180-gr. Nosler SP Partition	IMR 4064	37	2,315	
200-gr. Speer SP	H414	44	2,220	May not stabilize

NOTES: All cases are once-fired Winchester Super-X, all primers are Winchester 120.
Velocities instrumental at 12.5 feet and rounded to nearest five fps. Test rifle Model 99 Savage w/24-inch barrel, 1-in-12-inch rifling pitch. Temperature: 64 to 87 degrees F. Chronography on Oehler Research M33 Chronotach with Skyscreens.
These loads were safe in the test rifle, but may be too heavy in another rifle. Always work up carefully from at least ten percent below maximum. All loads in this table are intended for use in lever, slide, or autoloading actions, and with proper precautions they may safely be increased in a sound, modern bolt action such as the Winchester M70 or Remington M722.
These loads are listed for the information of readers only, and they do not constitute reloading recommendations. Neither the author nor *Guns & Ammo* can accept any responsibility for the use of this information, having no control over the conditions of such use.

.300 SAVAGE

Furthermore, because of the propellant powders available in the 1920s, the .300 Savage actually did come so close to .30-06 standard ballistics that the difference was negligible, for practical hunting purposes.

Originally introduced in the M-99 Savage (which was, in itself, considerably more advanced than its lever-actioned competition of the day), the new cartridge was a great success, providing unprecedented power in a light, handy, quick-firing deer rifle. It was subsequently offered in the Savage Models 20, 40, and 45 bolt actions and the Winchester M-54, and I've been told a few Winchester Model 70s also appeared in this chambering, although I've never seen one. Remington added the cartridge to the list of those available in the Model 81 autoloader and subsequently offered it for a time in their Model 760 slide-

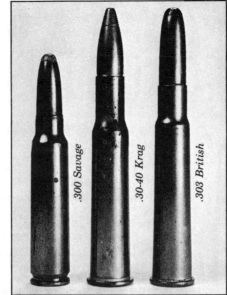

The author's Savage M-99EG was his standard whitetail deer rifle for a decade, helping him bag about two dozen deer.

Although much smaller than the .30-40 Krag or .303 British cartridges, the .300 Savage fully equals both when it comes to killing effectiveness on game.

Remington once chambered its M-760 slide action (above), M-722 turnbolt and M-81 autoloader in .300 Savage.

With modern powders, both the .308 and .30-06 are ballistically superior to the .300 Savage cartridge.

The .300 Savage (left) had the sharpest shoulder of any factory case until the advent of the .284 WCF, and still ranks only second to the .284 in this respect.

The current deluxe version of the Savage M-99 is offered in .300 Savage plus other, newer rounds.

action and M-722 turnbolt guns. There may have been other models so chambered as well, possibly including some of the post-war imports. Obviously, there are a lot of rifles of various kinds floating around with .300 Savage chambers. A few are collector's items, but the majority are just good, solid shooters, available at reasonable prices because of the chambering. These may be real sleepers for the deer hunter who simply wants a practical sporting rifle and who may be a little shaken by the prices of factory-new hunting guns.

If he springs for a second-hand .300 Savage, what is he getting? For one thing, he's probably getting a smoother, more solidly built firearm than twice the price would bring in a newly manufactured piece today, but that's beside the point. Ballistically, he's getting a rifle flinging a 150-grain bullet from factory loads at a nominal 2,670 feet per second (fps), or a 180-grain slug at 2,370 fps. In fact, my chronography indicates that the .300 Savage factory stuff delivers the same bullet weights at only 100 to 150 fps less than the .308 commercial ammo when fired from identical barrel lengths. Not bad, considering the SAAMI

COMPARATIVE BALLISTICS

CARTRIDGE	BULLET WEIGHT (GRAINS)	MUZZLE VELOCITY (FPS)
.300 Savage	150	2,630
	180	2,350
.30-40 Krag	180	2,430
.308 WCF	150	2,820
	180	2,620
.30-30 WCF	150	2,390
	170	2,200
.303 British	180	2,460
.30-06	150	2,910
	180	2,700

NOTE: These figures are from the latest published ballistics tables for factory-loaded ammunition. Barrel lengths are not specified.

specs call for a maximum working pressure of only 46,000 pounds per square inch (psi) in the Savage while 52,000 psi is permitted for the .308!

That difference in maximum breech pressures must, of course, be respected even by the handloader, *if* he happens to be working with one of the lever or slide actions, or the autoloader. Some of these lack the inherent breeching strength of a good bolt gun, and all of them lack the primary extraction power necessary to deal with hot loads. When one of the good turnbolt rifles is involved, however, there is no reason why the reloader cannot safely push pressures to 50,000 psi or slightly higher, which will deliver velocities approximately equal to the .308 factory ammunition. Let it be understood that I'm not touting the .300 Savage as the full equal of the .308. It is not, and never will be, because there is a difference in powder capacity between the two cases of about four grains. When loaded to equal pressures with the same bullets, the .308 cartridge will always be a little faster . . . but hardly enough to make a detectable difference in trajectory or killing power.

I should add that the comment above does *not* mean that maximum .308 loads can merely be cut four grains of any powder for a safe max in the .300. That reference was simply to volumetric capacity, and bears no direct relationship to actual weights in handloads.

The .300 Savage case is, of course, just as strong as any other which is based, as it is, upon the .30-06 design. From the reloader's viewpoint, it suffers the deficiency of too short a neck, but then, so do the modern .243 WCF, .284 WCF, 6.5, 7 mm, and .350 Rem. Magnums, .300 Win. Magnum, and the .308 itself! This is a mechanical problem, not only offering a doubtful grip and guidance to the bullet, but requiring that bullet bases be seated deeply into the powder space and thus reducing the velocity potential. It is not, however, a fatal flaw, and will not bother a reloader of the .300 Savage if it doesn't bother him in those other, newer hotshots listed above. Likewise, no special problems arise in loading for the .300 Savage in the lever, pump, or semi-auto actions which are not also common to other cartridges in the same actions. Standard dies will serve most of the time, but individual rifles may require the use of a special "small base" or even an "extra small base" full-length sizing die if standard sizing results in chambering or extraction difficulties.

The .300 Savage uses all standard .308-inch diameter bullets, naturally, which means that the handloader has an exceptionally wide choice of weights, makes, and styles from which to select. However, all .300 Savage barrels with which I am familiar have a 1-in-12-inch rifling pitch, which

means that normal .300 Savage velocities may not be sufficient to stabilize spitzers of more than 180 grains. Round noses up to 200 grains will probably work okay at velocities of 2,200 fps or a little more, but I'm not certain what their utility would be . . . unless you were seized with an uncontrollable passion to shoot a moose with your .300 Savage. Plenty of moose have been shot with this cartridge, but I suspect a good, strong 180-grain slug would serve as well, even for such an unconventional application. The limited powder capacity and slow rifling twist (especially in a non-turnbolt repeater) suggest that the bullet weight range from 125 through 165 grains will be most useful for the American deer hunter. I've shot most of my whitetails with this cartridge with the 150-grainer, and a few with slugs of 180 grains, and the lighter bullet seems a little more effective to me. It is my standard deer bullet in the Savage cartridge (just as it is in the .308 WCF), loaded to about 2,600 fps or a little more. That and all other velocity and pressure references hereafter refer to use in a lever, slide, or auto action; velocities from 100 to 200 fps higher *may* be possible with careful work-up in a sound bolt gun.

The 125- and 130-grain spitzers and round- or flat-nosed bullets available may be satisfactory for small deer and excellent for smaller game, but they tend to be unreliable for run-of-the-mill deer hunting, even though they can be driven to at least 2,800 fps from this cartridge. Penetration is likely to be a bit dicey and expansion, premature. A fair rule might be to never shoot a deer with a handloader's bullet which doesn't have a cannelure. The 165-grainers on the market work just fine on deer, at around 2,500 fps, but no better than the 150s, as far as I can tell.

IMR 4064 is the classic powder in the .308 WCF (among the extruded numbers, at least) and, because it and the Savage round are so similar, it is not surprising that 4064 is also the usual recommendation for the latter. In my early days of reloading, I worked with it and with IMR 3031 almost exclusively. In researching this article, however, I had powders available of which nobody had ever heard back in the 1950s, and I was curious as to whether any of them might prove to augment the potentials of the .300 Savage startlingly. Alas, powders such as Hodgdon's H322 and H335, or Winchester's 748 or 760 Ball proved interesting and useful but not revo-

lutionary. H322 did deliver the highest velocity with 150-grain bullets, within my self-imposed pressure limitations, but not by much, and 760 Ball did top the old reliable IMR 4064 with the 180-grain bullets by a few feet per second, but the margins were so slim that the results might easily be reversed in a different rifle. Nevertheless, we now have half a dozen or more propellants with which to experiment in the .300 Savage, whereas we once were limited to only two or three for big-game bullets, and that's a step forward. H322 might be a very good place to start for .300 Savage loads with all bullet weights from 110 through 165 grains.

Accuracy is very rarely inherent in a cartridge case design, usually being a function of good barrels properly bedded and good bullets. The .300 Savage, in good bolt actions, has proved itself to be at least as accurate as the .308 WCF, which is by no means damning with faint praise, since the latter holds a good number of benchrest records. Shooters are often surprised at the accuracy potential of the ancient Savage M-99 lever action, especially when the forearm is removed so that excess pressure is not exerted on the barrel as it heats up under repeated firings. In any case, I've rarely tested a 99 in .300 Savage persuasion which would not group within two inches (often less than 1½), and that's not all that different from run-of-the-assembly line turnbolt sporters these days, despite what you may read. With a little careful tuning of the ammunition, excellent hunting accuracy is to be expected routinely from most rifles chambered to the .300 Savage.

In most of them, the short magazines rigidly restrict overall cartridge length to 2.60 inches. None uses a tubular magazine, so spitzer bullets are both safe and correct for most hunting purposes. Case length should be monitored regularly and kept trimmed, not to exceed 1.87 inches. Care should be taken that the full-length sizing die does not set the shoulders of the cases back abnormally, although the springiness of some of the older actions may require repositioning of the shoulder with warmish loads. This, of course, can be expected to reduce case life somewhat, but the problem is not peculiar to the .300 Savage; the same actions do the same things with the .243! Overall, the old .300 Savage is no more temperamental than any other fat, short-necked case being fired in non-front-locking actions. It is, in fact, still a remarkably "modern" cartridge, in spite of its 1920 vintage, which seems to have been underrated by shooters.

Everybody, that is, except the hunters who have been knocking over whitetails and game of similar size with it for more than 60 years! It was ahead of its time when it was introduced . . . and it's not so far behind the times, even today.

OF ALL THE Savage cartridges, the old .303 receives the least acclaim. At best, it is usually regarded as one of the cartridges in the .30-30 class. But originally it was considered much more than that. Actually, the .303 Savage was its own kind of pioneer and it became the favorite of many woodsmen and big game hunters. In those avenues it received high acclaim and had a multitude of admirers.

The .303 began as the .30 Savage, born about the same time as the .30-30 Winchester. Winchester records indicate that W.R.A. first loaded .30 Savage ammunition in 1896 with 190-grain softpoint or full-metal-cased bullets. That ammo would have been for the Model 1895 Savage lever action rifle, and I'm sorry to say that I have no ballistical data for the old .30 Savage round.

Smokeless powders were still in the developing stages in those years close to the turn of the century. So was the use of metal-jacketed bullets. In Europe, it was believed that barrel life would be increased if the bullets were a couple of thousandths undersize, supposedly reducing wear. On this side of the Atlantic, we felt that the erosion from gas passing these undersize bullets would show increased barrel wear. Hence came the theory of using a jacketed bullet with a diameter greater than the groove diameter of the barrel.

The Savage people did just that, and Winchester ammunition records show that W.R.A. Co. began loading ".303 Savage" cartridges in 1897, and included the "new" cartridge in its catalog printed in December 1896. And, contrary to many written statements I've seen about this round, the .303 Savage was a true .303, firing a .311-inch diameter bullet.

Today some loading manuals recommend that .303 Savage owners slug their barrels before attempting to reload for the rifle. This advice usually says that while no barrels over .308-inch have been encountered, they might exist!

Fact is they don't exist. The .303 Savage was always made with a standard .30 caliber barrel and the ammunition was loaded with the larger .311 bullet. The early Savage catalogs make quite a point of this. In the 1904 catalog it was said of the rifle/cartridge combination that "the tight fit of the metal cased bullets gives increased velocity and accuracy." It was also pointed out that the .303 Savage had greater killing power at 150 yards than a .45-90, a statement based on foot pounds of remaining energy.

Not all the loading companies, however, used .311 diameter bullets for the .303. In Philip Sharpe's *Complete Guide to Handloading* is an interesting table as an appendix which shows the diameters of factory loaded bullets, a list compiled in 1948. The diameters listed for the .303 Savage are: .3088 inch by Western, .3085 by Winchester, .3085 by United States Cartridge Co., .3084 by Peters (prior to the Inner-Belted), and .311 by Remington. Savage brand ammunition is not listed, but since most Savage ammo was made by Remington, a .311-inch bullet can be expected.

Ammunition for the .303 Savage varied with the company that made it. Savage cartridges were loaded with a 190-grain softpoint bullet or a 180-grain full-metal-cased slug. Winchester had 190-grain bullets in both styles and Remington-U.M.C. used a softpoint of 195 grains and a full patch of 182 grains. All of these bullets were blunt, roundnosed and the use of the oversized bullets was a way to increase the pressures up to 43,000, which in turn would increase the velocity. Savage claimed

2,000 feet per second with its 190-grain load and Remington-U.M.C. listed a 195-grain bullet at 1,950 fps.

This was at the time when the .30-30 had a muzzle velocity under 2,000 fps with a bullet weighing 20 to 25 grains less. The difference in power and penetration were in favor of the .303 Savage, and the .303 was considered a much more reliable cartridge when used on big game. Townsend Whelen wrote in 1917 that the .303 was very satisfactory for all but the very largest game. At the same time, Whelen recommended the .30-30 only for game up to and including deer and black bear.

Whelen also told about a hunter in British Columbia who took a .303 Savage into the mountains on a hunt with one box of cartridges. With those twenty rounds he took eighteen head of big game, including two grizzlies. That's a tale of good hunting, good shooting, and a good reliable cartridge. I believe Jack O'Connor also quoted this story in an article he wrote about Savage rifles more than 20 years ago, and he said that the hunter still had one cartridge left after accounting for those eighteen animals.

The .303 Savage had to be a better performer than the .30-30 just to compete with the Winchester cartridge. After all, the very success of the Savage Model 1895 rifle was hinged on the .303 Savage since that model was made in no other caliber, unless you count the .30 Savage separately. The Winchester Model 1894 had a price tag nearly half the cost of a Savage, and it would only be natural for the buyer to expect something more for the extra money. The "more" was recognized in range and power. Accuracy was another recognized extra, and the Savage has always been known for its rigid mounting of the stock which makes it a "stiffer" rifle than the Winchester or

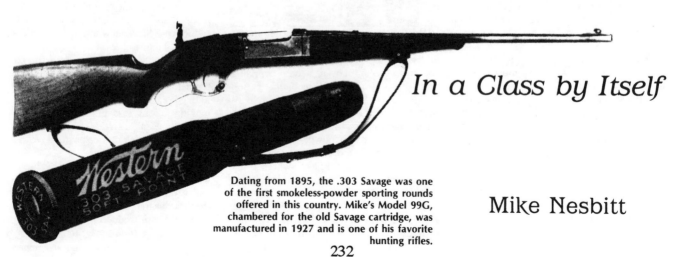

In a Class by Itself

Dating from 1895, the .303 Savage was one of the first smokeless-powder sporting rounds offered in this country. Mike's Model 99G, chambered for the old Savage cartridge, was manufactured in 1927 and is one of his favorite hunting rifles.

Mike Nesbitt

Marlin lever action. The hammerless Savage rifle looked more streamlined and modern as well, and that could have been a factor which helped the .303 become the success that it was in those early years, but I'm more prone to believe it was the performance of the rifle/cartridge combination.

Another hunter who used the .303 Savage was William T. Hornaday. In his book, *Camp-fires in the Canadian Rockies*, he mentions specific firearms only a few times but he clearly points out a .22, the .405 Winchester, the .33 Winchester, and the .303 Savage. Hornaday took quite a few head of game with his .303 on the trip described in his book, including mountain goat, bighorn sheep, and grizzly bear. He didn't however, claim the skills of marksmanship that the hunter Whelen told about, and he needed more than just one box of cartridges.

"Cougar Pete" Peterson, the first government hunter in the Pacific Northwest, used a .303 Savage. One thing he would do with his 99s was remove the safeties, which apparently got in his way. Pete would carry the rifle with a round in the chamber, but the striker would not be cocked. To get ready for a shot, Pete would just begin to open the lever and then close it again. That would cock the action and he was ready to fire. His reason for this might have been for speed, although I don't really see how his method would be much faster.

One time he was after a big bear, around 1919, near North Bend, Washington. He fell behind as his dogs ranged ahead of him and in the distance he could hear the dogs doing battle with the bear on the ground. One of Pete's dogs was a big Airedale and it was included with the hounds just in case a bear wanted to fight. When Pete approached there was a big tree

Over the years, .303 Savage cartridges have been produced by several different manufacturers.

The great variety of factory loads and loading components which have been available to .303 Savage shooters from the beginning is indicative of the round's early popularity.

MAY-JUNE 1985

The .303 Savage was well-known in the old British Empire. Both Eley and Kynoch made cartridges for it. Note the English crimp marks near the base of the bullet on the Kynoch round next to the box in the photo at right. The bullets were cannelured near the base to accept the notches.

Understanding the
.303 SAVAGE

"Understanding the .303 Savage," *Handloader Magazine*, May-June, 1985, by Mike Nesbitt, Prescott, AZ: Wolfe Publishing Co., Inc. Reprinted by permission.

between him and the ruckus. All of a sudden the bear came around the tree with Pete's Airedale in its mouth. Pete snapped the .303 to his shoulder and shot the bear in the head, which stopped the fight for good. That bullet also cut some of the whiskers on the Airedale's snout.

Cougar Pete liked the .303 Savage cartridge so well he had a Winchester Model 94 saddle ring carbine in .30-30 rechambered for the Savage cartridge. The barrel wasn't set back when this was done and the fired cases came out of the chamber with a double shoulder. That really didn't matter to Pete since he didn't reload; I would guess that he used either .30-30s or .303s in the "dual chambered" rifle interchangeably. It would be interesting speculation about how popular the .303 Savage might be today if Winchester and Marlin had adapted it to their lever action rifles and carbines.

The brand of ammunition or the bullet style those early hunters used was not mentioned but Savage tried to make the .303 attractive to everyone. The 1900 catalog listed several loads available for the .303 in addition to the regular softpoint or full patch loads. One used the regular 190-grain full metal case bullet loaded over 40 grains of black powder. This was said to have an accuracy range of 600 yards and that was probably quite true for a clean barrel. The rate of twist in the .303, one turn in twelve inches, was rather fast for black powder and I dont' know how well the jacketed bullet would have plowed through the fouling left by previous shots. To my knowledge, the .303 Savage is the only cartridge designed for smokeless powder to be available in factory-made black powder loads, other than the .32 Winchester Special.

The black powder load in the .303 was not made very long. It's understandable that it wasn't popular. The black powder load was still shown in the 1903 catalog, but not in the catalog of 1904.

Another curious load in the 1900 Savage catalog was called the target load, featuring a lead paper-patched bullet. This bullet was roundnosed and apparently hollowbased with a listed weight of 185 grains. Savage's load description for the paper-patch cartridge states only that it was designed for target shooting up to 200 yards and that the bullets were not to be crimped. The paper-patch load, like the black powder load, was not listed after 1903. U.M.C. also listed the .303 paper-patch load and catalogued it as late as 1913.

The paper-patch cartridge intrigued

me, I'll admit, so I got a mould from Northeast Industrial to make paper-patched .30 caliber bullets. I haven't tried too many powder charges with that bullet at this time and progress on developing a load is going slow. I haven't had any real luck with it and have turned my attentions back to standard cast bullets. Maybe soon I will use the paper-patch again since the mould is an excellent one and other people have had good luck with them.

Listed separately in the 1900 catalog is a load consisting of a wire-bound bullet, and the bullets themselves were available for reloading. These were called the lubricated wire-patched bullets and they were made in 160, 180 and 200-grain weights. The loaded cartridge contained 18 grains of No. 1 Model 1899 Savage smokeless powder; the catalog also shows that the wire-bound bullets could be loaded over 40 grains of black powder.

Various .303 loads: (1) U.M.C. 100-grain Short Range; (2) U.M.C. 195-grain softpoint; (3) Peters 180-grain full-jacketed roundnose; (4) Western 190-grain softpoint; (5) Remington-U.M.C. 195-grain roundnose; (6) Winchester 190-grain Silvertip; (7) handload with Speer 180-grain roundnose; (8) handload with Lyman bullet 311291 and (9) a short-range handload with NEI bullet 95.308.

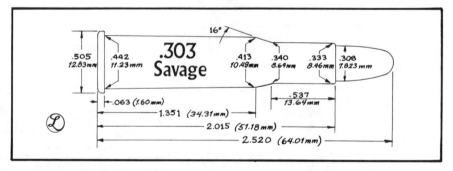

Author's Loads for the .303 Savage

bullet	weight (grains)	powder	charge (grains)	velocity (fps)	remarks
NEI No. 95.308	95 cast	Unique	5	1,000	For small game and indoor/outdoor target
Lyman No. 311291	170 cast	IMR-4895	28	2,100	Powerful cast bullet load
Lyman No. 311291 (long heel)	190 cast	IMR-4320	33	1,980	Accurate load, duplicates factory 190
Jacketed	180	IMR-3031	29	2,150	Listed as factory duplication in *Cartridges of the World*, very pleasant and accurate

Be alert — Publisher cannot accept responsibility for errors in published load data.

The description of the wire-bound bullets gives them a hearty recommendation, saying that the bullet expanded well on flesh and gave fine accuracy. In actuality, the lubricated fiber-covered wire must have been cut by the rifling and if the wire patch began to unwind in flight, these bullets could have easily been dubbed a "howling success." Successful or not, the wire-bound bullets and loads had disappeared before Savage printed the 1903 catalog.

Savage's No. 1 Model 1899 smokeless

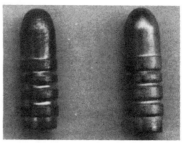

Lyman's famous 311291, on the left, is slightly shorter than the old 190-grain version, on the right.

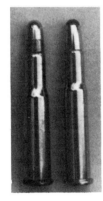

A .303 Savage cartridge, on the left, compared with a .30-30. The .303 was the shorter of the two, although its neck was longer than the Winchester's.

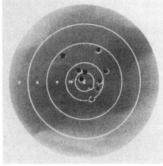

At right, a fairly representative group fired from a kneeling position at 50 yards. Not bad for tang sights and well-used eyes.

This group was made with Speer 180-grain .308 roundnoses over 29 grains of IMR-3031. Range was 50 yards.

235

.303 Savage
Old Loading Data Taken from
Lyman/Ideal Handbooks No. 38 & No. 40 and
The Belding & Mull Handbook of 1949

powder	charge (*grains*)	velocity (*fps*)	remarks
80-grain Jacketed (.32-20 Hollowpoint)			
2400	27.0	3,000	Maximum
2400	24.4	2,840	
Unique	15.2	2,590	
Unique	11.0	2,120	
Hi-Vel 2	38.0	3,100	
Hi-Vel 2	31.0	2,445	
IMR-3031	38.0	2,500	
IMR-3031	33.0	2,175	
110-grain Jacketed			
2400	22.5	2,400	Maximum
2400	22.0	2,350	
2400	17.0	1,940	
Hi-Vel 2	34.0	2,540	
Hi-Vel 2	26.0	1,990	
IMR-3031	36.0	2,330	
IMR-3031	30.0	1,940	
150-grain Jacketed			
Hi-Vel 2	31.5	2,300	
IMR-3031	31.0	2,400	
IMR-3031	29.0	2,050	
170-grain Jacketed			
IMR-3031	30.0	2,200	
IMR-3031	28.0	1,940	
180-grain Jacketed			
Hi-Vel 2	30.5	2,150	
Hi-Vel 2	25.0	1,950	
IMR-3031	32.0	2,200	
IMR-3031	29.0	2,000	
190-grain Jacketed			
2400	19.0	1,800	
2400	17.9	1,660	
IMR-4198	27.5	2,000	
IMR-4198	20.0	1,498	
Hi-Vel 2	30.0	2,000	
Hi-Vel 2	25.0	1,720	
IMR-3031	33.5	2,090	From B&M book
IMR-3031	33.0	2,040	
IMR-3031	30.0	1,840	
IMR-4320	36.5	2,145	Top load in all books
IMR-4320	32.0	1,850	
Unique	11.3	1,390	From B&M book
Unique	8.0	1,012	
No. 80	14.0	1,250	
No. 80	10.0	765	
Lightning	25.8	1,990	
Lightning	24.0	2,065	From Ideal No 38, max.
Lightning	12.0	900	From B&M book
Sharpshooter	17.6	1,695	
Sharpshooter	13.0	1,335	

Be alert — Publisher cannot accept responsibility for errors in published load data.

.303 Savage

rifle powder was used in all its smokeless cartridges prior to 1903. But that's not exactly true, because before 1899 Savage had two powders on the market, identified only as Savage Smokeless No. 1 and Savage Smokeless No. 2. Number 1 Model 1899 powder took the place of both of the earlier propellants. With the regular 190-grain jacketed bullets in the .303 Savage, the normal charge of No. 1 1899 Model powder was 22 grains. The wire-bound bullets received 18 grains and the paper-patched loads were backed with 12 grains of this same powder. The two miniature loads for the .303, one with a lead bullet and the other with a full-metal-cased bullet, used either 6 grains or 10 to 12 grains of No. 1 1899 Model powder respectively. Use of this powder in the miniature loads was discontinued when the faster burning Savage Rifle Powder No. 2, 1903 Brand, was introduced.

This might be a case of saving the best for last; the factory loads which I want to describe now are the short range loads, or as Savage called them, the .303 Miniatures. These fired a bullet weighing about 100 grains at only 1,000 feet per second. The uses for such a load are countless and they should have been a great aid to trappers and cowboys who had to depend on just one rifle for all purposes. Short range loads could be used on small game, the finishing shot on big game, dispatching an animal in a trap, or for simple fun and target practice at reduced cost. The main strike against the short range loads was that they were really not much cheaper than full power factory ammunition and the short range loadings were dropped about World War I. The last reference I have seen for the short range loadings is in the Remington-U.M.C. catalog of 1918-1919 and only the 100-grain metal cased miniature is listed. It is fairly safe to assume those were stocks on hand and not items in actual production. Now the only way to duplicate the short range load is by reloading and loads will be discussed here.

Savage had two miniature loads for the .303 and the same loads were duplicated in .30-30 cartridges sold under the Savage brand. These can be recognized by the cannelure around the neck of the case. One of the miniatures used a lead bullet of 100 grains, .303 Savage No. 4, and the other load fired a full-metal-cased bullet of the same weight, .303 Savage No. 6. Other ammunition makers also loaded short range cartridges for the .303 Savage, and U.M.C.

used a lead bullet weighing 103 grains. Winchester also loaded short range .303s and in a way it's too bad these useful loads have not survived.

The only factory-loaded miniatures I have had any experience with were the Savage No. 6 cartridges, the load with the full metal case bullets. It was several years ago and I had a number of loose rounds. I would fire those, sparingly perhaps, but they would be good collector's items now. I don't specifically recall bagging any game with the factory miniatures, but I did like them and now I enjoy shooting duplicates of that load.

Handloading for the miniatures was recommended very early. Savage used to claim that the velocity of the full load in the .303 and the rapid pitch of the rifling would strip the lead even with a hard alloy. At the same time, the company encouraged reloading the miniatures and could provide bullet moulds to make the miniature bullets. Those moulds, I'm sure, were made by Ideal and the number of that bullet was 31110. I've been looking for one of those moulds for quite a while; someday I'll find one.

Savage Rifle Powder No. 2, 1903 Brand, was intended for use only with miniature loads in either the .303 Savage or the .30-30. Loading instructions and recommended charges came on each can. Bullets for the miniature loads were available from Savage as well; the old catalogs indicated that 10 grains of black powder could be used instead of the smokeless powder.

I've never tried to duplicate the miniature loads by using black powder, but that information is good to know. What I have used, and used quite a bit, is five grains of Unique beneath a bullet weighing between 95 and 115 grains. The bullet used for most of this is Northeast Industrial's No. 95.308 and it works very well. Velocity is right around 1,000 fps and it has plenty of accuracy for small game out to 100 feet without having to re-adjust the sights. Another plus for this load is that the cases never seem to wear out.

My first experiences in loading for the .303 Savage came in my mid-teens. I had a .30-30 Model 94 Winchester at the time. One of my close friends wanted a rifle but even a used Winchester was beyond what he could afford. Used Savage 99s were fairly cheap in the older standard versions, and my friend bought a 26-inch barreled .303 for a twenty dollar bill. For a couple of more bucks he picked up a Lyman 310 tool and dies to go with his .303, along with some ammunition which cost him a dollar a box. He had no reloading experience and we spent

several hours applying what I knew about reloading at the bench to hand-loading out of the cigar box with his nutcracker tool.

Most of the old loading manuals contained no data for the .303 Savage with cast bullets, only the note to use the loads as for the .30-30 Winchester. That's just what we did, mostly with Lyman's cast bullet No. 311291. Many of the cast loads listed, however, did not develop the velocity we desired, so we took a powder charge listed for a jacketed bullet, reduced that by a couple of grains, and topped the cartridge off with a cast bullet of similar weight. This procedure had proven itself in the Model 94 .30-30 I was using at that time with 28 grains of 4895 under the 170-grain gas check. That same load was tried in the .303 Savage and if there was any difference in performance, the .303 would have come out the better.

Hodgdon's surplus 4895 was a powder we used a great deal in those days. It was, and still is, a good powder for high velocity cast bullets, but we used it for reasons of cost. One of the gunshops used to buy this powder in barrels and then sell it in one pound paper bags. The price for a bag of powder was 69 cents, meaning that a pound of powder was cheaper than a box of primers. The same shop would sell surplus 4831 for 49 cents a pound, also in bags, but that powder was too slow for our rifles. Life seemed pretty simple in those days. The only things I needed money for were primers, powder, a couple of bucks for gas, and a box of gas checks now and then.

Bullet lead would have been another expense if we'd had to buy it. Our bullets were made out of wheelweights and most gas stations would give the old ones away to anyone who'd ask. Wheelweights were a bit harder than they are now but I still regard them as a very good source for bullet material.

My own interest in the .303 Savage didn't surface until a couple of years later and when it did, it was a case of the cart before the horse. A gunsmith offered me three full boxes of .303 ammo plus a whole cigar box filled with loose rounds. I took it, thinking I'd do my friend a favor. But he had all the ammo he wanted, and I was stuck with more .303 Savage cartridges than I had in any other caliber. The obvious solution was to buy a .303 Savage rifle.

The rifle I bought had seen better days. It was an 1899A made between 1920 and 1927 with a 26-inch heavy barrel, crescent buttplate and a grooved trigger. The bore was pitted and dark, but the lands of the rifling were still sharp. This well-worn treasure set me back twenty bucks and I spent another five to equip it with a used Redfield peepsight.

That .303 proved to be quite accurate. As soon as I had gathered enough loose change, I toted home a gleaming set of RCBS dies complete with shellholder. The load of 28 grains of 4895 under Lyman's No. 311291 bullet was immediately put into service and I was pleased to see that load hitting very close to the impact of the 190-grain factory-loaded Silvertips.

I quickly developed an unending fondness for the Savage 99, and a deep respect for the old .303 Savage. One reason was accuracy. I'll admit that accuracy was not my primary concern at the time, but groups with cast bullets that measured under three inches at fifty yards were something that I'd never experienced with my .30-30 Model 94. With the long-barreled Savage, such groups became commonplace and I was rapidly becoming spoiled.

Contributing to this accuracy was probably the .303 Savage cartridge itself. It does resemble a .30-30 Winchester in general, but there are differences. The body of the case is a little fatter and the cross-sectional burning area of the powder is greater than in the .30-30. With some powders, that could contribute to more consistent burning. The biggest difference, however, can be noticed in the necks of the cases; the neck of the .303 is quite a bit longer than that of the .30-30. This allows the .303 to support a cast bullet better than the .30-30, especially heavy cast bullets whose bases would protrude into the body of the case if loaded in the .30-30 and seated to the proper overall length. All in all, the .303 proved to be a very good cartridge for cast bullets.

There was rather little variance in the loads I used in that first .303. The only jacketed bullets I tried were in factory ammo; all reloading was done with cast slugs. Another mould had been added to my little array, a hollowpoint version of No. 311291, and bullets from that mould were also loaded over 28 grains of 4895. Lighter loads were made up with Lyman's pointed 115-grain gas check No. 311359, and a .32-20 bullet (No. 3118 style) was tried over five grains of Unique or a similar charge of AL-8 for short range shooting. The .32-20 bullets were cast from an original Winchester mould that a friend of my father's had used to cast fishing weights.

All of these loads worked well and no others were tried until I got my second rifle. It was a Featherweight takedown made sometime between 1910 and WW I, with a 20-inch barrel. This one was in excellent condition with a bright, shiny bore.

With that rifle came an urge to duplicate full power ballistics with cast bullets, and that meant a bullet weighing 190 grains. The mould I got to do this was Lyman's No. 311334, a bullet design with a reputation for good performance, but it wasn't designed for the .303 Savage. I would seat this bullet over 30 grains of 4895 and in the gravel pit it had the punch to really show those tin cans a thing or two. This is a pointed bullet, however, and to be able to work the loaded cartridge through the magazine, the bullet had to be seated very deeply. That put the base of the bullet into the powder area of the case; bullet support was lost. Some of the gas checks might have even fallen off. When I tried this load on paper, keyholing was prominent — so I gave up on that bullet style.

Another .303 came into my hands after that, an early 99H, the carbine without a barrel band. It was very accurate, and the only scoped .303 I've ever fired.

A short time later I was approached by a Savage collector and I sold all my .303s, the dies, and all my ammunition just so I could afford something I thought I would rather have. What that might have been, I don't recall.

My shooting with cast bullets continued but the results fell off sharply. Maybe that was an excuse, but I missed not having a .303. One evening while talking to a friend, I mentioned that I wanted another .303 Savage, namely a 99G. He had also been looking for old Savage 99s and knew far better than I that they were getting harder to find. All he said in reply was, "Good luck!"

G Models in .303 are fairly scarce, at least in the Northwest corner of our country. I've seen only two. The one that I bought could be described, in negative terms, as not as accurate as my old 99A and not as pretty as the little Featherweight. On the positive side, this rifle is in good condition and had the original sights still on the barrel. The only modifications were a refinished stock and the addition of sling swivels. Both of these treatments had been tastefully done.

This rifle was made in 1927, one of the first G Models made with the ramp front sight, and I installed a Marbles flexible tang sight on the back. I was very satisfied with this .303, I still am, and it inspired me to look at loading for the .303 again.

My first need was ammunition. I called every sporting goods and hardware store in town before I located a single box. The old days of buying shop and shelf-worn boxes at a dollar each were forever gone. I was able to build up a good supply by hitting small town stores. It's not easy to make .303 Savage brass out of other cases, and the best bet is to start with existing ammo.

I still had the bullet moulds, so loading could be resumed. The loads I began to assemble were the same ones I had both started and left off with, bullet No. 311291 and 28 grains of 4895. That's a fairly powerful load. I've chronographed it when loaded in a .30-30 and found the average velocity to be about 2,100 fps out of a 24-inch barrel. The same velocity or something very close to that could be expected from the .303 Savage. My hope, however, was still to duplicate the 190-grain load with cast bullets.

My main requirement to realize that load was a new bullet mould, which I got somewhat by accident. Lyman had a sale on rejected mould blocks and I sent for a double cavity version of No. 311291. I could see why they were classed as rejects — they had been cherried too deeply and the bullets that dropped from those cavities were regular 311291s, yes, but with especially long gas check heels. Out of curiosity, I weighed a sized and lubricated bullet complete with gas check and was delighted to find that it weighed 190 grains. That was the very bullet I had been looking for.

A good powder charge to put behind the 190-grain cast bullet left me wondering for a while. Memories of the 4895 load with No. 311334 made me want to try something else, perhaps a slower burning powder. In *The Fouling Shot*, the publication of the Cast Bullet Association, Frank Marshall Jr. has a column called "Speaking Frankly," and he had mentioned the .303 Savage several times. I wrote to Frank, asking him to recommend a good load with the 190-grain bullet. He said to use 33 grains of 4320 with the heavy cast bullet, and that for woods-use it would be as effective as the factory load.

Before that letter had floated to the floor, I was at the loading bench. Older loading manuals recommended 4320 for jacketed bullets weighing 190 grains and if all things followed the general rules, a slightly reduced charge would work well with cast bullets of similar weight. In this case it did. At fifty yards the bullets cut a very comfortable group through the ten and X rings, clocking 1,980 fps across the Skyscreens of the Oehler 330. The combination using 33 grains of 4320 is now my standard cast bullet load with 311291.

I haven't mentioned the diameter of the sized cast bullets. When I started loading .303s I sized the bullets to .311 inch and that was the recommended practice for all .30 caliber rifles at the time. Later I began to size the bullets in a .308 die and I now prefer the smaller size. I've never made an accuracy comparison between the two sizes, and I honestly don't think any real conclusions could be made with the rifles I am using. In reloading, however, the .308 bullets load into the cases easier and with less deformation and that in itself should aid accuracy by being more consistent.

Jacketed bullets in the .303 Savage make a whole different story and I've loaded very few store-bought bullets. One reason is that I've always favored heavy bullets and that's especially true for the .303. There are plenty of 170-grainers available along with some good updated data for use in the .303 which makes it very usable, but just like another .30-30. I'd rather shoot loads which contain more characteristics of the .303 Savage, hence, heavier bullets.

Hornady makes good bullets for the .22 Savage High Power and for the .33 Winchester. The .22 H.P. bullet is primarily intended for the European market, but I'm awful glad it's available whatever the reason. I contacted the company with the idea of making 190-grain roundnose bullets for the .303, bullets that could also be used in the .30-30. Lyman's No. 45 manual gives data for using the 190-grain Silvertip in the .30-30 along with comments of very fine accuracy. (The same manual gives no data for the .303 Savage with bullets heavier than 170 grains — strange.) Hornady listened to my request, then kindly said my train was about to stop and told me where to get off. I can't say that I really blame them.

Speer used to make a roundnose .308 caliber bullet that weighed 200 grains. I tried those in the .303 Savage with 35 grains of 4320. That load did not display high pressure signs, although I believe it to be about maximum, and it shot accurately. I only loaded one batch of those bullets because they are probably too heavily constructed to expand on deer-size game. That would make them less effective than the cast bullets, and the idea was given up.

Several 180-grain roundnosed .30 caliber bullets are available, but many of these have a taper that begins too soon to be properly adaptable to the .303 Savage. Speer's .308 180-grainer would work well but, again, it is designed to be launched at higher velocities than the .303 is capable of. The .303 Savage is in a class by itself when compared to other .30 calibers because even though it is of such a common bore size there is no bullet available that will allow the cartridge to perform as intended.

Factory loaded ammo is still available but that is subject to stocks on hand. It would be a lucky find to locate some 190-grain Silvertip bullets or 180-grain Core Lokts on the shelf, and the handloader should be aware that the Winchester-Western Silvertips are .308 inch diameter, but the latest Remington softpoints are still .311.

For loading data with jacketed bullets weighing over 170 grains, the old manuals must be consulted. The properties of the powders can change over the years, however, and the loads listed in the old books could easily give higher pressures today; those loads should be approached cautiously. It would certainly be the best idea to begin with the suggested load rather than the maximum charge. The .303 Savage is not a speed demon anyway, but it has always been a cartridge with a reputation for delivering the goods.

My G Model 99 has done its delivering well. I've taken both deer and black bear with it while using factory loads. The deer fell to a 180-grain Remington load backed up by a short range load to make doubly sure. For the bear, the rifle's magazine was loaded with old 190 and 195-grain softpoints by Western and Remington respectively. The aged cartridges fired like they were made yesterday, which made the hunt a good one. Very good actually, because I was the back-up man and the bear, a young adult male, was getting away.

While the .303 Savage receives little regard today, it was Savage's cornerstone cartridge. The very success or failure of that company rested on the performance of the .303 in the early years, and the .303 performed well enough to establish Savage Arms on solid ground. Over the years, the .303 Savage has never been updated ballistically and it could be said that it reached its zenith of performance at the time it was introduced. In the same breath it would have to be said that the .303 never lost any of its punch over the years either. No rifles for it have been made for over 40 years, but many of the old rifles are still in service and they will probably remain in service as long as there is ammunition.

The .303 Savage has some unique characteristics, enough that it can stand in a class by itself. Those characteristics, plus the history and the way the .303 performs, make it one of my very favorite cartridges. ●

Reprinted by permission of the author

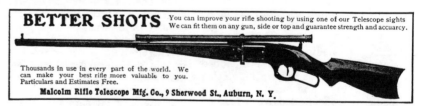

Source: OUTDOOR LIFE   Aug. 1909

SAVAGE ARMS

A collection of Savage and Stevens firearms, both production guns and prototypes, is displayed at the Savage Arms, Inc., plant located in Westfield, Mass.

THE most famous product of Arthur W. Savage and the company he founded is, undoubtedly, the Model 1899 rifle that came to be called the Model 99. Because of that, some think that 1999 will mark the centennial of Savage Arms.

The Model 1899, however, was only a Model 1895 with slight modifications, so Savage now says that 1995 will be its centennial. Why, then, since the 1960s, has Savage claimed that it had more than a century of gunmaking experience behind it? Simple.

In 1920 Savage acquired the J. Stevens Arms Co. that was for years one of America's largest arms producers. Savage began coupling its name with that of Stevens and, later, with that of the A.H. Fox Gun Co. that it absorbed in 1929. As the Stevens firm was originally founded in 1864, it followed that the Savage/Stevens/Fox operation could have celebrated full-century status quite legitimately in 1964, making it 128 years old today.

Since its formation in Utica, N.Y., as Savage Repeating Arms Co. on April 5, 1894, the firm has had many changes in its names, owners and locations. It was incorporated as Savage Arms Co. in 1897, was sold to the Driggs-Seabury Corp. in 1915 and became Savage Arms Corp. in 1917.

In 1946 Savage transferred its production to Chicopee Falls, Mass., the base of its Stevens facilities, and, in 1959, it was bought by The American Hardware Corp.

Savage's current factory, originally the base of a pre-fab house manufacturer, was built in Westfield, Mass., in the 1940s, and Savage took ownership in 1960. In 1964, the firm became the Savage Arms Division of a large conglomerate, the Emhart Corp.

In 1981 some local businessmen bought the division's assets from Emhart, and Savage Industries, Inc., was born, only to be transferred to another set of private owners in 1986.

None of the postwar foster parents of Savage treated it with much love or respect, and the firm was forced into bankruptcy in February of 1988 with debts exceeding $14 million.

Immediately the word went out that Savage was finished, but, in March of 1989, a Bermuda-based,

SAVAGE
REACHES FOR ITS CENTENNIAL

A new management team, having rescued the company from bankruptcy, moves ahead with a few key guns to keep the name prominent in the sporting arms marketplace.

By Pete Dickey
American Rifleman, January 1992

Savage Reaches For Centennial

Savage President and CEO Ronald Coburn (c.) is flanked by his management team (l.-r.), Richard Hamre, Stanley Kruszyna, David Barker, David Tolly, Clayton Pilz, Jerry Stock and Thomas Humphrey. Pilz has the critical sales/marketing portfolio.

American-owned, publicly traded company, Challenger International Ltd., signed a letter of intent to acquire certain assets of Savage Industries. The bankruptcy courts approved the program, and today's corporation, Savage Arms, Inc., was formed by Challenger on Nov. 1, 1989.

At the 1991 NRA Annual Meetings, Savage's exhibit included not only its Model 99 lever-action, but the popular and popularly priced line of Model 110 center-fire bolt-action rifles, the Model 24 rifle/shotgun combination and an over-under shotgun line made for Savage by Italy's Marocchi.

Several new variations of the Model 110 were shown, but Savage's newly patented Passive Bullet Traps were the central point of the display and were being examined not only by club and range officers but by competitive firearms manufacturing firms, some of which have already placed orders.

The traps are made in sizes to accept bullets of all constructions, weights and velocities. The principle of the steel trap is to direct bullets into a "snail" drum where they spin until they lose their momentum and then drop to be washed out by a water/oil mixture that is continually sprayed within the snail. The liquid mixture is filtered and recirculated and the bullet particles can be salvaged. A main benefit of the "wet" trap is that lead dust at the impact point is virtually eliminated.

With the great emphasis put on the traps at the NRA exhibit, we asked if Savage was shifting away from firearms production. Savage's president, Ronald Coburn, responded with a definite "no" and an invitation to visit the Westfield factory, which was gladly accepted.

The factory stands as it was built, but the gun operations no longer occupy all or even most of its vast space. As part of its recovery strategy, Savage decided to downscale its scope of operations to a profitable level by dropping the manufacture of guns that were netting little or no profit and concentrating on a few best-sellers.

The Model 110-series rifles and the Model 24 rifle/shotgun combinations were chosen as the line leaders. The considerable space that had been devoted to .22 rifles and pump-action, single-shot and side-by-side shotguns etc. was freed and the Model 110 and 24 operations were concentrated in a relatively small area.

The 150,000 sq. ft. "surplus" space achieved is leased to other firms, bringing in the welcome cash needed to continue and expand operations and the work force (re-duced from 1987's 400 to 160 today—but growing) is made up of what every manufacturer dreams of: skilled artisans who have stuck by the firm over the rough times.

Many other space- and labor-saving programs have been adopted. Prominent has been the installation of the most modern CNC (computer numerically controlled) machinery to supplement or replace some of the older, more conventional equipment, and the outside pro-

Model 99 evolution was shown in a 1980 NRA museum exhibit. Savage is rebuilding with guns that have been successful.

curement of all wood and Rynite stocks.

The Model 99 rifle was threatened with extinction, despite its high demand, because the firm's previous ownership had inexplicably let its forged receiver program die. One of the new team's very first moves was to ship the remaining parts to Gabilondo/Llama in Spain, where new receivers were investment cast, and the barreled actions were re-

turned to be stocked and sold by Savage.

The 99-C is, then, back in Savage's line in limited quantity, but full U.S. production of the durable hammerless lever-action is planned to coincide with Savage's elected centennial, 1995.

That, to many dealers and customers, is the best news to come from Savage recently, but there is more. If all goes as planned, the rotary magazine/shell counter versions of the Model 99 may return as well; so may some of the ultra-popular Savage/Stevens/Fox shotguns of the recent past.

In addition to the Savage name, Challenger acquired those of Stevens and Fox and, while neither is used at present, it is obvious that a Fox double-barreled shotgun would get instant market recognition, as would a Stevens single-barrel or Stevens-branded .22 rifles or pistols. Coburn, who is not only president and CEO of Savage, but one of the

five board members of Challenger, says *all* the above product prospects are being considered.

The new management team seems dedicated to, in Coburn's words, "breathe new life into Savage" and, judging from the spirit and activity shown during the Westfield visit, this may already have been accomplished in good measure.

Gun shipments in 1991 totaled over 80,000 pieces and, as said, each piece netted a profit, as did each square foot of previously unused or unprofitably used factory floor space.

A visitor to Savage's compact operations comes away with the assurance that bullet traps are only a sideline (as were such other products as washing machines, refrigerators and lawn mowers in the past), but one with great potential. Guns are Savage's main business as they have been since 1899, or '95 or '94, or was it 1864? ■

Savage's new bullet trap, while only a sideline, attracted much shooting industry interest at the NRA Annual Meetings.

American Rifleman, January, 1992
Reprinted by permission.

SAVAGE REACHES FOR ITS CENTENNIAL

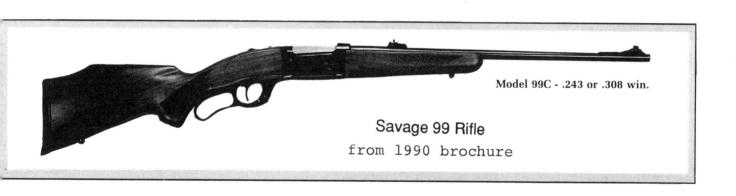

Model 99C - .243 or .308 win.

Savage 99 Rifle
from 1990 brochure

High Quality Firearms — at Moderate Cost

APPENDIX A

SAVAGE ARMS

Recent Chronology of Savage Arms Ownership and Trends

On September 21, 1981, Emhart Corporation sold the assets of its Savage Arms Division to third party private investors. These investors formed a new corporation called Savage Industries, Inc. to purchase all assets of the previous Emhart division.

On February 2, 1988, Savage Industries, Inc. filed for protection under Chapter 11 of the U. S. Bankruptcy Code in the Federal District Court of Massachusetts. While the Chapter 11 is still pending, however, Savage Industries is now out of business.

On November 1, 1989, Savage Industries, Inc. pursuant to a Bankruptcy Court order sold many of its assets to Challenger International, Ltd. Challenger International is a publicly traded corporation with its shares traded on the NASDAQ Exchange (Symbol CSTIF) and on the Toronto Exchange.

Challenger formed a new corporation called Savage Arms, Inc. to purchase selected assets from Savage Industries. Savage Arms, Inc. purchased only the following product lines:

Model 110   Bolt Action Rifle
Model 24   Combination Over/Under Rifle/Shotgun
Model 99   Lever Action Rifle
Model 72   Falling Block Rifle

All other product lines manufactured by Savage Industries were discontinued March 1, 1988 as a result of the bankruptcy. Tooling for the discontinued product lines has been sold to a number of different replacement gun parts manufacturers/distributors throughout the country. All discontinued products will not and cannot be manufactured by the new company and will pass into Savage history.

The tradenames and tradestyles: "Savage," "Stevens," "Fox," and the "Indian Head," including all copyrights and patents were sold to Savage Arms, Inc. and the heritage will continue in the name of Savage Arms, Inc. and its various products.

The new Savage Arms, Inc. has been producing the Model 110, Model 24, and the Model 99. There are no current plans to produce the Model 72 at this time. The company also has introduced a new Model 312 Over/Under shotgun in trap, skeet, and sporting clays versions.

Source: Savage Arms, Inc. October, 1990.

APPENDIX B
The Savage Line Circa 1971

Single Barrel Shotgun
Savage-Stevens Mod. 94-Y, Youth Mod. 20 and 410 ga Reg. and Mag.
$42.50

Bolt Action Shotgun
Savage-Stevens Mod. 58. 410 ga. 2 1/2 " & 3" Clip
$46.95

Bolt Action 22 Magnum
Savage-Stevens Mod. 34-M. 5-shot clip
$44.95

Bolt Action 22 Long Rifle
Mod. 65. Monte Carlo stock 5-shot clip
$46.95

Bolt Action 22 Magnum
Mod. 65-M Monte Carlo stock, 5-shot clip
$49.95

Single Barrel Shot Gun
Savage Mod. 220-L. Hammerless, 12 16, 20, 410 ga.
$47.95

Bolt Action Shotgun
Savage-Stevens Mod. 51. 410 ga. Single shot
$37.95

Lever Action Center Fire.
Mod. 99-F. Featherweight. 300 Savage, 243, 308.
$159.95

Bolt Action 22 Long Rifle.
Key Lock Mod. 63-K. Built-in Key Lock.
$33.95

Bolt Action 22 Long Rifle.
Savage-Stevens Mod. 73. Also, Youth Mod. 73-Y.
$26.95

Automatic 22 Long Rifle.
Savage-Stevens Mod. 88. 15-shot tubular magazine
$49.95

Single Barrel Shotgun.
Savage-Stevens Mod. 94-C. World's most popular single barrel shotgun. 12. 16, 20, 410 ga.
$41.25
36" Barrel.
$42.50

Bolt Action 22 Long Rifle.
Savage-Stevens Mod. 34.
5-shot clip.
$39.95

Bolt Action 22 Magnum. Key Lock Mod. 63-KM. Built-in Key Lock.
$36.95

Bolt Acion 22 Long Rifle.
Savage-Stevens Mod. 46. Tubular mag. Long rifle, long, short.
$44.95
4X Scopegun Mod. 46/S.
$50.50

Anschutz Target Rifle.
1407 Match 54. 22 Long Rifle. Sights extra.
$179.50
Left-hand Mod. 1407-L. Sights extra.
$192.00

Automatic 22 Long Rifle.
Mod. 90. Carbine. Monte Carlo stock, barrel band. 10-shot tubular mag.
$54.95

Bolt Action Shotgun.
Savage-Stevens Mod. 59. 410 ga. 2 1/2" & 3" Tubular mag.
$56.95

Slide Action Shotgun.
New Mod. 30. Field grade. Interchangeable barrels. 12, 20, 410 ga Reg. and Mag.
$96.95

Anschutz Match Air Rifle.
New Mod. 335. Caliber .177. Open sights.
$58.95
Mod. 335-S. Micrometer Sights
$81.00

Combination Rifle/Shotgun
Mod. 24-S. 22-LR or 22 Mag. Gauges: 10 or 4410. Reg. and Mag.
$63.95

Slide Action Center Fire.
Mod. 170. World's fastest 30-30 action.
$99.95
Scopegun 170/S. 1.5X-4X var.
$137.95

Automatic 22 Long Rifle.
Mod. 60. Monte Carlo stock 15-shot tubular mag.
$57.95

Anschutz Target Rifle.
1413 Super Match 54. World's most accurate rifle. 22 Long Rifle. Sights extra.
$350.00
Left-hand Mod. 1413-L. Sights extra.
$365.00

Savage/Anschutz Target Rifle.
Mod. 64. Sights extra. 22 Long Rifle.
$79.95
Left-hand Mod. 64-L.
$89.95

Slide Action Shotgun.
New Mod. 30. Slug gun. Adjustable rifle sights. 12, 20 ga.
$99.95

Bolt Action 22 Long Rifle.
Savage/Anschutz 164 Sporter. Anschutz action.
$98.50

Combination Rifle/Shotgun
New Mod. 24-D. Monte Carlo stock. 22 Long Rifle/ 20 or 410 ga. or 22 mag./20 ga.
$77.95

Combination Rifle/Shotgun.
Mod. 24-V. Monte Carlo stock. 222/20 gauge.
$99.95
4X Scopegun Mod. 24-V/S.
$130.50

Fall Block Action 22 Long Rifle.
Stevens Favorite. Serialized. Limited Edition. Collector's Mod.
$75.00

Bolt Action Shotgun
Savage-Stevens Mod. 58 Clip 12, 16, 20 ga.
$55.95

Savage/Anschutz Target Rifle.
Mark 10. Target Sights included. 22 Long Rifle.
$75.00

Slide Action Shotgun.
Model 30-AC. Adjust. choke. Interchangeable bbls; 12, 20 ga. Reg. and Mag.
$99.95

Bolt Action 22 Magnum.
Savage/Anschutz 164-M Sporter. Anschutz action.
$105.50

Bolt Action Center Fire.
Mod. 340. 30-30, 222.
$89.95
4X Scopegun Mod. 340/S.
$108.00

Slide Action Shotgun.
MMod. 30-D. Deluxe. Interchangeable bbls., vent rib. 12, 20, 410 ga Reg. and Mag.
$116.95

Bolt Action Center Fire.
Mod. 110-E Magnum. 7mm Mag.
$136.95

Bolt Action Center Fire.
Mod. 110-D. 30-06, 243, 270
$144.95

Over-and-Under Shotgun.
Mod. 440B. Selective trigger; 12, 20 ga.
$239.95

Bolt Action Center Fire.
Mod. 110-C. Ejector clip 25-06, 30-06, 243, 270.
$146.95

Bolt Action Center Fire. Left-hand
Mod. 110-DL. 30-06, 243, 270.
$149.95

Side-by-Side Shotgun.
Savage-Fox B. Vent rib. 12, 16, 20, 410 ga.
$139.95

Bolt Action Center Fire. Left-hand
Mod. 110-EL. 30-06.
$127.95

Bolt Action Center Fire. Mod. 110-D. Varmint.
Med. Hvy., 24" chrome-moly steel barrel. 22-250.
$144.95

Lever Action Center Fire.
New Mod. 99-A 250-3000 Sav., 300 Sav., 243, 308.
$154.95

Bolt Action Center Fire. Left-hand
Mod. 110-DL. Varmint Med. Hvy., 24" barrel. 22-250
$149.95

Slide Action Shotgun.
Mod. 30-T. Trap gun. 2 3/4"-3" chamber
$124.95

Side-by-Side Shotgun.
Sav.-Stevens 311. World's most popular double. 12 16, 20, 410 ga.
$109.95

Bolt Action Center Fire. Left-hand
Mod. 110-EL Magnum 7mm, Mag.
$142.95

Bolt Action Center Fire.
Mod. 110-E. 30-06, 243.
$121.95
4X Scopegun 110-E/S. 30-06.
$145.95

Lever Action Center Fire.
Mod. 99-E. Carbine. 300 Sav., 243, 308.
$135.95
4X Scopegun Mod. 99-E/S.
$160.95

Bolt Action Center Fire. Left-hand
Mod. 110-DL Magnum. 7 mm, 300 Mag.
$164.95

SAVAGE ARMS, INC.
Springdale Road
Westfield, MA 01085

Bolt Action Center Fire. Left-hand
Mod. 110-CL. Ejector clip 25-06, 30-06, 243, 270.
$152.95

Bolt Action Center Fire.
Mod. 110-D Magnum. 7 mm, 300 Mag.
$159.95

Lever Action Center Fire.
Mod. 99-C. Ejector clip 243, 284, 308.
$159.95

Side-by-Side Shotgun.
Savage-Fox B-SE. Vent rib. auto. ejectors; 12, 16, 20, or 410 ga.
$164.95

Anschutz Target Rifle
1411 Match 54. Prone stock mod.22 L.R. Sights extra.
$179.50
Left-hand Mod. 1411-L. Sights extra.
$192.00

Over-and-Under Shotgun.
Mod. 444B. Deluxe. Selective trigger. Ejectors. 12, 20 ga.
$289.95

Bolt Action Center Fire. Left-Hand
Mod. 110-CL Mag. Ejector clip. 77mm, 300 Mag.
$167.95

Anschutz Match Air Rifle.
Mod. 250. Caliber .177 Sights extra.
$155.00

Lever Action Center Fire.
Mod. 99-DL. Deluxe. Monte Carlo stock; 243, 308.
$164.95

Side-by-Side Shotgun.
New Savage 550. Monobloc construction. 12 and 20 ga.
$172.95

Over-and-Under Shotgun.
Mod. 330 Selective trigger; 12, 30 ga.
$199.95
Mod. 330 Set. 12 ga. 330 plus extra 20 ga. bbl.
$287.95

Over-and-Under Shotgun.
Mod. 440B.T. Trap gun. Select. trigger.
$284.95

Bolt Action Center Fire.
Mod. 110-C Mag. Ejector clip. 7 mm, 300 Mag.
$161.95

Bolt Action 22 Long Rifle.
Sav./Anschutz 54 Sporter. World's most accurate smallbore action.
$157.50

243

STEVENS CATALOGS

Issued	Cat. No.
1875	
1877	
1889	4
1894	11
1896	14
1898	
1900	
1902	50
1903	50 Spec. Ed.
1903	Telescopes
1904	51
1904	51 English
1907	52
1907	Shotguns
1908	52 (1st)
1909	52 (2nd)
1909	Demi-block Shotguns
1910	52 (3rd)
1911	53
1912	53 Revised
1912	Shotguns
1914	54
1919	54 Revised
1920	55
1925	56
1927	57
1929	57 Revised
1931	58
1933	59
1934	60
1935	61
1939	39
1940	40
1941	41
1942	42
1946	43

Source: Robert Sears
"Stevens Arms Catalogs"
NRA Gun Collecting
Newsletter, Wtr 81/82

A MODERATE priced gun—that shoots well, looks well, wears well, handles well—is a STEVENS SINGLE or DOUBLE BARREL MODEL. Made in all standard lengths and gauges in Hammer and Hammerless styles.

For sale by all Merchants. If you cannot obtain, we ship direct, express prepaid, upon receipt of Catalog Price.

Send for 160-page Illustrated Catalog describing entire output. Has attractive cover in colors Mailed for 5 cents in stamps to pay postage.

J. STEVENS ARMS & TOOL CO.
P. O. BOX 77,
CHICOPEE FALLS, MASS.

STEVENS' RIFLES ARE USED BY PERFORMERS IN THE WILD WEST SHOW.

Source: William F. "Buffalo Bill" Cody program pamphlet, circa 1887

244

HILL PLANT

RIVER PLANT

SAVAGE & STEVENS ARMS

SAVAGE · STEVENS · FOX

Chicopee Falls

Savage Arms Corporation is one of the largest producers of sporting arms in the world. Pictured here are the firearms plants of Savage Arms Corporation located in Chicopee Falls, Massachusetts. These plants have a total floor space of more than 500,000 square feet devoted almost exclusively to the manufacture of 27 distinct and different models of shotguns and rifles. Up-to-date manufacturing methods, combined with skilled engineering and experienced workmanship, maintain the Savage reputation for quality and value.

CONSUMER CATALOG
NO. 1-53

SAVAGE

SAVAGE · STEVENS · FOX Rifles and Shotguns

SAVAGE · WORCESTER Power and Hand Lawn Mowers

APPENDIX E

Annie Oakley with Stevens used in Buffalo Bill Wild West Show
The Sure Shot Stevens Rifle was named in honor of Ms. Oakley.
It was Sitting Bull who nicknamed her "Little Sure Shot"
See: *Custer, Cody & the Last Indian Wars* by Jay Kimmel

INDEX

SAVAGE &
STEVENS ARMS

Calamity Jane (Martha Jane Cannary) shown with Stevens Hunter's Pet pistol with detachable wire stock. An infamous character of the Old West, she was periodically employed as a packer, mule skinner, and was associated with Wild Bill Hickok and the roaring wild west mining town of Deadwood in the Black Hills of present South Dakota. Photo by Charles Petersen. Courtesy of Hebard Collection, University of Wyoming. *[To order book contact CoryStevens Publishing, Inc.]*

STEVENS

N EVER before has as much been written about physical culture as now. It is advocated by doctors and all classes of people, and there is no subject which should receive more attention among young people who are fast growing to maturity. What prospect has a person starting out in life unless he has a strong constitution? And what better way to acquire it than an Out-of-Door Life? There is no sport quite as fascinating, to both old and young alike, as *Shooting*, but to enjoy it fully you must have a **Reliable FIREARM.** The Fall Season is here with all nature at its best, game is plenty, the laws off, and nothing to prevent the fullest enjoyment of a Grand Sport. We manufacture a large and varied line of

Rifles	*from*	**$3.00**	*to*	**$150.00**
Pistols	*from*	**$2.50**	*to*	**$25.00**
Shotguns	*from*	**$7.50**	*to*	**$25.00**

And have many Models for all kinds of shooting. Our popular styles of **Rifles** for younger shooters are the "**Stevens Maynard, Jr.,**" "**Crack Shot**" and our celebrated "**Favorite,**" while for older shooters our "**Ideal**" in its various Models has no equal. In **Pistols** we have our "**Tip-Up,**" "**Diamond,**" "**Lord,**" "**Conlin**" and "**Gould**" Models, all the **Best** of their class. No Shotgun ever introduced has become in as short a time such a favorite as our **Single Barrel** in Hammer and Hammerless Models.

Every boy should have a good Rifle and Shotgun in his Outfit and be taught how to handle them. The publishers of this paper offer an easy way for all to secure one of our High-Grade FIREARMS. Read what they say about it on page 533 of this issue.

Any dealer in Sporting Goods can furnish our **FIREARMS,** but if you cannot find them don't accept a substitute. Write to us and we will ship direct, express prepaid.

Every one at all interested in Shooting should have a copy of our new 128-page Cata. It is full of valuable information. Mailed to any address on receipt of two 2c. stamps.

J. Stevens Arms & Tool Co.,   Box 538,   Chicopee Falls, Mass.

STEVENS SINGLE SHOT PISTOLS

No. 35 STEVENS "OFF HAND"
Single shot.   Caliber: .22 long rifle.

Barrel	6 in. or 8 in. length. Round with octagon breech. Blued.
Action	Single shot. Stevens famous Tip-up action, blued, positive extractor.
Sights	Adjustable flat top rear with elevation, and bead front.
Stock	Selected black walnut.
Weight	6 in., 24 ounces; 8 in., 27 ounces.

For over sixty-five years the J. Stevens Arms Company has manufactured single shot pistols that have become world famous for their accuracy, finish, workmanship and durability.   The No. 35 pistol is one of the most practical models ever designed as a hunting side arm and has been sold in every part of the world.

It has an excellent "man size" grip, clean trigger pull, and sufficient weight in frame and barrel for extremely accurate shooting.   The Tip-up action is quickly operated for reloading.

Its compact size and weight makes it particularly appealing for a trapper or big game hunter to carry—the .22 long rifle cartridge is sufficient to account for all small game and birds.

No. 35 STEVENS "AUTOSHOT"
Single shot.   .410 gauge shot shell.

Barrel	8 in. or 12¼ in. lengths. Choke bored, round with octagon breech.
Action	Single shot. Stevens famous Tip-up action, blued. Positive extractor.
Sights	Shotgun front.
Stock	Selected black walnut, checkered.
Weight	With 8 in. barrel, 23 ounces; with 12¼ in. barrel, 25 ounces.

The Stevens No. 35 Autoshot has been designed to supply the increased demand for a single shot arm chambered for the efficient .410 gauge shot shell.

The increased barrel length, checkered stock, and other changes has made a compact light arm that is very efficient for all small game and birds up to 25 yards. A .410 gauge shell loaded with a single ball may be used, making a powerful single shot arm for protection.

The No. 35 Autoshot, chambered for this small gauge shot shell, is recommended to those desiring a side arm for quick shots at small game where a rifle is not practical.

SAVAGE MODEL 99
Styles A-B and E-F

MODEL 99-A. Solid Frame. 24 in. tapered round barrel. Raised ramp front sight base. Rifle butt plate. Weight about 7¼ pounds.

MODEL 99-B. Takedown. Same specifications as above with takedown feature. Weight about 7½ pounds.

CALIBERS: Models A-B. .30-30, .303 and .300.

The Model 99-A Solid Frame Rifle is the original design through which the fame of the Savage Model 99 was developed. The 24 inch barrel in all calibers, the rifle butt plate and straight stock appeals to the sportsman who prefers the longer barrels for assistance in steady, accurate aim, improved cartridge ballistics and reduced recoil.

Model 99-B Takedown is the same rifle as Model 99-A with takedown feature added.

MODEL 99-E. Solid Frame. Tapered round barrel. Raised ramp front sight base. Shotgun butt. Weight about 7 pounds.

MODEL 99-F. Takedown. Same specifications as above with takedown feature. Weight about 7¼ pounds.

CALIBERS: Models E-F, .22 Hi-Power, .30-30, .303 and .250-3000 with 22 in. barrel. .300 with 24 in. barrel.

Model 99-E Solid Frame and 99-F Takedown are the featherweight designs, so called, because the shorter barrel and straight stock with shotgun butt plate makes a quick handling, easy to carry rifle chambered for the most powerful cartridges.

Model 99-A   Model 99-E

SAVAGE MODEL 99
Styles G and K

MODEL 99-G. Takedown. Tapered round barrel. Raised ramp front sight base. Shotgun butt, full pistol grip, checkered stock and forearm, checkered trigger and corrugated steel butt plate. Weight about 7¼ pounds.

CALIBERS: .22 Hi-Power, .30-30, .303 and .250-3000 with 22 inch barrel. .300 with 24 inch barrel.

MODEL 99-K. Takedown. Same specifications as Model 99-G with following refinements: Selected American Walnut stock and forearm—special fancy hand checkering on forearm, panels and grip. Receiver and barrel artistically engraved. Action carefully fitted and stoned. Lyman rear peep sight, folding middle sight and white metal bead front sight.

CALIBERS: Same as the Model 99-G.

The outstanding high power rifle of today is the Savage Model 99, style G. It is our most popular rifle and is selected by sportsmen who want a moderate weight rifle uniting fine finish with extreme efficiency. Especially adapted to high concentration cartridges because of the exceptional strength and safety of the action, this rifle is ideal for any American game shooting.

The Model 99-K is our finest finished rifle and is a beautiful specimen of high class rifle making. The checkering and engraving are unusually rich and makes the rifle an appealing possession to the discriminating sportsman.

Model 99-K   Model 99-G

SAVAGE ARMS

The Definition Of Accuracy

By Carolee Anita Boyles

From Riches To Rags To Honors, This Company Is A Study In Commitment, Vision And Innovation!

In early 1988, Savage Arms was bankrupt. The formerly proud American company was days from being dissolved and its assets sold to pay creditors.

Fast forward to 2003. Savage Arms is voted the Manufacturer of the Year by the Shooting Industry Academy of Excellence. Just as significant, the Savage 12BVSS with the new AccuTrigger is honored by the academy as the Rifle of the Year.

What happened between 1988 and 2003 to transform Savage Arms from a doomed company to one celebrated by the industry? This is a story of one man's commitment, and a company that wouldn't die. It's a story of vision and innovation.

The Savage story is a long and honored one. Formed in 1894 by Arthur Savage, the company marketed the first "hammerless" lever-action rifle with the action enclosed in a steel receiver. By 1915, Savage Arms was manufacturing high-powered rifles, rimfire rifles, pistols and ammunition.

During World War I, Savage merged with the Driggs-Seabury Ordnance Co., and made Lewis machineguns. Savage purchased J. Stevens Arms in 1920, and later acquired the assets of the Page Lewis Co., Davis-Warner Arms, Crescent Firearms, and A.H. Fox. At the time, according to company history, Savage was the largest firearm company in the free world.

During World War II, Savage made heavy munitions and when the war ended, it again manufactured consumer products, including the first motorized lawnmower.

But in the 1960s Savage's fortunes took a downturn. A New York conglomerate purchased the company. Two additional sales later, Savage was on its deathbed.

Enter Ron Coburn. Coburn started his career at Smith & Wesson where he was director of engineering in the early 1980s. He was the president of Case Knives when the owners of Savage Arms hired him as the senior vice president "to straighten out the company."

"Their concern was two-fold," Coburn said. "First, they didn't have any money to change anything, and second, they had orders that they couldn't fill because of the lack of capacity. Plus, they had quality issues in the factory."

The owners thought the answer was "make more product."

"Making a product at a loss isn't the way to run a business," Coburn said. "The situation was just impossible. Just totally out of control. So within a few months, I resigned."

When Coburn resigned, the owners filed for bankruptcy. They pleaded with Coburn to return and either rebuild the company or liquidate it.

In February 1988, Coburn went to the bankruptcy judge.

"He was actually very good about it," Coburn said. "He really didn't want to

lose the name or the employment in the area, because we were one of the few manufacturers left in that part of Massachusetts. So he gave me 60 days to stop the bleeding."

With the permission of the owners, Coburn fired the president and the chairman. The owners named Coburn president and CEO and gave him free rein.

"I had to revamp the company from top to bottom," Coburn said. "I had more than 500 employees on the day we filed bankruptcy. By the end of that week we were down to 101. I took out all the VPs and all the administrative levels, and dropped nine out of 11 individual product lines in one day. I decided we weren't going to continue to make more than 400,000 units a year at a loss. We had way too many products, each of them in dire need of re-engineering. I kept two products in the line that I felt were the focus of the company."

The two firearms he chose — though he says he did it without any real market information and with nothing to go on but his intuition — were the Model 110 bolt-action rifle and the Model 24 over-and-under combination shotgun-rifle.

After the drastic reductions in products and employees, Coburn started to rebuild Savage.

"Within five months we had stopped the hemorrhaging," he said. "Within a year, we were able to come out of bankruptcy. We paid off all of our prior debts, and all the vendors we owed money to. We paid off all the back taxes we had accumulated. I'm very proud to say that we paid everyone off. That's one of the reasons we not only survived, but grew during that period. We took care of all the people who had taken care of us prior to bankruptcy. If we'd taken the easy way out, we'd have had a much harder time buying materials and staying alive afterwards."

The Rebuilding Begins

At that point, Coburn applied his engineering background to determine the direction of Savage Arms. He says he treats the manufacturing of firearms the same way automobile factories manufacture cars.

"You just start something at one end of the factory and keep it moving," he said. "You don't put it down, if at all possible. So, I put the equipment in line and kept the material flowing from machine to machine, and took the day-work approach. That was major culture shock to the company, but it got us focused on quality. Slowly but surely, we built up the company."

However, Savage Arms' troubles weren't over. In 1995, the company's owners decided to sell the company. While another firearm company was interested, Coburn believed Savage should remain independent. He told the owners that whatever they were offered, he'd match it. They agreed. Coburn raised his own money and attracted a group of investors.

"We bought the company in November 1995," he said. "Now, the company is privately owned by management and some silent investors."

The Innovative Stage

In the late 1990s, Savage reached its "innovative stage." Drawing once again on his engineering experience, Coburn started looking at new ways to manufacture firearms.

"It's all part and parcel of

Over the years, firearms manufactured by Savage include sporting arms and those used on the battlefield. In addition to firearms, Savage at one time made exercise and washing machines, and lawn mowers.

Photos By Paula M. Iwanski

Savage stepping up to the next level," he said. "First, we've corrected our problems of the past. Second, we've added a focus to the company: accuracy and value. Third, we wanted to improve on our product. The only way to do that is to see yourself as better than your competition, even if you're not, and drive yourself toward innovative improvements. So we strive to do more than anyone else."

That striving created a new generation of muzzleloaders.

"I didn't want to be in the regular black powder market and be a 'me, too,'" Coburn said. "I wanted something better or not at all."

For five years Coburn watched the black powder market grow, but stayed out of it until he had what he felt was a better idea that offered the consumer something he couldn't get anywhere else: a muzzleloader that uses smokeless powder.

"Is it creative thinking or better marketing?" he asked. "It's more opportunism than anything else. It's watching what everyone else is doing, and getting out ahead of them."

Savage's smokeless powder muzzleloader is not without controversy. Longtime black powder shooters either love it or hate it.

"I'll never be able to change their minds," he said. "There will always be controversy when there's something new and unusual."

Ron Coburn, Savage president and CEO, is credited with saving the company.

The Savage AccuTrigger Is Born

Coburn's vision and drive also resulted in the AccuTrigger. However, Coburn said, he only pointed the way.

"The engineers came up with it," he said. "They just needed someone to point them in the right direction."

The seeds of the AccuTrigger actually were sown in 1988, when Coburn decided to concentrate on manufacturing bolt-action rifles. As the company reinvented itself, the Savage rifle became an exceptional value. But Coburn still wasn't satisfied.

"People began to see Savage as comparable to anything else out there for the performance, but they still complained about the trigger. Not just of our rifles, but of everyone's," Coburn said.

In the late 1990s, that complaint reminded Coburn of something he had promised himself years before.

"I always felt very strongly that at some point, when I got the product to the point that I could go toe-to-toe with anybody in the industry, I would do something about the one thing we all suffer from, and that's a hard-pull trigger," he said. "I shoot other companies' rifles regularly, and I know that we all tug on triggers today."

Coburn got the company's two best engineers together and told them, "We're going to fix this. Redesign my trigger group and give me a crisp, no-creep trigger."

The engineers, Bob Gancarz and Scott Warburton, came back with an enormous amount of data about creeping and mushy triggers. Plus, they had a redesigned trigger group. It was just what Coburn had in mind. He then gave them another challenge: Take the trigger down to a pound and a half pull.

"They said, 'No, you don't want to do that because it's dangerous,'" Coburn said. "I told them, 'Then find a way to do it so jar-off isn't an issue.'"

Gancarz and Warburton went to work —

Savage
AccuTrigger

for almost a year. When they came back, they had a trigger that was not only creep free, it was adjustable from 6 pounds to a pound and a half.

"It had a feature built into it so that if it ever did jar off at the low setting, it would hang up on a secondary sear safety that wouldn't let the firing pin go," Coburn said. "I said, 'Great!'"

He then he gave the engineers another challenge: Allow the customer to change the trigger pull, safely.

"Think about it," he said. "When we sell our rifles, every one of us has a little blurb in the manual telling the customer not to adjust the trigger pull himself, but to take it to a reliable gunsmith. That's something the customer has to pay for. I think it's an insult. I didn't want to insult the consumer any more. I wanted to give him the mechanical means to adjust his own trigger, at will, at any range he wants, and safely."

Gancarz and Warburton succeeded, and the AccuTrigger was born. To prove its safety, Coburn, with an AccuTrigger-equipped rifle in hand, stood onto a pallet and had a forklift raise him up 20 feet off the ground. He dropped the rifle three times to a concrete floor to be sure it wouldn't go off accidentally. It didn't. Once he was satisfied, Coburn applied for a patent for the AccuTrigger.

"Now we have patent protection and it's the state of the art: A factory trigger that's fully adjustable with absolutely no safety issues attached to it," he said.

That gained Savage an enormous amount of publicity in late 2002 and resulted in the Rifle of the Year Award from the Shooting Industry Academy of Excellence.

Savage engineers Bob Gancarz (left) and Scott Warburton developed the AccuTrigger.

Photo By Paula M. Iwanski

Savage *12BVSS with AccuTrigger*

Manufacturer Of The Year

Rifle Of The Year

A Company Honored Looks To The Future

The Manufacturer of the Year award cut to the heart of the goals Coburn always had for Savage. The company was honored for originating the value-priced package concept, which allows the consumer to buy a rifle, scope and sling as a unit, while at the same time continuing to develop new products and innovations that provide true service to customers. The AccuTrigger was one of those innovations.

Upon accepting the Manufacturer of the Year award, Albert F. Kasper, Savage president, promised move innovation in the future.

Savage Arms
The Definition of Accuracy

Photo By Jim Spelios

Brian Herrick (left) and Albert Kasper display the 2003 Manufacturer of the Year and Rifle of the Year awards.

"On behalf of all 350 hard-working Savage employees who have really made a lot of this happen, I can tell you that you will continue to see the innovation in Savage grow in the years to come. Ron Coburn has given us the environment in which all this has taken place. I thank you very much."

Brian T. Herrick, Savage vice president for Marketing and Sales, also emphasized innovation when he accepted the Rifle of the Year award.

"It took us years to reclaim our place in the industry. Our latest phase is we've become a very innovative company, as the AccuTrigger suggests. I think historically, when you look back, it will probably be one of the most important innovations the company has ever had."

Driving this innovative attitude is Coburn.

"Now that we're in our stride, we stand to look at ourselves as the innovators," Coburn said. "We've taken on an innovative role, and now we must perpetuate it. We'll continue to look at the way products are made, and continue to look at price points."

Coburn says the company will focus on the technology of guns, and look at what the consumer wants and needs that's not already available.

"We're working on some things right now," he said. "I can't tell you what they are yet, but they're different, they're new and they're consistent with where this company has been going for the past 10 years." ◎

Savage employees gather to celebrate receiving two awards from the Shooting Industry Academy of Excellence.